1978

STUDIES IN PUBLIC COMMUNICATION

A. William Bluem, General Editor, 1966–1974

STUDIES IN PUBLIC COMMUNICATION

MASS MEDIA AND COMMUNICATION
Edited by Charles S. Steinberg

THE LANGUAGES OF COMMUNICATION
A Logical and Psychological Examination
by George N. Gordon

TO KILL A MESSENGER
Television News and the Real World
by William Small

INTERNATIONAL COMMUNICATION
Media—Channels—Functions
Edited by Heinz-Dietrich Fischer and John Calhoun Merrill

THE COMMUNICATIVE ARTS
An Introduction to Mass Media
by Charles S. Steinberg

PERSUASION
The Theory and Practice of Manipulative Communication
by George N. Gordon

MASS MEDIA AND THE SUPREME COURT
The Legacy of the Warren Years
Edited by Kenneth S. Devol

THE PEOPLE'S FILMS
A Political History of U.S. Government Motion Pictures
by Richard Dyer MacCann

THE IMPERATIVE OF FREEDOM
A Philosophy of Journalistic Autonomy
by John Calhoun Merrill

CONGRESS AND THE NEWS MEDIA
Edited by Robert O. Blanchard

AMERICAN BROADCASTING
A Source Book on the History of
Radio and Television
by Lawrence W. Lichty and Malachi C. Topping

STUDIES IN PUBLIC COMMUNICATION

AMERICAN BROADCASTING

A Source Book on the History of Radio and Television

By
LAWRENCE W. LICHTY
and
MALACHI C. TOPPING

COMMUNICATION ARTS BOOKS

HASTINGS HOUSE, PUBLISHERS · NEW YORK

For HBS

Second Printing, October 1976

Library of Congress Cataloging in Publication Data

Lichty, Lawrence Wilson, comp.
  American broadcasting.

  Includes bibliographical references.
  1. Radio broadcasting—United States. 2. Television broadcasting—United States. I. Topping, Malachi C.,
joint comp. II. Title.
HE8689.8L5   384.54'0973   74-2024
ISBN 0-8038-0362-1
ISBN 0-8038-0370-2 (pbk.)

Published simultaneously in Canada by
Saunders of Toronto, Ltd., Don Mills, Ontario

Designed by Al Lichtenberg
Printed in the United States of America

CONTENTS

CHRONOLOGICAL
TABLE OF CONTENTS

The readings are arranged generally in chronological order
in this additional Table of Contents.

THE 1930s

THE 1940s

THE 1950s

LIST OF TABLES

At ends of Parts (other than Tables included in articles in text)

PREFACE

THE MATERIAL that follows was selected by use of a number of different criteria. Above all we tried to give as complete and accurate a picture of broadcasting as possible within our knowledge and the material we could gather, study, digest and use.

We considered material from varied sources—choosing, when possible, those with the best primary data. We tried to balance scholarly articles with the journalism of the times. For every article reprinted in this book there were 20 articles or more reviewed and we hope that the selections give a sense of the variety and breath of broadcast research. What was chosen is a reflection of our own image of broadcasting history and reveals, at least to us, many gaps in our knowledge. We hope that broadcast historians will not only correct our errors of fact and interpretation but broaden the scope of research to fill in the blank spots.

Some items that might have been used were not because they are widely available in other collections. Examples are sources of such articles as the Langs' report on MacArthur's Chicago parade or various legal documents. We present less on social effects than is deserved because there are a number of anthologies of this nature already in print. The most editing of articles was done on the early historical selections. To the authors of articles published here for the first time we are particularly grateful for their work and editing through many versions. All other selections are reprinted with permission, except for those for which neither author nor publisher could be located. The major editing focus was to reduce redundancy, a task in which we were not completely successful. In a few cases we added material to account for later information. Most of the punctuation and spelling was left as original with corrections only for typographical errors and inconsistencies in form or grammar. The original style remains.

Much of our work was made easier by the editing skills of Bob Summers, Mike Kittross and Chris Sterling, editors of the *Journal of Broadcasting*.

Sandra, Claire, Gabrielle, Belinda and Laurel gave up nearly every holiday for "the book." Many students sent us in search of answers with their questions; some spent long hours themselves picking academic nits. Many helped us compile hard-to-get pieces of information but four who must be mentioned are Hal Niven of the National Association of Broadcasters and Broadcast Education Association, the late Leonard Weinles at the Federal Communications Commission, Larry Frerk and the A. C. Nielsen Company, and Ken Lichty. Authors and publishers graciously allowed us to borrow both part and parcel of their works.

The Graduate School of the University of Wisconsin-Madison and the Oklahoma Broadcasters Association provided financial aid.

Most of all we thank the broadcasters, journalists, and scholars whose work we have tried to present as truthfully as we know how; and Bill Bluem, Russell Neale and others of Hastings House who saw our eight-year project through to the end.

For our readers we hope this is only the beginning of their understanding of the history of that indefinable thing called American broadcasting.

LWL
MCT

A. WILLIAM BLUEM

A *Tribute*

This is the last book in the series of *Studies in Public Communication* under the general editorship of A. William Bluem. Bill died in April 1974. This space was reserved for his Introduction. His teaching and writing will stand for that Introduction.

Bill was the blithe scholar. His knack at finding the gaps in information about communication was matched by his courage in publishing to fill those gaps. His work as author and editor attests to his insights into the needs in the study of communication. He was continually hammering at the supports for a bridge between the business of broadcasting and the academic study of communications.

As scholar, founding editor of *Television Quarterly* (1962), general editor of this and a companion Hastings House series, *Studies in Media Management,* he gentled both academics and broadcasters, assuring each that the other was acting in good faith.

To us he was the best kind of editor. He had faith in our project and encouraged us when no one else did. He gave us support but left us alone.

Likely, his outlook is best expressed in his own words:

> If we possess the technology by which to obliterate ourselves, we also have the capacities to harness technology in the responsible service to mankind—seeking not only an essential betterment and a new level of harmony among men and nations, but the individualation of man. Even the most skeptical detractors of the mass media will admit that television, in its greatest moments, has served both goals. For all can sense that the images on the TV screen help to create, for the first time in human history, *communicating man*—a creation which underlies both a social and individual view of life.

As he said others must, his work was "an unceasing attempt to seek and transmit the inherent, and fundamental, relationships between the field of broadcasting and the whole of human knowledge."

LWL
MCT

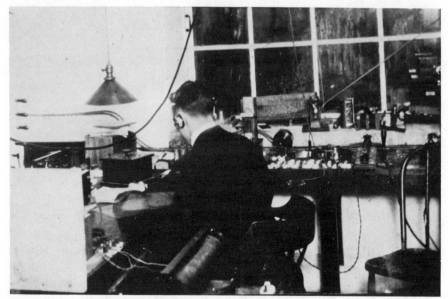

The wireless station at the University of Wisconsin, Madison, 1917.

August 8, 1974

August 9, 1974

PART ONE

TECHNICAL

. . . The child born today in New York City, when in middle age, shall visit China, may see reproduced upon a screen, with all its movement and color, light and shade, a procession at that moment passing along his own Broadway. A telephone line will bring to his ear music and the tramp of marching men. While the American pageant passes in the full glare of the morning sun, its transmitted ray will scintillate upon the screen amid the darkness of an Asian night. Sight and sound will have unlimited reach through terrestrial space.
—Charles H. Sewall, *Harper's Weekly,*
December 29, 1900.

Perhaps no other branch of science enjoys the romance and the spirit of adventure ever present in Radio.
—*Radio Broadcast,* 1922.

THE PERSONALITIES of the magnificent pioneers in broadcasting technology were as inventive as some of the tubes and wiring schemes they designed. Imagine Lee De Forest driving the streets of New York in the back of a car while he sparked out noisy messages on a dummy transmitter. Think of the very creditable Christmas program devised by Reginald Fessenden on that first voice broadcast in 1906. And when they were not promoting and publicizing their passion for the ether, they were defending their patents against the curious usurpers.

The invention, the men and the times cannot be separated and keep a true flavor of the history of broadcast technology. Broadcasting developed in an era when men believed that technology would solve the world's problems. From the boy who took the balls off his brass bed posts at night to send his messages, to the sophisticated researcher in Westinghouse laboratories there was a religious fervor around the invention of this device. Herbert Hoover was expressing the feelings of many men when he wrote:

. . . the ideal of universal communication, which has long aimed to inter-relate everyone possessing the necessary equipment anywhere on this earth, is in its realization predictable and must be accepted

1

as an augury of better understanding and of swifter means of accomplishment throughout the world.[1] *

Popular radio magazines of the 1920s were packed with stories about new receiving and sending techniques; but also, in each article, the writer stressed the personality of Marconi, De Forest, Armstrong, Fleming or Jenkins as part of the story. The pages of *Radio Broadcast, Radio News, Electronic World, Radio Digest, The Wireless World and Radio Review, Scientific American* and even *American Boy* told about radio and television. Inventions abounded. Every tinkerer was hearing the message: Invent something, get a patent, get rich, save the world.

As late as 1929, *The Annals* used an article that declared "the most fruitful field for improvement [in radio] . . . is . . . in the design of the antennas." [2] The history of technology and programming are linked. The electrical transcription made spot announcements feasible and changed programming as did the introduction of wire and tape recording.[3] Color changed the economics of television. Early broadcasters also affected early programming. Technicians such as Dr. Conrad, Dr. De Forest and others selected the programs for early radio and their vision (or lack of vision) in this was surely responsible for some of the ideas that carried through the days of early programming.

While De Forest called himself the "Father of Radio" historical research reveals that he had little understanding of his "invention." Unfortunately much of what is known about the invention of what he called the "audion"—actually the triode—was reported by De Forest, himself. To say he was immodest is understatement.

His undergraduate education has been described as "undistinguished" but he earned a Ph.D. writing what might have been the first dissertation closely related to wireless telegraphy. His academic credentials, compared with the bizarre backgrounds of other radio tinkerers, added to his credibility.

Summarizing the early history of the "audion" Robert Chipman wrote:

> DeForest's legend of the triode insists that each step in his experiments brought a marked improvement and that he immediately found the grid-triode to be the most sensitive device of all. The fact is that all the versions except the final grid-triode must have been extremely poor detectors. The impression, implicit in popular accounts and nurtured by DeForest, that the grid-triode was immediately recognized as a miraculous achievement is also contradicted by a number of facts.[4]

Thus, Chipman concludes that De Forest "invented" only in the "cut-and-try" sense of the word a method with "no scientific under-

* Footnotes are at the end of the book.

standing of what he was doing." After 1912 De Forest and many other inventors and experimenters would perfect the triode. However, in 1934 the courts officially declared De Forest to be the principal inventor and the beneficiary of the triode and its various applications. This is the "justification for his eminent position among U.S. inventors".[5]

Publications before 1930, naturally, were more concerned with the technical aspects of radio than its programming. David Sarnoff in 1922 was worried that broadcasting would not meet the challenge of providing service after the novelty wore off.[6] In 1904 when John Ambrose Fleming wrote Marconi that he had been receiving signals on an aerial with nothing but a mirror galvanometer and his "device," (thermionic vacuum diode) it was the medium, not the message that was dominant.[7]

No single inventor was more responsible for the development of radio than Edwin Howard Armstrong. As an undergraduate at Columbia University he perfected the concept of the feedback circuit. Two decades later he developed FM and spent his life promoting its high frequency, quality signal. Armstrong began working nearly full time in 1928 to perfect frequency modulation. In 1930 he filed his first basic FM patents. In 1933 Armstrong demonstrated his work to David Sarnoff of RCA and in 1934 Armstrong installed an experimental FM transmitter in the Empire State Building working with RCA's research labs. But RCA, and others, were more interested in television.[8]

In 1936 the FCC issued Armstrong a permit to build an experimental FM station. His station W2XMN, went on the air in 1938, and in July 1939 began a regular schedule of programs. The next year the first FM and AM-FM combination sets were available to the public. There seemed to be great interest and there were a number of applications for commercial FM stations, but there also were many FCC hearings and rule changes.[9] World War II stopped the progress of FM. About 50 commercial FM stations remained on the air during the war but more than 400 applications for stations were on file with the FCC. In June 1945 the FM band was moved up the spectrum to 88–108 megacycles. This made obsolete all existing FM receivers and required changes in transmitting equipment. With a second start FM was again on its way as applications for stations poured into the FCC.

Maybe as important as the inventors were the prophets. In 1912 S. C. Gilfillan wrote:

> There are two mechanical contrivances, one now taking its first unsteady steps in the commercial world, the other still in inventors' laboratories, each of which bears in itself the power to revolutionize entertainment, doing for it what the printing press did for books.

They are the talking motion picture and the electric vision apparatus with telephone.

. . . home theater has been a dream of Bellamy, Wells and other prophets, but now it is a thing invented twice over.

. . . some evening of 1930 we may find in the newspaper such a program as the following:

Tschaikowsky's "Pathetic Symphony," by the Eighth Telharmonic Orchestra. Popular Music, telharmonic, instrumental and vocal. "Coppelia," by the National Corps de Ballet of South America. "Francesca of Rimini," grand opera. "Antony and Cleopatra," by William Shakespeare. Thirty dramatic sketches. A reading . . . Los Angeles at the Moment; glimpses from various viewpoints in the city, with Ciceroni. Winnipeg vs. Gary, championship baseball game. "The Management of Monopolies," by Y, candidate for the Presidency.

If the industries, political included, which the electric theater threatens, do not forbid it to be born, as they endeavored to stangle the telharmonium, it ought to appear in a few theater buildings about five years from now, and be in the majority of homes within twenty.[10]

The fate of the telharmonium remains obscure but C. Francis Jenkins demonstrated his spinning disk for an eyewitness from *Radio Broadcast* in 1924. By 1928 Jenkins was demonstrating 48-line television.[11]

In *Radio Digest* four months later he reported that "already radio movies are giving pleasure to thousands of Radio amateurs and Radio shortwave fans." John Baird in England was also working along the lines of Jenkins struggling with the problems of the spinning disk.

In the 1930s television seemed to stop dead, in part held back by those best able to promote it because of their growing economic success with radio just turning commercial.

Articles in national magazines were asking "Where's television" throughout the 1930s. A writer in *Collier's* soothed the impatience however, after visiting the RCA TV labs with a prediction "you can prepare yourself for a surprise, because television, when we get it, is going to be good." [12]

The revolution that magnetic tape brought to broadcasting and other fields was not foreseen by the rather lukewarm interest that wire recording generated in 1924. An early article praised the use of thin iron wire in recording "the very shading of a speaker's voice." Records were being made on wire of important addresses including those of President Coolidge.[13]

From some of the same pioneers of radio and television, and those who walked in their steps, would come sound motion pictures, facsimile, radar, transistors, coaxial cable, communication satellites, laser, fiber optics, and . . .

WIRELESS SIGNALS
ACROSS THE OCEAN

Marconi Says He has Received Them From England.
Prearranged Letter Repeated at Intervals in Marconi Code.
The Italian Inventor Will Now Leave St. John's, N. F., and Will Go to Cornwall to Continue the Transantlantic Experiments from His Station There.

ST. JOHN'S, N. F., Dec. 14—Guglielmo Marconi announced to-night the most wonderful scientific development of recent times. He stated that he had received electric signals across the Atlantic Ocean from his station in Cornwall, England.

Signor Marconi explains that before leaving England he made his plans for trying to accomplish this result, for, while his primary object was to communicate with Atlantic liners in midocean, he also hoped to receive wireless messages across the Atlantic.

The Marconi station in Cornwall is a most powerful one. An electric force a hundred times greater than at the ordinary stations is generated there. Before he left England, Signor Marconi arranged that the electrician in charge of the station, which is located at Poldhu, should begin sending signals daily after a certain date, which Signor Marconi was to cable to him upon perfecting the arrangements here. Signor Marconi arrived here eight days ago. He selected Signal Hill, at the entrance to the harbor, as an experimenting station, and moved his equipment there. Last Monday he cabled to the Poldhu station orders to begin sending signals at 3 P.M. daily and to continue them until 6 P.M. these hours being respectively 11:30 A.M. and 2:30 P.M., St. John's time.

During these hours last Wednesday Signor Marconi elevated a kite, with the wire by means of which signals are sent or received. He remained at the recorder attached to the receiving apparatus, and, to his profound satisfaction, signals were received by him at intervals, according to the programme arranged previously with the operator at Poldhu. These signals consisted of the repetition at intervals of the letter "S," which in Marconi's code is made by three dots or quick strokes. This signal was repeated so frequently, and so per-

New York Times, December 15, 1901, pp. 1–2.

fectly in accord with the detailed plan arranged to provide safe-guards against the possibility of a mistake that Signor Marconi was satisfied that it was a genuine transmission from England.

Again on Thursday, during the same hours, the kite was elevated and the same signals were renewed.

This made the assurance so complete that Signor Marconi cabled word of his success to his principals in England, and also made it known to the Govenor of Newfoundland, Sir Cavendish Boyle, who apprised the British Cabinet of the result of the experiments.

Signor Marconi, though satisfied of the genuineness of the signals and that he has succeeded in his attempts to establish communication across the Atlantic without the use of wires, emphasizes the fact that the system is yet only in an embryonic stage. He says, however, that the possibility of its ultimate development is demonstrated by the success of the present experiments with incomplete and imperfect apparatus, as the signals can only be received by the most sensitively adjusted apparatus, and he is working under great difficulties owing to the conditions prevailing here. The Cornwall coast is 1,700 miles from St. John's.

In view of the success attending these trials, Signor Marconi will for the present disregard the matter of communicating with transatlantic steamers. He will return to England next week, and will conduct the experiments from Poldhu. He explains that the greater electrical power there will enable him to send more effective signals. He will undertake this work himself, leaving assistants here to erect a mast and receive the signals as he forwards them. It is not possible to send return signals from here until a powerful electric battery shall have been installed.

Premier Bond of Newfoundland offers to Signor Marconi every facility within the power of the Colonial Government for the carrying out of his plans.

Signor Marconi intends to build a large, fully equipped experimental station near St. John's, beside the Lloyd station at Cape Race. The former will have the same equipment as the Poldhu station, and will play the same part on this side of the Atlantic as Poldhu does on the other side. It is expected that the St. John's station will communicate with New York on one side, and Cornwall on the other, being midway between the two. This establishment will probably cost about $60,000, and is intended to perform the same work as a modern cable station.

Signor Marconi announced that he will remain in England until after the coronation of King Edward next Summer, and that he hopes to send the news of that event across the Atlantic by the wireless method, so as to prove the capability of the system for such purposes. He will probably in the meantime equip all vessels of the leading lines of steamers with his apparatus.

TALK WITH MARCONI'S LAWYER
Edward H. Moeran Says He is Sorry the
Inventor Has Given the Infor-
mation out So Early.

Edward H. Moeran, senior counsel in New York for the Marconi Wireless Telegraph Company, when seen at his residence, 55 Irving Place, last evening, and informed of the dispatch from St. John's to the effect that Signor Marconi had, received wireless signals from England, said:

"Marconi is one of the finest fellows that ever breathed, but I fear that he is talking too soon. If he has succeeded in getting signals from England, and I am inclined to believe that he has, it marks a new era in the history of the world. This morning I received a message from Signor Marconi and from it I was led to infer that his ambition had at last been gratified.

"I say that I am not certain that Marconi had got signals across, though, as his counsel in New York, I will say that I have every reason to believe that he has, but any information on the subject that I may have received is of the most guarded character."

Mr. Moeran was asked what was the message that he had received in the morning.

"It was a message," he answered, "that seemed to indicate that Marconi had communicated with the other side. I knew that he was trying to get in communication, but I was surprised to hear that he had done so. However, if Marconi says he has got signals across you can be pretty sure that he has done so, but I wish he had kept the news to himself a little longer."

Mr. Moeran declared that the Marconi Company was in excellent shape financially, and was not in need of funds. "We have not tried to advertise our company," he said, "and we are not in the habit of telling anything, unless we know it to be absolutely true. That's why I am sorry Marconi has given this information out just at this time."

SIGNOR MARCONI'S CAREER.
Early Discouragements Followed by
Success—The Inventor Not Yet
Twenty-eight Years Old.

Guiglielmo Marconi was born near Bologna, Italy, on April 25, 1874, and so is not yet twenty-eight years old. In 1900, when but twenty-two years old, he first flashed into prominence. Prior to this time he had demonstrated in Italy the possibility of signaling without wires by means of the Hertzian waves. His experiments in his native country came to but little so far as attending popular attention or even that of scientists. It was not until he went to England, in 1896, that he secured scientific and financial backing. Since that time both in this country and the United Kingdom he has received unstinted encouragement.

When first reaching England, however, Signor Marconi received a setback. His instruments were mistaken by Custom House authorities for bombs and infernal machines, and were accordingly broken up. This was discouraging, but Marconi, who had successfully used them the year before in telegraphing a distance of two miles on his father's estate, had unbounded confidence in his system. He had another set of instruments made, and conducted his first experiments in London, at Westbourne Park. He was introduced to Sir William Preece, then at the head of the telegraph department of the British Postal Service.

For years Sir William had been working on the problem of wireless telegraphy, but by a different system to that of Marconi. He promptly recognized the superior merit of Marconi's plan, and gave him material aid in developing the new system. Experiments were made both on an open plain, as at Salisbury, and in crowded city districts, filled with great buildings, and were in both cases successful. The penetrating power of the form of vibration used by Marconi was proved beyond a doubt before the close of 1907. In May of that year the apparatus was tried in the Bristol Channel, and signals were easily transmitted through space between Lavernock Point and the Flat Holm, and afterward between Lavernock Point and Brean Down, a distance of nine miles.

Subsequently, Signor Marconi went to Rome upon the invitation of the Italian Government, and gave a series of exhibitions of his system at the Quirinal before the King and Queen of Italy and high officials. A station was erected on land at the Arsenal, and two Italian battleships were kept in constant telegraphic communication with land up to a distance of twelve miles. The Italian Government, anxious to make amends for earlier neglect, now conferred upon Marconi the honor of knighthood.

In 1898 Marconi steadily carried on experiments in England. Regular wireless service was established between Alum Bay, Isle of Wight, and the mainland at Bournemouth, a distance of eighteen miles. Early in 1899 two more advances were made. The first message across the English Channel was sent in March of that year. In the following Summer a series of tests were made with warships.

The French naval vessel Vienne communicated with both France and England when at a distance of forty-two miles from France and twelve or fourteen from England.

Signor Marconi came to America in September, 1899, and engaged in a series of successful tests for the United States War and Navy Departments. His system had so far progressed that he was able at the time to flash messages a distance of eighty miles. Soon thereafter his system was adopted by a number of the foremost European Governments for the purpose of signaling at sea. He used the signal in reports of the races between the Columbia and Shamrock with great success.

Italy and France have adopted the system for use in their navies. On May 15 last the naval board at Washington recommended its adoption by the United States Government for use in the Navy Department. The use of wireless telegraphy to communicate with approaching ocean steamers at distances up to 100 miles from Nantucket or Sandy Hook is a recent development. Increasing distances have been conquered, but in an interview a few weeks ago Signor Marconi expressed the fear that he would never be able to successfully signal at a greater distance than 300 miles.

All important feature of the Marconi system is a wire arranged vertically near the sending apparatus and a similar one near the receiver. Without this attachment the system gives much inferior results. Wires ranging from eighty feet to 150 feet in height have been generally used in the experiments. The elevation to which the wire is to be carried bears a definite relation to the distance to be covered, although the latter is also dependent upon the "induction coil" of the telegraphic apparatus. If this be powered enough to compel a spark to leap across a gap of twelve or fifteen inches it will transmit Hertzian waves for thirty miles or more.

In discussing his system not long ago Signor Marconi said, "To Mr. Hertz, of course, belongs the distinction of having discovered the electric waves, and by his experiments he proved that electricity, in its progress through space, follows the law of optics. Many others have made experiments in the same direction as I, but so far no one has obtained such results at anything approaching the distance as I have done with these Hertzian waves.

"Fog has no effect upon the signals, nor has even the most solid substances. The waves can penetrate walls and rocks without being materially affected."

"Is it possible," was asked, "to send many messages in different directions at the same time?"

"It is," was the reply, "but care must be taken to time the transmitters and receivers to the same frequency or 'note.' I mean they must be in sympathy, and this tuning is effected by varying the capacity and self-induction of certain conductors which are joined to the transmitting and receiving instruments, so that the message intended for a particular receiver is thus rendered quite undecipherable on another."

Signor Marconi then referred to the uses of his invention in case of war. "Let us imagine," he said, "a small detachment of Europeans, say during one of these frontier wars, is stationed in a rather lonely spot. They, of course, set up telegraphic communication with wires. The enemy is not likely to allow this state of things to continue, and one night the little band is surrounded and the wires are cut down. Frequently this results in fatalities. Now, with the new system there would be nothing to give notice to the enemy that these small outlying parties were in communication with the main body, and all the time the electric waves are in use, and perhaps ten miles off they are anxiously reading, by the ticking of the receiver, messages of paramount importance. It will be possible to communicate with besieged fortresses, and, indeed, to use the system in many ways in field operations where it is impossible to lay telegraph wires. Wireless telegraphy is a possibility anywhere, and it will, I think soon be a reality in many places."

NIKOLA TESLA'S RESEARCHES.

Nikola Tesla, in discussing his theories and discoveries some years ago, hinted at the possibility of "telegraphing through the air and earth." He said:

"In pursuing this line of work I have had the good fortune to discover some facts, which are certainly novel and which, I am glad to say, have been recognized by scientific men both here and abroad. I think the probable result of these investigations will be the production of a more efficient source of light, thus supplanting the wasteful processes of light production.

"My experiments have been almost entirely confined to alternating currents of high potential. An alternating current is a current changed periodically in direction, and the word potential expresses the force and energy with which these currents are made to pass. In this particular case the force is very great. The fact that a current vibrates back and forth rapidly in this way tends to set up or create waves in the other, which is a hypothetical thing that was invented to explain the phenomena of light.

"One result of my investigation, the possibility of which has been proved by experiment, is the transmission of energy through the air. I advanced that idea some time ago, and I am happy to say it is now receiving some attention from scientific men.

"The plan I have suggested is to disturb by powerful machinery the electricity of the earth, thus setting it in vibration. Proper appliances will be constructed to take up the energy transmitted by these vibrations, transforming them into a suitable form of power to be made available for the practical wants of life.

"The outlook for wireless telegraphy is problematical. But one thing is certain, we shall be able to send very important short messages from centre to centre."

T. C. MARTIN'S VIEWS.

T. C. Martin, editor of *The Electrical World*, when seen last night, called attention to an editorial which he had written for the Nov. 30 issue of the paper, and in which he expressed the belief that Marconi's experiments would prove successful. Mr. Martin said further:

"I believed that Marconi would be successful, but did not anticipate it so soon. In a book which I published some eight years ago on Tesla's work is embodied one of his lectures, in which he gives wireless telegraphy considerable attention. He expressed his belief in the matter so clearly that he made up my mind for me. I am only sorry, therefore, that Mr. Tesla, who has given the matter so much thought and experimentation, and to whose initiative so much of the work is due, should not also have been able to accomplish this wonderful feat. I have talked with Prof. Fessenden, who is now engaged on the subject for the United States Government, and with Dr. Kennelly, at one time expert for Mr. Edison, and they agreed as to the feasibility and near possibility of the achievement.

"Although Mr. Marconi is to be heartily congratulated on his magnificent results, the idea is not to be jumped at that cables are any less useful than heretofore. So far as is known, there is no means of preventing successfully the interference of wireless signals, and until they become automatically selective it would seem that only one station on each side of New York Bay, would engage in the business. Even during the recent yacht races the wireless telegraph signals were in utter confusion until peace was patched up enabling each party in rivalry to send messages for a few minutes at a time. Even should this difficulty be overcome, as it doubtless will be, I find it hard to believe that it will be so entirely removed as to involve the complete supercession of cables."

John Bottomley, who is a nephew of Lork Kelvin and an attorney of the Marconi Company here, said:

"I am delighted at the news and very much surprised. It establishes a new scientific fact—that the electric current follows the curvature of the earth."

TO COMPETE WITH CABLE LINES.

H. Cuthbert Hali, the English manager of the Marconi Company, when seen at the Waldorf-Astoria late last night, said that he had received a message from Signor Marconi in the morning announcing his success in obtaining signals from England.

"Do you think that if wireless messages can be sent across the ocean it will affect the business of the cable companies?" was asked.

"Yes," was the reply. "I think that on account of our comparatively inexpensive methods we can compete successfully with them."

"Do you intend to take immediate steps in that direction?"

"Yes. Plans were formulated some time ago in anticipation of the successful outcome of Signor Marconi's experiments, but I do not care to make them public just now."

2

Thorn Mayes

HISTORY OF THE
AMERICAN MARCONI COMPANY

THE AMERICAN MARCONI Wireless Telegraph Company was the first wireless company to be formed in the United States. When it was incorporated in 1899, Marconi had received signals a distance of 30 miles. When Radio Corporation of America took over American Marconi just 20 years later, wireless was a worldwide communications media. Of the many wireless companies formed over this period, only the American Marconi lived for the entire time and for the last seven years had a virtual monopoly of wireless communications in this country.

In July 1897 Marconi formed the Wireless Telegraph and Signaling Company in England for the purpose of building and installing wireless on lightships and in lighthouses along the English coast for by then he had demonstrated that he could work over a distance of 15 miles which was sufficient for this duty.

In the fall of 1899, he brought equipment to New York to report the American Cup yacht races. By this time he felt so sure that he could span the Atlantic, with a more powerful transmitter, that he formed the American Marconi Wireless Telegraph Company under

The Old Timer's Bulletin, Vol. 13, No. 1 (June 1972), pp. 11–18.

the laws of New Jersey, with an authorized stock of two million shares, five dollar par value. 600,000 shares went to Marconi with 350,000 held by the English company. The company was formed for the purpose of using Marconi patents in the United States.

The first equipments installed by the American Marconi Company were made in mid-1901 on the Nantucket Light Ship and a shore station at Siasconset on the east coast on Nantucket Island. The sets consisted of battery powered 10-inch spark coils and coherer receivers. First messages were exchanged between these stations, which were 40 miles apart, August 12, 1901. Siasconset first gained fame when it reported the collision of the ships Republic and Florida in dense fog off Nantucket Island, January 23, 1909 with Jack Binns the operator on the Republic.

During 1902, duplicate antenna systems were built at South Wellfleet, Poldhu and Glace Bay, Canada. They were inverted cones of 200 wires each, supported by four lattice towers 215 feet high. Tests were carried on between these three stations for several years.

While in New York in 1899, Marconi met a prominent lawyer, John Bottomly who was interested in wireless. When the company was reorganized in 1902, Bottomly became General Manager, Secretary and Treasurer. He held the General's position until it was taken over by E. J. Nally in 1913 and continued as Secretary-Treasurer thru 1918. Bottomly's broad experience and good judgment were responsible for carrying the company thru the trying times of 1913. The Annual Report for 1910 states that the company had lost money each year.

David Sarnoff was hired as office boy in September 1906. Later he stated that when he arrived, the company was operating four land stations and had their equipments on four ships with a total of less than 25 employees.

American Marconi used British designed gear until 1910 when they started to originate their own parts arrangements but as they had no manufacturing facilities, most of the parts came from England.

As there had been flagrant infringements of the Marconi wireless patents, the Marconi Company in 1910 initiated several suits. The decision reached in the famous case, Marconi Wireless Telegraph Company vs. British Radio Telephone and Telegraph Company, handed down in December 1910 by Lord Justice Parker, was used as the basis for settling many other world wide similar court actions.

The Marconi Company claimed the defendant's use of autotransformers for connecting to the aerial and ground circuit was an infringement of their patent number 7,777. Lord Justice Parker after hearing a number of technical witnesses, stated that he felt the Marconi patent was being infringed.

A suit had been filed against the United Wireless Company and the English decision was applied in this case. The following notice from the April, 1912 issue of *Modern Electrics* gives the result:

> As a result of a merger which has been brought about between the Marconi Wireless Telegraph Company and the United Wireless Telegraph Company, when the suit of the former company against the latter company for alleged infringement of patent rights came up in the United States District Court on March 25th,1912, the United Wireless Company entered no defense and consented to the granting of a decree in favor of the Marconi Company.
>
> As a further result of the merger, all stations and contracts of the United Wireless Company will be taken over by Marconi. This involves about 500 ship and land stations in the United States.

From 1912 to 1919, the company developed a total of 21 receivers, number 101 to 121, but only the main production sets will be covered here.

The first of these improved receivers, the 101, was built in 1913 for use in major land stations equipped with 5 KW transmitters. It covered the range of 200–7500 meters. The design was copied from the United E turner but with the loose coupler behind the panel with all controls coming to the panel front. Approximately 25 sets were produced.

WAR DECLARED APRIL 6, 1917

All commercial and amateur wireless stations were closed or came under Navy control on April 7. The Navy took over 53 coastal stations from American Marconi and immediately closed 28. Of their 540 ship sets, 370 were on ocean going vessels so were taken by the Navy. Approximately 170 installations on small coastwise vessels and tugs were left with the Marconi Company.

ARMISTICE SIGNED NOVEMBER 11, 1918

Of the 370 ships taken over by the Navy in April 1917, 40 had been sunk by November 1918.

Special Order number 73 of December 3, 1918 addressed to all officers in charge of American Marconi Telegraphs, stated:

> The American Marconi Wireless Telegraph Company has sold to the United States Navy Department all of its coastal stations as listed below—45 in number. This company has also sold to the United States Navy Department its wireless apparatus on ship stations as listed—a total of 330. The sale of the above named ship and coastal stations is effective November 30, 1918. After this date, the United States Navy Department will own and operate the stations above mentioned and will furnish and employ the necessary person-

nel. Signed David Sarnoff, Commercial Manager American Marconi Company.

The company was paid $789,500 for the above stations.

The American Marconi Company was left with its three high power stations Bolinas, Marion and New Brunswick, all being operated by the Navy, plus equipments on 170 small ships and its plant at Aldene, New Jersey.

Wireless Age for February, 1919 carries the following item:

> The War Trade Board has lifted the ban on the use of radio by commercial vessels in the Pacific and Atlantic Oceans west of the 40th meridian. This restores the use of radio to conditions existing before the war.

The President on July 11, 1919 approved the return of radio stations to their former owners effective March 1, 1920. Most of the land stations were never returned as many were no longer needed and by that time the commercial companies had built new modern stations. Most of the shipboard sets had been converted so the Navy scrapped the majority of the stations that were taken over at the start of the war.

Wireless Age of November, 1919 carried an article on the proposed formation of R.C.A. which included a memo to the American Marconi stockholders from John W. Griggs president since 1905. This memo in part follows. It explains company objectives and why it should be merged into R.C.A.

> The principal aim and purpose of the Marconi Wireless Telegraph Company of American during all the period of its existence has been the establishment and maintenance of transoceanic communication. Although the company has done no inconsiderable business in minor branches of the Wireless art, such as the equipping of vessels, the operation of ship to shore traffic, the collection of royalties, and the manufacture of wireless apparatus, yet these by the management have always been considered as incidental to the greater and more profitable business of long distance communication.
>
> We have found that there exists on the part of the officials of our government a very strong and irrevocable objection to your company because of the stock interest held by the British Company. Consequently your company has found itself greatly embarrassed in carrying out plans for an extensive transoceanic traffic, and unless the British Marconi interest in your company is eliminated, your President and Board of Directors believe it will not be possible to proceed with success on the resumption of its preparations for a world wide service when its stations shall be returned to it, as they will be in the near future.
>
> In a word, we are satisfied and convinced that in order to retain

for your company the proper support and good will of our own government it is necessary that all participation in its stock, as well as in its operations on the part of any foreign wireless company must be eliminated.

Having these considerations in mind, your officers have lately undertaken to remove the objections of the government and to do away with the threatened embarrassment of which we have spoken.

Certain long distance and other radio devices and systems have been developed by General Electric Company. Some of these devices and systems promise to be of great value in transoceanic radio communication.

A corporation has been formed called the Radio Corporation of America which has entered into an agreement with General Electric concerning present and future patent rights, the manufacture of patented apparatus and devices exclusively by General Electric for R.C.A. and the exclusive right of R.C.A. to sell patented radio apparatus of General Electric.

General Electric has appropriated two and a half million dollars, a portion of which is to be used by G.E. under an agreement satisfactory to your Directors in the purchasing of the shares of stock in your company now owned and held by Marconi Wireless Telegraph Company of Great Britain.

Each stockholder of Marconi Wireless Telegraph Company of America will have the privilege of exchanging his stock in the company for an equal amount par for par, of the preferred stock of R.C.A. and in addition shares of common stock of the new company equal in number, to the shares held in the present company.

A shareholders meeting of the American Marconi Company was held November 20, 1919 at which time the proposed agreements were passed and a five percent dividend was declared.

Besides its operating organization, Aldene plant, patents, etc. American Marconi transferred to R.C.A. ownership of its three high power land stations and installations on approximately 350 ships.

Wireless Age of May 1920 carried this note:

Stockholders of the American Marconi met April 6th and voted to dissolve the company. This concludes the plan whereby the assets of American Marconi Wireless Telegraph Company are to be taken over by R.C.A.

We are in great haste to construct a magnetic telegraph from Maine to Texas; but Maine and Texas, it may be, have nothing important to communicate.   --Henry David Thoreau, *Walden*.*

---

*Quotes at end of articles edited to fit available space.

3

Elliot N. Sivowitch

A TECHNOLOGICAL SURVEY OF BROADCASTING'S PREHISTORY, 1876–1920

IN THE PERIOD prior to 1876, the telegraph, in its various forms, was the principal rapid news conveyor throughout the world. The transmission of information in this manner can be construed as "broadcasting" only if one interprets the usual definition ("the dissemination of radio communications intended to be received by the public, directly or by the intermediary of relay stations") in the sense of "wide dissemination of information, not necessarily at the same point in time." For the purposes of this paper, we will use a very broad definition and will include experiments that might more properly be related to point-to-point communication than to current definitions of broadcasting.

WIRED BROADCASTING

The telephone's introduction in 1876 forced a revolution in communication capability with wide ranging social and economic implications. Not only could more words per minute be transmitted, in both directions, but anybody could use the telephone without special training in code. This magic of voice transmission over wire led 19th century innovators to serious thoughts concerning the transmission of news and entertainment simultaneously and instantaneously to multiple receiving points. Although broadcasting by wire was hampered by equipment limitations with regard to fidelity and amplification, the idea was sufficiently intriguing to be explored by engineers both in this country and in Europe. Commercial development, however, was considerably greater abroad, where sound "rediffusion" (analogous in many ways to CATV) still exists in many places.

The beginnings of wired broadcasting can be traced to a "pre-telephone" transition period after 1860, when a number of experimenters were developing methods for transmitting musical tones over telegraph wire lines. These activities may have culminated in the work of Elisha Gray, who conducted several tests of "electroharmonic" broadcasting to audiences in 1874 and 1875.[1] Following a successful demonstration by Alexander Graham Bell of the speaking telephone at the 1876 Philadelphia Centennial Exposition, the possi-

Journal of Broadcasting, Vol. XV, No. 1 (Winter 1970–71), pp. 1–20.

bilities of using it as a broadcast instrument were apparent. In the Fall of 1876, experimental "concerts" were transmitted over wire line by Bell from Paris to Brantford, Ontario, utilizing a "triple mouthpiece" telephone transmitter to accommodate several soloists. From 1876 through 1880 a variety of transmissions were conducted, both in this country and in Europe. The carbon transmitter, co-invented during this period by Edison, David Hughes and Emile Berliner, enormously increased the power output of the telephone. In 1881, Clement Ader, in France, conducted intensive investiga-tions of wired stereophonic broadcasting at the Paris Electrical Ex-position, and by 1895 various European Opera Houses were equipped with either stereo or monophonic telephone systems. In 1893 a commercial broadcasting system called the Telefon-Hir-mondo (Telephonic Newseller) began operation in Budapest, Hungary, and shortly afterward the Electrophone Company started service in London. The Budapest operation was a highly sophis-ticated system that provided regular news and music programming up to 12 hours per day.[2] Although the European activities were rea-sonably successful, the United States did not see similar develop-ments until the Cahill Telharmonium broadcasts more than a decade later.[3] However, there were frequent occasions here of subscribers being "wired up" for specific church service broadcasts or special events. Of more than usual significance was the broadcasting of Con-gressional and local election returns by the Chicago Telephone Company on Nov. 6, 1894. It was estimated that more than 15,000 persons were reached by this novel transmission method.[4]

LOOMIS-WARD AERIAL CONDUCTION TELEGRAPH

19th century thoughts on broadcasting were not limited to land line experimentation. On April 30, 1872, William Henry Ward of Auburn, New York, received a patent for a telegraphic tower (No. 126356) that might be said to embody the earliest conception of transmitting signals by wireless from a single antenna to a multiplic-ity of receiving aerials. In the wording of the patent:

Different towers may be erected on the different continents, and if they are all what is technically called hooked on—that is to say, connected to the earth—a signal given at one tower will be repeated at all the towers, they being connected with each other by the aerial current.

No mention of the telephone, of course, at this early date. How-ever, a word of caution should be mentioned here. The "wireless" system described is that of *conduction transmission*, a technique de-veloped by telegraph engineers after 1838 when it was discovered that two wires were not necessary to complete a circuit. One could be eliminated and a return made through the ground. All sorts of intriguing possibilities were then thought of, including the idea of communicating across bodies of water. The particular technique which Ward envisioned involved the elimination of both wires, the use of the ground and bodies of water as a substitute for one wire, and the "conducting atmosphere" in place of the other wire. The inspiration for communicating through the atmosphere in this manner appears to have developed from observations of the effect of the aurora borealis on telegraph lines. Auroral storms created all sorts of havoc on domestic telegraph circuits including the freak ability to send messages over wire line with induced currents, entirely eliminating the need for batteries. If such electricity in the upper atmosphere could be harnessed, what a tremendous boon for global communications! We have no evidence, however, that Ward actually built a tower (which, by the way, looks in the patent application drawing very much like the modern space-satellite communications antenna in Andover, Maine—although, of course, operating on entirely different principles) and conducted experiments. Ward was principally an independent inventor in mechanical technology, with a concentration in railway car coupling devices. However, during the 1850s and 60s he developed a rather sophisticated semaphore signalling system for maritime communication, and published a book describing his coded symbols in some detail.[5] Sometime during this period he appears to have made the acquaintance of Mahlon Loomis and possibly was influenced by the latter's thoughts on conduction telegraphy. Loomis (1826–1886), a Washington, D.C. dentist, was the principal 19th century exponent of aerial conduction communication. Loomis' thoughts on wireless transmission date back to the great auroral storm of 1859 which was particularly vexing to telegraph operators in the Northeast United States.[6] Loomis seems to have conducted several tests in the Blue Ridge and Catoctin mountain ranges of Virginia and Maryland in the 1866–72 period but a detailed account of the equipment used and persons present is lacking. However, he obtained considerable support in Congress and probably would have received an appropriation had not the financial panic of 1873 struck.[7] The most important question, of course, from the engineering point of view, is whether the Loomis-Ward system could have worked in terms of the the design theory assigned to it. The answer is "no," with the qualification that under certain unusual conditions in the ionosphere, some deflection of the receiving galvanometer might be noticed. What is more likely is that Loomis radiated some electromagnetic energy from discharges of atmospheric electricity at the transmission end. Again, firm evidence is not at hand. Loomis was granted a patent for his system July 30, 1872.[8]

Although the aerial conduction scheme passed into obscurity, systems involving conduction through the ground appeared over the next few decades and have been revived in modern times. These, however, were viable systems without any question, though only over limited distances. So far as our broadcasting story is concerned, however, ground conduction becomes intertwined with certain other related phenomena in the developing telephone technology.

We mentioned earlier the experimental telephone "concerts" promoted soon after the instrument was introduced. In 1877, a telephone "broadcast" was made from New York City to Sarasota Springs, New York, using a newly developed Edison transmitter. The musical programming was heard accidentally in both Providence and Boston due to electrical leakages between adjacent sets of wires on trunk lines north of New York City. Although conduction leakage through the ground was the principal cause, *induction* through the air also was involved. Within both phenomena lay mechanisms for a new mode of communication: suppose one were to purposely cause induction of energy with large loops of wire, or conduction with stakes buried in the ground—would not a useful communication device result? This line of development appealed to several late 19th century personalities, though considerable thought toward wireless techniques of this general type was in evidence even prior to 1850.[9] The crucial point to remember, however, is that the scientific base for induction-conduction communication was a natural outgrowth of conventional telegraph and telephone technology, and was not directly related to the Hertz-Marconi approach to wireless. The latter method employed *radiated* waves of high frequency which had the capability some distance. However, there are certain interrelationships between these various systems which we will describe in the following critical review of the work of one early "wireless broadcaster."

NATHAN STUBBLEFIELD

Nathan B. Stubblefield (1860–1928), of Murray, Kentucky, was a self-taught tinkerer-experimenter. He is more in the tradition of Daniel Drawbaugh than Edison or any of the university savants.[10] However, he had a persistent vision of the success of his method of communication and influenced several businessmen to finance commercial exploitation. His first claim to fame, however, came via local "acoustic telephone" hookups in Murray circa 1890.[11] Following investigations into induction and conduction telephony, he developed several types of apparatus and performed some public demonstrations prior to 1900. In March 1902 he succeeded in transmitting speech from a boat in the Potomac River to shore-based receivers.

Inspired by this operation he boasted of the practicability of sending simultaneous messages from a "central distributing station" and of conveying the "general transmission of news." [12] However, commercial thoughts were directed toward point-to-point communication. The Wireless Telephone Company of America was formed and an active stock promotion plan put into operation. Although the stock prospectus was quick to point out the virtues of a cheap wireless system versus the expensive Bell Telephone lines, the fact of the matter was that induction/conduction telephony was too marginal in distance capability to offer any serious competition to Bell. The Gordon Telephone Company of Charleston, South Carolina, did purchase some equipment to communicate with off-shore islands, but this was about the extent of the operation's success.[13] Stubblefield became disillusioned with the stock promotion schemes of his financiers and withdrew to seclusion in his workshop. He did receive identical United States and Canadian patents in 1903 for the induction system [14] and an examination of the basic principle may prove useful.

A battery and telephone were to be connected in series with a very large coil of wire (i.e., transmitting "antenna"). Upon speaking or singing into the microphone, audio frequency currents would flow in the loop, and an alternating current induction field would form in the vicinity of the "antenna." A pickup-loop mounted atop a moving vehicle would act as the receiving aerial and feed a simple telephone receiver. Now here is the critical point: most of the energy in the induction field is contained in the vicinity of the transmitting loop. The field, however, is varying at an audio-frequency, so far as this is concerned it obeys the same law as any varying field in space, regardless of frequency. Why isn't this radio? It turns out that we can determine from electromagnetic theory that there are three components of a varying electromagnetic field in space, one whose electric field intensity varies inversely as the cube of the distance, $1/R^3$ (static field), one inversely as the square of the distance, $1/R^2$ (induction field), and one inversely as the distance, $1/R$ (radiation field). Some energy is *radiated* away from the antenna at any frequency, but at *low frequencies* (i.e., voice and music) most of the energy is confined to the vicinity of the wire.[15] The induction field is the principal component of the Stubblefield system, and this limited the transmission range of the system to something less than three miles. (This is not to be confused with the case where we superimpose voice or music on a higher radio frequency and make full use of radiation capability, as in modern broadcasting.) [16]

The mathematical processes and field theory outlined above were known in 1908, but at this stage of the game, the fine points of difference between the various wireless systems were not appreciated; after Marconi's work became known in this country many were quick to point out that Stubblefield had transmitted voice (not just Morse Code) via "wireless" as early as 1892

EDISON, DOLBEAR, THOMSON AND STONE

More than a decade before Stubblefield's first experiments, there was a line of development in which double-winding induction coils similar to the types employed in early telephone work and in physics laboratories were utilized. In some circuit configurations an induction field would predominate, and in others radiation capability existed, but the state of the art was such that most electricians and physicists failed to recognize the capability of the induction coil in the production of high frequency waves. Several persons were on the fringe of exciting discoveries but "missed the boat" by narrow margins. Included in this group were Thomas Edison and Elihu Thomson, who conducted a variety of investigations in the 1870s in which electrical sparks produced by a generator could be detected at a distance.[17] Only Heinrich Hertz, in Germany, really understood what was going on. His brilliant experimental proof of Scottish physicist James Clerk-Maxwell's theoretical predictions took place in 1888. However, the most significant work from the wireless telephone standpoint was performed by Amos Emerson Dolbear, Professor of Physics at Tufts College.[18] Dolbear, in the early 1880s, conducted a number of experiments with induction coils, carbon and condenser telephone transmitters, and batteries in a wireless set-up with grounded wires at both ends of a communications link. The system was fully described in the *Scientific American* of Dec. 11, 1886 and a patent was awarded (No. 350299). Transmission range (mostly induction field) was limited to something less than one mile. Following the development of true radiation wireless telegraphy more than a decade later, it was realized that Dolbear's circuit configuration created a borderline situation in which he probably radiated electromagnetic energy to greater distances but lacked a suitable detector. The Dolbear patent was later used by the DeForest radio interests in an attempt to prove priority over Marconi.[19]

By the mid-1890s a variety of experimentation in induction telegraphy and telephony was in evidence. However, the concept of modulating a high frequency carrier wave with voice perhaps can be ascribed to John Stone. Stone who, in 1892, utilized both induction coils and alternating current generators in experiments designed by AT&T to communicate by telephone with ships at sea. Although the inspiration for this series of investigations came from the work of Hertz and Tesla, and preceded Marconi by several years, Stone fell short of "inventing" radio partly by reason of the aforementioned confusion of induction with radiation, and partly by lack of appreciation of the need for such appliances as antennas and modulation detectors.[20]

REGINALD FESSENDEN

The credit for a major breakthrough in super-imposing voice or music information on a high frequency "carrier" goes to Reginald A. Fessenden (1866–1932) whose persistence along these experimental lines culminated in what many regard as the first broadcast using a reliable continuous wave generator (the high frequency alternator) from Brant Rock, Massachusetts, on Christmas Eve, 1906.

The high frequency alternator essentially was a type of alternating current generator that produced "continuous waves" in the radio frequency range. The term "high frequency" is a misnomer by modern standards, since the device operated under 100 kHz. Although developed by Elihu Thomson and Nikola Tesla in the late 1880s, Fessenden probably was the first to apply it to radio communication.

Fessenden became interested in wireless during the embryo period of the 1890s, but realized very soon that conventional spark oscillators used for radiotelegraphy created too high a distortion level to make the radio-telephone practical. However, he conducted some tests along these lines in December, 1900, at Rock Point, Md. (Cobb Island, 50 miles south of Washington, D.C.) where distances up to one mile were bridged.[21] He seems not to have had a really adequate detector on the receiving end, but the system was patented in 1902 (No. 706747) and constitutes the earliest registered invention in the United States for a ratiotelephone system employing Hertzian waves. Some commercial radiotelephone sets using the spark system were marketed by Fessenden.

At the turn of the century, another development occurred which proved crucial for the growth of experimental broadcasting. This was the application of the high frequency arc to wireless. The oscillating arc was basically a circuit arrangement that included two carbon electrodes activated by high voltage and shunted by suitable inductance and capacitance. Investigated by Elihu Thomson in 1889, it was not until further work after 1900 by William Duddell in England and Valdemar Poulsen in Denmark that frequencies high enough for radio transmission could be realized. Although the arc did produce "continuous waves" and was a favorite of other experimenters, Fessenden felt uncomfortable with it because of its high distortion level and instability.[22] As a result, he asked Charles Steinmetz of the General Electric Company to construct a 10,000 cycle alternator for him that would have some capability for modulation with voice or music information. Tests with this machine were made at the Washington, D.C. laboratory of the newly formed National Electric Signalling Company in 1905. Results were encouraging enough to construct a higher frequency machine for the use at NESCO's Brant Rock, Massachusetts, installation. The engineering team at Schenectady was headed by E. F. W. Alexanderson, a talented young Swedish electrical engineer. An alternator was delivered to Fessenden in 1906, and after many technical difficulties made ready for its debut. On Nov. 21, 1906, a variety of scientific dignitaries, including Greenleaf W. Pickard and Elihu Thomson, witnessed tests in which speech was successfully transmitted 11 miles between Brant Rock and Plymouth, Mass.[23] A phonograph was on hand and was used to transmit music over the airwaves. On Christmas Eve, 1906, Fessenden and his group at Brant Rock presented a program of varied content for the holiday occasion; this was advertised to ship operators of the United Fruit Co. three days in advance. A similar schedule was presented on New Year's Eve. Ship reports of reception came from points as far away as Norfolk and the West Indies. The programming was described by Fessenden:

> First a short speech by me saying what we were going to do, then some phonograph music . . . the music on the phonograph being Handel's "Largo." Then came a violin solo by me, being a composition by Gounod called "O Holy Night," and ending up with the words "Adore and be still" which I sang one verse of, in addition to playing the violin, though the singing, of course, was not very good. Then came the Bible text, "Glory to God in the highest and on earth peace to men of good will," and we finally wound up by wishing them a Merry Christmas and then saying that we proposed to broadcast again New Year's Eve.
>
> The Broadcast on New Year's Eve was the same as before, except that the music was changed and I got someone else to sing. I had not picked myself to do the singing, but on Christmas Eve I could not get any of the others to either talk, sing or play and consequently had to do it all myself. On New Year's Eve one man—I think it was Stein—agreed to sing and did sing, but none of the others either sang or talked.[24]

NESCO continued experimental work on the radiotelephone in July, 1907, and obtained distances up to 180 miles. The following excerpt from the log of wireless enthusiast Francis Hart shows the description of the transmission as received in the New York harbor area on Feb. 11, 1908, at 1:16 p.m.:

> Wireless phone at Jamaica and other must be at Brant Rock, Mass. Phone very clear except for a rasping noise that mingles with the voice . . . I managed to get the following and could probably have obtained more except for "9" and etc.
> "How's that now" "open up a little more"
> "You came in louder than that yesterday"
> Could hear music as clear as voice from weaker station but

couldn't make out words from other station although they came in fair.[25]

Although NESCO's wireless telephone activities continued for a time, the company ran into economic and administrative difficulties. The Bell System was quite impressed with Fessenden's wireless telephone, but AT&T suffered a major reorganization following the financial panic of 1907 and interest cooled. Fessenden and his financial backers also were on poor terms for several years, and the inventor was forced to leave the company in 1911. The following year NESCO went into receivership, though the organization continued in research and development activities until its purchase by Westinghouse in 1921. The alternator, for all its wizardry in wireless telephony, was too cumbersome a machine and the engineering fraternity preferred to endure the higher distortion level in the more portable Poulsen arc. The alternator's significance in radiotelegraphy would overshadow other use, as would its political effect in the battle over control of the early radio industry in the period during World War I and thereafter.

DeForest and the Arc Radiotelephone

Of all the members of the early wireless engineering fraternity, perhaps Lee DeForest, more than any other, had some vision of the broadcasting potential of the wireless telephone. Although possessing a Ph.D. in physics from the Sheffield School at Yale (1896), DeForest basically was an experimental electrician in the tradition of Edison rather than a mathematician such as Maxwell or Kelvin. He foresaw, at an early date, the application of the high frequency arc to modulated radio frequency transmission. In December, 1906, he succeeded in transmitting voice across his laboratory room in the Parker Building (19th Street and 4th Avenue, Manhattan) to a receiver employing a vacuum tube detector.[26] A number of experimental broadcasts were made early in 1907, and were picked up by ship operators in New York harbor.

In the summer of 1907 DeForest and his assistant, Frank Butler, went to Put-in-Bay on Lake Erie to report the Interlakes Association regatta from a radiotelephone installation aboard the *Thelma*. The Navy Department watched these activities closely and became aware of the potential of voice transmission as a tactical communication device. It should be noted, incidentally, that to promote this new invention the DeForest Radio Telephone Company was organized earlier in the year and a subsidiary, the Radio Telephone Company, was formed for the purpose of developing DeForest's patents. In September, the Navy ordered two complete transmitting and receiving units for installation aboard the *U.S.S. Connecticut* and *U.S.S. Virginia*.

Trials were held in Cape Cod Bay, and were so successful that the Navy ordered another two dozen sets for installation aboard Admiral Evans' "Great White Fleet," which was scheduled to depart for an around-the-world cruise on December 16. DeForest and his co-workers slaved night and day to get the equipment ready. Due to hasty procedures and other technical problems, some of the transmitters were inoperable, but several vessels, including the U.S.S. *Ohio*, continued to experiment for the duration of the voyage.[27] By January, 1908, the arc aboard the Ohio was made sufficiently stable to operate for several hours at a time. Radio-telephone broadcasts were made to the assembled U.S. and Brazilian fleets and later to British and Chilean vessels as the expedition moved along the South American coastline. In April, while the fleet anchored at Long Beach, Calif., the radio crew aboard the Ohio procured a phonograph and proceeded to entertain local radio operators. The inspiration for these broadcasting activities may have come from some of DeForest's tests at the Brooklyn Navy Yard prior to the sailing of the Connecticut and the Virginia for New England waters. It was here that contralto Madame von Boos Farrar sang "I Love You Truly" and "Just-a-Wearyin' for You" to the radio operators in the port. On April 23, 1908 the DeForest Company gave a banquet in Los Angeles for the Fleet wireless telephone crew. Roscoe Kent, one of DeForest's assistants, casually mentioned to the assembled group that this was the "first meeting of radio broadcasters."

Admiral Evans' fleet continued its cruise to the Orient where additional radiotelephone programs were "beamed" to the Japanese Fleet at Yokohama harbor, and upon continuation of the journey eastward similar activities were conducted near ports in Ceylon, Arabia, Egypt, Greece, Turkey, and Gibraltar. Broadcasts also were made to several ocean-going liners. Upon return to the Brooklyn Navy Yard in March, 1909, the equipment was placed in storage. The Navy was not again equipped for wireless telephony until 1917.

A corollary episode was taking place about this time in New York City that has some bearing on our story. Dr. Thaddeus Cahill, a scientist from Holyoke, Mass., demonstrated a sophisticated musical tone system before a meeting of the New York Electrical Society in September, 1906. The new device was called a "Dynamophone" or "Telharmonium," and consisted of a bank of alternating current generators controlled to give musical tones of varying combinations. The Cahill Telharmonium Company occupied a large building at 39th Street and Broadway. The musical transmissions were played on an organ-type console and fed from the generating plant to distribution lines leading to various halls and restaurants where receiving telephonic speakers were installed. The system can well be termed the first serious venture into a background music system in this country.

However, owing to the Bell Telephone Company's reluctance to give permission for use of conventional telephone lines (fearing damage to equipment), plans to extend the service to individual subscribers were seriously hampered. The Cahill Company was intrigued by DeForest's wireless telephone and gave permission for a trial broadcast of Telharmonium music over the air waves.[28] The programs took place in February and March of 1907 but apparently were not extended further. One can only conjecture that the audio quality left much to be desired. DeForest at this time was using Poulsen's version of the arc, but attempting to improve performance by substituting steam for hydrogen.

While Admiral Evans' "Great White Fleet" was on its round-the-world trip, DeForest traveled to Europe and conducted several spectacular wireless telephone demonstrations from the Eiffel Tower, Paris, in Spezia, Italy and in Portsmouth harbor, England. Upon return to the United States, he occupied himself with several matters relating to his equipment manufacturing activities, though the radiotelephone was still operated almost daily. He returned to an intense interest in musical broadcasting during the winter of 1909. Then he made the acquaintance of Andreas Dippel, assistant director of the Metropolitan Opera House and, outlining the past experiences with the Telharmonium and phonograph, persuaded the management to allow experimental broadcast of grand opera. The principal event occurred January 13, 1910, when *Cavalleria Rusticana* and *I Pagliacci* were transmitted, with several famous soloists including Ricardo Martin and Enrico Caruso. This activity actually was conducted in conjunction with the National Dictograph Company, whose president Kelley M. Turner had designed a new "acousticon" pick-up microphone for stage use. The tests were arranged both to determine the feasibility of broadcasting opera to telephone subscribers over wire line, and to check out the similar capability of wireless. Although the broadcasts were reasonably successful, and repeated again later with staff from the Manhattan Opera Company, one can safely conclude that limitations in audio fidelity and instability problems with the arc made commercial exploitation premature. The Radio Telephone Company became the victim of early stock promotion schemes and went bankrupt in 1911. DeForest then transferred his activities to the West Coast and went to work for the Federal Telegraph Company.

In 1915, the American Telephone and Telegraph Company conducted significant tests in radiotelephony at the site of Navy station NAA, Arlington, Va. Using banks of vacuum tubes in oscillator and modulator circuits, signals were transmitted across the Atlantic and were heard as far away as Honolulu.[29] Possibly with this event as the stimulus, DeForest picked up his broadcasting activities again, this time from High Bridge in the Bronx. A new company backed the venture, the DeForest Radio Telephone and Telegraph Company, bolstered with 5 years of advance in technology and a firmer patent position. Of particular interest was the manufacture of "oscillion" transmitting tubes, now being produced with power ratings up to 125 watts. DeForest installed a transmitter at the Columbia Gramophone Building on 38th St. and began daily broadcasts of phonograph music with the Columbia company as the sponsor. The transmitting site was later moved back to the High Bridge tower. On election night, November 7, 1916, DeForest broadcast the Hughes-Wilson election returns for some six hours—erroneously proclaiming at 11 p.m. (as did several newspapers) that the winner was Charles Evans Hughes.[30]

The U.S. entry into World War I shut down all non-Government radio operations in 1917, but two years later DeForest set up operations again at the High Bridge location with call letters 2XG.[31] Phonograph records this time were supplied by the Brunswick-Balke-Collender Company, which acted as sponsor. Richard Klein, of the DeForest sales organization, was the program director. In December, 1919, concert singer Vaughn de Leath appeared as soloist and made several broadcasts. The station later moved its facilities to the World Tower Building at 46th and Broadway to utilize better antenna facilities, but DeForest neglected to get a Government permit for the new location and the operation was ordered closed by the district federal radio inspector. This, together with other vexing legal troubles, prompted the inventor to once again head West. In San Francisco, the High Bridge transmitter was re-installed in the California Theater Building and daily broadcasts were made with Herman Heller's orchestral group. From this point on the story of the DeForest broadcasting activities becomes involved with the attempt of a group called the Radio News and Music Company to interest newspaper owners in the purchase of DeForest radiotelephone transmitters. The Detroit *Daily News* did so, and herein lies the start of the story of WWJ, whose predecessor 8MK began operation August 20, 1920.

WEST COAST RADIOTELEPHONY

The critical role of the high frequency arc and alternator in the growth of radiotelephony has been stressed. These devices were "continuous wave" generators, and were only reliable tools for voice modulation techniques prior to development of the vacuum tube oscillator. However, Marconi-type "damped wave" transmitters didn't necessarily preclude telephony if distortion caused by the spark irregularity and low spark frequency could be minimized. In practice this was difficult to do, though Fessenden, as we have indicated, made some efforts in this direction.

In 1902, an amateur operator from San Francisco, Francis Mc-Carty, began to experiment in spark telephony with a view toward development of a commercial system. The Henshaw brothers, influential bankers of Oakland, California, were persuaded to invest some capital in the new venture. However, McCarty was fatally injured in a motorcycle accident in 1906, and the project was temporarily interrupted pending the search for new engineering advice and leadership. In 1908, Cyril Elwell, an electrical engineering student at Stanford, was persuaded to join the McCarty Wireless Telephone Co. as a consultant.[32] He proceeded to set up experimental broadcasting with a phonograph supplying the program content. Elwell realized that the McCarty system worked best when the transmitter spark gap was so narrow that the system operated as a quasi-arc, providing nearly continuous waves. Experiments were continued from the Company's Palo Alto laboratory until early 1909. At that time, Elwell advised the management that it would be useless to play around further with spark gaps, and that the Poulsen arc held the real future for wireless engineering. Elwell discovered that the U.S. patent rights for Poulsen's invention had not yet been granted. An inquiry to the Danish inventor revealed that something in the neighborhood of one-quarter million dollars was considered the proper "ball-park" figure. The Henshaw brothers were, however, disinterested in putting further investment capital into such new and uncertain ventures, and sold the laboratory to Elwell for a low figure. The account of how a young Stanford graduate then proceeded to buy the U.S. rights to a significant invention is a fabulous story that we have insufficient space to treat here; suffice it to say that Elwell formed the Poulsen Wireless Telegraph and Telephone Co. with support from the Stanford faculty and a certain amount of good fortune perhaps possible only in the first decade of the 20th century. A considerable amount of experimental broadcasting and point-to-point radio telephony with stations at Stockton and Sacramento formed the principle wireless telephone "menu" of the day, with much of this work done for stock selling and promotion purposes. However, as with the alternator, the Poulsen arc's principle use would come with radio telegraphy, and Elwell's successor company, the Federal Telegraph Co., catered primarily to customers desiring high-powered telegraphic communication.

In the meantime, however, the "fall-out" from the arc technology spread to other experimenters. San Jose's Charles Herrold was the principal West Coast exponent of wireless entertainment in the 1920 era. In Seattle, Washington, William Dubilier performed a variety of "broadcasts" in 1911–1912 using modulated sparks and arcs. Back in the East, A. Frederick Collins of Philadelphia, under the auspices of the Collins Wireless Telephone Co., marketed equipment of short range capability, but including spark and arc oscillators. In New York City, Alfred Goldsmith, Professor of Electrical Engineering at CCNY, operated a broadcasting station at the College in the 1912–14 period under call letters 2XN.[34]

The above description of arc/spark events prior to 1914 indicates that quite a bit of activity was taking place apart from the work of Fessenden or DeForest, though these two personalities were still the most prominent on the wireless telephone scene. Between 1912 and 1915 there were some critical advances in electronic engineering, including the audio frequency amplifier (DeForest), regenerative amplifier and feedback oscillator (DeForest and E. H. Armstrong), and vastly improved high-vacuum triode radio tubes (Bell Laboratories and General Electric).

SARNOFF AND THE "RADIO MUSIC BOX"

Early in 1914, the American Marconi station in New York's Wanamaker Building was refurbished with a low power vacuum tube transmitter for experimental broadcasting of phonograph music. David Sarnoff, Contract Manager for the Company, had sailed aboard the S. S. *Antilles* for New Orleans to attend a convention of Railway Telegraph Superintendents. By advance scheduling, the Wanamaker station was tuned in while the vessel was about 60 miles away from New York. This incident appears to have influenced the young executive, and coupled with some fast breaking technical developments (such as E. H. Armstrong's feedback circuit and the Bell Company's radiotelephone tests) led to the famous "Radio Music Box" memorandum of Sept. 30, 1915, addressed to Edward J. Nally, Vice President and General Manager of the Marconi Wireless Telegraph Company of America:

> I have in mind a plan of development which would make a radio a "household utility" in the same sense as the piano or phonograph. The idea is to bring music into the house by wireless.
> While this has been tried in the past by wires, it has been a failure because wires do not lend themselves to this scheme. With radio, however, it would seem to be entirely feasible. For example, a radiotelephone transmitter having a range of, say, 25 to 50 miles can be installed at a fixed point where instrumental or vocal music or both are produced. The problem of transmitting music has already been solved in principle, and therefore all the receivers attuned to the transmitting wavelength should be capable of receiving such music. The receivers can be designed in the form of a simple "Radio Music Box" and arranged for several different wavelengths, which should be changeable with the throwing of a single switch or pressing of a single button.
> The "Radio Music Box" can be supplied with amplifying tubes and a loudspeaking telephone, all of which can be neatly mounted in one box. The box can be placed in the parlor or living room, the

switch set accordingly, and the transmitted music received. There should be no difficulty in receiving music perfectly when transmitted within a radius of 25 to 50 miles. Within such a radius, there reside hundreds of thousands of families; and as all can simultaneously receive from a single transmitter, there would be no question of obtaining sufficiently loud signals to make the performance enjoyable. The power of the transmitter can be made 5 kilowatts, if necessary, to cover even a short radius of 25 to 50 miles, thereby giving extra-loud signals in the home if desired. The development of a small loop antenna to go with each "Radio Music Box" would likewise solve the antenna problem.[35] *

A typical transmitter of 1915 or 1916 would be a vacuum tube oscillator (or a Poulsen arc, if one could stand the noise) with necessary speech modulation equipment. The home listener could use a simple crystal set or perhaps one of the single-tube receivers then available to amateur radio operators.

An obvious question would be: If all the necessary appliances for radio broadcasting were here in 1915, why wasn't broadcasting itself?

As so often happens with benefit of hindsight, we may be able to deduce more from the evidence than really applies to the situation. It would seem, however, that Sarnoff's proposal was perfectly reasonable, considering the state of the art as well as the past experience of DeForest and the Bell System engineers not to mention the full gamut of wired and wireless telephony development since Alexander Graham Bell's demonstrations of the telephone 40 years earlier.

The answer, it would seem to us, is two-fold: (1) a lack of appreciation of the entertainment and information capability of the radio-telephone ("the time isn't ripe yet" cliché); and (2) a turbulent patent situation leading to all sorts of manufacturing difficulties.

In September 1916 the courts ruled that DeForest had infringed the two-element Fleming Valve patent, and the Marconi Company had infringed the three-element DeForest "Audion" tube patent. Nobody could manufacture triodes—absolutely essential for vacuum tube transmitters and for tube-type receivers. Then the General Electric Company and AT&T became involved in patent interferences on the "feedback circuit" used with the triode.[36] Although there was a Navy-inspired truce for the purpose of aiding the war effort during World War I, this paralysis was not really resolved until the post-war cross-licensing agreements between the industry giants. Then broadcasting really had a chance to flourish.[37]

---

* Sarnoff also said that sales of the "Radio Music Box" would "mean a gross business of about $75 million." RCA's actual sales from 1922 to 1924 were $83,500,000.

4

Thomas W. Hoffer

NATHAN B. STUBBLEFIELD
AND HIS WIRELESS TELEPHONE

NATHAN B. STUBBLEFIELD was a Kentucky melon farmer who spent much time tinkering with coils of wire, electric batteries and telephones at a time when wireless telegraphy was still in an experimental stage. After 1892 Stubblefield worked on several devices enabling the transmission of voice without wires. In 1902, following a successful public demonstration, he predicted that his "invention" would be used "for the general transmission of news of every description." [1]

The first documented demonstration occurred in 1892. Stubblefield invited a friend to his farm home on the edge of Murray, Kentucky. He handed Rainey T. Wells a device and asked him to walk some distance away from a small shack he had erected near his house. Wells, doubting Stubblefield's claims, followed the instructions.

> . . . I had hardly reached my post . . . when I heard, "Hello Rainey" come booming out of the receiver. I jumped a foot and said to myself, "This fellow is fooling me. He has wires some place."

Wells moved to the side a few feet, and as he later reported,

> . . . all the while he [Stubblefield] kept talking to me . . . but there were no wires, I tell you. [2]

Wells' recollection and the documentation of other public demonstrations about Stubblefield's wireless voice transmissions were used to support the claim that the Kentuckian "invented radio" as early as 1892. In 1930, the citizens of Murray, Kentucky, erected a monument commemorating Stubblefield and his wireless telephone. The inscription stated, in part,

> Here in 1902, Nathan B. Stubblefield . . . inventor of radio—broadcast and received the human voice by wireless. He made experiments 10 years earlier . . . [3]

Marconi, Fessenden and DeForest have also had similar titles claimed for them.

The important question is whether his wireless telephone contained elements forming the basis for wireless voice transmission, as

Journal of Broadcasting, Vol. XV, No. 3 (Summer 1971), pp. 317–329.

it evolved into radio broadcasting.[4] Or, whether his system was based on wireless "techniques" generally known by other experimenters of his time, and subsequently discarded in favor of other wireless theories. The evidence in favor of the former position is very sketchy, indeed. Stubblefield's story is also important because his experiments were conducted when wireless telegraphy was in an embryonic state. His 1892 wireless *telephony* conversation with Rainey Wells antedated Marconi's wireless *telegraphy* demonstration by three years.

EARLY LIFE AND EXPERIMENTATION (1859–1901)

Nathan B. Stubblefield was born in either 1859 or 1860, and was the son of William Jefferson Stubblefield.[5] A self-educated experimenter and a farmer, he left school at 15 and, according to reminiscences of friends,[6] spent much time reading scientific journals at the newspaper office in Murray, Kentucky. By 1887, at the age of about 27, Stubblefield had achieved a local reputation for building "vibrating telephones," some of which were used by the townspeople.[7] The device was patented by Stubblefield in 1888.[8] Four years later, Stubblefield demonstrated his wireless telephone for Rainey Wells. Very few Murray residents were allowed entrance into Stubblefield's experimental sanctuary during those years. Stubblefield treasured his privacy.[9]

> . . . His home was so wired that a stranger approaching within a half-mile set off a battery of bells. If the trespasser was unidentified, Stubblefield waved him away.[10]

Among his several children only Bernard participated in his father's wireless experiments.[11]

After 1898 Stubblefield circulated a brochure on his electric cell which provided an energy source for the telephone. The steel rods used in the 1892 apparatus appeared to function in the same manner as the advertised use of Stubblefield's electric cell. The cell or the rods were inserted into the earth at the points of transmission and reception.

The transmitter device was comprised of a modified Bell-type telephone connected to a large circle of metal which looked very much like an antenna. Wires led from that to a "black box." Years later, in 1908, when Stubblefield built another wireless system, the circular steel "antenna" at the telephone transmitter was eliminated in favor of a long elevated antenna extending over several hundred feet. One device was demonstrated for a small group of Murray citizens in 1898.[12] Stubblefield told the group that he was finally going to patent his invention but an application was not filed until 1907. Those 1907 papers described a different wireless system contrasted with the verbal descriptions and occasional photographs of the 1892, 1898 and 1902 devices.

THE PUBLIC DEMONSTRATIONS (1902–1903)

On January 1, 1902, two weeks after Marconi demonstrated wireless telegraphy across the Atlantic, about 1,000 Murray, Kentucky, residents witnessed Stubblefield demonstrate his wireless telephone. Later, Stubblefield told a reporter from the *St. Louis Post Dispatch* that the successful results of the demonstration in Murray took 10 to 12 years of development.

> . . . I have solved the problem of telephoning without wires through the earth as Signor Marconi has of sending signals through space. But, I can also telephone without wires through space as well as through the earth, because my medium is everywhere.[13]

A private demonstration was given for the reporter during the second week of January 1902. Information was transmitted and received between a fixed transmitter and mobile receiver.[14] Bernard played a few bars of music on his harmonica. One mile away from the Stubblefield house, the pair secured the rods about thirty feet apart and listened. Bernard's harmonica music was heard again.[15]

The January 1902 *St. Louis Post Dispatch* story created more interest in Stubblefield's invention. Two months later, he traveled to Washington, D.C. for another public demonstration. On March 20, 1902, aboard the steamer Bartholdi, off the Virginia bank of the Potomac, opposite Georgetown, Stubblefield sent wireless messages to receivers ashore.[16] A test was also made on land and proved much more successful, ". . . with the voices of the speakers being more plainly heard . . ." [17] After the demonstration, Stubblefield said:

> . . . as to the practicality of my invention—all that I can claim for it now is that it is capable of sending simultaneous messages from a central distributing station over a very wide territory . . . Eventually, it will be used for the general transmission of news of every description.[18]

Stubblefield's March 1902 statement about news broadcasting was particularly noteworthy. Although such uses of wired telephone systems were made in Hungary four years earlier, the emphasis in utilizing wireless telegraphy or telephony was put on point-to-point transmission, not broadcasting. Additionally, Stubblefield's insight into the potential utilization of such wireless telephone systems provided interesting perspective to the often quoted 1915 memorandum by David Sarnoff, who urged his superiors at American Marconi to manufacture a "Radio Music Box" for home use. Later, Stubblefield "directionalized" the transmission characteristics as part of what he called "perfecting" his apparatus.

Between 1898 and 1902 two stories concerning offers Stubblefield received for his devices were circulated among the Murray townfolk. Dr. Will Mason told newspaper reporters that he had seen a written $40,000 offer to Stubblefield for the patent rights to his system.[19] Another offer was apparently made after Stubblefield's Washington, D.C. demonstration. Stubblefield told an old schoolmate that he had turned down an offer for $500,000.[20] The hearsay about those high-flying offers was consistent with speculation fever gripping potential investors. By 1901 reports of Marconi's wireless telegraphy experiments increased investor interest.

> . . . Every amateur intentor who had ever tinkered with a telephone at once became of major importance.[21]

THE WIRELESS TELEPHONE COMPANY OF AMERICA

In January 1903 Stubblefield agreed to participate in the commercial exploitation of his device. Incorporation papers for the Wireless Telephone Company of America (WTCA) were filed in Prescott, Arizona, on May 22, 1902.[22] Stubblefield was a director but he held no office. After some additional testing in New York City,[23] the company undertook promotion of the Stubblefield wireless telephone in Pennsylvania. On May 30 and 31, 1902, Bernard assisted his father in the Philadelphia demonstrations held in the vicinity of Fairmont Park.[24]

The Washington and Philadelphia demonstrations maintained the momentum needed to sell stock in the new company. A four page prospectus, extolling the investment opportunity in WTCA compared the Stubblefield device with Marconi's wireless telegraphy system by stating that both systems utilized ". . . for transmission what are termed Hertzian electrical wave currents . . ."[25] The technical details were not disclosed since the prospectus was designed to sell stock, and perhaps deliberately avoided specific evidence on the points of comparison or contrast. The use of steel rods thrust into the ground and large coils indicated that Stubblefield's 1892, 1893 and 1902 systems were based upon an induction principle. This principle was demonstrated by Professor Amos Dolbear of Tufts College, Massachusetts, in March 1882.[26] Stubblefield insisted that a more "powerful" apparatus would "transmit" unlimited distances.[27]

After the Philadelphia tests, some unknown events occurred which caused Stubblefield's withdrawal from the Wireless Telephone Company of America. He had previously signed over all patent rights to the company in exchange for stock. On June 19, 1902 he wrote the secretary of WTCA charging that one of the stock promoters was ". . . practicing fraud or deception as usual . . ." Stubblefield's letter indicated that he was obviously disturbed about an undisclosed incident, indicating that the practice was swindling him ". . . out of my inventions, and the defrauding of the public . . ." [28] Another incident possibly related to Stubblefield's letter occurred during the Washington, D.C. demonstration. He told an old friend that someone wanted Stubblefield to use a wire connection between the transmitter and receiver during the tests on land. ". . . They said they could sell more stock that way. I wouldn't do it." [29] Stubblefield returned to Murray referring to the New York "crowd" as "damned rascals." [30]

REFINEMENTS, PATENTS AND DISILLUSION (1903–1928)

Stubblefield went back to work in Murray, Kentucky, perfecting his device. With the financial backing of seven Murray residents, he filed a patent on April 5, 1907, which was granted on May 12, 1908. His system was now limited to wireless voice communication between moving trains and way stations, moving highway carriages and way stations, and ship-to-shore communication. It was a "land-mobile" system instead of a "broadcasting" one. The letters patent specifically included the use of a stationary "transmitter" and "antenna" with receiver equipped mobile vehicles passing adjacent to the elevated "antenna." In principle, Stubblefield's 1907 device envisioned the transmitter operator, speaking into a telephone transmitter and through the circuit, producing

> a varying current corresponding to that passing through the coil of great magnitude [which] . . . will be inducted in the coil [in the receiver] and the speech or other sounds will be transmitted to the operator on the boat.[31]

A similar system was depicted in what appeared to be an earlier design located among the Stubblefield Papers, and involving a Trans-Atlantic Oceanic system using a submerged wire. The idea was to induct signals to ships on the surface. The 1908 Stubblefield letters patent were quite vague technically except with respect to the point on the use of electrostatic inductance to accomplish voice transmission. This has been corroborated by Stubblefield's son, Bernard. At age 82, Bernard recalled that his father used two systems of wireless telephony. One was based on "ground radiation" and another on some kind of "magnetic radiation." He could not recall the details of each system precisely. But he stated that the devices used in the early wireless experiments did not contain an apparatus enabling the production of sustained and high speed oscillations.

After the 1908 patent was granted, nothing significant occurred in the technical development or commercial exploitation of Stubblefield's wireless telephone. In 1913, some officials of WTCA were convicted of mail fraud.[32]

Except for an occasional experiment, observed by some of Stubblefield's neighbors at a distance, he quietly lived out his existence in a small shack about nine miles north of Murray. Some observers reported seeing mysterious lights and hearing weird sounds in the vicinity of Stubblefield's home. Two weeks before his death, Stubblefield visited with a neighbor, Mrs. L. E. Owen. He asked her to write his life story.

> I've lived fifty years before my time. The past is nothing. I have perfected now the greatest invention the world has ever known. I've taken light from the air and earth as I did sound.[33]

About two weeks later, on March 30, 1928, a neighbor discovered Stubblefield's dead body in the shack which was locked from the inside. Nothing else was discovered except a few scraps of paper and portions of his apparatus.

On March 28, 1930, Murray citizens and two of Stubblefield's daughters unveiled a small monument to his memory. Since then several prominent Murray citizens and others interested in gaining recognition for Stubblefield have gathered evidence to support the claim that he "invented radio." Patent papers, correspondence, newspaper materials, affidavits, parts of the original coils and equipment are open to the public at Murray, Kentucky.

Conn Linn and one of Stubblefield's sons, Nathan, Jr., traced the wireless patents with a view of filing an infringement suit. Linn told a newspaper reporter that the lawsuit ". . . would have upset the financial structure of the radio world and required an accounting of profits worth millions since radio began its career."[34] An undisclosed New York law firm told Linn that their claims were in order and could be verified ". . . to the final detail." But the statute of limitations for the filing of a claim had passed. In 1950, Linn wrote to Vernon Stubblefield, a cousin of the early experimenter:

> I went with him to Washington, and helped secure his initial patents. Had I stayed there, and helped him finish the job, he might have been living today as a world renowned inventor, and both of us rich enough to make John D. Rockefeller look like a piker. Don't you think I am right about it?[35]

COMMENT

Stubblefield did transmit voice without wires as early as 1892. There is enough corroborative evidence in the form of affidavits, letters, newspaper accounts, photographs and drawings indicating that the Stubblefield devices did work. The important question was whether his devices contained elements which might have been a basis for, or consistent with, a new and slowly evolving wireless technology dealing with radio frequency oscillations and so-called

"Hertzian secrets." According to Stubblefield's onetime attorney, a case could have been made in support of this allegation. But the available technical evidence about the 1892, 1898 and 1902 devices was sketchy and hardly conclusive. The development of radio telephony evolved from the experiments of R. A. Fessenden and others dealing with radio frequency oscillations. Stubblefield's 1908 letters patent did not contain descriptions or drawings indicating capability for radio transmission and reception. Instead, his system utilized an audio induction technique. This was a great difference from the production of sustained radio frequency oscillations with superimposed modulated information.

The competence of persons testifying about Stubblefield's experiments cannot be challenged. But their competence about what was in Stubblefield's "black box" is certainly subject to question. Only Bernard, Stubblefield's son, had access to such information. Bernard Stubblefield has stated that his father's devices did not involve the generation of radio frequencies. Any litigation had to turn, in part, on that question. Interestingly, Bernard was not involved in the plans for litigating Stubblefield's claimed rights after his death. He would have been the most informed participant. There may be more evidence about the 1892, 1898 and 1902 devices but it has not been brought forward. Based upon the available material, and the fact that wireless voice transmission evolved from the experiments of several persons widely separated by time and geography, it is clear that Nathan B. Stubblefield did not "invent radio."

Stubblefield's story also illustrated how the devices of an ambitious experimenter could be absorbed by the heavy promotion of investors seeking to repeat a windfall like that of the commercialized Bell telephone. The Wireless Telephone Company of America had a long way to go to match the headline accomplishments of Marconi and other experimenters. Stubblefield concluded that the emphasis of the company was simply selling stock.

Stubblefield was a self-educated technician who developed his own telephone used by a few Murray, Kentucky, residents in 1887. He invented and utilized an electric battery in his wireless telephone experiments. Unlike Marconi and other researchers, Stubblefield continued his experiments with only his own financial resources and those of his friends. His vision of "broadcasting news of every description," while not sensationally unique for the time, did reinforce the mystery about the technical capabilities of his early devices. And, Stubblefield's public demonstrations did involve voice transmission without wires. Beyond those documented facts, the "Hertzian secrets" of his "black box" used in those experiments, if there were any, most likely died with him.

5

Edwin H. Armstrong

THE STORY OF THE SUPER-HETERODYNE

THE INVENTION OF the super-heterodyne dates back to the early part of 1918. The full technical details of the system were made public in the fall of 1919. Since that time it has been widely used in experimental work and is responsible for many of the recent accomplishments in long-distance reception from broadcasting stations. While the superiority of its performance over all other forms of receivers was unquestioned, very many difficulties rendered it unsuitable for use by the general public and confined it to the hands of engineers and skilled amateurs. Years of concentrated effort from many different sources have produced improvements in vacuum tubes, in transformer construction, and in the circuits of the super-heterodyne itself, with the result that early in the month of April there has been made available for the general public, a super-heterodyne receiver which meets the requirements of household use.

It is a peculiar circumstance that this invention was a direct outgrowth of the failure of the vacuum tubes constructed in the United States to meet a very important problem confronting the American Expeditionary Force. This problem was the reception of extremely weak spark signals of frequencies varying from about 500,000 cycles to 3,000,000 cycles, with an absolute minimum of adjustments to enable rapid change of wavelength. The technical difficulties of this problem are now so well known that it is not necessary to consider them. H. J. Round in England, and Latour in France, by some of the most brilliant technical radio work carried out during the war, had produced substantially aperiodic radio-frequency amplifiers covering the band from 500,000 to 1,200,000 cycles and though covering a much more limited band, amplifiers operating on 2,000,000 cycles had been constructed. These results had been accomplished by the use of vacuum tubes and transformers of a minimum capacity. As this apparatus was used in the highly important intelligence services, all information was carefully guarded. When the United States entered the war, the fact that it was necessary to produce extremely sensitive receivers for short wavelengths and that tube capacity would prove the bar to a straightforward solution of the problem was not known in this country. As a result, no attention was paid to the capacity in the type of vacuum tube which was adopted

Radio Broadcast, July 1924, pp. 198–207.

and while the tube met the requirements of the lower frequencies admirably, it was impossible to use it effectively for the frequencies of importance in the direction finding service.

How the Super-Heterodyne Originated

During the early part of 1917, I had made a careful study of the heterodyne phenomena and their effect on the efficiency of rectification. With these experiments freshly in mind, the idea occurred to me to solve the problem by selecting some frequency which could be handled by the tubes available, building an effective amplifier for that frequency, and then transforming the incoming high frequency to this readily amplifiable value by some converting means which had no low limit; preferably the heterodyne and rectification.

The Armistice ended development at this point, but in the fall of 1919, for the purpose of determining results which could be obtained by pushing the super-heterodyne method of reception to the limit, a resistance-coupled intermediate-frequency amplifier consisting of five high mu tubes was constructed.

Paul Godley Used a Super-Heterodyne to Copy American Amateurs in Scotland

The sensitiveness of the super-heterodyne was demonstrated during the winter of 1919–1920 when the spark signals from amateur stations on the West coast and telephone signals from destroyers in Southern waters were received in the vicinity of New York on a three-foot (one-meter) loop. Probably the most striking demonstration of the capabilities of the method occurred in December, 1920, when Paul F. Godley, at Ardrossan, Scotland, received the signals of a large number of amateur stations located in the United States, many of them being spark stations. The super-heterodyne used by Godley consisted of a regenerative tube for the first rectifier, a separate oscillator, four stages of resistance-coupled intermediate-frequency amplification, a second rectifier, and two stages of audio. While it is difficult to state definitely the actual voltage amplification obtained, it appears to have been between 3,000 and 5,000 fold.

With the coming of broadcasting and with the great increase in the number of stations and the consequent interference, the super-heterodyne began to take on a new importance—an importance which was based not on its superior sensitiveness nor on its selectivity, but on the great promise which the method offered in simplicity of operation. It was, and still is, the standard practice to furnish the public with receivers equipped with a variety of tuning adjustments for the purpose of amplifying the desired band of radio frequencies and excluding all others. As a matter of fact, many more adjustments are on receivers than should be used—more than could be placed in the hands of the average user. It would obviously be of the greatest importance if in some way these tuning adjustments could all be made in the laboratory by skilled engineers and sealed, leaving some relatively simple adjustment for the hands of the operator. The super-heterodyne offered the ideal solution. This solution lay in the construction of an intermediate-frequency amplifier which would amplify a given frequency and a band 5,000 cycles above and below it and which would cut off sharply on either side of this desired band. The adjustments necessary to accomplish this could all be made by skilled men, and the only operations left for the user would be the two adjustments necessary to change the incoming frequencies down to the band of the amplifier—adjustments which are not dependent on each other, which are of extreme simplicity, and which can be made equally well by the novice or the engineer. To determine just what could be accomplished along these lines, the writer, working in conjunction with Mr. Harry Houck constructed during the spring of 1922, a set designed for the maximum usable sensitiveness and selectivity.

The First Model

The set-up consisted of one radio-frequency stage (non-tuned transformer) a rectifier tube, an oscillator tube (used as a separate heterodyne), a three-stage iron-core transformer coupled intermediate-frequency amplifier designed to cover a band of 20,000 to 30,000 cycles, a second detector tube, and two stages of audio-frequency amplification UV-201-A tubes were used. To prevent the intermediate-frequency amplifier from oscillating, each stage was shielded separately. The use of a radio-frequency stage ahead of the first detector possesses a number of advantages but the chief one is in eliminating the reaction between the loop circuit and the oscillator circuit. Experience with the original type had shown that when an oscillator of ordinary power was used, it was necessary to couple it rather closely with the loop circuit in order to insure a sufficiently strong heterodyning current. This close coupling affected the tuning of both circuits, an adjustment of one changing the setting of the other. To avoid this trouble and to produce a system wherein a station could always be tuned-in on exactly the same settings, a single stage of radio-frequency amplification (using a non-tuned transformer) was used, and the oscillator was coupled into this transformer. This arrangement eliminated the reaction, reduced the radiation to a minimum, and, in addition, removed the damping of the first rectifier from the loop circuit and improved its selectivity.

The results obtained with this set were about as expected. On a three-foot (one-meter) loop, the factor determining the reception of a station was solely whether the signal strength was above the level of the atmospherics. The selectivity was such that stations which had never been heard before on account of blanketing by local stations, were received without a trace of interference. While the performance of the set was much superior to any other receiver, it was apparent that the cost of construction and maintenance was prohibitive. The single item of a ten-ampere filament current will give some idea of the size of the storage battery and auxiliary apparatus required.

With the coming of the low filament consumption, or dry battery type of tube, the possibilities of producing a super-heterodyne for household use were tremendously improved. The set was remodelled for the WD-11 tube and its sensitiveness was brought to about the same value as obtained with the storage battery tubes. This was a long step forward but still its cost was prohibitive.

Why the Second Harmonic Principle Was Developed

It had been apparent ever since the question of the application of the super-heterodyne to broadcasting had been considered, that there were too many tubes performing a single function which were quite capable of performing a double one. The most outstanding case is that of the separate heterodyne oscillator. In view of our knowledge of the self-heterodyne, it appears quite obvious to perform the first rectification by means of a self-heterodyne oscillator and thereby save a tube. As a matter of fact, this was one of the very first things tried in France, but, except for very short wavelengths, it was never very successful when a high intermediate frequency was necessary. The reason was this. If a single tuned oscillating circuit was used, the detuning to produce the proper beat caused a loss of signal strength which offset the gain of a tube. If two tuned circuits were used on the oscillator, one tuned to the signaling frequency and the other arranged to oscillate at the heterodyning frequency, then on account of the relatively small percentage difference in frequency a change in the tuning of one circuit changed the tuning of the other. The solution of this problem was made by Houck, who proposed an arrangement so simple and so effective that it completely solved the problem. Houck proposed to connect two tuned circuits to the oscillator, a simple circuit tuned to the frequency of the incoming signal and a regenerative circuit adjusted to oscillate at such a frequency beating with the incoming frequency produced the desired intermediate frequency.

When this development had been completed, improvements in the design of the intermediate-frequency transformers made it possible to obtain with two stages all the amplification which could be used.

On account of the high amplification, signals from local stations overload the second rectifier and introduce distortion. Control of the amount of intermediate-frequency amplification is essential. While there are numerous methods equally effective, the simplest one appears to be the control by means of the filament temperature of the second intermediate-frequency amplifier.

The features just described were all incorporated in the receiver which measured 16″ x 10″ x 10″ and was completely self-contained— the batteries, loop antenna, and speaker mechanism being enclosed in the box. The results were highly satisfactory and loud speaker signals (at night) in the vicinity of New York were obtained from stations in Chicago and Atlanta. It demonstrated that not only could a household receiver of the super-heterodyne type be built, but that the first practical solution of the portable set was at hand.

From the Laboratory Model
to the Commercial Product

In this form, the capabilities of the set were brought to the attention of the Westinghouse Electric and Manufacturing Company and the Radio Corporation of America a little over a year ago. Its possibilities were instantly visualized by Mr. David Sarnoff, who immediately took steps to concentrate the resources of the research laboratories of the Radio Corporation of America, the Westinghouse Electric and Manufacturing Company and the General Electric Company on this new development. Many improvements and some radically new ideas of design have been introduced, but it is the privilege of those responsible for them to present these. In the final development of this receiver, an additional stage of audio-frequency amplification was added in order to insure operation within steel buildings, particularly those within the city limits where signals are relatively very weak compared to suburban locations. This makes a six-tube set but six tubes can be readily operated on dry batteries and the increase in sensitiveness is well worth the extra tube.

Some idea of the sensitiveness and the ease of operation of the set may be gathered from an incident during the *Radio Broadcast-Wireless World* transatlantic broadcasting tests of November and December, 1923. On December 1st, two women, neither having any technical radio knowledge received loud speaker signals from station 2LO, London, England. This was accomplished at Merrimac, Massachusetts, and perhaps constitutes a record for the first radiophone reception from Europe with a portable receiver. With the same set and a three-foot (one-meter) loop, loud speaker signals from broadcast stations on the Pacific Coast were received in the vicinity of New York on an average of three or four times a week. The sole criterion of reception was whether the signal strength was above the level of the atmospheric disturbances.

The type of super-heterodyne described herein is now available to the public. Each of these sets incorporate the arrangements herein described. Their sensitiveness is such that, with a two-foot loop and an unshielded location, the atmospheric disturbances are the criterion of reception. Here we reach a milestone in the development of broadcast receivers for no increase in the distance of reception can now be obtained by increase in the sensitiveness of the receiver. Unless the power of transmitting stations is increased we are about at the limit of the distance which can be covered. Future improvement of this receiver will lie along the line of increasing its selectivity and simplifying its construction. Aside from the development of the super-heterodyne but few recent radio receivers have improved in other than their mechanical arrangement and cabinet work.

It is perfectly apparent at the present time that the tuning of a large number of receivers in a congested area to the same signal results in a weakened signal for practically everybody. If every house-top were fitted with several antennae, the question arises as to how much energy the man in the center of the city would find left if everyone ahead of him had absorbed as much from the wave as possible by using as high and efficient an antenna as he could erect. The sole solution to this and all the other troubles is the use of an antenna of the loop type whose effect on near by receiving stations is negligible.

Of course, this necessitates more sensitive receivers with an increase in amplifying power commensurate with the relative receptive powers of an antenna versus a loop. At first sight, it might appear that the cost of this change would be prohibitive but with our present rate of development, I believe that it is going to be possible to build loop sets as sensitive as our present type antenna sets with but relatively little increase in cost. At the same time, the situation can be improved from another angle. The power of transmitting sets will gradually increase both because of the fact that there is no way to eliminate the effects of atmospheric disturbances, elevator induction, X-ray machines and all the other types of interference which exist in a large city except to ride over them with high power and because of the fact that from the program standpoint, it is economically better to concentrate talent at one point.

All these factors point to the elimination of the present type of antenna which will disappear in the same manner as the overhead telegraph, telephone, electric light and trolley wires have disappeared in the last twenty years.

6

TELEVISION ON THE WAY *

FRENCHMEN HAVE PRACTICALLY PERFECTED A MACHINE FOR SEEING
The Announcement of A German Inventor Forces
French Scientists to Disclose Their Progress ·
on a Machine That Sees as the Telephone Hears.

THE DAY is very near when one can sit comfortably in his own room and not only listen to the voice of a friend miles away, but see him as distinctly as though the friend were sitting in a chair beside him, and when from his palace a monarch or president can inaugurate some public exposition thousands of miles distant being both seen and heard by the assembled people.

The very interesting experiments in "television" that have just been made at La Rochelle by a young French scientist, M. Georges Rignoux, aided in his work by the advice of M. Fournier, director of the Municipal Laboratory of that city, gives strong hope that these dreams will soon be realized. Some weeks ago, the famous German electrician, Ruhmer, successfully carried through for the first time an experiment in "television" or seeing at a distance. Similar researches had been made for a long time in France, but these trials had always been surrounded by a mysterious silence. The French inventors were waiting the moment when their apparatus would be perfected before giving to the world their discovery. Professor Ruhmer's publication of his experiments obliged them to break their silence and the first trials of these two French scientists have been much more conclusive than those made by the German.

Under the ancient porticos in the historic old street, Manage, at the back of a dark and narrow court yard, Rignoux and Fournier have installed their laboratories. The first room as one enters contains the transmitting apparatus. A couple of rooms beyond is a darkened chamber, the tomb-like blackness being increased by the aid of great rolls of black paper which cover the whole wall. Here one finds the receiver.

Kansas City Star, January 30, 1910, p. 20C.
* This same issue of the *Star* carried advertisements for a new Ford Roadster at $900. and a Cadillac for $1,600, an item indicating that the University of Kansas Board of Regents had almost voted to prohibit football but settled for new rules to make the game safer. And a group of men from Kansas City attending the University at Lawrence "are trying Communism" having formed a "cooperative homekeeping scheme" for room and board.

"It seems very rudimentary and yet we have been working on it for more than two years," said M. Rignoux. "We have called our apparatus 'telephote.' As the telephone transmits by wire, variations of sound, the 'telephote' transmits the luminous scales, variations of shadows and lights. The transmitting apparatus is very simple. A concave mirror projects a beam from a Nernst lamp of 3,000 candle power on the object of which one wishes to transmit the image. Each point of the object thus lighted is projected by a lens on a surface formed of sixty-four cells of selenium.

"As you see, we use sixty-four cells while Ruhmer has only twenty-five on his demonstration apparatus, and the number of figures or combinations of signs that we can send is much greater. The cells of selenium constitute, really, an artificial retina. The selenium acts under the influence of the light and each lightened cell sends into the wire a current of intensity proportionate to the force of that corresponding to the luminous point. The variations of the lighting of the object, its play of light and shadow thus transform themselves into electric variations that travel along the sixty-four wires and arrive at the receiving point. At the receiver each one of these currents acts on the little galvanometers that are placed in the interior of a great electro magnet, that light or cover up a series of tiny mirrors and form on a screen the image of the object."

To newspapermen present the scientists gave some most interesting demonstrations. Different letters were placed before the transmitting telephote and instantly appeared on the screen in the nearby room. Then images of a bottle and a lead pencil were in turn instantly and accurately transmitted.

"We hope soon to transmit the colors as well," said M. Fournier.

7

David T. MacFarland

TELEVISION: THE WHIRLING BEGINNING

IN 1926 there was television. That statement comes as a surprise to many who do not know that the technical history of workable apparatus for "seeing at a distance" extends back to 1875 in theory, and to 1926 in practice. In 1926, "television" did not mean the elaborate system for broadcasting that we know today, nor did it mean a computer-assembled set bristling with tubes or transistors. For, until the electronic camera tube invented by Vladimir Zworykin came under intense development and into considerable use in the late 1930s, television transmission and reception was possible only through mechanical and electrical—rather then electronic—means.

SPECULATIVE PERIOD: 1875–1890

Much of the inventive art that eventually culminated in the mechanical systems that were tried in the late 1920s and early 1930s were attempts to improve the process of scanning, in which a given scene is broken into discrete units for sequential transmission to a receiver which then reassembles them into a unified picture again. Exactly this basic process is still used today in photo-facsimile systems. The early period of mechanical television development grew directly from experiments in facsimile technology.[1]

A facsimile (but not photo-facsimile) device was first proposed by Scotsman Alexander Bain in 1842. It used conducting brushes which made electrical contact as they passed over raised metal letters, with the current transmitted by telegraph line activating at the receiving end a similar set of brushes which moved over a chemically-treated paper, discoloring it when electricity flowed.[2] While the system was slow and needed a separate circuit for each contact, it did embody synchronous scanning. Five years later, Englishman F. C. Bakewell devised his "copying telegraph" which employed synchronous *sequential* scanning, the basis of all modern television systems. Bakewell's machine, which featured a single contact tracing a spiral over foil on a rotating drum, was sequential because it sent all its information in sequence on *one* circuit rather than simultaneously on several as Bain's had done.[3] In 1862, Abbé Giacomo Casselli, an Italian-born priest living in France whose experiments were backed by Napoleon III, used a system much like Bakewell's to send the first picture over a long distance by wire, from Amiens to Paris. Casselli even opened stations in France from which messages could be received and sent in handwriting.[4] All such systems for sending images required the conversion of the given still photograph into an electrically-conductive form such as a metal or foil plate. Under these restrictions, pictures of live, moving objects were out of the question.

Then, in 1873, a British telegraph operator named May observed that sunlight falling on selenium resistors in some of his Atlantic Cable circuits changed their electrical resistance. The Society of Telegraph Engineers that same year made it public knowledge that selenium was photo-resistive,[5] setting the stage two years later for electric picture system proposals by George R. Carey of Boston and Ayrton and Perry of England. These were to use a mosaic of cells and corresponding lamps, and were the first systems theoretically able to show movement of animate objects, a requisite of true television. But to yield a picture of adequate resolution, thousands of separate circuits would have been required since no scanning was involved. This drawback, plus the slow reaction time of selenium, predestined the proposals for failure, although the same basic configuration is used today in moving electric signs such as at New York's Times Square.

In 1877, French physician M. Senlecq's Telectroscope was able to transmit *projected* images by tracing them on a screen with a selenium stylus.[6] In 1880 Senlecq invented a system using a synchronous commutator/distributor and banks of transmitting cells and receiving lamps. A very similar arrangement would be used 50 years later in the early 1930s to achieve large-screen mechanical-system televiewing. In 1880, Maurice Leblanc proposed a full system for scanning, with a rapidly-vibrating mirror for horizontal movement and a slowly-vibrating one for vertical motion, but he did not mention a means of electrical light detection and reception, and he never built a model.[7] Leblanc's scanning method was used in several mechanical television systems of the 1920's and was rivalled for simplicity only by the rotating scanning disk proposed by German Paul Nipkow in 1884. Nipkow realized that moving objects could be optically scanned, point-by-point and line-by-line, through a number of small holes arranged in a spiral pattern along the outer edge of a rotating disk. Focus the scene through these holes onto a selenium cell and you have a transmitter; connect it to a controlled light source behind the holes in another disk and you have a receiver. If the two are in synchronization and rotate fast enough to take advantage of persistence of vision, you have television. But there was not television for Nipkow and a host of others who for the next 40 years wrestled with systems that lacked powerful, fast-acting light-sensitive cells for the transmitter, easily controlled light sources for the receiver, and adequate amplifiers for both.

HIATUS: 1890–1920

One by one, the problems were solved. In 1890, the first photo-*electric* cells were produced,[8] these being tubes which rather than slowly changing resistance in the presence of light, generated their own electricity. In the same year, the Englishman Sutton proposed a television receiver using as the controlled light source a Kerr Cell, a tube in which polarized light is regulated by passing it through certain liquids to which a variable electric field is applied. The Kerr Cell would be used 35 years later in many mechanical television receivers. In 1904 the Germans Frankenstein and Jaworski proposed a system for mechanical color television. The Frenchmen Rignoux and Fournier introduced the "flying spot" scanner which reversed Nipkow's process by scanning with a powerful light source beamed through the rotating disk onto the darkened scene, thus allowing multiple cells to be used for pickup of a much brighter image.[9] And in 1907, Russian Boris Rosing built a cathode ray tube for television reception. The tube failed because of insufficient amplification, but the system which Rosing designed (after Dieckman and Glage in 1906) [10] included the first fool-proof method of synchronization. And it employed magnetic horizontal and vertical deflection much as is used in today's sets. In 1908 A. A. Campbell-Swinton wrote a letter to the British journal *Nature* [11] which advanced much of the theory for an all-electronic system such as Zworykin would design in the 1930s, but Campbell Swinton admitted that the hardware to accomplish his scheme was lacking. In 1909, the field of phototelegraphy yielded a taste of things to come when Han Knudsen sent the first wireless phototelegraphs from London.[12]

By the end of the second decade of this century, the marketplace was already glutted with more miraculous gadgets—such as the phonograph, telephone, telegraph, and radio—than the public had ever been confronted with at once. This fact alone might have made the later part of the period an unfavorable time to innovate television had its component parts been ready, but it was also a time of general financial uncertainty, with little monetary backing available except from the inventors themselves. Thus it is not surprising that during the three decade span between 1890 and 1920, only a very few new mechanical television systems were proposed.

EXPERIMENTAL PERIOD: 1920–1925

Until 1926, television transmission and reception remained unrealized even though the field was filled with good ideas, important discoveries, and workable components for various inventions. The diffusion of information about these systems was agonizingly slow, and was probably spurred only by World War I and the growth of radio and its attendant technologies. In view of all the work that had already been done in developing television, it is ironic that a man such as John Logie Baird of Great Britain should be the one to stumble onto the right combination of factors that would give him the honor of being the first to send "true" television pictures (that is, pictures of animate objects, and with gradations of light and dark), the first public demonstration being on January 27, 1926. In a very short time, Baird was elevated from being a dreamy experimenter using darning needles and bicycle lenses in his rickety machines to the chief "scientist" of a string of companies which were committed to making mechanical television a roaring commercial success, in spite of such obvious shortcomings in the Baird "Televisors" as lack of synchronization, very poor resolution, flicker, low brightness, and picture size of only a few square inches. With these limitations, Baird's early mechanical television could not truly offer entertainment value, and was looked on as a mere novelty even by potential set manufacturers who were glad to let the Baird companies make the few they could sell.[13] Baird's backers wanted to get their system adopted in sufficient numbers to make it more difficult to supplant it with a better one in the future, and thus the honing and improvement of the instruments was hardly the object.[14] But the public was not fooled. It saw the many drawbacks of the Baird system and returned to listen to their newly-beloved radios. Even had early mechanical television been excellent, radio's act would have been a hard one to follow while satisfaction with the aural medium was so high.

But public apathy may have spurred more private experimentation. Among other prominent figures in mechanical television development was Charles Francis Jenkins of the United States, who had been experimenting with the Nipkow disk since 1890, and who *broadcast* the first motion pictures (but not live figures) by radio in June 1925 while Baird was still using wires.[15] Jenkins was only a few months behind the Baird companies in developing his mechanical system, and one that was technically much more sophisticated, using such devices as prismatic disks and quartz light transmission rods.

INNOVATIVE PERIOD: 1925–1933

Like Baird, Jenkins had plans for commercial introduction of his system, and until the stock market crashed, was preparing for set production and regular programming to begin in 1930. The period after 1925 saw many attempts to "cash in" on this next novelty that seemed to promise a business boom as big as radio had provided. Yet, while profiteers flourished, disappointing and hardening the public to the new medium with their inflated claims for shoddy equipment, some inventors were still at work trying to perfect— rather than just promote—mechanical television. Dr. Herbert E. Ives of Bell Telephone Laboratories developed a technique for making photocells many times more sensitive, solved problems of television relay by coaxial cable and radio, and developed a camera for televising outdoors (while everyone else was tied to the darkened room required by the "flying spot"). Ernst Alexanderson of General Electric invented a theater projection process using variations on the Kerr Cell. Ulysses A. Sanabria of Chicago had much to do with the development of large-screen mechanical television receivers using banks of lights and commutators (after Senlecq), a scheme Baird also tried.

A Los Angeles inventor named Gardner in 1923 developed a scanning drum called a "mirror screw" which consisted of a stack of mirrors arranged like a spiral staircase on which an image was viewed directly.[16] Concurrently, Baird was making only slight detail improvements on his commercial television system while again in the news with a series of promotional "firsts." He was the first to televise in the dark, using infra-red rays. This "Noctevisor" was eventually developed as a means of spotting ships, planes, or enemy troops in a dense fog. In August of 1923 Baird demonstrated color television, using a single disk with three spirals and glow tubes of various colors, and stereoscopic television which used two spirals and an ordinary stereopticon. He also developed "Phonovision," a simple phonograph recording of the electrical impulses from the photocells which could be stored or played back at will—the first television recordings. In 1931, Baird showed his version of "zone scanning," [17] an early attempt at "wide-screen" picture enlargement that is much analogous to the original Cinerama segmented wide-screen film system. Since Baird's pictures were only a few inches square, he attempted enlargement by using three separate side-by-side scannings and three separate channels of transmission. While this made the picture wider, it did nothing to increase its resolution and clarity.

During the period in the early 1930s when his system was being tested over radio wavelengths by the BBC without much public enthusiasm, Baird resorted to an intermediate film process in which movies of the scene are shot, developed, dried, and run through a "flying spot" scanner all in less than a minute. Because a much brighter light could be used with film than with live subjects, the unwieldy process did provide a better gradation of whites and blacks. But even this—and such other heroic stopgap efforts as running the scanning disk in a vacuum to get the highest possible speed—still could not raise resolution above 240 lines. In 1933, in the face of competition from the new electronic EMI-Marconi system which used all-electronic scanning and could even then offer twice the resolution of any mechanical method, Baird doggedly began again to develop a new higher definition mechanical system. Even Baird's apologists could see that he was doomed to fail, for in comparison with electronic methods, mechanical television systems were too bulky, too noisy, too prone to go out of adjustment, too hard to synchronize, too dim, too small, and most of all, too lacking in resolution. Baird's financial backers, always after short-term profits, realized in 1933 that mechanical systems would not be adopted if electronic ones were available and began to develop Farnsworth's electronic image dissector system as well. But it was already too late to start.

Conclusion

So mechanical television development came to an end, to be partially revived in only one form since: the CBS color wheel hybrid system which saw brief broadcast use in the early 1950s. Recently this system which employs a whirling three-color disk in front of a normal electronic scanner, has been used only in such specialized fields as medicine and in the cameras carried on Gemini and Apollo space flights. But mechanical television did not die without leaving electronic television a legacy of important technical discoveries, perhaps chief among which was the realization of the need for sequential scanning and a method of synchronization. Because mechanical television was far from perfect technically, and came along too soon after radio, it was not accepted by a large segment of the population. Lack of viewers caused programming to be extremely limited, with the few forms that were seen in the early 1930s over the scattered experimental stations in England, the United States and Germany being adapted directly from radio. Most prevalent were lectures and demonstrations, variety, drama, and actuality programs. The commercial aspects of modern-day television—such as advertising, networking, syndication, set manufacturing and so forth—were also prevented from blossoming, partly by lack of audience, partly by the economics of the depression, and partly by the vested interests of radio operators. Even in production and engineering, because of differences in lighting, field-of-view and aspect ratio, size and shape of the equipment, and the jumble of experimental line and field standards, there was little experience with mechanical television that could be carried over to the emerging electronic system. Yet mechanical television did one great service for the electronic television that followed: despite the scepticism its failure engendered, it stimulated the desire of engineering departments of electronic manufacturers to bring to the public a really good television system, one that would make possible and practicable the promise envisioned by so many for so long. And that desire, with the funding, research, and development based on nearly a century of trials, finally gave us the electronic television system we are so smitten with today.

```
Advertiser investment in TV to 1970       $33,400,000,000
Public investment in new TV sets to 1970  $43,200,000,000
    Advertiser daily cost in TV per home                 17¢
    Public daily cost to run TV sets per home            25¢
                    --Television Advertising Bureau, 1969.
```

8

Vladimir K. Zworykin

THE EARLY DAYS: SOME RECOLLECTIONS

I OWE my own lifelong interest in television to Dr. Boris Rosing, my physics professor at the St. Petersburg Institute of Technology. I was privileged to assist Dr. Rosing many an evening in his private laboratory, setting up a great variety of experiments on apparatus for the generation of television signals and for electrical picture reproduction.

Rosing employed rotating mirrors and a photocell in his transmission equipment, much as did several of his predecessors. On the other hand, he sought to accomplish picture reproduction with the aid of a primitive Braun tube or cathode-ray tube, a technique which had been employed up to then—unknown to him—only by his contemporary, Dieckmann. Furthermore, Rosing was firmly convinced not only that television was coming but that, when it came, it would be electronic television. And he managed to pass on this conviction to me, his student and assistant.

My association with Rosing was terminated upon my graduation in 1912, when I accepted a scholarship to engage in x-ray research under the well-known French physicist Paul Langevin. But World War I deferred for many years any possibility of pursuing my interest in television. In fact, even after I had come to the United States in 1919 and had joined the laboratory staff of the Westinghouse Electric and Manufacturing Company in Pittsburgh the following year, I found it difficult to persuade my superiors to let me work in a field of such questionable prospects. Only upon returning to Westinghouse after an interim with a mid-western oil development company was I given a sufficiently free hand to test some of the television ideas which had been maturing within me.

The most immediate problem appeared at the time to be the invention of an electronic generator of television signals, since the work of Rosing and Dieckmann had already established the feasibility of reproducing television images with the cathode-ray tube. Such an electronic picture generator, or "camera tube," could be endowed, as I saw it, with two important advantages: first, it did away with the need of high-speed mechanical scanning devices; and, second, it permitted the use of signal storage—i.e., the utilization for the picture signal of charge accumulated photoelectrically by a picture element throughout a picture period.

Television Quarterly, Vol. 1, No. 4 (November 1962), pp. 69–72.

An electronic picture signal generator had indeed been proposed by A. A. Campbell-Swinton in a lecture before the Roentgen
Society in London as early as 1911; this, however, did not come to
my attention until after its publication in the *Wireless World and
Radio Review* in April, 1924. Campbell-Swinton's picture signal generator, while incorporating a number of features essential to any
practical camera tube, possessed several other aspects which made
its practical realization impossible. Necessarily, my approach to the
problem had to be quite different.

The very first tube which permitted me to demonstrate the principle of all-electronic television is still in existence. Its most important component is a very thin aluminum oxide film supported by a
thin aluminum film on one side and a photosensitive (potassium
hydride) coating with high transverse resistance on the other. The
picture was projected through a fine-wire collector grid, in front of
the aluminum oxide film, onto the photosensitized side of the film,
while a high-velocity electron beam scanned the opposite side. Illu-
minated portions of the photosensitive "mosaic" which charged up
negatively by photoemission to the collector between successive
scans were momentarily shorted to the aluminum coating or signal
plate by the scanning beam penetrating to the insulating substrate.
This resulted in a signal pulse proportional to the illumination of the
scanned element in the signal plate and collector circuits. The
process as described depended on bombardment-induced conduc-
tivity, a phenomenon investigated at a much later date by Pensak.

With this "camera tube" and a cathode-ray tube as picture reproducer, the essential terminal elements of an electronic television
chain had become available to me. Further more, De Forest's invention of the audion, or vacuum tube amplifier, enabled me to amplify
the weak signal currents provided by the camera tube to a level at
which they could modulate effectively the beam current in the
cathode-ray tube employed as picture reproducer. Thus I could not
only describe the operation of my all-electronic television system,
but could also demonstrate it.

By present standards the demonstration, which was made to a
group of Westinghouse executives toward the end of 1923, was
scarcely impressive. The transmitted pattern was a cross projected on
the target of the camera tube; a similar cross appeared, with low contrast and rather poor definition, on the screen of the cathode-ray
tube. The performance indicated not only the fundamental
soundness of the system but also the tremendous improvement in
the components which had to be realized to create a useful television
system. In particular, the preparation of satisfactory thin-film targets
for the camera tube exceeded the capabilities of the technology of
that day. The first practical television storage camera tubes, built

some seven or eight years later, departed, in fact, from the original design by employing targets which were scanned on the side upon which the picture was projected. These tubes with a relatively thick "one-sided" target I named "Iconoscopes."

However, I am getting ahead of my story. Apart from general studies of modifications and extensions of the television system, my attention was first directed toward the problem of improving the cathode-ray tube as a viewing device.

In the tubes employed in the early demonstrations, the electron beam was defined simply by apertures and relied on gas focusing— i.e., the attraction of the beam electrons by positive ions formed by impact on inert gas atoms—to hold it together. This technique, however, imposed severe limitations on the sharpness and brightness of the scanning spot employed to trace the image on the viewing screen.

Accordingly, I set about focusing the electron beam in a highly evacuated, "hard," tube by means of electrostatic field between apertured diaphragms and cylinders at suitably chosen potentials, centered on the axis of symmetry of the tube. The general feasibility of this approach was suggested by the proof brought by Hans Busch in 1927 that axially symmetric electric and magnetic fields acted on electron beams in the same manner as glass lenses acted on light beams.

By 1929 I could demonstrate, at the Eastern Great Lakes District Convention of the Institute of Radio Engineers (November 18, 1929), a television receiver employing a viewing tube with the essential properties of a modern television viewing tube: a hard vacuum, an indirectly heated oxide cathode, an apertured grid as beam current modulator, and a first and second anode with their voltage ratio adjusted so as to form a sharp image spot on the fluorescent screen of a minimum beam cross section, or crossover, near the cathode. I called this tube a "Kinescope." The television signals employed for the demonstration were obtained by the mechanical scanning of motion picture film by means of an oscillating mirror.

Shortly before this time an event occurred which vitally affected the further development of my work in television. This was a meeting with David Sarnoff, then Vice-President and General Manager of the Radio Corporation of America, in which I had an opportunity to explain my ideas and hopes for electronic television. Sarnoff quickly grasped the potentialities of my proposals and gave me every encouragement from then on to realize my ideas.

In the course of a reorganization in 1929 of the activities of the General Electric Company, Westinghouse, and RCA, I was transferred to the RCA Victor Company in Camden, New Jersey and was made Director of the Electronic Research Laboratory. This enabled me to concentrate entirely on research on basic electronic processes and devices essential to electronic picture signal generation and picture reproduction. Assisting me was an adequate staff of engineers and scientists. In addition, I enjoyed the close cooperation of other research teams in Camden, Harrison, and New York which specialized in investigations of television system principles, circuitry, high-frequency tube design, signal propagation, and studio technique.

Progress now was rapid. By 1931 Iconoscopes had been built which demonstrated clearly the advantages of the electronic camera tube with storage over the earlier mechanical television pickup techniques. Within a few years all-electronic television replaced earlier mechanical efforts. Although tremendous efforts of a technological and organizational nature were still needed to establish television as an essential part of our culture, the main roadblocks to further progress had been removed.

9

Robert H. Stern

TELEVISION IN THE THIRTIES

THE STATUS OF television during the mid-Nineteen Thirties was in marked contrast to its condition at the beginning of that decade. Earlier the impulse to exploit it commercially had overmatched its technical capabilities; now the pressure to commercialize was temporarily lessened.[1] By this time the development of electronic methods for the scanning and reproduction of the televised image had reached a level of performance capability superior to that of any of the mechanical scanning systems upon which much of the earlier developmental and promotional effort had been spent. The future of the art technically, it was now clear, would follow the course along which Philo Farnsworth and Vladimir Zworykin had been moving in their separate experimentations since the previous decade. The work of these men on the design of basic instruments and techniques had provided the essential elements of electronic television; now steady progress was being made in the improvement of such instruments and techniques looking to their practical application.

American Journal of Economics and Sociology, Vol. 23 (1964), pp. 285–301.

Closely associated with the technical advances being made, the outlines of a patent-holding pattern were emerging, and strategic positions in the future industrial structure were being thus established. The shift of emphasis in technical development from mechanical to electronic methods was accompanied by a marked change in the status of individuals and companies relative to it. Some who in the earlier period had been in the forefront of experimentation and developmental work on mechanical-scanning systems now relinquished their positions of leadership. Others, whose work had seemed in the earlier period to be outside the main line of advance, now were in the vanguard of development and had sizable investments staked upon the pay-off prospects of their achievements. Yet others who previously had played no role of consequence in the developmental process, came forward during the period of the middle Nineteen Thirties thenceforth to have a part of some consequence in it.

In the sphere of government, also, certain changes of consequence had taken place during the years of television's retreat from overpublicity. The Radio Act of 1927 was replaced by the Communications Act of 1934, ending the life of the Federal Radio Commission and establishing as its successor the Federal Communications Commission, with jurisdiction extending over both wire and wireless communications services. Most of the provisions of the earlier statute, it is true, were with little or no modification incorporated into the 1934 Act, so that the statutory basis for the regulation of television, with respect to the basic powers and functions of the regulatory agency, remained unchanged in broad outline and also largely in detail. Television would continue to be dealt with, therefore, by the application of a law that nowhere explicitly indicated legislative awareness of its existence.[2] More significant than changes in the legal and organizational bases of regulation, perhaps, were certain barometric changes in the regulatory atmosphere. In particular, there were rising pressures upon the regulatory agency to do more than it had been doing to implement the legislative intent, which had been made explicit in both the 1927 and 1934 enactments, that competition in the radio industry be preserved. These pressures, although they were felt most immediately in regard to the situation of aural broadcasting, did nevertheless affect the climate in which determinations important to the development of television would soon be required.

What immediately follows relates to certain technological, industrial and governmental events mainly in the middle and latter Nineteen Thirties which were in the background of television's development during that period. It is intended as a prologue to an account that will be presented subsequently of what took place in the regulatory process proper respecting determinations as to when television should be permitted to begin as a commercial broadcasting medium and as to the adoption of standards controlling the technical characteristics of the transmission-receiving system to be used in the broadcast service.

I

The technical development of electronic television was already well begun when it became evident that mechanical-scanning systems would be incapable of achieving performance standards adequate for public broadcast purposes.

In 1928 Vladimir Zworykin had been a member of the Westinghouse research staff for most of a decade. There he had received some initial encouragement to pursue his interest in television, but only very limited support by way of facilities or staff assistance. The development of the iconoscope, therefore, was more a personal than a corporate achievement.[6] His successful demonstration of this device was followed by a marked change, both for him and for the pace and character of the developmental process.

Influential in this result was David Sarnoff, then vice-president and general manager of RCA. Sarnoff, highly impressed by the potentialities of the new device, persuaded Westinghouse, an RCA associate in the Radio Group, to give Zworykin what he needed to carry forward and intensify his developmental work.[7] Then in 1930, as part of an important change in the internal setup of the Radio Group, RCA took over from Westinghouse and General Electric research activities and manufacturing operations in the radio field, and Zworykin was transferred to the RCA staff.[8] Determined to assure its future as a leader in television at a time when public broadcasting in ths medium was widely thought to be at hand, RCA mobilized a sizable research corps to work with him. Among the major activities of this group were further work on the iconoscope to improve its efficiency, developmental work on the cathode-ray receiver (a model of which Zworykin had demonstrated in 1929), and work on circuit and synchronization problems.

In 1932, with about 60 persons thus occupied, RCA's developmental efforts reached a peak of intensity. Soon afterward, when it appeared that any technically adequate public programming service was still some years away from being born, or at any rate being given a birth certificate of authorization by the government, pressure on the research group for immediate results was lessened, and the staff around Zworykin was considerably reduced in size. A steady advance was made, nevertheless. By 1935 the results that Zworykin's group had achieved in their laboratory demonstrations was considered by RCA management to justify going on to a further stage in the developmental process. Preparations were begun, accordingly, for making experimental transmissions from a new transmitting station to be built atop the Empire State Building in New York City.[9]

Philo Farnsworth outlined a scheme of electronic television in 1922. The presentation was made to his high school chemistry teacher in Rigby, Idaho. In 1926, when he was nineteen, Farnsworth set out to make his conception work. He was confident that a year's time and the $25,000 financial backing that had been subscribed from their personal funds by a group of bankers in California would enable him to produce a television picture of satisfactory quality.[10] Early in 1927 the young inventor filed his first patent application, broadly covering his transmission-reception system, and later that year he was able to obtain with it a crude image reproduction.[11] The following year Farnsworth was ready to give a first demonstration of his "image-dissector" system to his financial backers. At this time, it is reported, he could transmit a motion picture of 100- to 150-line definition at a frequency of 30 pictures per second. "This gave a creditable television demonstration if great care was taken in the selection of the subject matter." [12] But the outlay of funds already had run to more than double the original estimate. When by early 1929 the total developmental expenses had mounted to well over $100,000 and Farnsworth's system obviously was still far from commercially practicable, his financial backers grew restive to the point of insisting that steps be taken to get outside support for the venture. At that time the enterprise was incorporated as Television Laboratories, Inc., with half the capitalization of 20,000 shares going to Farnsworth, his original partners and early financial backers. Since television was receiving a good deal of publicity at the time and Farnsworth's early backers were generally known around San Francisco as shrewd, hardheaded businessmen, there was no difficulty finding takers for the additional 10,000 shares.[13]

At the close of 1932 upward of an additional $200,000 had been expended, and Farnsworth had not yet demonstrated a near-marketable product.[14] But by the same time it had become pretty clear that when eventually television should emerge as a practical communications medium it would be through the development of an all-electronic system. And by then Farnsworth had accomplished much toward building a strong patent structure in this field.

Through the middle Thirties Farnsworth remained RCA's strongest competitor in developmental process. By 1935 they were both able to produce in their laboratories a picture much superior to anything seen three years earlier. The technical performance of Farnsworth's image dissector was in some ways unable to match that of the iconoscope, but in other ways superior.[15] In the patent rivalry both had gained strategically important positions. Victory by Farnsworth in a series of interference proceedings involving competing claims by RCA gave him a stronghold; but RCA also controlled many important techniques.[16] After several years of on-again, off-again negotiations a cross-licensing arrangement was worked out by these two companies. The aim of the Farnsworth organization was to obtain an agreement that would give it access to those RCA techniques which it needed to improve its own system and which would result also in the payment by RCA of substantial royalties for the use of Farnsworth patents. It looked to such royalties as a potentially important source of income.[17] RCA, while recognizing that its system would benefit by the use of Farnsworth patents, had no stomach for the prospect of breaking a long tradition not to be on the paying end of license royalties. It wanted rather to purchase the patents outright. The Farnsworth management, reports Everson, refused to countenance such a suggestion. "At first the two sides seemed so far apart that it looked utterly hopeless. Only the clear underlying fact that neither company could get along without the other kept the discussions alive." [18] In the end, after strenuous negotiations continuing from May to September, 1939, RCA capitulated on the question of royalty payments and an agreement was reached covering a very large number of techniques basic to electronic television. Everson finds poignancy in the scene of capitulation.

> The contract in its final form was brought in. All of the men were tired, but all were pleased that a satisfactory arrangement for both companies had been reached. When Mr. Schairer, RCA Vice President in charge of patents, finally signed the agreement there were tears in his eyes. It was the first time that his signature had been placed on a contract whereby the Radio Corporation had to pay continuing royalties for the use of patents.[19]

II

The situation of Philco in relation to television's technical development was quite different from that of RCA or Farnsworth.

Philco reacted more positively than did most other companies similarly situated when it appeared as the Nineteen Thirties began that television might have near-term commercial possibilities. It did not immediately attempt to launch a research and development program of its own, but it did agree to help finance the work of Farnsworth in return for license privileges on some of his patents.[20] Part of its intention apparently was to avoid becoming as subservient to RCA patent domination in television as it was in radio.[21] An arrangement through which Farnsworth conducted his research in the Philco laboratories in Philadelphia was initiated in the summer of 1931 and continued for about two years. Then it became clear, according to Everson, that "Farnsworth's aim in establishing a broad patent structure through advance research was not identical with the production program of Philco." [22] Upon the termination of its arrangement with Farnsworth the Philco company established its own research program (continuing, however, as a Farnsworth licensee). If this research was not notable for accomplishing major breakthroughs of technique, it did help bring television nearer to commercial quality.[23]

In connection with the Philco research activity during this period there occurred a bizarre episode in the history of intercorporate relationships in the communications industry. Philco brought a complaint in 1936 against RCA, alleging that the latter, attempting to learn Philco research secrets, had engaged in devious and unfair practices, including espionage. It charged that RCA undercover agents had even sought to play upon the frailities of Philco's female personnel. After striking up acquaintances among these employees, the complaint stated, the RCA agents

> did provide them from time to time with expensive and lavish entertainment at hotels, restaurants and night clubs . . . did provide them with intoxicating liquors, did seek to involve them in compromising situations, and thereupon and thereby did endeavor to entice, bribe, persuade and induce said employees to furnish them . . . confidential information and confidential designs, all in breach of the duty of trust and confidence which said employees owed to the plaintiff.[24]

It does not appear that this action proceeded to decision in the courts or other resolution of public record; the actuality of the threats to the personal and corporate chastity of Philco's females and their steadfastness of resistance if the threat was indeed substantial therefore remain uncertain. However that may be, there was reason for RCA to be disquieted by the prospect of competition from this quarter. Philco had proved to be a highly aggressive, successful and troublesome competitor in the radio-set manufacturing field. Also, it was one of RCA's more quarrelsome licensees, being frequently a party to litigation over patent royalties during the Nineteen Thirties. At the end of the decade it was to prove quarrelsome also in respect to the technical standards desired by RCA for official authorization as the basis upon which to initiate commercial television broadcasting.

The Columbia Broadcasting System, foreseeing the uncertainties of television's eventual impact upon its field of radiobroadcasting, was in a position roughly analogous to that of Philco in manufacturing. Organized in 1927, in five year's time CBS had gained a considerable stake in network broadcasting, with an impressive growth in volume of network time sales and a position almost matching RCA's subsidiary, the National Broadcasting Company, in number of station outlets.[25] It was not, in those early years, basically a research-minded organization; yet it could ill afford to ignore the possible consequences to itself of technological innovation brought about by the research and experimentation of others. Thus by 1931, a year of great expectancy that a full visual broadcast service (based upon mechanical-scanning systems) was nearly to begin, CBS was prominent among "dozens of eminently sound and respectable corporations [that had] decided to get into television." [26] The summer of that year it commenced experimental operations from a station in New York, offering a rather extensive program schedule. This station remained on the air for about a year and a half, until CBS was convinced, as were many others who at the beginning of the decade had projected an early entry into television, that prospects for its early commercialization had been illusory.[27]

Columbia did not, during the years of television's retreat to the laboratories, attempt to do significant independent work in technical systems development. Its posture was rather that of an interested bystander, awaiting evidence that the progress that others were making in electronic systems technology warranted a commitment to renewed experimental broadcasting operations based thereon.[28] In the spring of 1937 it did so commit itself. Plans were announced for the expenditure of about two million dollars within the next few years on experimental field óperations, a substantial portion of which was to go for the installation of transmitter facilities atop the Chrysler Building in New York. In this, CBS was about two years behind its major rival in network radio broadcasting. RCA had actually begun field tests from its new transmitter on the Empire State Building in the previous year. According to contemporary reports, many radiobroadcasters and set manufacturers welcomed the news of the CBS undertaking. Concerned over the possibility of domination by RCA of both broadcasting and manufacturing operations in television, they were pleased at this indication that a degree of competitiveness would exist.[29] A particular reason for the interest which the CBS venture aroused, apparently, was the anticipation that Columbia, with no vested interest in the promotion of a particular electronic transmission-reception system, might as a free agent provide objective information on the relative merits of the systems that others were developing. "CBS might, for example, be able to put RCA's iconoscope camera and Philo Farnsworth's dissector tube equipment to identical tests that would yield the first comparative data on the operating efficiency of these two principal rival systems." [30]

In contrast to the part they had earlier played as leading experimentors with mechanical-scanning methods, such major firms as the General Electric and the American Telephone and Telegraph Company were not major contributors to electronic systems development. General Electric, which along with Westinghouse had dropped television research upon agreeing in 1930 to relinquish manufacturing rights in the wireless communications field to RCA, reentered the field in the middle of the decade after the agreement was nullified by terms of the government antitrust decree.[31] Four years after reentry it had spent an estimated two million dollars on developmental work in television, in an effort to obtain leadership in receiving-set manufacture when commercial television should get under way.[32] No very radical technical advances resulted from its work during this period, and its activities do not seem to have had any pronounced effect upon this phase of the developmental process, except in adding to its momentum.

The American Telephone and Telegraph Company, in the face of the shift of emphasis to electronic television systems, did not continue to occupy the leadership role it had held in the development of mechanical-scanning methods. Nevertheless, with its wonted alertness to the implications of innovation bearing upon its own major sphere of interest, it did concern itself actively with one important phase of the latter developmental period. This had to do with supplying signal-transmission facilities essential for network television. In connection with radiobroadcasting, A. T. & T. enjoyed a lucrative business based upon its near-monopoly of wire facilities suitable for the relay of network programs. Since the existing wire facilities would not be technically capable of transmitting a high-definition television picture, the operation of a television network service after the fashion of radiobroadcasting would require the development of a new relay system. It appeared that a coaxial cable, which A. T. & T. was developing with a view to other uses also, might be used suitably for this purpose. In February, 1936, A. T. & T. was granted permission to install an experimental cable of this type between New York and Philadelphia.[33] This enterprise of the Telephone Company represented more than merely a desire to be ready with facilities for commercial television when it should arrive and more than a desire to head off possible competition for that particular type of business. It was an action, rather, which might be said to have derived from the Telephone Company's determination to hold its place as the master of the field of domestic wire communications against threats posed by the rapid progress of wireless communications technology. For RCA, an old adversary, was at this time already investigating the feasibility of low-power ultra-high-frequency point-to-point radio relays as a possible alternative to the coaxial cable method of carrying television signals and other kinds of messages as well. This held potentially ominous meaning for A. T. & T. Just as a coaxial cable would have many potential uses in addition to television (one such cable could carry one high-grade television transmission, or alternatively it could carry simultaneously about 250 telephone messages, or more than 2,000 telegraph messages, or many still-picture and facsimile reproductions), so would the radio relay. The development of an elaborate radio relay system, therefore, even if originally designed mainly for use on television relay, would potentially threaten the wire communications system which was A. T. & T.'s dominion.[34] The Telephone Company, with its usual resourcefulness and effectiveness, responded in a manner that alleviated the threat and turned challenge to profit. In doing so, of course, it was hastening the solution of a major technical (and economic) problem in television—the efficient distribution of programs to audiences beyond the receiving radius of the original transmitter.

III

Among the smaller companies in the radio industry that had worked on mechanical systems of television, there was little activity in the field after the promotional fanfare of the late Nineteen Twenties and beginning Thirties proved premature. It had become clear that the developmental process would require heavy outlays before any substantial returns could be hoped for—not a condition likely to stimulate activity by a firm of quite limited financial resources, especially during depression years. At any rate, the engineering personnel of these largely sales-minded firms were kept so busy making minor but showy improvements calculated to improve the consumer appeal of their companies' products in a highly competitive market that they had little opportunity to engage in research of a type needed for significant innovation.[35]

Meanwhile, newer phases of electronic technology did create some opportunity for new entrants to make their way into the field. The role of the Allan B. DuMont Laboratories is an instance in point. DuMont had become interested in television while employed by the DeForest Company at the end of the Nineteen Twenties when that concern was concentrating on mechanical-scanning techniques. In 1931 he went into business for himself on a shoestring. For the next several years he specialized in the development and manufacture of cathode-ray tubes and cathode-ray oscillographs, mainly supplying them to laboratories at universities and elsewhere for use in programs of research and experimentation.[36] At about mid-decade he ventured directly into television research on a small scale. Although DuMont's contribution on television systems development cannot rank with that of Farnsworth or Zworykin, he did make material contributions through his work on cathode-ray tube development and in synchronization techniques.[37] DuMont was to figure significantly in events of the period shortly preceding the FCC's authorization of commercial television. His was the first American company to offer electronic television sets for sale to the public—in 1939, before the regulatory agency had adopted a set of uniform engineering standards for television or authorized commercial service based thereon. At the time DuMont was not a party to licensing agreements with the major patent-holding firms, having developed a system that differed in significant respects from that of RCA or Farnsworth. Moreover, he was to be a leading critic of the system standards which most of the industry supported in 1940 as the basis upon which the agency should authorize the initiation of a regular television broadcast service.[38]

In yet another way DuMont deserves attention. Through this firm an important motion picture company first negotiated entrance into an industry of growth of which might clearly have great effects upon its own. In the late Thirties Paramount Pictures Corporation entered into an arrangement with DuMont whereby the latter was to get backing for its work in television, in return for which Paramount would acquire a large block of its stock over a period of years.[39]

While the response of the movie interests overall was certainly not as decisive as the potential magnitude of television's challenge would seem logically to have warranted, there was not an utter lack of industry-wide initiative. Two surveys were made by important industry organizations which dealt with the subject, and one of them presented a plan of action the central feature of which was that Hollywood interests gain an entering wedge into television by first obtaining control of a national radio network.[42] Although at a later period such a connection was established (American Broadcasting Company-Paramount Theatres, Inc., organized through merger in 1953), that can hardly be said to have realized any possible industry-wide hope earlier held of making the course of television's development conform to its own designs.

IV

By effecting a consolidation of governmental authority over both wire and wireless communications services, the Communications Act of 1934 may be said to have established a precondition, at least, for the achievement of a rationalized overall communications structure in this country. Authority for regulation of wire services, which formerly had been lodged in the Interstate Commerce Commission, was transferred by this legislation to the newly established Federal Communications Commission and enlarged in the process. For wireless services, Title III of the 1934 Act gave to the new agency regulatory powers generally similar to those that had been held by the Federal Radio Commission. As noted earlier, this meant that television would continue to be regulated under a statute that nowhere explicitly provided for its development and control as distinguished from that of aural radio.[43] The absence of differentiating provisions for television can be taken plausibly to mean that to the extent that the existence of the new medium may have been given specific notice at all in legislative deliberations preceding the 1934 Act, there was a disposition not to attempt to have television guided or controlled in the regulatory sphere in ways significantly different from those known to radio. Indeed, evidence is lacking that any serious legislative discussion occurred regarding the possibility of making such differentiations.

Nor were basic patterns of activity in the wireless field much disturbed as a result of the replacement of one regulatory agency by another. As Congress had seen fit to retain with slight alteration the legal framework fixing the scope and incidence of federal supervision, so the new Commission was initially disposed to respect existing regulatory arrangements and follow policies initiated by its predecessor. Generally speaking, the established commercial broadcasting interests continued to enjoy favorable treatment under these policies and arrangements.

Continuity of basic powers and policies did not bespeak an atmosphere of regulatory tranquility, however. The FCC almost immediately became as its predecessor had been, a frequent target of congressional criticism and was to live thereafter under almost constant threat of legislative investigation. Many facets of regulatory activity were thus subject to surveillance; but of particular importance in shaping the environment in which the development of regulatory policies for television would proceed was the degree of legislative concern with issues relating to the concentration of economic and social power in the communications industry.

In the hearings and debates preceding the enactment of the Communications Act of 1934, as in those which had preceded the original 1927 statute for the control of radio, the monopoly issue was much discussed. Both statutes contained provisions expressing the intent of Congress that competition in this field be preserved.[44] During the Thirties there was mounting congressional concern over monopolistic tendencies in the radio industry and increasing legislative criticism of the FCC for its apparent complacency in the face of these tendencies. In 1937 there were pending in Congress four resolutions calling for the investigation of monopolistic practices. Domination of the air by the major broadcasting networks, newspaper ownership of radio stations, widespread trafficking in broadcast licenses, concentration of control in the radio manufacturing industry, all were condemned on the floor of Congress.[45] Senator White of Maine, an authority on the affairs of the industry and the problems of regulation (he was prominent in the authorship of the Radio Act of 1927), was among those asking for an investigation of these matters and of

FCC's regulatory practices. If it could be shown that the Commission had done less than exercise to the full its power to preserve competition, the Senator suggested, this would be evidence of failure to comply with the congressional intent. "I do not view with complacence administrative disregard of legislative purpose," he said.[46] In 1938, after a period of internal reorganization following the appointment of a new chairman, Frank McNinch, the regulatory agency did undertake to investigate thoroughly one of the industry situations that was worrying monopoly-conscious legislators: the dominant position of the large networks in the entire broadcasting structure. From this time may be said to date the agency's own hyperconsciousness of the monopoly issue.

All of this was an important part of the background against which FCC had to confront certain issues in respect to the development of television, determinations on which could be of the greatest importance in shaping not only the technical character of the new medium but its industrial structure and social role as well. Particularly, in its duty to prescribe technical standards for industry-wide adoption as the basis upon which to inaugurate a public broadcast service, the agency would be facing a decision difficult enough because of the technical complexities involved, but made more so because of the economic interests at stake with the industry, the social consequences to be reckoned with, and the political reverberations that might be expected to ensue. How to achieve the necessary technical uniformity and yet not foster a dominance of the industry by interests which might, because of their control of the key techniques upon which such a uniform system was based, gain undue advantage and, using that advantage to impede further technical progress. thereby deprive the public of the benefits of it, and how to make such a policy appear to be their further particular advantage—these were considerations very much before the Commission as television was once more in the latter Nineteen Thirties brought out of the laboratories and proffered as ready for regular exposure to the public view.

Estimates place the cost of a television show at ten times that of a radio show or about $2,000 an hour, exclusive of talent costs. Because advertisers will not get their money back until they reach an audience of several hundred thousand people, the telecasting companies are going to have to make and pay for their own programs for some time to come.

—*Life*, February 20, 1939.

10

R. E. B. Hickman

THE DEVELOPMENT OF MAGNETIC RECORDING

ONE OF THE earliest published works dealing with magnetic recording was by Oberlin Smith in 1888, although some early experimenters had been using iron wire in primitive recording machines as long as twenty years before this. Oberlin Smith considered that a homogenous material such as iron wire was unsuitable for use as the recording medium, and suggested that better results would be obtained from a ribbon or thin tape made of cotton or silk into which small particles of a magnetic material had been woven. The difficulties of making such a ribbon proved to be just as intractable as the making of the recording itself.

In 1898 Valdemar Poulsen's experiments in Denmark culminated in his production of the first practical magnetic recorder which he called the "Telegraphone." Poulsen first investigated the use of a magnetised steel plate, but later results of this work led him to propose the use of a continuous steel wire as the recording medium. Poulsen took out his original patent in Denmark in 1898, followed by applications in the U.S.A., U.K., Germany and elsewhere in 1900, and this date may be considered as the starting point of practical magnetic recording. In 1903, with an associate Pedersen, he formed the American Telegraphone Company and in the ensuing years a number of Telegraphones were manufactured and used for commercial purposes, but development was very much retarded by the cumbersome nature and general unsuitability of the amplifiers of his day. There was also no ready source of the special type of iron wire required.

Few published works appeared dealing with magnetic recording between Poulsen's early work and the late 1920s, but it is of interest to recall that in 1917 an article describing the Telegraphone forecast the use of magnetic recording for sound films. It was suggested that a strip of pulverised iron filings could be deposited directly on to the film itself. Although magnetic recording has been used as a film production practice in studies, both in this country and in the U.S.A., for some years, it is only very recently that sound in the ordinary cinema has been reproduced from magnetic tracks.

As the efficiency of amplifiers and magnetic materials was im-

Magnetic Recording Handbook: Theory, Practice and Servicing of Domestic and Professional Tape and Wire Recorders, London: George Newnes Limited, 1956, pp. 1–7, 170–172. By permission of The Hamlyn Publishing Group Ltd.

proved in the late 1920s and early 1930s, recorders of better performance and quality were produced. Notable advances were made in
Germany by such workers as Stille, Begun and Hormann.

THE FIRST COMMERCIAL RECORDER:
THE MAGNETOPHONE

In 1928 Pfleumer took out a patent covering a method of coating
a plastics or paper tape with a magnetic material. In 1931 Pfleumer's
patents were taken up by the A.E.G. Company in Germany, who developed the coated tape, and who, in 1935 at the German Annual
Radio Fair, introduced the "Magnetophone"— the first commercially
available recorder to use this medium. This instrument was first described by Volk in *A.E.G. Mitteilungen* in September 1935. Also in
1933, two Japanese engineers Kato and Takei published, in the *Journal of the Japanese Institute of Electrical Engineers,* an account of
their method of preparing a magnetic material by the mixing of
various metallic oxide powders.

The Magnetophone was characterised by the high speed at
which it was necessary to run the tape, and the very cumbersome
reels which were consequently needed to give a reasonable recording time. The early oxide-coated tapes had poor magnetic qualities,
and instruments of this type which were being manufactured as late
as 1939 had very poor signal-to-noise ratio. None the less, since the
chief purpose for which they were supplied was for use as dictating
machines they served quite adequately.

THE BLATTNERPHONE AND
MARCONI-STILLE RECORDERS

Also in use at this time in Germany was the "Blattnerphone,"
and in England the "Marconi-Stille" recorder. Both these machines
used steel tapes: in addition to the difficulties associated with the
tape-transport system mentioned above for the Magnetophone, they
also suffered from the serious additional drawback of self-demagne-
tisation.

The Marconi-Stille apparatus was used by the B.B.C. principally, for the recording of events of national or sporting importance
for later transmission during evening listening hours. One of the
original machines can now be seen in the Science Museum at South
Kensington. It will accommodate up to 3,000 metres of 3 mm.-wide,
tungsten-steel tape, which at the normal operating speed of 90
metres per minute gave a programme capacity of approximately half
an hour per reel.

Development during the
Second World War

The onset of the Second World War stimulated intensive activity in magnetic recording. Both in this country and in the U.S.A. considerable advances were made in the production of wire recorders, culminating in the Camras wire recorder of 1943. But it was not until the Allied Forces occupied Germany that it became apparent that considerable advances had been made by German recording engineers. The use of oxide-coated tapes, and more significantly, the technique of using high-frequency bias during recording, enabled the Germans to produce recorders capable of giving very acceptable results.

The basic principles of high-frequency biasing were formulated in Carlson's patent applied for in 1921. Carlson and Carpenter—in a patent granted in 1927—described the application of an A.C. bias to the steel tapes and wires then in use. Poulsen, many years earlier, had recognised the advantages of some form of pre-magnetisation of the medium, but his experiments were confined to the use of D.C. bias. A German patent, taken out in 1940 by Braunmühl and Weber covering the application of high-frequency bias to the oxide-coated tape used on the Magnetophone, is generally recognized as the most potent factor in advancing magnetic recording from a back-room science to commercial importance. All present-day magnetic-recording machines may be considered to stem from the German designs of the war years.

Post-War Developments

In the post-war years developments in magnetic recording have concentrated chiefly on improving the reliability, and increasing the sensitivity, of recording and reproducing heads. In parallel with this work, much research has been applied to the improvement of the magnetic and physical properties of magnetic tape. Whereas in 1947 it was necessary to run a tape through a recorder at a speed of 30 in. per second to obtain high-fidelity reproduction, modern high-coercivity tapes give completely adequate results when operated at a speed of 7½ in. per second, and many recorders are now on the market which operate at speeds of 3¾ in./sec. or 1⅞ in./sec. and even less, but which produce quite acceptable results.

A development in magnetic recording which has had far reaching effects on television broadcasting is the development of systems of recording the complete television waveform on to a magnetic tape. Such recording is now widely used in television studios, in studios producing television commercials, and is beginning to be used, in certain applications, in location filming.

It has several times been stated by enthusiastic manufacturers that domestic video recorders may soon be available, permitting the television viewer to record any programmes transmitted at inconvenient times, so that they could be played back at leisure. At the time of writing, however, such equipment has not broken out of the laboratory stage.

A logical development of video recording would encompass the magnetic recording of both picture and sound in a television or film studio—without the use of conventional film—and again hopes are held out that this process will eventually be at the disposal of the amateur film maker.

TELEVISION RECORDING

An advance of technique of outstanding importance to the whole art of magnetic recording was the development in 1954 by engineers of the Radio Corporation of America of the first practical system for recording the complete television waveform onto magnetic tape.

A complete television signal contains components with frequencies ranging from 50c/s to 5 Mc/s, representing a spread of nearly 18 octaves. Due to the inherent 6 dB per octave drop in output of a magnetic reproducing head it is found that about 10 octaves is the maximum bandwidth that can be recorded and reproduced by a magnetic tape system. Additionally, the theoretical tape speed which would be needed to record a 5 Mc/s signal, with a head gap of 0.1 mil (0.001 in.) would be of the order of 500 inches per second.

The RCA recorder operated at a tape speed of 360 in./sec., and one of the major problems the designers had to tackle was to limit speed changes in the transport system to less than one part in a million.

Despite the disadvantage of the large quantity of tape which was required to record even a half hour programme, the particular timing and networking conditions under which the American television stations operate made the RCA system tolerably attractive. At the same time there was a great stimulus towards the development of an alternative system which permitted greater economy of magnetic tape, and at the same time permitted a less demanding mechanical specification.

In 1958, the British Broadcasting Corporation demonstrated, and for a limited period used in its own programming, a recorder known by its initials as VERA (Vision Electronic Recording Apparatus). This equipment was also a high speed machine, working at 200 in./sec. Using precision three-track heads of B.B.C. design and manufacture VERA was capable of very satisfactory results, but was soon made obsolete by the introduction of the "Videotape" recorder developed and manufactured by the Ampex Corporation of America.

Ampex Videotape recorders are now in use in practically all the television systems throughout the world, and the excellence of their performance is attested by the fact that the viewer is often unaware when he is in fact watching a recorded programme.

11

Lynn A. Yeazel

COLOR IT CONFUSING: A HISTORY OF COLOR TELEVISION

COLOR TELEVISION systems are based on theories traced back to the 1670s and Isaac Newton who devised a prism that divided light into color. Later Newton used persistence of vision to prove that white light is made up of a blend of colors. All these were pioneer color television experiments.[1]

John L. Baird, British TV pioneer, first demonstrated a mechanical color system in Glasgow in July of 1928.[2] His mechanical system used color filters to break light into color components by scanning the scene in sequence through red, then, green, then blue filters.

Later in July of 1929 Dr. Herbert Ives of Bell Labs demonstrated a flying spot scanner with three banks of photocells—one each for red, blue, and green. The receiver was a synchronized scanning disc with three tubes that discharged separate red, green, and blue images which were superimposed.[3]

On February 6, 1940, RCA demonstrated to the FCC an electronic color system.[4] Its pictures were colored, but this demonstration was so shaky, RCA skipped a public demonstration and went back to the Princeton Labs drawing boards. In August, CBS struck the first blow in what was to become a long game of "one-upsmanship" with a public demonstration of a sequential color system. The demonstration of Kodachrome slides and films was the result of one man's research. The man, Dr. Peter Goldmark, broke the scene down into red, green, and blue using three filters.[5] A scene projected through a blue filter registered only the blue elements on the pickup tube. The filter removed all tints except those of the filter. This scene on an ordinary black and white receiver viewed through a set of filters spinning in synchronization with those of the camera caused shades of gray to appear in color.[6]

In 1941 CBS made information on its system available to the FCC and to other electronics companies. FCC Chairman Fly encouraged other manufacturers to take advantage of the system and begin colorcasting. He urged the other companies to do six months of testing and report back to the FCC. CBS was the only organization to file such a report. On May 3, 1941 the FCC decided color was still in the future and allocated the black and white spectrum dropping channel 1, setting a 525-line standard, and adopting FM sound for TV. The Federal Telephone & Radio Corp. had built the transmitter for the 1940 CBS color experiments and needed an 18mc bandwidth for color. They used the high frequency experimental band in which at that time only a few others were interested. The need to transmit three signals necessitated the 18mc bandwidth for color and this too was against the system as present bandwidths were only 6mc in width. The apathy of other manufacturers and the shortage of technicians forced CBS to discontinue its color experiments during the war.

In 1944 John Baird, in Great Britain, developed a three gun receiving tube (Telechroma). It consisted of a two-sided mosaic screen in a glass envelope. One side was blue-green, the other red. Each side was scanned separately and it produced fairly good color, however the red was always too strong and Baird never achieved truly full color pictures. He was still using mechanical scanning for pickup.

Six months after V-J day at the 1946 NAB convention Richard Thomas displayed a color system that consisted of a three element lens on the camera and the receiver. This lens filtered the scene into red, blue, and green components. The actual transmission consisted of the grey scale equivalent of red, blue, and green. As in the CBS system only shades of grey were transmitted but the three element lens on the receiver converted these shades of grey back into their corresponding colors. This additive color system (Thomascolor) was originally intended for movies and printing but Thomas claimed it could be adapted to VHF television without major changes.[7]

In November 1946 RCA demonstrated a new electronic color receiver. An old flying spot scanner with photocells was used for pickup for the experimental receiver with three picture tubes. Color was fairly true, there was no flickering, but any movement caused color blurring. RCA engineers claimed three more months of work would cure the problem. RCA's Dr. Joliffe predicted that, "this all-electronic color system is so superior to any mechanical system as to take the issue of color completely out of the range of controversy." [8]

Despite this claim, in late November CBS petitioned the FCC to allow its color system to be used commercially. In December the FCC opened hearings on the matter. CBS's Dr. Frank Stanton claimed colorcasting could begin immediately. Goldmark was working on a one-tube electronic sequential color system that would improve the quality of CBS's color and, he said, outdate the proposed RCA three-tube system just announced.[9] For the hearing at the U.S. Court House in New York City, CBS, RCA, and DuMont planned elaborate demonstrations. In January 1947 CBS signals from the Chrysler Building were received on a CBS lab set and a proposed production receiver built by Bendix Aviation. The CBS demonstration consisted of fashion model Patti Painter displaying bright gowns, a boxing match, and an artist painting. The demonstration was criticized by Allen DuMont for distorted pictures and reflections caused by the magnifying lens. He claimed that the CBS screens were too small and could never be larger than they were because of the scanning disc. Dr. Goldmark, in defense, stressed that the CBS system was not inherently mechanical and that sequential selection can be applied to electronic scan. DuMont claimed the CBS picture was too dim. CBS engineers said contrast was more important than brightness. CBS wrapped up its demonstration by showing a yellow scarf in the courtroom and on TV for color accuracy. The color reproduction was judged extremely true.[10]

Two days later RCA televised from Penn's Neck Community Club in Princeton, N.J. The demonstration included a color newsreel, color slides, and color stills taken at the hearings on Monday. RCA engineer Engstrom stressed that it was a lab demonstration using lab devices and it wasn't the method that would eventually be marketed.[11] This lab device was the old flying spot scanner. CBS's Murphy criticized RCA's uneven color, poor registration, and inaccurate hues.

In March 1947 the FCC denied CBS's petition for color standards. The FCC stated that the refusal was based on: (1) inadequate testing, (2), and a belief that there may be other systems of transmitting color which offer the possibility of cheaper receivers, narrower bandwidths, and proven methods.[12] Vice President Murphy said CBS was merely seeking standards not trying to block future electronic color. He added that brighter pictures, compatibility, and replacement of the scanning wheel were in the near future.[13]

The Freeze

On September 30, 1948, the FCC froze all applications for television broadcast licenses pending further study.

The freeze didn't stop CBS's determination. From 9:00 a.m. to 12:00 noon when no network programs were scheduled, CBS telecast regular color programs from Channel 2 New York. It was the first time the CBS system operated in the 6mc bandwidth of VHF. Up to this time the three color impulses had each required 6mc bandwidth for transmission. This necessary 18mc bandwidth was only available in the new UHF band. Although the CBS system was now refined to operate in the present VHF spectrum, the system was still incompatible. Regular black and white sets received the color program either as a series of rolling horizontal bars or four small multiple images.[14]

The FCC announced plans for a hearing on VHF, UHF, and color. In May 1949 CBS again petitioned for their standards in the UHF band.

With the coming of the hearings new developments and developers appeared. Dr. Charles Willard Geer of the University of Southern California requested permission to demonstrate his system. It used a three-gun receiving tube with the appropriate electron gun firing its beam at phosphorous deposited on the serrated screen of the picture tube. A week later RCA announced it was ready with compatible color in the present spectrum. Sleeper's Color TV Inc. asked for time for further field tests before they demonstrated their line sequence system.[15] New York color photographer Leon Rubenstein filed his system of all-electronic color based on screens similar to an engraving process.[16] Skiatron announced a subtractive color system like Technicolor and Kodacolor. They also asked for time to do more testing before demonstrating the system.[17]

CBS's new image orthicon (I.O.) camera employed electronic sequential scanning using the disc only to avoid registration problems and light loss. The black and white compatibility problem was cured by an adaptor that increased line scanning frequency. It plugged into existing tube sockets of present black and white sets and used the displaced tubes in the adaptor, cost—about $10.[18] Another $35 and a color converter could be added to make the set receive color. Goldmark added that the CBS system would increase station cost less than 10% for cameras and gear, about three% overall.[19]

Demonstrations were in Washington, D.C. CBS began with Patti Painter and Jody Mill, Miss District of Columbia of 1948. The signal was sent via cable to New York and back to demonstrate compatibility with present AT&T lines. There was loss on the line but otherwise the pictures were reported as excellent. Special CBS "crispening" circuits showed excellent color that didn't wash out easily. Contrast was excellent and there was very little break up as dancer Betty Cannon performed; however, cameras were quickly capped when she lost her skirt. The FCC commissioners then turned their attention to studying black and white receivers which just happened to be tuned to the World Series.

RCA's equipment was in operation only 12 hours after arriving in Washington and had been produced in 77 days. The first pictures were poor. The system used three I.O. pickup tubes, one each for red, green, and blue with the same arrangement at the receiver; however, RCA said a new tri-gun picture tube would be available in six to 12 months. The next day RCA signals were sent from WNBW-TV's studios. To prove compatibility RCA ran demonstrations right up to network time for *Kukla, Fran, and Ollie*. They didn't warm up black and white cameras but fed the color signal to the full network. Compatibility was definitely proved with some affiliates reporting clearer black and white pictures than usual. Registration, resolution, and red smearing were RCA's main problems.[20]

The final member of the color triangle was Color Television, Inc. This system used a conventional I.O. camera with a three element dichroic lens placed between the camera lens and the pickup tube. The dichroic lens produced three two-inch images side by side on a modified projection receiver with a modified picture tube of red, green, and blue phosphor sections. Three lenses were mounted one above the other after the tube. These lenses threw pictures on an 11 by 14 inch screen with the pictures converging. CTI claimed registration to be simple, smear and carryover impossible.[21] CTI lacked brightness and uniformity and had registration problems; however, they had extensive line voltage problems. RCA's color was uniform and constant but not very faithful. CBS's color was excellent.

September 1, 1950, the FCC announced it favored the CBS system and asked manufacturers to report whether they could incorporate "bracket standards" of both 525- and 405-line systems into their sets. The "bracket standards" were a means of delaying the FCC's final decision while they did further study. Manufacturers informed the FCC that they could not meet a future deadline for the "bracket standards." Nevertheless October 11, 1950 the FCC "Second Report" adopted the CBS system and standards effective November 20.[22]

RCA filed against the FCC decision in U.S. District Court, Chicago. Seven manufacturers and many servicing companies did the same. The Chicago District Court issued a temporary restraining order four days before adoption. The changes would destroy a working machine before its replacements were built.[23] Without the proposed "bracket standards" TV sets currently on the production line would be as useless as older models. On November 20, 1950, an *ad hoc* committee, the National Television System Committee, was formed. It consisted of an all-industry group of engineers appointed to study compatible color standards. RCA's case was dealt a blow when the Chicago District Court upheld the FCC's decision, pending a U.S. Supreme Court ruling, on December 22, 1950. RCA appealed January 26, 1951, and on May 28th the Supreme Court unanimously (8–0) upheld the lower court and the FCC.[24] The Supreme Court ruling backed the FCC statement that any other system must incorporate drastic improvements over the CBS system before future petitioners will be considered. Many large and small manufacturers began to market converters for the new system.

The first network color program using the new CBS standards was telecast June 25, 1951. It featured FCC Commissioner Wayne Coy, William Paley, Frank Stanton, Arthur Godfrey, Ed Sullivan, Faye Emerson, Garry Moore, Sam Levinson, and Patti Painter, now "Miss Color TV." Sixteen sponsors picked up the tab for the "Pre= miere" telecast from WCBS-TV. In terms of significance to the television public the event was less notable since there were only 25 color sets in the U.S. Fifteen of them were in the New York studios with the remainder in Boston, Philadelphia, Baltimore, and Washington, D.C. Sponsors were impressed and color TV appeared to be headed for a harmonious future.

Then on October 19, 1951, Director of Defense Mobilization Charles Wilson called a halt to color receiver production for the duration of the Korean War. CBS and other manufacturers agreed but CBS maintained a rapid pace in its labs. They developed a new 17-inch tube without the magnifying lens and devoted much of their effort to military and medical uses of color TV.

The National Television System Committee (NTSC) remained busy during this time. In November 1951 they approved signal specifications for compatible color and began field testing. NTSC chairman Baker of General Electric claimed the proposal contained the best of all proposed color systems.[25] In January 1952, final specifications were approved.

In March 1953 color TV was back in the government arena as Senator Ed Johnson (D-Colorado) charged that powerful interests were seeking to delay the introduction of color. Republican Charles Wolverton, chairman of the House Interstate and Foreign Commerce Committee, announced an inquiry into the status of color TV. On March 26, 1953, the National Production Authority revoked the ban on color TV equipment manufacturing.[26]

RCA Asks Approval

Once again it was demonstration time with RCA, CBS, and Chromatic TV labs showing their wares to the FCC. On June 25, 1953, RCA petitioned the FCC for adoption of their NTSC approved standards for compatible all-electronic color TV. The petition said RCA has spent $21,000,000 on researching the system, that upon approval RCA would expedite equipment production, and that NBC would begin colorcasting to its 41 affiliates.[27] On December 17, 1953, the new system was approved by the FCC.[28]

Up to this point the CBS system had received the most attention by the FCC, broadcasters, and the press, creating the impression that

RCA didn't have an alternate system at the 1940, 1946, 1948, and 1950 demonstrations. The entire RCA system was based upon simultaneous color scanning. A separate pickup tube was used for red, blue, and green. Dichroic mirrors divided the incoming light into red, blue, and green components and reflected each component to the appropriate pickup tube. All three colors were transmitted simultaneously. The RCA system receivers were changed from a set with three picture tubes in the early demonstrations to the tri-color shadow mask picture tube. This picture tube made the RCA system practical, but production for home receivers was not realized until 1953. The beam was guided by razor-thin cuts in the shadow mask to the correct dot on the phosphor plate.

CBS Stays in Color

After millions of dollars of cost, court fights, years of experimentation, and many demonstrations the CBS sequential color system was junked. CBS ordered a number of three tube RCA cameras and began colorcasting. They soon learned that the cost of purchasing and maintaining color cameras with three I.O. tubes was staggering. A fourfold increase in studio lighting made productions uncomfortable and heavy bulky cameras made them cumbersome.

Color Makes Haste—Slowly

On March 14, 1954, RCA color set production began with a basic 15 inch set selling for $1000. There was no talk of converting existing receivers as there had been in the 1953 petition. CBS and NBC were each telecasting more than 22 hours of color per week.[29] In March 1955 AT&T color cables were ready to service over 90 per cent of the U.S. At the local level 46 stations could telecast color slides, 45 color motion pictures, and 15 live studio colorcasts. The equipment was ready but the public was not. Only one percent of the U.S. had color sets. CBS was colorcasting *Climax, The Red Skelton Show, Shower of Stars,* and others totalling less than seven hours a week in 1956. NBC began to cut back also with *Matinee Theatre, Howdy Doody, Milton Berle,* and others totalling 16 hours a week. By 1957 CBS had cut back to four hours with NBC doing 21 a week.[30] Set manufacturers were not producing enough receivers for easy availability and the limited production kept prices high. Despite the networks' attempts to sustain color programming color was only slowly gaining. The second half of the 1957–58 season saw CBS colorcasting only *The Red Skelton Show.*

CBS announced suspension of colorcasts for the summer of 1953, and dropped it in the fall. Admiral went back into color set production but other manufacturers delayed.

Total Color

From 1958 to 1964 only NBC telecast an extensive regular schedule of color programs.[31] CBS did one or two "Bowl" parades. ABC did no color telecasting until 1964 when they began two weekly cartoons, *The Flintstones* and *The Jetsons*. CBS did not regularly schedule any color programs between 1958 and 1966. In 1965 CBS telecast a multiple-episode *Lassie* in color and an occasional *Red Skelton Show* and one *Perry Mason*.

All but one and a half hours of NBC's 1965–66 prime time programs were in color. The 1966–67 season brought total color from all three networks to prime time viewing.

The total network color programming brought about a boom in color receiver sales. Lower prices and more reliable sets had started color set sales rising in 1964 but the full network color provided the boost.

During the complex history of color television there were charges and countercharges by CBS and RCA and beneath all of the fighting there were undoubtedly some villains. Despite their differences RCA and CBS stand out equally: RCA as the developer of a compatible system that works; CBS as the organization most responsible for promoting colorcasting out of the laboratory and on the air.

In February 1926 Hugo Gernsback offered this mystifying scientific entertainment. In the 1970s radio built-in headphones became popular. The "Father of Modern Science Fiction" the Hugo awards are named after him. © 1926 Ziff-Davis Publishing Company. Reprinted by permission of *Radio News* Magazine and the Ziff-Davis Publishing Company.

DIAGRAMS BY MAX GSCHWIND

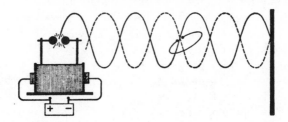

1888: With the simple apparatus above, Heinrich Hertz, a young German physicist, made the epochal discovery of electromagnetic or radio waves. Electrical sparks oscillating between the two metal balls, at left, sent out waves of high-frequency alternating electricity into space. The invisible waves were detected a few feet away by the open copper-wire loop, at right, which sparked in resonance with the metal spheres when properly positioned in the wave train.

SPARK-GAP TRANSMITTER   COHERER RECEIVER

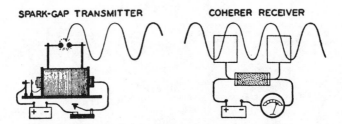

1896: Guglielmo Marconi, a young Italian-Irish experimenter, succeeded in transmitting Hertzian waves over a distance of two miles with the apparatus above. He added to Hertz' spark-gap transmitter a high earth-grounded aerial, which sent the waves rippling out over the earth. He substituted for the wire-loop receiver a more sensitive device called a coherer—a tube of loose metal filings that cohered and passed a weak current when struck by electromagnetic waves. In 1901 Marconi sent the first wireless message across the Atlantic.

EDISON EFFECT   **FLEMING VALVE OR DIODE**

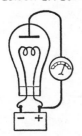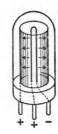

1883–1904: Thomas Edison, experimenting with his early incandescent lamp, stumbled on the basic principle of the electronic vacuum tube. Seeking to find out why filaments burned out, he inserted a metal plate in the lamp *(diagram upper left)*, connected it with a battery and discovered that a tiny but measurable current flowed across the empty gap from hot filament to plate. In 1904 Ambrose Fleming, an English physicist and consultant to Marconi, discovered that this tiny current, known as the Edison Effect, could be used to detect wireless signals. He curved Edison's plate into a cylinder around the filament and called the device a valve or, as it was later known, a diode. When the plate was coupled with an aerial, as shown in the circuit diagram above, it was rapidly alternated from positive to negative by the incoming waves, causing it alternately to attract and repel the tiny current from the filament, thus reproducing the signals in direct current to the headphones. But the Fleming valve, like the crystal detector, had no means of amplifying these signals.

"The Progress of Radio" from Lawrence Lessing, *Man of High Fidelity: Edwin Howard Armstrong* J. P. Lippincott Company, 1956, pp. 107–114. Diagrams by Max Gschwind.

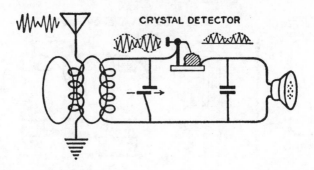

1906: Two Americans, H. H. Dunwoody and G. W. Pickard, almost simultaneously invented the famous crystal-and-cat's-whisker receiver shown in circuit diagram above. In the widespread search for a more powerful wireless receiver, they discovered that single crystals of quartz, galena and other substances had the power to detect wireless waves and pass them on as direct current to headphones, more efficiently than the coherer and other devices. The crystal detector came to dominate all wireless and early radio, but it lacked any means of amplifying the signals, for which the search went on.

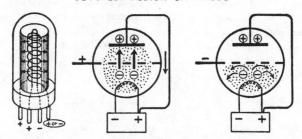

1906: The American inventor Lee de Forest added a third and controlling element to the Edison-Fleming vacuum tube device—a spiral wire or grid placed between the filament and plate, as illustrated above. This was called an Audion tube or triode. When the tube's grid was coupled to an aerial, as in the circuit diagram at right, the grid acted as a control shutter under the alternating positive-negative charges of the incoming waves, alternately passing and shutting off the current flowing from filament to plate to produce a replica of the incoming signals in the plate-to-headphone circuit. In some way this slightly strengthened the signals, but the triode's action was so little understood that initially it was little used.

REGENERATIVE CIRCUIT

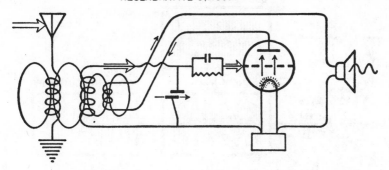

1912: Edwin Howard Armstrong, an undergraduate at Columbia University in New York, invented the regenerative or feedback circuit, diagramed above, in which de Forest's tube was suddenly revealed as a powerful amplifier as well as generator of electromagnetic waves. Closely studying the tube's action, Armstrong discovered that if part of the plate's output current was fed back and tuned into the grid *(arrow-marked loop at top of diagram)*, it reinforced and built up the strength of incoming signals to the grid as much as a thousand times. He also discovered that when the feedback was adjusted beyond this point of maximum amplification, the tube suddenly changed from a receiver to a transmitter, rapidly oscillating the current from filament to plate to send out electromagnetic waves of its own. With this dual-purpose circuit, still the basis of all radio transmitters, modern radio was born. The historic patent diagram is shown below.

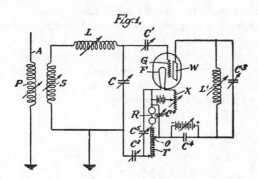

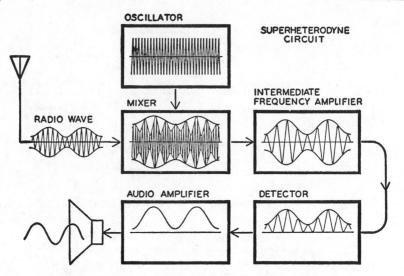

OSCILLATOR

SUPERHETERODYNE CIRCUIT

MIXER

INTERMEDIATE FREQUENCY AMPLIFIER

RADIO WAVE

AUDIO AMPLIFIER

DETECTOR

1918: Armstrong invented a second radio receiver, the superheterodyne, while serving as Major in the U.S. Army Signal Corps in France. Designed to get much greater amplification of weak signals than was possible with the regenerative circuit, the superheterodyne operates as shown in the block diagram above, each block representing a stage of one or more vacuum tubes. Stage 1: the incoming signal wave is mixed or heterodyned with a wave of slightly different frequency from a local oscillator tube, producing a signal wave of intermediate frequency equal to the *difference* in frequency between the two mixed waves. Stage 2: the wave of intermediate frequency is amplified three or four thousand times. Stage 3: the amplified wave is detected and converted to direct current by lopping off the lower or negative part of the wave. Stage 4: The detected wave is amplified into the audio frequencies and converted at the loudspeaker into sound waves. Highly stable and selective, the superheterodyne is the basis of nearly all present radios.

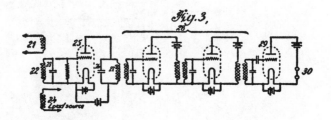

Fig. 3.

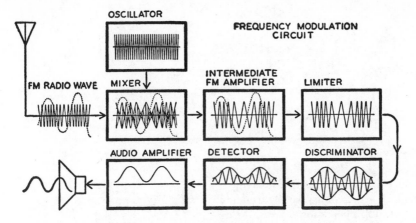

1933: Armstrong invented the frequency modulation or FM system at the end of a twenty-year search for a means to eliminate static. Most static is an amplitude phenomenon, mixing inextricably in the amplitude-modulated waves of ordinary radio. He therefore devised an entirely different radio system in which FM waves, modulated over a wide band of frequencies, are sent out and received by sets responding only to frequency variations. Key to the system is the receiver circuit shown in block diagram above, which is in all respects a superheterodyne except for the two additional stages labeled Limiter and Discriminator. The FM wave, with some static acquired in transit *(dotted lines),* is heterodyned and amplified in the first two stages. Then the limiter clips off any amplitude variations (static) and passes on the clean FM wave to the discriminator, which converts its frequency variations into amplitude variations for detection and amplification into sound at the loudspeaker. The result is a nearly static-free, high-fidelity radio system, still the last word in radio development.

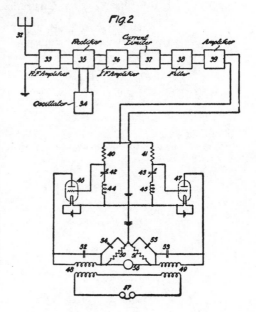

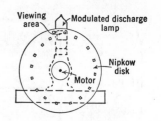

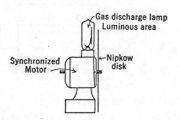

1884: Paul Nipkow used a light source and a spinning disc to create a picture by scanning with a rotating wheel. (top illustration) Synchronized discs could pick up and reproduce a "picture."

1907: Dr. Boris Rosing at the St. Petersburg Institute of Technology, Russia, demonstrated the electronic, rather than mechanical, creation of simple images using a Braun tube. Deflecting plates were used to direct a narrow beam of cathode rays and a scanning pattern was created by "sawtooth" current waves. This was the basis of the kinescope or "picture" tube. (Bottom illustration)

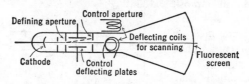

Illustrations from V. K. Zworykin and G. A. Morton, *Television: The Electronics of Image Transmission* John Wiley and Sons, 1940.

Illustrations from *Television: Collected Addresses and Papers on the Future of the New Art and Its Recent Technical Developments* RCA Institutes Technical Press, July 1936.

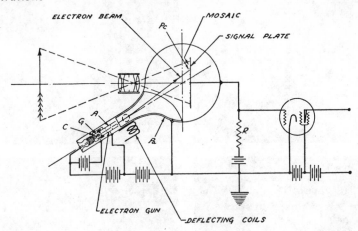

1923: Vladimir K. Zworykin filed a patent for the iconoscope (top illustration) Later in describing this device he wrote: "The inconoscope is a vacuum device with a photo-sensitive surface of a unique type. This photo-sensitive surface is scanned by a cathode ray beam which serves as a type of inertialess commutator . . . In its application to television the iconoscope replaces mechanical scanning equipment and several stages of amplification. The whole system is entirely electrical without a single mechanically moving part. The reception [Bottom Illustration] of the image is accomplished by a kinescope or cathode ray receiving tube." In 1931 RCA began experimental telecasts from a transmitter atop the Empire State Building using the Zworykin system. In 1939 both RCA and General Electric had regular, though limited, telecasting schedules.

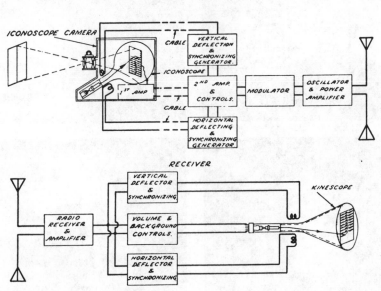

Walter Cronkite reported the launching of the Alan Shepard sub-orbital flight "crouching from the back of a station wagon" at Cape Canaveral. CBS had a 15-man crew in a nearby mobile unit. Eight years later he said "Oh boy" as Apollo XI landed on the moon. It was estimated that it took 1,000 people to produce this coverage on the three networks. A. C. Nielsen Company estimated that Neil Armstrong's first steps on the moon were watched by 40,130,000 (65%) U.S. households.

Live coverage via satellite of President Nixon's trip to China in February 1972 fulfilled, though reversed, Charles Sewall's 1900 prediction that we would watch "the American pageant . . . amid the darkness of an Asian night."

PART TWO

STATIONS

. . . at the present time two wave-lengths are assigned for broadcasting—the wave-length of 485 meters for Government reports, such as crop and market estimates and weather forecasts furnished by the Department of Agriculture; the wave-length of 360 meters for important news items, entertainment, lectures, sermons, and similar matter.

—*Radio Service Bulletin,*
April 1, 1922.

THE STATION is the basic structural unit of broadcasting. It links the broadcasting industry to audiences.

Stations vary in many ways. The typical television station in a major market employs 150, has revenues of $10,000,000, and profits of 20%. The typical radio outlet is in a one-station market, has a staff of 10, grosses $170,000, and earns a profit of 7%. In 1972 2,025 (47%) of all AM and AM/FM radio stations were in 265 standard metropolitan statistical areas; 2,314 (53%) were outside metro areas. One-third AM radio stations (1502) were in one-station markets.

The idea of distributing news and entertainment to a wide audience was introduced in Europe as early as 1880. This system, using wires in the same way community antenna television would 70 years later, was known as the Telephonic Newspaper in Budapest and had attained a subscriber list of 6,185 by 1896.[1] A few years later "Doc" Herrold's station in San Jose, California began broadcasting regularly.

Station KDKA in Pittsburgh, whether or not it was the first station to start continuous service is festooned in historic "firsts." Efforts by researchers to clear up which station, including WWJ, Detroit, and WHA in Madison, Wisconsin was on the air regularly the earliest have been clouded by faulty records.[2]

Everything that a station did in the infancy of broadcasting was an experiment. The idea of broadcasting caught on quickly in this country. By 1922 there were 570 licensed stations. Of these, 141 were still on the air in 1970 usually owning the best frequencies and the highest power in the largest markets. It would have been hard to predict in 1923 which broadcasters would survive. The most stable stations seemed to be connected with educational institutions, churches and radio manufacturers.

The first National Radio Conference in 1922 in Washington, D.C. was concerned with the conduct of stations. The group recommended that the Department of Commerce set aside two wave lengths—one for private broadcasting and one for toll broadcasting. Toll broadcasting was to be operated commercially on a basis similar to the telephone company. Messages would be paid for by individuals. Seven months later a real estate dealer paid WEAF to broadcast a message about the joys of country living in a New York subdivision and commercial broadcasting was under way. It would be a few years before the terms "sponsor" and "commercial announcement" would label the transaction. In the early 1920s wave lengths of stations were continually changed both by the government and by the individual station which found its assigned frequency unsatisfactory. There were nights when stations in one community would stay silent allowing local dial twisters to listen-in to distant signals. The equipment at both ends of the communication chain was unreliable. If the listener-in was able to tune in a station with a minimum of interference there was a very good chance that the station or the set would malfunction during the "program." It was a remarkable feat for sets in Kansas and Oklahoma to pickup eastern stations since the early power of most stations was about 100 watts.

KDKA and others began to increase their power as technological bugs were worked out of the transmitters. By 1925 most of the stations were broadcasting at 100 to 500 watts. However, 20 big stations were radiating 1,000 to 1,500 watts and WEAF was booming out with 2,000 watts. Stations had been experimenting with power up to 50,000 watts and there was talk of "super-power" above that.

Equipment in this period was limited. Microphones were inverted megaphones and tubes were subject to breakdowns. Stations were heavily draped to deaden sound—the idea originating with KDKA which had found its temporary roof "tent studio" acoustically satisfactory. The studio was usually draped and outfitted to look like a pretentious living room of the time.

Austin C. Lescarboura described a typical radio-phone broadcasting station in 1922 as a long, narrow room.

At one end stands a beautiful piano of the reproducing variety, with its long bench. This piano may be played by a flesh-and-blood pianist, or by Grainger, Godowsky, Rachmaninoff or Hoffman, not in person, of course, but in the form of a perforated paper roll. Then there are several phonographs of various makes for the broadcasting studio does not play favorites. Along one of the long sides of the room is a small table, with a silk-shaded lamp to add a touch of home atmosphere and to reassure the performers, followed by an automatic organ, several desks, and plenty of chairs. It is just a plain room, with very little embellishment except some draperies which can be placed over the bare walls . . .[3]

According to Lescarboura the drapes would be artistically arranged and potted plants and flowers added before pictures were taken. The transmitter was usually located near the studio—often on the roof near the antenna.

It was not uncommon to disguise the microphone in a birdcage or a lamp. Stations were using many techniques to gain status. WEAF transported actors and singers to the studio in a rented Rolls Royce. Many stations were not so extravagantly appointed. Following is a description of the WDAF studio in Chicago in 1921 and 1922:

A dear friend of ours was experimenting with the advertising business on the floor below, so we appropriated the front half of the office and moved in a piano and a few yards of drapery. We overcame the microphone problem by packing a four-button carbon affair into a fibre waste basket and hanging it on a pale blue parrot-cage support. I shall never forget the general effect. On top of the piano sat a loud speaker, connected to a hand microphone in the operating room. When the operator—it required just one to run the transmitter and the concert—would announce the station and the next number, it would be fairly audible to those in the studio. Then he would turn and bellow—"All right, *shoot!*" and the temperamental talent below would recover as rapidly as possible and do its best at the waste basket. It was a great way to run a station and I wish we could return to it.

WDAP, located on the Wrigley Building, Chicago, Illinois (it's a wonder we left off the U.S.A.), ground out her closing quotations and her three concerts a week all through the winter and up to July, 1922, steadily growing worse. It is a curious thing, that process of natural decay which a station, put up by the inexperienced, always undergoes. It just gets worse, despite your increasing knowledge and your violent efforts, and nothing will save it.[4]

The early prediction of high stability for educational stations backfired after 1927 when the new Federal Radio Commission ordered stringent restrictions on equipment. Nearly 100 educational stations went off the air unable to finance the new electronic requirements. Fifty other stations also left the air rather than meet the requirements. Other regulations or station operations required they broadcast only on assigned frequencies and during hours specified by the government. The plan by the FRC was to set up 40 "clear" channels with one station each at 50,000 watts, 35 channels with two or three regional stations each at 500 to 1000 watts and six local channels with station powers ranging from 10 to 100 watts and 25 stations on each local channel. The plan never was completed.

The increase in stations was gradual—from 700 to 800—between 1927 and 1940. Power of stations gradually increased, too, particularly in "regional" type stations which increased from 30 to 100 stations with 5,000 watts over the 13-year period. Other changes occurred in the 1930s: the number of daytime-only stations increased; the number of stations sharing time on the same frequency decreased; and at least one directional antenna was introduced into use in 1932. An experiment using 500,000 watts by WLW in Cincinnati was abandoned in 1939 after five years. The idea was technically sound but caused considerable economic objection from competing stations.

In September of 1940, 777 of the 862 radio stations in the United States changed their frequencies 10 to 30 kilocycles in agreement with the Havana Treaty. Of more immediate significance to 33 licensees was a duopoly ruling which had owners divest themselves of all but one AM station in a market.

The Federal Communications Commission, already aware of the concentration of control of the media, also proposed that newspaper publishers be barred from station ownership.

President Roosevelt whose second term was opposed by most newspapers and who had used radio to go directly to the people also urged the FCC to bar newspaper ownership of stations. The commission adopted such a rule but reneged after heavy congressional pressure.

The public was well aware of television by the early 1940s. There had been a widely publicized demonstration of TV at the New York World's Fair in 1939. There were 38 experimental television stations on the air in 1932.[5] In 1941 the FCC established technical and channel standards for commercial TV, five stations were so licensed by December 1941.

Radio station growth was small but steady during the 1930s and into the 1940s. The government allowed several stations building permits as essential industries during the war and by 1945 there were 950 stations in service. Stations were asked to decrease their power about 10% during the war to conserve power for other industry. After the war the Federal Communications Commission was flooded with requests for station licenses. The agency, allowing for less separation of signals and recognizing the use of directional antennas permitted the radio station population to double in two years. Prospects for radio looked very good. The stations which had been on the air through the war had made a handsome profit and there was expansion in advertising predicted. Most of the new stations were in the lower power group with sites in small markets—many times introducing broadcasting on a local basis to a community for the first time. By 1956 there were about 3,000 stations—five times the number 10 years previously. Along with the establishment of new stations the FCC was encouraging the licensing of frequency modulation stations. Many broadcasters felt that FM was the station of the future and sacrificed to acquire a station. Once getting the license it was not used for a great deal of original programming. The average AM station was beset by the addition of four new hungry AM radio competitors, and, on the horizon, the threat of television.

A portent of the future occurred in June of 1946 when the Gillette Company sponsored the Joe Louis-Billy Conn fight on television. The "network" for the fight was reminiscent of the early days of radio with several large eastern cities hooked up for the event. Within five months NBC had sold a network series to Bristol-Myers. Still for AM radio there was time to adjust. Only 50 TV stations were on the air and in 1948, with authorizations for a little more than 100 stations, the government "froze" new station authorizations while the idea of color and allocations of channels was discussed. The television licensees on the air in 1948 and which continued to operate during the freeze are the chosen people. Four years later the *Sixth Report and Order* thawed out the television situation and 1,300 communities were allocated 2,000 stations including educational and ultra-high frequency (UHF, 14 to 83) channels. About 10% of these allocations were reserved for educational, non-commercial stations—mostly UHF.

Radio station aspirations were changing as revealed by changes in the studio facilities. Early broadcasters had considered themselves part of the live entertainment business. Many small stations in the 1930s had full programs of live entertainment throughout the day. Others were tied in with the networks which were, in turn, broadcasting live material. However, the new stations were being constructed without facilities for live performance. The traditional "Studio A" with its music stands, grand piano and old sound effects equipment was not in the new plans for broadcasting stations. Large auditoriums which had been part of the earlier station layout were being sliced up into office space and record libraries. Probably the most important contribution to this revolution in broadcasting was the tape recorder which made live performance on radio unnecessary, except in programs where time was important. Programs on the network were mostly on tape, as were local and network commercials. The next step was automation, with every segment of the broadcast on tape. This became common, particularly for FM operations, in the 1960s. After January 1, 1967, FM stations in communities of more than 100,000 could according to new FCC rules duplicate only up to 50 percent of an AM station's programming. But by 1970 with 2,000 FM stations in the country, many still were automated for background music and only a few were striking out into programming for themselves. But for the first time FM stations in some markets were achieving ratings among the top stations.

Sound broadcasting audiences were being fragmented to local AM and FM and regional station audiences. Advertisers zeroed in on local markets with improved buying techniques. The big stations, booming out over miles and miles of farm country were losing their economic impact. They were unable (or unwilling) to finance programming which was a great deal different from that of their local and regional competition. The role of the 50,000-watt, clear channel station was difficult. Powerful enough to serve millions, yet the general interest programs so common in the 1930s and 1940s no longer were economical. The revolution in radio during the 1950s left no station untouched.

The role of the stations still was not completely clear in the 1970s. The total number of AM stations had reached 4,300 with half of them daytime-only. Only one station in 15 was authorized to operate at full power day and night without a directional antenna.

In the 1960s arguments continued over the cross-ownership of broadcasting stations and other media. The FCC adopted a policy further limiting one owner to only three TV stations in the top 50 markets—but those with more were grandfathered. This further restricted the total of seven AM, seven FM, and seven TV (a maximum of five VHF) stations that any one firm could operate. This controversy was extended to cable television, newspaper and other media ownership. The FCC prohibited CATV and TV station ownership in the same market area.

Minorities sought more ownership of media. Blacks owned more radio stations than ever, but the number still was less than one percent of the total licenses in the U.S. Some blacks saw the new media, such as CATV as their last chance for ownership of mass communications outlets.

From those few experimental transmitters half a century before had come 8,500 broadcasting stations: 700 commercial television stations, more than 200 non-commercial TV outlets, nearly 7,000 commercial radio stations and more than 600 in the non-commercial FM category.

12

Gordon R. Greb

THE GOLDEN ANNIVERSARY
OF BROADCASTING

THE REAL PIONEER of broadcasting is Herrold's Station of the Garden City Bank Building in San Jose, California.

This station began so early in the 20th Century with its broadcasting activities that it was not even required to have any call letters but simply identified itself by using the name of its founder, Charles David Herrold, principal of the Herrold College of Engineering and Wireless, San Jose, California. In January, 1909, it had its first successful broadcast.[2]

What began back in 1909 has continued in straight-line continuity to the present broadcasting of KCBS, the 50-thousand watt key station of the Columbia Broadcasting System, San Francisco, the direct lineal descendent of the small 15-watt spark transmitter with which "Prof" Herrold experimented so many years ago.[3]

"On January 1, 1909, I opened my School of Radio in San Jose," Herrold wrote Lee De Forest. "From the first, broadcasts were a part of my routine. I never employed a Poulson arc in broadcasting, nor did I use the so-called 'peanut whistle' type of spark of Charlie and Jack McCarthy in Oakland. I experimented with practically all the existing types of sparks and arcs, with the exception of the Alexandersen (sic) high frequency generators, which were very obviously outside the reach of my pocket book. When I opened my school I kept some sort of wireless telephone equipment hooked up all the time. The output was always small up to late in 1911, and the distances covered were small . . . In spite of continual changes in apparatus, there was always music of some sort coming from my station. It was real broadcasting—how do I know? Because I had to make my own audience. I went out through the valley and installed crystal sets so that people could listen to the music." [4]

These first broadcasts were more than three years before Congress enacted the Radio Act of 1912, which required licenses and call letters from "voice" transmitters.[5] Until then, Herrold's operators simply announced, "This is San Jose calling," gave a vocational school identification and went into their news and music. Operating the station continuously was a logical way for him to gain publicity for his wireless school among an audience most likely to enroll, the

Journal of Broadcasting, Vol. III, No. 1 (Winter 1958–1959), pp. 3–13.

teen-age amateurs. Herrold recalled that he used the call letters FN early in his experimental broadcasting. He also used experimental land station licenses 6XE (portable) and 6XF on variable wave length assignments. By 1913, the call letters SJN were heard on the air. And in 1921, after licenses finally were issued under the classification of broadcasting, Herrold's station became KQW. The call letters were changed to KCBS in 1949.

Herrold, a classmate of Herbert Hoover at Stanford University before the turn of the century, died in 1948 at the age of 72 in a rest home at Hayward, California.[6] So his letters, personal records, newspaper clippings, and other collected materials are the principal documents of his story.[7] But these private papers are not all. There are his contemporaries, too, who can verify what happened in these early days and the author sought them out.

One of the first to associate himself with Herrold in San Jose was a young man named Ray Newby, the professor's assistant and wireless code instructor. This 16-year old experimenter taught the half-dozen students enrolled in the fifth-floor classes of the Herrold College in the Garden City Bank Building, First and West San Fernando streets, San Jose. Newby had a natural bent for tinkering with electrical gadgets, as did his mentor. In an interview, Newby told what happened.[8]

Q. "Is this the same Ray Newby who with Charles D. Herrold successfully broadcast by radio from the Garden City Bank Building in San Jose in 1909?"

A. "Yes, sir! Definitely! I'll never forget it."

Q. "Can you tell us about that?"

A. "Well, it was experimental at that time and it was quite a thrill to everyone. All the crystal detectors in San Jose and for miles around were not only thrilled but shocked to hear voices coming over when they were really listening to the spark code . . . The voice was a shock to almost anyone that heard it the first time."

Q. "You told me earlier that it was on a little set you built that the first successful broadcast was made."

A. "Yes, when he (Herrold) put this school in operation he had built an umbrella, fan-type antenna from all corners of the building, out over the whole town, practically for a block in every direction . . . I think what started the whole thing—so far as putting the voice out over this large antenna was when I brought in a little one-inch spark coil and he had a microphone and we connected the thing into a storage battery and talked into this microphone and rattled out some voice. And right away we began to hear some telephone calls that they had heard us."

The antenna Newby mentioned created quite a stir in downtown San Jose the year it was installed. It was an enormous carpet aerial containing over 11,500 feet of wire, fanning out from the top of the seven-story bank building to the adjoining buildings on two sides, each three stories high, and to a pole atop a third three-story structure. Herrold preserved a detailed drawing of the "old aerial" among his personal papers. The October, 1910, issue of *Modern Electrics*, a publication for amateurs, is known to have called attention to the San Jose aerial.[9]

The claim that Herrold made for his 1909 station and its inauguration of broadcasting was never that he was the first man to talk over the wireless instrument or to transmit music over it. Those credits, he was first to admit, belonged to other men.

"I have never claimed such a distinction," Herrold told a radio interviewer on Jan. 15,1934. "I question whether any American has such a distinction, unless Amos Dolbear can be said to be the first man in America to talk to a receiving station at a distance without connecting wires of a telephone line. He did this at a distance of one mile, ten years before Marconi's time. In Europe such men as Count Arco and Professor Slaby; Reumer Vlavimir Poulsen, the Danish Edison; Simon; Dudell; and Thompson were far ahead of Americans in evolving wave-producing devices modulated by the voice. In America we had Collins and Francis McCarthy in San Francisco who talked from Twin Peaks to San Francisco, about three miles, using a spark telephone. Dr. Lee De Forest in this country did considerable development work on experimental wireless telephones before I did my work at San Jose . . ."

What Herrold established with his operating wireless-telephone station atop the Garden City Bank Building was, in one word, "broadcasting." The early definition of the word was, "A casting or scattering in all directions, as seed from the hand in sowing." Herrold contended no one actually used the instrument deliberately in this fashion until he created his station in 1909, even though one or two others may have speculated about its possibility. The great excitement that others found in using the wireless-telephone in the early years, Herrold maintained, was in trying to improve point-to-point communications. The household telephone still was incapable of spanning long distances and many experimenters were concentrating solely on ways of tying radio into direct-line equipment. This was not broadcasting but narrowcasting.

"A narrowcast," said Herrold on the same 1934 program, "is a message sent from one transmitting station to one certain receiving station and intended for none other . . . There is not the slightest evidence to show that Collins, McCarthy, De Forest, Poulson, or any of these early experimenters had in mind the use of their experimental radio telephone for entertainment purposes."

Herrold did more than think about broadcasting. He began pro-

grams of news and music on a regular schedule, starting in 1909, and
he continued the schedule without interruption, except for manda-
tory silencing of all civilian stations during the first world war. When
licenses were issued again, Herrold was back on the air, programming entertainment as usual.

There is ample evidence that Herrold operated on a daily schedule from 1910 forward.[10] Most members of the older generation living within a 50-mile radius of San Jose know about it and contemporary wireless operators testify to it.

Ray Newby, who participated in the broadcasting station's earliest activities, answered direct questions on this point:

Q. "You went into radio programming on a regular schedule?"

A. "Oh, yes. It got to be a habit with everybody. They would
even call us up and want to know when we were going to test some
more. And it was not long until we got into a prearranged schedule so
that we would have listeners that could report to us . . ."

Q. "When would you broadcast regularly . . . ?"

A. "Oh, daily! The first I remember . . . it was a habit to go on
Wednesday evening and broadcast news, records, and voice for one-
half hour. And sometimes we would run longer if the microphones
and everything didn't get too hot." [11]

Herrold's first wife, Mrs. Sybil M. True, of San Jose, answered
the same question with the same information—"every Wednesday
night." In fact, she herself was a pre-World War I disc jockey on
what she called her "Little Ham Program." She recalls that her program attracted teen-age amateur set enthusiasts and that weekly contests encouraged them to listen regularly.

"I really believe I was the first woman to broadcast a program,"
Mrs. True said, explaining how she would borrow phonograph
records from a local music store "just for the sake of advertising the
records to these young operators with their little galena sets. And we
would play up-to-date, young people's records. They would run
down the next day to be sure to buy the one they heard on the radio
the night before . . . We would ask them to come in, and sign their
names, where they lived, and where they had their little receiving
sets . . . And we would give a prize away each week." [12]

To encourage the public's interest in radio, Herrold established
a listening room in the Wiley B. Allen Company store in downtown
San Jose just prior to 1912. There he installed comfortable chairs and
two dozen pairs of telephone receivers, hanging from the walls, each
of which fed "concert" programs from two master receiving sets.
This store loaned Herrold "hit tune" phonograph records so that the
musical programs could be changed to suit listeners' tastes. Mrs.
True said she always acknowledged audience requests.

Mrs. True verifies the beginning of her broadcasting activities by virtue of the fact each Wednesday she needed a baby-sitter for her oldest son, Robert. He was an infant at the time she conducted her weekly programs. Motion picture film shows Mrs. True holding the baby in front of a microphone while Herrold tested the effects of crying on the meters.[13]

Soon after the station began broadcasting in 1909, Herrold became dissatisfied with the voice quality of the "spark" method because it was not distinct enough. So he began experimenting with the "arc fone" system, trying to exaggerate the factors that made the streetlamp arcs hum and sing. By causing the arc light to oscillate fast enough, the tone frequency could be increased to the point where the ear could not perceive the high-pitched "singing" but a carrier wave would be created to carry voice and music.

By 1912 Herrold had so improved his arc system that he interested the National Wireless Telephone and Telegraph Company in it. He became the company's chief engineer with the primary task of building and supervising the installation of his arc systems for the U.S. Navy at Mare Island and at Point Arguello, California, while still maintaining his college and regular broadcasting operations at the Garden City Bank Building. Assisting him in this were operators Emile A. Portal and Kenneth Sanders. Frank Schmidt, who also worked from time to time at the University of Santa Clara, also served as Herrold's mechanic.

The success of the Herrold station in San Jose in the early years was measured in many ways. There was a pickup truck which one of Herrold's students drove around the countryside, stopping at designated places to test reception. A laboratory also was built in a cabin, high in the Santa Cruz mountains, above which a 500-foot long aerial was strung from the peak of one mountain to another. A vertical wire dropped down from this to the receiving set in the shack. Herrold tested the signal from San Jose by taking equipment deep into the New Almaden mines; or by immersing rubber-coated wires in the Alum Rock creek; or by having his students fly kites with aerials attached from various locations.

One letter in Herrold's files from Leslie F. Sherwood states that when he was a wireless operator on the S.S. City of Sydney, sailing out of San Francisco from 1911 to 1913, he often heard the transmissions of the San Jose and San Francisco stations.

"The greatest distance I received good speech was abeam San Pedro . . . ," Sherwood wrote from Miami Beach, Florida in 1933. "As to quality, the signals were as clear cut and smooth as the present day transmitters. Laying at the dock in San Francisco, I many times heard your tests as follows, 'Hello, San Jose. Hello, San Jose.' etc., followed by a phonograph record more enjoyed with the head phones than with a standard Victrola of the time."

The San Francisco station was atop the Fairmont Hotel and was an N-W-T-and-T company station in which Herrold had great interest, because it was his ambition to be the first man to build a workable two-way radio communications system by talking to it from San Jose.

On June 20, 1912, with company stockholders looking on, Herrold succeeded in his plan to talk back and forth from the Garden City Bank to the Fairmont Hotel. Sanders and Portal operated the San Jose outfit while Schmidt and another student, Henry V. Anzini, operated the other. He used two transmitters and their water-cooled microphones at each location, enabling the operator to switch to the second unit if the first one failed. "This communication," said Herrold, "was continued uninterrupted for over 8 months." His personal file contains notarized documents to prove it.[14]

During 1912 the government wireless station on Point Loma complained about considerable interference from an unknown wireless-telephone operator who insisted on singing, "Oh, You Beautiful Doll" on the air waves. But a search failed to pinpoint the vocalist other than in the vicinity of San Jose.[15]

Another complaint not only illustrates the power of Herrold's station but proves as well that his operators were required to complete their scheduled tours of duty, not shut down whenever they felt like it. The following letter from G. E. Baxter, an operator for the Marconi Company, finally reached the U.S. Radio Inspector's office.[16]

"Dear Sirs;
    At one thirty PM to-day, the wireless telephone station of the National Wireless Telephone and Telegraph Co., at San Jose, started talking to the amateur station 'LQ' (Mr. K. Saunders, San Jose). (sic) At about the same time, the steamer (sic) 'Nann Smith' started calling this station with a message, but the arc from the San Jose wireless telephone station cut his signals down considerably and they were unreadable at times. At one thirty four PM, I told 'SJN' (San Jose Telephone) to 'break' and started the 'Nann Smith.' All this time 'LQ' was sending to 'SJN' but I could tune the Nann Smith in loud enough to read through him. 'SJN' stayed out for a minute or so, and then broke me right in the middle of a message.
    "Mr. Portall (sic) was using the telephone and wanted Mr. Saunders (sic) to come up there and relieve him, as he wanted to go some place on a car and they held me up until one forty two PM arguing the point with one another. As soon as they arrived at a conclusion, I called 'SJN' and he answered immediately, showing that he could hear me OK, and I told him it was bad enough for him to use the telephone arc when he had to without using it to talk across town with. His talk was entirely unnecessary, as they could have used the wire telephone just as well."

The long-distance capabilities of the Herrold-built stations bordered on the spectacular for the time. At Mare Island, using a Herrold outfit, operator Sanders got confirmation from the U.S. Naval wireless station at Bremerton, Washington, that his transmissions were "great." The message also said, ". . . the record, 'Trail of the Lonesome Pine,' you played came in extra good." On the same day, George Hanscom, civilian engineer for the government, got a dispatch saying the Mare Island station was being heard by the U.S. Naval station at Arlington, Virginia, three thousand miles away.[17]

In early 1914 Herrold left the N-W-T-and-T company but continued to operate the Garden City station as his own. In February, he accomplished what was up to that time the longest two-way conversation between two wireless-telephones yet reported. He succeeded in communicating back and forth with Point Arguello from San Jose.[18]

With the opening of the Panama Pacific Exposition in San Francisco in 1915, Herrold got an unusual opportunity to demonstrate the dependability of his arc system of broadcasting. Lt. Ellery Stone, the U.S. Radio Inspector, personally invited Herrold in San Jose to establish a lengthy schedule of programs to be picked up by receivers at the government's booth at the World's Fair.[19] Herrold provided no less than six to eight hours of musical programs daily from his San Jose station. Dr. De Forest, who also had an exhibit, found that his tube-transmitter would not work; so his booth operator tuned in the San Jose station to demonstrate De Forest's receiving set.[20]

Said Herrold long afterward, "Now if there was any other Broadcasting Station in the World at that time and if there was any other inventor who had perfected a reliable radio telephone capable of transmitting undistorted music and clear speech day after day in actual broadcasting, I certainly never heard of such. I read every scrap of scientific literature on the subject and read claims on 3000 U.S. and Foreign Patents so as to be thoroughly familiar with every inch of progress made by every known experimenter in the world.

"Now the very vital question will be put to the witness—'Why did you not immediately profit by all this development?' The answer is a very simple one—The Herrold System of Radio Telephony would not work on wave-lengths under 600 and the allocation of 360 meters by the Government was fatal. Over two decades of work, and expenditure of over $80,000 and a lot of patents went on the scrap pile. My Broadcasting Station . . . passed into the hands of those who could install the most modern High Powered Western Electric Equipment . . . And so we rest our case, a case which will be carried eventually to the highest court—the Court of Public Opinion of the whole world." [21]

Some years after Herrold issued this ringing call for recognition, apparently to a local newspaper, there came to him an unusual tribute in an extraordinary way.

It was Lee De Forest Day at the San Francisco World's Fair at Treasure Island, Sept. 7, 1940. Dr. De Forest addressed a banquet of the Veteran Wireless Operators Association. He said: "Very appropriately, the re-birth of my earliest broadcasting began here on the Pacific Coast when, during the Panama Pacific Exposition, Pioneer Station KQW at San Jose maintained regular transmissions which were daily heard in the Palace of Liberal Arts. That station, KQW, can rightfully claim to be the oldest broadcasting station of the entire world . . ." [22]

13

HISTORY OF
BROADCASTING AND KDKA RADIO

THE WORLD'S first scheduled broadcast was made from Westinghouse's KDKA, the pioneer broadcasting station of the world, in Pittsburgh on Nov. 2, 1920.

Much of the early history of KDKA is actually the early history of radio—many of its notable firsts are "firsts" for the industry as well. Outstanding on this list, in addition to the first scheduled broadcast, are:

> The first regularly broadcast church services and the necessary remote pickup.
> The first regular broadcast of baseball scores, first play-by-play baseball and football, first blow-by-blow boxing, first heavy-weight championship and first World Series.
> The first market reports from which grew the first complete farm service and, later, the first barn dance.

Establishment of KDKA and presentation of its inaugural broadcast came about as the result of several strange and seemingly unrelated circumstances; among them:

> Westinghouse experience with the vacuum tube while working on World War I radio contracts for the United States and British governments.

Public Relations Department, Westinghouse Broadcasting Company, news release, no date, pp. 1–34.

A $5.00 bet on the accuracy of a $12.00 watch.

An engineer's determination to save his voice by using phonograph records for amateur radio tests.

An alert department store's merchandising initiative.

Construction of KDKA, begun only one month prior to the election, was entrusted to Dr. Frank Conrad, then assistant chief engineer of Westinghouse and one of the participants in the watch wager and an intensely enthusiastic radio amateur. First KDKA license was issued October 27, 1920, and call letters were assigned from a roster maintained to provide identification for ships and marine shore stations, these being the only regular radio services then in operation under formal license by the Federal Government.

NEWSPAPER PROVIDES RETURNS BY TELEPHONE

Assisting Dr. Conrad was his long-time friend and co-worker, D. G. Little, former Kalamazoo radio "ham" later Assistant Manager and Consulting Engineer in the Westinghouse Electronics Division at Baltimore. Little had been tinkering with vacuum tube radio as early as 1910 and had come to Westinghouse after association with the Company and Dr. Conrad on government work while in the Signal Corps during World War I.

Arrangements were made with the *Pittsburgh Post,* to secure election returns by telephone. To increase audience, the late Dr. L. W. Chubb—then manager of the Radio Engineering Department and one of the little band of pioneers—was delegated to install a receiver and loudspeaker system, using two horns borrowed for the occasion from the Navy, in the main ballroom of the Edgewood Club, a suburban Pittsburgh community center where many Westinghouse people and other local residents gathered.

The broadcast originated in a tiny, makeshift shack atop one of the Westinghouse manufacturing buildings at East Pittsburgh. There was no studio. A single room accommodated transmitting equipment, turntable for records, and the first broadcast staff: William Thomas, operator; L. H. Rosenberg, announcer; and R. S. McClelland and John Frazier handling telephone lines to the newspaper office. Newspaper accounts of the broadcast were written and released by W. W. Rodgers. On hand as chief engineer, although the title was not known at the time, was Little.

Oddly enough, although it was Dr. Conrad's interest, stimulated by the bet on the watch, which had paved the way for KDKA, he was not present when the station went on the air. Fearful lest the new equipment fail, he was standing by at his own experimental station, 8XK, five miles away in Wilkinsburg, ready to carry on in the event of trouble at East Pittsburgh.

Broadcasting began at 6 o'clock election night and continued until noon the following day, even though Candidate Cox, hours earlier, had conceded the election to Senator Harding.

Broadcast Huge Success, Causes National Sensation

Throughout that stormy night, while the usual crowds stood in a driving rain before outdoor bulletin boards to see returns, a fortunate few early radio fans—equipped with crystal sets and earphones—were hearing the same returns in the comfort of their homes.

In addition, between returns and occasional music, they heard this request over and over again: "Will anyone hearing this broadcast communicate with us, as we are anxious to know how far the broadcast is reaching and how it is being received."

The broadcast was a national sensation, acclaimed by newspapers all over the country.

Dr. Chubb's Edgewood Club audience whooped and cheered and phoned the station from time to time demanding "more news and less music;" and even after the first flurry of excitement—when KDKA had settled down to the regular schedule of programs, mail continued to pour in telling of reception here, there, and everywhere.

One such report came from H. W. Irving, who later was transmitter supervisor at KDKA. Working as Merchant Marine radio operator assigned to the U.S. Army Transport, ANTIGONE, he heard the program off the Virginia coast while en-route with troops from Puerto Rico to New York.

Receiving the returns by earphones he hastened to deliver them to the captain expecting them to be posted on the ship's bulletin board for all to see. But the skipper, victim of a "radio" hoax several months before, was dubious and would not permit the returns to be posted.

$5 Bet On $12 Watch Spurs
First Radio Interest

Dr. Conrad first had become interested in radio in 1915 when—to settle a $5 bet on the accuracy of his $12 watch, made with his friend, and co-worker Thomas S. Perkins, manager of Detail and Supply at the Westinghouse East Pittsburgh plant—he had built a small receiver to hear time signals from the Naval Observatory at Arlington, Va.

Fascinated by his new hobby, Dr. Conrad turned next to construction of a transmitter which he installed on the second floor of a garage at the rear of his residence at Wilkinsburg. First official record of this station, licensed 8XK, appears in the August 1, 1916, edition of the *Radio Service Bulletin* issued monthly by the Bureau of Navigation of the U.S. Department of Commerce, radio licensing agency of that day; and it is from this station that KDKA stems and with it, radio broadcasting as it is today.

Security precautions brought cancellation of 8XK along with all amateur licenses April 7, 1917, one day after the United States entered World War I. However, the station's facilities were used from time to time during the war, under special authorization, to test military radio equipment manufactured by Westinghouse. The amateur ban was lifted Oct. 1, 1919, and the Bureau of Navigation bulletin of May 1, 1920, shows the station relicensed 8XK.

Its programs were heard in widely separated locations, and Dr. Conrad was kept busy answering mail—some from fans who merely wished to tell him they had heard his station, others from fellow operators reporting on the quality and strength of his signals. Although the former were welcome, it was the latter which interested Dr. Conrad more because they enabled him to plot the efficiency of his transmitter and plan improvements.

Radio messages, in that early day, were chiefly discussions of the kind of equipment being used and results obtained. Bored by this monotonous routine Dr. Conrad, on October 17, 1919, placed his microphone before a phonograph and substituted music for voice.

WILKINSBURG MUSIC STORE
FIRST RADIO ADVERTISER

The music saved Dr. Conrad's voice, but more—it delighted and amazed "hams" all over the country. Mail, heavy previously, now became a deluge with requests that records be played at special times so that the writer might convince some skeptic that music really could be transmitted through space.

Specific requests were played as long as this could be arranged, but so heavy was the demand that within a few days, Dr. Conrad was forced to announce that instead of complying with each individual request, he would "broadcast" records for two hours each Wednesday and Saturday evening. This is the first recorded use of the word "broadcast" to describe a radio service.

These broadcasts soon exhausted Dr. Conrad's supply of records, and the Hamilton Music Store in Wilkinsburg offered a continuing supply of records if he would announce that the records could be purchased at the Hamilton store. Dr. Conrad agreed and thus gave the world its first radio advertiser—who promptly found that records played on the air sold better than others.

This two-a-week program schedule was continued with live vocal and instrumental talent added from time to time and with Dr. Conrad's two young sons—Crawford and Francis, who was later Director of Radio for the Western Division of the American Broadcasting Company at Hollywood—acting as radio's original masters of ceremonies.

By late summer of 1920, interest in these broadcasts had become so general that the Joseph Horne Co., a Pittsburgh department store, ran this ad in the *Sun*, Wednesday evening, Sept. 29:

AIR CONCERT "PICKED UP" BY RADIO HERE

Victrola music, played into the air over a wireless telephone, was "picked up" by listeners on the wireless receiving station which was recently installed here for patrons interested in wireless experiments. The concert was heard Thursday night about 10 o'clock and continued about 20 minutes. Two orchestra numbers, a soprano solo—which rang particularly high and clear through the air—and a juvenile "talking piece" constituted the program.

The music was from a Victrola pulled close to the transmitter of a wireless telephone in the home of Frank Conrad, Penn and Peebles Avenues, Wilkinsburg. Dr. Conrad is a wireless enthusiast and "puts on" the wireless concerts periodically for the entertainment of the many people in this district who have wireless sets.

Amateur Wireless Sets, made by the maker of the set which is in operation in our store, are on sale here $10.00 up.

To H. P. Davis, Westinghouse Vice President who had been an ardent follower of the Conrad ventures, the ad was an inspiration. If this was a fair example of popular reaction to Dr. Conrad's broadcasts, the real radio industry lay in the manufacture of home receivers, he reasoned, and in supplying radio programs which would make people want to own such receivers.

Convinced that here was a great new business opportunity, Mr. Davis set about winning other Westinghouse officials to the same view, and so persuasive were his arguments that a station was authorized, license application submitted October 16, and election night—then only a little more than two weeks away—selected for the grand opening.

On January 15, 1921, Herbert Hoover, wartime food administrator and president-to-be, made his first radio address from KDKA. The occasion was a speech on behalf of the European Relief Fund at Pittsburgh's Duquesne Club.

February 18, 1921, brought the first remote pickup from a hotel when speeches of Col. Theodore Roosevelt, Jr., and Oklahoma Congresswoman-elect Alice M. Robertson were broadcast from a banquet of the Pittsburgh Press Club in the William Penn Hotel.

On March 4, 1921, KDKA scored another first with a broadcast of the inaugural address of Warren G. Harding as he became the 28th

President of the United States. A copy of the Harding text was obtained in advance and read on the air while the new President was speaking in Washington.

KDKA's First Studio Is
Tent on Factory Roof

For the first six months of its existence KDKA was a radio station without a studio. There had been little need for one, since all programs were originated either as phonograph records played on turntables in the tiny transmitter penthouse atop the East Pittsburgh plant; or from churches, theaters, hotels, or other remote points.

However, in mid-May 1921 it was decided that the program structure should include live band and orchestral talent as well as recordings and the services of several excellent musical organizations of Westinghouse employees were secured. First programs were broadcast from an auditorium at the plant, but room resonance was so great that engineers immediately set about finding other facilities.

As an experiment they pitched a tent on the roof next to their transmitter-penthouse. This tent-studio served admirably all summer long and—even after it had been blown down in an early-autumn gale—left its lessons to guide engineers in the uses of drapes and acoustical board in building its ever-so-much-more dignified indoor successor which was opened the following October 3 at East Pittsburgh.

These were days of endless, and frequently amusing, "growing pains" at KDKA.

Early fans still recall the whistle of a passing freight train which, in the days of the tent studio, became a regular 8:30 p.m. feature, no matter what the program.

Insect In Tenor's Mouth
Puts Station Off The Air

Singing in the tent studio one evening, a well-known tenor opened his mouth wide to sing a full, high note and almost swallowed an insect. His comments, which came in a torrent of angry words as soon as he caught his breath, were not in good radio taste— and a vigilant operator took the station off the air in a hurry.

On another occasion, after the first indoor studio had been built, a stray dog raced into the studio while Announcer Harold Arlin was presenting baseball scores, upset the microphone—scrambling scores, notes and announcer—then added his excited barks to the pandemonium.

The radio debut of Economist Roger Babson was another memorable occasion for Mr. Arlin. At great pains to reassure his guest, somewhat nervous at his first venture on the air, Mr. Arlin learned, after five minutes of Mr. Babson's speech, that the transmitter was not operating, and the entire program had to be repeated.

Testing some of KDKA's earliest shortwave equipment for remote pickup, Engineer Little had the embarrassing experience of breaking into the Lord's Prayer during a broadcast from Pittsburgh's Point Breeze Presbyterian Church with a monotonous "one, two, three . . . testing." Both regular wire and shortwave link pickups had been installed and someone, inadvertently, opened Mr. Little's shortwave "mike" while services were being broadcast via the wire pickup.

A broken wire at a tense moment in the memorable Dempsey-Firpo fight and an announcer's zeal to keep the station on the air combined to produce another pioneering chuckle.

The break came just as the excited ringside announcer was shouting "Firpo lands a terrific blow knocking the champion . . ."—and the standby announcer in the studio, snatching up the first convenient bit of copy, continued almost without interruption "With hogs up two cents a pound . . ."

By an unfortunate circumstance he had picked up a market report instead of late news flashes.

Heavyweight Championship, World Series
Early Broadcast Features

Much of the early history of sports in radio was written by KDKA during the summer and autumn of 1921.

On July 2 KDKA broadcast the four-round World's heavyweight Boxing Championship between Titleholder Jack Dempsey—who had defeated Jess Willard at Toledo just two years before—and French Challenger Georges Carpentier, blow-by-blow from Boyles' Thirty Acres at Jersey City.

In early August KDKA broadcast play-by-play details of Davis Cup Tennis Matches in which the Australian team defeated British netmen at Pittsburgh's Allegheny Country Club in suburban Sewickley.

Baseball's first play-by-play radio coverage came August 5 when Announcer Arlin described the Pittsburgh Pirates' 8-5 victory over the Philadelphia Phils from Forbes Field.

The 1921 World Series was an all-New York affair with the Giants meeting the Yankees at the Polo Grounds. The opener came October 5 and KDKA, with a direct wire to Pittsburgh, broadcast play-by-play details by Grantland Rice. The Giants lost the opener 3-0, but came on to take the series five games to three.

Other Yankee celebrities included: Babe Ruth; Waite Hoyt; Bob Shawkey; and Carl Mays, who won the opener.

To Pitt and West Virginia goes the honor of sharing radio's first play-by-play football. The occasion was Pitt's 21-13 victory over West Virginia October 8, 1921, and it was another first for Announcer Arlin.

"Repeater Station" Opened In Nebraska

In July 1923, a new short-wave station, 8XS began regular broadcasts of KDKA programs several hours each evening, and the following month reception was reported in England. When this reception continued in good quality the British Broadcasting Corporation arranged to rebroadcast special greetings from KDKA to Great Britain the following New Year's Eve.

On November 22, 1923—the earlier KDPM "repeater" tests having proved the feasibility of radio relay operation—a third Westinghouse shortwave transmitter was placed in service. It was KFKX at Hastings, Neb., especially designed as a "repeater station" to receive and rebroadcast shortwave programs from KDKA. Purpose of the installation was to increase KDKA program coverage. The Hastings location was chosen because it is not far from the geographical center of the country, and as a result of the experiment millions of new listeners throughout North and South America—many of them living on remote farms and ranches—joined KDKA's already sizable audience.

First Popular-Priced Home Receivers Built In 1921

From its earliest days Westinghouse officials regarded broadcasting as a public service and, as such, one which should be made available to the widest possible audience. This meant a serviceable popular-priced receiver and thus it was that while the KDKA staff was busy with its trailblazing, other Westinghouse engineers were designing a radio receiving set for homes—a set simple enough for the non-technical fan to operate, and inexpensive enough to be afforded in every household.

This new model was ready in June 1921.

It was the Aeriola, Jr.—first popular-priced home radio receiver—a tiny crystal set, six-by-six-by-seven inches in size. It employed earphones, had a range of from 12 to 15 miles, and sold for $25.

With this first model launched, engineers turned at once to refinements and by December, two new and improved models were ready—Aeriola, Sr., first home radio receiver to use a vacuum tube; and Aeriola Grand, first self-contained home radio receiver.

Aeriola, Sr., was of about the same size and appearance as its predecessor. It used dry batteries and one vacuum tube and sold for $60.

Aeriola Grand represented a greater advance. This was a table-cabinet model 12 by 15 by 16 inches, with a built-in loudspeaker and several vacuum tubes. It was with this model, which sold for $175, that radio receivers first began to take on the familiar appearance of today's sets.

At the site of Dr. Conrad's former home in Wilkinsburg, a plaque was dedicated on November 2, 1957, the 37th anniversary of that first broadcast.

It reads:

> BIRTHPLACE OF RADIO BROADCASTING
> Here radio broadcasting was born, At this location, Dr. Frank Conrad, Westinghouse Engineer and Scientist, Conducted experimental broadcasts Which led to the establishment of KDKA and modern radio broadcasting, And to the world's first scheduled Broadcast, November 2, 1920
>
>   Dr. Frank Conrad
>   1874–1941

14

R. J. McLauchlin

WHAT THE DETROIT *NEWS* HAS DONE IN BROADCASTING

THE DETROIT NEWS was the first newspaper in the United States and, so far as is known, in the world, to perceive the possibilities of increasing its usefulness by furnishing the public with radio service. When the broadcasting was inaugurated nearly two years ago, wireless telephony, although it had reached a commercial stage and was already the hobby of a few enthusiastic experimenters, still remained a mystery to the community in general and was looked upon by many as possibly a familiar source of enjoyment to their grandchildren but of no particular interest or importance to the present generation. This sentiment was changed virtually overnight, when in August, 1920, the Detroit *News* installed its first transmitting station and commenced its regular broadcasting.

The original apparatus consisted of a De Forest Type OT-TO

Radio Broadcast (June 1922), pp. 136–141.

transmitter, using a 200 meter wave length. Its range was limited, being, under the best of conditions, not more than 100 miles, and at this time there were approximately only 300 operators in the territory thus covered. The transmission set was in place ready for operation on August 20, 1920, but no announcement was made to the public until a series of experimental concerts had been conducted over a period of ten days. These concerts were enjoyed by no one save such amateurs as happened to be listening in. Everything was found to be successful and satisfactory, and on August 31, which was the primary day, it was announced that returns from the local, state, and congressional primaries would be sent to the public by means of the radio.

The *News* of September 1, carried the following announcement:

"The sending of the election returns by the Detroit *News* Radiophone Tuesday night was fraught with romance, and must go down in the history of man's conquest of the elements as a gigantic step in his progress. In the four hours that the apparatus, set up in an out-of-the-way corner of the *News* building, was hissing and whirring its message into space, few realized that a dream and a prediction had come true. The news of the world was being given forth through this invisible trumpet to the waiting crowds in the unseen market place."

It was August 31, then, which marked the beginning of wireless telephony as a social service. On that day the dream of actual vocal communication between points far distant and without any physical union came true on an astonishingly large scale. The public of Detroit and its environs was then made to realize that what had been a laboratory curiosity had become a commonplace of everyday life, and that the future held extraordinary developments which would affect all society.

In December, 1921, the present ambitious programme was inaugurated. By this time the radio department occupied the entire time of a programme manager and two technical men, which staff has now grown to eight persons.

To-day phonograph music occupies an incidental place on the daily schedule, and the programmes are filled by stage celebrities, prominent clergymen, musicians and public figures of various sorts, many with national reputations. Among the noted stage persons who have made their debut in the *News* transmitting room are Frank Tinney, Van and Schenk, Percy Wenrich, and Lew Fields.

Another point in last December's expansion of programmes was the securing of Finzel's Orchestra and other musical organizations with numerous members. These orchestras furnish music of various kinds, including dance music, and it is common for Detroit families to hold parties in their homes and dance to the music played by their favorite orchestra. The second Christmas concert presented by the *News* last year consisted of songs by carolers and addresses by Gov.

Groesbeck of the State of Michigan, Mayor Couzens of Detroit and the Rt. Rev. Fr. John P. McNichols, president of the University of Detroit.

In February of this year [1922] the first concert by the Detroit Symphony Orchestra was broadcasted. Now every programme presented by that splendid organization is sent to music lovers not only in Detroit but over half of the United States. Expressions of enthusiastic appreciation from persons in all walks of life have followed this development of the *News* radio service. Contributions for the support of the orchestra have come from grateful people in a score of states who have thus been enabled to hear much finer music than could ever before be heard in the small towns where they make their residence. The radio has opened new worlds of melody to music-hungry folk throughout the Middle West.

The *News* has received letters from Honduras, from Alaska, from Saskatchewan and Alberta, from Cuba, from officers on vessels on the Atlantic Ocean, from a ranchman in Wyoming, and from scores of other remote places, expressing thanks to the *News* for bringing across the great spaces such splendid music, such first-class theatrical entertainment and such rousing and stimulating messages from the leaders of the country's thought. All this has been extremely gratifying to those behind the project and has persuaded them that the great expenditure which the radio service has entailed has been amply rewarded in the consciousness of enhanced public usefulness.

A curious thing in connection with the broadcasting has been the reaction of stage artists to the undemonstrative little receiver into which they pour their songs and remarks. Frank Tinney refused to believe that he was not the victim of a hoax and that he was in reality not talking for the sole entertainment of the persons in the tiny auditorium where the transmitting apparatus is located. He was not convinced that a trick was not being played upon him until he heard music relayed back by telephone from Windsor across the river. This has been noticed in the case of almost every artist who is accustomed to applause as occasional motive power.

The *News* of December 18, 1921, commented on this as follows:

"The receiver is not a very appreciative instrument, at least in appearance. One can't tell from the looks of the telephone whether his number is liked or not.

"This was quite baffling to Ernie Ball. He sang one or two of his most popular numbers, heard no applause and finally looked at the telephone in a manner that registered blind rage. And then he stuck out his tongue at the instrument which seemed to relieve his feelings a lot, for he swung immediately into another selection.

"In the case of Mr. Tinney, it was hard to convince that personage that his phenomenon was actually happening. Again and again he demanded to know if the thing were on the square it was that uncanny. Of all the entertainers who appeared last week, Mr. Tinney probably suffered the most because of the absence of applause. The nature of his offering was such that it was almost necessary for him to have some demonstration of how folks liked what he was saying. This demonstration in all cases was not long in coming, for at every concert, some of the appreciative listeners in flashed back their thanks and asked for more."

On the first of February of this year the installation was completed by the Western Electric Company of a 500 watt, 300 to 600 meter broadcasting set of the same type now being completed for the American Telephone and Telegraph Company on the roof of the Walker Lispenard Building, New York. Its power comes from two generators, one of 1400 and the other of 1500 volts, harnessed to a 5 H.P. DC motor. It is equipped with a specially high quality speech input arrangement, such as that used by President Harding at Arlington Cemetery last November, in which two No. 212-250 watt Western Electric vacuum tubes were used as oscillators and two more used as modulators.

One peculiarity about this set is the fact that, although it is only of 500 watt power when not in use, its power rises to 750 watts when subject to conversation or music. Another feature is the fact that the power panel is entirely devoid of live points on its surface. All of the switches are concealed.

Since the transmitter used in the speech input section of the device is not as sensitive as the ordinary type, a Western Electric amplifier is used, which magnifies the voice about a hundred thousand times without producing any distortion.

This installation has an ordinary broadcasting radius of 1,500 miles, but reports have been received from points 2,300 miles away telling of successful receiving. The set was built to the special order of the *News* and is the only one of its kind thus far completed by the manufacturers. With this splendid equipment the *News* plans future radio activities on an even more elaborate scale than has thus far obtained.

Dear Ann Landers: I applied for a job at a TV station and went to work last week. This TV job is so different that I am having a difficult time getting accustomed to it. Everyone around the studio kisses everyone else good morning and good evening. There's a lot of nose tweaking, cheek pinching, lap sitting and fanny patting. Do you think I ought to leave or try to be "one of them?"
                    --Square Peg, *Indio News*, April 3, 1967.

15

R. *Franklin Smith*

"OLDEST STATION IN THE NATION"?

WHEN WE SPEAK of the beginning of broadcasting, do we mean the date the *first* broadcasting station began operation, or do we mean the date the *oldest* broadcasting station began operation? Are these dates identical? Then if we can decide these matters, what is to be done about the conflicting claims of the leading contenders for historical honors? Any school child "knows" that broadcasting began with KDKA's broadcast of the Harding-Cox election returns in November of 1920. Yet WWJ, Detroit, claims it is the "world's first radio station." WHA, Madison, calls itself "the oldest station in the nation." Gordon Greb's scholarly work attempted to show that broadcasting began in 1909 with Charles Herrold's station in San Jose. Finally what is meant by the term *broadcasting?* The historical problem, then is a complex one. As E. P. Shurick stated in the preface to his book, "the radio industry . . . is an industry that hatched from a thousand eggs." [1]

This paper is concerned with problems posed by two of the above questions: (1) An attempt will be made to formulate a workable definition of the terms, *broadcasting station.* Though such a definition necessarily is conceived after the fact, it is hoped this definition might act as a guideline to help researchers probe their way back into the confused early days of *broadcasting.* (2) An examination will be made of WHA's claim of "oldest station in the nation" in terms of its broadcasting activities.

First of all, what are the characteristics of a *broadcasting station?*

(1) A *broadcasting station transmits by wireless.* The broadcast message is carried through space from the sender to the receiver by electromagnetic waves, or by wireless. Stations engaged in an activity in which the message is carried by wire would not be broadcasting. For example, closed circuit television is not broadcasting. Wired college campus stations are not considered broadcasting stations.

(2) A *broadcasting station transmits by telephony.* Broadcasting means that the message transmitted will be composed of sounds instantly intelligible to the general listener, such as music or speech.

Journal of Broadcasting, Vol. IV, No. 1 (Winter 1959–1960), pp. 40–55.

The Communications Act of 1934 says that broadcasting means the dissemination of communication by *radio*. These communications may include, "writing, signs, signals, pictures and sounds." "Signals" would include telegraphic signals. However, as far back as May of 1922 , the *Radio Service Bulletin* of the Department of Commerce defines "broadcasting" under the heading of "radio telephony." The *Encyclopedia Britannica* (1953 edition) states that the most common meaning of the term "broadcasting" excludes telegraphy, saying, "in its most common form, broadcasting may be described as the systematic diffusion by radio of entertainment, information, educational and other features. . . . Sound broadcasting in this sense may be said to have come into being about 1920." To the average American, the broadcasting message means a sound that can be immediately perceived through language or musical symbols without the necessity of having to decode telegraphic signals.

The *Britannica* does consider broadcasting in another sense: ". . . a less familiar usage of the term, broadcasting, still extant at mid-twentieth century, applied to the transmission by a radio telegraph or telephone station of messages intended for general distribution to other radio stations, such as for example, the broadcasting of weather reports to ships at sea."

A closer examination of this second statement reveals, however, that the intended recipient of the message is a specified group of individuals, not the general public, or a special public such as children, teachers or farmers. This point leads to another characteristic of a broadcasting station.

(3) *A broadcasting station transmits to the public.* The Communications Act defines broadcasting as the "dissemination of radio communications intended to be received by the public." The *Britannica* says that broadcasting is aimed at "simultaneous reception by a scattered audience, individually, or in groups, with appropriate receiving apparatus." According to the Communications Act, broadcasting is a distinct form of communication different from communication by common carriers like telephone or telegraph services. These services are not considered broadcast services since their facilities are available to any individual for the transmission of private messages to any other individual. Special radio services, such as amateur, safety, aviation, marine and industrial services are not broadcast services since their messages are intended for specific individuals that may be differentiated from the general public or special publics.

(4) *A broadcasting station transmits a continous program service.* A broadcasting station offers something which occurs over a period of time this *something* is a series of programs interconnected

into a pattern recognizable as a program service. The *Britannica* describes broadcasting as transmitting messages (in the sense here, programs) on the basis of "systematic diffusion."

A broadcasting station intends to maintain this service. Though a station may not necessarily transmit a program service twenty-four hours a day, it does, nonetheless, operate on a day-to-day basis. Even in the earliest days of broadcasting, many stations, though operating perhaps on a one-or-two-days-a-week basis, nonetheless, had developed some sort of patterned program service.

Circumstances beyond the control of a broadcasting station may interfere with the continuity of its program service. Thus, an educational broadcasting station may be said to offer a continuous program service, though the station may close down for certain specified vacation periods when student personnel are away from the campus. A station may be said to be operating continuously though its program service may be temporarily interrupted by a mechanical or electronic breakdown, a strike of station employees, a national emergency such as war, or an "Act of God" such as a flood, earthquake or hurricane.

(5) *A broadcasting station is licensed by the government.* Broadcasting stations are licensed today as broadcasting stations. All legally constituted radio stations, regardless of their functions or types of services, have been licensed by the government since the Radio Act of 1912. But while today a station license is a necessary part of its identity as a broadcasting station, a broadcasting station may not necessarily be identified by its license at the time it first began its operation. There are factors stemming from a stations' early licenses which give rise to confusion when one attempts to find the precise date that a broadcasting station began its operations.

(a) Early stations and their antecedents had different sets of call letters at different times. WHA was once 9XM; 8XK preceded KDKA; WWJ was formerly WBL; KCBS was predated by KQW.

(b) Early stations were classified at different times in different ways. Not until March 1, 1922, did the Department of Commerce report stations as "broadcasting stations" under a separate category. On that day the four main contenders for broadcast primacy, KDKA, KQW, WHA and WWJ, were all listed as "broadcasting stations." Before that date these stations were listed as "commercial land stations." WHA was first listed as a "commercial land station" on February 1, 1922; KQW, on January 3, 1922; KDKA on November 1, 1920. WWJ was never reported as a "commercial land station," but WBL was so reported on November 1, 1921.

(c) Ownership of early stations varied. The early 9XM at the University of Wisconsin was licensed to an individual, first, Professor Edward Bennett, and later, Professor Earle M. Terry. 9XM was later licensed to the University. 8XK was licensed to Dr. Frank Conrad; KDKA, to the Westinghouse Corporation. KQW was owned in its early history solely by Charles D. Herrold. The Detroit *News* was listed as licensee for both WBL and WWJ.[2]

It is unsound, then, to base a station's historical claims on the basis of dates and other information contained in the station's license. This is not to say that station licenses do not have some utility in a gross historical sense. One can, for example, distinguish a broadcasting station from some other radio station, by the station's license in the late twenties, thirties, or forties.

Thus, one can conclude that a broadcast station today has five characteristics. It is a station that (1) utilizes radio waves (2) to send non-coded sounds by speech or music (3) in the form of a continuous patterned program service, (4) intended to be received by the public, and (5) is licensed by the government. Only the first four of these characteristics are valid bases for verifying historical claims of broadcast primacy.

For example, suppose we are attempting to determine the *oldest* broadcasting station. We would find that radio station today which has these four valid characteristics, and trace its history back to that point in time where it first had these characteristics. At that point we would find the *birth* of that station. If we traced the history of this station back to the point where it had three or two or one of the characteristics we would be going beyond the period of *broadcasting*, though perhaps not beyond the period of some type of radio operation.

We might also use these characteristics to find the *first* broadcasting station. For example, one might argue that Fessenden's hour long radio program on Christmas Eve of 1906 marked the beginning of broadcasting with the world's *first* broadcasting station. Applying our characteristics to this historic event, we would be forced to ask: Was this program intended to be received by the public, or was it an experimental program? And was this program part of a continuous program service of a *broadcasting* station?

The formulation of a workable definition of a *broadcasting station* is needed if validity is to be attached to the increasing amount of historical research in *broadcasting*. Any historical research is fruitless unless we know what we are tracking.

II

On November 24, 1958, an historical marker proclaiming WHA "the oldest station in the nation" was unveiled and formally dedicated at the annual WHA Family Dinner. Imprinted on the marker are these words:

9XM-WHA
"THE OLDEST STATION IN THE NATION"

On this campus pioneer research and experimentation in "wireless" led to successful transmissions of voice and music in 1917, and the beginning of broadcasting on a scheduled basis in 1919.

Experimental station 9XM transmitted telegraphic signals from Science Hall until 1917, when it was moved to Sterling Hall. In that year, Professor Earle M. Terry and students built and operated a "wireless telephone" transmitter.

In 1918, during World War I, when other stations were ordered silenced, 9XM operated under special authorization to continue its telephonic exchange with U.S. Navy stations on the Great Lakes. After the war, programs were directed to the general public.

The WHA letters replaced the 9XM call on January 13, 1922. Thus, the University of Wisconsin station, under the calls 9XM and WHA, has been in existence longer than any other.[3] *

There is little doubt that the entity, WHA, today, is the culmination of the development of the entity, 9XM, that was conceived in the physics department in 1915. Thus, we can conclude that we are dealing with one and the same station. There is no problem here of determining whether the present station is sufficiently different so as to distinguish an earlier entity as an *antecedent* station, or a separate station. In other words, there is no problem of determining whether we are concerned with one station or two stations. (The problem of whether a present station is the same entity as that with which it is associated in its earliest days, or actually an off-shoot of some other antecedent station *may* or *may not* be the essential complicating factor in tracing the historical claims of KDKA, KCBS and WWJ. This problem depends at least partially on the full meaning of the claims made. To tackle such a problem is outside the scope of this paper.)

The question to be considered here is: when did the station, 9XM-WHA, cease to be solely a radio station and become a *broadcasting station* as well? In other words when did 9XM-WHA begin to (1) utilize radio waves (2) to send non-coded sounds by speech or music (3) in the form of a continuous program service (4) intended to be received by the public?

Professor Julian Mack of the University of Wisconsin physics department was in charge of making contacts with individuals affiliated with WHA in the early days, and inviting them to the Family Dinner in 1958. Professor Mack asked each person to search his memory for clues to the answer to our question.

L. L. Nettleton, of Houston, Texas, wrote, "When I came to the

* Now at Vilas Communication Hall, University of Wisconsin-Madison.

University in the fall of 1919, the station was operated as a spark transmitter. For a short time that fall, Professor Terry assigned me the task of sending out market reports in Morse code . . . Somewhat later in the year, or in the spring of 1920, Malcolm Hanson took over the operation and development of the station." [4]

C. M. Jansky, Jr., who delivered the main address at the Family Dinner, commented on Nettleton's letter. "Since Malcolm Hanson left Madison before April 3, 1917, and did not return until June 30, 1920, he had nothing to do with the construction of the first vacuum tubes which were used in 9XM when radio telephone tests were conducted in 1918 and regular radio-telephone broadcasting began January 3, 1919." He added that since he left Wisconsin on January 1, 1920, he had no knowledge of what Hanson did upon his return. Jansky said that daily weather reports were begun on January 3, 1919, through the medium of wireless telephony. He said the broadcasts were intended for anyone who wanted to listen, and that they were sent out by telegraphy also. He said the station had been closed down while he was here for only a day or two at most.[5]

Conflicting with Jansky's statement that daily weather forecasts were begun in January of 1919 is the statement from a copy of a telegram sent by Eric Miller, of the Madison weather bureau, dated February 15, 1923. Miller reported that, "Regular radiotelephone broadcasting of weather forecasts was begun here January 3, 1921," [6] exactly two years after the date given by Jansky.

Commenting on activities during this period, the *Press Bulletin*, on March 5, 1919, reported under a headline, "SEND RADIO TELEPHONE MESSAGES 100 MILES," that

> "Wireless telephonic communication with Great Lakes Naval Training station is now carried on by the University of Wisconsin wireless station after some months of experimentation. The first clear speech was transmitted last week.
>
> The university station talks to the Great Lakes station by radio telephony, but the latter answers by radio telegraph since it does not have the radio telephone sending apparatus.
>
> These are the only stations in this locality permitted by government authorities to operate at the present time. The university radio station, which is operated by the physics department, is well equipped for all sorts of experimental work in radio telephony or telegraphy, and extensive research work is being carried on.
>
> A vacuum power bulb which is said to be better than any commercial bulb for use as oscillator or modulator in regulating the aerial waves has recently been devised by Professor Terry of the university and is an important factor in certain research work." [7]

Malcolm Hanson considered the radio work during 1919 as experimental. He wrote,

"The radio telephone transmitter which was constructed in
1920 was not the first one placed in use at the university, as experimental work, partly with home made tubes, had perceded this in
1919; this work I believe had been carried on under Professor Terry
by C. M. Jansky, Jr., who obtained good results on a number of
broadcasts. In 1920 I worked under Professor Terry constructing a
permanent station to be ‚employed for regular broadcast programs. . . ." [8]

The *Press Bulletin*, on January 21, 1920, reported, "A plan is
now being worked out by the weather bureau to send telephonic
reports to farmers." [9]

On March 10, 1920, the *Bulletin* added,

"The sending of daily weather reports by wireless to Wisconsin
farmers and others was started last week by the physics department
of the University of Wisconsin in cooperation with the U.S.
Weather Bureau stationed on the campus. During the first week the
reports were sent out only by wireless telegraph but within a few
days they will be sent both by wireless telegraph and by wireless
telephone." [10]

The *Bulletin*, which is the official news source of the university
for papers throughout the state, reported no further news about 9XM
until September 29, 1920, when it stated,

"The sending of weather reports by wireless from the United
States Weather Bureau at the University of Wisconsin has been resumed after having been discontinued during the summer. . . . The
Continental Morse Code is used in the messages and copies of the
code may be secured from any Western Union Telegraph office." [11]

No mention was made of wireless telephony.

In a letter to Mrs. Terry, Hanson said, "In regard to the early history of WHA . . . about everything we did was written up succes-
sively in Grant Hyde's press bureau column at least weekly. Especially so since his reporter Marion Moore was a good friend of
ours." [12]

The *Press Bulletin*, then, in March of 1920, said that wireless
telephonic reports "will be sent out within a few days," not that they
"are now" sent out, and no mention was made about any transmissions until September of 1920, when only telegraphic reports were
mentioned. If Hanson's statement that close liaison existed between
the station and the *Press Bureau*, is valid, it would seem that there
were no telephonic broadcasts as such on a scheduled basis at least
up to September 29, 1920.

On the other hand, the *Press Bulletin*, in January of 1921 stated,
"That the wireless telephone and telegraph weather reports sent out
from Madison at 12:30 daily are heard in Texas, Kansas, New Jersey

and on the Canadian border is indicated by letters received at the wireless experimental station of the physics department. . . ." [13] According to the *Bulletin*, then, scheduled telephonic broadcasts began sometime between September 29, 1920, and January 19, 1921.

In a letter to his mother written September 27, 1920, Hanson referred to his work on the station. "The radio work is also a wonderful chance, I am in full charge, and can do what I want with the station. Wireless telephone will be the main work, very interesting, and if successful, it will give us a name over the whole country. I expect to have it done in about three weeks." [14]

In 1930, W. H. Lighty, the station's first program director, wrote to Hanson, who was at the time a radio engineer with the Byrd Polar Expedition. He said,

> "I am endeavoring to gather up some of the background facts in connection with the radio station development in the University of Wisconsin. With the sudden death of Professor Terry last year, and your absence from all means of communication, it has not been possible to collect any data as to the earliest dates of broadcasting from the University of Wisconsin." [15]

In 1931 Hanson wrote to Andrew Hopkins, that

> "The further promise (referring to the *Bulletin* article of March 10, 1920) that wireless telephone reports would be started in a few days refers to some low powered experimental equipment which the physics department had previously used in some tests with the Great Lakes Naval Training Station. Whether this service was actually tried and how long it was continued I do not know, but when I returned to Madison in the summer of 1920, the radio telephone equipment was somewhat disrupted and there were no reports of any regular telephone broadcast. Permanent broadcasting equipment was not completed until late in 1920, and I remember definitely that the regular daily weather broadcasts by telephone were instituted on or about 2 January 1921. If there were telephone broadcasts as early as March, 1920, they were highly experimental and lasted only a short time. . . . Our first regular broadcasts, which employed a wave length of 800 meters, took place at about the same time as the Westinghouse station KDKA." [16]

In response to a questionnaire Hanson replied to the question, "When did telephonic broadcasting begin at the University?" by commenting that music was broadcast in November or December of 1920, with the daily weather forecasts commencing January 3, 1921.[17]

In 1922 Hanson referred to "the regular scheduling of broadcasts" that began the year before.[18] He also said in his letter to Hopkins,

"We were the first station in the country to broadcast daily reports by the U.S. Weather Bureau by radio telephone. . . . These early broadcasts were with the approval of the U.S. Radio Inspection Service carried on under our old experimental call letters 9XM, but after January, 1921, were carried out on a regular daily schedule." [19]

Most of the papers of Professor Terry, the founder of the original 9XM, were destroyed after his death in 1929. However, a copy of one of Terry's letters was found in the WHA files. Writing to the Federal Radio Commission in a defense of the right of WHA to remain on the 570 kc channel in October of 1928, Terry said,

". . . The University of Wisconsin insists that, because of its long record in broadcasting work, it is entitled to a desirable channel. It desires to point out to the Commission that it has been a pioneer in the broadcasting field. Of the broadcasting stations now in operation in the United States, KDKA alone antidates WHA, and that by a few months only. Before power tubes were available, the writer developed the glass blowing and high vacuum technique in the laboratories of the University and for three years manufactured all of the power tubes used in the transmitter. The University station was the first to broadcast market and weather reports regularly. . . ." [20]

Other information is available concerning the beginning of broadcasting at the University of Wisconsin. One paper is entitled, *Notes on the University of Wisconsin Radio Station, WHA, Madison, Wisconsin,* dated February 26, 1925. Unfortunately the writer of the four-page typed document is not identified. However the paper stated,

"The early development of the University station was attended with communications, tests, and activities characteristic of that stage of radio development. The radio telephone broadcasting began on January 3, 1921, and has been carried on consecutively and regularly since. On September 17, 1921, began the regular broadcasting of market reports which we conducted from the university station for several years." [21]

Another paper entitled, *Background and Status of Administration and Financing of Radio Station WHA,* dated April 2, 1937 presented a brief outline of "Radio Beginnings at Wisconsin."

I. Radio Beginnings at Wisconsin
    A. Telegraphic
        1. Experimental, 1909. Professor Edward Bennett.
        2. First telegraphic station 9XM, 1916.
          a) weather reports (regularly)
          b) market reports (regularly)

B. Telephonic (9XM) (WHA)
   1. First successful telephonic transmission, early 1917. Professor E. M. Terry.
   2. Continued experimentation, 1917–1920.
   3. Regular service started January 1, 1921.
      a) weather (first regular in U.S.)
      b) market reports (Sept. 20, 1921)
      c) talks and entertainment
C. Educational Consciousness (Social Aspects)
   1. Social use of radio envisioned by Professor E. M. Terry and Professor W. H. Lighty, 1920.
   2. Professor Lighty, first program director, 1922.
   3. Professor A. W. Hopkins guided development of radio for agricultural extension, 1921.[22]

When did 9XM-WHA begin *broadcasting?* Jansky says broadcasting began in 1919. Hanson, Terry, the *Press Bulletin,* and certain unidentified documents indicate that broadcasting began, at the earliest, approximately the same time that KDKA went on the air. The most specific information from these sources is that broadcasting began on or about January 3, 1921. The weight of the evidence seems to tip in favor of these latter sources.

Applying the definition of a *broadcasting station* proposed at the beginning of this paper, one could conclude that 9XM-WHA, at least by January 3, 1921 was, in actuality, a broadcasting station. Its transmissions, from this date onward, were *telephonic.* For some time its transmissions had been by *wireless.* The evidence indicates that the programs were *intended to be received by the public.* Presumably the weather reports broadcast were intended for use by anyone or at least by some special public such as farmers. Finally, such phrases as "regular scheduling" and "consecutively and regularly" would indicate that 9XM had developed a *continuous program service* from January 3, 1921.

Prior to this date (or possibly late fall of 1920) the evidence would indicate that there was not a *continuous telephonic program service,* though telephonic programs had apparently been transmitted on an experimental basis. For several years programs had been transmitted on the basis of a *continuous program service,* but by *telegraphy, not telephony.* Apparently these telegraphic programs were *intended to be received by the public. Wireless* activity had been a part of 9XM's operation since 1916.

If, however, *all four* characteristics of a broadcasting station proposed in this paper are valid essentials for such a station, and these characteristics are applied to the early days of 9XM-WHA, the evidence strongly suggests that 9XM became a *broadcasting station* no earlier than November or December of 1920, and no later than January 3, 1921 (in spite of the fact WHA received its *broadcasting* license on January 13, 1922). The station's activity prior to this period suggests, though the station was evolving toward a broadcasting station, that the station had not yet fully developed into a broadcasting station.

There are other dates and events of great historical import to which WHA might validly lay claim. It has been established, for example, that experimental voice transmissions were conducted in 1917.

Perhaps as Professor Terry himself stated, the station was the first to broadcast market and weather reports regularly. Perhaps WHA may claim to be the "oldest educational broadcasting station." One statement records,

> "In the early part of 1922, after some time of discussing and deliberation, the university began purposeful educational broadcasting. This, as far as we know, was the first educational institution in the country to develop its own wireless station and systematically to broadcast definitely planned educational programs."[23]

Another paper mentions,

> "On Friday evening, March 25, 1922, the first lecture in a series, upon the Appreciation of Music was given which continued regularly on Friday evenings. . . . On May 5, 1922, daily noonday ten-minute addresses by members of the faculty were undertaken, and a Tuesday evening lecture course was begun. . . . The University of Wisconsin was one of the first, if indeed, not the first radio station to regularly broadcast consecutive and organized educational and informational addresses with a distinct educational as well as entertainment object in view." [24]

Perhaps WHA might even claim to be the "oldest *radio* station in the nation," though it might be well to wait until all other claims have been thoroughly and completely investigated.

In any event, it would seem that WHA's claim of "oldest station in the nation" needs some qualification.

III

Will students of radio history ever uncover sufficient data to validate once and for all, *oldest* and *first* claims?

In a letter to Professor Mack in November of 1958, Mr. Shurick said,

> "In compiling historical data for my book . . . I was shocked and somewhat discouraged to find that early records of this important industry were sadly inadequate and conflicting. . . . The first reference I received (in regard to WHA) was the year 1917 which

indicated that WHA was making experimental broadcasts (including weather and farm reports) with music. . . .

A communication was received from San Jose, California, indicating that what was later to become KQW began broadcasting in 1912 as a radio telephone transmitting station, presenting programs on a regular basis of broadcasting. If 1917 was the historical date, then, there is, of course 8XK of Dr. Conrad (broadcast start about summer of 1916) to consider. I realize it is most difficult to nail down an absolutely accurate and reliable chronological order of radio's early beginnings. . . . You might be interested, too, in the fact that I tried to distinguish between early experimental broadcasting and what was later to become the system as we know it today, by referring to all stations prior to KDKA's Harding-Cox election returns as *radio* and considering from November 2, 1920 on as *broadcasting.*"[25]

David Sarnoff, in a letter to the writer in December, 1959, had this to say:

"At various times many people have attempted to reconstruct history with the aim of finding a specific date when the 'oldest' station started. Although some historians award the palm to one station, while others bestow it on a different one, I have never been satisfied with the findings, nor do I believe that any of them has won acceptance. . . .

". . . In the absence of definitive records, the only existing 'proof' is in the form of unsubstantiated claims based on pride of ownership or promotion. All of these apparently were put forth only after broadcasting became a going industry. Nobody kept an authentic verifiable record right from the first sign on and sign off. Too many people worked in the dark, and when the lights went on, nothing was too clear about what had happened previously.

". . . I believe that the answer . . . is lost beyond recall in the early unrecorded days of broadcasting." [26]

16

WHO WILL ULTIMATELY DO THE BROADCASTING?

There Were 570 Active and 67 Discontinued Broadcasting Stations in the United States as of December 1, 1922. Radio and Electrical Manufacturers and Dealers, and Educational Institutions Seem to Be the Most Permanent in the Broadcasting Field. Statistics by Months and by Businesses.

Radio Broadcast, April 1923, pp. 523–526.

TABLE NO. 1 shows the monthly growth in the number of broadcasting stations during the past year for the entire United States, including Alaska, Hawaii, and Porto (sic) Rico. The deletions were deducted each month so that the figures given represent the total active stations at the beginning of the month. It seems that the point of saturation in broadcasting stations as determined by present conditions has about been reached. As of December 1st, there were 570 active and 67 discontinued stations, *but during the month of*

TABLE 1

REPORT OF RADIO BROADCASTING
STATIONS FOR YEAR 1922

Total Number of Stations as of	Active Stations	Deleted Stations
Jan. 1st	28	—
Feb. 1st	36	—
Mar. 1st	65	—
Apr. 1st	133	4
May 1st	217	4
June 1st	314	8
July 1st	378	12
Aug. 1st	441	14
Sept. 1st	496	16
Oct. 1st	539	22
Nov. 1st	554	44
Dec. 1st	570	67

December alone, 22 stations were deleted. The last four months of 1922 show a distinct decline in the net monthly gain in stations as follows:

	Oct. 1st	Nov. 1st	Dec. 1st	Jan. 1st
New Stations	48	38	38	33
Discontinued	6	22	23	20
	42	16	15	13

Many broadcasting stations were continued in operation up to September 1st, last year with the expectation of another "boom" similar to that of the previous year. When the sale of receiving sets was seen to follow a more healthy and less spectacular growth, these stations began to drop out of the broadcasting field in increasing numbers. Another cause for discontinuance of stations is the fact that large stations of superior quality have now been installed in many territories, these making unnecessary and inadvisable the continuance of small, poorly equipped stations—unnecessary from the standpoint of stimulating receiving set sales and inadvisable from the standpoint of relations between the owner and the radio public.

Table No. 1 shows also the number of stations that were deleted in this country, beginning April 1, 1922, before which time there were no deletions. It will be seen that 570 stations were still active as of December 1, 1922, a total of 67 stations having been discontinued up to that date.

TABLE 2

BUSINESS ENGAGED IN BY OWNERS OF BROADCASTING STATIONS

Business	Number	Percent
Radio & Electronic Manu-factures/dealers	231	41%
Newspapers & Publications	70	12
Educational Institutions	65	11
Department Stores	30	5
Auto & Battery Cos./Cycle Dealers	17	3
Music & Musical Inst. & Jewelry	12	2
Churches & Y.M.C.A.s	10	2
Hardware Stores	8	1
Police, Fire and City	7	1
Banks and Brokers	5	1
Stock Yards, Poultry, and Grain	4	1
Clubs and Societies	4	1
Mine Supplies, Marble, Oil Cos.	4	1
Railroad & Power Companies	4	1
Tel. & Tel. Cos.	4	1
Parks and Amusements	3	1
State Bureaus	3	1
Theaters	2	—
Laundries	1	—
Unknown	86	15
TOTAL	570	101%

Table No. 2 is particularly interesting and significant. It shows the businesses engaged in by the various broadcasters in each state, with the totals for states and businesses. Those broadcasters classed as unknown include individuals and companies whose businesses were not evident from their names or from other available sources. The radio and electric manufacturers and dealers make up 40% of the owners of stations, with publications and educational institutions coming second and third, although with totals far below that of the manufacturers and dealers.

TABLE 3

STABILITY OF VARIOUS LINES OF BUSINESS
IN BROADCASTING FIELD

Business	Active Stations	Deleted	Total	Percent Deleted
Educational Inst.	65	5	70	7.1%
Churches & Y.M.C.A.s	10	1	11	9.1
Radio & Elec. Mfg. and Dealers	231	26	257	10.1
Plumbing & Hardware	8	1	9	11.1
Newspapers & Public.	70	12	82	14.6
Unknown	86	17	103	16.5
Clubs & Societies	4	1	5	20.0
Parks & Amusements	3	1	4	25.0
Railroads & Power Cos.	4	3	7	43.0

In Table No. 3 is indicated the stability of various lines of business doing broadcasting, with the percentage of the total in a given line of business who have discontinued the use of their station. From this table, it will be seen that radio and electrical manufacturers and dealers, and educational institutions are apparently the most permanent in the field of broadcasting.

17

PIONEER STATION W9XK

IT WAS JUST an ordinary spring evening in the year 1933. Across the land most children had finished dinner and were outside playing, while parents were gathered around their radios listening to the news, wondering what might happen next as the nation sank deeper into the depression.

However, for some families—in Omaha, Nebraska; Rock Port, Missouri; Duncan, Oklahoma; DeWitt, Iowa; and other towns and cities throughout the Midwest—this night was quite special. It was "television night"!

In those days the "head of the house" was always considered the

On Iowa, May-June 1960, pp. 4-5.

expert on tuning the radio, and this was especially so on "television night." About 7 o'clock, Dad would begin to spin the radio dials until he received strong reception from Radio Station WSUI, broadcasting from the campus of the State University of Iowa.

He would then turn his attention to tuning the separate television set, while Mom called the children in from play and arranged chairs in the living room to face the four-inch-square television screen.

At 7:30 the telecast would begin with the announcer in Iowa City saying:

"Good evening, ladies and gentlemen. Station WSUI now joins facilities with television transmitter W9XK to bring you a program of both sight and sound. WSUI is operating on its regular broadcast frequency of 880 kilocycles, while W9XK is transmitting television images on a frequency of 2050 kilocycles with a power of 100 watts."

A typical program, with student and faculty performers, might begin with a short musical selection, followed by a lecture on astronomy, and conclude with a dramatic skit.

Although the programs were short and the screen was tiny, the devoted viewers who tuned in W9XK twice a week were in on something big—the beginning of educational television.

By virtue of being one of only three educational institutions holding a full-time experimental television license, SUI became a pioneer in using the new medium as an educational tool.

During the early 1930's, Station W9XK was the only television station in the world operated by an educational institution to transmit combined "sight and sound" educational programs. The other two educational stations—at Purdue University and Kansas State—broadcast pictures alternately with sound on the same wave length and, therefore, the picture had no sound accompaniment.

Station W9XK's regular schedule of telecasts built up a large group of faithful viewers. There weren't any television "rating" services in those days, of course, but Professor Edwin B. Kurtz, Head of Electrical Engineering at SUI and Director of Station W9XK, says it wasn't long after each program before letters from viewers would arrive at the studio.

Professor Kurtz includes comments from some of the viewer's letters in his book, *Pioneering in Educational Television,* a thorough documentary account of Station W9XK.

A Chicago viewer wrote: "The woman you have on the air appears very well over television. My set shows the waves in her hair. I could also see her eyes and white teeth."

A letter from Duncan, Oklahoma, said: "This is the first picture we have been able to get. Many people have watched the pictures, and it was given some publicity in the local paper."

A viewer in Bloomington, Illinois, wrote: "I think I get the most consistent results from W9XK. When I have someone in to see a picture I can always depend on W9XK. I doubt very much if your monitor showed up any better."

Another loyal viewer of the SUI telecasts was Sidney Mandelbaum, founder of Younkers department store in Des Moines. Professor Kurtz recalls that one day Mandelbaum drove up to the Electrical Engineering Building in his Rolls Royce. He stepped out, rushed to Professor Kurtz's office, and came straight to the point:

"I want to know if the picture I get in Des Moines is as good as it should be."

Professor Kurtz showed him some photographs taken from a studio monitor and said they represented a good picture.

"My reception is much better than that," huffed Mandelbaum as he spun around and headed back to his Rolls Royce.

Explaining why viewers as far away as Texas could receive programs telecast by W9XK, Professor Kurtz said the long wave length used, which is immediately below the commercial broadcast band, has very good carrying power.

There was another difference in television in the days before the development of the kinescope tube and the electronic picture tube. The television image was produced with a whirling metal "scanning disc" pierced by 45 holes arranged in spirals. A similar scanning disk in the receiver turned at 900 revolutions per minute.

Many photographs of the television equipment used in the pioneer station and images from the studio monitor are included in Professor Kurtz's book, which gives a detailed account of Station W9XK from its birth in 1931 to its last broadcast in 1939.

Interest in television at the University began in 1931 when the Department of Electrical Engineering decided to design and construct an elementary closed-circuit television demonstration unit for the University's State Fair display. The display encouraged SUI engineers to apply for a television broadcasting permit, which was granted in 1932.

The first formal combined broadcast of the SUI radio and television stations was viewed by SUI President Walter A. Jessup, nine SUI deans, and Extension Director Bruce E. Mahan.

Professor Kurtz gave an illustrated lecture about the University on the first broadcast. He showed a picture of Dean Carl E. Seashore and explained that the same picture was the first to be transmitted by wirephoto from New York to Chicago in 1925—a distance of 931 miles in 7½ minutes.

To the amusement of Dean Seashore, Professor Kurtz reported, "It is now being done in 1/15th of a second, which is 6,750 times as fast."

The first public demonstration was held in connection with a Baconian Lecture by Professor Kurtz. Reported *The Daily Iowan:*

"More than a thousand persons saw history in the making last night as they jammed a south corridor in Chemistry Building to witness the first public demonstration of television broadcast by Station W9XK.

"News flashes from *The Daily Iowan,* broadcast by its editor, Frank Jaffe, made up the first regular sight-sound program. The broadcast, lasting 15 minutes, was announced by Carl Menzer, Director of Station WSUI.

"A hubbub of conversation, with here and there an excited, half-suppressed giggle, greeted the appearance of the picture on a tiny screen. So great was the crowd that attendants were forced to keep people moving, allowing them only a few minutes to see the television display."

In 1934 Professor Kurtz was invited to report on sight-sound broadcasting at SUI to delegates attending the Institute for Education by Radio at Ohio State University. Finding almost no support among the skeptical delegates attending the Institute, Professor Kurtz debated the merits of SUI's educational television station with radio commentator H. V. Kaltenborn. He only ran into another non-believer. Said Kaltenborn:

"I doubt if television has much value at the present time. There is nothing that you have shown us which could not be more definitely shown by lantern slides, moving pictures, or sound movies. Engineers who have worked on television for commercial concerns seem convinced that there is nothing to it."

Replied Professor Kurtz: "I have witnessed sound-sight broadcasts sitting at home, and I have felt just as though I were sitting in a classroom with the professor facing the class, stepping aside to write something on the board, turning again and speaking in a natural tone."

Professor Kurtz recently sent Kaltenborn a copy of his new book, but he says, "I haven't heard from him yet."

A total of 389 telecasts, including programs on scouting, home planning, first aid, art, astronomy, physics, nnd shorthand, were made from Station W9XK before it went off the air in 1939 to make way for W9XUI, an electronic station using the newly developed iconoscope and kinescope tubes.

"It is no wonder that W9XK with its cumbersome disc had to give way to its fleet-footed successor and thus pass into oblivion," concludes Professor Kurtz. "However, it shall always be remembered as a station that helped prove that the theory was sound and that the system was practicable. This, together with the fact that it pioneered especially in educational television, should be glory enough for any station."

18

Christopher H. Sterling

WTMJ-FM: A CASE STUDY IN
THE DEVELOPMENT OF FM BROADCASTING

W9XAO (LATER WTMJ-FM) went on the air in January of 1940. The station's history divides into two distinct parts, which parallels the overall development of FM broadcasting. Prior to 1948, the station and the medium were in a period of experimental expansion; after that date FM development faltered (and WTMJ-FM left the air) until the late 1950s when momentum was again achieved (and the *Journal* station returned to the air, this time as but one of many trend-following operations). In addition to this varying role, WTMJ-FM illustrates special problems faced by newspaper owners of broadcast facilities.

Initial Development: to 1940

Prior to the early 1930s, there seemed to be no method of eliminating static in AM radio telephony reception. In 1933, however, Edwin Howard Armstrong, professor of physics at Columbia University and holder of a number of basic radio patents, filed application for four patents covering the basic elements of a static-free broadcast system.[2] Based on five years of extensive research, the new system utilized frequency modulated (FM) radio waves to which static did not "adhere."

For the next two years, the inventor worked closely with RCA engineers to further develop the FM system, but when RCA turned its research facilities full time to television, Armstrong decided the general public must be made aware of FM's capabilities.[3] Accordingly, he publicly demonstrated FM in the fall of 1935 to the New York meeting of the Institute of Radio Engineers. In 1936, Armstrong persuaded the Federal Communications Commission to allocate a few channels for experimental FM stations, and made plans to build a station of his own.[4] Located just north of New York City, Armstrong's W2XMN went on the air with FM broadcasts in early 1938.[5] In 1939, two mountaintop FM transmitters were installed by the Yankee Network in New England,[6] and an FM station began broadcasting in Hartford, Connecticut. These four FM operations represented the full extent of FM's visible growth more than five years after the basic patents had been applied for by Armstrong.

Journal of Broadcasting, Vol. XII, No. 4 (Fall 1968), pp. 341–352

Milwaukee's Journal Company had been involved in broadcasting for nearly 18 years by 1939.[7] The company operated standard (AM) radio station WTMJ (an NBC regional affiliate) and company engineers had been engaged in various types of experimental broadcasting—mechanical television, facsimile, and "apex" high frequency radio—since the beginning of the decade. WTMJ's general manager, Walter J. Damm, had long been interested in high-fidelity broadcasting. In 1934, WTMJ established an experimental AM station on the very high frequency of 42.2 megacycles. Learning about the possibilities of FM from Armstrong and officials of the Yankee Network, Damm and WTMJ engineers applied in June 1939 to the FCC for a construction permit for an experimental FM station.[8] Construction of the station began in September of 1939 on the top floor of a tall downtown Milwaukee office building. Armstrong himself helped with some of the technical problems of installation of equipment.[9] On January 15, 1940, station W9XAO went on the air with initial transmitter tests. With the granting of a license for experimental broadcasting, the station began a regular schedule of music and sound-effects tests on February 23, 1940. As mentioned earlier, W9XAO was the fifth FM station in the country.[10]

Satisfied with the results of initial testing, the next step was to "sell" the idea of FM to the Milwaukee public. Few people had heard of frequency modulation, and fewer still were aware of the static-free fuller range of sound the medium could present. The W9XAO engineering staff purchased 21 FM receivers from Stromberg-Carlson, one of the few manufacturers making FM equipment, and located them on a rotating basis in various public places to acquaint people with the new broadcast sound.[11] Service clubs and other meetings witnessed special demonstrations, and many thousands in Milwaukee were reached by the end of the year. In March of 1940, company management began a campaign to interest radio dealers in stocking FM receivers. On April 22nd, W9XAO began an expanded and regularly publicized schedule of music from 1:00 p.m. to 10:15 p.m. Most programming was music, using selections from transcription services. There were a few newscasts simulcast from WTMJ. This buildup of publicity among dealers and public was said to be the first time any organization tried to interest a mass audience in FM.[12] The attempt worked fairly well, for by the middle of 1940, the station's programming was being picked up on more than a thousand FM receivers, and more sets were selling all the time.[13]

Growth, War and Hiatus: 1940–48

Across the country, public interest in the few FM stations on the air sparked interest among broadcasters; by March of 1940, there were 22 stations authorized by the FCC. In March and April, FCC hearings investigated the need for more spectrum space for FM. The new medium was assigned the 42–50 mc band in which there was room enough for 40 channels, or nearly 2,000 stations across the country.[14] Authorizations had increased to 67 by the time of Pearl Harbor when the processing of applications was "frozen" for the duration of the war.

When the FCC approved final FM rules and standards in July of 1941, the *Journal's* application for a commercial license [15] was one of the first five received.[16] In October, the first fifteen commercial FM applications, including the *Journal's*, were approved by the FCC and the stations were "authorized to commence operations as soon as they were able to do so." [17]

The number of commercial FM stations actually on the air, only 18 in December, 1941, climbed to 46 by the end of the war as stations approved and under construction by the beginning of the war finished building and went on the air. FM receiver construction was halted by the war, however, so that audience growth for the medium was stymied, even though approximately half a million receivers were in existence.

Part of the commercial authorization for new FM stations was a new system of FM call letters. FM stations from January of 1941 on were to be known by call letters that identified both frequency and location. Originally known as W9XAO while licensed for experimental operation, the *Journal* FM station became known at the beginning of 1941 as W55M. The 55 indicated the frequency on which the station was assigned, 45.5 mc. As all stations were in the 42 to 50 mc range, there could be no confusion because only numbers 21 (42.1 mc) through 99 (49.9 mc) were used. The last letter, or letters, of the call indicated the city in which the stations were located—in this case "M" for Milwaukee.[18] By August of 1943, however, this call system had become too cumbersome, so FM stations reverted to an all-letter system and stations were given some choice as to which letter combinations they wished to use.[19] The *Journal's* W55M became WMFM (for "Milwaukee FM"). The station held those call letters until mid-1945, when the FCC announced another minor change: FM or TV stations affiliated with standard AM stations would all be allowed to use the same basic call with the suffix "FM" or "TV" added as needed. WMFM, therefore, became WTMJ-FM at the end of 1945.[20]

As the newly approved commercial FM stations pushed studios and transmitters to completion in early 1941, those operations owned or controlled by newspapers were dealt a hard regulatory blow. Under FCC Chairmen McNinch and Fly, the Commission had been investigating monopoly practices in the broadcasting industry since mid-1938.[21] In the case of FM radio, the FCC was very concerned about the increasing number of stations controlled by newspaper publishers. In March of 1941 the FCC issued Order No. 79 in order to put a halt to further newspaper ownership of FM radio while the commissioners decided on any possible new rules.[22] The freeze, "prompted primarily by Chairman Fly" [23] lasted but a short time, although the investigation itself, which came to no conclusions, was not closed until 1944. When the order was originally announced, however, it halted construction of all newspaper-owned FM stations (about a fourth of all FM applicants in early 1941), the *Journal's* included, at a critical period. As the war in Europe worsened and Lend-Lease increased, it became harder to obtain construction materials. With this time and material shortage in mind, *Journal* company management petitioned for permission to continue construction on its new transmitter site as originally approved by the FCC in late 1940.[24] After over a month of legal wrangling, the FCC gave W55M permission to continue work on the site located near Richfield, Wisconsin, about 22 miles northwest of Milwaukee. By early 1942, W55M was fully operational with a new 50,000 watt transmitter which effectively covered the more than half of Wisconsin's population within its 80 mile range from Richfield.[25] By August of 1942, W55M studios (as well as those of WTMJ) were moved to the newly built "Radio City," said to be the first structure built exclusively for AM and FM radio as well as projected television operations.[26] Visiting Milwaukee in 1943, FM inventor Edwin Armstrong termed the Milwaukee and Richfield facilities the "finest, most modern FM plant in the country." [27]

W55M programming was much like that of experiental W9XAO. Recorded music, primarily popular and light classical works from transcription services, remained the staple. Throughout the war, W55M programming remained primarily musical with the addition of four short newscasts and special Office of War Information programs in the noon-to-midnight seven-day-a-week schedule. With the exception of occasional NBC war coverage, which W55M simulcast with WTMJ, all programming was original to the FM operation. By mid-1942, W55M was programming to an estimated potential of 21,000 FM receivers, but with war-time production limitations, the listening audience remained much the same throughout the war period.[28] More and more people were exposed to FM radio, however, by the continuing series of FM reception demonstrations staged by station engineers and by sharing of duplicate receivers.

By the winter of 1943-44, the FCC began to examine the radio allocations picture in preparation for the eventual end of war-time restrictions on stations and receiver construction. The Commission asked the broadcasting industry to set up a Radio Technical Planning Board to examine allocations for all broadcast services.[29] Panel Five of that Board, the group concerned with FM, suggested that FM be given the band 41-56 mc, an increase of 7 mc over the then existing commercial FM allocation. When it was suggested that FM radio service should be "kicked upstairs" and expanded in the 100 mc area of the spectrum, Armstrong decided that an actual test would clearly demonstrate the drawbacks to this plan.[30] He approached WTMJ engineers to set up such a test. They interested the FCC in the proposal and persuaded the Zenith Radio Corporation to help. For a three month period in mid-1945, WMFM programs were broadcast on both the regular 45.5 mc channel, and on an experimental channel of 91 mc. Zenith engineers and Armstrong established a listening post 80 miles south of the WMFM transmitter, on the fringes of the regular listening area, to compare signals on the two frequencies. The final report to the FCC, submitted by a group of Zenith engineers in September 1945, supported Armstrong's position against any major move upwards in FM frequency allocations. Specifically, the tests showed a good signal about 90 per cent of the time on 45.5 mc, but only about 30 per cent of the time on 91 mc.[31]

By June of 1945, however, the FCC had nearly 430 FM applications on file awaiting the end of the war.[32] If the Commission were going to make any major changes in FM frequencies it would have to do so before the end of the war brought an end to wartime construction limitations. Available (possibly inaccurate) technical information on possible interference conditions in the 42-50 mc band convinced the Commission to order FM radio shifted to the 88 to 106 mc band, with the 88 to 92 mc segment of the band reserved for educational broadcasting.[33] The 106 to 108 mc band was assigned to facsimile with the provision that FM would use those channels if facsimile didn't develop, which turned out to be the case.[34]

The immediate problem facing FM broadcasters was that no transmitters or receivers existed for FM radio in its new home. For the 46 stations on the air at the time of the FCC decision, changeover meant modification or disposal of transmitter equipment only three or four years old. Listeners had to purchase new receivers as an estimated half-million FM sets were made obsolete by the FCC ruling.[35] Because of the need to re-tool for the higher band, and because of the manufacturers' rush to fill five years of suspended demand for AM equipment, FM radio did not show any appreciable growth for nearly 18 months after the war. Only in 1947 did FM begin to pick up steam across the nation as new equipment became available.

In Milwaukee, WTMJ-FM had to change from 45.5 mc to 92.3 mc by the end of 1945.[36] By making temporary use of materials left over from war-time FM experiments, WTMJ-FM engineers were able to have the station on its newly assigned frequency by December 30, 1945—one of the first FM stations on the air to complete conversion to the new band.[37] The FCC allowed a number of stations, including WTMJ-FM, to continue temporary operations on the old band so that listeners with old receivers would have service during the transitional period. WTMJ-FM kept up such two-frequency transmissions until February, 1947.[38] In the meantime, construction was begun for a new 50 kw transmitter and a higher antenna tower at Richfield so that WTMJ-FM, operating on temporary low power, could reach something of its old 80-mile coverage radius. In September of 1948, the station began broadcasting with its new equipment and 349,000 watts of effective radiated power. For a short time it was the most powerful FM station in the country.[39]

In mid-1946, a critical programming change was made when WTMJ-FM began simulcasting programs from WTMJ, originating no separate FM programming whatever. Station management cited costs of operating two temporary transmitters, plus contracting for a third, as primary reasons for the change from original to simulcast programming.[40] When the new high-power transmitter went into operation in the late 1948, the FM program schedule was expanded to a full 19-hour broadcast day, longer than ever before, but made up entirely of simulcast programming. With this inception of simulcasting, WTMJ-FM lost its separate identity, its separate advertising revenue, and its importance as a pioneering FM operation.

Decline and Rebirth: 1948–66

As 1948 began, the Journal Company was starting another new media service that was grabbing the imagination of Milwaukee: television. WTMJ-FM went on the air in late 1947, and the station's management undertook another major effort to sell the city on the new medium, much as had been done with FM eight years earlier.[41] Money, personnel, and interest of the company's broadcast division were focused on television while WTMJ continued to serve as the major broadcasting breadwinner to offset early television expenses. FM, with disappointing receiver sales and no advertiser interest (partly because of simulcast AM programming), became at best a tolerated third service. The effect on the FM operation of the Journal Company was felt in a short time. By early 1950, with increasing interest being directed to television, and apparent minor listener interest in FM, WTMJ-FM was cut to but seven hours a day. Few complaints were received and a straw poll appealing for listener interest printed in the *Milwaukee Journal* got no strong response either. It appeared to broadcast that there was "a decided lack of interest in FM." [42] Finally, on April 2, 1950, WTMJ-FM left the air, just over a decade after it had begun to pioneer the medium. All transmitter equipment and the antenna and tower were sold to the University of Illinois.[43]

Across the country, 1950 marked the first time the total FM authorizations, as well as stations actually on the air, declined from totals of a year before. In general, FM became more and more of a losing investment in the early 1950's as television swept industry and listener interest. Few people wanted to get into FM (except for educational stations which grew steadily in number) and an increasing number got out. Two other Milwaukee FM stations, which had first aired in 1948, closed down in 1953 leaving the city with no FM service until a classical music FM station came on the air in late 1956.[44] Stations which remained on the air in the 1949–59 decade were either those affiliated with AM stations (which usually meant simulcast programming), or independents which supplemented their thin FM revenue with supplemental music services to retail stores. The low point came in 1956.

By 1957–58, the outlook for FM radio began slowly to change. Authorizations were higher for the second year in a row, and for the first time since 1949, the number of stations on the air increased over the year before. A number of factors led to this renewed interest in the medium: income from supplemental services, possibilities of using multiplexed signals, better FM receivers (many with an automatic frequency control feature) and more of them, and a consequently larger potential audience for FM stations.[45] Limitations of an ever more crowded AM band also contributed to FM's growth potential as AM stations applied for FM licenses in order to increase coverage or broadcast during night-time hours.[46] Interest in high-fidelity music developed rapidly, fed in part by the introduction of stereo recordings. Across the country, FM stations grew in number, and by May of 1958 there were 20 FM stations in Wisconsin including two in Milwaukee, and more applications were being filed at an increasing rate.[47]

By early 1958, Journal Company officials began to seriously contemplate a return to the medium they had left nine years earlier. This feeling was prompted both by the fear that good frequencies in Milwaukee would rapidly be taken as well as by a desire to experiment with automated broadcasting.[48] Plans were made to use a Schafer Electronics automatic time-sensor system which used recorded tapes and timing units to fully automate the FM broadcast schedule. WTMJ-FM returned to the air in June of 1959 with an all-music format supplemented by two daily 15 minute newscasts, all of which were original to the station. A slight 1960 power increase to 5,000 watts gave the station about a 50 mile coverage radius (this with new equipment purchased in 1958–59). Just a month after going on the air, the station began weekly AM-FM stereo broadcasts with WTMJ. Late in 1961, WTMJ-FM began stereo multiplex transmissions, and by 1965, the station's musical programming was fully in stereo.[49] Over the 1959–66 period, the potential FM audience in the Milwaukee area increased from a 30 per cent FM set saturation to more than 50 per cent, or about 211,000 homes.[50]

Across the country, the story was similar. As FM began to shed its image of being a money-loser, programming mostly for classical music minorities, authorizations began to pick up in larger urban areas. Sets sold at an increasing rate, expecially after the 1961 introduction of stereo multiplex FM broadcasting, and FM became an increasingly viable medium.

COMMENT

WTMJ-FM history divides into two periods, both of which parallel the medium's general growth. At first, from 1939 through 1948, the station was a leader, exhibiting the experimental approach of the pioneer. Important innovations in technology and programming came from the station. On the other hand, from 1948–1966, WTMJ-FM illustrated the role of an average station in a medium; one which gives service to a local area but which considers balance sheets more important than pioneering. Both of these periods are important to the media historian, because both illustrate key elements in the growth of FM itself. When the medium was new and attracting attention, WTMJ-FM and a few other stations carried the ball. When the medium slipped in the face of a frequency change and television competition, WTMJ-FM and many other stations left the air. When FM revived in the late 1950's, WTMJ-FM and other stations, riding with the tide this time, came back on the air. While the specific importance of any one station such as WTMJ-FM is questionable (although it varies with the period), the story of WTMJ-FM is an excellent case study or focusing indicator of the trends in FM development in the United States over the past thirty years.

(On November 27, 1974, the call letters were changed to WKTI and the format to automated rock. According to the program manager, "It's a music machine.")

19

Robert Pepper

THE PRE-FREEZE TELEVISION STATIONS

WHEN THE FIRST two commercially licensed television stations in the United States went on the air July 1, 1941, they were met with pronouncements of television's great importance and predictions of television's quick growth. All this would have to wait however, for by the end of the year the nation was engaged in World War II. Although commercial television development was virtually frozen by the war, by the end of 1945 there were nine commercial television authorizations: six already on the air and three with outstanding construction permits (CP's). In addition, four future television stations were broadcasting under experimental authorizations while two more were in the process of building their "experimental" stations.[1] With the end of the war however, the number of television applications and authorizations mushroomed so rapidly that the FCC realized that its existing allocation plans were inadequate. As a result, the FCC issued its "freeze order" halting any further television authorizations. At the time of the freeze there were 108 stations authorized that eventually went on the air. In understanding the post-freeze development of the television industry and the patterns of control that developed, it is important to examine these 108 pre-freeze stations in light of their ownership, their investment, and their returns.

Pre-Freeze Development

As soon as World War II ended, the number of applications and authorizations for commercial television licenses increased at an incredible rate. Between the end of the war (when there had been nine authorizations) and June 1946 (the end of fiscal 1946), there were an additional 21 CP's authorized. One year later there were a total of 66 authorizations. During this two-year period however, no new licenses were issued; all stations (except the original six) were on the air under their CP's. The first post-war full commercial license was issued in January 1948 to WNBW, NBC's Washington station. By then the total authorizations had grown to 107 (7 licensed, 14 CP's on the air, and 86 CP's outstanding) and pending applications had grown to 191. The existing allocation plan, issued May 25, 1948, provided for 13 commercial television channels (6MHz wide) to be distributed over 140 markets enabling 405 stations. By the fall of 1948 the FCC realized that this plan was inadequate in that it left a good part of the country without any television service at all and most of the country receiving only one channel. Thus, on September 20, 1948, with 123 television stations authorized (12 licensed, 25 CP's on the air, 86 outstanding CP's) and 303 applications pending, the FCC issued its "freeze order" halting any further television authorizations while the FCC investigated an expanded plan for television allocations utilizing the UHF frequencies.

Although the freeze halted any new allocations, the FCC was very careful to note that the freeze did not apply to previously issued construction permits or other television authorizations. Thus, until the freeze was lifted three and one-half years later, in April 1952, the pre-freeze authorized stations would be able to operate without any competition. Although 123 stations were authorized, 15 never made it on the air. By the end of the freeze there were only 108 authorized television stations, all on the air, 96 of which were fully licensed. Twenty years later, in 1972, 106 of these original 108 were still telecasting under their commercial authorizations; two of the stations were taken over by educational broadcasters WHYY in Wilmington (Philadelphia) and WNET in Newark (New York). These 108 were distributed in 63 markets ranging from New York City to Ames, Iowa (pop. 23,105 in the 1950 census). All but three of the stations were in the top 100 markets, yet even some of the major markets were without any television service at all: Portland, Oregon (21st market), Denver (26th), and nine others in the top 50 markets.

While these pre-freeze licensees were shaping the medium, there were 716 applications pending awaiting the end of the freeze and entry into the the new industry. Who owned the original 108 pre-freeze television stations, how much did they invest, and how much did they make?

OWNERSHIP

The licensees of the 108 pre-freeze television stations that began commercial telecasting, for the most part, fall into four categories: radio licensees, publishers, electronics (radio and television) manufacturers, and motion picture interests.[2] As these interests are not mutually exclusive, there is naturally some overlapping of interests. An additional ownership characteristic of the pioneer stations, subsequently developed more fully, is that of the group owner. Close to half of these stations were owned by television group owners setting an increasing pattern for post-freeze industry growth. Although several stations changed owners before the end of the freeze, in order to simplify examination of ownership, the last licensee before the end of the freeze will be examined.

Radio Licensees

Of the 108 pre-freeze television licenses, 89 (82%) were held by parties (either individuals or companies) that also held radio licenses in the same market. Sixty-three of these joint licenses (58% of the total 108) had both AM and FM licenses in the same market. Twenty-one (19%) had just AM licenses in the market, while only five (5%) had just an FM license in the same market with their television license.

Not only was there a high percentage of joint radio-television licensees, but a close examination of those licensees indicates that, for the most part, the radio licensees involved in pioneer television had also been radio pioneers. Of the 89 radio licensees holding television licenses, 73 (68% of the total 108) were on the air by the end of 1930; 60 (56%) were on the air by the end of 1925; and 33 (31%) were on the air before the end of 1922. Thus, well over half of the 108 pioneer television licenses went to radio pioneers.

TABLE 1

OWNERSHIP OF PRE-FREEZE TELEVISION STATIONS: OTHER BROADCAST INTERESTS

N = 108

TV Station in 1952 Owned by: *	Number	Percent
With AM on the air before 1925	60	56%
With AM on the air 1926– 1930	13	12
With AM on the air 1931– 1940	7	6
With AM on the air after 1941	4	4
With AM only in same market	21	19%
With FM only in same market	5	5
With AM and FM in same market	63	58
Total with radio station same market	89	82%
3 groups with 5 TV stations each	15	14%
2 groups with 4 TV stations each	8	7
4 groups with 3 TV stations each	12	11
9 groups with 2 TV stations each	18	17
Total owned by TV station groups	53	49%

* Ownership defined as 10% or more.

The single greatest ownership interest in the 108 pre-freeze television stations was that of radio licensees. With 82% of the television stations owned by licensees of radio stations in the same market, there can be no doubt that the radio broadcaster played a major role in the early development and growth of television; they invested a lot of money and, as will be seen, they made a lot of money.

Reflecting the heavy radio licensee involvement in the pre-freeze television stations, it is interesting to note that the licensees of 30 of the 80 radio stations listed as having "questionable programming practices" in the FCC's *Public Service Responsibility of Broadcast Licencees*, ("The Blue Book"), received pre-freeze television licenses (28% of the total 108). These 30 "blue book stations" that received television licenses emphasized the fact that the FCC was not going to enforce the report's recommendations. As one observer has said, when the FCC gave WBAL—"a major exhibit of horrors in the Blue Book."—a television license without a hearing, "the Blue Book has indeed been bleached." [3]

The radio industry, that so heavily invested in the pioneer television stations, was itself heavily invested in by other interests. Reflecting the substantial influence of radio, one of the major interests behind the pioneer television stations, as in radio, were publishers of newspapers and magazines.

Publishing Ownership

Fifty-two of the pre-freeze television licenses (48%) were issued to publishing firms, or to companies that had substantial interests in publishing. A total of five licenses were held by two magazine publishers while 47 licenses were held by newspaper publishers. Both magazine publishers and eight of the newspaper publishers were television group owners while an additional five (owning only one television station) were radio broadcasting group owners. Of the remaining 24 newspaper owned television licensees, all but two (the Baltimore *Sun*, WMAR-TV, and the Los Angeles *Times*, KTTV) also owned radio stations in the same market.

With close to half of the pre-freeze television licenses being held by publishers, it is plain that publishing money, especially newspaper money, was important in financing the development of early television. In addition, the pattern of this newspaper/television ownership reflected the increasing tendency in the patterns of radio ownership, the move towards group ownership: ten publishers were television group owners owning 24 television stations (22% of the total). This tendency towards multiple ownership by one licensee was not unique to publishing licensees; rather it was a growing industry pattern and will be more fully examined later.

Motion Picture Interests

In addition to publishers, another group interested in the new television industry was the motion picture industry. Fearful that television would cut into movie revenues, motion picture companies began hedging bets (as broadcasters are doing with CATV 20 years later) and began applying for television licenses. One of the earliest moves into television was made by Paramount Pictures Corp., a major producer, distributor, and exhibitor owning more than 650 theatres across the country. Paramount owned two of the stations that were telecasting before the end of the war. They also owned 29% of Allen B. DuMont Laboratories Inc. owner of the DuMont network and the three DuMont television stations. In addition, when the freeze order was issued, Paramount had applications pending for television licenses in Detroit, Des Moines, and Boston. In addition to Paramount, three additional pre-freeze television licenses were held, at least in part, by movie exhibitors in Miami, Utica, and in New Haven.

Electronics Manufacturers

An important source of capital for early television experimentation and development came from electronic manufacturers. Nine such manufacturers owned 18 of the pre-freeze stations. It should be noted that four of these companies, Philco, RCA, G.E., and DuMont, had stations authorized and telecasting during World War II. RCA, G.E., and Philco had been engaged in television experimentation since the late 1920's and early 1930's and had experimental stations on the air with regular schedules as early as 1931. Of the original 108 pre-freeze television stations, RCA (NBC) owned five, DuMont owned three, and G.E. and Philco each owned one. In addition, five other electronics firms owned eight more pioneer television stations. These electronics firms were an important source of television ownership: they experimented with their facilities and, especially in the very early days, developed new equipment and techniques that benefitted the entire industry.

Other Interests

In addition to television pioneering by radio licensees, motion picture interests, publishers, or electronics firms, several other interests, both corporate and individual, invested in pre-freeze television. Several licenses were held by retailers and three licenses were held by insurance companies. In addition, one license was held by Wayne Coy, the FCC chairman who announced the freeze order in 1948. He resigned from the FCC less than two months before the freeze was lifted to become a partner, with Time Inc., in KOB-TV, Albuquerque. Another licensee was John Fetzer, director of domestic radio censorship for the O.W.I. during World War II. And, the only college to hold a pre-freeze television license was the Iowa State College of Agriculture in Ames.

Group Owners

Because of the high cost of building a television station, and because of the high return from television investments (as will be seen), those who could afford to build a television station could usually afford to build two or more—and often did. Eighteen such multi-television licensees owned 53 of the 108 pre-freeze television stations (49%). Of these 18 groups, 10 were publishers who owned 24 stations. The remaining 8 multi-television group owners held 29 television licenses (27%). In addition to the multi-television group owners, 14 television stations were owned by broadcasting (radio) group owners that owned only one station. Thus, a total of 67 television stations (62%) were owned by 32 broadcasting group owners.

Nine multi-television group owners were small group owners: they owned only two television stations. Seven of these small group owners were publishers. There were nine major multi-television group owners (three or more television stations), three of whom were publishers, owning a total of 35 television stations (32%).[4]

TABLE 2

OWNERSHIP OF PRE-FREEZE TELEVISION STATIONS: OTHER COMMUNICATIONS INTERESTS

N = 108

	Percent Interest in Licensee			
TV Station in 1952 Owned By	*10–49%*	*50–89%*	*90–100%*	*Total* *
Licensee of AM and/or FM in the same market	1	4	84	89
TV station group †	2	3	48	53
TV or radio group	4	3	60	67
Motion picture interests	4	–	4	8
Electronics manufacturers	–	–	18	18
Publishing interests	–	5	47	52
Licensees with *no other* ‡ communications interests (1952)	–	–	3	3

* Total does not add up to 108 as some categories overlap.
† In 1972 92 of the 108 (85%) were owned by TV station groups.
‡ In 1972 only one of the 108 was owned by a firm with *no other communications interests*.

Twenty years later, in 1972, the trend towards group ownership, thus concentration of ownership, has increased to the point where 92 (85%) of the 108 pre-freeze television stations are group owned. Three group-owned stations in 1952 are no longer group owned; however, 42 non-group-owned stations in 1952 are now group owned. One of the primary reasons for this dramatic increase is that most of the pioneer television licensees have subsequently bought more television properties with money they made from their pioneer station. The growing concentration of ownership can be illustrated in yet another way: in 1952 three of the pioneer television stations were owned by non-communication industry interests (no broadcasting or publishing interests); in 1972 only one such licensee exists (Lamb Communications) and it exists only because the licensee was forced to sell his broadcasting and publishing properties.

One very important set of television group owners, both in 1952 and in 1972, are the television networks. By the end of the freeze there were four networks, ABC, CBS, NBC, and DuMont that owned 16 pioneer television stations in eight different markets. Twenty years later, of the three remaining networks' 15 owned and operated television stations, 14 were pioneer stations; the ABC and NBC stations were the same, however, CBS sold its Washington pioneer and bought one in Philadelphia and one in Chicago.

INVESTMENT AND RETURN

The initial capital investment by the 108 pre-freeze television stations and the four television networks was substantial, amounting to over $124 million. This figure does not include the AT&T coaxial lines used by the networks, nor does it include operating expenses for either the networks or the stations; it is just the *initial* capital investment in buildings and facilities needed to get the stations on the air. The average initial expenditure of the 93 non-network stations [5] was $678,602 per station. As the market size increased so did the capital expenditure: stations in markets of between 100,000 and 250,000 spent an average of only $345,327, while non-network stations in markets over one million initially spent, on the average, $1,001,893. The networks and their 15 owned and operated stations spent more than $61 million of the initial $124 million.

Although the television industry sustained losses of $25 million in 1949 and $9 million in 1950, it more than made up for those losses in 1951 with profits of $41.6 million. By 1952 the profits for the 108 pioneer stations and the four networks reached $55.5 million. Of the 108 stations, 94 (87%) made money. All of the stations in the 40 single station markets made money in 1952; an average of $650,000 before taxes. Of the 14 stations still losing money in 1952, nine were in either New York or in Los Angeles where there were seven stations on the air competing for the advertising dollar. Even including the losing stations, in 1952, the average station made a profit of over $500,000 before taxes.

The total gross revenues in 1952 for television was $324.2 million, an increase of 38% over 1951 revenues. The profits of $55.5 million were more than 33% greater than in 1951. Seventeen stations made more than $1 million. Even though 14 stations were still losing money in 1952, the vast majority, 87%, were making money. The average non-network television station had cost $678,602 to put on the air. In 1952 the average depreciated cost of this investment was $412,597. Thus, the average non-network television station income of $492,351 was able to pay off the depreciated cost in less than one year.

By 1952 there was no question, television was already a very profitable business—and its profits were increasing. The original investors, the broadcasters, publishers, electronics firms, and others did not have to carry their pioneer television stations very long. They were soon able to reuse their investment capital and new television income to further expand their television, and other holdings.

SUMMARY

The patterns of ownership and control that developed among the first 108 pre-freeze television licensees set the trends for ownership in the ensuing post-freeze television proliferation. These lucrative stations were owned, for the most part, by radio licensees, including many of the early radio pioneers, publishers, electronics firms and motion picture interests. The high cost and the high return of the pre-freeze television stations encouraged the rapid growth of television group owners, a phenomenon not nearly as developed in radio, at the time, as it would become in television. The group owner developed out of successful broadcasting ventures financing new broadcasting investments; the profits from the first television station paid for more television stations. These patterns of ownership, among the very profitable major market television pioneers, set during the freeze, began a process of television ownership concentration that has continued.

Television became more frank but still had taboos. In April 1970 CBS would not show Abbie Hoffman's American flag suit. A 1971 commercial of a man and woman rolling in the surf was reminiscent of "From Here to Eternity." Faye Emerson's lowcut dresses attracted viewers and controversy early in TV's history—but at the 1971 academy awards Sally Kellerman went farther. In 1974 the fad was streaking and TV covered it.

Table 1.

BROADCAST STATIONS

Figures show the number of broadcasting stations for various categories, and the number of safety and special stations; not shown citizen band which in 1970 totaled 886,951.

YEAR	COMMERCIAL STATIONS				EDUCATION		TOTAL	TRANSLATORS & BOOSTERS		AMATEUR & DISASTER	OTHER SERVICES[2]
	AM	FM	F-II	TV	FM	TV		TV	FM		
1913										1,312	701
1920										5,719	1
1922	30						30			NA	NA
1925	571						571			15,000	1,905
1930	618						618			18,994	2,474
1935	685						685			45,561	4,254
1940	765	50[a]					765			56,295	10,013
1945	933	46	[5]	6	6		991			60,000	17,978
1950	2,144	691	[86]	104	62		3,001			87,967	66,717
1955	2,732	540	[38]	458	124	11	3,865	41[b]		142,387	158,465
1960	3,483	741	[218]	579	165	47	5,015	233		228,206	145,506
1965	4,025	1,343	[338]	589	262	92	6,311	1,762		280,343	431,855
1970	4,288	2,126	[689]	691	416	190	7,711	2,482		283,461	674,183
1974	4,395	2,502		705	633	233	8,468	2,933	54[c]		

Source: FCC. [1]FM "independent" stations; included FM stations operated by non-AM licensee in the same market (to 1968) and those plus FM stations associated with an AM but reported separately (since 1969). [2]Includes aviation, industrial, land transportation, and public safety. [a]Experimental. [b]1957. [c]FM translator service created September 1970, first three licenses granted December 21, 1971.

Table 2.

AM STATIONS ON SELECTED CHANNELS

Figures show the growth of stations assigned to
selected AM channels in each of the four classifications.

FREQUENCY	1925[a]	1935	1940	1945	1950	1955	1960	1965	1970
CLEAR									
700	2	1	1	1	1	1	1	1	1
750	2	2	2	4	7	7	7	8	8
1160	11	2	3	2	2	2	2	2	2
1170	16	1	1	2	8	8	10	10	18
1530	--	2	2	2	3	4	3	25[c]	40
REGIONAL									
550	2	9	9	9	16	21	25	25	22
630	3	6	6	6	18	25	28	29	28
950	4	3	3	8	19	33	38	43	45
1280	9	8	9	9	30	43	55	63	60
1590	--	--	--	3	20	34	60	69	73
LOCAL									
1230	16	35	62	83	159	159	161	168	168
1240	16	44	61	77	138	146	146	144	155
1340	10	48	59	84	164	158	159	168	171
1400	7	44	71	87	153	159	160	168	172
1450	3	42	55	75	158	162	161	171	171
1490	--	33	59	67	155	156	157	160	168
TOTAL LOCAL		246	367	474	927	940	944	979	1005
FOREIGN CLEAR									
Can 690	1	--	--	1	12	15	20	22	23
Mex 730	--	--	--	2	23	23	29	30	30
BI 1540	--	--	--	1	23	20	18	29	47
TOTAL		634[c]	752[c]	958	2309	2909	3608	4058	4327
% LOCAL	20%[d]	46%	49%	50%	40%	32%	26%	24%	23%

Source: Compiled from Bureau of Navigation and Broadcasting Yearbook 1926, 1936, 1940, 1951, 1956, 1961, and 1971 by Lichty and Topping with C. H. Sterling. [a]In 1925 there were class A stations-- 278 to 200 meters or 1080-1500 kHz--with no more than 500 watts; class B stations--545 to 280 meters or 550-1070 kHz--expected to stay on frequency, be technically superior with 500 watts as a minimum. Further, B stations were to have their programs "carefully supervised and maintained to insure satisfactory service to the public." In 1925 there were about 11 stations per channel between 1080 and 1500 kHz (less than 10% used over 500 watts). From 580 to 1070 there were about two stations per channel (62% used more than 500 watts--most 1,000 or 5,000 watts). [b]Prior to September 15, 1940, local channels were 1200, 1210, 1310, 1370, 1420, and 1500 kHz. Under the North American Regional Broadcasting Agreement (NARBA), nearly all American broadcasting stations changed frequencies but only the six local channels were completely re-allocated. The earlier frequencies are shown for 1925 and 1935. [c]Totals for 1935 and 1940 included four stations assigned channels above 1500 kHz--in 1935 the four stations (two each at 1530 and 1550) were designated as experimental but by 1940 the same four were referred to as high powered regional outlets. [d]In 1925 about 80% of all stations were classified B.

Table 3.

AM STATIONS BY CLASSIFICATION

Figures show the number and % of stations in the four classifications
for standard broadcast (AM) stations. All I-A and I-B stations are
listed as clear dominant. Class II stations, operating on U.S.
clear, shared clear, or clear channels assigned to other North American
countries are listed as clear secondary.

YEAR	Clear Dominant	Clear Secondary	Regional	Local	TOTAL
NUMBER:					
1935	38	56	226	260	580
1945	44	86	351	430	915
1960	52	596	1,905	947	3,500
1970	97	1,098	2,131	1,002	4,328
PERCENT:					
1935	7%	10%	39%	45%	101%
1945	5	9	38	47	99
1960	1	17	54	27	99
1970	2	25	49	23	99

Table 4.

AM CHANNELS AND STATIONS ON EACH CHANNEL

Figures show the number of channels and the average number of stations
on each channel in 1935 and 1970. Spectrum used in 1935 was 550 to
1500 kHz; in 1970 it was 540 to 1600 kHz.

	Number of Channels		Average Stations/Each Channel	
	1935	1970	1935	1970
U.S. Clear	40	36	1	3
Other Clear	6	24	9	46
Regional	44	41	5	52
Local	6	6	43	167
TOTAL	96	107		

Source: Compiled by Don R. LeDuc and L. W. Lichty from Broadcasting
Yearbook. The total number of stations varies slightly from FCC data.

Table 5.

AM STATIONS BY POWER CLASSIFICATION

Figures show the number and % of stations operating in various power classifications for fulltime and other (sharetime, parttime, daytime, specific hours, local sunset). Shown is the general growth of stations in power as well as number. In 1928 about three-fourths of all stations used 250 watts or less. In 1965 about one-half used 1,000 at least during the daytime. It is hard to compare but certain that in later years more power was needed to cover even a smaller area because of increased interference from other stations and other electromagnetic radiation, buildings, neon lights, cars, etc.

YEAR	50,000 Watts[1] Fulltime	Other	5,000 Watts[2] Fulltime	Other	1,000 Watts Fulltime	Other	250 Watts[3] Fulltime	Other	100 Watts[4] Fulltime	Other	TOTAL
NUMBER:											
1928	8	2	35	30	36	49	65	131	151	113	620
1935	23	5	26	18	119	57	79	73	85	95	580
1940	34	5	114	26	89	56	270	62	60	38	754
1965	73	45	351	631	176	1,832	233	678	6	1	4,026
PERCENT:											
1928	1%	--	6%	5%	6%	8%	10%	21%	24%	18%	100%
1935	4	1%	4	3	21	10	14	13	15	16	101
1940	5	1	15	3	12	7	36	8	8	5	100
1965	2	1	9	16	4	46	6	17	--	--	101

Source: Compiled by H. B. Summers and L. W. Lichty from FRC Second Annual Report and Broadcasting Yearbook.
[1]Includes WLW in 1935 with 500,000 watts.
[2]Includes some stations with 10KW or 25KW--in 1965 80 (9%) with 10KW; 1 with 25KW.
[3]Includes stations with 500 watts.
[4]Includes some stations with less than 100 watts--especially before 1970.

Table 6.

AM STATIONS BY POWER, OPERATING HOURS AND DIRECTIONAL ANTENNAE

Figures show the number and % of fulltime and daytime in different power and directional antennae categories.

YEARS	FULLTIME STATIONS				DAYTIME		TOTAL	
	Same Power D & N	Lower Power[1] Night	DA D & N	DA Night Only	No DA	Use DA	Full time	Day time
Number								
1935	358	202	NA	NA	74	NA	560	74
1940	498	186	NA	NA	68	NA	684	68
1945	800	80	NA	NA	78	NA	880	78
1950	1010	48	176	415	649	11	1649	660
1955	1016	46	262	507	1017	61	1831	1078
1960	979	62	264	600	1484	215	1905	1699
1965	279	832	252	694	1666	335	2057	2001
Percent								
1935	56%	32%	NA	NA	12%	NA	88%	12%
1940	66	25	NA	NA	9	NA	91	9
1945	84	8	NA	NA	8	NA	92	8
1950	44	2	8%	18%	28	1%	71	29
1955	35	2	9	17	35	2	63	37
1960	27	2	7	16	41	6	53	47
1965	7	21	6	17	41	8	51	49

Source: Compiled by C. H. Sterling from Broadcasting Yearbook. Directional antennae information not available prior to 1950. Daytime includes all stations that are not fulltime--including day only, sharetime, local sunset, specific hours, etc. However, in 1970 more than 1,500 daytime stations had authorization for pre-sunrise operation (usually beginning at 6:00 a.m.). The change in the number of fulltime stations using lower power at night in 1965 indicates the FCC's granting 1 KW day; 250 night to many formerly fulltime 250-watt stations.

Table 7.

FM AND TV STATIONS ON SELECTED CHANNELS

Figures show the number of stations operating on each of the channels listed.

YEAR	FM CHANNELS[1]			VHF CHANNELS				UHF CHANNELS[2]			
	91.5	93.5	93.7	2	3	7	8	15	30	50	75
1945	1	--	--	1	2	--	--	--	--	--	--
1950	5	--	6	6	6	10	2	--	--	--	--
1955	11	1	10	30	34	29	28	5	1	2	--
1960	16	4	16	44	46	46	45	10	5	1	--
1965	24	16	28	49	50	50	47	10	10	3	--
1970	42	39	34	51	54	50	52	16	10	5	--

Source: Computed from Broadcasting Yearbook. [1]91.5 mHz channel 218 educational non-commercial. 93.5 mHz channel 228 class A. 93.7 mHz channel 229 class B-C. [2]Except for two assignments in the 1960, since changed, the FCC has made no assignments of regular stations above channel 69. However; these channels have been used for low power translator stations.

Table 8.

AM, FM, AND TV STATIONS BY COMMUNITY

Figures show the number of communities with one station, two, three and four or more stations for AM and AM/FM, FM independent, and TV stations.

COMMUNITIES[1] WITH:	AM and AM/FM						FM[2] 1970	TV		
	1945	1950	1954	1960	1965	1970		1950	1965	1970
4 or more stations	43	113	123	143	198	202		3	25	49[b]
3 stations	31	68	75	120	91	106	63[a]	7	81	85
2 stations	57	174	229	319	318	321	54	12	57	96
1 station	435	897	970	1,660	1,481	1,611	280	40	111	60
TOTAL	566	1,252	1,397	2,242	2,088	2,240	397	62	274	290

Source: FCC and computed by Lichty and Topping. [1]Definition of community has varied. [2]Independent FMs and FMs associated with AMs but reported separately. [a]Three or more stations for FM. [b]25 of these were markets with only three VHF stations.

Table 9.

AM STATION OWNERSHIP

Figures show the number and % of owners of broadcasting
stations in various categories for 1922, 1925, and 1930.

	NUMBER OF STATIONS			PERCENT OF STATIONS		
	1922	1925	1930	1922	1925	1930
Broadcasting companies	10	21	223	3%	4%	36%
Newspapers/publishers	48	33	36	13	6	6
Radio stores/service	126	91	37	33	16	6
Educational institutions	45	110	52	12	19	9
Churches	6	50	30	2	9	5
Other	147	266	234	38	47	38
TOTAL	382	571	612	101%	101%	100%

Source: Willey and Rice, Community Agencies and Social Life, p. 196;
compiled from Radio Service Bulletin and FRC.

Table 10.

TV STATION GROUP OWNERSHIP

Figures show the % of television stations owned by groups with two to seven stations.

Number of Stations Owned	1952	1956	1964	1967	1972
7	--	--	--	2%	2%
6	--	3%	5%	8	7
5	14%	4	11	19	18
4	7	5	20	21	24
3	11	22	36	34	31
2	17	46	65	63	48
Percent of All TV Stations Group Owned	49%	45%	69%	75%	61%

Sources: 1952 Robert Pepper; 1956 and 1964 FCC; 1967 Rucker The First Freedom; and
1972 computed from Broadcasting Yearbook.

Table 11.

AM, FM, TV AND CATV OWNERSHIP

Figures show the % of AM, FM, and TV stations owned by newspapers/publishers and by groups, the % of AM station owners that operate FM stations in the same market, the % of FM station owners that operate AM stations in the same market, the % of TV station owners that operate AM and/or FM stations in the same market, and the % of CATV systems that are owned by broadcasters, telephone companies and newspapers/publishers.

	NEWSPAPER[1]			GROUP[2]			AM STATIONS % AM-FM	FM STATIONS % AM-FM	TV STATIONS AM &/or FM	CATV SYSTEMS[3]		
	AM	FM	TV	AM	FM	TV				Brdcst	Phone	Newspr
1922	11%											
1925	5											
1930	6											
1935	20											
1940	31			14%[a]								
1945	28	32%	11%									
1950	23	37	42	11[b]	15%[c]	54%[f]			82%[f]			
1955	17	31	34			56[g]						
1960	12	20	33	23		50						
1965	10	12	29	31[d]	31[e]	69[g]	35%[g]	90%[g]	61[h]			
1970	9	11	27	31		52[i]				37%	6%	8%

Sources: [1]C. H. Sterling, Journalism Quarterly, 46:2, p. 227. [2]Owned two or more stations. B. Rucker, The First Freedom, pp. 189-193. Data from W. Agee, Journalism Quarterly, December 1949, p. 414; Activities of Regulatory and Enforcement Agencies Relating to Small Business, Part I, p. 88. a1939. b1951. c1949, Agee. d1967. e1967 (82% of these are AM-FM in the same market). fR. Pepper, 1952. g1956 and 1966 from United Research Inc., The Implications of Limiting Multiple Ownership of Television Stations, or see Cherington, et. al. Television Station Ownership, the % differs some from figures reported in Television, February 1966. h1967, Broadcasting, March 25, 1968, p. 23. [3]Television Factbook, 1970-1971. iFCC 12/31/68 annual report 1970 differs from % in Rucker (Table 10).).

George Burns and Gracie Allen.

Jack Benny.

Ernie Kovaks.

Jackie Gleason and Art Carney.

Red Skelton.

Mr. Ed and Alan Young.

Sally Field as the Flying Nun.

Phil Silvers as Sgt. Bilko.

PART THREE

NETWORKS

(o) "Broadcasting" means the dissemination of radio communications intended to be received by the public, directly or by the intermediary of relay stations.

(p) "Chain broadcasting" means simultaneous broadcasting of an identical program by two or more connected stations.

—Communications Act of 1934,
DEFINITIONS

THE DEVELOPMENT of broadcasting networks (or chains) in the 1920s contributed more to the quality of American radio than any other structural innovation. The notion of a national radio broadcasting company was suggested by David Sarnoff in the spring of 1922. Sarnoff warned that when the novelty of radio had worn off audiences were going to expect more than they had of any media to that date. He foresaw a "specialized organization with a competent staff capable of meeting" the task of "entertaining the nation." [1] Within six months of the memo the World Series was broadcast over both WJZ in Newark and WGY in Schenectady inter-connected by telegraph lines.

Early networks were informal and non-binding associations, but were involved in matters of great importance. In June of 1924 stations in 12 cities joined to carry the Republican Convention. The impact of this coverage and that of the Democratic Convention a few weeks later spurred the sales of radios. In the fall, the election returns from WEAF in New York were carried on a 32-station network. The concept of network broadcasting was linked to the idea of program quality and cost of good programs. Some listeners and broadcasters thought that a few super-power stations in the spectrum would bring quality programming to the nation.

WEAF was the dominant network "flagship station" during the

1925–26 period, a program originator and a potential super-station. A number of stations in the northeastern section of the nation carried the same commercial programs from WEAF in a loosely defined network. Eveready radio batteries in a magazine advertisement in April 1925 listed six stations as the "Eveready Group" every Tuesday at 9 p.m. The network for the program had grown to 13 stations broadcasting the *Eveready Hour* in February of 1926.

The formation of NBC in 1926 was announced to "provide the best programs available for broadcasting in the United States." [2] The idea of the chain of stations was firmed up with the announcement that this new network would provide these programs for "other broadcasting stations throughout the country so far as it may be practicable to do so and they may desire to take them." Sale of WEAF to Radio Corporation of America and the organization of the National Broadcasting Company was heralded by a radio network program which was a four-hour and 25-minute extravaganza of stars.

> I put on my stiff shirt and went down to the Grand Ballroom of the Waldorf-Astoria Hotel to attend the inaugural program of the National Broadcasting Company. There were perhaps five hundred other stiff-shirted gentlemen were, and as many ladies in evening dress. Down in front was Walter Damrosch with his orchestra, playing the accompaniment for Titta Ruffo, Metropolitan Opera star. Harold Bauer, the famous pianist, came in a few minutes later. His ship had been delayed, and a special tug had been sent down the harbor to hurry him to the dock, so that he might appear on this program at the exact minute announced. Following his performance was a second's pause, and then suddenly, as clear and strong as though the voice were there beside us, the announcer—"Ladies and gentlemen: We are in the Drake Hotel, Chicago, in the parlor of Miss Mary Garden. Miss Garden will sing." And Miss Garden did. Another second's pause, and again a different announcer—"Ladies and gentlemen: We are now in Independence, Kansas, in the dressing-room of Mr. Will Rogers. Mr. Rogers will speak."
>
> And out of the air came the unmistakable tones of Will, who said he was traveling around the country as "God's gift to those who had failed to see Queen Marie." [3]

The use of colored pencils to draw network lines on a map, as asserted below, gave the two NBC chains their names. Other explanations have been advanced such as colored phone jacks used by the telephone company for switching. In any case the tradition would stick and later there were Orange, Green, and Gold networks as well.

> Although when NBC was formed a single program service was contemplated, the widespread demand for network service led almost immediately to the establishment of a second network, on January 1, 1927. NBC engineers named the two networks Red and Blue as a convenience when drafting maps of network coverage.

Initially, 25 stations constituted the Red Network, six others the Blue. In actual practice, several of the stations listed as Red were available to supplement the "basic" stations of either network. By the time the first NBC advertising rate card was published (September 1, 1927) all supplementary stations were listed separately from basic Red and Blue stations, and were offered as an optional adjunct to either network.

A Pacific Coast network of seven stations was also created in early 1927. Although the first coast-to-coast network program transmission by wire was achieved on New Year's Day, 1927, (a play-by-play description of the Rose Bowl game in Pasadena), transcontinental network operations did not become economically feasible for another two years. NBC commenced regular operation of a leased wire between New York and San Francisco in December 1928.[4]

Although the networks negated the possibility, there was still discussion in radio magazines about super-power stations. The idea was attractive to ranchers in 1928 since there was not one network affiliated station in the mountain time zone. However, in the large markets the listeners were satisfied and the idea of super-power was lost to the local station serving the metropolitan markets. NBC got started as a network a few months before CBS and because of a number of circumstances was the dominant broadcasting organization in the 1930s. It had the audience, the performers, and the business wrapped up in two networks. Other networks, with less decisive early management and lacking early ties with engineering innovations, were left at the gate in the nationwide broadcasting race between CBS and NBC. The inaugural program for the Columbia Broadcasting System was September 18, 1927. A year later the organization was acquired by a Philadelphia family one of whom, William Paley, became its president. The accounts of procedures in the early days of network radio broadcasting were hectic and extremely personal in nature. By 1931 the nation was deep into the depression and the major networks—NBC Red and Blue and CBS—still were not out of the red ink, but they were big business. NBC's operating costs for two networks were nearly $30 millions. CBS spent about a third of that in the same year.

A number of networks were formed in the wake of the NBC-CBS successes. One attempt—the Quality Network—started in 1929 with WLS (Chicago), WLW (Cincinnati) and WOR (Newark) later forming—with WGN substituting for WLS and the addition of WXYZ, (Detroit)—the fourth national network, Mutual Broadcasting System. Two famous radio shows were important to the success of MBS, *The Lone Ranger* and *Lum 'n' Abner*. Mutual gained a great number of affiliates and became the "world's largest radio network," but never was able to get power and prestige since it could not attract the full cooperation of powerful and prestigious affiliates. One of the most flamboyant attempts to establish a national network was financed by stage, radio and film comedian Ed Wynn—the Amalgamated Broadcasting System. ABS held its inaugural program at New York station WBNX September 25, 1933. It was a disaster for Wynn, who could not get enough affiliates do make the network viable. Meanwhile his resources were extended to near bankruptcy as he tried to meet salary and debtor demands. He gave up the efforts in October announcing that he had not only lost his shirt but also his job with NBC.[5] Other networks also proved successful regionally but never gained national hookups.

One regional network was formed November 21, 1936, by the McClatchy Broadcasting Company and by two firms owned by William Randolph Hearst publishers—the California Radio System. Its six stations in 1936 were scattered between Los Angeles and San Francisco. Affiliates provided facilities to the net for certain periods of time at half the regular rate for the period. Net sales in 1938, after agency commissions, amounted to $109,848.[6]

On the east coast, the Yankee Network, Inc., was organized in 1936 absorbing another smaller firm which had been in operation since 1930. The Yankee became a joint enterprise with the Colonial network, sharing the same telephone chain. In 1938, Yankee had 17 affiliates, three of them owned by the network, including stations in Maine, New Hampshire, Connecticut and Massachusetts. Colonial consisted of about the same group with the addition of WAAB (Boston) and was a participating member of Mutual, feeding MBS programs to its affiliates. Both Colonial and Yankee had option on affiliates' time, giving about 30% of the network rate to the stations. Colonial had network times sales in 1938 of $190,758. Yankee ceased operation in 1967.

The Don Lee Network was formed by two stations owned by Don Lee on the West Coast in 1929. By 1933 five McClatchy stations had joined the network giving coverage throughout most of California and Reno, Nevada. After becoming a CBS representative, the chain took in stations in Oregon and Washington. Don Lee continued relationships with CBS and McClatchy until 1936 when McClatchy joined the California group and Don Lee became a participating member of Mutual. The new Don Lee organization hooked up with Pacific broadcasting in Washington and Oregon bringing its total number of affiliates to 28 stations. The network furnished some original programs in addition to Mutual's service which was exclusive on the West Coast. Don Lee got two hours a week free time from stations. It had individual contracts with affiliates. Pacific's contract gave it 85% of the network revenue and all of the revenue Don Lee received for use of Pacific outlets until the telephone bills were paid. Net sales in 1938 after commissions were $853,333.

An investigation of network practices by the FCC began in 1938 and resulted in a report on networks, and a number of court battles which ended in 1943 with the Supreme Court of the United States upholding the FCC ban on operations of two networks by one company. As a result of the ruling by the high court Edward J. Nobel bought NBC Blue for $7,000,000 and renamed it the American Broadcasting Company. The investigation resulted in much more rigid rules concerning network relations to stations. The Commission eased the right of a network to control station time, exclusivity of contracts, length of affiliation contracts, exclusivity of territory and the right to reject network programs.

After the NBC Blue was sold, network structure remained about the same until the mid-1940s. There were some major network changes by stars for various reasons. Bing Crosby, who had been with NBC since the early 1930s moved to ABC in 1946 where he was allowed to pre-record his program. Two years later "Bill Paley's check book" was the popular conception but capital gains deals were the real reason for many of the most popular NBC stars to leave for CBS. Among those moving were *Amos 'n' Andy, Jack Benny, Burns and Allen, Ozzie and Harriet Nelson, Red Skelton* and (from ABC) *Bing Crosby*. A few month's later similar deals brought Groucho Marx and his *You Bet Your Life* programs from CBS (previously taken from ABC.) Five years later the stolen stars were the nucleus of television program offerings, particularly for CBS.

Television networks developed out of the radio organizations of NBC, CBS, and ABC right after World War II. A fourth network, DuMont using WABD in New York as its flagship station, began to search for affiliates as did the more familiar organizations but few markets had more than three stations. Stations, staff, and programs were "converted" to television. Some programs were simulcast on radio and television, others produced two versions for a time. Some—*Truth or Consequences*, for example—improved with the addition of video. Affiliates were not long in coming into the network associations. NBC signed its St. Paul outlet KSTP in March 1948. Since there was no coaxial cable to St. Paul the affiliate used kinescope (film) recordings of the network programs which were shipped to the station.

In 1948 both CBS and NBC operated eastern and mid-western television networks reaching out as American Telegraph and Telephone laid coaxial cable from east to west. January 12, 1949, the link between Cleveland and Philadelphia was completed. The network then reached from Boston and Schenectady to Richmond and west to Chicago, Milwaukee and St. Louis. The 1948 presidential campaign had been confined to local television coverage with some eastern network connections. September 10, 1951, Harry Truman, the last president to be elected mainly with radio and newspaper coverage, addressed the Japanese Peace Treaty Convention in San Francisco—linked nation-wide by 94 television stations carrying the program live. Thirteen other stations still were getting their programs by kinescope. DuMont fought to get outlets in major markets, but faltered in spite of the end of the "freeze" in licensing new stations from 1948 to 1952. In the 1954–1955 season there were 15 DuMont programs still being regularly scheduled. There were none the following year.

No network has dominated television as did NBC dominate radio in the 1930s. CBS, however, continued to maintain the highest ratings and the largest revenues of the three major television networks, NBC was a close second with ABC-TV continually a poor third in affiliates, audiences, revenues and profits. From 1958 to 1960 ABC, using very popular action-adventure shows as a base, began to catch up with the other two networks in ratings. They called this new programming "cultural democracy."

NBC was the first network to offer a complete schedule of programs. In 1952 it started offering *Today* early in the morning and ending with *Tonight* at 1:00 a.m. eastern time. All networks expanded their service during the 1960s. By 1969 all three were trying late night low-budget talk shows. CBS switched to movies in 1972. ABC still had not programmed an early morning show by 1973–4.

The trouble that DuMont had in establishing outlets for programs was duplicated 11 years later when a network which would exploit the accumulated talents in Las Vegas nightclubs had a brief fling.

ABC Radio West and the Columbia Pacific Network, regional interconnections, were maintained by ABC and CBS into the 1960s. But for the most part it was a decade of searching for ways to attract use of their programs over and above five-minute news reports.

The last of the surviving radio network entertainment programs were cancelled—Don MacNeill's *Breakfast Club* (December 27, 1968) and Arthur Godfrey (April 30, 1972). The era that ended in the mid-1950s finally died two decades later.

The most inventive radio network effort was by ABC which in 1967 began offering four separate services (with special FCC permission): Contemporary, Entertainment, Information and FM. From 1967 to 1973 ABC increased from about 300 affiliates to more than 1,200.

As broadcasting advanced into its sixth decade still other specialized radio networks were being created—for blacks and Chicanos, for example.

In the 1970s networks of cable systems were just developing and there were experiments with direct satellite to home transmission.

20

David Sarnoff

LETTER TO E. W. RICE, JR., HONORARY CHAIRMAN OF THE BOARD, GENERAL ELECTRIC COMPANY, JUNE 17, 1922

LET US ORGANIZE a separate and distinct company, to be known as the Public Service Broadcasting Company or National Radio Broadcasting Company or American Radio Broadcasting Company, or some similar name.

This company to be controlled by the Radio Corporation of America, but its board of directors and officers to include members of the General Electric Company and the Westinghouse Electric Company and possibly also a few from the outside, prominent in national and civic affairs. The administrative and operating staff of this company to be composed of those considered best qualified to do the broadcasting job.

Such company to acquire the existing broadcasting stations of the Westinghouse Company and General Electric Company, as well as the three stations to be erected by the Radio Corporation; to operate such stations and build such additional broadcasting stations as may be determined upon in the future. . . .

Since the proposed company is to pay the cost of broadcasting as well as the cost of its own administrative operations, it is, of course, necessary to provide it with a source of income sufficient to defray all of its expenses.

As a means for providing such income, I tentatively suggest that the Radio Corporation pay over to the broadcasting company 2 per cent of its gross radio sales, that the General Electric and Westinghouse Companies do likewise, and that our proposed licensees be required to do the same. . . .

While the total . . . may be regarded as inadequate to defray the whole of the expense of the broadcasting company, yet I think it should be sufficient to provide for a modest beginning. Once the structure is created, opportunities for providing additional sources of income to increase the "pot" will present themselves. For example, if the business expands, the income grows proportionately. Also, we may find it practicable to require our wholesale distributors to pay over to the broadcasting company a reasonable percentage of their

Looking Ahead, New York: McGraw-Hill, 1968, pp. 41–44.

gross radio sales, for it will be to their interest to support broadcasting. It is conceivable that the same principles may even be extended in time to the dealers.

Since the broadcasting company is to be organized on the basis of rendering a public service commensurate with its financial ability to do so, it is conceivable that plans may be devised by it whereby it will receive public support and, in fact, there may even appear on the horizon a public benefactor who will be willing to contribute a large sum in the form of an endowment. It will be noted that these additional possibilities of income are merely regarded as "possibilities" and do not in themselves form the foundation upon which the broadcasting company is to operate.

Once the broadcasting company is established as a public service and the general public educated to the idea that the sole function of the company is to provide the public with a service as good and extensive as its total income permits, I feel that with suitable publicity activities, such a company will ultimately be regarded as a public institution of great value, in the same sense that a library, for example, is regarded today. . . .

21

Jennie Irene Mix

GOOD NATIONAL RADIO PROGRAMS PROVE "WHAT THE PUBLIC WANTS"

THE LINKING of a sufficient number of stations to carry to uncounted listeners the WEAF programs of outstanding musical quality will do more to bring about a reform in the general character of all radio music than any other attempt that has yet been made with such an end in view. Not that the powers that rule WEAF had this in mind when establishing this wide connection through the country. Quite the contrary. With those officials it is wholly a matter of business, as all who are familiar with the firms who are putting these programs on the air through WEAF well know. But one could scarcely ask the American Telephone and Telegraph Company to give this well-nigh

Radio Broadcast, May 1925, pp. 62–65.

priceless opportunity to the public for nothing. So, as the intricate question "Who is to Pay for Broadcasting?" apparently remains as far from being answered as ever, we may well be thankful that we have this present development which makes possible the hearing of real artists at stated times, instead of, as before, being almost always nationally swamped by mediocrity or worse.

The much-discussed question of having a few very high-powered stations in this country that would ultimately control all the broadcasting has met with violent opposition from the hundreds of stations conducted for the purpose of advertising the products of the business firms operating them. The majority of these stations are far below any commendable standard so far as their programs and the manner in which they are presented are concerned. Will this new development in radio, which is bringing the best in radio music to far distant points, in time put these stations out of business? There would be nothing lost and a good deal gained for the public were this to come to pass.

Does it not look as if this linking of stations is but another way of having the broadcasting within the power of the few? Be this as it may, developments along the right line are coming so rapidly that all who have deplored the quality of radio programs in this country are beginning to grow optimistic. Whether the methods used to bring about this change will be permanent, no one can say. But of one thing we may be absolutely assured. Radio music having had this upward trend, can never again sink to the low level that has so widely obtained.

Of great interest are the statistics given by John A. Holman, broadcasting manager of the American Telephone and Telegraph Company relative to his opinions of the change in the musical taste of radio listeners during the past two years. In January, 1923, approximately seventy-five percent of radio fans favored jazz. In the same month of 1924 this percentage fell to thirty five and in January of this year to five per cent. These figures tell their own story.

Among the fine programs regularly featured through WEAF are those given by the Atwater Kent Company. Have you noticed that the singers of the quartet heard in these programs are never announced by name? That should be qualified by saying that we have never heard them so announced. "The tenor of the Atwater Kent Quartet will now be heard in the solo, "Onaway, Awake, Beloved!" And when you hear him sing you know that he is not an amateur looking for publicity through the microphone; indeed if he were, he would insist on having his name announced, "before and after." We are quite willing to hazard the guess that this quartet is made up of paid professionals—and admirable ones at that—who do not want their names sent out as "radio artists," a position that can be under-

stood considering the present chaotic conditions prevailing in broadcasting. If this guess is a wrong one, we stand ready to be corrected.

22

Federal Communications Commission

EARLY HISTORY OF
NETWORK BROADCASTING (1923–1926) AND
THE NATIONAL BROADCASTING COMPANY

I. EARLY HISTORY OF NETWORK BROADCASTING
(1923–26)

A. The A. T. & T. Network

STATION WEAF was constructed in New York by the American Telephone & Telegraph Co. and was licensed on June 1, 1922. It was
operated as a "toll" station, available for hire by those wishing to
reach the public by radiotelephony.

At that time the Telephone Co. claimed the exclusive right,
under certain patents and patent-licensing agreements, to sell radio
time and operate "toll" stations.[5] This right was asserted under a
cross-licensing agreement dated July 1, 1920, between the General
Electric Co. and the Telephone Co. and an extension agreement of
the same date under which RCA and Western Electric were added as
parties. The Westinghouse Electric & Manufacturing Co. was
brought within the purview of these agreements of June 30, 1921.[6]
They gave the Telephone Co. and its manufacturing subsidiary, the
Western Electric Co., the sole rights to make, lease, and sell commercial radiotelephone transmitting equipment. This provision, the
Telephone Co. insisted gave it the exclusive right to sell time over a
"toll" station. The assertion of these rights was a substantial factor in
giving it a position of leadership during the early days of broadcasting.[7]

The Telephone Co. inaugurated network broadcasting on January 4, 1923, with a program broadcast simultaneous over station
WEAF and a Boston station, WNAC, owned by John Shepard III.[8]

Report on Chain Broadcasting (Commission Order No. 37, Docket 5060, May 1941),
pp. 5–20.

The second network broadcast occurred on June 7, 1923, and involved, in addition to WEAF, stations WGY in Schenectady, KDKA in Pittsburgh, and KYW in Chicago.[9] The first continuous network broadcasting occurred during the summer of 1923, when for a period of 3 months station WEAF in New York programmed Col. Edward H. R. Green's station WMAF at South Dartmouth, Mass.[10] During the summer of 1923 the Telephone Co., through one of its subsidiary companies, constructed station WCAP in Washington, and thereafter WEAF and WCAP were frequently connected for network broadcasting.[11] These two stations became the nucleus of the network built up by the Telephone Co.

From 1924 to 1926, the Telephone Co.'s network expanded its operations rapidly. Early in 1924, the company produced the first transcontinental network broadcast, utilizing station KPO in San Francisco.[12] By the fall of 1924, the Telephone Co. was able to furnish a coast-to-coast network of 23 stations to broadcast a speech by President Coolidge.[13] At the end of 1925 there was a total of 26 stations on the regular Telephone Co. network, extending as far west as Kansas City (station KSD).* [14] The company was selling time to advertisers over a basic network of 13 stations at $2,600 per hour,[15] and was deriving gross revenues at the rate of about $750,000 per year from the sale of time.[16]

B. *The RCA Network*

Meanwhile, RCA was making a start in network broadcasting. In the spring of 1923, RCA acquired sole control of station WJZ in New York City,[17] and later that year it constructed and started to operate station WRC at Washington. The first network broadcast by RCA occurred in December 1923, and involved only WJZ and the General Electric Co.'s station WGY at Schenectady, N. Y. The connection was made with Western Union telegraph wires.[18]

Although there was keen rivalry between stations WEAF and WJZ during this period, the vigorous network competition which RCA might otherwise have offered was hampered because of two factors. In the first place, RCA was prevented from reaching numerous outlets and developing its network because of the Telephone Co.'s policy with respect to the use of its telephone lines by others for network purposes.[19] The telegraph wires which RCA was thus compelled to use were quite inferior for this purpose. Secondly, RCA was prevented from developing the business aspects of broadcasting and network broadcasting by its inability to sell time to advertisers; for the Telephone Co. claimed, under the cross-licensing agreement

* KSD was licensed in St. Louis.

of July 1, 1920, the exclusive right to sell time for broadcasting purposes.[20] Hence RCA stations made no charge for the use of time.[21]

Largely because of these obstacles, the RCA network did not grow as rapidly as the Telephone Co.'s network. Thus, while the Telephone Co. was able, in March 1925, to broadcast President Coolidge's inauguration over a transcontinental network of 22 stations, the RCA network carried it only over WJZ, WBZ, WGY, and WRC.[22]

C. Sale of WEAF and the Telephone Company Network to RCA

In 1926, the Telephone Co.'s direct participation in the broadcasting business, in which it had pioneered and attained a dominant position, came to an abrupt end. As part of a general readjustment of relations between the Telephone Co. and the so-called "Radio Group" (RCA, Westinghouse, and General Electric), the Telephone Co. withdrew from the broadcasting field, and transferred its properties and interests to the "Radio Group".

In May, 1926, the Telephone Co. had incorporated a subsidiary corporation, the Broadcasting Co. of America, to which were transferred WEAF and the network operations. On July 1, 1926 a contract was entered into, which became effective November 1, 1926, under which RCA purchased the assets of the Broadcasting Co. of America.[23] The purchase price was $1,000,000 and the transaction included WEAF and the entire broadcasting business of the Telephone Co. except the Washington station, WCAP, which was closed.[24] As a result of this sale, the way was cleared for the sale of broadcasting time by the "Radio Group". The Telephone Co. also agreed to withdraw from the broadcasting business and covenanted not to compete with RCA in this field for a period of 7 years, under penalty of repaying $800,000 of the $1,000,000 purchase price. The Telephone Co. also agreed to make available its telephone lines to RCA for network purposes, and an understanding was reached that RCA would use only Telephone Co. lines, unless they were not available.[25]

D. Formation of the National Broadcasting Company

On September 9, 1926, RCA formed a corporation, the National Broadcasting Co., to take over its network broadcasting business, including the properties being purchased from the Telephone Co.[26] In October 1926, RCA assigned to NBC its rights to purchase the Broadcasting Co. of America, and in November NBC paid the purchase price of $1,000,000 and took over the operation of WEAF and the old Telephone Co. network.[27]

The outstanding capital stock of NBC was owned by RCA, General Electric, and Westinghouse in the ratio of 50, 30, 20, percent, respectively, from the date of incorporation to May 23, 1930. On that date RCA acquired the NBC stock previously owned by General Electric and Westinghouse.[28] Thus NBC became a wholly owned subsidiary of RCA.

The sale of station WEAF to NBC and the withdrawal of the Telephone Co. from the broadcasting business marked the end of an era. The pioneer stage of network broadcasting was drawing to a close. The Telephone Co. had been well on its way toward financial success in the operation of WEAF as a "toll" station. The technical and social practicability of network broadcasting had been clearly shown as early as March 4, 1925, when the Telephone Co.'s 22-station network carried the inaugural address of President Coolidge to an audience estimated at 18,000,000 listeners.[29]

RCA could not fail to assume a dominant position in the field of network broadcasting as a result of its purchase of WEAF and the Telephone Co. network. Following the purchase the only two networks in the country were under the control of RCA. The purchase has had a lasting effect on the structure of network broadcasting; for NBC's present operation of two networks—the "Red" and the "Blue"—stems from its ownership of both WEAF and WJZ in New York City, and from its acquisition of the Telephone Co.'s network organization in addition to RCA's original network system based on WJZ. For some time after the purchase, RCA had a practical monopoly of network broadcasting, and NBC is still by far the largest network organization.

B. The National Broadcasting Co.

RCA's broadcasting activities after 1926 concentrated in its subsidiary, NBC, which took over WEAF and the old Telephone Co. network. Thereafter, NBC, pursuant to its understanding with the Telephone Co., discontinued the use of telegraph lines and used Telephone Co. long lines exclusively for connections between stations. On the business side, NBC continued to sell time to advertisers, a policy which had been inaugurated by the Telephone Co. at station WEAF, and since that time about 90 percent of its total revenues has come from that source.

1. Increase in Number of NBC Outlets

On November 1, 1926, there were 19 stations regularly on the NBC network. The number has steadily increased since that time. By January 1, 1928, there were 48 outlets. On December 23, 1928, the first permanent transcontinental network was instituted by NBC, composed of 56 permanent network stations. There were 154 outlet stations as of September 1, 1938, and as of December 31, 1940, the number had increased to 214.

Since the time of its organization NBC has operated two networks, the Red and the Blue. In many cases they use the same facilities and stations. As of September 1, 1938, when there were 154 NBC outlets, 23 composed the basic Red network and 24 composed the basic Blue network. Supplementing these basic networks were 107 stations, of which one was available only to the basic Red network, six were available only to the basic Blue network, and the remainder available to either.

2. Stations Owned or Controlled by NBC

NBC acquired station WEAF by purchase from the Telephone Co. in 1926, and WEAF became the key station of NBC's Red network. Prior to 1926, RCA had constructed and was operating station WJZ in New York and WRC in Washington. NBC's other network, the Blue, was based on WJZ, although title to WJZ and WRC was not formally transferred from RCA to NBC until 1930. Since 1926 NBC has purchased or leased, and has become the licensee of 7 other stations located in important radio markets. The 10 stations of which NBC is now the licensee, all but one of which (WENR) operate with unlimited time.

At the time of the committee hearings five other stations were "programmed" by NBC under management contracts with the licensees. These stations were WGY, licensed to the General Electric Co. at Schenectady, N.Y., and four Westinghouse stations—KDKA at Pittsburgh, KYW at Philadelphia, WBZ at Boston, and WBZA at Springfield, Mass. All of these stations except WBZA [49] were licensed to operate with 50,000 watts.

The contracts under which NBC obtained the right to program these stations were made in November 1932, at the time of the consent decree [50] under which the General Electric Co. and Westinghouse agreed to dispose of their stock holdings in RCA. The contracts transferred to NBC control over the operations of the stations, insofar as the listening public was concerned, and raised serious questions under section 12 of the Radio Act of 1927 (sec. 310(b) of the Communications Act of 1934), since the Commission's consent to a transfer of the licenses was not applied for nor obtained. Accordingly, in January 1940, the applications for renewal of the licenses of these stations were designated for hearing.[51] Shortly thereafter the management contracts were rescinded, and the five stations entered into contracts of affiliation with NBC.[52]

3. Increase in Business and Income of NBC

Except for the first 14 months of its existence NBC has earned substantial profits every year. Both the volume of business and the profit have increased materially and with great regularity since that 14-month period.

4. *NBC Artists' Bureau and Concert Service*

Within a few months after it commenced operations in 1926, NBC organized an artists' service as a department of the company for the purpose of managing concert artists, actors, announcers, writers, and other talent. In 1931 NBC acquired a 50 percent interest in Civic Concert Service, Inc., which was engaged in the business of organizing and managing concert courses throughout the country, and in 1935 NBC acquired the remaining 50 percent. In 1928 the business of the NBC artists' service amounted to slightly over $1,000,000, while in 1937 the gross talent bookings came to $6,032,274, which included the gross receipts of the Civic Concert Service, Inc., amounting to $306,099. On November 1, 1938, the NBC artists' service had more than 350 artists under management contract. Civic Concert Service, Inc., had membership concert courses in 57 cities when NBC acquired an interest in the company in 1931; by 1938 the list of cities served by Civic Concert had grown to 77.

As agent for artists, NBC is under a fiduciary duty to procure the best terms possible for the artists. As employer of artists, NBC is interested in securing the best terms possible from the artists. NBC's dual role necessarily prevents arm's-length bargaining and constitutes a serious conflict of interest. Moreover, this dual capacity gives NBC an unfair advantage over independent artists' representatives who do not themselves control employment opportunities or have direct access to the radio audience. Many of these independent artists' representatives have complained to the Commission of NBC's unfair control over the supply of talent and have filed briefs in the proceeding. This problem will receive the continuing attention of the Commission and may warrant further inquiry.

5. *Transcription Business of NBC*

NBC entered the transcription business in 1934, but did not get under way commercially in this field until about a year later. It has since engaged in the three principal phases of that business. The first is a library service, called the Thesaurus, a collection of transcribed musical selections leased or licensed to individual stations. This enables the station to produce programs by merely adding its own announcements. The second is the so-called custom-built transcription service, consisting of full programs produced by NBC or by sponsors or advertising agencies. Such transcriptions are delivered as a complete package at a unit price to radio stations and to commercial sponsors. The third is the "simultaneous wire line recording," or recording of a program while it is being broadcast, usually for the purpose of later rebroadcast.

In its transcription business, NBC cooperates with RCA Manufacturing Co., its affiliate, also owned by RCA. NBC arranges the programming and sells the transcriptions, while RCA Manufacturing makes the recordings. It is estimated that the total transcription business carried on in the United States in 1938 amounted to something less than $5,000,000, of which NBC-RCA accounted for $1,300,000.

Prior to April 1, 1941, NBC refused to permit any transcription company other than its associate, RCA Manufacturing Co., to make a "simultaneous wire line recording" of an NBC network commercial program. Even when the sponsor who was paying the entire expense, the agency in charge of producing the program, and an independent transcription company had come to an agreement for the transcription of an NBC network program, NBC refused to permit the independent company to come upon the premises for the purpose of making the transcription in accordance with the agreement. Independent transcription companies appeared in this proceeding and complained of this unfair competition. However, in March 1941, following the committee report and the oral argument, NBC publicly announced a change in its policy; [53] after April 1 the prohibition against the transcription of NBC network programs by independent companies would be removed and the advertiser allowed the transcription company of its choice.

C. Summary of RCA's Scope of Operations

RCA was originally founded to utilize wireless techniques for the transmission of messages; today it bestrides whole industries, dwarfing its competitors in each. Every new step has not only increased RCA's power in fields already occupied, but has enhanced its competitive advantage in occupying fields more and more remote from its beginnings.

Thus, for example, RCA's control of thousands of patents, and its experience with and ownership of prebroadcasting wireless transmitters, as well as its support from General Electric and Westinghouse, gave it a running start in the infant radio-broadcasting industry. Later, RCA's position as the leading distributor of radio receivers enabled it to enter the business of selling radio-phonograph combinations in cooperation first with Brunswick and then with Victor, and subsequently to acquire Victor, the leading phonograph and phonograph recorder manufacturer. This step-by-step invasion of the phonograph business, in turn, gave RCA entering wedges into the transcription and talent supply businesses; RCA-Victor artists broadcast over NBC and made RCA transcriptions, while NBC artists recorded for RCA-Victor. The result was to give RCA and its subsidiaries a marked competitive advantage over other broadcasting companies, other radio manufacturers, and other phonograph and phonograph record companies. RCA's entry into the motion picture field, first through RCA Photophone and then through RKO, was also a step-by-step process, and similarly buttressed RCA's competitive position in other spheres. Today, with its patents, managed artists, manufacturing plants, distribution facilities, personnel, experience, and financial strength, RCA has a tremendous competitive advantage in occupying such newly opening fields as frequency modulation (FM) broadcasting and television—an advantage which may, indeed, discourage newcomers in fields where RCA has become or seeks to become dominant.

A glance at RCA's last annual report [54] is convincing of the multifarious and pervasive character of its operations:

RCA's international radio-communication service is now "world-wide" and "globe circling," with direct circuits to 43 countries. Despite the suspension of service to half a dozen German-occupied countries, the volume of traffic handled in 1940 was "the greatest in RCA history." In addition, RCA's domestic radio-telegraph service "links 12 key cities in the United States."

The use of the international radio circuits is not restricted to message traffic. Newspapers receive many of their radiophotos from abroad through RCA. Foreign programs, particularly news, are transmitted over RCA circuits for broadcasting on domestic networks.

In the field of marine communication, RCA has "maintained its leadership," furnishing some 2,200 ships with radio equipment, and operating coastal and lake port stations.

RCA's manufacturing subsidiaries operate factories in New Jersey, Indiana, and California, and also in Canada and South America. The products include many types of radio and phonograph sets, radio tubes, broadcasting transmitters and studio equipment, Victor and Bluebird phonograph records, transcriptions for broadcasting, sound equipment for motion picture studios and theaters, and public address systems, to say nothing of motion picture and radio equipment for amateurs, electron microscopes, electronic pianos, television equipment, communications equipment and so on. Manufacturing is now the largest single phase of RCA's business.

RCA is active in technical education, and through RCA Institutes, Inc., conducts schools in New York and Chicago which offer "training in all branches of radio." Its laboratories and research organizations are extensive.

NBC's position in broadcasting is comparable to the situation of the parent company in the broader field. There are four national networks; NBC owns two of them. Approximately one-quarter of all stations in the country, utilizing nearly half of the total night-time power, are NBC affiliates. In the newer fields of international broadcasting, frequency modulation, television, and facsimile, NBC may be expected to play a major part.

The larger enterprises carried on by RCA do not blind its management to the smaller ventures which offer profitable opportunities. If broadcasters need transcriptions, NBC makes them. If broadcasters need talent, NBC will not only hire them, but is also glad to manage the artists and act as their agent in the concert as well as the radio field. Lately, with other members of the industry, it has embarked on a venture in musical copyrights (through Broadcast Music, Inc.—BMI).

It is significant that these numerous and, for the most part, critically important activities require a capital investment which, in other fields of enterprise, would not be regarded as staggering. The assets of RCA barely exceed $100,000,000; many a railroad, utility, bank, insurance company, or industrial establishment of relatively secondary importance has assets double or treble this amount. This tends to make RCA comparatively independent of the money market.

RCA, like many other giant enterprises today, is a "management corporation." It has nearly 250,000 stockholders. No one owns as much as half of 1 percent of its stock. In such circumstances, stockholder control is practically nonexistent. RCA's funded debt is small, so there is no substantial creditor influence on the management. As a result, the management is essentially self-perpetuating, and the responsibility of the executives and directors is largely intramural.

In short, RCA occupies a premier position in fields which are profoundly determinative of our way of life. Its diverse activities give it a peculiarly advantageous position in competition with enterprises less widely based. Its policies are determined by a management subject to little restraint other than self-imposed. Whether this ramified and powerful enterprise with its consistent tendency to grow and to expand into new fields at the expense of smaller, independent concerns is desirable, is not to be decided here. We have thought it proper, however, to call the attention of Congress and the public to the broader problems raised by this concentration of power in the hands of a single group.

An executive's success in NBC largely depends on his ability to bend his talents and his efforts to the advancement of the corporation's broad interests as much as to the advancement of his own immediate concern.
                         --Basic Executive Responsibilities,
                           NBC Memo, n.d. [1950s]

23

John Wallace

WHAT WE THOUGHT OF THE
FIRST COLUMBIA BROADCASTING PROGRAM

SUNDAY, the eighteenth of September, witnessed the début of the long heralded Columbia Broadcasting System. The evening of Sunday, the eighteenth of September, witnessed your humble correspondent, tear stained and disillusioned, vowing to abandon for all time radio and all its works and pomps. We have since recovered and will go on with our story. The broadcast divided itself into three successive parts, descending in quality with astounding speed.

Part One: the Vaudeville

This program came on in the afternoon, after a half hour's delay due to mechanical difficulties—a heinous sin in this day of efficient transmission, but excusable, perhaps, in a half-hour-old organization. This opening program, at least, was auspicious. The performers were of superlative excellence. Bits from a light opera were well sung. A quartet gave a stirring rendition of an English hunting song. A symphony orchestra played some Brahms waltzes. A soloist sang "Mon Homme" in so impassioned a fashion that she must have swooned on the last note. Then a dance orchestra concluded the program with some good playing. The offerings were of such high quality that it was doubly disconcerting to have them strung together with a shoddy "continuity"—especially with such stupid and overdone continuity as the "and-now-parting-from-Paris-we-will-journey-to-Germany" type.

Part Two: the Uproar

"Uproar," let us hasten to explain is Major J. Andrew White's way of pronouncing Opera. We seek not to poke fun at this announcer; he is one of the best we have. (Though we think both Quin Ryan and McNamee outdid him in the recent fight broadcast.) But his habit of tacking R's on the end of words like Americar and Columbiar doesn't fit into the high-brow broadcast as well as it does in a sports report. The Uproar was "The King's Henchmen" by Deems Taylor. Evidently no effort was spared to make the broadcast notable. A good symphony orchestra was utilized, capable singers were employed, and Deems Taylor himself was entrusted with the duty of

Radio Broadcast, December 1927, pp. 140–141.

unfolding the plot. But after all it was "just another broadcast." Musical programs into which a lot of talk is injected simply will not work. One or the other has to predominate. Either make it a straight recitation with musical accompaniment—or straight music with only a sparing bit of interpretative comment.

Mr. Taylor's music for this opera is delightful, the singing was admirable, but the total effect was disjointed and unsatisfactory. The composer outlined the story, but, enthralling as it may be on the stage, it was impossible to visualize the action with any degree of vividness from his words. We felt continually aware that there was really no action taking place, and the effort at make believe was too strenuous and detracted from an enjoyment of the music. It was less effective, even, than a broadcast from the regular Opera stage. Here the piece is likely to be more familiar and it is possible to conjure up its pantomime from remembrances of performances seen.

It is our humble and inexpert opinion that program designers are barking up a wrong tree and wasting a lot of energy in their unceasing attempts to fit spoken words into musical programs. But if they will persist let us suggest that they are going about the job in a blundering way with no proper realization of its difficulty. All present essays in this line fall into two classes: those which attempt to relate starkly the necessary information in a minimum number of words, and those which attempt to give a spurious arty atmosphere by the meaningless use of a lot of fancy polysyllables.

Neither method works. The first is distracting and effectively breaks up any mood or train of thought that may have been induced by the music. The fancy language system, besides being obviously nauseating, takes too much time.

Program makers may as well realize soon as later that the simple possession of a fountain pen doesn't qualify a man for writing "script" or other descriptive text. It is a job calling for the very highest type of literary ability and one that can't be discharged by just anybody on the studio staff. The properly qualified writer should be able to state the information tersely, *but,* with all the vividness of a piece of poetry. Each word he uses must be selected because it is full of meaning, and of just the right shade of meaning. Any word not actively assisting in building up a rapid and forceful picture in the listener's mind must be sloughed off. A further complication: the words can't be selected because they look descriptive in type, but because their actual *sound* is descriptive. Altogether an exacting job; it would tax the ability of a Washington Irving.

It is highly improbable that a genius at writing this sort of stuff will ever appear; the ether wave is yet too ephemeral a medium to attract great writers. But there is no question that scriveners of some literary pretensions could be secured if the program builders would pay adequately for their services. This they will never do until they realize the obvious fact that the words that interrupt a program are just as conspicuous as the music of the program itself. It is incongruous, almost sacreligious, to interrupt the superb train of thought of Wagner or Massenet to sandwich in the prose endeavours of Mabel Gazook, studio hostess, trombone player and "script" writer.

Part Three: the Effervescent Hour

O dear! O dear! Whither are we drifting!

You have all heard the ancient story of the glazier who supplied his small son with a sack of stones every morning to go about breaking windows. Comes now a radio advertiser who deals in stomach settling salts with a program guaranteed to turn and otherwise sour the stomach of the most robust listener. The Effervescent Hour was the first commercial offering of the new chain and far and away the worst thing we ever heard from a loud speaker. We thought we had heard bare faced and ostentatiously direct advertising before, but this made all previous efforts in that line seem like the merest innuendo. The name of the sponsoring company's product had been mentioned ninety-eight times when we quit counting. An oily voiced soul who protested to be a representative of the sponsoring company engaged with announcer White in sundry badinage before each number, extolling the virtues of his wet goods and even going so far as to offer the not unwilling announcer a sip before the microphone. Stuck in here and there amidst this welter of advertising could actually be discovered some bits of program! But such program material it was. First the hackneyed "To Spring" by Grief. Then "Carry Me Back to Old Virginia." Next some mediocre spirituals followed by a very ordinary jazz band and culminating with a so-called symphony orchestra which actually succeeded in making the exquisite dance of the Fée Dragée from the "Nutcracker Suite" sound clumsy and loutish— no mean achievement.

One long interruption occurred while special messages were given to soda jerkers the country o'er, inviting them to enter a prize contest for the best enocomium to the advertiser's wares. But the most aggravating interruptions were the frequently spaced announcements: "This is the voice of Columbia—speaking." This remarkable statement was delivered in hushed and reverential tones, vibrant with suppressed emotion, a sustained sob intervening before the last word. It was positively celestial. We have given a rather complete résumé of this program, but it may be warranted by the fact that probably not a dozen people in the country, beside ourself, heard it. No one not paid to do so, as we are, could have survived it. Perhaps this indictment of Columbia's opening performance is unkind in the light of subsequent offerings. Our stomach is still un-

settled. Furthermore we will *not* make use of any of the Effervescent
Hour's salts to settle it!

24

Federal Communications Commission

THE COLUMBIA BROADCASTING SYSTEM

A. *Formation and Early History*

THE ORGANIZATION which later became the Columbia Broadcasting
System was incorporated in New York on January 27, 1927, under
the name of United Independent Broadcasters, Inc. Its purpose was
to contract for radio station time, to sell time to advertisers, and to
furnish programs for broadcasting. Of its original four stockholders,
two, Arthur Judson and an associate, were managers of concert artists
primarily interested in creating a new market for their managed talent; a third, Edward Ervin, was assistant manager of the New York
Philharmonic Symphony Society; and the fourth, George A. Coats,
was a promoter.

In April 1927, before United began actual operations, the Columbia Phonograph Co., Inc. became interested in the project
through the Columbia Phonograph Broadcasting System, Inc., which
was organized on April 5, 1927, to function as the sales unit of the
network. The outstanding stock of Columbia Phonograph Broadcasting System, Inc., was originally issued to Columbia Phonograph Co.,
Inc., which was active in its financing and to four individuals.[1]

The effective date of United's contracts with its original network, some of which were signed as early as March 1927, was September 5, 1927, but United experienced some delay in getting under
way and the first program was broadcast over the network on September 25, 1927. United contracted to pay each of the 16 stations on
its original network $500 per week for 10 specified hours of time.
The sales company was unable to sell enough time to sponsors to
carry the network under this arrangement, and heavy losses were
incurred because of the definite and heavy commitments entered
into with the stations.

Report on Chain Broadcasting (Commission Order No. 37, Docket 5060, May 1941),
pp. 21–25.

Because of these losses, the Columbia Phonograph Co. and the four individual stockholders withdrew from the venture in the fall of 1927 and all the outstanding capital stock of Columbia Phonograph Broadcasting System, Inc., was thereupon acquired by United.[2] The name of the sales company was changed to Columbia Broadcasting System, Inc., and on January 3, 1929, when the sales company was dissolved, United took over its activities and its name. Columbia Broadcasting System, Inc., has been the name of the network since that time.

In November 1927 Jerome H. Louchheim, Isaac D. Levy, and Leon Levy acquired a controlling stock interest in United and controlled the network until September 1928, when William S. Paley and his family purchased 50.3 percent of the stock. In December 1927 the original affiliation contracts of March of that year were superseded by contracts which eliminated the commitment of United to pay for the station time under contract whether it was used or not. Under the new contract the station was required to pay United $50 per hour for sustaining programs and United to pay the station $50 per hour for broadcasting commercial programs.

B. Growth of CBS Network

The original CBS network (then United) consisted of 16 stations. At the end of 1938, CBS had 113 outlets.

The first station purchased by CBS was station WABC, its basic New York outlet, which was acquired in 1928. As of the time of the committee hearings, CBS was the licensee of nine stations, all of which were owned by it except WEEI in Boston, which it leased. In 1939 CBS sold one station,[9] so that it is now the licensee of the following eight stations, all of which operate with unlimited time: WABC, New York; WJSV, Washington; WBT, Charlotte, N.C.; WEEL, Boston; WBBM, Chicago; WCCO, Minneapolis; KMOX, St. Louis; and KNX, Los Angeles.

In addition, CBS now holds 45 percent of the stock of Voice of Alabama, Inc., the licensee of station WAPI in Birmingham, Ala., and it has a commitment to accept, by purchase of a new issue, 40 percent of the capital stock of Pacific Agricultural Foundation, Ltd., licensee of station KQW, San Jose, Calif.

In every year since and including 1929, CBS has operated at a profit. Both gross and net income have, with few exceptions, increased year by year.

C. Management of Artists by CBS

In December 1930, CBS acquired 55 percent of the stock of Columbia Concerts Corporation, which had been organized that year by the merger of a number of concert artist managements. Columbia

Concerts Corporation has been engaged in the business of managing concert artists in all fields of entertainment. Most of its business with respect to radio relates to the appearance of its managed artists on commercial programs over national networks. Practically all negotiations for the sale of its talent are carried on, and the contracts are made, with advertising agencies. The artists managed by Columbia Concerts Corporation have appeared frequently on commercial programs over NBC as well as CBS. Indeed, the total bookings of Columbia Concerts artists for appearances over NBC, from and including the 1931–32 season to January 1939, were greater than their bookings for appearances over CBS. For the fiscal year from June 6, 1937 to June 4, 1938, the total revenue of Columbia Concerts Corporation was $426,413, and the profit for that period was $94,038. For the 1938–39 season Columbia Concerts Corporation had under management contract approximately 120 artists and in addition about 17 dancing groups, special attractions, and ensembles.

Columbia Concerts Corporation, through a division of its business known as Community Concerts Service, engages in the business of organizing and managing concerts in various communities in the United States. As of the time of the committee hearings Community Concerts had concert courses in about 375 cities and towns. Its revenue from bookings for the fiscal year from June 6, 1937 to June 4, 1938, was $165,454, and the profit for this period was $20,418.

In addition to the concert artists managed by its subsidiary Columbia Concerts Corporation, CBS through another wholly owned subsidiary, Columbia Artists, Inc., also manages radio artists in all fields of entertainment. The income of Columbia Artists, Inc., comes from three sources: the booking of performances by managed artists, the sale of wires to hotels and night clubs from which dance bands are picked up, and income from the use of time by dance bands. At the time of the committee hearings, Columbia Artists, Inc., managed approximately 110 radio artists. For the 52 weeks ending January 1, 1938, the total revenue of Columbia Artists, Inc., was $194,757 and its profit $82,671.[10]

CBS' role as both employer of, and agent for, artists was the subject of complaint by independent artists' representatives just as in the case of NBC.[11]

D. Phonograph and Transcription Business of CBS

On December 17, 1938, CBS purchased from Consolidated Film Industries, Inc., the capital stock [12] of the American Record Corporation which had the following subsidiaries: Brunswick Record Corporation, American Record Corporation of California, Columbia Phonograph Company, and Master Records, Incorporated. Upon acquiring the American Record Corporation, CBS changed the name of that company to Columbia Record Corporation and that company has carried on the manufacture of phonograph records for home use.[13] In August 1940 it entered the transcription field.[14]

25

Charles Magee Adams

WHAT ABOUT THE FUTURE OF CHAIN BROADCASTING?

UNLIKE SO MANY other developments which have had their moment of the spotlight, and then passed off the stage, chain broadcasting has endured for four years—a longevity which has given it the rank of a near-permanent institution, as things in radio go. Moreover, it is at the present time just developing to the proportions which were promised from the beginning. Yet authorities whose judgments are too keen to be dismissed lightly, recognize in recent developments along two diverse lines—those of higher powered transmitters, and those in the field of the phonograph—potentialities which, if realized, may well relegate chain broadcasting to a place on the radio shelf.

The Merits of the System

What are the advantages of chain broadcasting to the listener? The answer to this is, of course, obvious.

First, the network system has enabled the presentation of much superior programs; not only through distributing the cost of engaging better artists among many stations, instead of saddling it on only one, but also through making available to much of the country broadcasts of events of wide public interest. Second, it has made possible the enjoyment of these programs under conditions of local reception, as against DX.

Anyone who remembers the caliber of programs which were outstanding four or five years ago need not be told that the first result alone represents a genuine advance in broadcasting. But, it seems to me, the reception is even more important from the listener's standpoint. The freedom from interference of all kinds which reception

Radio News, February 1928, pp. 869–871. Ziff-Davis Publishing Company.

from local stations offers is generally recognized; and contact with listeners discloses the astonishing extent to which set owners, who have ranged far and wide in quest of entertainment, now limit the bulk of their listening to local stations, chiefly outlets of the various chains, for this very reason of more satisfactory reception.

And its Demerits

Next, what are the disadvantages of chain broadcasting? The first, and the most serious from the listener's standpoint, is occasioned by the difference in time between the various zones into which the country is divided.

To eastern listeners this appears a detail of small importance. But for those living elsewhere it constitutes a real problem, since practically all network programs originate in New York and are scheduled according to New York time.

A difference of only one hour means an annoying conflict with the habits of listeners. For example, a chain program put on the air at 7:30 p.m. eastern time falls at 6:30 p.m. central time, when many listeners in the latter zone are not free to enjoy what is offered. A difference of two hours, as between eastern and mountain time, or eastern and central when the former is using daylight saving, entails a heavy loss in the western audience, unless the program is one of compelling interest; and the difference of three hours between the eastern and Pacific zones is such a prohibitive obstacle that the National Broadcasting Company has found it necessary to make the Orange network a separate unit, except for the airing of national events or daylight programs.

It is true, of course, that it has been possible to change the habits of listeners to some extent, by educating them to listen in at times to which they were not accustomed; and also to set programs at a compromise time acceptable to listeners in zones between which there is only one hour's difference. But a difference of two hours or more presents such complications that chain broadcasting cannot overcome the handicap, save in the few exceptions just noted, at least with key stations in New York; and the suggested solution of establishing a key station for each of the various zones would entail a sacrifice of the economy, in artists' fees which the network system effects.

Sectional or National Programs

The reference to event broadcasts leads naturally to a second disadvantage of the network method from the listener's standpoint—namely, its unwieldiness as regards programs with sectional interest.

Because they are designed first of all to serve the sponsors of commercial programs whose support makes them possible, the chains are organized on a scale as nearly national as practicable. From the standpoint of financing this is, of course, sound; and on the score of service to the listener it is also an advantage particularly, as far as broadcasts of national events are concerned. But, for material with only sectional interest, the network method discloses a serious weakness.

Lines connecting the member stations are planned for serving from a single key station, generally located in New York. No provision is made for breaking up the chain into regional units served from lesser key stations, for the good reason that, under the conditions of national operation which usually prevail, this would be uneconomical. Such an arrangement makes the airing of programs with a sectional appeal practically prohibitive; a disadvantage which has become more and more apparent to listeners of late.

Smaller Tie-Ups Desirable

Football games are an apt example. With few exceptions, notably the Army-Navy contest, they are of interest chiefly to listeners living in the states or sections represented by the teams taking part. It is true that most of them are put on the air by single stations. But these, it will be noted, are rarely of sufficient power to serve properly the entire area in which listeners are interested, especially under the handicap of daylight transmission. If a few stations, selected to cover the territory, could be tied together for such a broadcast, the resultant service would be keenly appreciated by listeners. But existing chain facilities are, for the sound reason just cited, not adapted to this purpose; and the leasing of lines for such a single event is, as a rule, too costly.

Many other events of interest to listeners in a section, larger than can be served by a single station of average power, could be mentioned—conventions, industrial gatherings, meetings of various kinds; and it is also true that many entertainment programs could be developed to a point of greater interest if aimed at simply a sectional audience. But, as chains are now constituted, what is put on the air must have a national appeal.

The question of whether chain broadcasting will survive accordingly resolves itself, from the listener's standpoint, to this: do recent developments in higher-powered transmitters or phonograph technique offer possibilities that would eliminate the disadvantages of the network method, at the same time retaining its advantages?

Super-Power Transmitters

First, as to higher-powered transmitters.

There is no question that a station with 50 or 100 kilowatts output, such as WJZ, WEAF, or the new WGY, can command an audience which, for part of the time, compares favorably with that of a sizable chain system. Therefore, a station of this power as a substitute for a chain would make feasible the presentation of superior programs by high-class artists, the first advantage of the network method.

Further, it is equally clear that a few such stations properly placed could eliminate the difference in time handicap under which the networks now labor (assuming, of course, that each operated independently); and also that they would lend themselves well to the airing of material with special interest to listeners in their respective sections.

So, as a substitute for chain broadcasting, the higher-powered transmitter scores on three of four points. But, on the fourth, that of service compared with local reception from a chain outlet, it falls short.

This is said with full respect for the fine results secured by those transmitters using 50 kilowatts or more. It is true that such stations have materially increased their service range by employing increased power. But it is also true that, as compared with that supplied by locals, the dependability of their service at any real distance has been considerably overestimated in many quarters.

Effect of Distance

For example, the writer lives some 600 miles from WJZ and there are nights when this big station "comes in like a local," to use the stock phrase; but there are also nights when it does not come in at all, because of static or other atmospheric obstacles. KDKA is about 200 miles away from my location, and at times this pioneer comes in better than local; but again there are times when it does not come in at all.

The still more serious error in popular discussion of recent super-power developments, particularly with respect to WGY's 100-kilowatt set, is the assumption that doubling the power doubles the effective range. At the time WJZ's present equipment was installed, engineers explained that because of the "square-root rule" which applies in such a case, it is necessary to increase the power four times in order to double the signal strength, which means 200 and not 100 kilowatts, is the next step in power increases, but one not expected in the near future.

In the light of all this it should be clear that, gratifying as the results have been, recent developments in higher-powered transmitters do not offer any present or near-future substitute for chain broadcasting in the vital matter of dependable service over a territory even approximating that served by present networks; and further that anything approaching a dependable nation-wide service from a single station is still only a hope; since a power of at least 1000 kilowatts and possibly as high as 10,000 would seemingly be required for this.

Chain Method Still Best

So neither the higher-powered transmitter nor the modern phonograph proves to be a completely satisfactory substitute for chain broadcasting just now.

It may well be, of course, that a combination of the two will, in the not too distant future, supplant networks to a large extent. Instead of being broadcast through a few score of stations linked by telephone lines, programs of the ordinary type may be recorded and transmitted by many locals, supplemented by a dozen or two truly super-power stations so placed as to supply regional service; and with chain facilities making possible the connecting of all for the airing of outstanding events. Such a compromise arrangement would afford maximum service to the listener and accordingly, is a possibility which can be anticipated with interest as developments take shape.

But, in the meantime, chain broadcasting as at present constituted seems certain not only to remain, but to continue its expansion, notwithstanding these promising substitutes.

26

Federal Communications Commission

THE MUTUAL BROADCASTING SYSTEM

THE MUTUAL BROADCASTING SYSTEM is organized along lines radically different from those of CBS and NBC. It does not own any stations, but is owned by several stations. Mutual has no studios, maintains neither an engineering department nor an artists' bureau, and does not itself produce any programs except European news broadcasts. The commercial programs are produced by the originating station or by the sponsor who buys time, and the sustaining programs are selected from among those put on by the stations associated with the network.

Report on Chain Broadcasting (Commission Order No. 37, Docket 5060, May 1941), pp. 26–28.

A. *Formation of Mutual*

On September 29, 1934, WGN, Inc., Bamberger Broadcasting Service, Inc., Kunsky-Trendle Broadcasting Corporation, and Crosley Radio Corporation, the respective licensees of stations WGN at Chicago, WOR at Newark, N.J., WXYZ at Detroit, and WLW at Cincinnati, entered into an agreement for the purpose of securing contracts with advertisers for network broadcasting of commercial programs over their stations and making arrangements with the Telephone Co. for wire connections between the stations. WGN and WOR were to contract with the Telephone Co. for wire connections between the stations and all four stations agreed to share the expenses thus incurred.

In a supplementary contract of the same date, WGN and WOR agreed to organize a new corporation for the purpose of contracting with the Telephone Co. for the wire facilities required under the contract between the four stations. Stations WOR and WGN guaranteed the payment of any indebtedness of the new corporation to the Telephone Co. The new corporation provided for in the supplementary contract was the Mutual Broadcasting System, Inc., which was incorporated in Illinois on October 29, 1934, and which entered upon the business of selling time to advertisers over the four-station network and of making arrangements with the Telephone Co. for lines between the stations.

The capital stock of Mutual consisted of only 10 shares, of which WGN, Inc., and Bamberger Broadcasting Service, Inc., each held 5. WGN, Inc., is a subsidiary of the Tribune Co., which publishes the Chicago *Tribune,* and the Bamberger Broadcasting Service is a subsidiary of L. Bamberger & Co., which in turn is a subsidiary of R. H. Macy & Co. Ultimate control of the new network, accordingly, lay with the Chicago newspaper and the New York department store.[1]

The arrangement among the four stations comprising the Mutual network was carried forward by a new agreement on January 31, 1935, but the network did not expand during that year. Under the new contract, Mutual agreed to pay the four stations their regular card rates for network programs broadcast over their facilities, deducting for itself a commission of 5 percent and such expenses as agency commissions and wire-line charges. Station WXYZ in Detroit left Mutual in September 1935 in order to join NBC, and was replaced by station CKLW, located in Windsor, Ontario, but serving Detroit as well, and owned by the Western Ontario Broadcasting Co., Ltd. On January 31, 1936 the four-station agreement was extended for another year, and Mutual's commission was reduced to 3½ percent.

B. Development of the Mutual Network

Prior to 1936, WOR, WGN, WLW, and WXYZ (replaced by CKLW in 1935) were the only stations which regularly carried Mutual programs. During 1936, however, a number of stations were added to the network, including 13 in New England and 10 in California associated with regional networks (Colonial and Don Lee).

Mutual continued to increase the number of its associated stations throughout 1938, adding a Texas regional network of 23 stations during this period. As of January 17, 1939, shortly prior to the date on which Mutual presented its testimony at the committee hearings, the Mutual network included a total of 107 stations, of which 25 were also associated with NBC and 5 were also associated with CBS, and at the end of 1940 there were 160 outlets.

As the number of stations on the Mutual network increased, the structure of the network grew more complex. During the period in which only four stations were regularly associated with the network each contributed one-fourth of Mutual's expenses and wire-line charges. As more stations were added, three classifications were set up: member stations, participating members, and affiliates. At the time of the committee hearings in February 1939, there were two member stations, WGN and WOR, which held stock control of Mutual. The four participating member organizations were the Colonial Network, the United Broadcasting Co. (licensee of WHKC at Columbus and WCLE and WHK at Cleveland), the Don Lee Network, and the Western Ontario Broadcasting Co., Ltd. The remaining stations associated with Mutual were affiliates.

All network commercial time sold by Mutual is sold at the card rates of the stations. The two members and four participating members pay Mutual a commission of 3½ percent, and share any network deficit, while the affiliated stations pay a commission of 15 percent. Stations associated with Mutual receive a 2-percent commission from Mutual on the proceeds of network time sold by them. The member stations underwrite all operating deficits and wire-line charges; and the participating members contribute in varying degrees toward the expenses of Mutual and their wire-line connections to Mutual's main line. The affiliated stations do not contribute toward the operating expenses or wire-line charges of Mutual as such, but, in addition to the commission of 15 percent they pay Mutual, in most cases they also pay the cost of the wire-line connection from their station to the Mutual main line.

Since the presentation of testimony by Mutual at the committee hearings during February 1939, several changes have taken place in its organization, as set forth in its brief of November 11, 1940. In

January 1940 Mutual, which at that time was entirely owned by WGN and WOR, issued stock to five additional companies: the Don Lee Broadcasting Co., the Colonial Network, Inc., the Cincinnati Times-Star Co. (licensee of WKRC at Cincinnati), the United Broadcasting Co. and the Western Ontario Broadcasting Co., Ltd.[2]

27

David T. MacFarland

THE LIBERTY BROADCASTING SYSTEM

OF ALL THE NETWORK organizations which have challenged the established chains, Liberty Broadcasting System was one of the most successful. Liberty depending on the great on-the-air talent of its president started as a baseball network but at its peak in 1951 it was serving 458 affiliates with 18 hours of sports and entertainment programming.

The network began on KLIF in Dallas in 1948 serving 42 stations with coverage of major league games. The announcer was "The Old Scotchman" Gordon McLendon, flanked by sound effects and furnished with information that made the games, many of which came into the studio on ticker tape, seem as if they were live. His coverage of games had created such high local ratings at KLIF that he received requests from other southwestern stations for feeds. In 1949 there were 100 stations on the Liberty network. He started 1950 with 238 stations in 33 states serving an estimated 30 million listeners from coast to coast.

McLendon had served in naval intelligence during World War II. He noted that his fellow soldiers were intensely interested in the broadcasts of baseball games over the Armed Forces Network. Standard thinking in broadcasting was that the only audiences that could be amassed for baseball would be for local teams and the world series. No major network carried team broadcasts on a regular basis. Recreations of games were not new. Western Union wires were available for every major league game. But the tradition was to give the game as it came over the line with the ticker obviously audible behind the announcer's voice.

The Old Scotchman programs created an atmosphere of the game.

He trained a staff of engineers to manipulate sound effects on four turntables. Many of the records had been made at the park where the games were being played. There were records of crowd noise including boos and roars for home runs. Other records had sounds of the bat hitting the ball, and local shouts of food and beer vendors. He even had local public address announcements with regional accents and slang varying according to the home team. The Old Scotchman had every ballpark mapped out with detailed information so that he could describe accurately which sign the "well-drilled drive over the left field wall" hit. Some of the games (about half of them) were presented live. Listeners were unable in most cases to tell the difference. One station complained that Liberty was operating the programming in violation of the federal regulations concerning recreations. The Federal Communications Commission ruled that notification that the programs were "reconstructions" before and after games met the requirements of its rules.

Organized baseball also was fearful of the broadcasts. McLendon as the programs became more popular began to broadcast a "Game of the Day" traveling to each city to broadcast the games live. Baseball owners began to place restrictions on the network. The network was prohibited from broadcasting at night and then was told not to broadcast any games in towns in opposition to minor league games. Most stations in the northwest and midwest were prohibited from broadcasting any "Game of the Day." Minor league attendance which had been dropping through the 1940s dipped to a new low in 1951 and, at the request of the smaller teams, 13 major league clubs cut back on their broadcasting commitments. Some banned Liberty broadcasts altogether.

Liberty responded to the embargo on broadcasts with an anti-trust suit against the clubs, leagues and baseball commissioners. The network asked treble damages of 12 million dollars. The 1952 season opened with McLendon allowed to carry only three major league teams. McLendon finally gave up the effort to broadcast the games in the spring of 1952. He made a settlement of $200,000 in the anti-trust suit.

The network had failed to bring a profit for McLendon, despite the popularity of the baseball broadcasts. Initially affiliates paid only their own line charges with Liberty getting 15% of local sales. As the coverage expanded Liberty adjusted its financial picture by charging stations from $450 to $10,000 a month depending on the market size. Liberty was most attractive to stations with no network affiliations. About 80% of the stations on the Liberty System were independent—many of which had gone on the air after the war. Smaller market affiliates of large networks also were attracted to Liberty since they received little or no compensation from the big chain organizations. Eighteen % of the Liberty stations were affiliated with ABC and two % were with NBC or CBS.

Liberty, like many networks that evolved since the beginning of broadcasting, developed around one program service. When that service, baseball coverage, dried up, McLendon was forced into bankruptcy. The network was growing at a time when the major networks were retooling for television. Liberty was offering a fare of quizzes, disc jockeys, minstrel shows and news and talk programs that was, at best, no better than the offerings of the major networks. It was unable, or unwilling, to offer its stations any big name comedy or drama. Coverage of sports programs other than baseball never gained audience interest.

Gordon McLendon, who later castigated the national networks for their "old, tired" programming, was unable to find the network program forms which would compete for a national audience. Much of his success with KLIF and other stations was in programs and formats specialized for local consumption. The Old Scotchman, a .400 hitter as a baseball broadcaster, failed to "hit 'em where they ain't" in other programs.

28

Hal W. Bochin

THE RISE AND FALL
OF THE DUMONT NETWORK

THE DUMONT Television Network was created by Allen B. DuMont, a colorful pioneer in the technological development of broadcasting. He was Westinghouse engineer in charge of tube production in the late 1920's and later as chief engineer at the deForest Radio Company plant he was able to increase their production significantly. But DuMont needed his own stage and in 1933 on $12,000 capital he started the DuMont Laboratories. The engineer led his firm into television research after a tour of Europe's broadcasting facilities in the mid-1930's. To involve the laboratories in television research DuMont sold half of his interest in the company to Paramount Pictures for $56,000 in 1938. Two years later he was given an experimental license for television in New York. Although the station was not licensed commercially he allowed sponsors to try out television commercials on his regular Sunday evening variety shows. The station was licensed commercially in 1944 as WABD (Allan B. DuMont) and two years later the thrust of DuMont's planning became apparent as he started the DuMont Television Network. The second network station was his experimental outlet in Washington, D.C., W3XWT later WTTG. The inaugural program of DTN included a statement by Mayor William O'Dwyer of New York and a demonstration of cooking, serving and eating one of the sponsor's products, macaroni. The program was fed to a third station by radio relay—KYW in Philadelphia. DuMont had converted the Wanamaker department store auditorium to a television studio. The facilities could seat an audience of 400.

DuMont, basically an innovative engineer, developed a method of using a light beam to transmit pictures from point to point, but like many earlier signalling ideas the concept was defeated by fog. He also perfected a direct viewing color television receiving tube called the trichromoscope. With this system he could receive both the mechanical sequential (CBS) pictures and the electronic simultaneous (RCA) signals. DuMont told FCC members visiting his Passaic laboratories that he preferred the RCA system.

DuMont was squeezed out of network television by a number of factors. He was never able to get his programs to the population centers on a regular basis. Stations in large communities were not particularly enthusiastic about clearing their program time for his low budget programs. He was unable to get his full complement of five owned-and-operated stations because Paramount, still part-owner of DuMont, owned KTLA in Los Angeles, KTLA did not clear DuMont programs. The established radio networks were using old affiliation ties to establish themselves in the population centers. DuMont had similar network costs but was unable to use the network effectively.[1] His efforts to get Paramount involved in production of programs fell short. His network was forced to produce inexpensive variety, quiz and sports shows. Meanwhile the other networks were channeling great resources into productions. DuMont's most outstanding programs were Bishop Sheen, Jackie Gleason and Monday Night Boxing. One of the great services to the country was DuMont's coverage of the Senate Army-McCarthy hearings.

DuMont doubled his sales from 1948 to 1949 but was still operating the broadcasting division at a loss. He offered the network as a closed circuit hookup for industrial and sales firms. The charge for an hour on the 21-city network was $11,000. There were few takers. The federal freeze in the authorization of new licenses for television between 1948 and 1952 probably helped DuMont, but new allocations of stations made it clear his network was in for

stormy weather. The FCC allotted four or more stations in only six of
the top 25 markets. With the affiliations which the three other networks already had, DuMont was in trouble. He made an alternative
plan of station distribution to the commission which made more stations available in the large markets. It was rejected. The year the
freeze on licensing ended, DuMont had an affiliation lineup of 80
stations and gross billings of 10 million dollars. He was the first
network to own a UHF outlet—KCTV in Kansas City. A month after
he took over the station he closed it. The Kansas City audiences
seemed satisfied with three major network outlets on VHF. Despite
the problem of outlets to major markets DuMont opened a new
$5,000,000 production center in New York in early 1953. Later in the
year he announced that his list of affiliates had reached 178 with 27
more stations linked with him by bills of agreement.

Despite this list of affiliates the costs mounted faster than the
revenue and DuMont began to try various economies. He developed
the Electronicam system which allowed the production of film and
live television with the same cameras. The idea was to send affiliates
the filmed versions of shows to cut coaxial cable costs. Despite economies the losses mounted. In 1954 he lost $4,000,000 and even more
in 1955. During the first six months in 1955 DuMont averaged billings of $2,900,000 a month. ABC the struggling network of the big
three was averaging $3,600,000. There was talk of merger but there
seemed no advantage for ABC to merge. The struggling DuMont finally separated the network and the DuMont Laboratories, with the
network serving out its contracts with various programs. The stations
and what was left of the network were sold to Metropolitan Broadcasting Company (Metromedia) ending the most valiant effort to start
a nationwide broadcasting network in 20 years.

Hosted by WABC disc jockey, Frank Kingston Smith, "Retro Rock"
is a historical retrospective on Rock 'n' Roll Music. The
program explores the sounds of the Rock era--Chuck Berry,
Little Richard, Bill Haley, et. al.--to the present, along
with insights and comments from the artists themselves.
"Retro Rock" qualifies as "Instructional" under FCC
definitions.   --American Contemporary Radio Network Schedule.

Table 12.

STATIONS AFFILIATED WITH NATIONAL NETWORKS

Figures show the number of affiliated stations for the national radio and television networks and the Keystone syndicate.

	1927	1930	1935	1940	1945	1950	1955	1960	1965	1970	1974
NBC Red/NBC	22	22	27	53	150	172	208	202	209	223	232
NBC Alternates		32	41	69							
NBC Blue	6	17	20	60							
ABC					195	282	357	310	355	334	407
ABC Information										241	347
ABC Entertainment										213	317
ABC Contemporary										182	216
ABC FM											
CBS	16	60	97	112	145	173	207	198	237	246	248
Mutual			3	160	384	543	563	443	501	576	635
Mutual Black											90
Keystone System[1]				50	202	395	852	1100	1140	1154	1060
TELEVISION											
NBC-TV					9a	56	189	214	198	215	218
CBS-TV					3a	27	139	195	190	193	212
ABC-TV					6a	13	46	87	128	162	181
Dumont						52	158				
% OF TOTAL AFFILIATED WITH NATIONAL NET											
AM	6%	16%	21%	50%	94%	55%	49%	33%	32%	43%	52%
TV						92	82	86	88	82	87

Source: Compiled by Lichty with C. H. Sterling from Broadcasting Yearbook, FCC and the networks. Figures are usually for January 1. [1]Keystone not interconnected; but syndicated. [2]Excluding NBC alternates and ABC FM. a]1948.

Table 13.

STATIONS OWNED BY NETWORKS

Figures show the stations and the potential audience of the facilities owned by the three national networks, 1974. Call letters are given for TV stations and markets indicated for AM and FM stations.

MARKET Rank	ADI Households	% U.S. Homes	ABC TV	ABC Radio	CBS TV	CBS Radio	NBC TV	NBC Radio
1 New York	6,161,900	9.44%	WABC-TV	A/F	WCBS-TV	A/F	WNBC-TV	A/F
2 Los Angeles	3,415,100	5.23	KABC-TV	A/F	KNX-TV	A/F	KNBC	
3 Chicago	2,686,000	4.12	WLS-TV	A/F	WBBM-TV	A/F	WMAQ-TV	A/F
4 Philadelphia	2,209,900	3.39			WCAU-TV	A/F		
5 Boston	1,644,800	2.52				A/F		
6 San Francisco	1,535,500	2.35	KGO-TV	A/F		A/F		A/F
7 Detroit	1,529,800	2.34	WXYZ-TV	A/F				
8 Cleveland	1,304,300	2.00					WKYC	
9 Washington	1,183,500	1.81					WRC-TV	A/F
10 Pittsburgh	1,064,200	1.63		A/F				
12 St. Louis	915,100	1.40			KMOX-TV	A/F		
14 Houston	786,000	1.20		A/F				
TOTAL POTENTIAL U.S. HOUSEHOLDS			23%	26%	24%	28%	22%	18%

Source: ARB 1972-73, Broadcasting Yearbook, 1973. Number and percent of households are for the Area of Dominant Influence (ADI).

PART FOUR

ECONOMICS

> The fact of the matter is that social change in this country is usually ratified, not in the halls of legislature, or even in Gloria Steinem's salon, but in advertising.
>
> —Harry Reasoner, ABC TV,
> June 15, 1972

> They don't sell products, they sell prestige and security and ego-aggrandizement. . . .
>
> —Ken Kesey

THE PROBLEM of financing broadcasting was apparent as soon as interest in receiving programs became general. In February 1922 Secretary of Commerce Herbert Hoover noted that the question is "who is to support the sending stations."

Suggestions for paying the programming bills included donations of time by artists trading their talent for exposure, voluntary contributions by listeners and "pay radio" with a coin box on each receiver. In the early days of broadcasting, owners of the stations met the costs of programming, receiving in return indirect advertising value and attendant publicity. About a quarter of the nearly 500 stations listed by *Radio Digest* in 1925 were owned by manufacturers, retailers, firms including hotels, automobile related businesses, and newspapers. These businesses programmed the stations for their publicity. Another quarter of the stations in that period were owned by radio-related manufacturers, sales and repair shops which were providing programming in response to sales of batteries, tubes and parts. Educational institutions, radio clubs, civic groups, church, government and military interests accounted for 40% of the stations on the air in 1925. Fewer than 30 owners were "radio broadcasting companies" or groups in entertainment such as theaters and amusement firms. Nearly 90 licenses were given to individuals, some of whom supported the programming out of pocket.[1]

Call letters of stations became symbols of the trademarks of the owner's business. In Chicago WLS was owned by Sears Roebuck & Co., "The World's Largest Store;" WGN by the "World's Greatest Newspaper," the Chicago *Tribune*. Programs came from a number of sources, piano rolls, records and the like. Singing, dancing, and oratory teachers supplied their students for programs.

American Telephone and Telegraph's WEAF in New York broke the commercial ice in 1922. On August 28 a short essay on the joy and benefits of apartment living was read in behalf of a development in Jackson Heights, New York.[2] That sponsor, the Queensboro Corporation, purchased time for four afternoon 10-minute talks at $50 each, and one evening broadcast at $100. In two months WEAF carried three hours of commercial time totaling $550. Other sponsors included Tidewater Oil and American Express.

But a year later WEAF had no more than 30 advertisers.[3]

By 1923 B.F. Goodrich was presenting a weekly program for Silvertown tires. The program was typical of a pattern to be carried out through the 1920s with no commercial messages as such. However the star of the show was "The Silver Masked Tenor" and the music was supplied by the "Silvertown Cord Orchestra." The editor of *Radio News*, a radio magazine in 1925, commented on this form of advertising:

> "This is Station WZXY, broadcasting the Everlast Battery Corporation Symphony Orchestra." The advertising is contained in this announcement and if it is repeated week after week it must sooner or later impress the listener that the Everlast Battery must be a good battery, although the batteries themselves are never mentioned by name.[4]

Early broadcasting advertisers varied from area to area. WEAF had Macy Department stores, I. Miller & Sons shoe company, and Lily Cup Co., makers of paper cups. KQW in San Jose had Sperry Flour as a sponsor of a five-times-a-week cooking show. KFI had an opera series sponsored in Los Angeles by Standard Oil Co. of California. KLZ in Denver had Cottrelli's men's store sponsoring a news program. WSPD in Toledo was the first outlet proclaiming the virtues of Speeden gasoline which was owned by the licensees of the station. Cigaret companies, wines, automobiles, hotels, churches, and many others sponsored early radio.[5]

The reaction of listeners to broadcasting stations in 1925—reported by critics in the print media—shows acute sensitivity to the amount of advertising on stations. Few stations were selling ads and fewer advertisers were willing to take the chance in the new medium. Even the most important stations in 1926 had, at the most, fine commercial programs each week. WEAF had a list of rules for advertising that had been formulated in 1923 and that still applied:

(1) Entertainment on sponsored programs had to be up to the standard set by the station for its sustaining programs; (2) the commercial must be kept, so far as reasonably possible, to the mention of the sponsor and product; (3) direct selling and price mentions were forbidden; (4) if the sponsor failed to conform to these rules, the station could cancel his advertising.[6]

In 1926 WEAF carried the Jack Dempsey-Gene Tunney fight with Royal Typewriter Company sponsoring the program for charges reported from $25,000 to $35,000. The sponsor's name was not mentioned during the fight but it was "worked in" in pre- and post-fight commentary.

The problem of how broadcasting was to be financed was being settled as business began to support programming. In March of 1925 a Haverford, Pennsylvania man won $500 from *Radio Broadcast* magazine in the prize answer to the question: "Who is to Pay for Broadcasting—And How." [7] He proposed that some funds be raised by taxing tubes (since the best index of the range and value of the set was in the number and kind of tubes) and that super broadcasting stations should get the funds from the tube tax administered by the government. The idea had little support outside of the editorial rooms of the magazine. Herbert Hoover "did not believe that your prize-winning plan is feasible." The chairman of the National Association of Broadcasters termed the idea "obnoxious."

Hoover, opening the Third National Radio Conference in October of 1924 seemed to have no better ideas for financing broadcasting, but warned, "I believe that the quickest way to kill broadcasting would be to use it for direct advertising." Later in the speech he said, "Nor do I believe there is any practical method of payment from the listeners." [8] A year later David Sarnoff who was vice president of the Radio Corporation of America had started to see broadcasting as an advertising medium but with limitations:

At present it cannot be said that advertising over the radio is parallel in effectiveness with advertising in periodicals and newspapers. The standards of periodical and newspaper advertising should also apply to the standards of the air and no advertisement should be broadcast without the plain advertising label.[9]

The idea of "giving the listener-in the privilege of knowing that advertising is about to be broadcast" was suggested by the lively critic for *Radio Broadcast:* "You may listen quite a time before you catch on to the fact that Mr. Blank is telling you about these products because he wants you to buy them." [10]

Radio commercials were greeted with many misgivings. An unsigned editorial indicated disatisfaction with some ads:

> Aside from . . . senseless and meaningless technical appeals, most radio advertising confines itself to generalized boasts. The same charge may be made not only against the advertising of radio sets, but that of automobiles, iceless refrigerators, and any mechanical or electrical product.[11]

The writing was on the electronic wall in 1928 as Orrin Dunlap looked with trepidation at the image of radio as "a world-wide billboard." He reported on the activities of Henry Field of KFNF in Shenandoah, Iowa, the friendly farmer and "seller of seeds." Dunlap describes the "go-getter" broadcaster as sitting down in his shirtsleeves before the microphone and telling "millions" about his "seeds, bacons, auto tires, pig meal, fresh hams, radio batteries, prunes, paint, tea, coffee, shirts, shoes" and the like. Termed the "Roxy of the open spaces," Dunlap says:

> Henry Field has a voice personality and sincerity in his nasal twang. When he begins to sell this is what he says, "Howdy, Folks. This is Henry, Henry Field talking folks. Henry himself." [12]

The timing of a federal court decision in 1926 "anaesthetized" the old law of 1912 and removed all vestiges of government control over radio came at a time when Congress had "just gone home." The "immediate effect of the judicial decree was to give impetus to a growing belief in a more liberal interpretation of indirect radio advertising." [13] By 1930, nine out of ten stations were selling time for advertising. The depression had forced even the most reluctant broadcaster to begin accepting help in paying for programming.

During the depression, radio revenues grew steadily. Other entertainment industries suffered—in 1932 legitimate theaters grossed only 35% of 1929 and motion pictures theaters only about one-half.

It probably cost $5,000 to $10,000 a year to operate the average small or medium station in 1928 to 1930—some very small stations much less. Typical of larger owners was Crosley Radio in Cincinnati which lost more than $120,000 in 1928 in operating WLW and WSAI. The stations carried no local advertising and the only revenue was from carrying Blue Network programs. That year Crosley made profits of more than $3,000,000 on radio manufacturing. In 1930 Crosley Radio lost nearly a million dollars—WLW and WSAI like most other radio stations were soon commercial.

By 1930 advertising and subsidies of broadcasting stations were expendable luxuries. Despite the increase in gross income for broadcasting in the United States, most of the stations were losing money after 1929. In 1931 more than half of the stations grossed less than $3,000 a month, which was not enough to break even on expenses.

GROSS INCOME [14]

	1930	1931	1932
Radio Broadcasting *	$ 125,239,000	$ 130,543,000	$ 136,078,000
Total Recreation and Amusement	1,915,618,000	1,688,324,000	1,458,589,000

* Radio broadcasting includes manufacture of sets, tubes, not just advertising revenues.

The old WEAF ban on price mentions was finally broken by NBC in July of 1932—but for daytime only. Two months later the price bar was dropped after dark by both NBC and CBS—September 12 the A&P Gypsies program mentioned prices.[15]

In the period of 1926–1927 "the tradition—if not the actual rule—that 60 seconds was the optimum time for declamation was cemented into station and network practice." [16] The notion of direct "selling commercials" and the one-minute length were standard in the early 1930s. There were other innovations: so-called personal products began to sponsor programs—laxatives, deodorants and toothpastes; certain religious organizations, astrologers, medical quacks and many products of questionable value were advertised widely. Many of these "undesirable" advertisers were off the air by 1935 as the economy began to recover from the depression and the Federal Radio Commission and the American Medical Association applied pressure. One practice which was stopped was on-the-air prescribing with the sponsors splitting money orders per inquiry from listeners.

Broadcasting—particularly network broadcasting—was becoming big business. Sponsors were paying $200,000 to $500,000 a year to produce popular programs and paying an additional $4,000 a week for an hour hookup on the NBC Red network (with WEAF as the flagship station). Radio was spawned in a depression in 1920 to 1922 and was showing its greatest growth with businesses failing throughout the country, in 1929 to 1931. After 1929 entertainment suffered—vaudeville died. People saved their money for a radio set and sat around it listening to sponsored programs such as Show Boat, Rudy Vallee's Variety Hour and Amos 'n' Andy. George Washington Hill, president of American Tobacco Company, sponsored many programs on radio: the Metropolitan Opera, Your Hit Parade, Ben Bernie, Kay Kyser, Eddie Duchin, Jack Benny, Phil Harris, Wayne King, Information Please, and others. His ads featuring the "chant of the auctioneer" and such ideas as "Lucky Strike green has gone to war," were repeated to the extent that they became part of the American experience.[17]

Name talent like Eddie Cantor, Bing Crosby and *Fibber McGee and Molly* came to radio. The assignment to do a series of commercials for one of these popular programs was an advertising agency plum. But it was not until 1934 that an advertising copywriter was named to do radio commercials which till then were patterned after the print copy messages—for better or worse.

Network stations added another source of revenue in the early 1930s when they began to accept national "spot" advertising. Thus they were receiving money from national and local sales in addition to the money received for carrying network programs. National spot was enhanced by the development of high quality transcriptions which allowed the sponsor to control the delivery and add production values to his message. These were used during the 30-second chain breaks between network programs and later were quite common in local "spot carrier" shows such as homemaker, farm, hillbilly music and other inexpensive programs. Bulova watches brought a number of chain break spots announcing the "Bulova time."

The Federal Radio Commission found in a 1932 survey that 36% of the time on 582 stations was commercial with the remaining two-thirds being without sponsors (sustaining). At night (from 6 p.m. to midnight) 40% of the stations' time was commercial—15% network and 25% local.

Commercials took various forms. Dramatic situations were commonly presented in support of soap products. Singing commercials for such firms as Wheaties, Pepsi-Cola and Barbasol became rampant when transcriptions were established. Personalities were particularly important for programs on the networks which were each sponsored by only one firm. The voices of James Wallington, Ken Niles, Don Wilson and Ken Carpenter became readily identified with certain products. Integrated commercials—some spoofing the product, such as Ed Wynn, the Texaco Fire Chief—were common on the networks about 1935. Fred Allen, Phil Baker and Jack Benny all began to make pitches for the product. Premium offers, often redeemed by sending in the products' boxtop, started in 1933 and became exceptionally popular with women and children. The audience for *Clara, Lu 'n' Em* was asked to send a Super Suds boxtop and a dime to receive a package of gorgeous "Hollywood flower garden" seeds.[18] The response was a sales record of more than half-a-million packages of the soap in 10 days.

The Federal Communications Commission in 1935 sought to make the broadcasting of some commercials an object lesson by bringing several broadcast licensees into Washington to set up guidelines. The results were not clearly definitive to broadcasters.[19] There was no halting the booming radio broadcasting business. From 1935 to 1941 radio revenues nearly doubled. Network radio received about half of that money but there was aggressive growth in national spot advertising. Local advertising and national spot advertising accounted for about a fourth of radio revenues in 1939. Sponsorship was becoming more prevalent. About a third of radio broadcasts in 1938 were sponsored. However, the super stations—the 50,000-watt facilities—had more than half of their program time sold.

> The impact of broadcast was apparent to researchers and advertisers alike: A study made for a large broadcasting company shows that the purchase of radio advertised goods is 35 percent higher in radio homes than in non-radio homes; another study shows that radio advertised goods are used 29 percent more than corresponding non-radio advertised goods.[20]

Advertising on radio nearly doubled during World War II. One reason for the growth was the evasion of an excess profits tax by industry through the use of advertising which was available in radio but not in newspapers and magazines which were limited because of paper shortages. The tax was 90% on those profits over an individualized amount set by the government. Thus companies could buy advertising for about 10 cents on-the-dollar since the government considered advertising a legitimate expense. The unspent portion went to taxes. Most firms used institutional ads to create good will anticipating sales at the end of the war.

National spot advertising for various government programs and agencies was conducted by the War Advertising Council which acted in conjunction with the Office of War Information. The council was responsible for more than a 100 campaigns using advertising time worth millions of dollars.[21]

The business of broadcasting, showing life at all levels during the 1930s blossomed in the 1940s. More than a third of the stations in 1939 were reporting they were in the red. In five years less than five % were losing money. During that period the average ratio of income to revenues in broadcasting stations rose from 19% to 31%.

Radio revenues continued to grow after the war—about 10% a year—until 1949. Then came television. In 1950 TV time sales were a quarter of radio sales. Two years later the time sales for television networks surpassed those of radio networks. In 1954 total television revenues including local, national spot and network were greater than radio. If local radio was rapidly changing, there was revolution in the offices of the national networks. Program costs had caused many advertisers to participate with other advertisers in sponsoring programs rather than foot the whole program bill. This practice had started with networks in the late 1940s. In the 1950s struggling radio networks began to offer "co-op" ads for local sale within the programs. This was not effective in changing the course of events. Fewer and fewer radio network programs were sponsored—some were kept on the air on a sustaining basis, more were being dropped.

The increase in the number of stations added to the woes of local stations. The actual total radio advertising revenue was about the same each year from 1951 to 1956, yet the number of AM broadcasting stations had increased by nearly 50%. Radio sales were maintained as national spot and local advertising grew with more and more network money deserting radio for television. Radio revenue in 1954 failed to increase over the previous year—the first time since 1938. In 1956 networks accounted for about 10% of all radio revenues. Only six years before in 1950 about 60% of the network evening time was either sponsored by one or two firms per program. In 1956 three-fourths of the network programs were sustaining, participating or cooperative.

Not only was the type of sponsorship changing but so were the charges by the networks. NBC first proposed a rate decrease for radio affiliates in television markets, meeting heavy affiliate resistance. But in less than six months all four networks had chopped 10 to 15% off their rate cards. The next year the four networks dropped their rates another 25%. Trade magazines were full of plans to "save the radio networks." NBC revamped its radio schedule in the season of 1951–52, hoping to offset the impact of TV.

Another effort was made with NBC and WLW in Cincinnati experimenting in block programming. The station and network grouped show types, hoping to get viewers to abandon the tube at least a few nights each week to hear their favorite types of radio programs. The idea, which featured nights of mysteries and crime followed by nights of quiz shows, did not work. Several stations revived the notion of a quality radio group, which had been the start of Mutual in 1934, but this too, failed to head off the radio network toboggan slide.

The upheaval in radio in the 1950s left the sound medium stripped down for a new kind of commercial broadcasting. In the 1960s radio, depending on local programs sponsored by local and national spot advertising, began to show a steady increase. The typical AM station bounced off the ropes and was making about $10,000 on revenues of $125,000. A third of the AM stations were reporting losses. It was unusual for an FM station to report a profit in the 1960's.

Television was born amid dismal commercial predictions. *Life* magazine editors in 1939 predicted that TV could reach only six% of the land area of the United States with only seven stations able to broadcast in each city.[22] The magazine also said that the cost of $2,300 an hour exclusive of talent costs, 10 times that of radio, would be a dampening effect on television growth. Contrarily, the medium, after various struggles over color and assignment of frequencies, boomed into the mid-1950s. From 1953 to 1960, TV time sales increased about two-and one-half times. At every level of advertising—network, national spot and local—the growth was rapid; about twice that of radio.

Like radio, most early TV programs were sponsored by a single advertiser. As production costs rose and as 15- and 30-minute programs were replaced by longer formats, more and more shows were presented by alternating or dual sponsors. By the 1960s nearly all programs were sponsored by participating advertisers. Only a few companies purchased entire program series preferring to buy a huge volume of advertising on varied programs.

Increasingly in the 1960s television stations and sometimes the networks began selling eight, 20- and 30-second spots instead of full minutes—the "standard" commercial. In radio, especially, with the rise of "formula" the shorter spots were standard. In December 1970 the outlook for the TV networks was not good. After resisting growing advertisers and agency pressure for several years, CBS began "a two-for-one clearance sale that became a permanent part of the business." [23] In the last few days of broadcasting's 51st season the half-minute spot became the standard. Some advertisers purchased a one-minute spot with messages for several products—cutting the cost-per-thousand impressions. Networks, and some stations, charged premium rates for these "piggyback" commercials.

By 1970 46% of non-network national commercials were 30-second spots; that increased to 72% by March 1973.[24]

Broadcasting advertising still has its critics but nothing to compare with the magazine reviewer who wrote in 1927:

> This month's prize for the ugliest and most cacophonous coined name plastered on any troup of radio performers is hereby awarded by unanimous and enthusiastic vote to WOW's popular entertainers, the Yousem Tyrwelders Twins.[25]

```
I believe that the quickest way to kill broadcasting would
be to use it for direct advertising.  The reader of the
newspaper has an option whether he will read an ad or not,
but if a speech by the President is to be used as the meat
in a sandwich of two patent medicine advertisements there
will be no radio left.              --Herbert Hoover, 1924.
```

29

Joseph H. Jackson

SHOULD RADIO BE
USED FOR ADVERTISING?

NO ONE who reads this article will have to consider very long what broadcasting advertising implies, before the presence of the difficulty becomes apparent enough. The very thought of such a thing growing to be common practice is sufficient to give any true radio enthusiast the cold shakes. And he doesn't need to be a dyed-in-the-shellac radio man to see the point, either; the veriest tyro with his brand-new crystal set can realize, if he has listened in only once, what it would mean to have the air filled with advertising matter in and out of season; to have his ears bombarded with advertisers' eulogies every time he dons a pair of head phones.

Now suppose, for instance, that you are the maker of some household article used universally. There are a dozen others putting out the same kind of article; it is a home necessity—every family should have one. Competition is keen: you're anxious to get the name of your product before as many people as you can, as often as you may, and, naturally, as inexpensively as you are able to do it. It is budget time and you are face to face with the job of okaying next years' advertising appropriation. It looks like a pretty big chunk of money. You don't mind spending it—no-o-o, not exactly—but you sometimes wonder whether everybody who passes a billboard, picks up a newspaper, reads a magazine, or enters a store sees your dearly bought advertising and is influenced by it. You are wishing two things: that you could tell potential buyers what you have to tell them so you could be *sure* they heard you, and that you could tell them without spending quite so much in doing it.

Just as you are chewing over this thought and trying to resign yourself to the inevitable, along comes a man with a plan. He says to you:

"Suppose I guarantee to put over whatever advertising message you wish, to several hundred thousand people who have *got* to listen. All of them—since your product is a universal necessity—are potential customers. Suppose I promise to do this for you at a tiny fraction of the amount you pay for the usual advertising which may or may not be attracting attention. Suppose I tell you, in addition to this, that through my plan you can say ten times as much as you

Radio Broadcast, November 1922, pp. 72–76.

could through any other advertising medium with any hope of being listened to. Will you give me a hearing?"

Would you? And when you found that his plan was to utilize the practically national system of broadcasting radio messages; that he would syndicate your advertising so that it was distributed from coast to coast if you wished, or centralize it so that it was intensive in the localities where your distributing facilities were best equipped to handle massed sales: that he would guarantee you, in fact, what advertising salesmen call "one hundred per cent coverage" among a certain class of people who, *ipso facto,* have money to spend—*would you be interested?*

And if you didn't care in the least about radio and its future but were only concerned with putting over your advertising with the least possible cost and to the greatest possible advantage, *would you agree to use his methods?*

Supposing—just supposing—you are sitting down, head phones clamped to your ears, or loud-speaker distorting a trifle less than usual, enjoying a really excellent radio concert. A famous soprano has just sung your favorite song, and you're drawing a deep breath; sorry that it's over. Your thoughts, carried back to some pleasant memory by the magic of the radio, are still full of the melody. You are feeling sort of soothed and good-natured and at peace with the world. All of a sudden a gruff voice or a whining voice or a nasal voice or some other kind of voice says "Good Morning! Have you used Hare's Soap?" Or maybe a sweet, girlish baritone implores you "Ask for Never-Hole Sox. There's a Reason. You just *know* she wears 'em."

Well, how about it? Do you like the idea? Can you picture to yourself the horror of sitting down to listen to a good song or two, or perhaps a newsy chat on the events of the day, and then being forced to listen to a broadcasting programme that is nine tenths advertising matter?

There is one factor which may appear at first blush to lighten the situation; that is the attitude held at present toward such means of advertising by recognized, reputable advertising agencies and by men who govern the advertising policies of the larger manufacturers. *Most of these are openly arrayed against the exploitation of radio for advertising purposes.* Sensing the situation broadly, they realize what a drag upon the science its use for purposes of this kind would prove. But the danger is not from reliable firms and individuals, so that the disapproval of these folk, pleasant though it may be for us to know their attitude, does not help matters much. It is the irresponsibles who are to be feared. Fly-by-nights, plenty of them, unburdened by any sense of what is fair and right, are always ready and waiting to put public enthusiasm to work for them. The woods are full of opportunists who are restrained by no scruples when the scent of profit comes down the wind.

30

J. H. Morecroft

WHO WILL PAY FOR
THE CAMPAIGN BROADCASTING?

THE BELL Company's intention gradually to build up a group of high-class broadcasting stations, all modulated from one microphone when the occasion warrants, is gradually being worked out. On special occasions, large parts of the company's country-wide network of wires has been tied up for broadcasting control, but the arrangement has been temporary only. The connection between WEAF and WCAP is of course a practically permanent installation, and now we hear that six stations, WEAF, WCAP, WJAR, WGR, WCAE, and WGN, are to be tied together in a semi-permanent network. It may be only a matter of a year or so before this company will have available a nationwide service for those who have something worthwhile saying, and money enough to rent the broadcasting system.

A very large investment is tied up in such a wire and broadcasting chain. The stockholders have a right to a reasonable return on their money on this investment. Therefore the question of cost of broadcasting must necessarily be met in some fashion by those using it. How are the political campaigns to be carried on by radio? These radio campaigns sound logical and reasonable in so far as conserving the candidates' strength is concerned, but who is going to foot the bill? Someone is going to find out that it costs money, a lot of it, for the privilege of addressing a million or more listeners. The telephone company cannot afford to give the service for less than cost, and the cost will be pretty high, if the present ambitious plans of some campaigners are carried out.

One thing is sure; when a campaign manager has paid $10,000 or more for the use of the radio channel for an hour he is going to be careful who uses up his time—the days of the cheap ranter and phrase maker are over. For such a costly channel the manager will

Radio Broadcast, October 1924, pp. 470–1.

have to select men with brains who can present their arguments clearly and forcefully. Radio will probably do much good in improving the quality of pre-election oratory, and so give the people a better understanding of what the political issues really are.

31

WHO IS TO PAY
FOR BROADCASTING AND HOW?

A Contest Opened by RADIO BROADCAST
in which a prize of $500 is offered

WHAT WE WANT

A WORKABLE plan which shall take into account the problems in present radio broadcasting and propose a practical solution. How, for example, are the restrictions now imposed by the music copyright law to be adjusted to the peculiar conditions of broadcasting? How is the complex radio patent situation to be unsnarled so that broadcasting may develop? Should broadcasting stations be allowed to advertise?

These are some of the questions involved and subjects which must receive careful attention in an intelligent answer to the problem which is the title of this contest.

HOW IT IS TO BE DONE

The plan must not be more than 1500 words long. It must be double-spaced and typewritten, and must be prefaced with a concise summary. The plan must be in the mails not later than July 20, 1924, and must be addressed, RADIO BROADCAST Who Is to Pay Contest, care American Radio Association, 50 Union Square, New York City.

The contest is open absolutely to everyone, except employees of RADIO BROADCAST and officials of the American Radio Association. A contestant may submit more than one plan. If the winning plan is received from two different sources, the judges will award the prize to the contestant whose plan was mailed first.

Radio Broadcast, May, 1924, advertisement.

32

H. D. Kellogg, Jr.

WHO IS TO PAY·
FOR BROADCASTING—AND HOW

THE PLAN Which Won *Radio Broadcast*'s Prize of $500 Offered for
the Most Practicable and Workable Solution of a Difficult Problem
Radio broadcasting, to be placed on a sound economic basis, must
pay its way as do other forms of entertainment. It should be paid
because of, and in proportion to, the value of the entertainment provided. And the payment should be made by the consumer, that is,
the owner of the receiving set.

Under present conditions, what is entertainment for the radio
fan is a subtle source of advertising, in the great majority of cases, for
the broadcasting station. And advertising foots the bill. This inconsis-
tency between the purpose of the broadcaster and the radio listener,
and the differential between the source of payment and the actual
consumer, has led to recognition of the fact that the economic foundation for broadcasting must be rearranged.

While it is apparent that a certain proportion of the expense of
present-day broadcasting can continue to be borne by appropriations
for the advertising received, and that artists who wish to receive the
advertising that their performances bring them will perform free, still
the highest type of broadcasting cannot be financed indefinitely on
this basis. To secure the utmost excellence in talent, talent which
needs no advertising, the performers or artists must be paid. And further to insure that program directors shall secure the best entertainment possible, untrammeled by any commercialism or advertising
for the broadcasting station, the operating expense of the station
should be paid directly by the radio audience.

A Yearly Charge—to the Receiver

A charge, then, must be collected from each owner of a radio set,
on a yearly basis, sufficient to pay the annual expense of the broadcasting received. The fair and equitable way to apportion the sum
each owner shall pay is on the basis of the value and range of his set
and the amount it is used. We would not expect the owner of a crystal set with its limited range and sensitivity to pay as much to the
broadcasting fund as the owner of a many tube super-heterodyne.

The amount paid by the radio owner should be compulsory—in

Radio Broadcast, March 1925, pp. 863–866.

other words, it should be equivalent of a box office charge. No theatre could support the cost of regular performances open to the public in a sound and business-like way through voluntary contributions. A fixed and definite amount must be collected from each individual in the audience before entering the theatre. And likewise the owner of a radio receiving set, with his power to tap in on many sources of entertainment, should be made to pay his share of the entertainment received, commensurate with the range of his set and the amount it is used.

Probably the best index of the range and cost of a set lies in the kind and number of its tubes. In a crystal set it is difficult to pick out any one satisfactory index of its value or use. The crystal should no doubt be taken as the index here. A charge, then, on the tubes or crystals purchased, and included in the purchase price paid by the owner of the receiving set, is the method here suggested for meeting the cost of broadcasting.

The Government Should Administer the Fund

The most practicable administrator of the broadcasting levy outlined is obviously the Federal Government. It is inconceivable to require manufacturers and producers of tubes and crystals to collect a stamp tax and turn it into a pool or fund held as a monopoly for and by private interests. The problem is clearly national in scope. It is outside the control of individual states and if run by private interests would require the granting of dangerous monopolistic power. The work of administering a national broadcasting service is not particularly susceptible to political corruption. With full publicity of all accounts, mishandling of the funds in trust would certainly be difficult. And the public would be a daily judge of the quality of entertainment provided. The tremendous value to the Government of having broadcasting stations continuously under its control in times of emergency, or even in ordinary times, to crystallize and direct public opinion and thought, cannot be overemphasized.

Broadcasting under this plan would then be conducted from twenty-five or fifty high power stations throughout the country. How these may be financed can be indicated by a brief illustration. Tubes and crystals should be rated according to their quality, durability and service. A stamp purchased from the Government Division of Broadcasting should be affixed by the manufacturer to the article or its container. The amount of the stamp should be set, in accordance with statistics compiled, such that each tube will bear $2 of the broadcasting budget for the year. Similarly, the tax on each crystal sold may be apportioned so that each crystal will bear 50 cents of the broadcasting budget for the year. If we assume 4,000,000 tube sets with an average of two tubes each and 6,000,000 crystal sets in operation, the

returns from taxes set at this rate would be $19,000,000. Taking
$1,000,000 as the cost of collection, $18,000,000 would remain to be
distributed among some twenty-five or fifty stations, allowing each
$720,000 or $450,000 respectively, per year.

Is This the Solution?

The officials of the American Radio Association, under whose
auspices the contest was conducted, do not feel that this plan is the
final word in the matter of "who is to pay?" and neither do the editors of this magazine. The broadcasting problem cannot be settled as
easily as this plan proposes, although without doubt there is much to
be said for Mr. Kellogg's plan. One of the chief stumbling blocks is
the setting up of a federal bureau of broadcasting which seems to be
contrary to the entire trend of radio development. We believe that
anything which smacks of too centralized federal control or censorship would be resisted as much by the public as by all those administering radio to-day.   —The Editor

33

Hiram L. Jome

BROADCASTING AND ITS PROBLEMS

THOUGH TELEGRAPHIC broadcasting has been in use for more than a
score of years for sending such things as time and weather signals,
news items, and orders to ships at sea, only recently has the public
interest been aroused.

Individuals have established stations because the fever was in
the air. Radio manufacturers and dealers, department stores, hardware stores, newspapers, state experiment stations, universities and
colleges, churches, secondary schools, various associations—these
are some of the group which have entered this fascinating and mysterious field. Some have entered it to promote good-will, some to facilitate the sale of radio, still others for many various purposes. But a

Economics of the Radio Industry Chicago: A. W. Shaw Company, 1925, pp. 165–183.
This book was accepted as Mr. Jome's Ph.D. dissertation, University of Wisconsin,
1925. It was probably the earliest doctoral dissertation on the subject of broadcasting.
Parts of this chapter also were published as "Public Policy Towards Radio Broadcasting," *Journal of Land & Public Utility Economics*, April 1925.

large number have begun the broadcasting game for no ulterior motive at all. They have gone into it merely to satisfy their desire for a hobby, or because they wanted to learn the tricks of the new game, or as a method of giving vent to their pent-up enthusiasm and restlessness—the desire to reach out into space and explore the unknown.

On this point the replies received in response to the writer's questionnaire to broadcasters throughout the United States are suggestive. The results are given in Table 14. If this is a fair sample, most broadcasting stations were established for some private end and only incidentally to serve the public generally.

TABLE 14
PURPOSES OF BROADCASTERS

Purpose	Total	Number of Stations Reporting as the Only Purpose	Number of Stations Reporting as One of Two or More Purposes
To help maintain sale of receiving sets	31	2	29
To profit from advertising received and good-will developed	44	8	36
To profit by direct sale of advertising time	2	0	2
To serve public generally	146	46	100
To serve some special group or clientele	26	6	20
Research purposes	13	4	9
Police Information	8	2	6
University extension work	1	1	0

Table 15, prepared from answers to the questionnaire, indicates the relative importance of capital outlays among 106 stations.

It will be noted that 51 stations, or almost one-half, indicated a cost of $3,000 or less. These are almost entirely the stations of colleges and churches. Eight stations, or almost 8%, reported an initial expense of more than $50,000. These are, as a rule, constructed by large manufacturers or dealers in radio apparatus. Fifteen reported an original outlay of more than $25,000, while one dual station revealed an expense of $400,000.

Variations in the cost of installation are due primarily to the fact that some stations are built without the purchase of Western Electric sets; in colleges the parts are constructed in the physics department;

construction costs of buildings are not included in the case of stations housed in sheds or attics; and there is also the difference in the power and elaborateness of the machinery installed.

TABLE 15
EXPENSE OF INSTALLING
BROADCASTING STATIONS

Expenses of installing, in dollars	Number	Percentage
0– 1,000 Inc.	12	11.3%
1,001– 2,000	20	18.9
2,001– 3,000	19	17.9
3,001– 5,000	14	13.2
5,001– 10,000	11	10.4
10,001– 25,000	15	14.2
25,001– 50,000	7	6.6
50,001– 75,000	3	2.8
75,001–100,000	2	1.9
100,001–above	3	2.8

The cost of operation, is given in Table 16.

TABLE 16
ANNUAL OPERATING EXPENSES OF
BROADCASTING STATIONS

Operating expenses, in dollars	Number	Percentage
1,000–or under	39	42.4%
1,001– 2,000	11	12.0
2,001– 3,000	9	9.8
3,001– 5,000	8	8.7
5,001– 10,000	9	9.8
10,001– 25,000	7	7.7
25,001– 50,000	3	3.2
50,001– 75,000	2	2.1
75,001–100,000	1	1.1
1000,001–above	3	3.2

Among the reasons for the variations in the annual operating costs of the different stations may be mentioned:

1. Many stations, such as schools, churches, and hobby stations, operate only part time at irregular intervals, and the work is done by non-paid persons.

2. Only a few of the broadcasters are making any payment for the services of the artists and performers. Home talent is used, but the demand for compensation is increasing. A few pay regularly, others only occasionally.

3. Some must pay copyright royalty fees, usually $500 a year,

while colleges pay only a nominal fee of $1. Others are paying no fee at all.

Broadcasters of the type being considered have little or no direct income. Several stations are supported by interested business men or clubs. Church stations continually receive donations from the members of the congregation. Students and alumni help support their college broadcaster. Such contributions can, however, be considered as payments by the owners, be they congregations, student bodies, or business clubs. Though a small number of broadcasters indicated that occasionally they received a check from a far-off "listener in," only 3 out of 110 reporting stations stated that they received more or less regular contributions from their radio audiences. This business aspect of broadcasting is not often remembered by radio "fans." Up to a recent date, the American Telephone and Telegraph Company station was the only one which charged for advertising. For example, its station will permit any concern to broadcast a program and announce its name and position in connection with the rendition. For such advertising WEAF charges $10 a minute or $400 an hour. But even the American Telephone and Telegraph Company has stated that its broadcasting is unprofitable, "receiving a revenue of less than half the operating expenses" in 1923.[1]

The ordinary broadcaster has, then, no source of direct income. He relies on the indirect benefits, such as the building up of goodwill. But these indirect receipts are very uncertain. In his questionnaire the writer asked the broadcasters whether the average number of applause cards received after each program was considered satisfactory. Of the broadcasters replying, 36% answered in the negative. A considerable number of those added the comment that the response from their audiences is "not what it used to be." Only about one-fifth of the stations reported difficulty in obtaining talent, but of this small number three said the complaint was "lack of appreciation." The point is this: If a large percentage of the audience are not interested and appreciative of the programs rendered for them free of charge, there seems to be a good reason to believe that the indirect gain through the advertising and publicity may not be very great. With large sums of money going out, and uncertain and unmeasurable indirect benefits coming in, many stations are asking themselves the question: "Does it really pay?"

"Last winter," writes the proprietor of a middle-western 500-watt station, "our talent cost us $700 per month, besides $200 for an operator and many other expenses too numerous to mention. We have put about $50,000 of our money into radio during the past 12 months and we have never received back one dollar in cash returns. We no doubt have lots of good-will and are nationally advertised, but we cannot cash in on our advertising. Furthermore, we cannot see our way clear to withdraw; we have too big an investment to throw it away; yet, every day we stay with it, we put in more money without hope of cash return." [2]

The Sweeney Automotive and Electrical School, of Kansas City, Missouri (WHB), has adopted a very unique scheme, called the "Invisible Theater." The general plan is the sale of tickets of various classes—box seats, $10 per year; main floor, $3; loges, $5; circle seats, $2; second balcony, $1. The purchase of one of these entitles the holder to hear any programs which may be broadcast, besides receiving a monthly program and a year's subscription for the *Microphone*, the official paper of the Invisible Theater. In view of the voluntary nature of such contributions, the plan has so far been fairly successful.

A plan that is used extensively in foreign nations is the levying of a direct tax on the owners of receiving sets and the distribution of a large part of the receipts to the broadcasting stations according to some logical and equitable system.

34

Austin C. Lescarboura

HOW MUCH IT COSTS TO BROADCAST

RISING COSTS and strenuous competition have been responsible for the advent of commercialism in broadcasting. It costs plenty of money to keep the air filled with programs, especially on a daily basis. Figures? Well, there is a leading broadcasting station covering a large section of the country, which operates at a *monthly* cost of close to $30,000 including the bills of the musicians, staff, electric service and plant. Multiply that by twelve and you have $360,000 for the year! A department store, operating a powerful broadcasting station, estimates its *yearly* operating costs at close to $60,000. Even the modest broadcasting station, of limited power and mediocre programs, must cost upward of $25,000 a year. And then there is the heavy investment for the equipment which may run anywhere from $10,000 to a $1,000,000 or more for the latest high-power stations, at a rate of obsolescence which is positively appalling.

Radio Broadcast, September 1926, pp. 367–371.

Little wonder, therefore, that broadcasters, realizing the futility of collecting funds from the radio audience, despite several pleas at spasmodic intervals in the past, have sought to solve their economic problem by collecting at the microphone end. At first it was the general belief that the operating expenses of broadcasting stations could be derived from the sale of radio equipment, but unfortunately, no manufacturer and not even a group of manufacturers could afford to broadcast throughout the entire country day in and day out in return for the sale of radio receivers and radio accessories. Existing receivers, some of them several years old, have long since received their quota of broadcasting many times over. The situation is quite like that which would result if automobile manufacturers sold their cars at the usual prices, and then offered to build more and more roads and maintain them in the best condition as a perpetual obligation to the purchasers. But automobile manufacturers make no promises regarding roads and do not support the cost of the roads. Others pay for the roads. And so with broadcasting; others pay for the programs, so that the public may ride the air waves.

How Much Does It Cost?

But how about the dollars and cents involved? It is a matter of interest to note what the sponsors pay for broadcasting our musical programs.

The rates charged vary largely, depending on the power of the station, the importance of the area, the time of day, the day of the week, whether it is a single feature or a regular series, whether it is good music or simply talk, and so on. Let us not forget to mention, once more, that many leading stations do not charge for the allotted time, but insist on the best musical programs sponsored by others. At present we are dealing with the toll charges for the allotted time, with whatever charges there may be for the musicians.

New York rates lead the rest. It costs $600 per hour to broadcast a sponsored program from one of the leading stations in that city or $375 for half an hour, during the late afternoon and evening, which constitute the best part of the day so far as the largest and most attentive audience is concerned. The morning charges are $300 for an hour, $117 for half an hour. A ten-minute talk costs $130.

Chicago follows close on the heels of New York, with $350.00 for an hour and $218.75 for half an hour with a wire connection from the New York studio. Most of the other large cities command $200 or $250 for an hour and $125 or so for half an hour. The smaller cities drop down to $150 for an hour and $93.75 for half an hour. All these rates are based on chain broadcasting, operating from the New York studio. The rates of the individual stations, broadcasting from their own studios are considerably less. Take, for instance, a Buffalo station, whose chain rate is $200.00 for an hour and $125.00 for half an hour. The individual rate becomes $120 per hour and $60 per half hour, thus indicating the additional expenses involved in the chain operation. On the other hand, some stations charge the same rate whether engaged in chain work or individually. All these rates are, of course, exclusive of talent.

Getting down to some of the smaller stations of modest power, it is interesting to note that the prices are as low as $12.50 per hour. In fact, the rate cards—yes, they have rate cards, just like publications!—disclose an interesting analysis of the relative importance of the radio audience from early morning till late night, with corresponding charges. Thus, in the case of a Western broadcaster, his rates are: from 9–12 in the morning, $12.50 per hour; 12–3 P.M., $16.00; 3–6 $18.00; 6–8 $30.00; 8–11 (the cream of the program) $36.00; 11–12 M. $28.00.

Most broadcasters undertake to furnish the musical talent at what is purported to be cost. One broadcaster, for instance, on his very explicit rate card, charges $250.00 per hour from 6–8 P.M.; $400.00 per hour from 8–11; and $200.00 from 11 to 1 A.M. including the music. The choice of the following is offered:

1. Classical or semi-classical musical programs by string quintette. 2. Popular or semi-classical program by 4-piece concert orchestra and 2 singers. 3. Musical program by male quartette and pianist. 4. Musical program by quartette and solo numbers by mixed quartette and pianist. 5. Dance program by 6-piece jazz orchestra. Remote programs cost $35.00 more for the first hour.

As a general thing, the day rate runs about 40 per cent less than that of the evening.

All in all, the business end of radio publicity seems very well organized, following closely that of the periodicals in soliciting advertising. We have seen elaborate charts prepared by broadcasters, indicating just what territories are covered by strong, reliable signals, secondary territories covered by fair signals most of the time, and tertiary territories covered under the best possible conditions.

Paid broadcasting is here to stay, if we read all signs correctly. It is the logical way to pay for broadcasting under our present system. For the most part the public seems well satisfied to accept sponsored programs and to reciprocate by extending its good will to those who make possible the wonderful programs of to-day.

35

Orrin E. Dunlap, Jr.

WHO PAYS THE BROADCASTER?

MILLIONS OF DOLLARS are invested today in broadcasting stations in the United States.

Millions more are being spent yearly on programs broadcast from these stations.

Most of this vast sum is paid for the maintenance of the 500 or more broadcast stations that are supported for the purpose of creating good will on the part of the radio audience toward the concerns that pay the bills.

These concerns are paying the bills because they believe that they are thus building up what the psychologists tell us is "a subconscious buying attitude" toward the products, or toward the merchandise, or toward the professional or other services, or whatever it is that these broadcasters have to sell.

Many of the broadcasting stations (the number of which at the present time is probably over 100) are becoming frankly "toll stations." They are renting out time on a rate-basis that each station determines separately on the basis of the area that it covers, and its influence as gauged by its estimated audience, and other factors.

The year 1927 is destined to see a rapid growth in the number of these "toll" stations.

At present most of the program features of outstanding merit and popularity are supported by business concerns that not only pay the toll station charges, but the fees of the artists as well—to say nothing of the innumerable incidental expenses incurred.

From these large expenditures the radio audience benefits. It will continue to benefit as long as these programs are continued.

But the programs will be continued only as long as those who pay the bills have reason to believe that the large amount thus invested brings back returns from the radio audience.   —Editor

IT HAS BEEN found that different types of programs are more suited to be associated with certain products. The name "Happiness Boys" is synonymous to the name of the product they promote, as were Goldy and Dusty closely related to their cleanser. In the Eskimo Ensemble which entertains on Thursday nights with bright and sparkling music, the banjo is made to predominate because it creates

Popular Radio, Vol. XI, No. 1 (January 1927), pp. 11–15, p. 94.

a suggestion of the sparkling of the ginger ale which the particular troupe of Arctic residents represent.

What does a moving picture theatre gain from broadcasting? The Hertzian waves are employed to popularize the name of the show house and during the entertainment the theatrical program of the week is mentioned so that the public will be aware of the performance and who is acting on the screen.

But what does all this cost?

The cost of the programs aside from the station toll charges are matters of conjecture; information concerning the prices paid for broadcast artists varies greatly, and is generally regarded as confidential.

Perhaps the most costly programs are those of the Atwater Kent Hour, the A and P Gypsies, the Balkite Hour and the Eveready Hour which have been estimated as high as $500,000 a year, including the toll charges.

The total cost of the Eskimos, engaged for the Cliquot Club Company's program, is $202,800 a year; the performers probably cost about $400 an hour. Orchestras such as the Silvertown, which is sponsored by The Goodrich Tire Company and the Ipana Troubadours, sponsored by Bristol-Myers Company, manufacturing chemists, probably cost from $400 to $500 an hour. The popular Goldy and Dusty during their period of contract, are said to have cost the Gold Dust Corporation about $250 an hour. The Royal Orchestra, supported by the Royal Typewriter Company, must cost from $500 to $650 an hour. No figures have been given out about the costs of broadcasting the special concerts of New York Symphony Orchestra, but each appearance at the studio probably costs Fansteel Products, Inc., which maintains the Balkite Hour, from $3,000 to $4,000. The nine concerts of the Cleveland Symphony Orchestra sponsored by the Sandusky Cement Co., cost that company about $2,500 each. The Bristol-Myer program for some months cost at the rate of a total of $107,000 a year. The Happiness Boys are said to cost the Happiness Candy Stores, Inc. about $400 for each weekly appearance. Artists such as McCormack and Galli-Curci, who have appeared on programs sponsored by the Victor Talking Machine Company, would ordinarily charge about $5,000 for an appearance, although, because of their connection with the Victor Company, it is probable that they charged little or nothing, taking their remuneration in the form of commissions on the stimulated sales of their gramophone records. On occasions well known artists, such as appear on the Eveready and Atwater Kent Hours, for example, get fees ranging from $1,000 to $2,500 for an appearance before the microphone.

The Eveready Hour (which is said to be the oldest regular broadcast feature in the field, dating from December, 1923) costs the

National Carbon Company an average of from $5,000 to $6,000 a week; this sum includes the toll charges as well as the costs of employing regularly a sixteen-piece orchestra, six singers and occasional great artists.

It may be parenthetically observed that the value to the artists of a broadcast appearance is becoming an important factor in the economic scheme of the radio industry. The Happiness Boys, for example, are receiving $2,500 a week for their appearance in vaudeville—a value that has been created entirely by their popularity with the radio audience. And the Goodrich Silvertown orchestra unit, including the Silver Masked Tenor, is getting $3,000 a week on the Keith-Albee vaudeville circuit. These artists established their professional value through their appearances before the microphone. It is this creation of values that must be taken into account by the artists when they contract for appearance in the broadcast studio.

36

John W. Spalding

1928: RADIO BECOMES A MASS ADVERTISING MEDIUM

To serve its sponsors effectively as an advertising medium, radio had to satisfy at least four requirements. First, the technical facilities for broadcasting and for receiving broadcasts had to be of a quality that would transmit station signals dependably and would reproduce the signals in the home with reasonable fidelity. Second, an audience of considerable size was needed, an audience in the habit of listening to the radio. Third, acceptance of the advertiser as a partner in the production of radio programs was required of the operators of broadcasting stations. And finally, the radio industry had to devise vehicles for advertising by building program formats suitable for sponsorship. While the satisfaction of these four requirements did not occur at any one instant in the latter part of 1928 (nor can it be said that that year alone saw the satisfaction of all of the requirements), 1928 was the year in which the radio industry had solved enough of its problems of equipment, audiences, sponsorship, and

Journal of Broadcasting, Vol. VIII, No. 1 (Winter 1963–1964), pp. 31–44.

programming to enable an historian of broadcasting to identify that year as the one in which radio assumed the characteristics of the communications and advertising medium that it was to be until television became fully established.

Necessary Conditions

If a mass communications system is one which makes possible "the approximately simultaneous delivery of identical messages through mechanisms of high speed reproduction and distribution to relatively large and undifferentiated numbers of people," [3] then it was not until permanent networks facilitated simultaneous broadcasting across the country that radio achieved the status of a communication system worthy of consideration for the mass distribution of advertising messages. This occurred toward the end of 1928. Networking of radio stations had begun in 1924 with broadcasts of the *Eveready Hour,* sponsored by the National Carbon Company, over the stations interconnected with WEAF by the Long Lines Department of the American Telephone and Telegraph Company.[4] But the Telephone Company network of 1924–1926 was not entirely satisfactory. At best it covered only 16 cities in the northeastern quarter of the United States, and its circuits were not always up to broadcast standards.[5]

A step toward more satisfactory network operation was made in 1926, when the Radio Corporation of America abandoned the concept of the "super power station" implicit in its own WJZ and "endorsed the network concept" by purchasing WEAF from the Telephone Company.[6] A subsidiary, the National Broadcasting Company, was established to unify all RCA broadcast activities, permanent connecting wires were leased from AT&T as rapidly as they could be installed, and the new organization set about building a more substantial network than the one it had replaced. By the summer of 1927, at the end of six months of operation, NBC had in the East a "Red" chain of fifteen stations including WEAF, a "Blue" chain of ten stations including WJZ, and an additional group of eight stations which were affiliated with both chains. In the West, it had a "Pacific" or "Orange" chain of seven stations. Compared to the sixteen stations of the old AT&T network, the NBC total of forty stations could offer far greater coverage to the program sponsor. Moreover, in October 1927, the company was able to centralize its production activities in a new building at 711 Fifth Avenue in New York City, that gave it, for the first time, suitable studio facilities for large-scale broadcasting.[7]

Unfortunately, as late as 1928, some of the lines used to serve NBC were still temporary and not suitable for carrying music. There was no such thing as a weekly "coast-to-coast" program available to sponsors before September, 1928, and even then the connection from Denver to Salt Lake City was nothing more than a temporary one made by placing a long distance telephone call. Eleven sponsors reached the West Coast by means of this expedient during the next few months. Then, a few days before Christmas, AT&T engineers completed the last link in the cross-continent radio lines, and for the first time a truly national network was made possible. The *New York Times* reported that NBC, now grown to a total of fifty-eight affiliates connected by "permanent, specially engineered lines," theoretically could put a sponsor's program into 82.7% of the receiving sets in the United States. On Christmas Eve, 1928, the *General Motors Party* inaugurated "the twenty-four hour, coast-to-coast circuit of the National Broadcasting Company . . . regarded by engineers as an achievement of first magnitude." [8]

Network facilities making possible the distribution of programs to all parts of the nation would not have been sufficient to attract sponsors to radio, however, unless at the terminals of the network wires there were transmitting stations capable of putting out a broadcast signal on a regular basis with a minimum of interference. Prior to 1926, these conditions did not obtain; the consuming task at local stations was not the development of programming, but the problem of "keeping the station on the air." [9] After 1926, station transmitters were fairly dependable, but station schedules remained irregular because of the necessity in many cases of sharing wave lengths. Station WMAQ, Chicago, for instance, interrupted its broadcasting four times each day to give other stations air time as late as September, 1928. In fact, the hours of operation among Chicago stations were such that in order to reach that city with the programs of one network, the Columbia Broadcasting System had to sign affiliation contracts with three stations, and in order to reach it with two networks, NBC needed five stations. Furthermore, all local stations observed a "night of silence" on Monday to enable Chicago listeners to tune-in distant signals. [10] Thus, during the 1927–28 season, the advertiser could not have the broadcaster's assurance of a full, daily, stable program schedule.

It was the activity of the Federal Radio Commission in 1927 and 1928 that soon made it possible for broadcasters to give that assurance. In its first year, the FRC established a standard broadcast band, eliminated a few sub-standard and mobile stations, and severely restricted the number of stations authorized to operate at night. [11] In the second year it made even more substantial progress toward its goal of an interference-free national radio service. Radio stations were classified according to the size of the locality they were to serve, definite hours of operation were established, and nearly every station in the country had its assigned wave length altered in an attempt to reach the greatest number of people with radio signals.[12] These changes were effected on November 11, 1928, although Commissioner Orestes Caldwell warned that "on the first few nights there are bound to be 'strays', and heterodynes and crosstalk, as stations settle themselves into their new positions." [13] The arrangement apparently displeased some radio fans still prone to sit up late at night listening for a distant station, but the pattern of local service established across the country was soon reported to be satisfactory to most people.[14]

Just as problems of networking and transmitting signals tended to be solved by the end of 1928, so developments in receivers tended by that date to have reached a point at which the quality of the sound available to the listener might encourage an advertiser to take up radio program sponsorship. Loud speakers were available as early as 1922, but they were crude devices given to distorting sounds. Besides, they placed a drain on the batteries which still powered all receivers. The usual practice was to connect the set to earphones and, as Gleason Archer remarked in his history of radio, wearing earphones was "hardly a pleasant way to spend an evening." [15]

The "super-heterodyne" receiver of 1924 was powerful enough to put a relatively undistorted signal into a loud speaker, but the problem of the drain on the batteries was only aggravated.[16] Eventually, it became possible to attach the receiver to ordinary household electric current, and by 1928 sets using this source of power were giving reliable performance:

> A year ago receiving sets reached what was termed the electrical era. The circuits and vacuum tubes were designed to operate in direct connection with the lightsocket, dispensing with all batteries. Millions of electric sets have been sold. The manufacturers in many cases overlooked precautions to offset the danger of current fluctuations. The result has been premature burning out of tubes and grid resistances. So much trouble was experienced with some of the sets that they were withdrawn from the market and improved models substituted. A year has, therefore, taught radio designers valuable lessons based on practical experience. They contend that the 1928–29 receivers are designed so that no further trouble need be feared.[17]

Not only were radio sets greatly improved, their prices were lower than those of the earlier battery sets. The 1924 table model RCA "Radiola" had cost $245 without batteries or loud speaker.[18] The "Radiola" of 1928 could be purchased for $184.50 including the speaker, while Atwater Kent made a radio for as low as $77 and Freshman one for only $69.[19] Given the quality of reception available at lower prices, David Sarnoff concluded that:

> . . . radio now takes the easy chair at the fireside of the American home. The electrically operated set that feeds off light current is no

longer an experiment. It is a fact. Full volume reception is no longer a hope. It is an accomplishment. True tonal value has ceased to be a serious acoustical problem in the modern receiving set.[20]

The public had in its hands something that was no longer a novelty; radio was an instrument capable of satisfactory reproduction of sounds that could entertain and inform, if people would only listen.[21]

The Audience

The radio audience grew steadily during the 1920s, and as it grew, the broadcasters came to have a more sophisticated understanding of the conditions under which radio listening occurred. In 1922, a radio could be found in only 60,000 of the 26 million homes in the United States (i.e., in less than one home out of every four hundred), and the total audience was estimated at only seventy-five thousand persons.[22] By 1926, there were twenty million listeners in five million homes,[23] but the popular announcer Graham McNamee still had only a vague knowledge of his audience:

I am heard by millions of people from three to 3,000 miles away. I know you are sitting in little farm houses or city apartments with head phones over your ears, standing by loud speakers in the city, or massed in great concert halls, all listening to what we say in quiet syllables just as if we were talking to our wives. Yet we never see the vast audience, your massed faces, and you never see ours. We are voices out of the night.[24]

From such information as was available to them, the best that broadcasters could conclude about their audiences was that they were "folks who like what they are getting." [25]

During the 1928–1929 season, more precise information began to replace romantic conjecture. Professor Daniel Starch of the Massachusetts Institute of Technology was commissioned by NBC to undertake a survey of the audience. He conducted personal interviews east of the Rocky Mountains with "thousands . . . believed to be a representative cross-section of the country," and gathered information on radio ownership from the sales figures of radio set manufacturers. Starch reported that as of January 1, 1929, there were 11,032,855 receivers in 9,640,348 homes. This meant that one-third of the nearly thirty million homes in the United States were available to radio programming. Approximately 67% of the receivers then in use contained the five or six tubes necessary to put a satisfactory signal into a loud speaker, while an additional 8% were even more powerful. Some 20% contained less than five tubes, may or may not have been battery operated, and may or may not have been connected to earphones. Only 3% of the radios were crystal sets. The total number of people in the audience available to radio was

41,453,469. Daily radio listening was the habit of 80% of these people, the heaviest concentration of listeners occurring between the hours of 8:00 and 10:00 P.M. There was some evidence that loyalty to particular stations had replaced the novelty of listening to distant signals; three-quarters of the interviewees reported that they listened "regularly" to one or two local stations. Finally, Starch was able to make a few generalizations regarding program likes and dislikes. Rural areas tended to prefer religious services, crop and market reports, and children's programs more than other types, while metropolitan tastes ran to semiclassical and classical music and to broadcasts of grand opera.[26]

Rudimentary though they may have been compared to audience surveys that were to come, the findings of the Starch survey provided the kind of information regarding the radio audience broadcasters needed if advertisers were to be induced to buy time and programs. Advertisers are impressed by the wide circulation of a medium; radio could point to a sizeable audience at the end of 1928, and it could offer a limited knowledge of popular listening hours, tastes in programs, and conditions of reception.

Commercial Sponsorship

There remained a question of the acceptability of commercial sponsorship by the broadcasters themselves. In its first years, radio was distinctly not available for exploitation by advertisers. If the stations established in Chicago between 1920 and 1922 may be taken as an example, early radio programming was intended to reflect credit on station owners, to facilitate technical experimentation, to distribute information to farmers, to relay messages for the police, to promulgate the religious beliefs of the station owner, or simply to enable the owner to enjoy a hobby.[27] Radio seemed to have all purposes except the sale of time to advertisers. But as the opening announcement on the first broadcast of the *Eveready Hour* had noted, radio could grow as an integral part of daily life only as the quality of the programs improved.[28] Accordingly, some broader base of financial support for programming than the pocketbook of the station owner had to be found. David Sarnoff, general manager of RCA, suggested an endowment plan; Martin Rice of General Electric proposed that a tax be collected on receiving sets; and Secretary of Commerce Hoover wanted the radio manufacturing industry to subsidize programming.[29] In the end, however, it was an experiment by AT&T that showed the broadcasters of the United States where they might find an income.

In February, 1922, AT&T announced that radio, like the telephone, should be available to anyone willing to pay the cost of transmitting a message. As an experiment in "toll" broadcasting, the company would soon open "the first radio station for telephone broadcasting which will . . . handle the distribution of news, music, and other programs on a commercial basis for such people as contract for this service." [30] *Printer's Ink* immediately warned that commercial radio would "prove positively offensive to great numbers of people; . . . the family circle is not a public place." [31] Nevertheless, AT&T went ahead with its plans. On August 28, 1922, the Queensborough Corporation, a real estate firm, began the first of a series of announcements to the radio public over the Telephone Company station, WEAF. Six months later, at the end of February, 1923, WEAF had fourteen sponsors of talk or music programs. The station severely limited them to "indirect" advertising; they could not offer samples, quote prices, or even describe the color and shape of their products. For the most part, they were limited to whatever goodwill and sponsor identification they could secure from naming their "gift of entertainment" after themselves.[32]

As this experiment continued at WEAF, a debate on the wisdom of permitting advertising took shape. From the mild warning that the public would "resent" advertising sponsorship, opposition rose to charges of "insidious dangers" from spokesmen for traditional advertising media, condemnation as "perverse" and "pernicious" from broadcasters, and a fear that "there will be no radio left" from the Secretary of Commerce.[33] The public, fascinated by tuning-in distant stations, paid no attention to the controversy. By the end of 1924, enough stations had followed WEAF's lead that it was concluded "that the public has no strong objection to this practice; . . . the excellent quality of entertainment actually neutralized opposition from listeners." [34] Yet the issue was by no means settled; over four hundred of the 561 stations on the air still refused to accept sponsors.[35]

The establishment of the National Broadcasting Company in 1926 decided the argument. Its first president, Merlin Aylesworth, issued this prospectus:

> First, we'll find the programs giving the fullest measure of service to the public; next, we'll establish the best facilities for such service; and lastly, we'll make the structure self-sustaining. Obviously, if broadcasting is to be a success, it must stand on its own legs.[36]

Inquiring into what NBC had in mind with regard to becoming "self-sustaining," the *Literary Digest* got the answer:

> . . . it is expected to make advertising ultimately pay the entire expense for the elaborate programs to come. Thus, apparently, is solved the old discussion as to whether radio audiences should be made to pay for their entertainment.[37]

The rules against direct advertising NBC had inherited from AT&T with the purchase of WEAF in 1926 were "relaxed" in 1927,[38] but advertisers cautiously invested in less than four million dollars worth of time on NBC's two networks. The figure reached almost ten million dollars in 1928, and it would rise again to fifteen million in 1929, as more and more advertisers turned to radio.[39] Stations watching the progress of NBC in these years could only conclude that financial stability lay in accepting sponsors. In Chicago, for example, station WGN experimented with a few NBC offerings, and the income so pleased its owners that in the last months of 1928, WGN even began to carry locally sponsored programs.[40]

Summing up the attitude of the broadcasting industry, Merlin Aylesworth wrote in a *New York Times* article:

> The commercially sponsored program spells, in a large measure, the future of radio. Dispensers of woe, who foretold the death of broadcasting when stations began selling time, have been met with ever-improving programs, not in spite of time-selling, but because of it. The national networks, comprising a virtual magazine of the air, are able to give their best services just as do newspapers and magazines, as a result of the support of advertisers . . . Radio programs presented by advertisers not only furnish financial support to the radio station; they are, per se, some of the most desirable presented.[41]

The National Association of Broadcasters tacitly accepted advertising when it appointed a committee to devise ways of controlling commercial announcements. In January, 1929, the committee's recommendations became part of the first code of broadcast standards.[42]

Programming

What kinds of programs were to serve as vehicles for the now accepted commercials? The concept of the radio program as an identifiable entity with a title, musical theme, personality, and regular broadcast period of its own had begun to take permanent shape as early as the season of 1923–24. That winter, WEAF had broadcast the *Eveready Hour*, the *Happiness Boys*, the *Cliquot Club Eskimos*, the *Ipana Troubadors*, the *Gold Dust Twins*, the *Silvertown Cord Orchestra*, the *Lucky Strike Orchestra*, and the *A & P Gypsies*, programs which identified their sponsors as well as themselves.[43] The *New York Herald*, noting the development of an audience responsive to these programs, began to publish a magazine of weekly radio previews as part of its Sunday edition on January 20, 1924, and the *New York Times* began a similar listing a week later.[44] The next season, 1924–1925, WEAF inaugurated its small network and broadcast essentially the same programs as the year before throughout the northeast. Weekly regularity, ease of identification, and split-second timing became characteristic of programs, and programs became characteristic of radio.[45]

Admittedly, there was a marked similarity among sponsored programs, a similarity that continued throughout the 1920's. a breakdown of all the programming making up the two hundred hours broadcast weekly by the two NBC networks during the 1928–1929 season indicates a heavy preponderance of music and talks, an almost complete lack of drama, and no summaries of news. The two chains devoted 71% of their broadcast week to music (nearly half of it "classical"), 21% to talks, 3% each to children's programs and descriptions of events, and 2% to drama.[46] Moreover, sponsored programs were not distributed equally among the features on the broadcast schedule. While talks, drama, children's programs, and daytime concerts often were not sponsored, the evening musical programs were.[47] *Fortune* classified the latter as "studio programs" and explained the reason for their similarity:

> The Studio Program is essentially a concert. It is built around an orchestra, accompanied by soloists, and interrupted by an announcer. It is the oldest type of broadcast and was developed mostly by the National Broadcasting Company . . . The Studio Program, radio's experts will solemnly tell you, grew out of the sustaining program, that program which, at the station's expense, sustains the principle—sacred to all radio stations—that broadcasting must be continuous . . . So NBC played music from morning to night. When an advertiser came along and bought a program, he usually bought a concert. But his name was tacked on fore and aft and sometimes in the middle.
>
> So the early commercial programs were studio designed and studio staffed, and usually had a Made-at-711-Fifth-Avenue trademark.[48]

In spite of their sameness, these programs were regarded by advertisers as suitable for sponsorship. It was universal practice for the program title to include the sponsor's name, but it even became common to re-name soloists for further sponsor identification. Thus, Frank Munn and Virginia Rea appeared as "Paul Oliver" and "Olive Palmer" for Palmolive soap, Joseph M. White was known to his audience only as the "silver Masked Tenor" for the sake of B. F. Goodrich Silvertown Cord Tires, and Harry Horlick's gypsy orchestra was sponsored as the *A & P Gypsies*.[49] With rubber companies especially prevalent as sponsors, James Melton submitted to being called "Seiberling's Own Tenor" by the sponsor of the Seiberling Singers, while the Fisk Rubber Company made reference to a famous trademark by naming its program *The Fisk Time To Re-Tire Boys*.[50] Broadway musical comedy star Franklyn Baur was introduced to his audiences as "the voice of Firestone," a phrase that would remain as a program title for more than three decades.[51]

During the 1927–28 season, thirty-nine companies sponsored programs at NBC, and four sponsors were to be found at CBS. The following season, there were sixty-five nationally sponsored programs on the air.[52] Taking together the technical facilities, the audiences, and the programs available to advertisers, plus the welcome now extended to them by the broadcasters, it can be concluded that by the end of 1928 conditions in the radio broadcasting industry strongly favored provision for network program sponsorship in the advertising budgets of manufacturers of products with nation-wide distribution.

A significant development at the N. W. Ayer & Son advertising agency indicated that the favorable conditions in broadcasting were recognized. Ayer had been involved in radio production work for some years:

> Gradually, it developed a staff of workers especially trained and experienced in the work; and in 1928, when the possibilities of radio advertising were clearly established, this staff was separated from the firm's other publicity work and organized as an independent department. Its duties were to assemble information about all phases of broadcast advertising, build up programs, hire talent, direct production, and handle the leasing of station time and all other details connected with broadcast programs.[53]

The pattern and structure of the broadcasting industry had become established; advertisers were now expected to support it. Ayer's reorganization in 1928 implied that sponsors were preparing to accept that responsibility, even though the first commercial announcement was only six years in the past. Two years later, the president of another advertising agency expressed the relationship between sponsor and the broadcaster simply and forcefully:

> The public wants entertainment. The advertiser wants the public's attention and is willing to pay for it. Therefore, let the advertiser provide the entertainment.[54]

Strictly from the network's point of view a good soap opera is one that has a high rating, and a bad one is one that doesn't.
—Tony Converse, director of daytime programs,
CBS-TV, *Magazine*, May 2, 1974.

37

H. A. Bellows

BROADCASTING: A NEW INDUSTRY

THE BEGINNINGS of commercial broadcasting were rather ludicrous. In the spring of 1925, for example, I visited some 20 prominent stations to try and buy time for one of the largest of American advertisers. In most cases I was listened to with incredulity followed by indignation. "Sell time! Never!" But "never" is a dangerous word, and today nineteen of those 20 stations sell time with avidity; the other one has passed out of existence.

For better or worse, American broadcasting has entered the advertising field. In England, where commercial broadcast programs are unknown, broadcasting being supported as a government monopoly by taxation, they regard our system with profound disapproval. But, after all, these things are largely matters of taste. Last spring, in London, at a luncheon given by the British Broadcasting Corporation, I was asked repeatedly how we in America could tolerate the advocacy of a particular brand of tooth paste between the movements of a Beethoven Symphony, and so on. But the questions abruptly ceased when I remarked that between Southampton and London all the railroad stations I saw evidently belonged to a single vast suburb named "Bovril."

The broadcasters in general are fully aware of the perils of too much advertising, but they feel that the situation will automatically correct itself. No advertiser, and above all no advertising agent, will knowingly create public ill-will and disapproval by broadcasting programs the sole purpose of which is to create exactly the opposite.

The unanswerable argument is that broadcasting on its present advertising basis has been responsible for the fact that 13½ million radio receiving sets are now in use in the United States. In no other country in the world does broadcasting play so large a part in the national life; in no other country is there such a wide variety of broadcast service.

It is impossible to estimate accurately the total amount of money spent by advertisers on broadcasting, but a guess of between 80 and 100 million dollars for 1930 would probably not be far wrong. In 1924 this business was absolutely non-existent; most of its present volume has been the creation of the past three years.

With it has come the urgent need for a broadcast personnel fitted

Harvard Alumni Bulletin, December 18, 1930, pp. 382–386.

to manage a business of such scope. The early broadcast managers were an odd lot. As recently as 1927, when I was a member of the Federal Radio Commission, the broadcasters who appeared before us represented an appallingly low average level of business intelligence. Conditions are rapidly changing, but the broadcasting industry is still an open hunting ground to young men of real administrative capacity.

Of the 80 to 100 million dollars a year spent by advertisers on broadcasting, about one-third goes for mechanical operation, including the enormous item of telephone line service, one-third for salaries, fixed charges, office maintenance, profits (if any), and the like, and one-third for programs. It is in the judicious expenditure of this last item that broadcasting has met its greatest difficulties.

38

Herman S. Hettinger

SOME FUNDAMENTAL ASPECTS
OF RADIO BROADCASTING ECONOMICS

DURING 1929 AND 1930 the development of electrical transcriptions—programs recorded especially for broadcasting purposes—and the success of some companies in the use of short announcements placed over large numbers of stations, turned the attention of national and regional distributors to the possibility of advertising over individual stations, not bound together in networks.

This development placed new responsibilities upon the advertiser and the agency. Station selection, time buying, the development and production of programs, and the servicing of widely scattered stations presented considerably more complicated problems than those involved in the use of a single network. At the outset the agencies were not equipped to cope with these problems.

The time broker, historically the counterpart of the space broker in the early newspaper and periodical days, arose to meet the needs of non-network advertising. In addition to promoting the sale of stations' time, the more enterprising time brokers entered the program-building field, and becmae specialists able to render every service required by those engaging in national non-network advertising.

Harvard Business Review, Vol. XIV, No. 1 (Autumn 1935), pp. 14–18.

The tendency to buy time at the lowest price possible and to sell it for what the market would bear, rebating, the cumulation of commissions—in that transcription companies, the manufacturers of turntables used in the broadcasting of electrical transcriptions, and others, also demanded the traditional 15%—and the entrance into the field of inadequately financed and poorly managed organizations, contributed to the downfall of the time broker.

Accordingly, in 1932 the special representative entered the broadcasting field, supported by the advertising agencies and a number of the larger stations. He functioned as did his counterpart in the periodical field and received the customary commission on business originating in his territory. A number of leading time brokers shifted their activities to the field of representation, while the rest passed from the picture.

The rise of the special representative was hastened in part by the fact that agencies were beginning to equip themselves to deal adequately with all phases of this new medium. Leading agencies developed well-equipped radio departments. Smaller enterprising organizations won positions of leadership by concentrating upon the possibilities of broadcast advertising. Many of the general services of the time broker were assumed, quite logically, by the advertising agency, which became an integral part of the structure of both network and non-network broadcast advertising. It should be noted, however, that the number of agencies equipped to service adequately broadcast advertising is still relatively limited.

A satisfactory solution has yet to be reached as far as the development of national non-network advertising is concerned. The expense involved in the creation, production, and servicing of national non-network broadcast advertising programs has been such as to have caused many agencies to be reluctant to push this type of business, so that it has tended to lag. Moreover, the problems of selling broadcasting are only partly analogous to those of periodical advertising, a fact which raises serious difficulties for the special representative in radio. Broadcast advertising depends particularly upon freshness and originality of ideas, and upon programming and showmanship, rather than upon merely mechanical factors, such as layout and space buying. In addition, it is considerably more difficult to visualize a finished program from a bare idea than it is to imagine a final advertisement from a rough layout.

It is, therefore, highly essential that broadcasting be promoted as an advertising medium. Several attempts have been made to solve this problem, but none has been more than partially successful. One, Group Broadcasters banded together a number of important stations for the joint sale of time and promotion of national non-network advertising. The organization disbanded comparatively shortly after its formation. The World Broadcasting System, a large transcription company, has developed another attack on the problem by entering into an agreement with leading station representatives whereby it will build and audition programs in return for a commission ranging from 5% to 7% of the station card rate for the time used by the advertiser. This commission will come out of what the station usually pays the representative and will not constitute an additional charge to be deducted from the station's gross.[6]

It is difficult to venture what will be the final solution of this problem. It is probable, however, that either the special representative will assume additional promotional functions, or that some form of joint promotional organization finally will be successfully consumated. It also devolves upon the agency to give national non-network advertising possibilities even greater consideration than they have received to date.

Composition of Broadcast Advertising

There is a great tendency on the part of the layman to view broadcast advertising purely from the national network viewpoint. National networks accounted for but 58.5% of total gross time sales of the medium in 1934, while regional networks were responsible for 0.9% of radio volume. National non-network advertising—advertising placed over individual stations by national and regional distributors—represented 18.6% of the total of the medium. Local broadcast advertising, comprising mainly retailers and local manufacturer-distributors, represented 22.0%. National network advertising, has increased steadily in relative importance since 1931, when it represented 51.2% of total broadcast advertising. The increasing proportion arose from a more rapidly growing volume of network advertising, and not to decreases in other portions of the radio structure.

Marked differences exist in the volume and type of broadcast advertising placed over stations of various classes. National business tends to concentrate largely upon the higher powered stations and upon network affiliated stations. It is estimated [11] that 85% of all business placed over stations of more than 1,000 watts in power is national in origin.[12] Even when network advertising is eliminated from consideration and non-network volume alone is considered, approximately 60% of non-network business over stations of this class is represented by national and regional advertisers.

So-called regional stations, ranging from 250 to 1,000 watts in power present a different situation. Here national advertising, network and non-network combined, represents approximately 70% of total gross time sales. National business accounts for approximately 35% of the non-network volume of this class of station. In the case of stations in the 100-watt group, only about one-eighth of total advertising revenue comes from national business. These stations are not affiliated with networks to any appreciable degree so that this aspect requires no consideration.

There is also a concentration of business on affiliated stations as against those not associated with networks. It is estimated that slightly more than 75% of all broadcast advertising volume is placed on stations affiliated with networks. These comprise approximately one-third of the transmitters in the country. Network affiliated stations account for approximately two-thirds of national non-network business and 55% of total non-network advertising. Thus approximately one-third of the station structure of the country constitutes the backbone of the economic structure of the broadcasting industry.

Within the various classes of stations previously mentioned, advertising volume varies tremendously. The principal variation is on the basis of management, though there are some slight differences to be found on the basis of the size of community. Clear channel and regional stations in towns of more than 500,000 population tend to show considerably higher gross time sales than do those in communities under that size, though there is no important difference farther down the scale until communities of less than 100,000 are reached, when gross revenues again drop materially. There is practically no difference in the average gross revenues of 100-watt stations in any size of community. Program building and sales ability are the principal determinants of individual station advertising volume to a remarkable degree.

When the non-network field is examined with regard to the type of rendition employed by advertisers, additional interesting aspects of broadcasting economics are revealed. In the national field, 37.6% of non-network advertising in 1934 was represented by electrical transcriptions, 42.8% by live talent programs, 0.4% by records, and 19.2% by announcements. In the local field the proportions were as follows: electrical transcriptions, 8.1%, live talent programs 52.3%, records, 2.5%, and announcements, 37.1%.

There are decided differences by classes of stations in this respect. Electrical transcription volume is concentrated upon stations over 1,000 watts in power, where it represents 25.6% of non-network business. The influence of the national advertiser is the reason for this situation. Transcriptions thus far have made little progress on the local stations.

Live talent programs are concentrated upon the clear channel and regional stations. Financial resources, program and studio facilities, and type of advertisers appealed to, combine to produce this result.

Announcements constitute a fairly large proportion of the business of all classes of stations, increasing in relative volume as the power of the station declines. In the case of 100-watt stations they constitute approximately 46% of all advertising volume. Records are important only to this class of transmitter, and represent nearly 12% of all advertising volume. Since most programs utilizing records on these stations are participations, wherein announcements are inserted between numbers, there is little difference in the two classes of business. Thus nearly 60% of 100-watt station advertising tends to be in the nature of announcements.

Retail store advertising, when considered separately, shows marked differences in importance between classes of stations. In the case of stations over 1,000 watts in power it represents approximately 6% of total gross time sales. It constitutes about 16% of time sales over stations in the 250- to 1,000-watt group, and over 43% of those of 100-watt stations. The small retail establishment is therefore the economic backbone of the 100-watt group at the present time.

The bulk of retail advertising at present is broadcast over regional stations. It is estimated that in 1934 approximately $4,000,000 was spent by retailers over stations of this class, $1,750,000 over 100-watt stations, and $1,400,000 over clear channel and high powered regional stations.

Sponsors of Radio Advertising

Sponsorship of radio advertising by various product and service groups varies with the portion of the broadcasting structure under consideration as well as with power of station.

Convenience goods—small articles of low cost, mass consumption, and a high degree of repeat purchase—constitute the preponderance of national network advertising, and tend to assume a similar position in the national non-network field. In 1934 they constituted approximately 86% of national network volume and about 70% of national non-network volume.

The greatest rise in network advertising during the past two seasons, however, has been in the more expensive goods, particularly automobiles. A similar trend regarding household equipment and like products seems to be beginning.

The composition of local broadcast advertising reflects more of the retail picture, and is further characterized by a great variety of advertisers. Analysis of the accounts of 150 stations for several months in 1933 and 1934 revealed an average of more than 200 different types of business utilizing radio broadcasting.

Different types of business tend to concentrate upon various classes of stations. Amusements represent a larger proportion of the total business of 100-watt stations than they do of any other class of transmitter. Gasoline and accessories, drugs and cosmetics, confectionery, beverages, and tobacco are particularly important with regard to the higher powered stations. The influence of the national advertiser, and of the local manufacturer-distributor who imitates him, is responsible for this tendency.

Clothing and apparel advertising represents a larger proportion of the business of regional and local stations than of the higher powered units of the medium. Department and general stores tend to seek out the regional stations, and the smaller retailers the local stations. As the size of station decreases the variety of advertiser increases.

The Economic Position of Broadcasting

Broadcasting is a small industry, regularly employing probably less than 11,000 persons all told. It is comprised of but slightly more than 600 units, of which one-half are of any real economic importance, and one-third constitute the backbone of the medium. The business of broadcasting is concentrated to a large degree in this third comprising the higher powered stations and those affiliated with networks.

Viewing this structure from the operating side, greater economic stability could be desired. In 1931, which was the peak year of the medium prior to 1934, total expense of the medium exceeded revenues by $237,000.[13] The monthly gross revenues of more than half of the stations of the country were $3,000 or less. There seems to have been some improvement in recent months, but by no means sufficient to rectify the situation.

The development of national non-network advertising constitutes another important structural problem, structural because increased volume of this type of business is an important factor in promoting the stability and profitableness of certain classes of stations. No matter what the ultimate solution of the network-station problem is, the increased economic well-being of many network affiliates probably will tend to center largely in increased non-network business. Even more important is the desirability of developing the national advertising of stations not affiliated with networks. Some form of joint promotion undoubtedly will be required, the implications of this question having been discussed earlier in the paper.

Some progress has been made toward a standardization of practice with regard to items such as contract forms,[14] units of sale, discounts for broadcast series of given duration, and similar matters. Rates show considerable lack of uniformity, especially as to charges at different times of the day, with a seeming tendency toward a greater number of variations for specific time periods rather than toward a reduction therein. There is also a tendency toward the establishment of a single station rate and the discontinuance of the so-called "general-retail" rate system borrowed from the newspaper field.

The amount of merchandizing service which should be provided to advertisers by broadcasting stations and networks constitutes another important trade practice problem. Some stations have developed this service to such an extent that it has practically resulted in furnishing the program sponsor with supplementary advertising without additional charge. Undue extension of this service not only constitutes an important cost item, but introduces a potentially vicious price-cutting situation.

The lack of standardized information regarding station coverage and listener data has constituted an important problem in the sale of advertising. Notwithstanding the fact that radio has developed a fund of information equal to that of any medium, the newness of research in the field has resulted in a variety of approach and method which has seriously impaired the comparability of results with regard to individual studies. Steps are now being taken looking toward the creation of a cooperative bureau, to be maintained by the broadcasters, advertisers, and agencies, which will provide certain basic information regarding the medium and will function for radio in the same general capacity as does the Audit Bureau of Circulation in the periodical field.

39

David G. Clark

H. V. KALTENBORN AND HIS SPONSORS: CONTROVERSIAL BROADCASTING AND THE SPONSOR'S ROLE

LACK OF RELIABLE sources usually precludes study of the three-cornered interplay among the outspoken commentator on public issues, the financial backer who gives him access to the mass audience, and the audience that responds to what he says. Accounts of attempted suppression of controversial analysts tend to be dramatized and exaggerated by the participants, and the public is left to conclude that the truth lies somewhere in between.

Journal of Broadcasting, Vol. XII, No. 4 (Fall 1968), pp. 309–321.

But the papers of the late news analyst and commentator H. V. Kaltenborn, restricted until his death in June 1965, contain two striking examples of this interplay.[1] These examples seem strongly to reinforce the suggestion that successful airing of controversial public issues depends not so much on commentator or network willingness to speak out, as on sponsor willingness to stand the gaff. For as the price of admission to the marketplace of ideas has increased, the precepts of Milton and Mill regarding the speaker's commitment to the search for truth have been expanded to include a man seldom heard from in the public dialogue: the businessman-sponsor.

In December 1938, Kaltenborn signed with General Mills, makers of Gold Medal Flour and other food products. The contract called for a 15-minute Sunday night program for an initial period of 13 weeks, renewable upon exercise of an option. Kaltenborn's fee was to be $600 a week.[2] General Mills sponsored several other radio programs, all non-controversial. They included *Jack Armstrong, Hymns of All Nations,* and three soap operas. What the company needed, argued Henry Adams Bellows, its director of relations with the public, was an attempt at "institutional advertising, differing materially from product advertising in that its primary function is to create goodwill." Therefore, said Bellows, the company should have a link with a program which "renders actual service." Kaltenborn met this requirement very well, Bellows added.[3] The directors of General Mills embraced the suggestion, and when Kaltenborn took the air on January 1, 1939, Chairman James F. Bell introduced him via a special line from Minneapolis: "Everyone who has listened to his comments on the world's news . . . have [sic] come to regard him as a profound student, a keen observer and a wise interpreter of the world in which we live. . . . General Mills has pledged itself to preserve untrammeled that complete freedom of selection and expression which has been the basis of Mr. Kaltenborn's independence." [4]

Chairman Bell may have been sincere in what he said, but General Mills, at the behest of its advertising agency, had taken certain precautions. Chief among these was an insistence that Kaltenborn was to inform Bellows of the subject of each week's talk in advance. Written copies were to be sent to Bellows and to the Minneapolis and New York account men in the firm's agency of Batten, Barton, Durstine and Osborn. Never one to encourage incurrences into what he considered the territory of his editorial independence, Kaltenborn from the start seems to have ignored this contractual agreement.

The effusiveness with which General Mills greeted Kaltenborn lasted just over a week. On January 9, with two Kaltenborn broadcasts under his belt, Henry Bellows wrote the commentator: "Of course, we are beginning to get the usual crop of abusive letters.

Many of these we are not answering, but I will pass them along to you, not as having in any way influence on our own feelings, but simply as an indication of what people are expressing to us." A week after that, Bellows suggested that Kaltenborn have a talk with Board Chairman Bell, to clear up any misunderstandings which might be arising over Kaltenborn's denunciation of Nazi propaganda. The chairman, said Bellows, seemed a little bewildered by some of the "perfectly natural and inevitable" things that were happening.[5] Bellows was referring to angry letters of protest that came to the sponsor when Kaltenborn took his editorial stands. For the truth was, as Wilbur Schramm was later to demonstrate (using Kaltenborn as the model), a man could be at the same time the most popular—and the most unpopular—commentator on the air.[6]

Kaltenborn had his visit with Bell, smoothed things over, and for a short while matters seemed to go better. But on January 24, Bellows wrote that a boycott of Gold Medal Flour was being threatened by a bakers' association composed of Germans or German descendants who did not like the anti-Nazi position taken by Kaltenborn. Of course, said Bellows, "we none of us worry about such threats from the public, but we naturally have a real situation to face when state organizations of bakers take up the matter at their meetings." [7]

Another segment of the audience was beginning to react adversely to Kaltenborn's commentaries. Having spent several weeks in Spain both in 1936 and 1937, and having observed the war there from the front lines of both sides, Kaltenborn, knew how the Catholic Church in some areas supported the Republicans, and, in others, Franco. Gradually Franco gained the upper hand, both in the war and in the Church's sympathies. But his acceptance of aid from Hitler and Mussolini made him, in Kaltenborn's eyes, a Fascist. And when Franco began to execute members of the Republican government, Kaltenborn condemned him in strong terms. Many listeners apparently interpreted that criticism as anti-Catholicism. And, despite the fact that mail during this period ran approximately two to one in Kaltenborn's favor, the directors were inclined to pay attention.

Before long, there came to General Mills a letter from a priest who was associate editor of *Ave Maria,* a Catholic family weekly printed at South Bend, Indiana. The letter found its way to Henry Bellows, who composed an answer designed to turn away wrath. In return came another letter, this time addressed to Bellows, and this time three and a half pages of single-spaced typing in length. In it the priest first recited a long list of atrocities which he said had been committed by the anti-Franco forces. (This news did not surprise Kaltenborn; he had witnessed atrocities committed by both sides.) Next, the priest mentioned a figure—310—which he said represented

the total number of Catholic publications in the United States prepared to "fully reveal to their readers the true story of what has been
going on in Spain." Then the priest, as he put it, "frankly and with
genuine friendliness," continued:

> I fear very much, Mr. Bellows, that you and your organization will
> regret it for a long time to come if, as a result of any future broad-
> casts, your millions of Catholic customers get the idea that General
> Mills is ever so faintly associated with any activity supporting the
> Loyalist cause and what it represents in Catholic eyes. . . . You are
> not manufacturing lawn mowers or automobiles which go into the
> garage when the day's usefulness is over. You are manufacturing ar-
> ticles which go into the intimacy of Catholic homes where little
> children cluster around the breakfast tables. Articles admitted into
> these sacred surroundings, Mr. Bellows, must come there free from
> even the slightest taint of suspicion on the things about which we
> have been discussing.

If Bellows should read his letter in the "same friendly spirit in
which it was written," the priest was sure that a "sufficiently sympathetic and just solution can be found to obviate any future difficulties
with the resulting loss of Good Will which must inevitably follow." [8]

Bellows at once divined the spirit of the letter and that same day
fired off a telegram to Kaltenborn. No stranger to broadcasting, or to
the pressures encountered by broadcasters, Bellows was a former
manager of radio station WCCO in Minneapolis, and had been an
original appointee to the Federal Radio Commission in 1927.
Later he had served as a CBS vice president. He had known Kaltenborn since their Harvard days, when Kaltenborn was an undergraduate and Bellows a Ph.D. student. Bellows appeal thus contained, in
addition to its tutorial tone, more than a little ambivalence:

> In handling Spanish news this week please remember many list-
> eners sincerely and intensively believe Franco's victory a triumph
> for Christianity. While suggesting no limitation on your report or
> analysis of the news I believe this is a case where editorial com-
> ment or indication of personal bias should be avoided. [9]

Just what Kaltenborn's response to Bellows might have been
will never be known, though the commentator was usually predictable in these matters. In the past, he had always vigorously defended
his right to utter his own opinions on any subject he wished, even if
it meant losing his place before the microphone, which more than
once it had. But two days after Bellows dispatched his telegram,
Pope Pius XI died. The following Sunday, in a move that seemed
both opportunistic and appropriate to the magnitude of the news
event, Kaltenborn reduced his comment on other matters to deliver a
warm and lengthy tribute to the late Pope. [10]

But letters threatening boycott continued to arrive at the General Mills offices. And as they came, so too came conviction to the minds of the directors. On March 7 Kaltenborn received a telegram with the not unexpected news that the board had voted against renewal of his contract. To this day the corporate officers of the company remain reluctant to release minutes of the directors' meetings in which the decision to drop Kaltenborn was reached. The threatened boycott by bakers' organizations may have been the crucial element, though the Catholic question was certainly important, and many years later Kaltenborn expressed the opinion that Catholic board members forced the decision.[11]

Within a few days, Board Chairman Bell wrote to give ostensible reasons why General Mills could not renew. With masterful understatement, he declared that every board member was more than satisfied with Kaltenborn's performance. Nor, asserted Bell, was the decision to quit influenced by "such criticisms of your attitude on particular subjects as have come to us." It was just that the nation was approaching a time when "our national problems will be reflected in violent political emotions." And, said Bell, it was not a proper function for a company making products for general consumption to involve itself publicly in such emotions. But if General Mills could not sponsor Kaltenborn successfully no one could, Bellows chimed in, adding that a commentator should be no more subject to sponsorship than the editorials in a newspaper.[12]

Perhaps not, replied Kaltenborn, but the Pure Oil Company seemed willing to try. He had just signed with Pure for 52 weeks of Sunday and Tuesday night broadcasts, at a fee of $1,200 a week.[13] With that signing began a relationship that lasted 15 years, through many controversies on many topics. But where General Mills had not elected to support the commentator, Pure now did; and though Kaltenborn soon brought real miseries in the form of actual boycotts of Pure products, his sponsor never once tried to crack down on him, or even threatened seriously to do so.

Pure acquired, along with Kaltenborn, the audience which had been so responsive to his General Mills broadcasts. A student of Kaltenborn fan mail during the years 1939–41 (some 15,000 letters were addressed to Kaltenborn) has shown that many of the writers who sent letters to him in care of Pure had also written him at General Mills, and had assumed that their boycott threats had resulted in non-renewal of his General Mills contract.[14] As soon as he started for Pure, charges of anti-Catholicism began to mount against him, and against Pure. By June 8, 1939, the advertising manager of Pure Oil, Francis H. Marling, was writing of his concern that the "Catholic situation" was getting out of hand. Some district managers, especially in the Northwest, were reporting loss of business.[15] This time, however, international events stepped in to distract public and commentator alike. Kaltenborn went to Europe for the summer, and when he returned Germany was poised on the Polish border.

The early baptism Pure experienced on the anti-Catholic question proved valuable as time passed. This issue had shown what could happen; and likewise how fears might never be realized. It also developed a sense among Pure officials and Kaltenborn of having weathered a storm, of having stood together to resist pressures against criticisms Kaltenborn had voiced which neither they nor he considered unfair. The greatest testing of this alloy came not long after the United States entered the war.

If certain Catholics considered Kaltenborn a Communist, certain labor union members labeled him a Fascist. Kaltenborn's criticisms of labor grew from the fact that the American war production was slow getting underway after the country entered the war. At the heart of the problem, Kaltenborn thought, were the peacetime attitudes held by both labor and management, and the reluctance of the government to step in and lead effectively. Labor wanted to restrict production unless management granted increased benefits. Management thought labor should agree to suspend wage and hour demands for the duration. For a time Kaltenborn criticized the government-labor-management triumvirate about equally. But when he talked about manufacturers, or government, there was little organized response. Not so with unions. Response to criticism of their policies came swiftly and in great quantity.

By March 1942, Marling was worried. "It begins to look as though we have a real problem on our hands," he wrote Kaltenborn. Numbers of midwestern unions were threatening boycotts. As the company's trade area was primarily the Midwest, with some coverage of the deep South, this was serious. In addition, some unions could do more harm than simply call membership boycotts. Engineers, oilers and master mechanics frequently were able to recommend to employers the brand of oil and fuel to be used by their companies. The situation in Duluth, Minnesota, rapidly became so bad that Pure's local manager there asked to have Kaltenborn's program discontinued immediately. "If this sentiment from our field sales organization spreads," Marling wrote, "we will be up against serious trouble." [16]

The sentiment did spread. From the Northwest, it seeped through Wisconsin, into Chicago, and began to stain the South. By the end of May, Pure would hear from 59 different union organizations with members totaling many thousands. In his reply to Marling's March letter, Kaltenborn indicated that he would refuse to yield. "My course is set and cannot be changed," he wrote Marling. "Not since the Munich Crisis has anything I have done on the air met with such universal approval." He advised Marling to consult with Pure executives "and have it out," a reference to the fact that his contract was up for renewal. Kaltenborn realized, and certainly the Pure hierarchy realized, that through the fairly simple expedient of non-renewal, Pure could solve its troubles.[17]

The key man in the situation was the president of Pure Oil, Henry May Dawes. Brother of Charles G. Dawes, Coolidge's Vice President, Henry had served in the Harding-Coolidge administration as Comptroller of the Currency. He was as firmly Republican as Kaltenborn was Democratic, but his acquaintance with national politics had inured him to pressures, and he did not question the value of free speech, even in wartime. After all, that was one of the things for which the war was being fought. Dawes did, however, write a memorandum to Marling, which reads as if it were composed to be passed on to Kaltenborn, which it promptly was. Kaltenborn's recent broadcasts, not merely the ones which castigated labor, but those as well which accused management of obstructing the war effort and government of not doing all it might to lead industry, appealed powerfully to him, Dawes wrote. But those sentiments, continued too long, would convey to the public a note of scolding and defeat their own purpose. Mr. Kaltenborn would understand, Dawes wrote, "why we have been very nervous about his recent crusade, especially when he remembers the terrific pressure which is being brought upon us. But Dawes added that he thought the stockholders would be willing to take any losses Kaltenborn's remarks might occasion.[18] This moderate appeal for moderation, backed by a clear endorsement, was followed in a few days by renewal of Kaltenborn's contract, which put him on the air five days a week instead of three and which increased his weekly salary to $4,000.[19]

In taking these actions in positive support of Kaltenborn, Dawes was placing his company in jeopardy. As if Dawes did not have enough worries about boycotts by labor (with gasoline rationing soon to come, war plant workers would be the ones with priority to buy, or not to buy, petroleum products), Kaltenborn set in after Secretary of the Interior Harold Ickes, who was also petroleum coordinator. It was almost as if the commentator was consciously seeking to test the outer limits of his sponsor's tolerance. After a while, Dawes wrote directly to Kaltenborn, and said that in the main Ickes' administration had been good. "In addition to that, I do not hesitate to say that he is almost in the position of a dictator in the oil business, and it is not impossible that in some way at some time, we, as your sponsor, might be called to account for your comments." Although it seems reasonable to assume that Dawes' statement might be less indication of his fear than of Ickes' reputation as a curmudgeon, Kaltenborn replied that it was possible he had been "a little harsh in speaking of

Mr. Ickes. I have nothing against him, but he does do and say so many foolish things. However, I bear no man malice, and will seize a proper occasion to say a friendly word about him." Thus, the commentator's positions were to a certain degree negotiable. He would say what he thought, but he would add a propitiatory word later.[20]

Throughout these controversies, the networks which carried Kaltenborn's programs remained in the background. During the General Mills period, he was with CBS. He switched to NBC in 1940, but his shift was occasioned by the need to obtain a more favorable broadcast time and not by any disagreement over policy. Network executives frequently objected to remarks by radio commentators (the Cecil Brown-CBS case in 1943 is the best known example), but Kaltenborn enjoyed a unique position *vis a vis* his network. Not only was he the preeminent radio analyst during those years, he was thoroughly inured to controversy by a long career as a newspaper editorial writer and columnist in addition to his 20 years' experience in radio. He was fully prepared to face suspension from the air (as he had more than once during the 1920s). His reputation as a fighter for the right to express his opinion was great; and after NBC extracted from him an agreement to protect the network from libel suits, the broadcasting company sought no further real control. As long as Pure was happy, so was NBC. The sponsors who sometimes took Kaltenborn's programs in areas where Pure did not conduct business were secondary in importance and in no position even to attempt to exercise influence.[25]

When Pure Oil did finally terminate sponsorship of Kaltenborn in September 1953, the decision seems to have been made strictly on the basis of a cost analysis of the way in which the company allocated its advertising budget. Kaltenborn's program, like so many other news commentary shows, fell victim to television. In 1953, an average Kaltenborn broadcast reached 537,000 homes at a cost of $2.04 per thousand homes per commercial minute. A Pure-sponsored panel show reached 1,427,000 homes at $2.29 per thousand per commercial minute. The decision to drop Kaltenborn was, Pure's advertising manager wrote, a matter of economics. The commentator could, and did, accept that judgment. Moreover, the company had changed from the old days. Henry Dawes had died in 1952, and so had Francis Marling, the long-time advertising manager. Their passing changed the relationship Kaltenborn had enjoyed with Pure, and, as the commentator himself was nearing 75, retirement for him was slowly becoming a state of fact if not of mind.

But the basic question, why Pure consistently backed the commentator's outspokenness when General Mills shied away, does not yield to definitive answer. Perhaps the best answer is the old-fashioned one: commitment to principle. That point was put neatly by the vice president of the Xerox Corporation when he accepted an award given his company for its sponsorship of a controversial series of programs on the United Nations. "We firmly believe," he said, "that in the conduct of our business, and in chosing the vehicles we use to achieve our business goals, we must embody those values which hold free men in cooperative, peaceful association." [26]

At any rate, it seems clear that the mass media system in a free society requires not only money to assure that the marketplace of ideas receives a multiplicity of voices, but money—and a willingness—to underwrite company losses when pressure groups protest the speaker's message. Pure Oil's crisis, it now seems clear, came with the decision to resist pressure. That decision was made, and adhered to, and eventually troubles flew in the face of firm resolve.

40

Harvey J. Levin

COMPETITION AMONG MASS MEDIA AND THE PUBLIC INTEREST

COMPETITION IN newspaper publishing has declined noticably since 1910,[1] and a few giant producers and theater owners still dominate the motion picture industry.[2] It has been hoped that the growth of radio and television would provide alternative outlets for expression, especially in those communities with only one newspaper or one movie theater.[3] The entry of newspapers into the field of radio and the more recent entry of movie producers and theater owners into television have, however, dimmed these hopes. On January 1 of this year, about 19 percent of all standard stations, 33 percent of FM stations, and 37 percent of television outlets were affiliated with newspapers.[4] Though only about 20 radio-TV stations are actually run by the movie industry today, a far more extensive marriage seems pending.[5]

This growing number of cross channel associations is of special concern on at least three counts. *First* it accentuates the trend to

Public Opinion Quarterly, Vol. XVIII (Spring 1954), pp. 62–79. Also see *Broadcast Regulation and Joint Ownership of Media*, New York University Press, 1960.

fewer independent outlets of communication. One consequence is that fewer individuals select and interpret news or determine editorial policy. This may lessen the diversity of output in its own right. To be sure separate owners, often businessmen from identical social milieux, frequently see life so similarly as to produce similar contents. Nonetheless, occupational affiliation is not the only determinant of perspectives; two owners, though both businessmen, may vary sharply in outlook. Non-profit organizations would, of course, differ even more fundamentally from publisher or theater owner, than would independent commercial broadcasters.

Second, radio and television alone among the media are required by law to be fair and balanced in their coverage of controversial questions. Some quarters fear that the partisan tradition of newspapers may carry over into their electronic subsidiaries. Indeed, although abuses are not inevitable in newspaper owned radio, they have occurred and warrant precautionary measures.[6] Roughly analogous problems have also arisen in the movie industry over Paramount Pictures' "restrictive" policies vis a vis television and United Paramount's merger with ABC.[7] One broad issue here is whether the Federal Communications Commission should limit itself to reviewing programs at renewals, encouraging self-regulation and professionalism, and relying on *potential* competition to keep its licensees in line, or whether it should also seek to discourage the older media from entering the new. In the UPT case, the former were considered adequate safeguards, although FCC's main reason for approving the merger was to enhance competition between the major radio and television networks by allowing the UPT to bolster ABC's finances and programming. But the case for separate ownership of the media still stands.

Third, the diversity of expression which may result from diverse ownership, is seen as necessary to the democratic process. The different, insulated groups in society, each with its own outlook and perspective, must be interpreted to one another. The problem is especially thorny in a society like ours where owners of media are themselves members of a particular group and yet are expected to provide unencumbered channels through which all groups can exchange conflicting views.[8]

These largely theoretical advantages of diversity of ownership, subsume certain favorable economic conditions: namely, that preventing affiliations will have no adverse effects on finances. An effective, comprehensive coverage of social, political, cultural and other matters is expensive at best, and abundant resources are necessary for adequate performance. Moreover, financially unstable media appear more susceptible to pressures from organized groups in the community, and consequently less able to be fair and impartial.[9]

In this article we shall consider whether an anti-affiliation policy,[10] by encouraging competitive rivalry, might subject older media to financial blows which made them more susceptible to group pressures and less able to afford highest quality research, reporting, etc. If this is not true, the theoretical advantages of separate ownership already noted, may materialize and would seem consistent with widening and enriching the range of expression.

Next we shall examine and appraise from a social viewpoint, the adjustments in price and content which older media have had to make in jousting with their new rivals—especially where they do not consummate affiliations. Then we shall consider the bearing of such adjustments on the adequacy of the press in modern society.

Impact of New Media on Old

Publishers entering radio and television have apparently had abundant financial resources to facilitate entry whatever their *reasons* for affiliating. Given their wealth, however, one wonders why so many preferred to invest here and now in Facsimile—the electronic newspapers—rather than in equally profitable alternatives. Research shows, among other things, that publishers have feared the competitive inroads of these electronic rivals and have entered into affiliations as a "hedge" against the unknown.[11] Indeed, movie producers and theater owners as well as newspaper publishers, have recently come to view television with similar trepidation.[12]

Although the validity of these fears has long been assumed, we have undertaken a systematic analysis in order to appraise public policy.[13] If radio *was* the major cause of newspaperdom's troubles in the 1930s, and if television *is* the major threat to the revenues of other media today—as publishers and movie executives say—then the discouragement of cross channel affiliations might be criticized sharply on *social* as well as private grounds. The public would supposedly suffer from output of reduced quality.

Radio and Newspapers

During the worst years experienced by newspaperdom, radio was experiencing a rapid growth in coverage which apparently cushioned it from the sharp decline in national income, possibly at newspaperdom's expense.[14] Perhaps publishers were correct therefore to impute their severe losses to radio's growth, and to enter broadcasting in self-defense—as a business hedge. Or were other forces primarily responsible for their troubles?

Analysis of overall time series soon makes it clear that radio has not turned newspaper publishing into a declining industry since 1929. (1) Extensive losses in circulation and advertising revenues *did* occur during the 1930's, at a time when radio's share of total advertising revenues grew rapidly; (2) that circulation seemed to regain its average growth rate more quickly than did advertising; (3) circulation grew rapidly in the 1940's, apparently despite severe newsprint shortages, and then declined slightly after 1945; (4) that advertising revenues soared after 1945 and that publishers have steadily bettered their relative position vs. radio's since then. Other data show that newspaper circulation moves generally with changes in national income and general business activity.[15]

Granting that radio has not turned newspaper publishing into a declining industry, has it at least deterred the latter's growth? Was this especially true before 1943? What is the relative importance of radio growth and income change in explaining newspaperdom's difficulties since 1929? The possible impact of FCC's anti-affiliation rule, as it applies to newspapers and radio, must be viewed in this context. The results of our statistical analysis follow:

First, radio's adverse impact on newspaper advertising revenues seems to have grown noticeably between 1929 and 1940, and then virtually disappeared after the war. To a lesser extent, the same is true of its impact on circulation. Income levels, on the other hand, grow steadily as a factor explaining circulation and advertising levels: the sharp growth between 1940 and 1947 may reflect the diminution of radio's impact.[16]

Second, income change seems more important in 1929–1933 and 1941–1943 than during the period 1937–1940—when radio growth was apparently reaching the peak of its impact on circulation and advertising revenues.[17]

Third, the relative strength of income change and radio growth vary as between regions: income apparently played its most important role in the East, 1929–1933; radio growth in the East and South, 1937–1940, and in the Central States, 1941–1943.[18]

Fourth, newspapers in our largest cities were apparently hit more severely by income decline in the 1930's, than were newspapers in the country as a whole.[19]

Fifth, radio's impact on advertising revenues seems to have been greater than its impact on circulation, 1937–1943, though the reverse may be true in 1929–1933.[20]

Sixth, radio's growth does not seem to have been a factor causing suspensions of newspapers during the 1930's; but income decline may have played a limited role. On the other hand, during the war, suspensions occurred more frequently in areas of greatest radio growth.[21]

At this point, it is hard to say how large a role the affiliation rule played in encouraging competition. Whatever its impact the policy probably did not seriously subject newspapers to blows which might shatter their integrity, if only because such blows were apparently not delivered by radio even during the depression, let alone after the war. The main trouble occurred in the East, in the late 1930's.

Two additional questions now pose themselves: First, in view of radio's limited inroads on newspapers, from what other sources did its great growth in revenues come? Second, what factors explain radio's ability to take the limited revenues it took from newspapers during the depression and war, especially in view of the different basic appeals of the two media? What about the publishers' come-back after the war?

Answering the first question may make our statistical findings more plausible and so support the conclusions we have just tenta-tively drawn. For if radio's inroads really were as limited as they ap-pear, there must be another way to explain the rapid growth in its revenues during the depression. The second question, like the first, is important for public policy. For if radio's gains were due primarily to an inherent technological superiority—say its speed—then a pol-icy of maintaining competition between the media would seem in-evitably to subject the older medium to forces lowering its adequacy.

Sources of Radio's Revenues. The rapid growth of radio set ownership during the 1930's brought many families into radio's reach and widened the market for radio advertisements.[22] When radio entered a community for the first time we believe that existing advertisers increased their total outlays, and also diverted funds to radio from newspapers, magazines, car cards and farm papers. Many concerns that had never advertised before apparently started.

Advertising outlays on certain kinds of commodities may have increased with radio's advent simply because the new medium was especially suitable for promoting them. For example, the outlays on cereals, pharmaceuticals, tobacco, etc. showed gains; whereas, finan-cial, legal, and funeral parlor notices, medical, classified, automotive and display advertisements, remained the forte of newspapers.[23] Moreover, radio advertising, according to some authorities, stimu-lated newspaper advertising directly on a number of counts. First, there was simply the effect of introducing newcomers to the role of advertising, after which they simply "got the bug" and turned to other media too.[24] Then, there was the phenomenon of "competitive advertising" where outlays by one firm in a new medium forced its rivals to follow suit while maintaining their older appropriations, or to counter with increased outlays in established media.[25] Radio set manufacturers, moreover, poured millions into newspaper advertise-ments.[26] Furthermore, though there is no evidence that radio seriously deterred movie receipts, what inroads there were would seem to have brought new money into advertising. Lastly, newspa-pers turned to radio for promotion, which is not at all the same as saying that radio took revenues that would otherwise have gone to newspapers. But newspapers plugging their circulation over the radio may not have advertised at all in other newspapers or magazines.

Additional data somewhat support this hypothesis on new advertising money. The ratio of total advertising expenditures to national income remained relatively stable during the years 1935–1939.[27] Of course, a sharp growth in this ratio might strengthen our case. But the argument still stands. For in the years 1935–1939, radio revenues rose some $83,500,000, magazines and newspapers some $30,700,000 and $39,472,000, respectively. The fact that radio grew more rapidly than the others might be interpreted to mean that it took money which otherwise would have gone to printed media. But there is no way of knowing this. Perhaps when new markets opened to radio, advertisers simply increased radio outlays *more than other outlays.* Their increases might well include funds that would never have been spent on advertising at all.

How Radio Took Revenues from Newspapers Despite Their Different Appeals. Despite the different potential appeals of aural and printed media, and despite the new money which radio apparently brought into advertising, newspapers did suffer definite, if limited, losses to their new rival. One possible explanation, of course, is that the *potentially* different appeals of radio and newspapers, were not immediately exploited by publishers. For example, it took newspapers time to adjust to a new competitor. The publishers' adjustments to radio and television may explain in part the sharp post-war rise in advertising revenues and also the absence of evidence that radio was a deterrent in 1947.

The end of newsprint shortages and greater availability of advertising space, of course, are other factors which may explain the post-war trend. Likewise, existence of such shortages during the war may have induced advertisers to turn to radio in some cases.[28]

In any case, during the depression proper, radio's inroads appear to have been facilitated by a number of "accidental" factors—unrelated to any "inherent" technological superiority of an aural medium. These factors, moreover, must be viewed in a context of falling national income. No one of them by itself is likely to explain even the limited inroads we have observed. Even combined they may not present a convincing case. But when hard-pressed by a general decline in business activity, otherwise indifferent advertising agencies may well have weighed such factors carefully and then turned from newspapers to radio.

Radio's superior canvassing techniques with advertisers and more intensive audience research, the growing divergence between public opinion and the editorial position of most newspapers, free coverage in newspapers of radio programs and even of the products of radio advertisers, the fact that radio listening was considered a "free good" once a set was bought, as well as the rigidity of newspaper space rates, and the advantage of dealing with a single network radio official able to act for several hundred affiliated stations, as opposed to the cost and inconvenience of dealing with many newspapers separately all probably affected the change.

To sum up, advertisers diverted some outlays to radio during the depression and war. But no inherent technological superiority was involved; a number of temporary factors seem largely responsible. When many of these were later altered, the publishers made marked gains in their relative share of total advertising revenues.

There is no evidence, however, that all or even most of radio's spectacular growth came at the expense of newspapers. Radio probably brought much new money into advertising and also took revenues from magazines, farm papers, car cards and the movies.

Publishers owning radio stations obviously shared in radio's profits. But by and large they do not seem to have recouped money that would have gone to newspapers were radio non-existent. Anyway, they might also have stabilized their revenues by strengthening their own strong points, as they tended to do after 1945. In this context, it seems that FCC's policy of discouraging affiliations may have weakened newspaperdom's resilience against outside pressure groups somewhat during the 1930's. But it has probably *not* had this effect since the war. Indeed if anything, FCC's formal rule (1944) may actually have hastened the day when publishers would meet radio's threat squarely by developing their own strong points, rather than by buying stations as a hedge. Affiliations may actually have weakened the incentive to adjust.

Television and Other Mass Media

How great are television's inroads in the finances of its major rivals today? Does ultimate coexistence seem possible or likely? Will a policy to discourage television's rivals from affiliating with her threaten their financial stability? Such are the questions that now confront public policy makers.

Our statistical analysis of television's impact shows that it was apparently no deterrent to newspaper circulation in 1948.[29] Nor did the 15-fold growth in TV sets between 1949–1951 seem to play any significant role in the decline in newspaper circulation during that period.[30] Perhaps the new media are sufficiently distinctive in the eyes of readers, viewers, and advertisers, to warrant prosperous coexistence. Adjustments by publishers to TV in form, technique, and content may also be partly responsible for newspaperdom's resilience. These will be considered later.

On the other hand, television has apparently reduced radio revenues,[31] without yet putting radio seriously into the red.[32] The broadcaster's further adjustments to TV by exploiting his own special strong points, will determine the extent of future inroads.

A study of movie receipts in 1948 showed no serious adverse effect of television.[33] However, television's growth between 1946 and 1950 *was* a factor of at least some importance in explaining the decline in movie revenues in the same period.[34] Nonetheless, TV was of little importance as a factor causing *failures* of movie theaters.[35]

Further study of our findings suggests that television has hit movies and radio much more sharply than newspapers.[36] Indeed this is in line with many audience surveys published recently.[37]

Finally, there is weak evidence also that TV may be hitting radio somewhat more sharply than the movies.[38] This too is in line with several audience surveys.[39]

There are several possible reasons why television's inroads have not been more serious to date. By reviving old films television is paying Hollywood money that it might otherwise not receive.[40] Film shorts about attractions coming to local theaters are also being used by movie interests to stimulate attendance. Indeed some quarters believe that TV will eventually become a large consumer of new Hollywood productions made especially for home reception. Like radio, moreover, TV is probably stimulating newspaper circulation, both because TV is news itself and because it seems to make people more news-conscious.[41] Besides, manufacturers of TV sets are pouring millions into newspaper advertisements. And newcomers to advertising—the department stores—are finding TV demonstrations effect sales promoters. Indeed such developments (plus others already noted) may explain a part at least of the sharp growth in newspaper advertising revenues during the past few years. In any case, TV's general stimulating qualities seem of sufficient importance to the Dept. of Commerce to make "possible and likely" a successful long-run adjustment of the major media—despite short-run losses.

Differences in the basic appeals of TV and other media suggest merely that TV's impact *need* not be lethal—that after a period of adjustment, the older media may come to prosper side by side with TV just as newspapers have done with radio. Whether or not this happens, of course, is another question, and it is still too early for predictions. Hence, before adjustments in technique and form take place, TV's impact may well continue to increase its rivals' susceptibility to pressures from organized groups and in other ways to reduce their adequacy. An anti-affiliation policy would therefore have limited but definite social costs, in the short run—more in radio and movies, perhaps, than in newspapers. On the other hand, the possible long-run effect of vigorous price and quality competition on both the revenues and adequacy of television's rivals, is of paramount concern here.

Adjustments of Old Media to New

The second and final viewpoint from which we shall appraise FCC's anti-affiliation policy relates to the price and quality adjustments this policy may encourage older media to make in meeting the challenge of their newer rivals. So far as such competition stabilizes the revenues of older media, of course, it increases the latter's resilience to pressure groups. But adjustments in price and quality may also affect adequacy more directly as we shall see.

Adjustments in Price. Newspapers have reduced their operating costs to meet radio-TV competition. They have also begun reducing space rates.[42] Moreover, a major goal has been to offset network radio's system of discounts for long-term advertising contracts and discounts on a rising scale as more stations are included in the advertiser's coverage.[43] Publishers set up an American Newspaper Advertising Network in 1946, offering space contracts in 46 basic newspapers with progressive discounts.

Movie producers have also begun to reduce costs to meet TV competition. Less time is spent in shooting, there are fewer retakes, reductions in technical staff, less elaborate costuming, etc. So far theater admission prices have *not* been reduced. Lastly, network radio is cutting time rates, research outlays, and other costs too.[44]

Newspapers, adjustments in quality. A decade ago newspapers dropped the afternoon "extra," in the face of radio's rapidity with news bulletins; then they turned to greater commentary and evaluation where printed media excel. Thus, since 1930 we find marked increases in column space devoted to foreign news and features, Washington news, and smaller increases in editorials and special columns devoted to public affairs.[45] Newspapers may thereby have reacted to the great news consciousness stimulated by two world wars and the rise of radio and television.

Of course there have also been substantial increases in comics and picture news, possibly as newspapers felt the need to entertain, as well as inform, their readers. Perhaps the most important trend, however, is the marked shrinkage of *general* news and *general* features, as newspapers became functionally specialized. Special sections on labor, sports, theater, foreign affairs, etc., have become the rule.[46] Radio competition may well have stimulated this trend—for departmental specialization clearly enhances the newspaper's ability to comment and evaluate.

Newspapers now carry radio-TV logs and background materials on radio-TV programs, capitalizing on interest in the new media. Their fears of radio and resulting restrictive practices have largely disappeared. Special newspaper columnists review the performance of radio and TV; radio and TV, on the other hand, also review the press. Some authorities predict that newspaper techniques will change even more when most readers can be assumed to have *seen* most events reported on TV. The trend to greater commentary and interpretation can be expected to continue.

Lastly, newspapers have undertaken more systematic analysis of the impact of their advertising on the public. They have also intensified their canvassing campaigns of potential agency accounts by stressing differences in their appeals compared with radio and television.[47]

Movies. Movie producers have called on Hollywood for better films, not more or cheaper films, to cope with television's challenge.[48] Indeed columnists like Bosley Crowther and Leda Bauer, whose standards of adequacy are not those of Hollywood, have noted a marked improvement in recent movies.[49] They wonder whether TV competition may not be a partial explanation.

Theater owners, moreover, bring in more top-run foreign films to hold their audiences. And domestic productions like "The Well," "Streetcar Named Desire," "Death of a Salesman," "Detective Story," "Place in the Sun," etc., suggests what can be done with simple settings and more meaningful content. Some writers claim that the movies have begun to seek out specialized audiences, now as television takes the mass city following, although the success of this venture is by no means assured.[50]

On the other hand, the most recent adjustments to television have become more spectacular—featuring new techniques like three dimensional movies on giant-sized screens, where the epic sweep of *Quo Vadis* and *The Robe* replaces more intimate and simple settings.

Radio's adjustments. Similarly radio programming has begun to show greater diversification and a growing concern with minority tastes and interests.[51] It seems to be leaving varieties, quiz shows, and musicals to television—to some extent. And it is at least suggestive that classical music on sponsored network radio programs rose 100 per cent during 1950.[52] But as large networks divert research and production outlays to television, some observers believe their radio offerings must suffer from inadequate resources, at least in the short run.

How Adjustments Affect Revenues of Older Media. The adjustments just noted seem to strengthen the hands of older media in dealing with their new rivals, and thus strengthen their resilience to outside pressure groups. But it is hard to say *how* effective they have been. The publishers' comeback against radio, and their ability to stand up against TV, of course, are most suggestive. On the other hand, the adjustments of the movies and radio to TV may well be less successful, financially. Perhaps differences in appeals here are less fundamental than in the newspaper case.

One overriding factor which may limit the financial effectiveness of adjustments by older media to television today, is the ratio of total advertising expenditures to national income. Since 1947 this has averaged about 2.35 per cent, compared to a high of 2.74 per cent in 1935 and an average of about 2.62 per cent for 1935–1939. A serious question is how much of our national income can go to advertising without straining the economy. The chances for successful adjustment by older advertising media would seem weakened unless much of television's support comes from a rapidly expanding *total* of advertising revenues, or unless non-advertising funds (e.g. subscription fees) play a sizable role. Even the movies might face intensified competition where available advertising revenues for television reach a ceiling.

Social Significance of the Adjustments. Cost reductions may reduce quality if they entail reductions in research and technical staff. On the other hand, if lavish sets are eliminated, reliance on a few stars and expensive stories are lessened, and greater emphasis is placed on meaningful themes, simple settings, etc., perhaps better and not worse products will be produced on small budgets.

Criticism of the media by one another, limited as it is, seems directly in the public interest, and may be the most desirable adjustment from the community's viewpoint. Greater comprehensiveness of coverage of important issues may be a further by-product of the newspaper's turn to greater commentary and evaluation. So far as movies and radio seek out minority tastes hitherto neglected, different groups in society may be interpreted to each other more realistically.

Indeed most of these quality adjustments seem in line with the standards enunciated by the Commission on Freedom of the Press in 1946, with similar standards stated by FCC, and by the Supreme Court. In any case, of great importance is the absence of convincing evidence that quality competition has seriously intensified triviality, sensationalism, trends to crime, sex, horror, etc.—at least not among the older media that do the adjusting.

To sum up, FCC's policy of discouraging cross channel affiliations would seem to operate in the aid of inducing the adjustments in price and quality described in this section, and through these adjustments possibly to improve the adequacy of the press.

Conclusion

An anit-affiliation rule may aggravate the older media's sensitivity to organized groups, especially in the short run. But in newspaper publishing, long run adjustments in price and quality, developing the newspaper's strong points, seem to have helped the printed medium to hold its own. And though television's sharp blows on radio and the movies may well continue, there is some evidence that here too competitive adjustments may eventually help stabilize the older media. Indeed many (though not all) adjustments older media have made to their newer rivals, appear to enhance the adequacy of the press in their own right. Economic stability of media, lastly, may facilitate realization of certain theoretical benefits of separate ownership. It follows that FCC would do well to reconsider the meaning of its Newspaper Rule today and also ways of applying it to movie producers and theater owners.

At a January 11, 1964, press conference research showing smoking was harmful to health was presented. In June 1967 the FCC ordered stations to carry anti-smoking commercials under the "Fairness Doctrine." Finally, Congress passed a law, secretly supported by the tobacco industry, prohibiting all cigarette commercials—the last were broadcast January 1, 1971. A September 1973 law banned ads for "little cigars."

Table 14.

ADVERTISING DOLLARS

Figures show the total expenditures by advertisers for media and the % to each.

DOLLARS (Add 000,000)	1935	1940	1945	1950	1955	1960	1965	1970
Newspapers	$762.1	$815.4	$921.4	$2,075.6	$3,087.8	$3,702.8	$4,456.5	$5,745.0
Radio	112.6	215.6	423.9	605.4	544.9	692.4	917.0	1,308.0
Television				170.8	1,025.3	1,590.1	2,515.0	3,596.0
Magazines	136.3	197.7	364.5	514.9	729.4	940.8	1,198.8	1,323.0
Direct Mail	281.6	333.7	290.2	803.2	1,298.9	1,830.2	2,324.0	2,766.0
All Other1	397.4	525.2	874.5	1,540.1	2,508.1	3,175.4	3,843.7	4,862.0
TOTAL	$1,690.0	$2,087.6	$2,874.5	$5,710.0	$9,194.4	$11,931.7	$15,255.0	$19,600.0
PERCENT								
Newspapers	45%	39%	32%	36%	34%	31%	29%	29%
Radio	7	10	15	11	6	6	6	7
Television				3	11	13	17	18
Magazines	8	10	13	9	8	8	8	7
Direct Mail	17	16	10	14	14	15	15	14
All Other1	23	25	30	27	27	27	25	25

Source: McCann-Erickson. 1Other includes farm publications, business publications, billboards, and miscellaneous.

Table 15.

RADIO AND TELEVISION ADVERTISING BILLINGS

Figures show the net time sales by networks and stations.

BILLINGS (Add 000)	1935	1940	1945	1950	1955	1960	1965	1970
RADIO:								
Network	$39,738	$ 73,789[a]	$133,974[a]	$131,530[a]	$ 64,077[a]	$ 35,026	$ 44,602	$ 48,800
National Spot	13,805	37,140	76,696	118,824	120,393	202,102	247,942	355,300
Local	26,074	44,757	99,814	202,211	272,011	385,346	535,238	852,700
TOTAL	79,618	155,686	310,484	456,543	456,481	622,474	827,782	1,256,800
TELEVISION:								
Network				35,210	308,900	471,600	1,141,700	1,551,100
National Spot				25,034	222,400	459,200	795,900	1,102,600
Local				30,385	149,800	215,800	328,300	589,100
TOTAL				90,629	681,100	1,146,600	2,265,900	3,242,800
RADIO:								
Network	50%	47%[a]	43%[a]	29%[a]	14%	6%	5%	4%
National Spot	17	24	25	26	26	33	30	28
Local	33	29	32	45	60	62	65	68
TELEVISION:								
Network				39%	45%	41%	51%	48%
National Spot				28	33	40	35	34
Local				34	22	19	14	18

NETWORK TELEVISION BILLINGS (Add 000)	1950		1955		1960		1965		1970	
ABC-TV	$ 6,629	15%	$ 51,393	13%	$158,591	23%	$338,033	27%	$472,312	27%
CBS-TV	12,965	29	189,018	46	274,140	40	492,310	39	661,712	38
NBC-TV	21,186	47	103,385	40	249,640	37	429,977	34	599,692	35
Dumont	4,500	10	3,103	1						

Source: FCC for radio and television total billings. Network television billings for each network were not actual revenues but estimates based on one-time network rates; thus, these figures are higher than the network billings reported by the FCC. Individual network billings compiled by Publishers' Information Bureau (1949-1958), Leading National Advertisers (1959-1967), and Broadcast Advertising Reports (1968-) for TvB, Television Factbook.
aIncludes regional networks.

Table 16.

STATION AND NETWORK REVENUES AND INCOME

Figures show the total revenue and income for radio networks and owned stations, all other AM stations, FM independent stations, television network and owned stations, and all other TV stations.

	1930	1935	1940	1945	1950	1955	1960	1965	1970
REVENUE: (Add 000,000)									
Radio Networks & Owned Stations	$27.7	$50.1	$56.4	$100.9	$110.5	$78.3	$63.0	$74.4	$86.1
Other AM Stations[1]		37.4	90.6	198.3	334.0	374.0	534.7	702.4	991.3
FM Stations[1]					1.4	1.0	5.8	15.7	59.5
TV Networks & Owned Stations					55.5	374.0	640.7	1,023.8	1,457.1
Other TV Stations					50.4	370.0	627.9	941.0	1,351.1
INCOME:[2] (Add 000,000)									
Radio Networks & Owned Stations	$2.8	$5.9	$14.1	$23.1	$19.0	$5.9	$(3.0)	$3.0	$1.7
Other AM Stations[1]			19.1	60.5	49.2	40.4	48.9	78.0	102.3
FM Stations[1]					(2.6)	(0.4)	(2.4)	(3.3)	(11.1)
TV Networks & Owned Stations					(10.0)	68.0	95.2	161.6	167.4
Other TV Stations					0.8	81.5	148.9	286.3	286.4

Sources: FCC financial reports; Variety Radio Directory, 1939-1940 for 1930 and 1935.
[1] FM independent stations and FM stations associated with an AM but reported separately.
[2] Revenues less expenses before federal income tax, ( ) indicates loss.

Table 17.

STATION AVERAGE REVENUES AND INCOME

Figures show the average (mean) revenue and income for network owned radio stations, all other AM stations, FM independent stations, owned TV stations, and all other TV stations.

	1940	1945	1950	1955	1960	1965	1970
AVERAGE REVENUE:							
Net Owned Stations[1]	$545,161	NA	NA	NA	NA	$ 1,926,316	$ 2,568,550
Other AM Stations	123,433	$227,148	$151,268	$137,298	$145,735	179,092	236,635
FM Stations[2]		7,800	16,535	26,316	26,606	46,450	86,357
Net Owned TV Stns				NA	NA	15,680,000	20,833,333
Other TV Stations			541,935	880,523	1,219,223	1,642,234	2,013,562
AVERAGE INCOME:[3]							
Net Owned Stations	$180,645	NA	NA	NA	NA	$ 210,526	$ 358,900
Other AM Stations	26,022	$69,301	$22,283	$ 14,831	$ 13,279	19,888	48,292
FM Stations			(30,233)	(10,526)	(11,009)	(9,763)	(16,110)
Net Owned TV Stns				NA	NA	6,813,334	7,820,000
Other TV Stations			8,602	195,249	289,126	449,650	426,826

Source: FCC
1 Includes network owned AM and AM-FM stations, for some years this data is not available because information was reported only for stations and networks combined.
2 FM independent stations and FM stations associated with an AM but reported separately.
3 Revenues less expenses before federal income tax figures show the mean of all stations reported, ( ) indicates loss.

Table 18.

STATION REVENUES, EXPENSES, PROFITS AND COST

Figures show the average (mean) broadcast revenues, broadcast expenses, broadcast income, depreciated cost and original cost for AM, FM and TV stations.

| TYPE OF STATION | N= | AVERAGE FOR STATIONS | | | COST | |
		Revenue	Expenses	Income	Depreciated	Original
1940						
AM stations	756			28,968	40,079	
1945						
AM stations	891			73,513	38,721	
1970						
AM network owned	20	2,568,550	2,209,650	358,900	472,550	933,750
AM and AM/FM	4189	236,635	212,215	24,419	89,168	174,975
FM	689 [a]	86,357	102,467	(16,110)	54,501	90,260
TV network owned	15	20,833,333	13,006,667	7,820,000	2,562,267	5,246,200
TV	671	2,013,562	1,586,736	426,826	848,496	1,750,000

Source: FCC, An Economic Study of Standard Broadcasting, October 31, 1947 and 37th Annual Report/Fiscal Year 1971, Federal Communications Commission.

Original costs for stations which have been sold is that portion of the price assigned by licensee to property; depreciated cost is the original cost minus depreciation.

[a]464 independent FMs and 225 FMs associated with AMs but reported separately.

Table 19.

STATION REVENUES AND PROFITS

Figures show the average revenue and profit for stations in several
categories 1940 and 1972, and the number of employees and salaries for 1972.

	Total Revenue	Profit		Employees[4]	
		Dollars	%	Salaries	No.
RADIO-1940					
Local Unlimited	$ 43,800	$ 4,200	10%		
Regional	204,300	47,000	23		
50 KW Unlimited	856,100	296,300	31		
RADIO-1972					
Over 2,500,000[1]					
Fulltime-Large[2]	$2,948,700	$648,400	22%	$1,148,800	67
Fulltime-Small[3]	427,600	54,300	13	209,700	14
Daytime	295,700	10,100	3	144,100	11
500,000-100,000					
Fulltime	597,200	42,500	7	282,900	25
Daytime	258,500	14,500	6	106,000	12
100,000-250,000					
Fulltime	282,700	19,700	7	145,300	15
Daytime	136,300	7,600	6	68,200	8
25,000-50,000					
Fulltime	243,700	22,800	9	122,400	13
Daytime	161,100	13,300	8	74,500	8
Under 10,000					
Fulltime	119,200	9,600	8	57,200	7
Daytime	96,000	6,100	7	47,000	6
FM Stations					
Over 500,000	139,300	(9,700)	(7)	78,300	7
Under 100,000	62,200	(500)	(1)	33,400	4
50 KW Stations					
Over 1,000,000	2,196,400	424,600	19	875,300	43
Under 1,000,000	668,400	115,600	17	261,900	25
TELEVISION-1972					
Network Affils.					
1-10	$13,361,900	$3,945,800	30%	$3,427,500	197
26-50	4,176,700	1,159,500	28	1,173,400	135
76-100	1,617,200	223,800	14	556,700	55
126-150	1,061,900	80,500	8	414,500	41
201-209	632,000	117,900	19	232,900	25
Independents					
1-15	3,331,600	(564,700)	(17)	281,500	68
16-209	1,311,700	(69,000)	(5)	456,700	41
UHF					
1-50	1,617,600	(287,900)	(18)	359,800	49
101-209	666,400	(7,300)	(1)	272,700	34
Satellite					
54-155	192,500	18,300	(10)	64,000	9

Sources: 1940, FCC, An Economic Study of Standard Broadcasting, October 31, 1947; 1972, *1973*
Radio Financial Report and *1973 Television Financial Report*, National Association of Broadcasters.
[1]Market size for radio stations is population; TV is rank (ARB). [2]Stations with revenues over
$1,000,000. [3]Less than $1,000,000. [4]Fulltime.

Table 20.

STATION TRANSFERS

Figures show the number and average price for the transfer of radio and/or TV stations for selected years and the average for 1938 to 1946 and 1954 to 1971. The average transfer price is computed from dollar volume figures representing total consideration reported for all transactions, with the exception of minority-interest transfers in which control of the license did not change hands. In computing the number of stations, an AM-FM facility or an AM-only or FM-only was counted as only one unit.

| YEAR | NUMBER OF STATIONS TRANSFERRED | | | AVERAGE PRICE OF TRANSACTION | | |
	Radio Only	TV Only	Radio-TV	Radio Only	TV Only	Radio-TV
1940	12			$ 98,708		
1945	14			229,582		
TOTAL 1938 to 1946	228			$ 45,600,000[a]		
1955	242	29	11	$112,947	$ 806,712	$2,031,964
1960	345	21	10	150,039	1,091,915	2,464,840
1965	389	32	15	143,787	919,796	3,317,133
1970	268	19	3	321,988	4,602,846	346,155
TOTAL 1954 to 1971	5,882	463	231	$ 1,067,411,935[a]	$ 942,380,914[a]	$ 637,407,439[a]

Source: 1938-1946 data from FCC, An Economic Study of Standard Broadcasting, 1947, p. 88, 90. 1954-1971 data from FCC annual reports, Broadcasting Yearbook. [a]Total all transactions; not average.

Table 21.

AUDIENCE AND STATION INVESTMENT

Figures show the investment in broadcasting made by audiences in receiver purchases and repairs compared to the gross investment in broadcast station facilities. Add: 000,000

5-Year Period	R/TV Set Manufact.	R/TV Repairs	Audience Total Costs	R/TV Stations Gross Investment
1922-1925	$ 150.8		$ 150.8	
1926-1930	808.5		808.5	
1931-1935	452.6	$ 95	547.6	
1936-1940	777.1	129	906.1	$ 747.7
1941-1945a	336.8	302	638.8	411.5
1946-1950	4,513.4	923	5,436.4	1,059.9
1951-1955	6,625.1	2,164	8,789.1	2,491.7
1956-1960	5,834.0	3,601	9,435.0	4,401.3
1961-1965	8,043.0	NA	14,000b	6,075.6

Sources: Set production, Electronics Industries Association Year Book 1967. Radio/TV repairs, Chapin, Mass Communications, East Lansing: Michigan State University Press, 1957, p. 94 (to 1955). Based on Commerce Department figures which are source for 1956-67 figures ("Survey of Current Business"). R/TV stations gross investment, Statistical History of U.S., Government Printing Office, p. 491. aNo set manufacture April 1943 to October 1945. bLWL/MCT estimate.

Table 22.

BROADCAST ADVERTISERS BY PRODUCT CATEGORIES

Figures show the percent of advertising volume for various categories of products and services for radio in 1934 and 1958 and television in 1960 and 1970

	RADIO		TELEVISION	
	1934	1958	1960	1969
Food	19%	20%	21%	19%
Toiletries	14	7	14	15
Drugs	10	8	10	10
Gas, Oil	9	7	3	3
Candy & Soft Drinks	8	3	4	5
Automotive	6	10	6	7
Soap, Cleansers	5	5	11	9
Tobacco	5	14	9	8
General Household	4	1	6	5
Clothing	3	1	2	2
Finance, Insurance	2	1	--	1
Amusements	1	1	--	1
Other	14	22	14	15

Sources: Hettinger, Harvard Business Review, XIV:1, p. 14; TV-Radio Basics (Sponsor), 1958, p. 132; TV Basics (Sponsor), 1961, p. 51; Broadcasting, May 11, 1970, p. 48.

Buffalo Bob and Howdy Doody.

Kukla, Ollie, and Fran revived to introduce the CBS children's films.

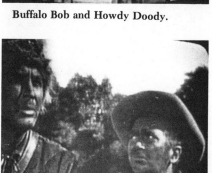

Fess Parker as Davy Crockett with Buddy Ebsen.

Art Linkletter.

In the fall of 1969 CBS brought in Merv Griffin to duel Johnny Carson.

That first night Carson countered with Bob Hope.

Joey Bishop walked off December 1969. Griffin lasted three seasons and was replaced by movies.

On the 20th anniversary of *Today*, January 1972, all of the hosts gathered: Jack Lescoulie, Dave Garroway, Frank McGee, John Chancellor, Hugh Downs, with newsman Frank Blair.

PART FIVE

EMPLOYMENT

> My entire life has been an endless battle against the faceless,
> the inscrutable, inhuman, callous establishment . . . corporate struc-
> tures, government, public apathy, non-involvement, permissive,
> submissive, the demographics that make a great bunch of numbers,
> and faceless people out of all of us.
> —Arthur Godfrey, CBS Radio Network
> April 30, 1972.

BROADCASTERS in the early 1920s were a collection of parttime
practioners. The firms owning radio stations were in it for motives other than entertainment and information. Employees were reluctant to go into a business with such a cloudy future. The first fulltime programming employee of a broadcasting station was Harold W.
Arlin, an engineer for Westinghouse assigned to KDKA as an announcer, who kept the job until he was assigned a better position in
another Westinghouse plant. Most employees of broadcasting stations were—like Arlin—interested in but not committed to broadcasting as a career. A former vice president of NBC recalls that in 1922 as
a reporter for the Chicago *Daily News* he was assigned to do a radio
column but was told ". . . this may not last long. It may just be
another fad like mahjong." [1] Graham McNamee describes his motivation for getting into broadcasting as:

> But I had scarcely heard of radio then; in fact, had never listened to
> a loud-speaker or handled a head phone.
> What prompted me to drift into the studio of the American Tele-
> phone and Telegraph Company (WEAF) on Broadway I do not
> know. [2]

Most of the early broadcasters got into the business first as technicians. It was a new business and most of the people in it in the

early 1920s were young and untried. In 1925 an 18-year-old college girl was termed by *Radio Age* as "radio's leading lady," labeling her as reaching a "pinnacle of career as America's premier 'radio theater' actress." [3] The goal of many programs was the promotion of some business including the famous "Roxie" Rothafel who conducted an intimate radio show each Sunday night from the New York Capitol Theater which he managed. His "gang" at the Capitol was interviewed and, in turn, entertained as part of the contract with the theater. Rothafel was an early student of broadcasting—never forgetting the primary audience.

> The studio at the Capitol is immense and is generally half filled with people famous in various walks of life who have come to see the Gang in person. Upon these celebrities Roxy literally turns his back. Over in the extreme corner he has set up his microphone, and when he talks to his Radio friends he stands facing the wall quite away from the spectators. [4]

Employment of men rather than women, particularly as announcers has continued to be a phenomenon peculiar to this country. A woman, commenting on this matter in 1924, wrote:

> Women, as a rule, when they speak over the microphone, are apt to make one of two mistakes. They either speak in a patronizing tone or they are precise to a point of exasperation. With the latter, it is as if they stopped to cross every T and dot every I. The effect in either case is disagreeable. And, so far as the present writer's experience goes, women radio speakers are lacking in humor. On the other hand, men are inclined to be preachy. Here is a choice of two evils, one as bad as the other. But there are some men heard via radio to whom it is joy unalloyed to listen.
>   There are a few announcers in this country—all men—who are beyond criticism. They are consequently an unfailing pleasure to hear, from their first greeting to their final, "good night." They know just how far to carry familiarity in their speech—a trait that is the final test of an announcer's adaptability to his position. The men who are continually "jollying" their listeners trying themselves to be entertainers, become extremely tiresome. A little of this sort of thing may be agreeable and effective, but more than a little becomes a surfeit. This is not an individual opinion, but one that has been expressed by large numbers of people. [5]

Very few employees on stations in the 1920s were being paid from station revenues—some announcers and a few musicians in studio orchestras on the most important stations. As stations settled some technical problems they offered prizes for original radio plays—a form of indirect pay. Very few artists were paid for performances on radio, which added to the lack of interest by big stars. As broadcasting stabilized and audiences grew, some artists began to use it as a song-plugging device, combining appearances on the air with local sheet music sales. A critic, writing in one of the most influential broadcasting magazines of the 1920s, urged that concert performers give up some of their fees to perform on radio in the public interest:

> The concert artist lives on public patronage, and public patronage can be obtained only through advertising. This advertising is carried on through two mediums. The straight out-and-out advertising which appears in newspapers and musical magazines, and the veiled medium in the form of stories which the publicity agent concocts and then persuades editors the public will eagerly devour. Both of these mediums cost an incredible amount of money. The reason why so many fine artists have passed into the obscurity of the teaching profession is because they have not had the money to keep up this advertising. Their names must be constantly before the public if they are to succeed. And even after success has come, the advertising must be kept up with equal vigor, or they drop to the rear of the procession, then soon are out entirely.[6]

A most heralded event was the broadcast January 1, 1925, by John McCormack and Lucrezia Bori, Metropolitian Opera star. The Victor Talking Machine Company reversed its ban on its stars appearing on radio and arranged the event to stimulate sagging record sales. One "conservative" estimate was that over 6,000,000 heard the broadcast.

The entrance of networks into broadcasting changed the employment picture. One radio magazine in 1928 jubilantly reported that Eddie Cantor was dividing his talent between the "stage and mike." [7] The division at the time heavily favored the stage. Other groups were under the spell of the "good will and friendly influence of broadcasting" as Keith and Orpheum vaudeville circuits featured an hour broadcast of their performers each week over NBC.[8]

By 1930 an estimated 6,000 persons were employed fulltime in broadcasting. It was the only amusement industry (in fact one of the few industries of any kind) to show an increase in employees during the period between 1929 and 1935. It had more than 12,000 fulltime employees by 1935 with an average pay topped only by the brokerage business.

Talent came to broadcasting as the depression widened. Entertainers of all kinds sought jobs, waiting for vaudeville to come back.

The biggest increase in employment in broadcasting occurred when radio and television expanded in the late 1940s. The industry employed 36,000 in 1945; 58,000 in 1950 and leaped to nearly 80,000 in 1956. Radio station staffs became smaller. The average station in 1945 employed 40 staffers. Ten years later the average station had only 15 employees. Television used men as extensively as it used money and materials. In 1955, 500 television stations and the networks employed as many persons as 3,000 radio stations and their networks.

Events of the early 1950s revealed the susceptability of broadcasting to pressures of all sorts. In 1950 all employees of CBS were required to sign a loyalty oath as a result of blacklists and suspicion throughout the country. A booklet entitled *Red Channels: The Report of Communist Influence in Radio and Television* was distributed to networks to uncover communists or lukewarm noncommunists. Litigation over blacklisting continued until 1962 when finally one former CBS employee was awarded three-and-a-half million dollars (later reduced to $550,000).

By 1970 about 120,000 were working in broadcasting stations and on networks. About 93,000 of these were fulltime. The period of the 1960s showed an increase of efforts by minorities, especially blacks, to get more persons into broadcasting and its allied fields. The decade featured a number of plans to train minorities for jobs both on and off the air. The period showed an increase in the number of women and minority persons as series stars, in commercials, and as news reporters and anchor-persons. The types of roles played by minorities were less stereotyped. Yet, complaints continued and some research studies actually showed little increase in better jobs for women and minorities.

Being a broadcaster had changed from hobby to a table of organization that listed hundreds of specialized professions, skills, talents, and unions. After a lifetime in broadcasting, most of it with CBS, on his last radio network broadcast Arthur Godfrey probably expressed the judgement of many.

> I have enjoyed every minute of it with CBS . . . the great *esprit de corps* that we once had here at CBS. Networks don't have it any more. No big corporation does I guess . . . in recent years I haven't seen . . . Paley or Stanton. I saw Doc Stanton the other day when we both got Peabody Awards. We were on the same dais and never spoke, never got a chance to. And it saddened me a little. He's become so involved in the gray, great huge corporation, conglomerate which CBS is now.[9]

In a 1963 speech to the National Association of Broadcasters, FCC Chairman Newton Minow clearly articulated the need for enlightened broadcasters.

> Finally, ladies and gentlemen, you chose a hard life when you chose broadcasting. You volunteered for public regulation and public pressure. In return, the people have placed in your hands and hearts the greatest gift possible in a free country, the extraordinary privilege of using the public airwaves to the exclusion of others who would welcome, and indeed have fought for, that privilege. Under

our broadcasting system, as I have repeated so often, your government does not decide what goes on the air. Acting as trustees for all of us, you private citizens made the decisions. We will continue to prod your consciences, to goad your ideals, to disturb your sleep.

As you meet your responsibility, you will remember to provide more news and public affairs programs where ideas are rubbed against other ideas into the friction of controversy. On such informational programs may rest the strengthening of an enlightened electorate, critical to the survival of freedom. But you will also remember that you need to do more than feed our minds. Broadcasting must also nourish our spirit. We need entertainment which helps us to grow in compassion and understanding.[10]

At the 1951 Kefauver crime hearings only Frank Costello's hands were shown.

Senator Joseph McCarthy. 1954 Army hearings.

From May 17 to September 26, 1973, there were 40 days of live TV coverage of Senate hearings on Watergate—10 on all three networks before a system of rotation was worked out. Two-thirds came in June and July and all were repeated each night on PBS. In his testimony beginning on June 25, John Dean said Richard Nixon was part of the Watergate coverup.

The networks also rotated coverage of House Judiciary hearings on the impeachment of Richard Nixon beginning July 24, 1974. On July 28, the committee approved the first article of impeachment on the Watergate coverup. A second on misuses of power was voted on July 29 (above) and a third passed on July 30, the sixth and final day of the proceedings.

41

Carl Dreher

MAKING RADIO YOUR BUSINESS

BROADCASTING HAS opened up a considerable number of new positions. The personnel of a first-class station may include a program
manager, who interviews prospective artists and makes arrangements
for out-of-the-studio broadcasting, several announcers, and a technical staff, consisting of control operators, transmitter attendants, and
out-side or pick-up men. The control operator monitors the outgoing
material and makes indicated adjustments, such as increasing or de-
creasing the amount of modulation, setting the accompaniment at the
proper loudness relative to the singer, and so on. The transmitter operator watches the tube set, checking the wavelength and antenna
current, and listening in at short intervals for distress signals at sea,
which necessitate immediate shutting down of the transmitter. The
outside men take care of acoustic exploration at theatres and halls
from which special-event broadcasting is contemplated, the setting
of the microphones, necessary tests, and supervision during the actual transmission. Of course in most stations there is not as much
specialization as this, and one man may handle most of the routine of
the studio. As soon as one gets into outside work, however, a good-
sized staff becomes imperative.

An ear for music and sensitiveness to cacophanous elements are
among the special qualifications of the broadcasting station operator.
The more he knows about the engineering end—the special features
of tube set operation, the technique of electrical voice reproduction,
and so on—the better, but in addition to these fundamental factors he
must be something of a musician and expert in practical acoustics. If
he lacks these qualities, he will often be in the position of knowing
less about the mechanics of his job than the performers in the studio,
many of whom have had experience in the closely related field of
phonograph recording. Social qualities are also of more importance
in the broadcasting field than in other branches of the art, since the
personnel of a station is in contact with outsiders of prominent position and good breeding. The broadcasting specialist, accordingly, has
to try to make himself a combination concert hall manager and engineer. This question of general cultivation and social ease is likewise
prominent in the selection of announcers.

The writer has had occasion recently to give counsel on the matter of taking up radio as a profession to several young men of high

Radio Broadcast, July 1923, pp. 190–196.

school age, and an outline of his recommendations may be of interest to readers in somewhat the same position. The first desirable step is to get into practical touch with the field through amateur activities—reading the periodical literature, building sets, joining radio clubs and becoming junior members of the engineering societies. It is best to go to a college or technical school, specializing in electrical engineering—not that a B.S. or an E.E., as such, makes an engineer of a man, but it affords him a good foundation, enables him to make pleasant and valuable personal connections and gives him, in later years, the satisfaction of feeling that he has not overlooked any good bets in preparation. This point is emphasized, it should be added, by associates of the writer for whom he has the highest respect, and who, lacking academic preparation, feel nevertheless that the time and capital is advantageously invested. During vacations, if it is at all practicable, the student should try to obtain temporary employment in commercial operating, as an apprentice or junior, or factory experience, less for the income obtainable in this way than for the value of coordinating practice and theory. Attention should be devoted to code practice and a commercial operator's license secured as soon as possible. Although radio's centre of mass may be shifting from telegraphy to telephony, the relations between the two will of necessity remain intimate; operators of broadcasting stations, for example, are required to have commercial telegraphers' licenses at the present time. On the other hand, it is clear from what has been said above that courses in the arts, such as a study of the history of music; and such experience as may be obtained in playing in a college orchestra, for example, will be quite valuable, even looking at the question from a narrow utilitarian viewpoint, without regard to humanizing and cultural influences.

42

James C. Young

BROADCASTING PERSONALITY

WHAT DOES the radio public want?
  "I don't know."
  Such was the answer of S. L. Rothafel, one of the most successful

Radio Broadcast, July 1924, pp. 246–250.

impresarios of the air. Sitting at his big desk in the Capitol Theatre Building on Broadway he confided some of the troubles which beset a radio director.

"No general reply will answer your question," he said, "but perhaps we can state the matter a little differently. It is the personality of the performer that sways or fails to sway the great unseen audience distributed over thousands of miles, but drawn together in a common thought by the pulsations of the air.

"This is the most appreciative audience in the world and also the most critical. Above all else, it is a sincere audience, and accurately measures the human quality of the performer before the microphone.

"When a man begins to speak, let us say, the audience in his vast theater instantly divines whether he knows his subject, whether he merely is speaking in the professional sense, or sends words worthwhile across the reaches of space. If the man is sincere, moved by high purpose, his audience hands over its confidence; if he is prosaic, indifferent, just talking to kill minutes, his audience is likely to tune-out with one accord.

"I am convinced that the radio performer's personality is more important than his voice, his subject or the occasion. Any of these may be poor or inopportune and still a speaker will succeed. But if his personality is flat, his purpose vague, he certainly will not command respect on the radio circuit."

Mr. Rothafel has a trick of catching one knee in two strong hands, then whirling this way and that in his swivel chair, as he talks. It is not difficult to see why he has caught the imagination of radio audiences. He has a sparkling eye and a moving vitality that impart confidence and enthusiasm. His Sunday night programs broadcast from WEAF, WJAR, and WCAP, are awaited by radio owners everywhere. Certainly there is nothing of the casual, hit-or-miss quality about these programs. They have all the finesse, the completeness and satisfaction of a theatrical performance that just strikes the nail of public favor.

The Capitol company—known to fame as Roxie's Gang—includes more than thirty-five performers and his programs range all the way from the severely classical to "Sally in Our Alley." Between times these programs dip into philosophy, poetry, folklore, and musical compositions of every possible shade.

How Roxie Turns on the Psychic Tap

Now just observe the impresario. He raises a finger, the girl watches his face, and at the sign of an eyelid she begins to sing.

As the first notes rise Mr. Rothafel "registers" for her benefit how she is getting on. Her eyes never leave his face. A wag of the head, a shake of the finger, a change of expression, govern her efforts. For the moment the director is her audience, taking the place of all that multitude perhaps listening to some old ballad. Mr. Rothafel is no mean actor. He conveys to the girl every emotion which she stirs. He has a plastic, expressionable face; for the moment his own personality drops away. He literally is the audience, sensing just how it feels and as the girl goes on he carries her over every bad spot in the road—if there happen to be any.

Perhaps her expression is a little over-drawn; maybe the pathos is a trifle too deep. Right there the director shakes his head and frowns and the expression comes down a key, into the more natural, easy mode which is needed. If the girl were singing by herself—on her own, so to speak—she never would know that she had reached a little too far, that her technique had faltered. But with a director at her elbow who literally turns on the psychic tap and interprets for her how the audience responds, she has a valuable aid to genius.

Roxie's Programs are Experiment

Radio programs still are a matter of much uncertainty. No station in the country has been able to decide what the public wants—and Mr. Rothafel says he doesn't know. But evidently the public knows and his guesses about its state of mind are remarkably accurate.

Looking over the Rothafel programs it is evident that he believes in variety; also that each program is something of an experiment. One of his recent successes was the offering of "Massa's in the Cold, Cold Ground." That is a song which but few Americans of this generation ever heard. It came from the pen of Stephen Foster, author of the many negro melodies which gradually have become American classics, perhaps our only distinctively American songs.

Mr. Rothafel, with the same sure instinct that prompted Foster to write the song, decided to test its possibilities by radio. Any one who has heard these plaintive notes will recall that it is sung almost in a monotone and is especially suited to a mellow voice.

When the singer in this case stepped up to the microphone Mr. Rothafel waited with considerable anxiety for the results from his psychic contact. But the song had not gone beyond the first bars until he signalled "all's well." Then, toward the end, he took the singer's arm and together they walked across the studio, the last melancholy notes gradually blending with the air—that insubstantial element which had just borne to an awed audience the story of an old slave's sorrow that his good master should lie "in the cold, cold ground."

Although without technical musical education this impresario directs orchestras by the sense of feeling, arranges all of his musical selections, devises scenic and lighting effects, and does a dozen other things that are supposed to require the strictest sort of technical training. He long since proved that he understood the public mind better than most men and his later success with radio programs has greatly broadened his field of effort.

43

Jennie Irene Mix

AT LAST—GREAT ARTISTS OVER THE RADIO

THE EXPECTED happened when the phonograph companies began to feature their artists over the radio. Many who are equally familiar with the music and the radio game knew that in time the phonograph manufacturers would relax from their autocratic attitude in forbidding any of their artists to broadcast and would realize that in refusing to use the microphone as a means of advertising they were neglecting a rich opportunity.

Still, the change came rather suddenly. To the Brunswick-Balke-Collender Company goes the credit of taking the initiative in what is the most significant development in radio programs since broadcasting was started.

To be sure, the Brunswick firm had somewhat prepared the way by making records of the chief hits of some of the popular radio singers and players, and advertising them as radio favorites, thereby selling many of the records. But that was quite different when that company suddenly sprung on the public the news that Florence Easton, one of the leading sopranos at the Metropolitan, Mario Chamlee, who holds a position as tenor of equal prominence at the same house, Elly Ney, pianist, and the Cleveland orchestra, would be heard in the first of three programs to be given by the Brunswick recording artists during December.

Then came the Victor Talking Machine Company with the announcement that on New Year's night they would present Miss Lucrezia Bori and John McCormack in the first of a series of radio programs to be given by their artists. One would have thought, in reading many of the papers after this performance that never before in the history of radio had the great stars in the musical world broad-

Radio Broadcast, March 1925, p. 880–882.

cast. This was a deep injustice to the Brunswick Company and the artists they had up to that time presented before the microphone. The first program of the Brunswick artists in all respects equalled and in some ways excelled the first Victor program. But then, no intelligent person was beguiled by the newspaper reports into the belief that the Victor program was the first one of its kind broadcast. We have no issue to raise with the Victor people regarding this matter. Our complaint is against the press, which did not state the case completely. We believe in fair play.

There has been no end of discussion in the papers regarding whether these artists who have so far been heard on the Brunswick and Victor programs, are or are not paid. The Victor Company has announced that all of their artists are giving their services for these initial experiments. But this is a matter with which the public has no concern. It is a business question to be decided between the recording companies and their artists. For this entire scheme of the Brunswick and Victor companies in putting their singers and instrumentalists on the radio is a business proposition, and it is quite right that it should be. They are out to sell records, and let us hope that they will sell so many more of them than ever before that they will feel they can never desert the microphone as a means of advertising. If, on the other hand, they do not find that the returns justify the expense involved, a large public will have had the opportunity to hear artists they could never have heard any other way.

True, with radio in its present uncertain state so far as good production is concerned, some may have failed in trying to hear the artists so far featured on these programs. But to one such person there are no doubt hundreds to whom the voice, the instrument, the interpretation, came through with a clearness that brought keen satisfaction.

But let us not lose our heads. It was amusing to read in *The New York Times* the day after this Victor program was broadcast, a wail from William A. Brady over the vacant seats in the theaters New Year's night. According to him, every one had stayed at home to hear this concert. The theater faced ruin. Even when great stars were not broadcasting, the theater crowd stayed at home to listen to the music broadcast!

If Mr. Brady thinks that any one who knows a good play when he sees it is going to stay away from the theater when a good play is on because he prefers to hear radio music, then Mr. Brady's knowledge of radio music is exactly equal to a cipher.

No, let us not lose our heads. These programs put on by the phonograph companies are going to help radio music tremendously. But they are not going to dominate.

It must be borne in mind that not all the programs put on by the phonograph companies will be given by famous concert and opera stars. Artists who make "popular" records will be heard as well—but then, when you are out to advertise your wares, if you are wise, you are going to advertise all of them and not just the *de luxe* variety.

44

F. G. Fritz

WENDELL HALL:
EARLY RADIO PERFORMER

DURING RADIO'S early years, 1920–1925, broadcast entertainment drew upon a rich tradition of vaudeville entertainment in America. It often reflected whatever was currently popular among vaudeville theater audiences. There were few attempts to develop programming designed specifically for broadcasting.

In those early days of radio entertainment, a hard core of seasoned, professional entertainers who had served their apprenticeship on vaudeville stages, behind store counters plugging songs, in cafes, and in church choirs were often the innovators. Most of their names are little remembered.

Wendell Woods Hall was born August 23, 1896 in St. George, Kansas, and at an early age moved with his family to Chicago. His musical training came first from his mother, then later developed at the various schools which he attended. Throughout high school he performed as soloist, in quartets—at lodge meetings, churches, and amateur theater. He learned to play the ukelele but commenced his professional career at the xylophone. He claimed to be the first person in vaudeville to sing and play that instrument at the same time. In 1917 he was doing three shows a day at the Rialto Theater in Chicago for $75 a week billed as "The Singing Xylophonist."

After six or seven months as a "small timer" on the circuit doing three to five shows a day, Hall returned to Chicago where he performed in clubs and began writing songs. By the time he entered the Army in August 1918 he had composed and published four tunes. He returned to vaudeville, plagued by poor routes, split weeks, long railroad jumps and low pay—not very different from most of his fellow performers. He left the tour; wrote and promoted his own compositions, and made records.

Song pluggers abounded in Chicago and other cities during this period. They were singers and musicians who were employed by publishing firms, and who travelled not only from counter to counter, but wherever the opportunity presented itself to promote their company's songs and sheet music. In the next few years numerous song pluggers, along with Wendell Hall and other performers, would form the vanguard of early radio entertainment.

> I was on State street in one of the music stores and somebody said, hear that stuff over there, that's radio. I said, what's radio? They had a little crystal set and I put on the earphones and started to listen. First time I ever heard radio. I thought to myself, why not go into radio and see what happens. If I could make my songs go behind a music counter, and radio, I imagine, covers many more people, then that's for me.[1]

The Westinghouse Corporation opened Chicago's first radio station, KYW on November 11, 1921, with studios located in the Commonwealth Edison building. The KYW program schedule for the 1921–22 season was, "entirely Chicago Civic Opera. All performances, afternoon and evening, six days a week, were broadcast—and nothing else." [2]

It appears that KYW built up a rather large audience by broadcasting the Chicago Civic Opera. The popularity of these programs meant that if the station was to maintain its quality image, it was imperative to engage competent personnel and professional entertainers.

Mr. Hall's first appearance before the microphone took place shortly after the close of the opera season about the first of March 1922. Commenting on Hall's debut over the air, Wilson Wetherbee, a director at KYW, said:

> One day a young red-headed singer and song writer came to our office and said he wanted to try broadcasting some of his songs. This chap saw he would have to make his songs go if they were to go at all and he decided to tackle the biggest of all audiences—the radio listeners. He got his chance, and in a very short time became famous.[3]

For a few months Hall sang and played two or three evenings a week over KYW. In time the expense and inconvenience of his six-foot xylophone led to substitution of the ukelele. He took a job as the station's first paid staff artist at $25 a week, working from 3:00 P.M. to 3:00 A.M.

At KYW, Hall tasted success and popularity and perfected his broadcast style. Throughout 1922 and up until his radio tour in June 1923, he was probably the best known and most listened to entertainer in Chicago. Wilson Wetherbee commented that the station received "more requests for songs by Wen Hall than for anybody else."

The new star saw the tangible results of radio as a promotion medium. In pre-KYW days his tunes were only moderately successful. His radio performances gained publicity for him and created a demand for his songs. Sales of his sheet music increased enormously. The idea of using radio to promote songs was quickly seized by other music publishers. Chicago stations in 1922 were overrun with song pluggers anxious to "work for nothing," according to Hall. He continued writing, and plugging, and in 1923 wrote "It Ain't Gonna Rain No Mo' "—the song would be associated with him for the rest of his life.

At KYW he also recruited other talent who would broadcast free. The lack of payment kept many artists from the air, and those with reputations would not risk their good names by submitting to the harsh fate that might await them over the air.[4] While the microphone might cause even the most seasoned performer to quiver and quake, the small timer had all to gain.

Hall was vaudeville trained but he adopted a new approach for an audience whose laughter and applause registered in the mail two or three days later. He chose songs and a style, worked on jokes and a monologue, and above all, learned the importance of personality and variety. Voice was all. ". . . The radio performer must feel his invisible audience; while the stage star gets continual stimulus from the listeners right in front of him, the mike entertainer must possess good imagination to picture his tuners-in." [5] Hall ruled that jokes could be used but once and that a new program was needed every night because a radio entertainer could never have a fresh audience. Vaudeville acts could be used for years on the circuit without change. Three decades later new TV stars would learn the same, again.

During the first three or four years of radio, a small group of professional artists developed the form, and set the style and pattern for radio entertainment.

Early midwestern radio artists from vaudeville included "The Harmony Girls," Edith Carpenter and Grace Ingram; "Happy" Harry Geise; Riley and Goss; Gosden and Correll who appeared over WEBH in 1924 and later became famous as *Amos 'n' Andy;* Carson Robison; the team of "Little" Jack Little and Tommy Malic; Ford Rush and Glenn Rowell; "The Whispering Pianist," Art Gillham; and "The Gaelic Twins," Eddie and Fanny Cavenaugh.

East coast audiences were listening to "The Original Radio Girl," Vaughn deLeath; "The Harmony Boys," Billy Jones and Ernest Hare; "The Sweethearts of the Air," May Singhi Breen and

Peter deRose; "The Silver Masked Tenor," Joseph White; and comedians such as Ed Wynn, Will Rogers, and Stoopnagle and Budd.

Future radio teams adopted the song-and-patter style of Jones
and Hare; the comedy patter of *Amos 'n' Andy;* the singing style of
Breen and deRose; the announcing manner of Cross and McNamee,
and many single acts copied the style of Wendell Hall.

THE GOOD YEARS (1923–1930)

Wendell Hall was first to "play" radio stations the way others had
played theaters. In June of 1923, driving his father's automobile with
built-in sleeping quarters, he set out on the first radio tour. He appeared on about 35 stations and covered 5,000 miles in four months.
Station managers who depended on local talent were delighted
when Hall asked for the opportunity to broadcast. Stations often adhered to no definite time schedules, so he would often sing and play
for a two- to three-hour period. When he wasn't performing he visited
music counters promoting his songs. He made sure the clerks knew
he was appearing over the local radio station, and that they had an
ample supply of his sheet music. In addition to singing and playing,
Hall would help station managers (though they often did not have
that exact title) plan future programs and inform them of news of
other stations. The tour started at WOC, Davenport, Iowa, and
reached WEAF, the premier station of the East coast. In New York
he discussed a recording contract with the Victor Talking Machine
Company and returned to Chicago via Philadelphia, Baltimore,
Washington, Pittsburgh, Cleveland, and Detroit, appearing at radio
stations in each city. "It Ain't Gonna Rain No Mo' " was the first
song to become a national craze because of radio.

Wherever he toured, requests for the "Rain" song led the rest.
Over the years the song sold close to 10,000,000 copies of sheet
music and records, with Hall's voice selling well over 2,000,000 recordings. From 50 verses in the original composition the number
grew to 1,000 and became one of the greatest novelty numbers in all
music publishing.

In November of 1923 Wendell Hall signed a contract to record
exclusively for Victor for one year with an option for at least two. He
was the first Victor record artist to broadcast.[6] Other Victor recording
artists could not go on the air for fear that broadcasting might slow
sale of their recordings.

Hall's success may have convinced the Victor Company that
radio stimulated record sales. On January 1, 1925, two Victor artists,
John McCormack and Lucrezia Bori made their debuts before the
microphone. The Victor Company realized the power of radio and, as
Gleason Archer said, ". . . decided in the spring of 1925 to conform

rather than perish." [7] Hall recorded for Victor until 1926 when he signed a $100,000 contract with the Brunswick-Balke-Collender Company.

In January 1924 Wendell Hall signed a national advertising contract with the National Carbon Company, and became the first entertainer to use radio under the wing of a sponsor. He appeared over WEAF in New York as a member of the *Eveready Hour*, sponsored by the National Carbon Company, makers of Eveready batteries.[8] The *Eveready Hour* reached only the territory covered by WEAF. Dealers of the National Carbon Company elsewhere, of course, desired radio publicity in their markets. Until network broadcasting made possible the delivery of the *Eveready Hour* to distant stations, the National Carbon Company sent out groups of artists to give broadcasts over stations throughout the country.[9] The first sponsored tour was led by Wendell Hall, because of his stature, ability as a performer, and competency as a salesman.[10] In Wendell Hall or "The Red-headed Music Maker" as he billed himself, the Eveready advertising agency found a showman with an act that had a "flavor" all its own, dominated by its star's dynamic personality.[11] He used a variety of songs, mixing the tempo of musical numbers and his pace was fast. The climax to his act came with the singing of "It Ain't Gonna Rain No Mo'." This was his trademark and listeners eagerly awaited it.

In late January 1924, Hall accompanied a salesman for the battery division of the National Carbon Company and a representative of the Victor Talking Machine Company on a series of trips that in three years would take him to every principal radio station in the United States. The first tour covered some 21 stations, as far west as Texas. Although there was no "direct" advertising (no written commercials extolling the virtues of Eveready batteries) it was a woefully inattentive listener who failed to get the message every time Hall was introduced as "The Eveready Redhead," "Eveready Red," the "Eveready Entertainer," or the "Eveready Red-headed Music Maker." These identifying tags were used not only at the beginning and end of each program, but between songs.

Hall usually spent a week at each station entertaining from 11 minutes to two hours nightly, depending on the number of telephone requests. During the day he again visited music stores pushing his sheet music and Victor records.

The tour was completed some time in late May. When he returned to New York and station WEAF, there were nearly 20,000 letters of appreciation, in addition to the thousands he received during the tour. At WOC, Davenport, Hall received more than 5,000 letters and tokens of gratitude. In the next years, he averaged close to 6,000 letters per week, and by 1927 adding machine slips showed that he had received close to 1,000,000 pieces of mail.[12] Wendell Hall had a national reputation. "The fact that battery sales increased wherever they appeared proved the commercial possibilities of broadcasting a program simultaneously from several stations." [13]

In 1924 there was a proliferation of artists touring the country. The more popular groups included: the "Mono Motor Oil Twins," John Wolfe and Ned Tollinger; the "Ray-O-Vac Twins," Russ Wildey and William Sheehan; and the "Shell Oil Twins," Bill and Bob. Artists touring for music publishers included: "Little" Jack Little; Ford and Glenn; "The Whispering Pianist," Art Gillham; the Barrel House Quartette; "The Gaelic Twins," Eddie and Fanny Cavanaugh; and "The Eiffel Tower of Radio," Lew Farris. In three years for National Carbon Mr. Hall appeared at some 300 stations throughout the United States, Canada, Hawaii, and Cuba.

In 1923 two stations had held radio weddings and later "so many other stations did the same thing that it almost became one of the standard publicity tricks." [14] Wendell Hall's radio marriage ceremony was unique in that, "it probably deserves the title of first network nuptials and first to be solemnized under advertising agency auspices." [15] The marriage ceremony between Wendell Hall and Marion M. Martin of Chicago was broadcast on June 4, 1924, as part of an *Eveready Hour* program over a four-station hookup originating from the WEAF studios in New York. Linked with WEAF were WCAP, Washington, D.C., WJAR, Providence, and WGN, Chicago. Shortly after the wedding, the Halls launched the "First Canadian Radio Tour" under the auspices of the Canadian National Carbon Company, including appearances in Winnipeg, Calgary and Vancouver. The couple then toured radio stations in Washington, Oregon, California and Hawaii where Hall entertained over station KGU, Honolulu. After two weeks in Hawaii they visited the Eastern section of the United States, covering over 50 stations including PWX in Havana, Cuba.

On October 7, 1925, Mr. and Mrs. Hall sailed for England on what has been described as the first European radio tour by an American artist.

Hall assumed he would walk in, introduce himself and go on the air. Under the British system, entertainers were auditioned, required to attend rehearsals, and finally "dated" for a performance. After six weeks he was auditioned. Hall broadcast several times over 2LO and was apparently well received.

Having spent more time than anticipated in London and anxious to complete the tour, which called for appearances in France, Germany, and Italy, the Halls left for Paris shortly after his final broadcast in late November.

In Paris, Hall broadcast several times from the Eiffel Tower station, but apparently the French people had some difficulty understanding the humor implicit in Hall's southern jokes and stories.

Originating and popularizing the expressions "Yes, suh;" "Hello folks;" and "Hey hey;" Hall in 1923 was the first to introduce what he called vocal squeals and throat noises to fill breaks of songs. This was the first step in what later became known as vocal orchestrations—somewhat like "scat" vocals. Ukelele Ike, John Marvin, and Phil Cook adopted the style and made even more peculiar noises. The Revelers Quartette and the Mills Brothers continued this style but it was Helen Kane who profited the most from the idea when she started the whole country "boop-boop-adooping." [16]

Hall also introduced on radio the "whispering" or "half-voice" style of singing—later known as crooning. The first record using this style was his singing of his composition "Land of My Sunset Dreams" in 1923; it sold over a million copies.

Wendell Hall composed exclusively for radio, and throughout the composer-radio conflict, vigorously defended radio. He joined ASCAP in 1935 but until then his compositions could be played over any radio station, regardless of whether or not the station had paid the music fee.

Throughout 1927 and 1928 Hall not only guest-starred on radio at $1,000 a performance, but headlined in practically all of the R-K-O vaudeville theaters at up to $2,000 per week. He was a star created by radio. The late 1920s listeners were dialing for programs rather than distance, and one of the favorites was the *Majestic Hour* (also known as *The Majestic Theater of the Air*), one of the big variety shows. In January of 1929, Hall was named director of broadcasting for the *Majestic Hour,* sponsored by the Grigsby-Grunow Company, manufacturers of Majestic receiving sets. The program originated in the studios of WABC (later WCBS) New York, and was fed to 58 stations coast-to-coast and Canada. As director Hall produced, directed, performed, acted as master of ceremonies, and selected the talent. When he left the *Majestic Hour* in February of 1930 production of Majestic radios had quintupled. "When I went to work for Grigsby-Grunow they were making 500 sets a day, and when I left they were turning out 2500 sets a day." [17] In 1929 Wendell Hall was at the peak of his career.

TWILIGHT OF A CAREER (1931–1940)

In the late 1920s a succession of events took place which changed radio. With the depression a swelling tide of vaudeville and movie actors, night club entertainers, and concert stars added luster and ingenuity to broadcasting. The struggle of Wendell Hall against the tide began. During the first few months of 1930 he was earning more money per week than at any other time in his career. But now artists from all areas of the entertainment field were eager to go on the air. Will Rogers remarked, "Radio is too big a thing to be out of."

Following the demise of the *Majestic Hour,* Hall went back to vaudeville as a headliner on the R-K-O circuit at $2,500 a week. In April 1930 he signed a contract with the National Broadcasting Company to host Shell Oil Company's *Sign of the Shell* program; a 26-week series originating from Chicago's WENR and broadcast over the NBC-Red network. According to the Akron *Times Press* this new Shell contract made Hall "the highest priced artist working out of the NBC Chicago studios." [18] Two years later Hall approached the F.W. Fitch Company in Des Moines, Iowa, with the idea of using radio to promote its products and in so doing, gave the faltering career of Wendell Hall a much needed boost. For the next three years, from 1933 through 1935 the *Wendell Hall Fitch Program* from WMAQ could be heard Sunday evenings over a 52-station hookup of the NBC radio network.

After the *Community Sing* program Hall went into semi-retirement for three years. During this time he conceived the idea of establishing his own commercial production company. From 1941 through 1948 Hall created, produced, and sold transcribed musical spot announcements or "adsongs" as he called them, to various advertising agencies in Chicago. In 1949 and 1950 he served as sales manager for the company that sold him his xylophone back in 1914.

Then, for two years Hall conducted a daily afternoon program over WGN called *Reflections.* This program marked the end of Wendell Hall's radio career; a career which began at KYW in Chicago and ended at WGN in Chicago—a few blocks away. Only one medium was left before the "Red-headed Music Maker" would leave broadcasting forever. On August 9, 1949 Wendell Hall made his television debut on a program over WGN-TV called *Silhouettes in Song.* Following several guest appearances over a two-year period, Hall was offered a regular show in 1951 over WBKB-TV in Chicago. For six months the *Wendell Hall Trio* appeared five nights a week.

By the autumn of 1951, Wendell Hall's career in show business was over. For two years he looked for a place to retire, choosing Fairhope, Alabama. Wendell Woods Hall died on April 2, 1969. Two years before his death he commented:

> Radio did it, of course. Never before had songwriters been able to plug their tunes on an entertainment medium that extended coast-to-coast. I made "It Ain't Gonna Rain No Mo' " and it made me. Yes sir, it and radio.

45

John Cogley

CLEARANCE AT CBS

THE AUGUST 1, 1955 Edition of the New York *Times* carried the news that Daniel T. O'Shea, a vice-president of the Columbia Broadcasting System, has been named president of RKO Radio Pictures, Inc. The *Times* reporter covering O'Shea's career at CBS was hard put to describe his exact job at the network. Mr. O'Shea, the *Times* said, "served as a corporate vice-president and general executive in a consultative and advisory capacity to all (CBS) divisions." To speak more plainly, Mr. O'Shea has served as chief "security officer" at the network between 1950 and 55. In the five years he was with CBS, O'Shea and another, lesser official, a former FBI agent named Alfred Berry, became to the radio-tv industry what Jack Wren is to advertising agencies.

Ironically, the role O'Shea and Berry played, at least in part, was an unforeseen byproduct of the very policies which have enabled CBS to keep up with, and in some respects overtake, its chief rival, the National Broadcasting Company. As *Fortune* magazine once told it, when in 1945 William S. Paley, chairman and principal owner of CBS, returned from military service, he formulated his strategy for a forthcoming battle with NBC.

"He had made two major decisions. The first was to concentrate on 'creative programming' . . . Instead of being merely a pipeline for the programs of others, CBS would become a programming organization, originating and putting on its own shows . . . Decision No. 2 was to seize leadership in radio by getting control of the talent."

The self-programming policy carried over into television. So did the talent policy, only not in the form of Paley's celebrated postwar radio talent raids. "While NBC drew on the great resources of RCA to gain its position in broadcasting, CBS, having less resources and having spent heavily to gain its position in radio, was forced to counter in TV with the strategy of low-cost programming. It worked hard to build a 'creative organization' that would substitute cleverness and imagination for dollars. The most notable example of CBS adroitness in this respect is 'I Love Lucy,' the hit that cost only $38,000 to produce."

Report on Blacklisting II Radio-Television New York: The Fund for the Republic, 1956. pp. 122–134.

The policy worked. But, when the need to apply the "controversy" standard in hiring arose, it also caused a major headache. First, in packaging more shows of its own, CBS has to take more responsibility for "clearing" material and talent. As the dispenser as well as creator of radio-tv shows, the network is more vulnerable to direct public criticism than an advertising agency.

Second, CBS, in foraging for all the "creative imagination" it could lay its hands on, neglected, or could not afford to inquire into, personal politics. Hence, as one executive put it: "We unknowingly hired a lot of questionable people."

When *Red Channels* appeared, CBS met the blacklisting problem by seeking to gain a solid reputation for patriotism with those who were counted as "anti-Communist experts," while at the same time it maintained its public reputation for "creative imagination" via the network's news division. The network set up a department to administer internal security but exempted its news division from the stern "security" provisions operating in other departments.

The security problem was at first given to Joseph Ream, a CBS executive, and Berry. Ream instituted a loyalty oath for all who were employed by CBS to sign under pain of losing their jobs. The oath remains the only one of its kind ever used in the industry. It required that the employee certify he had not belonged to any of the organizations listed as subversive by the Attorney General, or if he had, that he provide a convincing "explanation" his membership was not meaningful. The oath was kept sealed and confidential in CBS files.

The loyalty oath program however proved to be not quite enough. There may even be some dispute as to whether it ever amounted to more than a dubious public-relations gimmick. The first case in which it was questioned involved a producer-director named Danny Dare. Dare was among those named by Martin Berkeley, Hollywood screenwriter, as Communists or one-time Communists, before the House Committee on Un-American Activities. Like Berkeley himself, Dare denied the charge. He went to Washington, testified that he had not been a Communist and was kept on the employment rolls of CBS. Later, he asked for another hearing, stating that his first testimony was not truthful. At this second hearing, Dare told the Committee that after the people Berkeley named were listed in the newspapers "I became panicky . . . realizing that if I said 'Yes, that is true,' I would immediately lose my job . . ."

Similarly, Allan Sloane, a CBS writer who had signed the loyalty oath, later testified that he had been for a short time a member of the Communist Party but withheld this fact from the network. Neither of these experiences sat well with network officials.

When Ream, an executive of long standing in the industry, retired to Florida, his place was taken by Daniel T. O'Shea. A graduate of Holy Cross College and Harvard Law School, O'Shea had served as chief counsel for RKO Radio Pictures, Inc., had been vice-president of the Selznick International Pictures Company, and was leading executive at Vanguard Films in Hollywood before joining CBS in 1950.

Under O'Shea, CBS developed a vigorous screening policy. At BBD&O, the network seized on the realities of the moment and made the best of them. O'Shea and his assistant, Berry, even more than Jack Wren, made themselves available to anyone who wanted to see them. Ordinarily, they did not seek out the blacklisted, but any writer, director or actor who believed he was "not available" for CBS shows and felt he had a case could go to them and get a hearing. This policy has been the object of widespread criticism in radio-tv circles. "Clearance" at CBS was from the beginning overt and frank; hence O'Shea was an easy and obvious target for those in the industry who despised blacklisting. CBS and blacklisting have become almost synonymous. Sooner or later everyone hears that CBS is the place to go to "get rid of a problem." But it is not quite that easy.

Like Wren, O'Shea and Berry saw to it that they had adequate information on hand and kept up their contacts with the "anti-Communist experts." Berry took care of day-to-day details. O'Shea set the overall policy for the network and concerned himself only with difficult or especially prominent cases, like that of Lucille Ball.[1]

Like Wren, O'Shea and Berry were most concerned over whether or not they had a full accounting on which to base their judgment. The purpose of the interviews was, first, to elicit as much information as possible from the artist "in trouble," and, second, to determine *how* full an accounting the artist was giving of his own past activities. The "security officers" checked what they knew about the artist against what he volunteered to tell them about himself. That way they could judge whether he was holding back. If he was, his sincerity was open to question. If the artist did not make a clean breast of all the information they already had, he was dismissed with "It's been nice talking to you."

If he did come up with everything known and then some, indicating sincerity, O'Shea or Berry took on the case. The first thing that had to be decided was whether he was "defensible." He was "defensible" if there was enough positive "anti-communism" in his record to overshadow the charges made against him. In that case he would be "cleared." But even if there weren't enough to make him "defensible," the artist, after he finished the interview, would have some idea of where he stood and what he could do about getting out of "trouble." Here is where a good anti-Communist sponsor took over. The artist not yet "defensible" needed advice on what kind of "anti-Communist" acts would count with the people who counted.

The standards set for CBS "clearance" procedures are necessarily hard to fix. They depend largely on how the networks' "security officers" read the intentions and opinions of the accusers, be it the American Legion or AWARE, Inc. There are fluctuations from show to show, from client to client, and from one day's international news to the next. "Omnibus," which does most of its own casting, is exempt except where, in the word of one executive, something "outlandish" is planned. So are most public-service programs.

Yet CBS can't have it both ways. An example was provided when Winston Burdett, a CBS newscaster, appeared before the Senate Internal Subcommittee in the summer of 1955. Burdett testified that in the late Thirties he had belonged to the Brooklyn *Eagle* unit of the Communist Party, had gone to Finland on the Party's money and the *Eagle's* credentials, to do espionage work there. Burdett went on to name a number of his associates in the Party, some of whom were working newspapermen.

Then, with astoundingly precise timing, news broadcasts and newspapers announced that Senator Eastland, the Committee chairman, had written a letter to CBS asking that the network keep Burdett. The letter, which was addressed to O'Shea, plus a CBS policy statement, followed hard upon Burdett's testimony. On the face of it, both appeared to have been well-timed and well-coordinated with Burdett's appearance in Washington. The coincidence was striking enough to arouse public speculation as to how much rehearsing preceded the performance.

Still, not everyone was satisfied. The night the story broke, news commentator Quincy Howe on another network announced that Burdett had made his information available in a private hearing four years earlier. Howe saw no reason why Burdett's story should have been made public at such a late date. It was a lucky thing, he said, that Burdett could work on sustaining shows since no sponsor would hire him. But over on a third network, Fulton Lewis, Jr. only fifteen minutes earlier said the testimony had raised a lot of questions, one of which was why Senator Eastland felt obliged to write CBS on Burdett's behalf. Was there any reason to believe, Lewis asked, that CBS might have considered firing Burdett for his patriotic act in testifying?

Yet, CBS keeps trying to eat its own cake. Edward R. Murrow, who is considered beyond the pale in the anti-Communist power centers, goes on his way. Murrow's McCarthy broadcast caused a great deal of criticism (some of it merely professional). O'Shea is reliably reported to have disputed Murrow's use of J. Robert Oppenheimer on the celebrated "See It Now" program which kept the "radical-right" pot boiling for months. These instances alone would have been enough to upset most conscientious public-relations men. But CBS—villain to those who reject blacklisting—can always point to its Ed Murrow when the criticism gets too hot. When criticism of Murrow starts to mount, the network can point with pride to the tight shop its "security officers" run.

It is no secret that Murrow is something less than enthusiastic about his network's "screening" policies. By the same token, O'Shea was utterly convinced that there is at least some intrinsic worth in what the network's "security officers" do. Some distraught radio-tv people left O'Shea's office feeling less vindictive towards him than they were before they went in. One went so far as to characterize him as being "emotional" about the problem. All seemed to agree that O'Shea was, if nothing else, candid. He believed in blacklisting (though undoubtedly the word offended him), and he tried to practice it as judiciously as possible.

More likely than not, the performer "cleared" at CBS had sought help. His agent may have told him he was "in trouble" or he may have found out directly through a friend in the network that he had to be cleared before CBS would hire him. In any event, his chances for "clearance" were enhanced considerably if he came under auspices of an acceptable "clearance man." If he could come bearing credentials, or implicit agreement, from AWARE, Inc., *Counter-attack*, the American Legion, or George Sokolsky, so much the better.

The best way for the accused to go about getting "clearance" was, and still is, first to find someone who knows his way around. In the process the "victim" will almost certainly have to render an explanation of his past activities, often in the form of an affidavit. He should also divulge whatever information he has, whether or not he believes it useful, to the FBI. Depending on his record and auspices, he may have to certify his earnestness by other acts. Support of an AWARE-endorsed position in his union, plus, say, signing a petition against admission of Red China to the U.N., might turn the trick. The important thing is to "clear" himself as much as possible before seeing the network's "security officers."

In the Spring of 1955 the NBC network, wanting to clear a prominent performer for a top dramatic show, asked the actor to get two letters of endorsement, one from an officer of the Anti-Defamation League, the other from Godfrey P. Schmidt, President of AWARE, Inc. The network's request was recognition of the growing importance of AWARE, Inc., "an organization to combat the Communist conspiracy in entertainment-communications."

At one time the letter from the Anti-Defamation League official might have turned the trick, but in this case it took two endorsements. And of the two (as the actor found out), AWARE's was harder to get. For it is AWARE's position that a performer wanting to clear himself should not only prove he is not a Communist, or Communist sympathizer, but give ample evience that he is "actively" anti-Communist—or, in AWARE's own words, that he does not support "dangerous neutralism."

"No one can be neutral before the Communist challenge and peril," AWARE stated in one of its publications. "Its threat to our civilization demands that people stand up and be counted." Many radio-tv people feel strongly about AWARE because it is their general impression that those who wish to establish anti-Communist credentials must "stand up and be counted" on AWARE's side on any given trade-union issue. Certainly one who opposes blacklisting, for instance, would not be considered truly "anti-Communist" by AWARE. But it was largely because the organization supports blacklisting that members of the American Federation of Television and Radio Artists voted almost 2 to 1 in the summer of 1955 to "condemn" it—982 in favor of the condemnation, 514 opposed.

In practice, AWARE, though it urges universal political screening, has confined its efforts to the radio and television field. With blacklisting firmly established on Madison Avenue, AWARE's main function has been to uphold it and call for its extension. In the case of the entertainment industry, the size of the salaries involved is added to AWARE's general arguments for denying employment to "subversives."

AWARE has not published any public "lists," but its bulletins have cited the past political associations of radio-tv workers, *a la Red Channels*. These bulletins are treated with the utmost seriousness by some of the "security officers" on Madison Avenue. But "exposure" is not among AWARE's chief purposes. The organization, rather, has functioned as a pressure group within the industry. As individuals, however, certain prominent AWARE members have been deeply involved in the blacklisting machinery. The organization's prestige is an element in establishing their credentials as anti-Communist "experts." For instance, the actor NBC was trying to clear, did get a letter from Godfrey Schmidt and was given a lead on a dramatic show. When it was announced that he would appear a week later there were immediate protests. To the embarrassment of the network, Schmidt said he did not intend his letter, written in Christian charity, to serve as "clearance" and pointed out he wrote it as an individual, not as president of AWARE, Inc. But the interesting fact was the enormous prestige which Schmidt could bring to bear "as an individual." Armed with his letter, the network felt safe in lifting its ban against the actor.

Table 23.

EMPLOYMENT IN BROADCASTING

Figures show the number of radio and television employees at stations and networks and average salaries. Also shown for comparison number of persons employed in film production in Los Angeles.

Year	RADIO			TELEVISION			BROADCAST	SALARIES	Film L.A.
	AM, AM-FM, & Networks	FM Only	Total	Stations	Networks	Total	Total	Weekly	Average Employment
1930			6,000				6,000		
1935			14,600				14,600		
1940			25,700				25,700		26,479
1945			37,800				37,800	$ 60.05	31,468
1950			52,000[a]			14,000[b]		77.41[a]	21,292
1955			45,300			32,300	77,600		23,877
1960	51,723	1,266	52,989			40,600	93,589	120.74	23,732
1965	59,489	2,718	62,207	36,741	11,012	47,753	109,960	148.45	24,002
1970	64,939	6,109	71,048	45,228	13,197	58,425	129,473	145.86	25,600
1972	65,898	8,722	73,719	46,976	12,410	59,386	133,105		

Sources: 1930, Department of Commerce estimate; FCC.
[1]Included are fulltime and parttime employees based on selected weeks in either October or December.
[2]Salary information includes only fulltime employees in non-managerial occupations based on January each year.
[a]1949. [b]1952.

Table 24.

NETWORK TELEVISION PRODUCTION EMPLOYEES AND EARNINGS

Figures show the number of members of the American Federation of Television and
Radio Artists and Screen Actors Guild; the % of SAG members in two earning
categories; the earnings for SAG members from television, motion pictures, and
commercials; earnings of AFTRA, WGA and other Hollywood craft unions; and the
total program expenses of the three national television networks

	1962	1966	1971
MEMBERS OF			
AFTRA	15,506	17,565	22,752
SAG	14,365	16,791	24,996
% SAG Members earning:			
more than $10,000	11%	14%	10%
less than 2,500	75%	77%	74%
EARNINGS (Add 000,000)			
SAG from television	$21.6	$ 32.3	$ 20.5
SAG from TV residuals	6.4	8.2	13.5
SAG from movies	NA	23.7	20.6
SAG from commercials	NA	40.6	59.2
SAG TOTAL	$73.7	$104.8	$113.8
AFTRA members[1]	$ 37.9	$ 48.4	$ 69.3
Writer's Guild members	27	34	37
Hollywood craft union members	127	186	163
NETWORK PROGRAM EXPENSES	$491	$734	$925
(Add 000,000)			

Source: AFTRA, SAG, WGA, AMPTP, FCC reported in <u>Analysis of the Causes and Effects</u>
<u>of Increases in Same-Year Rerun Programming and Related Issues in Prime-Time Network</u>
<u>Television</u>, Office of Telecommunication Policy, March 1973. [1]Includes some AFTRA
members working for stations.

The team of David Brinkley and Chet Huntley was formed to cover the 1956 political conventions, with Billy Henry.

President Kennedy was on the first 30-minute *Huntley-Brinkley Report* September 1963.

Election night November 1968.

"Good night, Chet. Good night, David and good night for NBC News." October 29, 1956–July 31, 1970.

PART SIX

PROGRAMMING

I have in mind a plan of development which would make radio a "household utility" in the same sense as the piano or phonograph. The idea is to bring music into the house by wireless.

—David Sarnoff,
September 30, 1915

One of the planks in the platform of this polite if not pertinent purveyor of program piffle is that radio stations be constrained to specialize. Specialization will eventually overtake the radio industry just as surely as it has the magazine business, and every other entertainment dispensary. . . . WBAL has a definite weekly program schedule: Sunday night, Twilight music (whatever that is!); Monday, Concert night; Tuesday, Ensemble night; Wednesday, silent; Thursday, Concert night; Friday, Novelty night; Saturday, silent. . . . Of course we don't want all stations to specialize thusly, in highbrow manner—let it be in any manner they choose, as long as it is specialization. For this reason we are inclined to regret the passing of WTAS at Elgin, Illinois . . . a lowbrow station—and proud of it. WTAS had thousands of devoted and enslaved listeners. If you didn't particularly snap for its offerings . . . your next door neighbor sought them out and enjoyed his fill of peppy pieces and flip announcing. So no harm was done.

—*Radio Broadcast*,
March 1926, p. 579.

That's a WDEC oldie. We don't play all the oldies as some stations do. We play only the best ones. We spend, oh 20 or, uh 25 minutes a week picking only the best ones. We can't play anything we want. I thought you ought to know that.

—WDEC, Decorah, Iowa,
October 23, 1972

THE WORLD was never so ready for an invention as it was for radio. The idea of programs had been predicted nearly a half century before the first sparks of code shattered the ether in the Marconi orchards. A *Punch* magazine cartoon in 1850 depicted a woman seated before three clock-like devices bringing in three different musical concerts and captioned "Music by Electric Telegraph." [1] In 1887 the American novelist Edward Bellamy predicted a device which would bring music into the home. He even predicted a version of *Radio Guide:*

> The card bore the date "September 12, 2000," and contained the longest program of music I had ever seen. It was as various as it was long, including a most extraordinary range of vocal and instrumental solos, duets, quartets, and various orchestral combinations . . . this prodigious list . . . was . . . divided into twenty-four sections answering to the hours.[2]

The forecasts of the cartoonist and the novelist were quite correct in that music has been the mainstay of broadcast programming throughout the world. Most of the programming on experimental stations prior to 1921 was phonograph records with some speeches or talks and an occasional singer. Much of the programming was somewhat private in nature such as a Chicago phonograph record concert in 1919 which was "for the pleasure of convalescent soldiers at Fort Sheridan." A short article in *Popular Mechanics* entitled "Wireless Music Sends Joy in All Directions" said that this program was picked up by "more than 100 long-distance eavesdroppers in Detroit." [3]

In the early 1920s the attitude of broadcasters began to change— programming developed more general interest. Performers worked free and frequently lacked talent or polish. De Wolf Hopper, one of the great Broadway performers in the era, expressed frustration in performing over WJZ in Newark—"There was no way to tell whether I was pleasing my audience or not." [4] Announcers were often volunteers, many of who had regular jobs with the firm that owned the station. There were talks for children, some humorous, some lifted from newspaper serials and books.

On occasion no talent would arrive at a station to perform and it might not go on the air. There were other interruptions.

> . . . all stations were required to "stand by" or remain inactive for . . . three minutes every fifteen minutes in order to listen for distress signals from ships at sea. A prima donna from some well-known opera company had just rendered an aria . . . The announcer . . . stepped up to the small transmitter and said: "We will now stand by for three minutes to hear distress calls." [5]

Sundays were established as the time for religious services and many were broadcast from churches. Larger stations were programming in the daytime—mostly records with some news flashes, market reports and weather information. Religious broadcasting and sports made up most of the remotes. KDKA in Pittsburgh broadcast a religious service in January of 1921—only a few months after starting regular program service—and broadcast a boxing match in April. The famous boxing match broadcast, Dempsey vs. Carpentier, was fought in July. A special station, WJY, was erected in Hoboken. The description of the fight in Jersey City was relayed by phone, typed, and read over the air to an estimated audience of 300,000.

WJZ's announcer Tommy Cowan arranged for a remote from the Hotel Pennsylvania Grill in 1921. It was the start of the famous broadcasts of Vincent Lopez, his theme song "Nola" and his signature, "Lopez speaking." [6] Stations arranged with hotels to have remote studios for pickups of interviews, dance bands and banquets as early as 1923.

Other more prestigious programming was underway in the early 1920s. The wife of the owner of WOR radio paid $15,000 out of her own pocket for the first broadcast series of the New York Philharmonic.[7]

Music was dominating the programming of stations as early as 1923. A report on programming on WJZ from May to December in 1923 showed: 1798 musical programs; 998 talk programs; 17 talk and band programs; 88 banquets and church; 21 sports; 40 plays.[8]

WLW program director Fred Smith wrote in 1923:

> The nature of radio programs eventually will follow the demands of economic conditions, which in other words is but the demand of the public. . . . The public will demand of radio that it be a joy bringer. The basis of radio programs has established itself: it is music. Music is the most etheral of the arts, and can do more to stimulate spontaneous joy and happiness than anything which impresses human sensibilities. Music is audible sunshine.[9]

A study of nine important U.S. stations reported that three-fourths of their programming was music in the 1920s; declined to about two-thirds in the 1930s. On the national networks music shows were about 60% of all programming in the late 1920s, dropping to less than 20% in the 1940s and 1950s. Drama and talk programs were most numerous from the late 1930s to the early 1950s on the networks.[10] In the 1970s music accounted for three-fourths of all radio programming—news being the next largest category.

WJY, now permanently in New York, in 1924 attempted an early form of block programming called "Omni-Oral Productions." One such program was:

A Night with the Conquistadores
8:30 p.m.—Overture—Thomas Clive's Fraternity Tango Orchestra
8:35 p.m.—Prologue—by the announcer
8:40 p.m.—Episode I—Tangos—Clive's Orchestra.

9:00 p.m.—Episode II—Spanish Folk Songs—Mildred Delma, so-
    prano. Spanish Piano Selections—Vincent De Sola.
9:30 p.m.—Episode III—A Sunday in Caracas—Harry Chapin
    Plummer.
9:45 p.m.—Episode IV—Mexican Composition by Piedmont Trio
10:15 p.m.—Episode V—Music of the Incas—Carlos Valle Riestra,
    pianist
10:30 p.m.—Episode VI—"Bits from Carmen," sung by Glukerja
    Campanieskaja, soprano; Euminico Blanco, tenor;
    Paul Morenzo, tenor; Francesco Catalina, soprano.[11]

This type of programming was considered more desirable by critics
who found a disease called "radio-emotionalis" brought on by
"changing our mood as fast as the program director's whims." [12]

From almost every point of view the outstanding radio program
in the 1920 to 1926 period was the *Eveready Hour*. It began in December of 1923 over WEAF as a regular weekly program. It was on a
network and was highly experimental, combining different types of
material each week including musical presentations and "sketches."
The program was held up as an example of what is good in broadcasting. It was suggested that the program be used as a model:

When radio was new somebody perceived the need of a cue to
what the programs meant, and that brought in the announcer, of
whom great things were required. He has met the task well, but the
continuous program, built in dramatic sequence, will make his work
considerably easier for himself and the listener.

Instead of bobbing up every ten minutes, like those in a class,
he can make one announcement in an hour and try to do it in a
humanly interesting fashion. No tricks are required, just a plain
statement of what should be a few pertinent facts. Then the continuing theme must keep alive the interest created, constantly reminding the listener of the general trend, but steadily developing the
performance as it is done in the theater, on the screen—everywhere
the drama has an influence. This, in fact, is the true radio drama and
not a hybrid adaptation such as the reading of a play. Radio has developed every means of expression peculiar to itself and it is
thoroughly reasonable to suppose that its own kind of drama will be
the next step in evolution.

The stage is now opening before us, if we may believe the evidence furnished by one successful broadcaster, responsible for the
performance known to a national radio audience as the Eveready
Hour. Promptly at nine o'clock each Tuesday night the entertainers
in this group take over the air as controlled by WEAF in New York.
For the next hour, some millions of Americans are entertained in a
way distinctly new to radio. WEAF transmits the program to ten
other stations, WFI, WCAE, WGR, WEEI, WEAR, WCCO, WWJ,
WOC, WSAI, and WJAR. And for sixty intensive minutes an invisi-

ble audience equal to the population of many nations may enjoy a real radio drama.[13]

Dramatic programs were not being broadcast on a regular basis by any station in early 1922 but a number of stations had attempted "radio plays." WGY in Schenectady broadcast a drama from the studio in August of 1922.[14] However, most broadcasts were done live from the theaters. WGY began a weekly series of radio plays in October of 1922. WLW began a stock company for radio plays called Radarios on the station, and presented an original radio drama in April of 1923.[15]

Early radio took news as it came. One regularly scheduled treatment of the news was a weekly news analysis broadcast by H. V. Kaltenborn over WEAF. Other programs of a topical nature were broadcast by the Department of Agriculture and Weather Bureau as daytime services to farm listeners. A number of newspapers were providing news summaries and reports through the early years of broadcasting—particularly those papers which operated stations.

Early radio was not plagued with reruns but it changed programming during the summer. One reviewer complained:

> What a ridiculous thing it is for radio to have an off season! If there ever was an entertainment that should be free from temperament and maintain its equilibrium equally well in January and July it is broadcasting . . . this only proves how dependent is radio on outside events.[16]

Local stations were also severely criticized from time to time. The following note in addition to being critical also was somewhat prophetic of later broadcasts:

BROADCASTING FUNERAL SERVICES

> As one of the outstanding examples of bad taste in broadcasting that has come to our attention during the past month, we submit the broadcasting by a Mid-Western station of funeral services for one of its departed minstrels.
> Certainly the man was a most excellent entertainer and his death was regretted by those who had come to know him through the air. But we question whether their grief was so sincere as to justify their being, not merely invited, but forced, to attend his obsequies. And of course thousands of listeners-in had never even heard of him before. It is a doubtful mark of respect to the deceased to intrude his funeral eulogy into what may be a dancing party, a convivial dinner, or a poker session.
> Assuming that the whole nation was genuinely "bowed in grief" over the death of some great statesman or outstanding leader, a radio funeral service might be not only appropriate but almost im-

perative. In the instance cited the service was given an importance
all out of proportion to the importance of the deceased.[17]

Programming in 1926 was changing. A major change was pre-
saged by the formation of the NBC networks. The first season—1926–
1927—consisted of primarily musical variety and concert fare. There
were other programs—a once a week news commentary, and some
religious and informative talks. Drama, forums and discussion programs all were put on the networks in the next few seasons. Local
programming was dominated by music and some talk programs.

In 1928 *Radio Digest* conducted a poll of "listeners-in" to find
the most popular orchestra in the United States and found that radio
bands, including a group on WBAP (Fort Worth) called the "Seven
Aces," was the most well known and best liked.' [18]

WLS in Chicago had started the *National Barn Dance* in the
spring of 1924 and the next year the *WSM Barn Dance,* later to be
called the *Grand Ole Opry,* was underway from Nashville. The impact of these programs was tremendous. Units from Nashville and
Chicago soon were travelling throughout the Midwest playing theaters, dances and fairs with such stars as Uncle Dave Macon, "The
King of the Hillbillies," Uncle Ezra, The Hoosier Hotshots, Lulu-
belle and Scotty, and Fiddlin' Arthur Smith. A pair of blackface comedians appearing on the *National Barn Dance* and already known
locally as *Sam 'n' Henry,* were establishing the characters which
would make them nationally known. The pair, Charles Correll and
Freeman Gosden, which went on NBC Blue in August of 1928, had
been syndicated by WMAQ, Chicago, and the *Daily News* (owner of
WMAQ). Pepsodent, a Chicago-based firm, had been approached by
the network to sponsor a musical program. A member of the tooth-
paste company recalled:

> . . . musical programs were in the vogue; there was little else on
> the air. And, frankly, we couldn't get very enthused . . . we wanted
> something different . . . we found a program (and) went to the
> chain (NBC) . . . They had never broadcast any quarter-hour pro-
> grams before and they weren't sure they wanted to start doing so.[19]

During *Amos 'n' Andy's* second season on NBC, 1930–1931, the
Cooperative Analysis of Broadcasting reported a rating of 53.4. Thus,
more than one-half of all the radio homes in the nation were tuned to
this program during six nights the sample week in early Spring.

Song-and-patter teams, just off the vaudeville stage, such as
Jones and Hare, Pick and Pat, and Gene and Glenn, were being
programmed on both local and network shows. Although there was
some educational material being broadcast, the big educational interest in the late 1920's was college football broadcasts:

No question about it. Radio has been the salvation of many a waning sport in the past few years—not to intimate for a minute that football ever could be classed in that category. The man at the gate has been able to observe that during the last three and four years the out-school interest and attendance has increased from fifty to seventy-five per cent.[20]

Radio coverage of events was exciting. The Graham McNamee description of the Dempsey-Tunney prize fight in the fall of 1928 reportedly caused 12 fans to die of excitement.[21]

In addition to Kaltenborn and his weekly news analysis there was Floyd Gibbons.

Known as one of the greatest war correspondents . . . He has ridden with Pancho Villa, been torpedoed and sunk in mid-Atlantic, lost an eye in the great war, crossed the Sahara by camel, covered wars and events in all parts of the world.[22]

In the summer of 1930 Gibbons and his sponsor *The Literary Digest* parted. At CBS William Paley began looking for a substitute to offer the *Digest*—Gibbons was on NBC. Among those auditioned was Lowell Thomas, a war correspondent, author and lecturer. To prepare for the first broadcast CBS sent a staff of three. Thomas arranged for help from his publisher, Doubleday, who sent young manuscript reader, Ogden Nash. Also assisting was Dale Carnegie, a personal friend and former manager of one of Thomas's road company shows, and Prosper Buranelli, who had been a feature writer on the New York *World* and was to be Thomas's writer for many years. To an all-day meeting to plan the broadcast Thomas, "knowing something about the habits of newspapermen," also "brought a flagon of something that might refresh them"—it was still prohibition.

Late in the afternoon, seeing that we were getting nowhere, Prosper Buranelli and I quietly disappeared, the others not even missing us. We hurriedly put together some notes, and with these I went up to CBS and went on the air at six o'clock.[23]

That night, September 29, 1930, Lowell Thomas began a broadcast that would be on the air more than 44 years and reported: "Adolf Hitler, the German Fascist chief, is snorting fire. There are now two Mussolinis in the world, which seems to promise a rousing time."

The first five years of the 1930 decade saw an avalanche of new program types—particularly on the networks. The season of 1929–1930 introduced comedy variety. The pioneers of this type of show were *The Cuckoo Hour* and *The Nitwit Hour*. Eddie Cantor brought the first comedy variety show featuring a comedian as master of ceremonies to the networks. He was quickly copied with programs featuring Al Jolson, George Burns and Gracie Allen, Ed Wynn, Fred Allen, Jack Pearl, Ken Murray, the Marx Brothers and others. Probably the most successful of all the comedians to start on the air in 1932 was Jack Benny. His program was as carefully formatted as the production line for a model A Ford. He was a success in vaudeville in the 1920s and became one of the highest-priced comedians on radio.

Rudy Vallee brought a vaudeville variety show to NBC in the 1932–1933 season, introducing hundreds of performers to the country. A year later the *National Barn Dance* became truly national as it went on NBC each Saturday night. Chicago—the cradle of many original shows—was the first to broadcast a network daytime variety program, *The Breakfast Club*. In addition the concept of competition in entertainment—the amateur contest—was put on the air in this period: *National Amateur Hour* and Major Bowes' *Original Amateur Hour*.

Networks tried nearly every kind of dramatic format with both anthology and continuing characters, comedy drama, action-adventure, crime-detective, women's serial dramas (soap opera), Westerns and documentaries.

Gone were the days of early *Amos 'n' Andy* when the sound effects were incidental to the show. The first sound effects men were former movie pit band drummers who already had a number of sounds left over from their silent movie days.[24] Fidelity was so poor in the early 1930s that almost any sound suggested the effect needed for the show. Actually the drummers had to make many adjustments since stage sounds could be quite a bit louder than those needed when held close to a microphone, no matter how insensitive it is. The shaking of a can of buckshot by a sound man was found to sound more like "Niagara than rain" as it had on the stage.[25]

Radio programs were copied of other media. Sherlock Holmes— a success in novels, movies and plays—was on NBC in the 1931–1932 season. Out of the west came the thundering hoofs over Detroit's WXYZ early in 1933. In May, four months after the program had been inaugurated, *The Lone Ranger* announcer said that the first 300 children to write the station would get a free pop gun. Two days later the station had received 24,905 letters. Only Father Coughlin, on a coast-to-coast hookup had exceeded this response. That year *The Lone Ranger* and his faithful Indian companion went on a network which was later to join the Mutual chain. The program was carried in 1938 on 140 stations in the U.S., Newfoundland, Ontario, Hawaii, and New Zealand.[26]

A Chicago program, *Clara, Lu 'n' Em*, went on a regional network out of WGN in February 1931. A year later Colgate-Palmolive-Peet took it to the network allowing the nation's women to tune in NBC for their first rinse in the world of soap opera. Theories which learned psychologists and sociologists have applied to the daytime serial are as fast moving as many of the plots of those plays: *Against the Storm, Arnold Grimm's Daughter, Backstage Wife, Betty and Bob, David Harum, Helen Trent,* and so on. According to a study by Rudolph Arnheim the setting of most serials was small town and occupations were mainly either professional or housewife. The 15-minute serials were found to have more than three definitive problems per installment, most of which were personal involving courtship, marriage, family or friends. The next most important problem was economic or threat to professional status. The problems were found to be caused in most cases by the people themselves. Arnheim's analysis found that there were both good and bad characters in the soap opera but that there was also a group who were unpleasant but not evil. Weak men outnumbered the weak women by a third.[28]

> Chicago spawned the earliest soaps. Mrs. Gertrude Berg, Elaine Carrington, Irma Phillips, Paul Rhymer and Frank Hummert operated opera factories that got underway, mostly around Michigan Ave., in the late 20s and 30s. Mr. Hummert, flanked by Mrs. Anne S. Ashenhurst and Robert D. Andrews, sparked the Blackett-Sample-Hummert production line: . . . *Vic and Sade, Myrt and Marge, Pepper Young's Family, Rosemary, When a Girl Marries, Women in White, Right to Happiness, Young Dr. Malone, Guiding Light, Just Plain Bill, Lonely Woman,* and many others . . .[29]

Drama increased on the networks and musical programs decreased. But the local station—many using recorded songs—was increasing the amount of music that listeners heard on the air. Local stations hired, or traded time for plugs, with small musical groups including hillbilly entertainers. Stations arranged with hotels to use feeds of orchestra music from the ball rooms on a regular basis. Local station and networks both were experimenting with human interest interview programs.

Two events in the early 1930s stood out from the regular news coverage of stations—the Lindbergh kidnapping and trial of the kidnapper in the first two years of the decade and the political campaign in 1932. The Lindbergh sequence was so painful for the family—particularly press coverage of the trial of Bruno Hauptman—that the aviation hero moved to England. In later days the coverage of the kidnapping seemed overdone with various remote facilities, and hundreds of newsmen and technicians on the scene. The trial established the reputation of Boake Carter for his accuracy as a reporter and as a commentator for CBS.[30]

Senators and representatives by 1932 had started sending "reports to the people" via transcriptions to local stations. However, the star of the political broadcasters was President Roosevelt who seemed to know innately how to use the medium. He broke a tradition by flying to Chicago in the summer of 1932 to accept the nomination by the Democrats in person. His address was heard by millions of radio listeners. His major speeches, as were those of his incumbent opponent President Herbert Hoover, were broadcast. The master touch, however, occurred a few days after Roosevelt's inauguration when he quietly talked with the nation in the first of what would be called "Fireside Chats." President Roosevelt's simple, direct, conversation—at least in comparison with other politicians —described the banking crisis so that most listeners could understand it. From this first talk on banking, March 12, 1933, the President would make 28 "fireside chats" to June 12, 1944 when he opened the fifth war loan drive.

In an analysis of those chats, Waldo Braden and Earnest Brandenburg conclude with Robert Sherwood that radio was able to "bring the people right into the White House."

> Perhaps for the first time in American history the people of the nation were made to feel that they knew their President personally and that they were receiving inside information first hand on important events. They were stirred and stimulated by Roosevelt's friendly informal manner; they somehow felt that they had a direct part in shaping the policies of the federal government and that Washington was no farther away than the radio receiving sets in their living rooms. Unquestionably, his continued acceptance by the majority of the American people, despite the frequent opposition of the press and his occasional troubles with Congress, was due in important measure to Roosevelt's outstanding success whenever he carried issues directly to the people in his Fireside Chats.[31]

A better conceptualization may be to think of radio transporting Roosevelt to America rather than the opposite. Adolph Hitler, Roosevelt's contemporary master of the media, used radio and especially film not in an intimate manner but to sweep up audiences in the frenzy of crowds. Rather than Roosevelt's one-to-one approach, Goebbels and others planned huge, long rallies with bands, shouting speeches, and mass audience response. An interesting though simplistic, characterization is of Roosevelt putting himself in every American home by radio; while Hitler tried to transport all of Germany via radio and film to each mass meeting.

It was in one of these talks that Roosevelt made his famous statement that possibly was the key to his election in 1940:

> I have said not once but many times that I have seen war and that I hate war . . . I hope that the United States will keep out of this war and I believe that it will.

News broadcasts were becoming more and more important to broadcasters in the early 1930s. On-the-spot coverage of important events and trivia, as described in books by the news directors of the networks, made the listener see the drama of events in ways they had never felt before.[32] An outcome of these proceedings was various treatments of the news in ways more dramatic than simply reading copy. The most noteworthy of these was *The March of Time* which weekly treated the listener to dramatic versions of events in the news.

It was easy to see that the newspapers were not going to accept the new medium as a news channel without a fight. Print controlled the wire services and in an agreement decided to join the wire services to offer stations three news broadcasts a day. In the 1920s some papers had refused to even use the word "radio" in their columns.

Broadcasting of news was traumatic to the newspaper competition as it gathered momentum. Kaltenborn, Carter, Thomas, and Edwin C. Hill all were broadcasting five-times-a-week on networks in 1932. The Lindbergh kidnapping, the election of Roosevelt, and many lesser stories were no longer "scoops" for the listener who had already heard the news on radio. Broadcasters were using all sources for news including the columns of rival newspapers. The "barons" of print struck back at the upstart by banning the use of news wire copy on radio. A "press-radio war" was waged. It ended when networks expanded—and stations created—their news staffs.

Three major program types developed on the networks in the last half of the 1930s—the suspense-psychological thriller such as *Lights Out* and *Suspense*, the one-half hour situation comedy drama, and quiz formats with a number of variations. First there were studio quiz programs with audience participants—*Professor Quiz* and *Old Time Spelling Bee*. This last program being very similar to a later TV show called *College Bowl*. Then came quizzes with professional panel members (*Information Please* and *Quiz Kids*), telephone giveaways (*Pot o' Gold*), and comedy audience participation with contestants performing stunts (*Truth or Consequences*).

Networks were taking more and more of affiliates' time expanding news programming in response to international events and soap operas in response to advertiser demands.

CBS tried the first overseas roundup news program via short-wave on March 13, 1938—from London, Paris, Berlin, Rome, and Washington. By 1939–1940 all four networks had similar programs relaying the war's developments as part of nearly 20 hours of network news each week.

By January 1940, 60 different women's serial dramas—five of them repeated on two networks—totaled nearly 80 hours a week.

Live music on broadcast stations decreased as records increased.

The platter show with a disc jockey and multiple sponsors was part of the local station repertoire. Local news was reflecting the increased popularity of the national network news. However, in 1938 the FCC found in a survey that music accounted for more than half of the programming on the air—local, syndicated and network. The results of the survey showed the more powerful stations had the smaller percentage of music and a larger percentage of other program forms such as drama, variety and talk programs.

Special events had ceased to be promotionally oriented and had become items of real interest. In 1937 a combination of elements—a warm winter and heavy rainfall—brought on the worst recorded flood in the Ohio River Valley. Radio mobilized help for the disaster overnight. Announcers and engineers at stations in Portsmouth and Cincinnati, and at Louisville and Paducah stayed on the job relaying messages internally and to the nation whose entertainment programs were interrupted to broadcast direct from the scene instructing boats to pick up pregnant women and deliver blankets.[33] It was the nation's first living room disaster.

The other major special—the crash of the Hindenberg dirigible—was not broadcast live but was presented recorded on network radio.

All of this activity was just a warm up for the main event—the war in Europe. Within a few months the flamboyant memories of Floyd Gibbons and his trench coat were replaced as idols by the cool clear truth of Edward R. Murrow who was the link between this country and Europe for many listeners. A writer in *Scribner's* said Murrow "has more influence on Americans' reaction to foreign news than a shipful of newspapermen." [34] Kaltenborn wrote:

> Within a few hours after the first German troops crossed the Austrian Border in March, Columbia was on the air with an eyewitness description of conditions in the threatened capital, followed in swift succession not only from Vienna, but from London, Berlin, Paris, Rome and Washington, D.C.[35]

The nation listened as more and more news broadcasts brought information of invasions and death. Austria, Poland and France were overrun, with radio correspondents only a few minutes ahead of the troops. Some correspondents, William Shirer for example, stayed in occupied zones and kept sending out news. The nation got an eyewitness account of the sinking of the German pocket battleship *Graf Spee* off the coast of South America. Battle correspondents practiced their trade in mock war games held by our armed forces in Louisiana and Alabama in 1941.

A most revealing demonstration of mass persuasion involved another mock invasion—an invasion of Martians in a dramatization of

H. G. Wells' *War of the Worlds*. Thousands of persons, psychologically groggy from the information pouring over the air concerning war and invasion, were not prepared for the "prank" reporting of the fake invasion by Orson Welles and his *Mercury Theater* company. The result was an awareness of the power of radio and the suggestibility of many in the frightened audience.

Mobilization was underway in the United States with much emphasis on bringing the creative talents of the nation to bear on its patriotic spirit. One such effort, the first of many, was the dramatic series conducted by CBS entitled *The Free Company Presents . . ."* Ten well-known authors contributed scripts to the series based on various freedoms listed in the Bill of Rights.[36] There were a number of recruitments of outstanding talent for this kind of broadcast during the war.

For the first half of the 1940s the war dominated every phase of American life. Programming continued to include more and more news. There were reporters, commentators and analysts. The labels were used to define similar functions. Men were dismissed for defining the terms incorrectly and giving too much opinion. One definition of the commentator was that "the commentator interprets the news, thereby helping people to give meaning to the scattered news items of the day." [37]

A reviewer in 1942 reported that in the space of a week he heard 30 analysts.[38] In addition, a number of "propaganda" programs were broadcast with such titles as: *The Army Hour,*[39] *Our Secret Weapon, The Lands of the Free,* and *The Sea Hound.* The BBC sent *Britain to America* by shortwave with Leslie Howard as narrator. However, the introduction of more news analysts and the addition of a number of public service programs altered the structures of programming significantly according to reports by both CBS and NBC in 1943, resulting in music programs being less than one-third of the total program output of the two networks.[40]

Programs met the challenge of the war in various ways. For the Monday program after Sunday, December 7, 1941, Kato, the chauffeur for the *Green Hornet* suddenly changed from a likeable Japanese to a Philippino with a new accent. A number of programs began to originate from service camps, particularly the *Bob Hope Show. Spot Light Bands* was created to take shows to various training centers for young service men. Other new programs included *Meet Your Navy* and *Stage Door Canteen.* With the fright engendered by the Martian invasion hoax a few years before, the networks were careful of all sound effects, changing the opening of *Gangbusters* which had featured a number of aggressive marshal sounds including marching feet, whistles and the chatter of a machine gun. Measures were taken to avoid any chance that the enemy might hear ad lib talks by unauthorized persons, weather information and information about military troops.

From time to time there were special programs, many with name stars urging the public to save tires, buy bonds, work hard, and other patriotic activities. One of the most famous campaigns was the marathon fund appeal made by singer Kate Smith throughout the broadcasting day of February 1, 1944. She made 57 appeals over 134 stations in 18 hours to urge her listeners to buy bonds. The sales attributed to her appeals are said to have totaled $108 million.[41]

Government propaganda was generally under the Office of War Information. There was an intense awareness of the excesses of propaganda in the United States during World War I. Members of O.W.I. tried to avoid blatant lies and deceit.[42] Radio was under the direction of a section of the Office of Facts and Figures, headed by Archibald McLeish but was moved to Elmer Davis's O.W.I. in late 1942. The functions of both agencies seemed to be more of a clearing house nature than a fountainhead of propaganda ideas. Stations received "Radio War Guides" to aid them in presenting the right information at the right time. Networks were allocated spots of a certain nature to avoid inundating the nation in information without planning. The bureau produced programs only when a serious breach of general information was noted. The O.W.I. also was involved in short wave propaganda to friends and enemies oversea—the beginnings of the Voice of America.[43] All was not tranquil in the retooling of American broadcasting for wartime. Publicity expert Edward L. Bernays, noted "There is no well-planned approach to the problem of radio broadcasting's all-out conversion in total war." [44]

Radio war broadcasts brought numerous eyewitness accounts from overseas. Edward R. Murrow described the London air raids from atop a building. Later Murrow described some of his difficulties arranging this broadcast.

> I had to stand on a rooftop for six nights in succession and make a record each night and submit to the Ministry of Information in order to persuade the censors that I could ad lib without violating security. And I did it for six nights and the records were lost somewhere in the Ministry of Information so then I had to do it for another six nights before they would finally give me permission, after listening to the second take of six, to stand on a rooftop.[45]

Other correspondents made dramatic reports of war action including Bert Silen's description of the Japanese attack on Manila, recordings by George Hicks and Bill Downs on the landing in Normandy on D-Day, and Jim Cassidy facing the fury of the Wiermacht at the Battle of the Bulge. There were on-the-spot reports of Pacific island landings, from a B-25 bombing Tokyo, live coverage of the surrender of Germany as described by Charles Collingwood, the announcing of the dropping of the atomic bomb, and the description by Merrill Mueller of the Japanese surrender signing on the Battleship Missouri.

The war kept political campaigning to a minimum. Thomas Dewey, the Republican candidate, was considered a very effective radio campaigner—skilled in public speaking as a criminal prosecutor—but against the master, FDR, in 1944, he was unsuccessful. The President's health was failing and he devoted most of his campaign to radio addresses. Both parties made extensive use of five-minute programs—starting a new style in political use of broadcasting.

President Roosevelt's death, April 12, 1945, was announced to a stunned world. The networks and most stations cancelled all commercial programs till after his funeral four days later.

The introduction of television in the early 1940s brought on speculation that the nature of the programs would be the same as those on radio.[46] A token broadcast schedule of a few hours a week was maintained by television stations during the war, but the program budgets were infinitesimal.

Music accounted for 52% of radio programming time in 1938 and 48% in 1942. Four years later music was only 40% of radio programming. Large stations carried twice the drama as on small stations. For all station programming 16% was drama, 13% news and comment, seven % comedy, six % quiz and audience participation, and 18% devoted to other programs. About a third of all programs were sustaining but about half that number was commercial (spots and paid commercial announcements).

News still was a mainstay of radio despite the time for news dropping for a while after the war.[47] Never before and never again would radio carry so great a quantity of programs other than music as during the 1940s.

Network radio programs were starting their downhill slide in 1948. Comedy variety programs, by 1954, had slipped to one-sixth of the number on the air in 1947. Radio networks kept producing psychological thrillers (particularly science fiction), but every other type of program decreased except music.

The ban on recordings that the networks broke only for major stories such as the Hindenburg crash and the Normandy invasion was dropped with several disc jockey shows such as Martin Block, Paul Whiteman, and *The Amos 'n' Andy Music Hall*. More telephone quizzes came on in the late 1940s like *Stop the Music*, which offered large amounts of money to those who could give the correct answer to the telephone call question. Serial dramas continued on the air, but were beginning to fade away from radio.[48] Ma Perkins finally said, "Good-bye and may God bless you," November 1960. During the period that soap operas were on the wane, other types of programs were tried on the networks including drama of a more sophisticated nature and several light music programs. Research had shown that such programs were preferred by those listeners not interested in soap operas. But the audience was rapidly being attracted to the hundreds of new radio stations on the air and, where it was available, to television.

In the 1950s network radio programs were disappearing and not being replaced. Mutual was feeding its stations 50 minutes of music and 10 minutes of news an hour in 1955. The pestilence of TV reached epidemic proportions for radio in 1954 which has been called by one author the "signal year . . . that saw television ascend over radio." [49]

Each radio network met the crisis with a different panic button. The most successful solution was *Monitor*, the magazine idea of NBC's Sylvester L. (Pat) Weaver.[50] Monitor was a week-end *potpourri* of program tidbits including recorded and live music, talk, news, interviews, short dramatic and comedy sketches, commentary, sports coverage, and other elements. The program started June 12, 1955, running 40 hours, Friday night to Sunday; then was shortened to about 25 hours on the weekend. There were problems—particularly the rigidity of a vast number of pre-taped portions. The concept of "going places and doing things" was often "went places and did things," since so much of it was on audio tape. However, it was successful commercially and was imitated by both CBS and ABC. NBC imitated the program on weekdays with Mike Wallace and Margaret Truman as hosts. As time went on, *Monitor* changed its form and the early excitement of experiment gave way in the 1970s to a simple weekend of records, short interviews and news features.

After 1955 radio network programming was completely different from the period a scant seven years before. In 1957 NBC followed ABC and Mutual in presenting little more than news service. Each network made efforts to revive the interest in drama, national personalities, quiz programs and the like. The last dramas on CBS, which included *Gunsmoke*, went off the air in 1962. Don McNeill's *Breakfast Club* left the networks in 1968. A few network programs survived to 1970. Arthur Godfrey continued to broadcast seven days a week until 1972. ABC began using its network wires for four separate types of news services, for various local station formats. MBS in 1972 added two services to its news offerings, the Mutual Black Network and one for Spanish-speaking listeners. After seven months, problems with multiple dialects forced suspension of the Spanish service. In addition to the four national networks with 160 hours a week of news and talk, United Press International and Associated Press were offering audio services to stations and the educational radio network presented a news roundup of an hour-and-a-half each week.

Todd Storz at KOWH in Omaha was probably most responsible for beginning the evolution of what would come to be called "top 40," "formula," "modern," and "contemporary" radio. In 1949 Storz began to program mostly popular songs on his station. By 1956 this had evolved into the "top 40 formula" of a limited-play list. Of course, recorded music programs were the first and principal programming of many radio station before 1923. Al Jarvis had begun the original "Make Believe Ballroom" in California in the early 1930s. Also in the 1930s Martin Block was popular in southern California playing records from a Tijuana station—since U.S. stations did not have regular record programs. Block moved to KMPC, Los Angeles, then to New York. During the Hauptmann trial for the Lindbergh kidnapping he filled time playing records from the courtroom. This evolved into *Make Believe Ballroom*—Block apparently taking the title idea from Jarvis—and was the progenitor of "disc jockey" programming in the late 1930s and early 1940s. But it was Storz, closely followed by Gordon McLendon in Texas that would change radio. According to *Sponsor*, by 1953 the McLendon station in Dallas had "burst into national prominence with its formula of music and news plus razzle-dazzle promotions. . . . Through such flamboyant promotion, KLIF became the highest rated metropolitan radio station in the country." [51] Actually the year was 1954 and the innovator with McLendon was Bill Stewart, a former classical music announcer from Boston.

At the same time a new kind of music was emerging. Maybe the term was coined by Alan Freed a Cleveland DJ after hearing Bill Haley and The Comets sing, "we're gona rock . . . we're gonna roll . . ." What was part "race," part rhythm and blues, part country, part lots of other things became "Rock and Roll." Following Storz and McLendon, many other station-owning groups developed "top 40" formats in market after market and "promoted" them to the top in metro ratings—chief among them were Plough, Bartell, Crowell-Collier and ABC. Many of the early stars of rock and roll were country and the records were from Memphis—Elvis Presley, Carl Perkins, the Everly Brothers, Jerry Lee Lewis, Sam Cooke, and Johnny Cash. By 1960 nearly every medium-size and major radio market was dominated by a "rocker." Radio and TV, while competing, worked hand-in-hand to promote new pop music stars with TV dance programs and radio DJs. The appeal was broadened by black and other ethnic performers from Chicago, Philadelphia, New York, Los Angeles, Cleveland, Detroit, Nashville, and other cities.

In the late 1950s various stations began to use helicopter traffic reports as part of their service to the auto listeners in their areas.

WGN in Chicago did some helicopter reports in 1954. KMPC in Los Angeles began them the first day of 1959. This brought on experiments with more than one airplane and sexy-voiced female reporters. Some police became sky comedians while they gave traffic information.

Local radio programming was essentially music and news. A 1964 analysis of programming on 22 radio stations covering all the Los Angeles market indicated that 67% of the programming was music. News was 15%. Stations specialized, presenting primarily one type of music, or only news or talk. Twenty of the 22 stations presented one type of programming more than 50% of their broadcasting time; 13 of 22 broadcast one program type 80% or more of the time.[52]

In the largest markets sometimes 40 or more stations compete for listeners with specialized middle-of-the-road country, jazz, "good," album (so-called wall-to-wall background), soul or "Negro appeal," ethnic music and foreign languages, all news, conversation, telephone call-in, classical and concert, progressive-underground rock, or "free form" formats.

The radio station in the smaller markets—half of all radio stations were in a one- or two-station market—was likely to have more program diversity. It was a time of change—an effort to find an important place for radio in the face of the "money machine." One researcher found in 1960–1961 that more than a quarter of stations surveyed throughout the country had changed their programming in the previous 12 months.[53]

After 1965 FM radio began to capture a much larger part of the radio audience. More pop music formats on FM were partly the result of a 1965 FCC rule prohibiting more than 50% duplication of AM programming by FM stations in markets of more than 100,000. Also FM car radios were more available and were capable of better reception.

Early television took many programs from radio, some were simulcast. A number of vaudeville and comedy variety and sports programs were aired in the 1948–1949 season. The following season, drama became more prevalent, particularly action-adventure and detective. The networks were experimenting with new forms suited to viewing as well as listening. *Howdy-Doody* and *Kukla, Fran and Ollie* were among the foremost marionette and puppet programs. A number of ad lib courtroom dramas were attempted, including *Black Robe* and *Cross Question* (which was later called *They Stand Accused*). In addition several programs using silent films and a narrator were produced. The giant program maw of television was grinding up ideas faster than the producers of traditional radio programs could get them together. As in early radio, Chicago TV began to produce a number of outstanding fresh formats in the early 1950s. The center of television programming was shifted from New York to the West Coast. Eric Johnston of the Motion Picture Association of America wrote in 1948:

> Motion pictures, in my judgment, will be the sturdy backbone of television. I believe that a great spurt in film production and forward strides in picture-making techniques are inevitable.[54]

However, television at every level depended on feature films from the earliest days. Hopalong Cassidy films, cut down from their feature length, were used as both half-hour and hour programs. By 1948 NBC had begun producing films for television. However, most of the programs—even action-adventure such as *Martin Kane, Private Eye*—were live with some film inserts to set the exterior scenes. By 1952 a pattern of action-adventure, crime-detective and situation comedy drama was established which continued throughout the first 20 years of the medium. Daytime television duplicated radio with low-budget variety, and quiz shows. Soap operas too became a staple of daytime TV first as 15-minute programs taken from radio then as 30-minute episodes often more frank than their ancestors.

Dramatic programs in the first seven years of television were both very bad and very good.[55] Some good shows were the output of a whole cadre of new authors who came out of "nowhere." They included Reginald Rose and:

> . . . the following distinguished writers, Robert Alan Arthur (a partner in a small record company), J. P. Miller (an air-conditioner salesman), David Shaw (a struggling water-colorist), Rod Serling (a student on the GI Bill), Ted Mosel (an airline clerk), Horton Foote (an actor), N. Richard Nash (a school teacher), and Paddy Chayefsky (a sketch writer for night-club comics) . . . each able to write a script in spare time and sell it into an anthology show.[56]

Children's programs on the networks reached a peak of 37 hours a week in 1956 and for the next 15 years remained at about 20 hours a week.[57] News broadcasts were established on all four networks (ABC, CBS, Dumont, and NBC) five nights a week in 1948. Many observers failed to realize the flowering of television as a news medium was held up, while a style evolved from radio and motion picture newsreels.[58]

As with radio 30 years before live special events coverage was an early TV programming form and helped sell receivers. In October of 1947 network cameras went to the White House to cover Harry Truman in the first major television address by a President. The next year television reported the Democratic and Republican conventions from Philadelphia to about 10,000,000 viewers. In 1952 the TV audience was led on the first electronic tour of the White House by President Truman. The following year a coast-to-coast audience saw the

first television report of the "Oscar" ceremonies. Senate sub-commit-
tee hearings on crime chaired by Senator Estes Kefauver were televised in 1951. While crime figure Frank Costello was testifying only
his hands were shown but the nation's attention was riveted. Some
said that just seeing his nervous hands told the story better than any
other pictures. The West and other parts of the country saw kinescope film recordings.

That same year President Truman fired General Douglas Mac-
Arthur over the conduct of the Korean War. Television covered the
military leader's dramatic return to the U.S. with appearances in San
Francisco and New York, his "old soldiers never die" speech before
a joint session of Congress, and a parade through Chicago.[59] He
hoped that the coverage of his national procession would vault him
into the Republican nomination for the presidency. His hopes were
blunted in Chicago as General Eisenhower, another war hero, became the first to be nominated President before a national television
audience.

Traditions of politics had been shattered by radio coverage.
Television clinched the case for streamlining procedures with the
whole convention evolving into a program for home viewers. A 1952
case in point was the keynote address by Governor Frank Clements
which was said to have thrilled the delegates. But evaluations of the
Tennessee Democrat's address said it was "ho-hummed" by viewers.
In the 1952 campaign Richard M. Nixon made his famous "Checkers" speech explaining a special fund, retaining the support of General Eisenhower, and revealing himself to be the first master of TV
politics.

Like the Kefauver hearings, the televised Army-McCarthy hearings of 1954 filled daytime hours and gripped TV viewers. From this
came television's first major news controversy. On *See It Now* Edward R. Murrow challenged Senator McCarthy and questioned his
methods. The Senator asked for, and received, time to reply which
he used primarily to attack Murrow, showing documents that he said
supported his charges.

As on the networks, local news programming was limited in the
earliest years of TV but expanded steadily as it received good support from sponsors.[60]

The mid-1950s featured many general drama anthologies but
these dwindled as a result of the changing composition of the audience, lack of good scripts and rising production costs. There was
great interest in *The $64,000 Question* and other big-money quiz pro-
grams in the last half of the 1950s. The fad was running a natural
course, but it was killed quickly when the shows were revealed to be
rigged. This deception, and the additional revelation that DJs were
receiving "payola" to favor certain records and artists led to pressure

from the FCC and others for reforms. It was suggested that the networks take direct charge of more program production rather than leaving it to advertising agencies and program packagers and present at least one primetime hour of public affairs programming a week. The FCC view on program control was reversed later in attempt to break network "monopoly" on programming and to encourage local and independent packagers of shows. The pressure for more public affairs programs led to a period of one-hour documentaries such as NBC's *White Paper, CBS Reports,* and *Close-Up* on ABC (sponsored by Bell and Howell).

In 1962 two young doctors captured viewers and fan magazine attention as no two programs had before—*Dr. Kildare* and *Ben Casey.* Other programming fads included the addition of jazz music to crime-detective drama, teenage music shows, international spies, dramas concerning "social problems" and, above all, variations on situation comedy. Comedy situations included a flying nun, a beautiful genie, ghosts, ghouls, witches, a woman reincarnated as a car, a fun war in the Pacific, a Nazi POW camp, and ranged from a sympathetic treatment of blacks to blatant bigotry.

The prediction of Eric Johnson came true in the 1961–1962 season as NBC introduced *Saturday Night at the Movies.* Ten years later it was every night at the movies. More long programs, and fewer episodes of each series, were produced as production costs rose and the audiences leveled off. Blockbuster movies captured highest ratings—*Bridge on the River Kwai* (1966), *The Birds* (1968), *Ben-Hur* (1971), *Love Story, True Grit,* and *Patton.* The last three all had shares above 60% and reached more than 25,000,000 homes early in the 1972-3 season when all 10 network movie programs were in the top-35 shows in ratings. But the supply ran low. The solution—as suggested two decades earlier by Samuel Goldwyn—was to produce made-for-television movies. In 1971–72 about 100 TV movies were produced, mostly in Hollywood.

Programs were as new in form as they were in placement in the 1960s. Sports fare in primetime was changing. *Friday Night Boxing* went off the air in 1964 after 20 years of telecasting, but basketball, football, and baseball all were scheduled into primetime on networks. Professional football, which had been quite successful on Sunday afternoons became a formidable program block on Monday nights in the fall of 1970. Probably the most memorable sports in primetime in the 1960s was ABC coverage of the Olympics in Mexico in 1968 and Munich in 1972.

There were some flashy network successes including *Batman* which was a January replacement in the 1965–1966 season. In the next season *The Green Hornet* was also revived for television with other imitations of the Batman style—*Captain Nice* and *Mr. Terrific.*

A night soap opera, *Peyton Place,* became a hit in 1965. It was broadcast one-, two- and three-nights-a-week at various times. In 1972 it
returned as a daytime serial, only to die again in January 1974.

The decade of the 1960s featured so many specials that in some
seasons there was one nearly every night of the week. Both ABC and
NBC tried nights of specials including three and one-half hour documentaries on Africa, foreign policy and crime in America.

CBS introduced a new program idea in 1965—*The National Dri-
ver's Test*—in an effort to point out the need for safe driving.[61] The
network found the program important enough to give the audience
other "tests" on citizenship and health. The 1968–1969 season
brought two new programs which were magazine-type documentaries—NBC's *First Tuesday* (in 1971–72, moved to Friday as *Chron-
olog,* then returned to its day and title, then dropped) and CBS's *60
Minutes.*

The march of history on the television screen was by far the
most important happening in communications in the years after
1960. The coverage of an event by television became as important as
the event itself. Television reshaped the conduct of public affairs. It
became difficult to separate the following events from their television image: Soviet Premier Khrushchev's visit to the United States;
the "Great Debates" with John F. Kennedy and Richard M. Nixon,
the live press conferences of President Kennedy, integration of the
high school in Little Rock, the Russians in space, the United States
in space, the Cuban missile crisis, the integration of the University of
Alabama, a succession of civil rights marches (especially Selma), the
"poor people's" march on Washington, the assassination of President
Kennedy, the Vietnam war, pictures of Mars from Mariner I, summer
riots in Watts, Detroit and Newark, the Six-Day Israel-Egypt war, the
Tet offensive of 1968 and the beginning of "peace" talks, the invasion of Czechoslovakia, the murder of Martin Luther King and
resulting violence, the assassination of Senator Robert F. Kennedy,
the 1968 Democratic Convention in Chicago, Americans on the
moon, charges of bias in TV news, the controversy over CBS *Selling
of the Pentagon* editing, President Nixon in China and Russia, the
signing of a ceasefire in Paris, the return of the American POWs, the
Watergate hearings, another Mideast war, resignation of Vice President Agnew, a fuel crisis, Nixon in the Mideast and Russia, the judiciary committee hearing on the impeachment of the President, the
resignation of President Nixon, and. . . .

In the sixth decade after the debut of the *Eveready Hour,* television executives would argue that a new technical innovation—cable
television and especially "pay cable"—might change TV programming for the worse, just as TV had altered radio and the movies. It
was 125 years since a *Punch* cartoon predicted, and 100 years since
Elisha Gray tested, entertainment by wire.

46

C. E. Massena

HOW OPERA IS BROADCASTED

THE PROGRAMME for the evening has been announced through the press and by bulletin, and the thousands of radio fans are adjusting their headpieces at the scheduled hour.

The company arrives and is shown into the *sanctum sanctorum.* They take their places. The announcer explains that they are subject to certain radio traffic regulations, as other broadcasting stations are also operating and it would be discourteous to begin until the exact hour announced, when the air lanes are free. Now the usual running time for "The Impresario" is an hour and forty minutes, but in the tabloid version for broadcasting twenty-five minutes have been eliminated. Even an hour and a quarter in this musical straightjacket is enough to tire any artist. Movement is prohibited, whispering is little short of criminal, and even too deep breathing is forbidden. The announcer cautions all regarding these details and asks if they are ready. With a final admonition of "Sh-h," he closes the switch and then speaks into the microphone, while the members of the company stand silently by, with eyes dilated, enwrapped in a new experience. "This is the WJZ station at Newark, N.J." he begins, "broadcasting Mozart's opera comique 'The Impresario,' under the direction of William Wade Hinshaw. Announcer ACN.* I take pleasure in introducing Mr. Hinshaw." Mr. Hinshaw silently slides into the position promptly vacated by ACN and addresses his audience. Anxiety! Suspense! Yes, 100 percent! The nervous strain is intense, and all are glad when he concludes and they can do something. This tension acts as a stimulant. In most cases, radio singing and playing inspires the artists to do even better than their best. This is why the radio concerts are of such excellence.

What The Future Holds

To-day, that is true; to-morrow, it may not be true. There is too much variety, good and bad all jumbled together, in an effort to fill out the broadcasting time. Artists realize that it is detrimental to appear on a jazz programme, or to be sandwiched in between a comic singer and an anateur band. The time is coming soon when programmes will have to be planned with more skill. There must be an

Radio Broadcast, August 1922, pp. 285–293.

* Early announcers were often identified only by their initials. ACN was the acronym for Tommy Cowan—Announcer Cowan Newark.

"opera" night, a "popular" night, a "band" night, a "jazz" night, an "artist" night, a "juvenile" night, etc. The time is hastening when it will be necessary to engage artists and organizations precisely as is done in the regular concert field. A laborer is worthy of his hire, and as soon as programmes are made up with a view to their artistic value, and not with a view to securing something for nothing, then there will be proper cooperation and a mutual benefit for all partici- pants.

All the world wants music. The easiest and cheapest way to get it is by means of the radio telephone which affords opportunities to a vast multitude of persons who otherwise would be unable to hear any. The man in the lighthouse, the farmer in his kitchen, the lum- berman in his shack, the traveler at sea, literally thousands of per- sons hitherto isolated, are now able to relieve the monotony of their existence by introducing culture and entertainment into it by means of radio-telephony. Music is no longer confined within the four walls of concert halls and opera houses. Radio-telephony has freed the cap- tive bird from its prison, and it is now at liberty to soar and to sing for all who may care to hear.

47

Lawrence W. Lichty

RADIO DRAMA: THE EARLY YEARS

ACCORDING TO THE best available materials in 1944 Donald W. Riley reports that WGY, Schenectady, formed the first group "for the specific purpose of putting on plays." [3] The first radio play on WGY was "The Wolf," by Eugene Walter, broadcast on August 3, 1922. All three acts of the play were given without cuts. Music was played be- tween the acts just as in the legitimate theater.[4] WGY broadcast plays as a regular weekly feature beginning in October 1922.[5]

On April 12, 1923, KDKA broadcast the complete performance of "Friend Mary" from the stage of a Pittsburgh theater.[6] In the same month, WJZ, Newark, broadcast "Merton of the Movies" directly from the stage of the Court Theater [7] and also carried the first install- ment of "The Waddington Cipher," a detective story.[8] But Professor Riley notes that KDKA might have "heralded radio drama with its

The NAEB Journal, July–August 1966, pp. 10–16.

experimental programs prior to the granting of its license"[9] November 2, 1920.

On November 9, 1922, about a month after the first play had been presented on WGY, a program that was a "near drama" was broadcast on WLW. On this program the one-act play "A Fan and Two Candlesticks" by Mary MacMillan of Cincinnati, was read before the microphone by Miss MacMillan, Fred Smith, and Robert Stayman. According to the *Crosley Radio Weekly*, this reading "got over so well" that it was "decided to continue the broadcasting of playlets and one act plays."[12] More important, this article noted, "It is believed that the radio play has specific requirements such as simplicity and brevity, which must be given the most careful consideration."[13]

The following week, on November 16, 1922, Mary Sullivan Brown was presented on WLW "reading from the Balcony Scene of Romeo and Juliet." Fred Smith had heard plays broadcast on WGY, and decided to try them on WLW.[14]

On November 24, 1922, WLW broadcast its first real dramatic program. The play was "Matinata" by Lawrence Langer and was presented by permission of Stewart and Kidd, the publishers. According to *Crosley Radio Weekly:*

> We realize the radio play can only be made effective if it is put over in such a way that it may be readily visualized by the radio listener. With this end in mind, we are, for the present, having some of the parts taken by those of the Crosley staff who are accustomed to talking over radio, and who can work in effects which would not occur to professional players.[15]

WLW next presented a drama on December 15, 1922—a play entitled "What the Public Wants." On December 22, "The Shadowed Star" was presented with a cast of five. On January 5, 1923, another one-act play, apparently unnamed, was presented and directed by John R. Froome, head of the drama department of Cincinnati College of Music.

On February 6, 1923, a play written by Mr. Froome and starring himself and his student Emil Lewis was broadcast from WLW. Another original drama written by a Cincinnatian, Belle McDiarmid Ritchley, was given in the same month. It is not known whether these plays were written especially for the radio and for presentation over WLW or whether they were merely adapted for WLW.[16] Either might qualify as the first plays written especially for presentation on radio.

On April 3, 1923, "When Love Wakens" (note the W-L-W), an original play written especially for WLW by station director Fred Smith, was broadcast.[17]

By October 1923 about one year after its first drama, WLW had presented twenty-five different dramatic programs. In addition to presenting a drama about every other week, Mr. Smith and other WLW staff members were innovators of a specialized dramatic form for radio. In September, 1922, according to Mr. Smith:

> we began to think of plays for radio. But we were always of the opinion that the most effective production would be the one-act play. So far as we know there was no broadcasting station sending out one-act plays at the time. During the fall we put on several with good effect.
>
> Since this was pioneer work we made discoveries as we went along. We did incidental music to give atmosphere in a place where part of the action took place at a dance. . . . It then occurred to us that an artistic hour of entertainment would be the production of a foreign play with music of its own country surrounding it.[21]

These combined music and drama programs included plays by Benavente, Maeterlinck, and Ibsen. Mr. Smith's stay in Europe had developed in him an appreciation for European music and drama. In presenting these plays he condensed and adapted them for radio, and he added a "descriptionist" (now we use the word narrator) to give a synopsis of the play up to "the scene to be radioed." [22] This reduced the play to the brevity Mr. Smith felt was needed to hold the attention of the radio listener, and reduced the cast to two or three actors. The fewer actors the less confusing for the listener to separate the voices.

The next logical step—as we have seen—was to write plays especially for radio presentation; probably "When Love Wakens" was the first of these. Mr. Smith added background music and even included vocal and whistling numbers as part of the plots. When he started writing or adapting plays for WLW he then began to use the dialogue to carry all the action and eventually the "descriptionist" was eliminated. Sound effects were added. On one play the sound of an elephant walking was needed; Powel Crosley, Jr. made the sound by pounding his fists into the table.

To describe the radio dramas, Mr. Smith and Mr. Stayman coined the word "radario" (from radio and scenario), even applying for a copyright. But the word never caught on. The most frequently used term for radio dramas in the early days became "sketches."

Mr. Smith even tried musical comedy plays. The first of these was "When Madam Sings," written by Alvin R. Plough, associate editor of *Crosley Radio Weekly*. This was a story about a great opera star who would not appear before a radio microphone because her powder puff had been mislaid and she would not disgrace herself with a shiny nose.[23] A second "musical playlet," entitled "When

Betsy Ross Made Old Glory," was presented June 13, 1923—the night before Flag Day.

On September 26, "The Magic Journey," a specially written play for children was broadcast. It was written by T. C. O'Donnel, editor of *Writer's Digest,* who contributed a monthly play for children to *Child Life* magazine. The cast included "the most talented students from the Reulman School of Expression." [24]

Dramatic readings were added to the WLW daytime schedule on September 6, 1923. Fred Smith read stories with piano background from the "classics."

On October 4 came the announcement that Helen Schuster Martin, of the Schuster Martin Dramatic School, henceforth would direct all of the radarios. Further, she would form a WLW "stock company" of fourteen actors to be called the "Crosley Radarians." The staff included Thomie Prewitt Williams, of the Cincinnati Conservatory of Music, as musical director. Soon William Stoess, later WLW music director, provided music for the dramas. Mr. Stoess developed background music and montages and was recognized as one of the first to "develop this new art" as early as 1923.[25] By the fall of 1923 the Radarians were presenting dramas every week on Thursday evenings at 10:00 p.m.[26]

The nationally distributed magazine, *Writer's Digest,* and WLW held a contest beginning in May 1923, for the three best radarios.[27] The winner received $50, second $30, and third $20. All three plays were broadcast on WLW. This was one of the earliest national contests—maybe the very first—for dramatic radio scripts. Donald Riley reports that WGY held a contest "as early as 1923" but a more exact date apparently is not available.[28] E. P. J. Shurick says that WGY held a national contest in the spring of 1925.[29] In October 1923, WLW held a second contest for the best original radarios. Thus radio drama evolved at WLW from fall 1922 to fall 1923, and it was evolving at other stations in the U.S. at about the same time.

Radio cooperates rather than competes with newspapers and magazines. It supplements in a remarkable and delightful way the former means for filling leisure hours. Radio is not a suitable medium for direct advertising. The radio advertiser has no chance to catch the eye. Nor can radio, with its limited appeal to a single sense, compete with the many-sided appeal of the speaking stage. The great future of radio broadcasting lies in the field of education.
                    --H. V. Kaltenborn, associate editor,
                    Brooklyn Daily Eagle, 1925.

48

David G. Clark

H. V. KALTENBORN'S
FIRST YEAR ON THE AIR

WHEN H. V. KALTENBORN, associate editor of the Brooklyn *Daily Eagle*, began his first season as a radio news analyst in the fall of 1923, he felt a certain misgiving. Radio, he had told an audience not long before, was an unsatisfactory method of speechmaking, for "there is no comeback and you can't tell how it is received." [1]

When American Telephone & Telegraph began operations over WEAF, the added power of that experimental station and its greater convenience led *Eagle* publisher Herbert F. Gunnison to offer to supply a program over that facility. WEAF was delighted to have two hours of programming one night a week supplied by the *Eagle,* and an agreement was soon reached calling for programs to begin late in October and to run through the following May. Kaltenborn was to have roughly 30 minutes for his current events talks.[5]

Arriving at WEAF, Kaltenborn made the engineers laugh when he referred to the draped studio as the "torture chamber." But he found nothing humorous in the minutes just before he went on the air. The absence of a live audience provoked agonies of nervousness which its presence never had. And there was the discomfort of a neck clamp to keep him in front of the microphone. If his mouth came closer than 14 inches from the microphone, they told him, his voice would "blast"; if he moved farther back, it would fade out. Finally the light over the door flashed red, warning that he was on the air, and he began to talk.[6]

Just as he always had, he spoke from rough, topic notes jotted on cards five and a half inches by three and a half inches. He would use that system on the radio for nearly 30 years, rarely employing more than half a dozen cards with a few statistics and quotations jotted on them. His ability to extemporize led him to prefer that method, and as he delivered his talk he made the usual platform gestures, which helped relieve his nervousness. Extemporization would soon prove itself both a strength and a weakness: it made him difficult to censor, but it tended to allow mistakes to creep in.[7]

As reported in next day's *Eagle,* Kaltenborn's subjects that night were varied. He spoke first of Lloyd George:

> What a lively personality his is. He reminds me so much of our own Theodore Roosevelt. Lloyd George has a great faith in his own

Journalism Quarterly, Vol. 42, No. 3 (Summer 1965), pp. 373–381.

personality, in his ability to carry through what he believes is the union of the English-speaking people: England and America.[8]

Shifting to Andrew Volstead, who authored the act implementing prohibition, Kaltenborn told of having been a passenger with the Minnesotan the past summer on a voyage to Bremen. "I found him sincere in his views, but a fanatic on the subject of prohibition," Kaltenborn said. Then he told how he and his wife had persuaded Volstead and his daughter to dine with them at the famous Bremen Rathskeller. He had even managed to coax Volstead into tasting a thimbleful of the "Rosewein," reputed to be 200 years old. That glass cost a million German marks, Kaltenborn said, but the actual cost in U.S. currency was $1.60.[9]

With that smooth transition from prohibition to Germany, Kaltenborn touched on conditions in the Rhineland, which he had found abject. He said he looked for a communistic revolution in Germany, but did not think it would win because "Europe is anti-communist." Then he closed his broadcast with a resounding appeal for his listeners to appreciate America. Few Americans realize how much they have to be thankful for, he said, until they travel abroad.[10]

Kaltenborn stepped outside the booth unaware that WEAF's pianist, Winifred T. Barr, had been standing by in case he had faltered or run short. Now the talk was over, he felt curiously unfulfilled sensations. Had he really been heard by hundreds, perhaps thousands of people? Then someone thrust a radio-gram into his hands. It read, "We're listening. Good stuff. Keep it up—Captain Cunningham, Steamship George Washington." The Kaltenborns had sailed on Cunningham's ship that summer and had become friendly with him. At that moment, the George Washington was a thousand miles off the Atlantic coast.[11]

Other reaction soon arrived, showing both the popularity of Kaltenborn's type of talk and the strength of WEAF's signal. Letters came from as far away as Alaska. To further stimulate response, sometimes to help WEAF determine the pattern of its coverage area, Kaltenborn and the *Eagle* followed the general practice of offering incentives. On November 20, the offer of a guide to the New York subway system brought more than 100 requests to the *Eagle*. And on January 17, 1924, Kaltenborn read Walt Whitman's "Pioneers! O Pioneers!" and offered printed copies to his listeners. More than 1,000 requests flooded in, a tremendous response for that period in broadcasting. Thereafter, Kaltenborn knew that an offer of poetry would always elicit great response from his audience.[12]

49

George A. Lundberg [1]

THE CONTENT OF RADIO PROGRAMS

THE CONTENT of newspapers has, during the last two decades been the subject of a number of studies.[2] The reason for this type of research has been the recognition of the fact that before the mechanism of public opinion and other public reactions can be understood, a knowledge of the nature of the material upon which these reactions are founded is essential.[3] Recently, another means of communication has developed, namely, the radio, which has become almost as general in its appeal and contacts as the newspaper. What is the nature of the material of which it is the carrier?

"There are at present approximately 5,000,000 radio receiving sets in the United States, which means that there are probably 20,000,000 potential 'listeners-in' each night." [4] Much has been said about the probable social effect of this sudden development of a new means of communication and socialization. "These programs have stimulated the conclusions that we shall have a greater religious consciousness, that we shall take a greater interest in politics than we are wont to, that we shall find less apathy for education, and that we shall wake up one bright morning with an international consciousness, the result of worldwide broadcast programs, and the dawn of mutual understanding and world peace will have come." [5] Whether any or all of these optimistic expectations are justified or not, depends to a great degree on the nature of the material being broadcast through this device. As in the case of the newspapers, the quantitative analysis of radio programs is the first step in an estimate of their social influence.

As a preliminary attempt to get some light on the subject of the nature and probable influence of radio programs, an analysis of all the radio programs broadcast from the nineteen stations of New York City during the month of February 1927 was undertaken. The categories employed are admittedly general, but are regarded as sufficiently definite for the present purpose. While the proportion of time devoted to each type of subject matter varies considerably with different stations, the comparison of stations is not here exhibited, the purpose being merely to determine the general character of "what's in the air" for radio fans. The results are found in the accompanying table.

Social Forces, Vol. 7 (1928), pp. 58–60.

DISTRIBUTION OF TOTAL BROADCASTING
TIME FROM ALL THE STATIONS
OF NEW YORK CITY, FEBRUARY, 1927

Type of subject matter	Total no. of hours	Per cent of total
Educational	263.66	9.3%
Religious	150.40	5.3
Dance Music	743.66	26.2
Other Music	1,362.33	48.0
Children's Programs	32.83	1.1
Drama and Readings	74.50	2.6
Information	81.25	2.8
Sports	49.50	1.8
Miscellaneous	76.45	2.6
Total	2,834.58	99.7

The table shows that for the month of February 1927 programs aggregating 2,834.58 hours were broadcast from the stations of New York City. Three-fourths of this time was devoted to music, about one-fourth of the total time being devoted to dance music and about one-half of the total time to other music. Approximately five per cent of the total time is devoted to the broadcasting of religious services, Bible stories, and lectures on religious subjects. About nine per cent of the time is devoted to subject matter of a generally educational nature, chiefly lectures, travelogues, and talks. About three per cent of the total time is devoted to information—news, market and weather reports, police alarms, etc. About two and a half per cent of the time is devoted to drama (plays and readings), one per cent to children's programs, about two per cent to sports, and the remainder to miscellaneous unclassified material, including a small amount of material of a political nature (about 0.2 per cent of the total broadcasting time).

The general conclusion to be drawn from this analysis is that the radio is at present used almost entirely as an entertainment device for the advertising of the radio itself, and of the businesses which provide the programs. This advertising consists of the broadcasting of the name of a business as well as the short advertising talks which intersperse the items on the regular program. It is recognized, of course, that the time distribution for the month of February is not strictly representative of all months of the year. A similar analysis during a political campaign or during the football season would undoubtedly reveal a larger percentage of the time devoted to politics and sports respectively. As a sample of the time distribution during the greater part of the year, however, it is believed that the analysis for February is perhaps representative. The present direct influence of the radio as an organ of public opinion, therefore, would appear to be very limited.

50

Lawrence W. Lichty and Thomas W. Bohn

RADIO'S *MARCH OF TIME:*
DRAMATIZED NEWS

THE MARCH OF TIME may be remembered best by its opening with
those same words and the mellifluent voice of Westbrook van Voorhis. Yet it should be known as the prototype of many broadcast programs—dramatic and documentary, fact and fiction—that followed. A
broadcaster's idea and the support of a magazine publisher combined
to produce one of radio's most interesting programs.

In early 1922 Briton Hadden and Henry R. Luce quit their jobs
at the Baltimore *News* to found a magazine they would call *Time.*
That same year Fred Smith became director of radio station WLW,
Cincinnati. Just six years later an idea of Mr. Smith's with the backing of *Time* would produce the *March of Time.*

To promote the idea they had nurtured as undergraduate journalists at Yale and promoted while working in Baltimore, Hadden
and Luce formed Time Incorporated in 1922. On March 2, 1923, the
first issue of their new "paper" was published; it was to establish a
whole new class of "news magazines." [1] Just a year prior to the
beginning of *Time,* Powel Crosley Jr. had begun radio station WLW
in Cincinnati. [2] In August 1922 Fred Smith joined WLW as station
director. He joined two other parttime employees and was the station's only fulltime staff member. Mr. Smith's main interests were
music and literature, but he soon developed some of radio's earliest
and most inventive formats. He established a regular program schedule, including five-times-a-week financial market news, weather,
farm market reports, and phonograph record programs. He also pioneered some of radio's earliest dramatic programs, and probably wrote
the first original radio drama ever broadcast. [3]

Musical News

"Late news bulletins" from the Cincinnati *Enquirer* were included as part of WLW's inaugural program in March 23, 1922. However, news did not play an important part in the schedule of WLW
nor any other radio station in those early days. This was mainly
because there were no news gathering sources available to radio. Occasionally "bulletins" would be read and infrequently, special news,
such as election returns, was given. Some stations, especially those
owned by or associated with newspapers, had news programs, but
few on a regular basis.

Journalism Quarterly, Vol. 51, No. 3 (Autumn 1974), pp. 458–462.

In 1925 Mr. Smith hit upon a novel idea for a new program at WLW call *Musical News*. He reported news items he had taken—without permission—from various newspapers and magazines, interspersed with organ music. After each news item an "appropriate" musical number was played. A review of that program in a radio fan magazine was almost as unique as the show itself.

WLW is using a novel method to present the daily news, and while it may not be very exciting, as excitement is measured in these days of petting parties and uncovered feminine knees, it is pretty good for so young and yet so mossy a thing as radio broadcasting.[4]

By this time news programs were being added to some stations across the country. *The Political Situation Tonight* with Frederick William Wile was the first "news program" carried on the national radio networks in the season of 1926–1927. However, this commentary, broadcast only one time each week, was not very similar to the later-to-be-developed daily newscasts.

NewsCasting

In 1928 Fred Smith started a weekly news round-up on WLW. Mr. Smith re-wrote news stories from newspapers and magazines, including *Time*. In 1928 he wrote Roy Larsen, *Time* vice-president and general manager, requesting a weekly advanced "makeready" copy of the magazine from the printing plant in Chicago. From this Mr. Smith wrote a 10-minute daily summary of news. Apparently *Time* also purchased an announcement in each news program for $25 and Smith was required to mention *Time* three times in each broadcast.

Mr. Larsen and Briton Hadden in 1925 (or 1924?) had promoted the magazine via radio with what might have been the first radio quiz program called *Pop Question* game.[5]

Fred Smith's main goal now was to move to New York. His major interest was music and the promotion of his wife's career as a concert pianist.[6] They listed nearly a score of possible ways they might get to the East Coast—one far down was to create a network radio program.

Mr. Smith again wrote Mr. Larsen who recommended spending $750 for exploration of the idea for a new network radio program, and Hadden agreed. Time Inc. hired Fred Smith in May 1928 and during that summer he traveled over much of the Northeast and as far west as the Mississippi visiting radio stations. He made agreements with stations to carry the 10-minute summary of the news provided by *Time* once each day. On September 3, 1928, *Time* began publishing and syndicating the 10-minute news summaries to more than 60 stations.

The program, called *NewsCasting*, began in New York on October 1, 1928. It was carried from 5:50 to 6:00 P.M. Monday through Friday, over WOR. Smith himself read *NewsCasting* over WOR that first year. Scripts were airmailed to other stations. There were few other news programs on the air at this time. H. V. Kaltenborn's commentaries were carried on WOR and WNYC. On the 14 stations listed for the immediate New York area there were only three other news programs. These programs—*News Summary, Time, News, Weather,* and *News Flashes*—were usually one to five minutes in length.

Roy Larsen, according to Smith, suggested that the program be called *NewsCasting.* However, the *New York Times* in its radio log listed the program as *Newscasting.* Smith believes that this is the first time the word newscast—of course, from news and broadcast—had ever been used.[7] *O.E.D.* cites September 1930 as the first usage of the word;[8] the first *NewsCasting* releases were sent out two years earlier. It is easy to believe that Larsen made up the word, for *Time* had become known for its coined words, such as "cinemaddict," "radiorator," "radiowner" and "radiomanufacturer."[9] Smith, who also like to coin words, in 1923 had called the dramas he presented on WLW "radarios" (for radio and scenario) and his players were called the "Crosley Radarians."

By the spring of 1929 the 10-minute daily news summaries were being carried on as many as 90 stations. This very well may have been the first large-scale regular daily news broadcast carried in the United States—although it was never a network program. The first daily news program on the national networks, Lowell Thomas, began on September 29, 1930. In that same season, 1930–1931, *H. V. Kaltenborn, Editing the News* was carried three-times-a-week on CBS.

NewsActing

Prior to *NewsCasting* Smith had experience with dramatic programs at WLW and had written a number of radio dramas. One of his scripts from a serial story "Step on the Stairs" which appeared in *Radio Digest* in 1926 was produced in weekly episodes on 16 stations from coast to coast. This experience and two shows on NBC gave Smith a new idea. Those two programs were *Great Moments in History* and *Biblical Dramas;* two of the five dramatic programs presented on the national radio networks in the season of 1927–1928, the other three were light dramas.[10] There had been no dramatic programs on the national radio networks prior to that season; however, "sketches" had occasionally been included in some programs. Some local stations also had similar programs. For example. *Historical Highlights* which dramatized noteworthy events in history, was carried on WLW during the season of 1928–1929.[11]

Mr. Smith's idea was to dramatize the news of the day. This he considered "far more dramatic than history." Smith again took his idea to Roy Larsen, who was somewhat skeptical of the legality of voice imitation. Smith, Larsen and others refined the idea. In September 1929 Smith made a phonograph record of a five-minute "news drama" and submitted his audition program to a number of stations under the title *NewsActing*. By December, Smith with a crew of six or eight actors was producing a weekly five-minute transcription which was syndicated to about 20 stations. Two recordings were produced each week in the Brunswick recording studios, and Smith would choose the one that came out the best. It was copied and mailed to the stations. The programs could hardly be called full-scaled dramatic productions, but they did include sound effects and occasional music. Within a few months, *NewsActing* was being carried on more than 100 stations "from Florida to Hawaii and Alaska, and from Halifax to New Orleans." [12] This surely makes *NewsActing* one of the most widely circulated early syndicated dramatic programs. *Amos 'n' Andy* programs were syndicated on disc briefly beginning in the fall of 1928 from WMAQ but gained their real fame when they went on the NBC Blue Network August 19, 1929.

Time was not entirely satisfied with *NewsActing*. Mr. Larsen did not feel it had enough "publicity or promotional effect." In October 1930 Fred Smith wrote a long memo to Roy Larsen suggesting that dramatized news be done as a network show.

The March of Time

Batten, Barton, Durstine & Osborne (BBD&O) with CBS tried a 15-minute version—then tried 30 minutes. On February 20, 1931, Roy Larsen obtained Arthur Pryor Jr., head of the BBD&O radio department and son of the well-known band leader, to produce the program. The CBS production department and artists' bureau produced the programs written by Smith. These developmental programs were tried out on a number of small audiences listening in audition rooms. On February 6, 1931, an experimental program was "piped" in by telephone lines to Roy Larsen's home where he listened with a small group that included William S. Paley, president of CBS.

The title *March of Time* was suggested by the song chosen for the theme music. "March of Time" was from Earl Carroll's "Vanities" written by Ted Koehler and Harold Arlen, copyrighted July 14, 1930.[13] There are several versions but the most credible is that Howard Barlow selected the theme. It is not clear whether he selected the theme music after a search for a song with "time" in the title, or if the song was recalled and suggested by Jesse Butcher, of the CBS promotion department.

On the afternoon of March 6, 1931, a preview program was presented and carried to stations on the basic CBS Radio Network for radio editors and others to audition. This, according to Smith, was the first nationwide radio preview.[14]

That evening, the program, produced in Columbia's New York studios at WABC (later WCBS), was carried to 20 of the network stations at 10:30 P.M. (E.S.T) This seems like a very small number of stations; there were at least 80 in the CBS chain by this time. It ran between *Deutsch Orchestra* and *Sissle Orchestra*. That first program was written by Fred Smith.

> (Fanfare, orchestra, :05)
> The March of Time.
> (Fanfare up, :03)
> On a thousand fronts the events of the world move swiftly forward. (Music up :05, and end.)
> Tonight the editors of *Time,* the weekly newsmagazine, attempt a new kind of reporting of the news, the re-enacting as clearly and dramatically as the medium of radio will permit some themes from the news of the week. From the March of Time. (Fanfare, :03)
> A thousand new details, new facts from the world's history come into being every hour. In India at midnight nut-brown Mahatma Gandhi comes out of a conference with the Vice Royal Lord Irwin tells his followers that peace with England is approaching. In Peru three men . . . all have been president within the past week. From every corner of the world comes new facts about politics, and science, people, crime and religion, art, and economics. There is one publication which watches, analyzes, and every seven days reports the march of human history on all the fronts. It is the weekly newsmagazine, *Time.*
> Tonight, with the March of Time, a new kind of reporting of the news, let's review some of the events of the week. (Fanfare, single trumpet, :04).
> Chicago. In the executive offices of the fifth floor of the City Hall adherents of the Mayor have gathered to celebrate with their chief his victory at the polls . . .

William H. ("Big Bill") Thompson talks on the telephone with Governor Huey Long of Louisiana, Mayor Jimmy Walker of New York, and William Randolph Hearst in Los Angeles. This segment on Mayor Thompson lasted just over four minutes.

Next the story of the death of the New York *World* was dramatized. It lasted about six minutes and included testimony by Joseph Pulitzer and a scene in the *World* city room when it is announced that the *World* and *Telegram* will be merged. Then there was a three-minute segment on some French prisoners being sent to Devil's Island. For about a minute and a half King Alphonso of Spain "spoke" to Americans about the revolution in his country—he said there was none. There was a two-minute segment on prison reform by the King of Rumania and a round up of other news of royalty that lasted about 45 seconds. Segments on the auction in New York of Czarist possessions and the closing of the 71st Congress lasted two and one-half and three and one-half minutes, respectively. The latter included the Marine Orchestra lead by Fiorello La Guardia. The program's closing, which lasted about one and a half minutes, included questions about what might be the news of the next week and another short mention of *Time*. This and the opening were the only commercials. The program ended with the theme, "Time marches on," (Theme up and out) "the voice of time." (pause) "This is the Columbia Broadcasting System." Between the opening, each of the eight segments, and the closing there were short fanfares or bridge music. The entire production lasted 26:45 minutes.

Ted Husing did the "voice of time" for only the first 13 weeks of the program. In the fall of 1931 he was succeeded by Harry Von Zell. Westbrook van Voorhis was the other announcer on the program reading passages from *Time*. Soon van Voorhis's booming voice saying "time marches on" became the trademark of the program. Regular actors on the program included Bill Adams, Harry Browne, Frank Reddick, Charles Slattery, Herschel Mayall, Pedro de Cordoba, and Mr. Husing.[15] Howard Barlow (later Donald Voorhees) scored special music and directed the 23-piece symphony orchestra for the program. Andre Kostalanetz was first violin.

The *New York Times* made no special mention of the debuting program and did not review it the following day. However, the following week the *Times* listed the "sketch" "The March of Time on WABC" in a radio page box noting "Outstanding Events on the Air Today."

The *March of Time* ran for 13 weeks till June 5, 1931, and was carried to Great Britain via the BBC. Fred Smith wrote all or most of each script for all but one of those programs. Probably the most arresting feature of the program was the impersonation of a number of well-known personalities. Each program was usually rehearsed about 12 to 14 hours a week and cost about $6,000—high for the time. The new program was highly acclaimed; Walter Winchell called it a "thrill," *Variety* said it "represents the apex of radio showmanship," and *Broadcasting* said this "audible journalism made the radio world sit up and take notice." [16]

With the program off for the summer, the Smiths took a trip to Paris. In the fall, Mr. Smith returned and continued to write for the *March of Time* between October 1931 and February 26, 1932, when it was announced that the program was being cancelled.

Who Shall Pay?

In "The Press" section of its news columns *Time* announced that after February 1932 it would not continue the radio program because "further expenditure on radio at this time would not justify itself." [17] It was said that *"Time* bought the series . . . to acquaint a larger public than its own logical readers with the existence of *Time,* The Weekly Newsmagazine." [18] The theory was, it said, that a magazine profits from its general reputation. Commercials had been limited to short, simple announcements at the beginning and end of each program.

On the last broadcast, listeners were invited to write *Time* if they desired the program to be brought back. More than 22,000 letters were received, most asking that the program be continued.[19]

The *Time* editors argued that they could not afford the expense for advertising which was no longer needed, and asked "should a few (400,000 *Time* subscribers) pay for the entertainment of many (9,000,000 radiowners)?" [20] In its news columns, *Time* argued:

> For all its blatant claims to being a medium of education, radio contributes little of its own beyond the considerable service of bringing good music to millions. (Yet radio men sputter with rage when Radio is called "just another musical instrument.")
>
> Unlike a newspaper, which sells advertising in order to fulfill its prime function of giving news, the advertising is radio's prime offering.
>
> Thus was raised a question of responsibility: should *Time,* or any other business, feel obligated to be the "philanthropist of the air," to continue paying for radio advertising it does not want in order to provide Radio with something worthwhile? Or is it up to the Radio Chains to improve the quality of broadcasting even at some reduction of their fat profit? [21]

Not all listeners agreed with *Time*'s interpretation. One wrote the magazine saying "your article is disgustingly ungrateful and 'loaded propaganda'" and added "you top off your pound of flesh with sour grapes . . ." [22]

Time Marches Back

On September 8, 1932, *March of Time* was resumed as a sustaining feature (during the election campaign) carried over the CBS Radio Network.[23] On November 4, Time Incorporated resumed its sponsorship of the program.

After a summer hiatus the *March of Time* returned to the air October 13, 1933, sponsored by Remington-Rand. It was, according to *Time,* the first time that an advertiser "bought time on the radio to put on another advertiser's program." [24] In this season Westbrook van Voohis became "the voice of time" so synonymous with the program.

The program returned for its sixth season on CBS on October 5, 1934, after being off for the summer.[25] After another summer hiatus the program was again carried in the season 1935–1936 sponsored alternately by *Time* and Remington-Rand. Later the alternate sponsorship was assumed by Wrigley, and then Servel Electrolux. However, in 1935–1936 *March of Time* was presented five-times-a-week for 15 minutes but still at 10:30 P.M. (E.S.T.). There was a regular acting staff of 12 with about a score of others for special effects or particular characters.

In the 1936–1937 season *March of Time* returned to its original 30-minute once-a-week format, again sponsored jointly by Remington-Rand and *Time*.[26]

F.D.R. and Amelia Earhart

After a ban of 34 months, from January 1934 to November 1936, *March of Time* again began to imitate the voice of President Franklin D. Roosevelt. Earlier, the White House had felt that too many radio announcers were trying to imitate the president's style and had asked all to cease with no exception for *March of Time*. However, in the fall of 1936 when the president was running for a second term, the White House withdrew its objection and the role of Franklin D. Roosevelt was again heard on the *March of Time*.[27]

In July 1937 Amelia Earhart and her navigator, Fred Noonan, were trying to fly more than 2,500 miles from New Guinea to Howland Island in the Pacific as one leg of an around-the-world flight. (And "spying" for the U.S. at the same time?) They were apparently lost at sea about 5:00 P.M. on Friday, July 2. On Thursday evening, July 8, *March of Time* re-enacted the story of the Earhart-Noonan flight. Mistaking the radio program for a shortwave S.O.S. a radio man for Inter-Island Airways at Hilo, Hawaii, notified officials that he had heard a conversation between the lost aviatrix and ships at sea. He probably actually heard the CBS network's shortwave relay of the program from San Francisco to Hawaii. For a short time, at least, the little remaining hope of finding the two flyers was buoyed up. The next day the *New York Times* argued that the loss of Earhart proved the need for more powerful transmitters in airplanes. Also, the head of the F.C.C. unit concerned with amateur broadcasters suggested that there should be an emergency network of radio amateurs to intercept distress messages.[28] There were some unfavorable comments, but there was no major criticism of the program's dramatization of the event. A little over a year later Orson Welles, who had been an actor in *March of Time* programs and certainly influenced by the program would broadcast his now famous Halloween *Mercury Theatre* "War of the Worlds."

War Time

    After seven seasons on CBS, in the fall of 1937, *March of Time* moved to NBC's Blue Network for the seasons of 1937–1938, and 1938–1939. The program was not on the air from summer 1939 to October 1941 because of restrictions imposed on broadcasters after war came to Europe. However, in 1941, NBC relaxed these restrictions.

> In general since the war began radio has provided news reports and news comments but broadcasters have barred all dramatizations of controversial subjects (including war and politics) and all impersonations of important people. Without these two things March of Time could not resume. But the National Broadcasting Company recognizing the importance and value of the program, and trusting in the journalistic responsibility of Time's editors, agreed to make a special exception for the March of Time. The National Broadcasting Company also relaxed its rule on recordings not only of sound effects (such as falling bombs) but of music, singing, and speaking voices where necessary.[29]

    In October 1941 *March of Time* was carried over 110 Blue Network stations and for the first time was produced by Young and Rubicam instead of BBD&O.

    In July 1942 the format was changed, and only one or two dramatic scenes were given instead of a full half-hour. The rest of the program was made up of on-the-spot news and remote reports—24 foreign pickups between July 1942 and June 1943.

    Also a number of war songs were added to *March of Time* broadcasts—such as, "Praise the Lord and Pass the Ammunition." [30] And for the first time a number of well-known people appeared in person on the *March of Time* for various appeals and war-time campaigns. Of course, nearly all the dramatizations had to do with the war.

    In July 1942 when NBC split its two networks, *March of Time* was moved from the Blue Network to NBC's Red Network.

    For the season of 1944–1945 *March of Time* moved to the ABC Radio Network (earlier Blue). During this season *March of Time* was carried at 9 P.M. (EWT) on Thursday evenings. On April 12, 1945, just as the staff was completing the final rehearsal for their planned broadcast word was received that President Franklin D. Roosevelt had died in Warm Springs, Georgia. A new script was quickly prepared and *March of Time* dramatized highlights of Roosevelt's career utilizing recordings of his former speeches. The program ended with the reading of Walt Whitman's eulogy to Lincoln, "O Captain! My Captain!" [31] This was the thirteenth and last season on the air for *March of Time*. It had been on CBS, NBC Red, NBC Blue, or ABC intermittently from March 1931 to summer 1945 (except during the seasons of 1939–1940 and 1940–1941.

COMMENT

Fred Smith last worked for *March of Time* in 1934. He later worked for *Newsweek*, a *Time* imitator begun in 1933, doing similar news dramatizations, directed his wife's concert tours, was managing executive for the board of trustees of the Cincinnati College of Music, and was an investment broker.

Fred Smith and Roy Larsen, with many others at *Time*, CBS and BBD&O created *March of Time*.[32] Its prehistory saw the word newscasting coined by Roy Larsen. The program *NewsCasting*, 1928, may have been the first widely distributed daily news program. *NewsActing* was probably the first regular program of news dramatization and one of the earliest widely syndicated (on disc) dramatic programs. *March of Time* became the first news drama on the national networks in March 1931 and it helped inspire the newsreel and documentary versions of *March of Time*, 1935.

After *March of Time* there were many local versions of the program and imitations.[33] There was much experimentation on *March of Time*—sound effects, voices, stream of conscious, and other techniques. Erik Barnouw writes that "the *March of Time*—and the vistas it opened—may have been among the factors that, in the closing months of 1932, sharpened the split between the newspaper world and the broadcasting world." [34]

March of Time was only a small part of growing news and documentary coverage on radio in the 1930s.[35] Few who worked on later programs would ever know their debt to *Musical News*, *NewsCasting*, *NewsActing*, and *March of Time*.

51

Hubbell Robinson and Ted Patrick

JACK BENNY

"JELL-O AGAIN."
Every Sunday at seven a slender, pleasant-looking man murmurs those three words into a little black box in a radio studio in Holly-

Scribner's Magazine, Vol. CIII, No. 3 (March 1938), pp. 11–15, 73.

wood. And in 7,000,000 American homes the family draw up their chairs and prepare to hold their sides. For those are the words with which America's No. 1 Funnyman greets his huge radio audience, the biggest audience that ever pounded its palms for any one entertainer. The name of the miracle-worker who turns this trick once a week, thirty-nine times a year, is Jack Benny, born Benjamin Kubelsky.

Mr. Benny's employers think so highly of this feat that they pay him top funnyman salary—$10,000 a week, $390,000 a year—and add another $15,000 a week for time and additional talent. They spend this, not because they think laughter will help cure the country's ills, but simply because of the uplifting effect Mr. Benny has on the great god, *Sales Curve*. And that is what really counts in radio today—its ability to sell. No matter what you may hear of its educational, cultural and ethical place in modern life, the radio is a commercial instrument, pointed primarily toward the business of selling goods. Jack Benny is top man of radio because he has proven his ability to sell an ungodly amount of his sponsor's merchandise. And because, more than anyone else you can name, he is a *Business Man of Humor*.

How does he brew his magic, this suave-mannered, slick-tongued clown, born in Waukegan, Illinois, in 1895, fiddling futily with *The Bee* at the age of eight and, at forty-three, the highest-salaried employee of as great and serious-minded a corporation as General Foods? What has he got that impels a close-trading manufacturer to lay out $25,000 a week to keep him on the air and lures the public into spending $30,000 a week in electric current alone to listen to him?

There's an obvious answer—"He can make people laugh."

And that's the trouble with that answer. It's too obvious. The true answer lies much deeper. If you say, "He has the ability to induce friendly, sympathetic laughter," you're getting warmer, but you're still only flirting with the surface facts. To understand the phenomenon of this man who holds America's funny bone in the hollow of his hand, you must go back to some of Jack Benny's earlier experiences in the fine art of public rib-tickling. Benny was not born and nursed to his present competency by radio as were Amos 'N Andy. Nor is he an overnight sensation like Mr. Bergen's wooden-headed pixie, Charlie McCarthy.

Jack Benny has been on the air almost continuously for six years. His deft wit adorned the legitimate stage for four years before that, and he was one of vaudeville's darlings for fourteen years before that. It was in vaudeville that he learned the tricks that were to make him worth the princely pittance radio pays him.

In vaudeville, Jack achieved the ultimate goal, the Mecca of all vaudevillians, the final triumph of all who ever trouped the "five-a-day." He "headlined at the Palace." And New York's Palace Theater, on the corner of Broadway and Forty-seventh Street, was, in its heyday, the high temple of vaudeville. Whether you were a comic, a juggler, or head man in an animal act, you had to be the best in the business to play the Palace.

Yet Benny was conspicuously different from the other comics to whom the hypercritical Palace patrons awarded the accolade. Practically all the others got their laughs as much from some sort of physical high jinks as from lines.

But not Benny. He used no props, no funny suits, no stooge. He just walked on and "wowed" them. He was, in the technical language of the experts who gathered on the corner of Broadway and Forty-seventh Street, and who were to vaudeville what the Monday-morning quarterbacks are to football, a "smooth" comedian. To put it in plain English, Jack's humor could be propelled across the footlights by his voice alone.

That gave him a long lead on the other boys when radio burst into show business. His first Jell-O broadcast came on the evening of October 1, 1934. Before that, he was on for General Tires, Canada Dry, and Chevrolet. During his two years with these sponsors, he was a star, but not one of the top-flight stars. He was growing. His gags were "ear" gags rather than "eye and ear" gags. But that wasn't all. Benny, shrewd showman that he is, widened the lead by creating, for himself, on the air, a character aimed dead-center at the universal tendency to howl at the self-confident man who makes a fool of himself. Jack isn't the wise guy who tells all the jokes on his show nor the brightie who has all the funny lines. He's on the other end of the gun. He is the target of most of the jokes, most of the comic situations. You laugh at him, but you also sympathize with him because, almost inevitably, his best-laid plans blow up in his face.

Another of the invaluable foundation blocks of Benny's comedy structure is his uncanny ability to outline quickly a basic situation so that the listener can grasp easily its fundamentals. He doesn't depend on the conventional question-and-answer gag routine. He builds a crystal-clear picture of himself in a given situation, and because it is so clear, it is child's play for the audience to follow him through the laugh-provoking complications that develop out of that situation. This is because they understand completely the basic humor of the situation and his relation to it.

For example, when Jack gets into his rattletrap Maxwell he sets the situation so adroitly that he is no longer a comedian in front of a microphone beguiling you with inanities about a mythical jalopy. He is a guy named Jack Benny, a real person, engaged in a real struggle with a specific, tangible, worn-out, broken-down 1918 Maxwell automobile. It becomes a reality, not make-believe.

One of the ways he achieves this neat trick is by avoiding the temptation to fall in love with a joke. For instance, he might hear a highly entertaining joke about a fish, but he doesn't build a fish sequence into his next show just in order to use that joke. Instead, he stars with a situation that is in the show because it, in itself, is funny. Benny's situations are never contrived for the purpose of working around to a preconceived gag or a specific joke which might be funny in itself but does not properly fit into the idea of the show.

Pat examples of typical Benny situations are: the effort to sell his Maxwell, a car that nobody in the world would possibly want; the idea that he is a virtuoso on the violin; the absurdity of trying to palm himself off as a Western sheriff of the old school. Starting out with an idea that is basically comic, he gets his laughs largely by hanging additional embellishments onto his original idea. He not only tries to sell the Maxwell, but he demands a fantastic price for it. He not only demands a fantastic price, but flatly refuses to consider less. In a Benny show, the gags are not an end in themselves. They are a national evolution from the basic situations.

There are two reasons why this technique has contributed importantly to his success. In the first place, the laughs are so carefully planted, their climaxes so surely indicated, that they rarely fizzle. When Benny gets to the laugh line, he has set the reason and the events leading up to the "pay-off" so thoroughly you can't miss the point unless you're a half-wit. In the second place, one comedy situation lasts Benny a long time. He gets immense mileage out of his material, more, probably, than any of his contemporaries. That's why he's been able to sustain the pace so well, for so long.

Immediately after the rebroadcast of each week's show, Benny and his writers start on the next one. Each Benny program, like most of the other big-league network shows, is broadcast twice. The first show is broadcast from the N.B.C. Studio in Hollywood at 4 o'clock—7 o'clock Eastern Standard Time. This broadcast is for the East and Middle Western stations and is not heard on the Coast at all. Then at 8:30 Coast Time, there is a second or rebroadcast. This goes out over the Coast stations only. As soon as the rebroadcast is over and the usual rush of autograph seekers and people who "just wanted to shake hands" has been appeased, Benny, and his writers Beloin and Morrow go into a huddle on the studio stage. A million dollars' worth of comedy brains wheel into action. Each of them suggests his ideas for next week's show. They decide which ideas seem worth developing into script, and then go home—or if they don't, that's their business.

On Monday, Beloin and Morrow feed the grist into the mill, and on Tuesday they have a rough draft of the show you will hear next Sunday. They take this draft to Benny, and the three of them spend Tuesday, Wednesday, and Thursday polishing, changing, cutting, building it into a working rehearsal script. The actual hours they spend may run from eight to eighteen a day, depending on whether or not they're clicking.

Friday they rest, although the script is always with them, in their minds. Saturday, the entire cast is brought together—sometimes in the studio, sometimes in Jack's home—and Jack reads them the script. Any comments that Mary Livingstone, Kenny Baker, Don Wilson, Schlepperman, or Andy Devine or Phil Harris have to make on their own lines are duly noted. Sometimes, revisions are made with these comments in mind. Kenny Baker may feel he can't say a certain line they've written for him. He may have an idea that improves the line. That's true for all of them. Then they go over the script again. This time every member of the cast reads the lines written for him. Usually there are further revisions after this reading. Then they read it again—and again and again.

After this rehearsal, the cast is dismissed, and there's another conference. Sitting in, are Benny, Beloin, Morrow, Tom Harrington, and the producer for Young & Rubicam, the advertising agency which handles the show. They discuss the rehearsal, the suggestions, and all their own bright ideas. The Benny trio are intent on improving the jokes, Harrington on keeping them from being too good. They talk and write, and talk some more, and rewrite for hours. This ordeal usually lasts till after midnight Saturday, by which time they all heartily dislike each other, and depart convinced the show will be a flop.

Sunday morning at 10, the entire cast assembles again and rehearsal of the rewritten script starts. It lasts without interruptions till the first show goes on, at 4 o'clock.

PROGRAM	PRODUCTION	TIME	TOTAL
Chase & Sanborn Hour (Bergen)	$20,000	$15,900	$35,900
Jack Benny (Jell-O)	15,000	11,500	26,500
Kraft Music Hall (Bing Crosby)	13,500	17,100	30,600
Al Jolson (Lever Brothers)	12,000	10,400	22,400
Major Bowes' Amateur Hour	25,000	20,100	45,100
Royal Gelatine Hour (Rudy Vallee)	9,500	15,500	25,000
Burns and Allen (Grape Nuts)	10,000	10,600	20,600
Lux Radio Theater	15,000	17,300	32,300
	--*Fortune*, May 1938.		

52

Sammy R. Danna

THE RISE OF RADIO NEWS

NEWS, though it did not dominate in the early years of radio, did hold a fascination for many. It intrigued some newspaper owners to such an extent that it was often felt that a radio station could serve as an "arm," an extension, a supplement to the all-prevailing news-medium, the newspaper. Charnley said:

> In city after city, newspapers followed a similar course (getting into the radio station operation business). U.S. Department of Commerce lists of stations published in its monthly *Radio Service Bulletin*, showed eleven newspaper owned stations in May, 1922. At the end of the year there were sixty-nine.[22]

Before KDKA was a year old, it began newscasts from the old Pittsburgh *Post* newsroom from September 20, 1921, onward. The *Post* was the first newspaper to print a daily radio station program log, that of KDKA, beginning September 10, 1921. WJAG, owned by the Norfolk (Nebraska) *Daily News*, began a daily noon-time news broadcast on July 26, 1922, which is claimed to have been the oldest continuous service of its kind in radio.

On February 3, 1923, a 15-minute news resume was aired by the New York *Tribune* over WJZ, New York. KOIN of Portland, Oregon, began its "Newspaper of the Air" newscasts with music and advertising during 1925. "News every hour on the hour" described the extensive news broadcasting undertaken by WOMT, Manitowoc, Wisconsin, in the late 1920s; the station received a press service to aid in this presentation.

In 1922 the AP warned its members against broadcasting the service's news. The AP's rights in the reception of news from and the sending of it to all of its members gave validity to this protest. As the number of stations owned by publishers became more numerous, it became harder and harder to enforce this set of rules. However, by 1925 the AP regulations became slightly more relaxed, allowing news of "transcendent" national or international importance to be broadcast.

In order to prevent the growth of special news-gathering agencies—exclusively organized for radio—the three major press services (AP, UP, and INS) initiated a plan in 1928, giving radio two daily

Freedom of Information Center Report No. 211. School of Journalism, University of Missouri at Columbia, November 1968, pp. 1–7.

newscasts. This concession was enlarged the next year to permit fairly free sale of news to broadcasters. The early 1930s, however, saw this "liberal" practice come to an abrupt end, but the later 1930s also witnessed a gradual relaxation of the harsh news prohibitions the newspaper publishers forced on radio newscasting.[29]

On March 18, 1925, when Chicago's WLS was not quite a year old, a bulletin was read concerning a highly destructive tornado which hit southern Illinois and Indiana. The contribution bandwagon began almost immediately. Through all-night radio marathon appeals, the station succeeded in raising tens of thousands of dollars for relief of the unfortunate victims.

WGN made arrangements in the summer of 1925 to broadcast, live, from Dayton, Tennessee, to Chicago via phone lines, the major-interest parts of the Scopes "monkey" trial. (John Scopes, a young high school science teacher in Dayton High School, was convicted of illegally teaching evolution to his students.) Beginning July 13, the blow-by-blow courtroom happenings were broadcast by WGN. The trial ended on August 21. The broadcasts cost WGN $1,000 a day just for phone lines.[36]

AP, UP, and INS in the fall of 1928 agreed to furnish returns to radio stations of the Smith-Hoover presidential election. Local newspapers in many cases cooperated similarly with local broadcasters in this endeavor. Radio news of that election served both to whet the appetite of many millions of listeners and to increase radio's interest in making news of this and other types a regular part of the daily programming menu. For instance, KFAB of Lincoln, Nebraska, inaugurated two editions of its "radio newspaper." It hired George Kline away from his city editorship of the Lincoln *Star* to direct the newscasts.

Also, in late 1930, KMPC, Beverly Hills, California, not only opened a scheduled series of three 15-minute news programs daily, and organized a news-gathering service. The station's "Radio News Service of America" put 10 reporters on news beats, regularly covering the Los Angeles area. Soon publishers would adopt a strategy to "control" radio news. The radio stations often "pirated" news from the newspapers and news services' reports.

Floyd Gibbons was the most popular radio announcer of the early 1930s, pioneering an on-the-spot news report series, and delivering news at an average rate of 217 words a minute. One night in 1930 a young man named Lowell Thomas, a relatively unknown radio announcer at the time, substituted for Gibbons. Thomas was so good that he was hired permanently.

Broadcasting During the Depression

Network newscasting increased by 1930, with at least one network's five-day-a-week news program scheduled for a 15-minute period.[47] The depression by 1930 had taken its toll of the Brooklyn *Eagle* as was the case of so many newspapers at the time. In order for the *Eagle* to survive, it had to cut expenses and to fire with only two-weeks' notice its highest paid and best-known employee, H. V. Kaltenborn, associate editor for many years. He was almost immediately hired for $100 a week by CBS as a news commentator and announcer.

News reports came at various times of the broadcast day. For instance, Kaltenborn was aired at 6:00 p.m., Thomas at 6:45 p.m., Boake Carter at 7:45 p.m., and Edwin C. Hill at 10:15 p.m. (all Eastern Standard Time).

The competition in news broadcasting extended itself to international broadcasting. In 1930–31, radio brought to American listeners the comments of five prominent foreign leaders: King George V of Britain, Premier Hamaguchi of Japan, Benito Mussolini of Italy, Mahatma Gandhi of India and Pope Pius XI of Vatican City.[52]

A somewhat novel news broadcast took place in 1931 when WTAD of Quincy, Illinois, set up remote facilities in an airplane. The plane followed a car from the scene of a bank robbery for 100 miles before it was stopped by law enforcement officials.

The first news of the Lindbergh baby kidnapping was reported by radio, although the report was called into New York radio stations by Newark, New Jersey, newspapers in order to gain a credit-line at the end of the bulletin. WOR and CBS practically scrapped their regular program schedule in favor of extensive coverage of the tragedy. The night following the kidnapping NBC did *not* carry the story— even in bulletin form—for the network considered the news "too sensational" for radio. Soon, however, NBC changed its mind when the kidnapping story produced many false clues which consumed a large part of the broadcasting day on networks and stations.[57]

Boake Carter, a mellow-voiced announcer, became a news commentator in 1930. His coverage of the Lindbergh case for CBS catapulted him to almost immediate fame. Other radio newsmen also increased their prominence as a result of reporting the Lindbergh kidnapping.

The presidential election night in November 1932, was the "fateful" incident which would break the situation wide open. Radio, as a public medium, had broadcast the presidential elections since 1916. KDKA and WWJ aired the Harding-Cox returns. Succeeding presidential election races of 1924 and 1928 received far greater coverage.

In the 1932 campaign, CBS was prepared to throw aside all normal schedules and to devote the evening prime time to the reporting of the election returns. The network bargained with UP and finally emerged with a contract whereby the news service would supply results for a nominal sum of $1,000. However, a few days before the election, CBS's news director, White, received a phone call from Karl A. Bickel, UP president, who stated that the contract to supply the election results to CBS had to be broken. The newspapers who were the chief subscribers to UP's service put considerable pressure on the association not to deal with CBS.

In the meantime, Kent Cooper, AP general manager, had heard about the UP-CBS contract but did not know that it had been canceled. Accordingly, he informed both NBC and CBS that they could have the AP election return service free of charge. Later, the UP also contributed its services "in a more or less covert manner." [61] The nets already had the UP printer machines (Teletype) over which the bulletins were transmitted. Said White:

> On election night, these machines were "mysteriously" switched to the main news trunk service of UP. And at the last moment, INS machines were also installed. . . . Never before had it (radio) covered anything so fully. Newspaper "extras," long since doomed, that night became an anachronism. [62]

It was a great triumph for radio news, but it was a short-lived one. The AP board of directors, meeting in April 1933, voted to withdraw any kind of service to networks and ruled that stations owned by AP member newspapers could use the service only upon payment of an additional fee. UP and INS quickly followed suit, and by the spring of 1933, radio was without sufficient news services.

Radio beat newspapers to the story of the attempted assassination of Franklin D. Roosevelt in Miami just prior to his March 1933 inauguration. Ed Cohan, a CBS official, was vacationing in Florida and was cruising near the scene of a Roosevelt reception; his car was equipped with a shortwave receiver. He was listening to a local radio station's account of the assassination attempt. He phoned CBS headquarters in New York with the brief news bulletin that someone had attempted but failed to shoot Roosevelt, but did wound Chicago's mayor. The news was immediately broadcast over a nationwide hookup before any newspaper, anywhere, was on the streets with the story. [63]

The AP remained steadfast on its "no-sale" policy to stations, while UP and INS sold news to any station willing to pay. Some newspaper owners of radio stations—e.g. The Milwaukee *Journal*, Chicago *Tribune*, and the Hearst chain—frankly insisted that radio news was an integral part of their business.

Without the availability of the news services, radio newsmen had to use telegrams and newspaper clippings as news sources. Despite this, there still were some scoops over the newspapers. In the summer of 1933 a big steamer was grounded off Naushon Island near Massachusetts. The newspaper and press services were desperate for news reports of the disaster, but it was Walter Winchell who finally carried the "exclusive" account on his newscast the night of the big accident. A. A. Schechter Jr., NBC news director, tracked down the story by phone.

The AP at a New York City meeting in April 1933, voted: (1) not to release any of its news to radio networks; (2) to require member papers owning stations to confine broadcasts of AP news or their own local stories to "brief bulletins" put on the air by only one station; (3) to levy fees on AP for using news for radio. The so-called "brief bulletins" were to consist of 30 words.[72]

CBS Forms Own News Service

In the middle of the summer of 1933 the General Mills advertising manager made CBS's news director, White, a proposition to the effect that if the weekly cost of a CBS-operated news service were $3,000 or less, the milling firm would pick up half the tab. CBS formed Columbia News Service in September 1933. The Dow-Jones ticker service was purchased, giving a great deal of Washington news in addition to financial news. Other foreign and domestic "minor" news sources were tapped, as well as newly established CBS bureaus in New York, Washington, Chicago and Los Angeles—each of which had correspondents in every U.S. city of more than 20,000 population. These correspondents were paid higher space rates than the newspapers were willing to pay.

White stated that the news service provided material for commentators Carter and Kaltenborn, plus three news broadcasts a day, two five-minute programs every weekday for General Mills at the noon hour and 4:30 p.m., and finally, a broadcast at 11 p.m.

Some newspapers threatened to stop CBS' program listings. NBC would be left alone since Schechter's "scissors and telephone-call" approach to news gathering hardly constituted a threat to the newspapers. The future of the news service seemed in grave doubt.

CBS in 1933 applied for but was denied access to the press galleries of the U.S. Congress, on the basis that such activities were exclusively reserved for newspapers and news services.[80] It would take more than five years for radio to gain access to the Congressional press galleries.

Radio becomes Serious Rival

In November 1933 *Christian Century* commented:

> Radio stations as purveyors of news have become a serious
> rival, not to say menace, to newspapers. Out of this rivalry there is
> developing something which may assume the proportion of a war
> between the two interests . . . If radio news service is to be taken
> seriously, then in spite of being licensed (by the government) . . . it
> must have a degree of freedom comparable to that exercised by the
> press.[81]

Carskadon stated that "in the fall of 1933 radio had the newspapers licked. The broadcasters were operating independently of the established news services and they were getting on the air daily with spot news before newspapers could get copies on the street." The newspapers began, often subtly, to threaten the stations by reminding them that they had a form of monopoly by controlling "limited " airways (belonging to the public; but used for profit). There was no united front against the newspaper attacks, for, while CBS had a news service, NBC had nothing to remotely compare with it; thus, NBC was far more disposed to submit to negotiation with the newspaper interests.

All of this set the stage for the Biltmore Conference of December 1933. Carskadon stated:

> In smoke and hate-filled rooms in the Hotel Biltmore in New
> York City, radio and newspapers came to terms. . . . The two big
> networks must withdraw completely from gathering their own
> news; they must restrict their newscasters to 'interpretation' and
> 'Comment,' and the actual broadcasting of news must be confined to
> two five-minute periods daily, one in the morning and one at night.
> This news must be supplied free by the major wire services (AP,
> UP, INS) to the Press-Radio Bureau . . . and the broadcaster would
> bear the administrative and (wire) transmission costs of the Bureau.
> News announcements must not be sold commercially, must be limited to thirty words per item, and special bulletins were to be issued
> only on news of transcendent importance.[82]

Carskadon referred to the Press-Radio Bureau restrictions as follows:

> Such savage restrictions were an open invitation to revolt. It
> came. The two big networks dutifully signed the agreement and it
> was arranged that the Press-Radio Bureau would start operations on
> March 1, 1934, but the independent stations were howling bloody
> murder. . . . Distinguished affiliates, independent stations, regional
> groupings (networks), such as the Yankee Network and a Northwestern group centering around Seattle, all set out to gather their
> own news.

A number of independent news services were forthcoming, exclusively constituted to gather news for radio stations. Transradio

News Service, founded by Herbert L. Moore became the leader of the new radio news services.

For several hundred years, newspapers have worked hard for their freedom, their prestige and their general accomplishments. When radio, a new and generally faster means of disseminating news to the public, evolved, it was only natural that the press would react violently. After all, before radio emerged, the newspapers were virtually the sole means of daily mass news dissemination. During the time covered in this paper the newspapers' reactions to radio news were often unsure, hasty, panicky, unfair, and without precedent. The radio stations who "lifted" newspaper and press service news stories without paying for them were far from guiltless.

53

Sammy R. Danna

THE PRESS-RADIO WAR

THE ASSOCIATED Press took a major "offensive" against KVOS, Bellingham, Washington. In October 1934, the Bellingham *Herald* obtained an injunction forbidding the station to use news from the *Herald* and two other AP newspapers in Seattle, the *Times* and *Post-Intelligencer*. On December 18, however, a federal judge in Seattle dissolved the injunction on the grounds that the publication of news in the newspapers threw such information into the public domain. A year later, the North Circuit Court of Appeals in San Francisco reinstituted the original injunction, upholding the principle that a newsgathering agency retains a protectable property right to news during its commercial life. Nevertheless, on December 14, 1936, the U.S. Supreme Court, on a technicality, dodged the issue by declaring that the case was not within its jurisdiction, since the AP had failed to prove prospective damage of $3,000, the minimum sum necessary to establish a federal case.[2]

The Columbia News Service was a casualty of the Press-Radio Bureau's formation, this short-lived but significant newsgathering organization received much comment. Isabelle Keating, writing for *Harper's* said:

Freedom of Information Center Report No. 213. School of Journalism, University of Missouri at Columbia, December 1968, pp. 1–7.

Columbia did a thorough job. It made contacts with correspondents in most of the towns of more than 10,000 population (20,000 population is mentioned elsewhere) throughout the country, and it had news contacts in a number of foreign capitals. Its full-time personnel probably did not exceed 25 persons, but in addition, there were from 800 to 1,000 correspondents who were paid by the story. . . . Most of the full-time men associated with the service were newspapermen of long experience and high repute—men who know how to gather and how to present news.[9]

The formation of Transradio news service in March, 1934, attempted to fill the "news blackout gap" caused by the press-radio agreement.

Until the stipulations of the pact were put into effect on March 1, radio continued to "scoop" the newspapers. On January 17, 1934, Lowell Thomas carried a detailed story about the great Peruvian floods, and many newspapermen were mystified after hearing about the news broadcast. The press could not get any word from Lima concerning the big disaster, though it was common knowledge that a major flood had taken place. Thomas obtained his "exclusive story" from the Lima airport, via shortwave radio. Another exclusive about the escape of the notorious John Dillinger from the Crown Point, Indiana, jail added to Thomas's and NBC's news achievements. The fact that the sheriff, Lillian Holley, was a woman, added greatly to the human-interest appeal of the story.[11]

A feature story in March 1934 issue of *Popular Mechanics* described the elaborate means by which radio often gathered important news. Among other things, the feature depicted radio covering such events as the eruption of a Hawaiian volcano and yacht races. A description of NBC's remote-control panel truck and a "knapsack transmitter on the back of a radio reporter" were also featured.[12]

Despite radio's triumphs and lesser successes during January and February 1934 the inevitable was rapidly approaching, the March 1 date when network news would become hampered in its reporting efforts. Concerning the press-radio agreement, *Newsweek* asserted:

In his Barbasol broadcast Friday night of last week (early March 1934) Edwin C. Hill, the air reporter, observed sourly: "In these days a news commentator must kneel like Lazarus before the rich man's kitchen door." In this case the rich man must have been one of the newspaper publishers who had signed an agreement with Mr. Hill's bosses of radio.[13]

Despite the network prohibition on newscasts, independent stations offered news frequently all day and night.[18] During this time most of the public was unaware of the news-restriction agreement.[19]

The radio newscasters protested that the bureau reports were brief, colorless and too old to be useful. In the meantime, at least a half-dozen radio newsgathering organizations were born.[20]

Radio Forms Own News Service

With the discontinuance of the Columbia News Service Boston's WNAC hired the Boston *Transcript's* Richard Grant to build a newsgathering organization to cover New England for the regional Yankee Network. He spent $90,000 within a year, hiring reporters in 45 New England centers. On the Pacific Coast, Radio News Service of America—organized in 1930 by Los Angeles' KMPC—announced an expansion program. Two other groups worth mentioning appeared on the newsgathering scene in 1935: The American Newscasting Association and the American Broadcasters News Association.

However, on February 28, 1934, Herbert Moore began a so-called "cooperative service" to distribute radio news; actually, it was not until about a month later, March 21, that the former Columbia News Service news editor founded the Transradio Press Service. Some of the major clients included the Yankee Network, WLS in Chicago, KWK in St. Louis and KSTP in St. Paul. Long-term contracts were quickly acquired, enabling Moore to operate on a revenue of $100,000 a year. His original 20-client business grew to nearly 100 by summer and to 150 by December 1934. The news service sent from 5,000 to 30,000 words a day to subscribers, but about 10,000 words was the average distribution.

Thus, by the summer of 1934, there were four rival newsgathering agencies to compete with the Press-Radio Bureau, serving radio exclusively. There were about 170 stations subscribing to the expurgated bulletins sent out from the official bureaus in New York and Los Angeles. The services claimed, together, a newsgathering organization of 10,000 men, an investment of $250,000 and unlimited backing if needed. Transradio, was the biggest of the all-radio services, claiming an organization of 7,000 men throughout the world. It furnished its clients with as much news as the press associations formerly provided—before the press-radio pact was signed.

Transradio continued to grow as it began its second year of operation in 1935, but only 50 clients were listed in early 1935 (differing considerably from a previous figure given in this respect). The Press-Radio Bureau's list of clients numbered 200 at this time.[28] Transradio even added two newspapers in 1935 to its client list. In May, Herbert Moore filed a suit against all members of the Press-Radio Bureau Committee, including some 1,400 newspaper members of the AP and ANPA, asking a New York federal court for a judgment of $1.1 million and a permanent injunction, restraining the press from interfering with his business. Although the suit lasted over a period of many months, Moore never collected damages.

One consolation for radio was that as of March 1, 1935, one year after the signing of the press-radio pact, there were but 245 stations subscribing to the Press-Radio Bureau. This left some 360 stations as non-subscribers. At the April meeting, the Press-Radio group decided to continue operations for another year, but it did acknowledge that news broadcasting competition had become a "reality"; publishers approved the resolution allowing UP and INS to sell their news for broadcasting—should competition force the press services to do so. Also, the newspaper subscribers to AP who owned radio stations were authorized to make up four 15-minute press-radio broadcasts daily.

Within a month UP and INS announced their decision to offer news for broadcasting to any newspaper client owning a station or even affiliated with such an operation. There was to be no sponsorship limitation of news programs. Soon this "half-way" measure was extended to any radio station—no strings attached. The UP-INS decisions were prompted mainly by Transradio's success of more than 185 subscribers in mid-1934 (figures differ in various sources).

The year 1936 saw Transradio grow, but UP and INS also increased their client lists. By January, Transradio claimed nearly 190 subscribers. To add to the news service's luster, some 30 newspapers subscribed to its new facilities. Transradio, soon after its founding, instigated the Radio News Association, which developed and perfected the delivery of so-called flash news via shortwave telegraphy. This service was specially designed for the remote and less prosperous stations that could not afford the regular Transradio news service. Latham reports Transradio's client list in 1936 was 250.[41]

Carskadon wrote in 1936:

> After years of bitter opposition, newspapers are beginning to see the "light," and there is now a formidable movement toward ownership or alliance with radio stations. Hearst Radio now controls six stations outright; Scripps-Howard owns a station in Cincinnati and both Hearst and Scripps-Howard chains are embarked on active campaigns to build up radio alliances.[42]

Radio news took on an international aspect in the 1930s as the following story indicates. From across the Spanish border near Hendaye, France, in 1936, came news via American radio of things to come. H. V. Kaltenborn was in Hendaye when the Spanish rebels were battling the Spanish Loyalists in the frontier city of Irun. The conflict was finally drawn into farmland outside the Spanish city. Somehow, Kaltenborn managed to get his microphone and transmitting equipment to comparative safety—in a haystack—and from there he described the battle as it progressed nearby. With the sounds of bullets and shells in the background, and often interrupted by static, the pioneer newscaster was able to broadcast the blow-by-blow results of the battle, "live," to his American audience.

Other radio news of 1936 included the celebration of NBC's 10th anniversary, featuring a conversation between an NBC newscaster and radio's inventor, Marconi, while the latter cruised in his yacht off the coast of Genoa, Italy. During that year, NBC announced "first" to America the death of Britain's King George V. On December 11, King Edward VIII made a worldwide broadcast, the now famous "Woman I Love" abdication speech, a news event that drew one of radio's largest audiences for a speech.

Radio "Goes to War"

In September 1938 with Hitler and Germany threatening war in Europe, both CBS and NBC brought more than a thousand foreign broadcasts to America from more than 200 reporters. Notable reporters included Edward R. Murrow from London, William L. Shirer from Prague, John T. Whitaker from Paris and Max Jordan from Munich. In CBS's New York studio, Kaltenborn sat before the microphone virtually every hour for 20 straight days, broadcasting and analyzing the news of the European crisis. After the Munich crisis ended, foreign news reports naturally subsided for a while. According to James Rorty:

> American newspaper correspondents were almost continuously on the air, speaking from European capitals. The newspapers, an hour or two later, gave the eye a chance to read and digest what the ear had heard . . . In the network studios and offices, the technical and program staffs worked almost continuously, ate and slept where and when they could. One of the most overworked men in the country was Columbia's 60-year-old H. V. Kaltenborn, dean of American news commentators. . . . Kaltenborn hung up the almost incredible record of 50 hours on duty between September 10 and September 20.[52]

During this time, 443 separate news broadcasts, including "flash bulletins," were sent out over NBC's Red and Blue networks, taking 58 hours and 13 minutes of airtime.

CBS sent out a total of 54.5 hours of news broadcasts. During the Munich crisis, according to *Variety*, Columbia made 151 shortwave pickups from Europe while NBC's totalled 147. The Mutual Broadcasting System had to rely on the cooperation of foreign broadcasting stations in transmitting government news in English. This included unedited official news reports from Prague, Berlin, Paris and Rome. Mutual rebroadcast more than 130 of these European crisis programs.

Radio's correspondents seemed to be all over Europe during the major portion of the Munich crisis. Often, they broadcast from the scenes of the difficulties. For instance, Shirer of CBS traveled 2,950 miles by air, rail, truck, bus, car, and even horse-drawn army carts, averaging two hours of sleep daily, usually in his clothes. *Newsweek* reported:

> In Prague, Shirer broadcast intermittingly for two days. He later learned that Atlantic storms and government (radio) interference for official messages prevented reception in America on almost every occasion. . . . Despite many difficulties Shirer managed to contribute his share of the 2,847 minutes of European broadcasts, carried by CBS. Shirer said: "I've bellowed so long into the microphone and bad telephones that my doctor says that if I don't keep my mouth shut for a few days my voice will be gone entirely." [55]

NBC carried 118 broadcasts from abroad, many of them by Max Jordan. Although suffering from a very bad cold all the time, he made 40 airplane trips around Europe, hiring a substitute to broadcast for him when his throat became too sore to speak. He succeeded in beating the press services by 25 minutes in relaying the full text of the Munich agreement.

Finally, in May 1939 the AP lifted its ban on sponsored newscasts of newspaper members' stations. Direct sale of AP news to radio stations would come shortly. Meanwhile, the networks built up their foreign news staffs, and radio stations installed full-fledged newsrooms. The nets had started operations of this kind in their key stations even before the Munich crisis began. When the Germans stormed into Poland in September 1939 all these news preparations more than justified themselves.

In early May 1939 almost entirely due to the tireless one-man campaign of Mutual Broadcasting's 36-year-old Fulton Lewis, Jr., a Washington-based news commentator, the congressional press galleries were finally opened to radio newsmen. Early in 1939, Lewis had been turned down in this request by the Standing Committee of Correspondents, which controlled admission to the galleries. He took his case to the House and Senate Rules Committees, arguing that radio handled news just as did newspapers. Soon after this victory, Lewis scored another triumph in Washington when Stephen Early, White House Secretary, issued permission for accredited radio newsmen to attend White House press conferences, a privilege previously denied broadcasters.

Radio Scores in War News

December 17, 1939, James Bowen of NBC from Montevideo, described the scuttling of the *Graf Spee*.

When Germany received the conquered French on June 22, 1940, in the historic *wagon-lit* in Compiegne forest to accept their surrender, William Shirer of CBS and William C. Kerker of NBC were there to broadcast the events, giving America the news more than two hours before Germany and France received it. On August 24, 1940, Edward R. Murrow, Eric Sevareid, Vincent Sheean and J. B. Priestley put on what is considered a gripping picture of London under the Nazi blitz.[64]

Later, radio gave America the first news of the attack on Pearl Harbor. Cecil Brown made history with his descriptions of the fall of Singapore to the Japanese. Sevareid, turning a hand-crank to generate transmitter power, sent out for re-broadcast, the story of his parachute hop from a plane into the Indo-Burmese jungle in August 1943. Throughout World War II, American radio newsmen were at the scenes of action, often at great risk to their own lives.

In 1940, AP set up a subsidiary organization called Press Association, Inc. (PA), which went into operation in March 1941—with the prohibition of newscast sponsorship removed.

Thus, by the close of 1941, there were four fulltime news services available to radio newsrooms: Transradio, since 1934, the UP and INS since 1935, and finally the AP (as PA), since early 1941.

54

A. A. Schechter with Edward Anthony

THE FOURTH CHIME

RESOURCEFULNESS and planning have been responsible for most of the important NBC beats, but not even the stanchest partisans of our News Department would have the hardihood to say that without the fortuitous co-operation of Lady Luck we would have had our electrifying "exclusive" on the *Hindenburg* disaster. At that time, because the *Hindenburg's* regular schedule had ceased to be news, no radio news department was bothering to cover her arrival.

Herbert Morrison, announcer for WLS of Chicago, an NBC affiliate, was at Lakehurst to make a recording of the arrival of the dirigible. He was doing a routine job of telling how the great silver ship looked as he spotted her in the rain and she approached and he

I Live On Air, New York: Frederick A. Stokes Company, 1941, pp. 257–258.

became more and more conscious of her size—when, all of a sudden, as she neared her moorings, the explosion came. His complete description of the entire scene was transcribed by the recording apparatus.

Beginning with a calm description of the grace and beauty of the *Hindenburg* as she settled down to earth, the voice of Morrison continued:

"She is practically standing still now. The ropes have been dropped and they have been taken hold of by a number of men on the field. It is starting to rain again. The rain has slacked up a little bit. The back motors of the ship are holding her just enough to keep her. . . . She burst into flame!

"Get out of the way! Get this, Charley. Get out of the way, please! She is bursting into flames! This is terrible! This is one of the worst catastrophes in the world. The flames are shooting five hundred feet up into the sky. It is a terrific crash, ladies and gentlemen. It is in smoke and flames now. Oh, the humanity! Those passengers! I can't talk, ladies and gentlemen. Honest, it is a mass of smoking wreckage. Lady, I am sorry. Honestly, I can hardly—. I am going to step inside where I cannot see it. Charley, that is terrible. Listen, folks, I am going to have to stop for a minute because I have lost my voice."

Shocked by the horror of the tragedy, yet sustained by his announcer's habit of recording what he saw, Morrison went on:

"Coming back again, I have sort of recovered from the terrific explosion and the terrific crash that occurred just before it was pulled down to the mooring mast. I don't know how many of the ground crew were under it when it fell. There is not a possible chance for anyone to be saved.*

"The relatives of the people who were here ready to welcome their loved ones as they came off the ship are broken up. They are carrying them, to give them first aid and to restore them. Some of them have fainted. The people are rushing down to the burning ship with fire extinguishers to see if they can extinguish any of the blaze. The blaze is terrific, because of the terrible amount of hydrogen gas in it."

The Chicago announcer kept pouring his running account of the disaster into the microphone, even to brief interviews with the first of the survivors. In his explanation of a sudden break in the recording just as he announced that the ship had burst into flame, Morrison said that the terrific blast of the explosion had knocked the tone arm

---

* In fact 36 people—just 13 passengers—died and 61 survived. These were apparently the only passengers killed in 30 years of zeppelin travel. This one broadcast, and the still and newsreel photos were in part—probably a large part—responsible for the end of dirigible passenger service.

of the recording instrument clear off the disc and that Charlie—Charles Nelson, the Chicago radio engineer who operated the machine—replaced it almost instantly.

That evening—May 7, 1937—NBC's rigid network rule against broadcasting recorded programs was broken for the first time in the history of the company so that the radio audience could hear one of the most dramatic eye-witness broadcasts ever presented, a "wax show" that was in process of being recorded at the exact second that the famous "Zep" blew up.

55

William L. Shirer

1938 LONDON, MARCH 14

AT ONE A.M. this morning (eight p.m. yesterday, New York time) we did our first European radio round-up. It came off like this.

About five o'clock yesterday afternoon my telephone rang. Paul W. White, Columbia's director of public affairs, was calling from New York. He said: "We want a European round-up tonight. One a.m. your time. We want you and some member of Parliament from London, Ed Murrow of course from Vienna, and American newspaper correspondents from Berlin, Paris, and Rome. A half-hour show, and I'll telephone you the exact time for each capital in about an hour. Can you and Murrow do it?"

I said yes, and we hung up. The truth is I didn't have the faintest idea how to do it—in eight hours, anyway. We had done one or two of these, but there had been *months* of fussing over technical arrangements before each one. I put in a long-distance call to Murrow in Vienna. And as valuable minutes ticked away I considered what to do. The more I thought about it, the simpler it became. Murrow and I have newspaper friends, American correspondents, in every capital in Europe. We also know personally the directors and chief engineers of the various European broadcasting systems whose technical facilities we must use. I called Edgar Mowrer in Paris, Frank Gervasi in Rome, Pierre Huss in Berlin, and the directors and chief engineers of PTT in Paris, EIAR in Turin, and the RRG in Berlin.

Berlin Diary, New York: A. Knopf, 1941, pp. 104–107.

Murrow came through from Vienna; he undertook to arrange the Berlin as well as the Vienna end and gave me a badly needed technical lesson as to how the entire job could be done. For each capital we needed a powerful short-wave transmitter that would carry a voice clearly to New York. Rome had one, but its availability was doubtful. Paris had none. In that case we must order telephone lines to the nearest short-wave transmitting station. Before long my three telephones were buzzing, and in four languages: English, German, French, and Italian. The first three I know fairly well, but my Italian scarcely exists. Still, I understood enough from Turin to get the idea that no executives of the Italian Broadcasting Company could be reached at the moment. Alas, it was Sunday. I still had Rome coming in. Perhaps I could arrange matters with the branch office there. Berlin came through. The Reichs-Rundfunk-Gesellschaft would do its best. Only, they explained, the one line to Vienna was in the hands of the army and therefore doubtful.

As the evening wore on, the broadcast began to take shape. New York telephoned again with the exact times scheduled for each capital. New York's brazen serenity, its confidence that the broadcast would come off all right, encouraged me. My newspaper friends started to come through. Edgar Mowrer, Paris correspondent of the Chicago *Daily News*, was spending Sunday in the country. Much urging to persuade him to return to town to broadcast. But Edgar couldn't fool me. No man, I knew, felt more intensely than he what had happened in Austria. Gervasi in Rome and Huss in Berlin came through. They would broadcast if their New York office agreed. Not much time to inquire at the New York newspaper offices, especially on Sunday afternoon. Another call to Columbia in New York: Get permission for Gervasi and Huss to talk. And by the way, New York said, what transmitters and wavelengths are Berlin and Rome using? I had forgotten about that. Another call to Berlin. The station would be DJZ, 25.2 metres, 11,870 kilocycles. An urgent cable carried the information to the CBS control room in New York.

Time was getting short. I remembered that I must also write out a talk for the London end of the show. What was Britain going to do about Hitler's invasion of Austria? I telephoned around town for material. Britain wasn't going to do anything. New York also wanted a member of Parliament, I suddenly recalled, to discuss British official reaction to the *Anschluss*. I called two or three M.P. friends. They were all enjoying the English week-end. I called Ellen Wilkinson, Labour M.P. So was she.

"How long will it take you to drive to the BBC?" I asked her.

"About an hour," she said.

"I looked at my watch. We had a little more than two hours to go. She agreed to talk.

Gervasi's voice from Rome was on the line. "The Italians can't arrange it on such short notice," he said. "What shall I do?"

I wondered myself. "We'll take you over Geneva," I finally said. "And if that's impossible, phone me back in an hour with your story and I'll read it from here."

Sitting alone in a small studio in Broadcasting House, I had a final check-up with New York three minutes before one a.m. We went over the exact timings of each talk and checked the cues which would be the signals for the speakers in Vienna, Berlin, Paris, and London to begin and end their talks. Rome was out, I told our control room in New York, but Gervasi was on the telephone this minute, dictating his story to a stenographer. We agreed upon a second switchback to London from New York so that I could read it. One a.m. came, and through my earphones I could hear on our transatlantic "feedback" the smooth voice of Bob Trout announcing the broadcast from our New York studio. Our part went off all right, I think. Edgar and Ed were especially good. Ellen Wilkinson, flaunting her red hair, arrived in good time. New York said on the "feedback" afterwards that it was a success. They want another one tonight.

56

Ernest D. Rose

HOW THE U.S.
HEARD ABOUT PEARL HARBOR

DECEMBER 7, 1941

At "X" plus 1 hour and 5 minutes the Japanese carriers were taking aboard the last of their returning aircraft. (To simplify time zone difference, "X" denoted the time at which the bombing attack on Pearl Harbor ended; i.e., 9:45 A.M. Honolulu time, 11:45 A.M. PST, or 2:45 P.M. EST.) At that moment, an NBC announcer reread the following statement relayed a few minutes earlier from station KGU in Hawaii:

BULLETIN: We have witnessed this morning the attack of Pearl Harbor and the severe bombing of Pearl Harbor by army planes that

Journal of Broadcasting, Vol. V, No. 4 (Fall 1961), pp. 285–298.

are undoubtedly Japanese. The city of Honolulu has also been attacked and considerable damage done. This battle has been going on for nearly three hours. One of the bombers dropped within fifty feet of Tanti Tower. It's no joke—it's a real war. The public of Honolulu has been advised to keep in their homes and away from the army and navy. There has been severe fighting going on in the air and on the sea . . . (Then there was an interruption followed by this) . . . We have no statement as to how much damage has been done, but it has been a very severe attack. The army and the navy, it appears, now has the air and sea under control.

This early bulletin was not untypical of the on-the-spot accounts received in the U.S. during the first few hours after the bombing. Except for occasional lapses, such as the wishful remark which ends the above bulletin, these broadcasts tended as a whole to be reliable, to be comparatively brief, and almost always to be reportorial rather than interpretive in nature.

On the other hand, many of these messages contained small errors as to detail, which in retrospect might be judged as relatively minor in terms of the over-all context of the message. However, these small details were frequently picked up and amplified back in the states. Three such errors of detail are evident in the above example. First is a reference to the attackers as Japanese "army" planes. Actually they were all specially trained units of the naval air arm which had rehearsed the attack for weeks at a secret island base in the Kuriles where the terrain was similar to Pearl Harbor. A second inaccuracy is the statement that the battle "has been going on for nearly 3 hours." The subsequent examination of log books and records show that the first Japanese planes actually came over the harbor at 7:59 A.M. and the final wave departed approximately 1 hour and 45 minutes later. Since the planes were not pursued to their carriers, for all intents and purposes the raid ended at 9:45 A.M. A third point refers to the attack on the city of Honolulu and the considerable damage done. A congressional investigation later revealed that about 40 explosions occurred in Honolulu. All except one of these were the result of U.S. anti-aircraft fire and not enemy bombs. Total damage to the city was approximately $500,000.

While such factual errors seem minor in scope to us today, it is possible to trace some of the subsequent distortions in news programs at least in part to just such seemingly trivial inaccuracies. At the very least they added to the confusion of those at home who attempted to piece together the entire picture from the fragments and phrases that came from the scene of the disaster.

As the day wore on, however, direct on-the-spot news reports were heard less and less frequently as security measures were clamped into effect. Thus a considerably larger proportion of air time throughout the day was devoted to commentary by radio news analysts and military or political pundits.

One such personality was Upton Close,* expert on Far Eastern affairs and a nationally prominent radio news analyst. At "X" plus 1 hour and 10 minutes he went on the air from San Francisco.

Hello, fellow Americans. The most fantastic thing that has yet happened in this fantastic world is the bombing of Honolulu and the bombing of Manila and the sinking of several ships off this coast. We don't know yet what is behind this—there is more behind it than meets the eye. So far the reports that have been coming in have been entirely based on military sources and military understanding and military computation. I think I have just received the most interesting and perhaps the most important sidelight on what has happened . . .

I have just been in touch with the San Francisco Japanese Consulate General. The Consul, Mr. Yoshio Muto, was not able to talk but his representative and secretary, Mr. K. Inagaki, spoke to me from the home of Mr. Muto. He said that the attack is a complete surprise to the Consulate General here in San Francisco, that the first the San Francisco Consul General knew about it was hearing it over our radio and he implied that it was likewise a complete surprise to the Foreign Office in Tokyo and the Japanese government in Tokyo.

Now that may prove to be true. It is very possible that there is a double double-cross in this business. I suppose that if the attack on Honolulu had been made in such force as to destroy the American Naval Base there, we might believe that the Japanese government was behind it as a matter of policy. But, you notice that the news gives us every assurance that it is far from destroyed and that the only thing left there now as the result of the first attack are a few parachute troops wandering around on the sand on the north end of Oahu Island. They will soon be pulled in the bag and we'll find out who sent them. (Actually there were no paratroopers landed; only 2 or 3 pilots who bailed out of their damaged aircraft.)

It is possible, my friends, that this is a coup engineered by German influence and with the aid of German vessels in the Pacific. And again it is possible that this is a coup engineered by a small portion of the Japanese navy that has gone fanatic and decided to precipitate war. And still again it is possible that this is a coup engineered by the group in Japan that wants the group that wants the war kicked out of office. And that when the thing is brought home to the Tokyo government now it might be possible for the Tokyo government to repudiate the action, call upon the nation to repair the injury to America by agreeing to American terms and precipitating a complete revolution in the government in Tokyo. All these things are possible. You will have to wait and see what happens.

* Josef Washington Hill.

Now I will be glad to go on talking as long as they wish me to take time on various phases of this situation. It seems to me that if the coup is precipitated by those fanatics who have wanted America at war with Japan and visa versa it might have been done as an answer to the messages of Secretary Cordell Hull to the Envoy Kurusu and Nomura. You notice that we are told that Mr. Hull burst out in true Tennessee language and told the Japanese that their reply was crowded with infamous falsehoods and distortions.

I have been in many a Japanese brawl, I am sorry to say, and I have seen many an argument with Japanese, that would have ended just an argument, suddenly burst into violence because something was said by one of the so-called "white people" in the crowd that suddenly lashed across the Japanese face. Now it is possible that the Japanese completely lost face and descended to the status of being willing to engage in a violent brawl as a result of this answer, although it might be that this answer and Secretary Hull's message came at the same time. But it sounds like one of those Japanese arguments that suddenly descends into violence. (Announcer: One moment please while we attempt further contact with Hawaii")

Seventeen minutes later, at "X" plus 1 hour and 42 minutes, Mr. Close returned to the microphone. At that moment, thousands lay dead; four of the navy's 9 Pacific Fleet battleships were sinking or already on the bottom; 4 more battleships had been badly hit and disabled; 347 of Oahu's 394 military and naval planes had been destroyed.

Hello Americans. We have just had a flash from Tokyo saying that a state of war exists with the United States. Now we begin to see through things. It's obvious that the Imperial General Staff in Tokyo took affairs right out of the hands of the civil government and has precipitated an attack and now announces that that attack is official . . .

We are very interested in whether or not the attack on Honolulu would be called from a military standpoint a real serious attack. So far five civilians killed in the bombing of the city is certainly not what they would call a serious attack in London. We have at present two conflicting, possibly conflicting, reports about the damage done in a military sense. There seems to be no doubt that the air field at Hickman (actually Hickam) Field was hit and damage done which was not serious from the standpoint of flying but a tragedy in the shape of a direct hit on an American barracks which it is said killed 350 American soldier boys on the field. That's the worst thing yet.

There seems some uncertainty whether any real damage was done to the naval base. We have a report saying the USS *Oklahoma*, a battleship, one of our first class but not one of our newest, was set afire in the air attack, but it doesn't say whether it's seriously afire or not. There is another report, unconfirmed, that two U.S. warships, one of them the *West Virginia*, were sunk. I would take that just as a

rumor until we have further confirmation. Now, as I have said before, the whole thing is going to come clear after we get these
speeches from the Premier of Japan.

It's rather interesting to note the possibilities of the way in
which the attack took place. There is one rumor that the attack took
place from the south, that would be in the direction of the island of
Maui. It might be that a Japanese airplane was hiding out around
the little island of Maui or below Molokai. It might even have been
in connection with something going on in the island of Hawaii, the
biggest in the chain and the southern-most one. There's a port there
called Hilo where there are Japanese in dominance . . . We have
just had a flash saying that Japan has also entered a state of war with
Britain. Manila is ready now so we take you to Manila.

The general character of Mr. Close's remarks is by no means an
isolated example of the kinds of statements the American people
heard during the first eight hours of radio news broadcasting on Sunday, December 7th.

For instance, at "X" plus 3 hours and 15 minutes while rescue
operations continued to occupy the attention of every spare man in
the Pearl Harbor area, while fires still raged uncontrolled aboard the
battleships *West Virginia, Tennessee, Oklahoma* and *Arizona,* Major
George Fielding Elliott, syndicated columnist and author of several
widely read books on military strategy explained in his characteristic
monotone:

> . . . It should be emphasized that this attack is of a suicidal nature
> from which few of the ship's aircraft and personnel participating
> have any hope of returning. (Actual box score as close as can be de-
> termined from subsequent investigations: enemy planes claimed
> shot down by the U.S.—48; losses admitted by the Japanese—29;
> total number of Japanese aircraft participating in the attack—353.) It
> is a procedure entirely in keeping with the Japanese character. A
> sort of desperate and sudden blow which recalled the Japanese tor-
> pedo attack on the Russian fleet in Port Arthur Harbor in January
> 1904. But this is an attack against a far more formidable foe and under
> far less favorable conditions.
>
> What actual damage has been done is hard to ascertain at this
> moment. There are reports that two capital ships of the United
> States fleet have been damaged. Even if this is so, and these reports
> are unconfirmed, we have yet to see what the Japanese fleet will
> lose in the way of aircraft carriers. . . .
>
> When the President was talking to the governor of the Hawaiian
> Islands, the governor repeated that a second wave of Japanese
> planes was just coming over, which suggests that the Japanese
> planes, or some of them, had left, had time to return to their carrier,
> get a new load of bombs and fuel, and return to the attack. (Actually
> there were two separate waves, 183 planes leaving the carriers at

6:00 A.M. followed by 170 at 7:15 A.M. None came back a second time.) But this procedure will certainly lead the heavy American bombing planes to the carriers and the fact that the fleet has sailed from Pearl Harbor, (Actually the remnants of the fleet escaped from the harbor more as a safety precaution, although some units did set out in a fruitless search for the enemy.), as just reported probably indicates that an attempt to round up and destroy the carriers is now in full swing. . . .

None of these operations, however, can overcome the fact that Japan is cornered, surrounded by forces which she cannot hope to overcome and to which in the end she must succumb. We have heard so far of what the Japanese have done. We shall hear presently what has happened to the Japanese forces which have been engaged in these daring and distant raids. And that, we may be sure, will be a different story and one which will mark, in the opinion of well informed observers, the beginning of the decline of the Japanese empire from its present position as a world power.

Equally authoritative in tone, but less well supported, were the observations of John B. Hughes, distinguished radio news analyst, speaking at "X" plus 3 hours and 40 minutes over a rival network:

Good evening . . . It is obvious that the Japanese will attempt to develop in the South Pacific a triangular strategy. They will attempt to take either Singapore or Manila in order to establish a triangulation, as it were, a triangle of bases with Formosa, the island of Hainan and probably Manila. This is a Japanese naval strategy which has been planned and worked out in detail for a period of forty years and is to be found in all the naval books of warfare, as many of the Japanese militarists well know.

A member of the Japanese general staff told me less than a year ago that if it became necessary the Japanese militarists, rather than lose power to the conservatives of Japan, rather than sacrifice the leadership which they had succeeded in acquiring after ten years of deliberate planning and step by step procedure, would deliberately lead the nation into a war they knew they could not win.

Another very interesting point is the one made by Royal Arch Gunnison in his broadcast from Manila. He mentioned the fact that Russian planes and ships will be against the Japanese. The participation of Russia in the war against Japan on the side of the United States and Britain is a very important factor and a point upon which the Japanese have been making a tremendous effort to interfere. It was said in the past 10 days in Tokyo unofficially by a high official of the government that Japan was safe from Russia, that Russia would not fight against Japan with Britain and the United States. Royal Arch Gunnison's mention of Russia, particularly in this broadcast only ten minutes ago is very interesting, and on this side it is to be hoped that what he said is true because Britain and the United States must have Russian cooperation in order to wage the war effectively against Japan. (Actual date of Russia's entry into the war against Japan—August 8, 1945, six days before its surrender.)

Of all the commentaries none combined a greater mixture of false conjecture, exaggeration, wishful thinking, and rationalization than those of Fulton Lewis, Jr. Less inhibited than many of his colleagues, he spoke with the same zeal that has maintained for him a loyal following (and a steady list of sponsors) throughout the past two decades. For instance, at "X" plus 5 hours and 10 minutes, Mr. Lewis was observing:

> . . . First of all this attack took place under, to all intents and purposes, under the white flag of truce, because that's what it did. In their language it took place while Japan was using the integrity, the fairness, the peaceful intentions of the United States to stall for time, when as a matter of fact they were all the time, very obviously now, preparing for this attack on the island of Oahu, the Philippines, Guam and the United States in general. In other words while these peace conferences have been going on over the past two weeks they have not been peace conferences at all. They have been teachery, carrying the white flag of truce. They have been lies from the ground up and that has produced terrific and bitter resentment here in the State Department circles, in diplomatic circles, in general, among the administration leaders and in Congress.
>
> The second thing was the manner in which this was done today. The attack on the ships in Pearl Harbor, . . . a very very foolish thing, as a matter of fact, suicidal fool-hardiness as a matter of fact, because the Japanese must know, as all the rest of the world knows, and all the rest of the navies and military men of the world know, that Pearl Harbor is the one invincible, absolutely invulnerable base in the world. It's stronger even than Gibralter itself, and as far as an attack or siege of it is concerned there could have been no possible sane intention on the part of the Japanese to such an end.
>
> The great resentment comes from the fact that these bombing planes and battleships—rather these bombing planes, and the gun boat off Manila came in as they did to a peaceful, unsuspecting unwarned community, dropped bombs out of a clear sky, served no notice, gave no fair play of warfare, no decency, no fair respect. After all, a good many people may have questioned today, "Well, how was all this damage done if we had such an excellent navy and such an excellent army air corps?" Why anyone can walk in, ladies and gentlemen (laugh), to ships lying peacefully in the harbor without the slightest suspicion that attack may come—anyone can come in with bombing planes and sink anything under those conditions. And that's exactly what happened this morning at Hickman [sic] Field. Officers, pilots at the field were going about their usual everyday procedure—the planes out on the field, no preparation for war, no expectations of it, no advance warning of any kind—when into that peaceful situation comes attacking planes. It is of course a

one shot thing. They got away with it once—they will never get away with it again. The army and the navy privately have made that perfectly clear this afternoon, and the second attack later today on Hickman Field has proven that it isn't the same the second time. . . .

There is considerable mystery, as I told you earlier this evening, as to where these fifty bombing planes came from. . . . One of the great points of interest so far as the War Department and the Navy Department here are concerned is to find out who the pilots of these planes are—whether they are Japanese pilots. There is some doubt as to that, some skepticism whether they may be pilots of some other nationality, perhaps Germans, perhaps Italians. . . .

In the meantime, however, the American navy has steamed out under orders from Washington—has steamed out of Pearl Harbor, anchors away, and we may have more to that story of final results on these aircraft carriers and the Japanese fleet within a matter of a very few hours.

There is little question as to what will happen once there is an open engagement between the Japanese fleet and the American fleet, if it ever happens, on the high seas. A very high admiral of the United States Army—I mean the United States Navy told me not four weeks ago when I asked him how long it would take for an American victory under such circumstances, he said, "Well, Fulton, we'd be glad to do that any Wednesday morning." When I asked him—told him that I would like to have lunch with him that day because I would like to get a scoop on it, he said he would try to keep it in mind but he was afraid I wouldn't be interested because by noon that day it would be old news.

To be sure not all the broadcasts indulged in all the types of misleading statements and rationalizations. Indeed, some commentators exercised remarkable restraint in view of the shortage of information available to them and the pressure from an aroused public to inform. At "X" plus 7 hours and 10 minutes a voice is just barely heard above the din in the background:

This is Eric Sevareid reporting again directly from the press room in the White House. Here in the White House the vigil of reporters from all over the United States is still on. The phones are ringing . . . men are still working at the typewriters. Outside, a few yards away, in front of the main portico other reporters are still standing in a group, waiting for important personages to come in to the White House or to leave, trying to buttonhole all that they can for what information can be gleaned.

Out on Pennsylvania Avenue you can see the policemen walking back and forth, and then across the street in the dim street light, you can see from this porch a mass of faces all turned this way, a patient crowd standing there in the chill evening simply watching this lighted portico of the White House as the figures come and go. And

to me I must confess there is a very familiar look and feeling about
this whole scene. I've seen it in similar moments in Downing
Street, in the Quay d'Orsay in Paris . . . the same crowd as these
watching, waiting faces of ordinary citizens of those countries.

Now there is one report which I must give you which is not at
all confirmed—a report which is rather widely believed here and
which has just come in. And that is that the destruction at Hawaii
was indeed very heavy, more heavy than we really had anticipated.
For this report says that two capital ships of ours have been sunk,
that another capital ship has been badly damaged, and the same
report from the same source says that the airfield hangers there in
Hawaii were completely flattened out and that a great many planes
have been damaged. There is no speculation about the number of
planes. Now if the planes were dispersed on that airfield as they
normally would have been with piles of earth around each one, the
number of planes damaged probably was not great. But if the field
was overcrowded for a possible emergency, then no one knows how
many have been lost. Now I repeat, this report has not been confirmed but it has come in from a fairly reliable source and many reporters here indeed believe it.

It was in such tones that word of the real fate of Pearl Harbor began
finally to filter through to the American people toward the late hours
of that seemingly endless night.

DISCUSSION

In spite of cautious, simply stated observations by a few scattered commentators, one cannot escape the conclusion that in the
over-all pattern of radio news communication that day something
was drastically wrong. While on-the-spot reports were, for the most
part, reliable as to general content, errors of detail in many of them
led to misinterpretation and confusion back in the States. After censorship drastically curtailed reports from on-the-scene sources, the
bulk of radio news time was consumed by commentators and analysts trying to explain the meaning of situations without access to reliable first-hand information. Background to the news tended to be
overly conservative and evasive. Under pressure from the public, the
dominant tendency was to carry on regardless of the meager flow of
"hard" news. The result was that a good deal of early information
was stated and restated many different ways, and with varying degrees of indignation, throughout the day. But if that was all that happened to the news December 7th one would have only minor cause
for concern.

The truth is that a disconcertingly large proportion of news analysts went considerably beyond what available facts supported in
commenting on the events of that day. The result was a verbal pick-
me-up, a confused concoction of defensive and aggressive statements

ranging all the way from attempts to depricate the enemy's intelligence and minimize the danger on the one hand, to emotional appeals based on exaggerated retaliatory capacities or moral and intellectual superiority on the other.

It might be argued that such a position is justifiable, even desirable in a crisis. Such a commentator, it may be said, "reassures" the people, keeps them from losing all control, and lets them down easier to the blow that they must ultimately face up to. In a democratic society predicated on faith in the many, rather than an elite, superior few, such logic appears somewhat feeble. It is one thing to tell a person he has suffered a serious personal loss in a compassionate way and with rational concern for the consequences. It is quite another to imply that maybe the loss really didn't occur at all, or if it did its importance is after all questionable. If our system is based on the premise of freedom of information, that implies not only the freedom to express unpopular beliefs and minority viewpoints, but the responsibility to listen to and evaluate the unpopular and the unpleasant as well.

In opposition to the questionable policy of "soft-pedaling" or "playing-down" bad news, the broadcasts that day themselves suggest that those who were well informed, even though they were located in positions of greater danger, were far more rational than those, either on the spot or back home, who lacked what facts were known and who supplied their own answers via wishful thinking tempered by unexpressed fears of the worst. Those on the scene spoke mainly, and reliably, of *effects*. Those back home dealt principally, and often inaccurately, with the *causes*.

To understand the implications of this, one must consider the role of the news reporter and the news commentator in our society. The man on the spot who presumably has accurate information is, under the stress of the moment in a crisis, generally less able (and sometimes less qualified) to take the broad view of events required for intelligent interpretation.

This analytical role, it is usually reasoned, belongs to a commentator who, with additional facts at his disposal, can view events dispassionately and with greater perspective on the situation as a whole. In recent years an encouraging development has been the assignment of more and more analysts to overseas tours of duty so that they might broadcast their commentary from abroad. But when accurate information is lacking, the home based commentator's role becomes an extremely difficult one.

Most radio (and now TV) news analysts have always worked in a market where each is in competition with the other for an audience. The eye of a sponsor is usually somewhere in the background. If it does not often selectively scan the news content itself it is certainly

always focused on the size of the audience the commentator is drawing. With the development of the cult of the news "personalities" we
have come to regard our commentators as much entertainer as oracle.
In addition to his distinctive "delivery style" and his "audience appeal," the news analyst's reputation is based upon his ability to provide intelligent, rational, accurate assessments of problems and answers to questions *in the mind of his particular following*. When the
chips are down that audience expects him to live up to his reputation. Otherwise he runs the risk of temporarily relinquishing his
image (sometimes self-created) as the man who knows, the one capable of seeing beneath the issues on the surface.

On December 7th, surrounded by anxiety and uncertainities,
many of our commentators proved all too human in succumbing to
the temptation of having a right answer, reasonable sounding for the
moment at least. Some simply up-dated day dreams and kept passing
them on to the public almost as if the soap opera had never been interrupted by the momentous events of that tragic day.

From the hind-sight of twenty years it is easy now to sit back and
Sunday-quarterback. That is not the intended purpose in recalling
these events to mind. Nor will it be argued that our basic and long
cherished "right to know" may at times be overridden by factors of
greater magnitude such as our "need to survive." What is suggested
is that we may have missed the more subtle, yet equally important,
meaning of the Pearl Harbor disaster.

Looking back now one can easily fit together a dozen clues
which we knew about in advance of the attack but which were discounted or somehow never got to the right people quickly enough to
alter the course of events. The catastrophe of December 7, 1941, was
as much due to rationalization, inaccuracy, and lack of coordination
in our communications as it was to our inadequate preparedness for
surprise attack.

In a world where the pace has accelerated many fold in twenty
years the real message of Pearl Harbor may be that our "need to survive" is inextricably linked to, if not dependent on, our "need to
know." In any future war we may expect no "notice" nor any "fair
play of warfare" that Commentator Lewis denounced on December
7th. But the responsibility for averting such a war goes far beyond
improving our intelligence network or our military communications.
It resides as much with the sovereign people of the United States
and the other world powers as it does with their leaders. Few dicta-
tors have been able indefinitely to ignore the organized will of an
aroused people. In democracies, if the channels of mass communications are frequently utilized by our elected representatives to
bring us around to the course of action they have already decided

upon, let us not forget that it is within our power to use these same channels to inform them of our will in these matters.

In recent times there is some doubt whether the feedback aspect of democratic communications has been making any headway against a veritable deluge of information from the opposite direction. It is alarming, for example, to speculate on how little popular protest we probably would have heard even if the American people had known in advance the extent of this government's involvement in the ill-fated Cuba invasion. Such a response (or more precisely, lack of one) would probably have been due less to unflinching support of administration decisions—right or wrong, than to a lack of awareness of possible alternatives or limitations of the proposed course of action.

We live in an era when most of us get most of our information from one or another of the mass media. Super-speed and technical accuracy of communication are today commonplace both throughout this planet and beyond it. Yet years after Pearl Harbor we still accept as inevitable: (1) inaccurate reporting of critical events, (2) confusion as to what kinds of facts should be withheld for the common good and what information is needed by the public to exercise its legitimate role in government, (3) frequent misinterpretation or deliberate falsification of "facts" by special interest groups, and (4) a tenacious preference for the myth of "what could be" over the reality of "what is."

There is no simple answer for the problem here illustrated; no sinecure, no formula for eradicating human frailities overnight. Nor does the weakness lie only with the speaker and not his listeners in an era when all forces interact upon each other.

"Responsibility" is not a characteristic which can be legislated into existence. Like "wisdom," it must sometimes be acquired through a long and painful series of lessons that remain in our memory. In "remembering Pearl Harbor" it would be well to set out anew in pursuit of those two human goals. Perhaps in so doing we may find the clues we seek in this dilemma. For how to update the democratic handling of communications in a modern world is an inseparable part of our battle for survival.

The cooperation of wire and radio is undoubtedly a development which will prove of inestimable importance in putting the vast multitudes of this country in close touch with its important events.   --*Radio Broadcast*, September 1923.

57

Kenneth G. Bartlett

RADIO WAR PROGRAMS

THE OUTSTANDING public service program at this time, in my judgment, is "The Army Hour." The opening continuity describes it officially as, "A Military operation of the United States Army," and
from then and until sign-off it uses the documentary method to bring
us short glimpses of what the Army is doing. It moves from one Army
camp to another, from this country to foreign lands, from a discussion
by generals and cabinet officers to drafted and enlisted men. It is
documentary at its best and, assuming that its purpose is to give an
inside glimpse of Army operation, seems to succeed admirably. It is
authentic, generally significant, and paced to give a rapid sense of
movement. The official Army communiques followed by an analysis
by the head of the Public Relations Division of the Army was, to me,
the high light. A band ties diverse parts together. Oddly enough,
there is an audience, presumably in New York, that applauds periodically, and that we could easily do without. This, however, seems
like a minor fault in such a large and pretentious undertaking, it is
produced under the active supervision of Lieutenant Colonel Edward Kirby, Radio Branch, Bureau of Public Relations, War Department, and formerly director of public relations and educational ad-
viser to the National Association of Broadcasters.

CBS's "Our Secret Weapon," Rex Stout as moderator, does an interesting job of exposing Axis propaganda. The format is simple. It
utilizes German, Japanese and Italian accents as a method for reading Axis claims. Rex Stout breaks in to provide an answer and does it
in a strongly sarcastic manner which leaves you with the impression
that we are not dignifying an absurd claim with a formal answer. The
manner of all who appear on the program seems to be well calculated to prevent dial-samplers who hear only a part of the program
coming away with a wrong impression. "Our Secret Weapon" is
made timely be several research assistants who provide reports on
what the Axis is saying and its manner is quite different from the
usual talk, or drama, or discussion program.

"Pan American Holiday," "Lands of the Free," "Music of the
America's," and "The Sea Hound" are four programs that are related
in terms of central purpose, although they seek different publics.
The first was arranged at the suggestion of Vice President Henry A.

Quarterly Journal of Speech, Vol. XXIX, No. 1 (February 1943), pp. 100–103.

Wallace and has the direct cooperation of his office. "Lands of the Free" and "Music of the New World," are sponsored by NBC's Inter-American University of the Air, directed by Sterling Fisher. The fourth is a children's program broadcast by the Blue Network.

NBC's Inter-American University of the Air should receive the enthusiastic cooperation of colleges and universities. There have never been very many programs at the university level. The public schools have CBS's "School of the Air of the Americas," and the Blue network's "Victory Hour," and for many years had NBC's "Damrosch Music Appreciation Hour." The idea of an Inter-American *University* of the Air is new and because these programs are authoritative and at the university level they should receive more college and university support. With our immediate attention, so much on the Far East and Europe, it is possible that only the far-sighted will get excited now about informative or inspirational programs about Latin America. If the war were in the Southern Hemisphere, these programs would seem more vital. Yet, though their timeliness is more remote, they are a part of our international policy, and the world is now too small for us to concentrate our attention on only one or two spots. The rumba, American fashion, is not Latin American music and "Music of the America's" helps to keep the perspective right. "Pan American Holiday" is a novel and realistic way of learning customs and language. "Lands of the Free" provides historical background not easily available in other forms. Together, we can be proud that, through radio, the good neighbor can be brought into the home and made to seem a friendly as well as a formal policy of government.

"The Sea Hound" is a children's dramatic serial, with a concealed educational purpose. As a result of a give-away offer made on each program for three weeks, more than 90,000 requests were received. The giveaway was a specially prepared map of Latin America, about 36 × 24 in colors, showing products, and carrying on its border flags of all the Latin American republics and pictures of the outstanding heroes of each country. The program is planned in cooperation with the Office of the Coordinator of Inter-American Affairs. The Coordinator's Office also supplied the maps. Considering all the trouble caused by children's programs, and the additional criticism of daily serials, it is interesting to observe that here is one that uses the techniques of both, yet escapes the undesirable qualities of either. The fact that it is still attractive to children makes it strikingly unusual and worth attention.

"Report to the Nation" through CBS reviews the most vital news of the week and describes how it affects civilians and soldiers. Paul White, in charge of news for CBS, supervises the program. Bill Slocum edits it; and Earl McGill directs it. It is spectacular, yet a listener gets the impression that it is expressing an official attitude of the government. Although it is not as spectacular as the "March of Time" it has greater unity and more direction. It leans heavily on the narrator with periodic dramatic flashbacks.

"To the President" and "Britain to America" will be off the air, unless present plans are changed, by the time this review is published. Perhaps it is enough to say that it is too bad that Arch Oboler, who is a capable radio dramatist, finds it necessary to broadcast his best work, "To the President" on a Sunday afternoon whereas his "Lights Out" series gets an early evening week-day spot. It is not that one is bad and the other good. To me they are both good radio. I am only sorry that the better of the two has to be broadcast at a time when fewer people listen. As the title implies, "To the President" is a series of letters from people to their President and explains their common hopes and disappointments, and psychologically, has the effect of making it seem that the common man has found a spokesman who is interceding for him. The series could be better if Mr. Oboler did not have so much to do but it is still an interesting idea, well executed and should be continued—at a better hour.

"Britain to America" is a series of broadcasts presented by BBC and sent to this country by short wave. Leslie Howard acts as Master of Ceremonies. Each program presents in dramatized narration the picture of some one phase of Britain's war effort—the Commandos, British merchant seamen, British war workers, and the living problems of average citizens. It offers a listener an opportunity to contrast life in Britain with life here and it is this comparison, more than anything else, that makes it a real public service.

"The Victory Hour" is presented in cooperation with the War and Navy Departments, the U.S. Office of Education, the Civilian Aeronautics Administration, and the War Man Power Board as a radio program adjunct to the recently created High School Victory Corps. It is intended for reception in high schools, and has the general purpose of creating attitudes toward the war and toward military service. It is a variety program with a number of spots tied together by George V. Denny, Jr., Moderator of America's Town Meeting, acting as master of ceremonies. Each week the program includes music by one of the Service bands and, in addition, a short analysis of the military situation by a "name" commentator or a Washington newspaper correspondent. The program is being carried by more than 115 Blue Network stations—an unusual station acceptance for a sustaining program, particularly since a large proportion of the stations had to shift commercial programs to make room for this series.

Finally, a word about the more established radio forums. These public sounding boards have their biggest job to do when the war is over. Lyman Bryson, CBS's director of education, recently pointed out that it should be their function to sharpen issues so that we may not make the same mistakes that were made at the close of the First World War. If their function is to sharpen issues, it becomes mightily important that they be maintained during the War so that public confidence be continued and developed. "Town Meeting," "People's Platform," and "The University of Chicago Round-Table" seem pretty well established. They are well planned, although differently executed. I am not so well acquainted with the planning that goes into "American Forum" or "Wake Up America."

SUMMARY

A reviewer must doubt if many of the propaganda programs evaluated above get a very good Crossley rating. This does not mean that they are not good. It does, however, indicate that we have not yet begun to compete with the best entertainment. Radio is still a paradise for an escapist who wants to avoid his responsibilities as a citizen. In this connection I should point out that many commercial programs have added important government appeals to their program format, and many of the dramas have reshaped their plots to put emphasis on things that need to be done. Music programs, too, particularly the Waring Program, have stressed war songs, and in so doing helped to provide the victory spirit.

American radio has many good war-time programs. Furthermore, its news, even if there may be too much, still makes us one of the best informed peoples in the world. If our propaganda effort seems scattered, it may be because American radio has always been pretty scattered. That is a characteristic of freedom.

58

George A. Willey

THE SOAP OPERAS AND THE WAR

RADIO, unaccustomed to wartime service, required considerable time to re-tool. Except for the special broadcast of Franklin Roosevelt speaking before Congress asking for a declaration of war, the program logs on December 8 were identical to those of the previous

Journal of Broadcasting, Vol. VII, No. 4 (Fall 1963), pp. 339–352.

week and, indeed, strikingly similar to those of previous seasons. In addition to listening to Franklin D. Roosevelt's somber definition of the Nation's crisis, daytime radio listeners on December 8 had their choice of no less than fifty-four serials between the hours of 9 a.m. and 5 p.m.[1]

Radio's Three Approaches to Wartime Service

Radio quickly began to experiment with three approaches to public service with regard to the war, exclusive of brief announcements: (1) utilizing big stars in special mass audience appeals; (2) insertion of appropriate material within existing programs; (3) development of new program series.

Established stars adopted the practice of closing their programs with a reminder to buy war bonds, to grow victory gardens, to conserve scarce materials and in other ways to hasten the day of victory. The great exception to such casual participation was the phenomenal "Kate Smith Day" on CBS, February 1, 1944, on which occasion the singing star made 57 separate appeals throughout the day and was credited with a grand total of $112,000,000 in war bond sales.

Most of the popular entertainment shows turned immediately to wartime references. Within the first week Jack Benny was cautioning Rochester to check the Maxwell automobile carefully with an eye toward conserving gasoline, oil and rubber. Weekly dramatic programs demonstrated the efficacy of interchangeable parts in radio drama; heroines were still being kidnapped but the villains had become Nazi agents. The majority of radio's many adventure programs focussed their heroics upon wartime themes and locales.

The new radio shows which originated during the war years were divided primarily among documentaries, drama and variety programs. "This Is War" was among the first of the documentary series and remained the most ambitious in preparation and distribution. Norman Corwin wrote six of the thirteen half-hour programs and directed all thirteen, carried simultaneously over 700 of America's 924 stations through the facilities of all four networks. The purpose of the series was to stimulate national morale and to inform the public of wartime resources and policies. This same purpose was behind such individual documentaries as "Three Thirds of the Nation," "To the Young," "Report to the Nation" and "The Midwest Mobilizes."

New dramatic programs dealt predominantly with the war. "Counter Spy" was typical of such new titles; "Alias John Freedom" dealt with an intrepid hero who outfoxed the Gestapo week after week while "The 22nd Letter" dramatized stories of underground opposition in Axis countries.

Many variety programs were taken on tours of military camps, motivating the integration of thematic material within their formats. New "Hours" developed in time, the first of which was "The Army Hour" which began in April of 1942. "The Navy Hour" did not begin until July of 1945, followed by "The National Hour," which replaced "The Army Hour" in November of 1945. In addition to providing music and brief dramatic sketches, these programs included official messages to the civilian population and direct pick-ups from such distant locations as overseas army bases and the fleet in the Pacific.

Response of Daytime Serials

Shortly after the outbreak of the war *The New Yorker* magazine carried a Helen Hokinson cartoon in which a matronly woman, turning to two guests as they listened to the radio, asked, "Don't you think it's wonderful how 'John's Other Wife' is taking the war?"

Paul Lazarsfeld defined the basic choice whereby serial drama might render genuine service to wartime audiences, or, on the other hand, might allow the great potential of such service to remain undisturbed:

> Aside from casual references and the weaving in of actual information the war can enter the plots in two ways: It can either become an integral part of the stories, skillfully dealing with such problems as the home front, the post-war world, the nature of the enemy, or it can become just another trouble against which the experiences of isolated individuals are enacted. It is vitally important that the former alternative be taken. It would be unintelligent to obscure by happy endings the heroic tragedies of our war.[2]

Many of the daily dramatic series chose neither alternative, proceeding throughout the war with little or no acknowledgement of the fact that the country was locked in mortal conflict; the make-believe character of certain of radio's fictional small towns was virtually impervious to the great reality of the day. In other instances the war received token acknowledgement either by oblique references or by integrating war material into the stories with a minimum of disruption. Aunt Elmira baked a victory cake without sugar while chatting on about the war. Another radio heroine might think to collect fat and tin or send the youngsters out to collect scrap rubber but that was often the extent of it; a dab of khaki here and there was added to several of the stories without in any way adding to their over-all color. One critic, having listened steadily to the radio throughout the first Wednesday of June in 1942, concluded that the soap opera was doing virtually nothing to acquaint American housewives with global war: "With rare exceptions, our radio heroines never mention the war, rationing, hunger, poverty, minority problems, or, indeed, anything but their own febrile crises."[3]

On the other hand, perhaps by listening to an earlier or altogether different sequence of stories, it was possible for another critic to arrive at the opposite contention:

> The daytime serial has developed a social conscience. There's more emphasis on moral values and less on plot gyrations. Not one of the daily dramas is capitalizing on escapism, ignoring the fact that we're at war. Result is that the characters seem endowed with a sterner reality and more good sense than formerly. True, life is still a galling mood for most of them with trouble following fast upon trouble. But chins were never higher, determination never harder. For the first time in their not altogether distinguished history the daytime serials are setting an example of fortitude and courage.[4]

Special Audience Appeals

As was the case with radio in general, serial drama first became involved with the war by bringing forth various performers and special guests in order that they might appeal directly to large audiences, next by integrating appropriate thematic material into the framework of existing plots and, finally, by developing new stories specifically centered about the war.

A few of the serials brought guests before the microphones for interviews or statements before the dramatic portion of the program commenced. Miss Adet Ling, daughter of Lin Yutang, appeared on "Young Dr. Malone" to appeal for Chinese blood plasma. Miss Lin's appearance in 1943 coincided with the story line of the serial which at that time was not only laid in China but was also making a strong point for Sino-American cooperation after the war. Susan B. Anthony II went on "Bright Horizons" to talk about women in industry. Mrs. Theodore Roosevelt, Jr., spoke to the audience of "Aunt Jenny's Series." Eleanor Roosevelt discussed the wartime role of women with Bess Johnson, heroine of the serial carrying her name. "Woman of America," a new serial introduced during the war, presented guests in place of the opening commercial on twenty-seven different occasions. These guests were usually war heroes or women who were devoting their energies to the war effort in some particular capacity.

Utilization of Existing Stories

Although the war served as a backdrop for many of the stories it seldom became an integral part of the action for more than an occasional sequence. The leading characters in nearly every daytime series were women and none of these women went to war as members of an auxiliary service organization. Such enthusiasm, presumably, would have resulted in too narrow a range of dramatic material for too long a time. By staying at home the heroines could become involved in whatever part of the war best suited the purposes of the show and, by the same token, the war could be played down or discarded altogether from time to time. The majority of daytime serials looked upon their response to the war as one of interior decoration rather than basic change in architectural plan.

An examination of plot developments during this period reveals that certain programs and writers were more prone than others to use "romantic" aspects of war. Mary Marlin's long-missing husband turned up in Tunisia waiting for the bandages to be removed from his eyes. Walter Manning, fiancee of the heroine in "Portia Faces Life," was wrongly accused of being a Nazi as a consequence of his service to the American Intelligence in Germany; Portia was drawn into the court action under the same shadow of public prejudice. Later in the same series Walter became Portia's husband and, as a newspaper correspondent in Europe, was held and tortured to such an extent by the Nazis that he was returned to New York for intensive psychiatric care. The psychiatrist, as the luck of such stories would have it, was in love with Portia.

David Harum befriended a young woman who disclosed that she was once a member of the German underground, and in this manner the hero discovered that a new acquaintance was in reality a Nazi secret agent. "Young Widder Brown" introduced a doctor in the Medical Corps who, as the heroine's fiancee, played a significant role for a period. A Naval surgeon was also written into this story but the motivating force in this serial, as in most of its kind, did not deal with the war.

Another example was that of "Young Dr. Malone" which in 1942 sent its hero to England where he accepted a commission in the British Armed Forces. Soon enroute to Russia, he was shot down by the enemy and thought by his wife to be dead. Surviving as a prisoner of the Nazis, he eventually escaped to find that his wife had become enamoured of a Naval flier whom she had been nursing back to health after total disablement from shell shock.

The common denominator of all serials acknowledging the war was the departure of expendable male characters for active military service. Where the men were essential to the plot, as in "Pepper Young's Family," they failed to gain admission to the armed forces by virtue of a 4-F classification or a vital role in essential industry and thereby became the personification of another wartime precept: not all soldiers in the war would be at the front but on the production line as well.

Ma Perkins' son went off as an infantryman and was killed. The heroine of "The Right to Happiness" was married to a soldier wounded in action (who returned just as she was about to marry another man). The husband in "Backstage Wife" joined the Coast

Guard. Certainly the most true-to-life departure was that of young
Sammy in "The Goldbergs." Alfred Ryder played the role until
called into military service. When he left for duty, so did Sammy
Goldberg in a broadcast originated at Pennsylvania Station just before the troop train departed.

Cooperation with Governmental Agencies

Much was made in certain quarters of the fact that some writers
were working closely with governmental agencies and other responsible groups in selecting wartime themes and providing specific information which would be of maximum benefit to the listening audience. Elaine Carrington, author of "Pepper Young's Family,"
credited the Office of the Surgeon General in Washington for assistance in reassuring listeners about military medical attention. Although a new character in Miss Carrington's story was missing in action, other incidents involved the establishment of medical facilities
on front lines and beaches. Irna Phillips, author of three network
serials during this period,[5] told participants of the Third Regional
Conference on Broadcasting at Stephens College that she plotted her
stories with the help and advice of the American Legion, Association
for Family Living, Federal Council of Churches of Christ in
America, the American Medical Association, the Red Cross, the National Educational Association, the Office of War Information, the
War Department, the Navy Department and the Veterans Administration.[6]

The degree to which these and other writers may have solicited
or responded to the suggestions of various groups is not clearly dis-
tinguishable in programming. "The Guiding Light," for instance,
was one of Miss Phillips' serials which remained throughout the war
period a story that was chiefly concerned with emotional entangle-
ments. The fact that this preoccupation could remain unchanged
while the program drew upon wartime vocabulary can be illustrated
with one incident taken from the continuing drama in which the
heroine, loving nothing more in life than her adopted child, finds
herself drawn toward a Captain on leave from the Army. Loving her
in return, he became exceedingly fond of the child without realizing
that it was the child of his divorced wife who had put the youngster
up for adoption at birth.

Nearly every writer had access to Radio Background Material, a
series of pamphlets released periodically by the Office of War Information. Most of these were factual and statistical outlines dealing
with such matters of governmental concern as rumors, conservation,
productivity, absenteeism and inflation. Occasional editorial reference was made to our international responsibilities in the post-war
tomorrow. Background material was dispatched from the OWI to

radio script writers three times each month. There was no compulsion to use this material but several writers considered the basic objective of such communication: to use radio less as escape and more as guidance in adjusting daily lives to the war.

One theme in particular found its way into the serials. The OWI hoping to bring the shortage of manpower into public consciousness, recommended that serial characters be portrayed as working in war factories or training for war jobs. Sally Farrell, costar of "Front Page Farrell," was one of the first to go to work in a war industry. Kitty Foyle assumed leadership of a factory making small parts for munitions. David Harum became manager of a munitions factory so did Mr. Young of "Pepper Young's Family." Lora Lawton was loved by a man who managed a large shipbuilding concern. Stella Dallas took a job in a war plant (soon becoming involved with secret formulas and enemy agents). Although the war was seldom mentioned in "When A Girl Marries," two weeks were once set aside to feature the character of a lawyer who represented a war factory and made speeches to the workers on the necessity of sticking to their jobs.

Perhaps the most direct example of a daytime serial paralleling the interests of governmental agencies was "Front Page Farrell," a program which was less than six months old at the time of Pearl Harbor and which consequently was somewhat more flexible in format and characterization than the older and more established serials. Author Robert Shaw derived much of his plot material from consultation with the OWI and the War Manpower Commission. The format of the series lent itself to the involvement of current affairs inasmuch as the fictional hero, David Farrell,[7] was a newspaperman (the "New York Eagle") in contact with all contemporary problems with which the American people were faced. The events, facts and figures discussed in the episodes were accurate, all scripts having been checked in advance by the OWI. One of Farrell's first wartime assignments was to develop a story on women in defense. During 1942 various episodes were centered around or touched upon such diverse topics as President Roosevelt's trip throughout the Nation, the possible conscription of women, the employment of New York workers by Henry J. Kaiser, Vice President Wallace's speech on the people's war, the significance of the battle of Stalingrad, refugee problems and lendlease. In October and November of 1942 an eight week sequence was devoted to labor piracy and the problems which resulted when essential manpower became unstable.

While it was unusual for established programs to concern themselves directly with the war, three attempts were made to utilize some of these programs more effectively without disrupting their basic continuity. The first two of these, "Victory Volunteers," and "Victory Front," were identical in technique and objective. Presented in cooperation with the OWI by NBC and CBS respectively, both series intended to provide war information in the form of entertainment by utilizing existing serials and showing how these familiar radio characters coped with current problems created by the war. Selected radio serials were scheduled on a one-week basis to present complete stories within five episodes at an additional hour under the new title; there was no connection whatever with the story development of the regular series except the established familiarity of the characters and settings. The writers, production crews and advertising agency supervisory personnel as well as performers donated their services for the particular week in which their program participated.

Both networks planned to commence this operation on October 12, 1942. CBS was delayed five weeks but "Victory Volunteers" was introduced by NBC on schedule at 10 a.m. Eastern War Time. "Stella Dallas" was the first of the serials chosen for this unique purpose, followed in turn by "Portia Faces Life," "Ma Perkins" and "Young Widder Brown." Clifton Fadiman, moderator of "Information Please" and Chairman of the War Writers Board, served as narrator for the series and read the government messages at the end of each fifteen-minute broadcast. Although the initial implication was that the experiment would extend indefinitely,[8] the series was discontinued after seven weeks.

"Victory Front" was introduced by CBS at 9:45 a.m. November 16, 1942, and it too was destined to last just seven weeks. "We Love and Learn" was the initial serial chosen to develop its particular five-day variation on the theme of price control. The heroine in this instance was a small town schoolteacher attempting to combat the menace of inflation. So grave was her concern about this problem that she had an illuminating dream in which she was given a glimpse of what would happen to the town if inflation raged unchecked. Thus fortified, she showed the townspeople what was required of them to avoid the dire consequences of her dream. "Our Gal Sunday," "Big Sister," "Life Can Be Beautiful" and "Aunt Jenny" participated during the short life of the OWI experiment which concluded January 1, 1943.

The third and final such innovation occurred on May 4, 1945. Again under the auspices of the OWI, NBC combined two daytime serials by the same author, Irna Phillips, "Today's Children" and "Women in White." Inasmuch as both programs lay within the same hour paid for by a single sponsor (to advertise competing brands of soap) the author was free to experiment in consolidating for dramatic purposes two distinctly separate groups of characters.[9] The special broadcast was prepared to dramatize the work being undertaken to rehabilitate war wounded.

New Serials

A similarly brief attempt was made to convey specific war information via serial drama by developing an original serial, "Give Us
This Day." Sponsored by the Department of Agriculture, this one-
week dramatization was designed to persuade listeners that food was
an important weapon of war, that farmers and food producers were
important, and why the rationing announced by Secretary Wickard
was so essential. The resulting five episodes were crowded with dramatic references to farm labor problems, the evils of the black market
and hoarding, the manner in which shortages of pails and fertilizer
can affect farmers and the importance of regulations on consumer
prices.

During the period between the bombing of Pearl Harbor and VJ
Day there were approximately thirty-one new daytime serials added
to the network schedules.[10] Of this total the majority conformed to
the stereotype of romantically discordant adventures, exemplified by
such titles as "Amanda of Honeymoon Hill," "We Love and Learn,"
"Lonely Women," "Now and Forever" and "This Life is Mine."
Only five of the thirty-one new serials concerned themselves with
the war in anything more than a superficial manner. The remainder,
if they employed wartime thematic material at all, repeated the simple technique of applying a slightly khaki tint to the dramatic structure. Even such specific innovations as "The Soldier Who Came
Home," beginning in 1942 with the adjustment problems faced by a
discharged serviceman, soon began sinking in melodramatic quick-
sand. By the Spring of 1945, under the new title of "Barry Cameron,"
the plot had become centered around Barry's wife, Anna. Anna was a
model for a large fashion magazine. The editor's son fell in love with
her despite the possessive tendencies of his mother who threatened
to put an end to Anna's career, etc. etc.

"Bright Horizons," on the other hand, represented change in the
opposite direction. Beginning about the same time as "The Soldier
Who Came Home," "Bright Horizons" initially ignored the war in
favor of plots and sub-plots involving homebreaking secretaries, am-
nesia, sudden illnesses requiring perilous operations and similar dramatic cliches typical of daytime radio. Late in 1944 the advertising
agency decided to revitalize the ailing series with an entirely new
story. Shifting locale from a small fictional town to Chicago, the emphasis was placed upon such contemporary problems as the returned
war veteran. The new hero became a tail gunner with a stiffened arm
whose mother wanted him to show off his medals and whose father
was clearly disappointed in his refusal to discuss war strategy. The
new format succeeded neither in attracting a larger audience or in

keeping the serial on the air; it was discontinued altogether at the end of the year.

Procter and Gamble introduced "Brave Tomorrow" in 1943, intending to provide war background from the standpoint of someone in the service. The story began with a rebound marriage in which the heroine accepted the proposal of a soldier about to be sent to a combat zone. He was sent instead to a succession of military camps, dutifully followed by his wife. Considering the competition from other daytime serials, this story of domestic hardship was later recalled by one Procter and Gamble executive as "the most ghastly dismal failure you ever saw." When the story became stalled in Texas for eight weeks during which time the heroine was unable to locate a set of dishes, the disgruntled P & G representative wired the advertising agency handling the program: "For God's sake, tell her there is still Sears and Roebuck!"

"A Woman of America," introduced in January of 1943 by the same sponsor, represented a more original approach to patriotic material in daytime drama. The story was set in 1865 and centered around the character of Prudence Dane, a young widow determined to travel west in search of opportunity and happiness for herself and her two sons. The long trek from Pennsylvania to Kansas occupied more than two years of 10-minute installments. Each episode was introduced by the contemporary character of Prudence Dane's great-granddaughter, Margaret (played by the same actress), observing that "today the women of America are once again fighting side by side with their men in the factories, farms and homes." Aided by a good cast which included Anne Seymour, Santos Ortego, Ken Delmar, Everett Sloane, and Julia King with singing portions by Dorothy Kirsten, "A Woman of America" attracted sufficient audience interest to remain on the air throughout the war. Immediately thereafter the format was completely revised to a twentieth century story about Prudence Dane Barker, a lineal descendant who was the editor of the *Danesville Courier* in the town founded by the original heroine. An entirely new cast became embroiled in a problem with the local mining syndicate, from which it proceeded to a succession of problems sufficient to keep the series on the air for another nine years.

The fourth serial, "Lighted Windows," represented perhaps too obvious an effort to portray the 100% American family in wartime. Father found his labor to be a source of great pride, working as he did in an aluminum plant (the new serial was, by small coincidence, sponsored by the Aluminum Company of America). Mother devoted all her spare time to the Red Cross. The 19-year-old son was an Army trainee at State College and Sister was a Nurses' Aid. Even little Brother delivered packages after school for the corner drugstore, thereby releasing a man for essential war work. Apparently more successful in communicating War Effort than in demonstrating dramatic effort, the series was concluded in five months despite a 52-week contract.

"Against the Storm" was the first radio serial to address itself to the war. It originated in October of 1939, and almost immediately included reference to what was happening in Europe. The series, which author Sandra Michaels referred to as a "radio novel," initially dealt with a woman married to a professor but soon shifted to one of the daughters, also married to a professor. The concerns of these various individuals extended far beyond the mythical boundaries of Harper University, beyond the customary small towns constituting the current state of daytime radio to include the world events and their possible significance to Americans. Despite winning a 1942 Peabody Award for radio drama, this unusual extension of story line was not uniformly applauded. A question was raised as to the efficacy of wandering far afield for subject matter; specific criticism held that a vast number of listeners wanted no part of the war. The program was cancelled Christmas day, 1942, replaced by "Snow Village." During its three-year tenure the series had attracted further attention by having Edgar Lee Masters read from his "Spoon River Anthology" on one occasion, and on another, John Masefield was picked up from London, supposedly reading his poetry to assembled students at Harper University.

In December of 1943 NBC added "The Open Door" to its weekday schedule. Sandra Michaels, having won more attention than job security as a result of the daytime serial's only Peabody Award, was given another opportunity to experiment with a responsible theme treated in serial fashion. For her central character she chose a college Dean with a purposeful interest in the problems facing young people in wartime. Dean Eric Hansen [12] was conceived as an intellectual-liberal who fought for various convictions. From time to time the script involved visiting soldiers who had returned from action, adding stronger appeal and a greater sense of urgency to the Dean's philosophy. Each broadcast of the series opened with a statement expressing its basic theme: "There is an open door to a good way of life to all men, for all men. This open door is called brotherhood, and over its portal are these simple words: 'I am my brother's keeper'."

CONCLUSION

In 1940, during the air raids on Britain, the BBC introduced a daytime radio serial entitled "The Blitzed Family Robinson." In addition to undergirding the morale of its listeners the objective of the serial was, via shortwave, to show the rest of the world the human side of Britain's crisis. Immediately after the war the popular program continued on the Home Service as "Family Robinson," utilizing its characters and dramatic format to educate the public to the new rationing system, veterans' benefits and related information.

The objectives of American radio serials were, in contrast, to sell consumer goods. Within this highly competitive area of commercial responsibility the producers of various daytime serials weighed the advisability of relating their popular programs to the war. Some chose not to do this at all, seeing no advantage and possible harm in changing the structure of programs which had so clearly demonstrated status quo success. The majority of producers and writers experimented with characters and episodes involving the war from time to time. At the very least these programs included messages urging housewives to cooperate with the war effort. Only a few serials attempted to concern themselves deeply with the war and, with even fewer exceptions, those which did so were not successful in attracting audiences sufficiently large or responsive to remain on the air.

In evaluating the relationship of soap operas to the war the conclusion must be that daytime radio drama fell far short of its potential to inform, inspire or motivate. At the same time it becomes apparent that audiences which listened to the most popular serials were provided with a considerable amount of information which was accurate and important. Through the presentation of guests, the occasional involvement of high-priority information within existing dramatic situations and the less frequent creation of special episodes centered around the war, the daytime radio serials rendered a substantial service to their listeners during World War II.

November 25, 1963.

"I've been to the mountaintop." April 3, 1968.

June 5, 1968.

May 15, 1972.

59

Edward R. Murrow

"ORCHESTRATED HELL" AND "BUCHENWALD"

December 3, 1943

> *Before dawn on December 3, 1943, Murrow returned to England from a bombing mission over Berlin. The same afternoon he reported the flight by short wave to America.*

Yesterday afternoon, the waiting was over. The weather was right; the target was to be the big city. The crew captains walked into the briefing room, looked at the maps and charts and sat down with their big celluloid pads on their knees. The atmosphere was that of a school and a church. The weatherman gave us the weather. The pilots were reminded that Berlin is Germany's greatest center of war production. The intelligence officer told us how many heavy and light ack-ack guns, how many searchlights we might expect to encounter. Then Jock, the wing commander, explained the system of markings, the kind of flare that would be used by the Pathfinders. He said that concentration was the secret of success in these raids, that as long as the aircraft stayed well bunched, they would protect each other. The captains of aircraft walked out.

I noticed that the big Canadian with the slow, easy grin had printed "Berlin" at the top of his pad and then embellished it with a scroll. The red-headed English boy with the two weeks' old moustache was the last to leave the room. Late in the afternoon we went to the locker room to draw parachutes, Mae Wests and all the rest. As we dressed, a couple of the Australians were whistling. Walking out to the bus that was to take us to the aircraft, I heard the station loudspeakers announcing that that evening all personnel would be able to see a film, *Star Spangled Rhythm*, free.

We went out and stood around a big, black, four-motored Lancaster *D for Dog*. A small station wagon delivered a thermos bottle of coffee, chewing gum, an orange and a bit of chocolate for each man. Up in that part of England the air hums and throbs with the sound of aircraft motors all day. But for half an hour before takeoff, the skies are

Edward Bliss, Jr. (ed.) *In Search of Light: The Broadcasts of Edward R. Murrow 1938–1961*, New York: Alfred A. Knopf, 1967, pp. 70–76 and 90–95; also available on "Edward R. Murrow, A Reporter Remembers, Volume One: The War Years" Columbia LP album 021 332.

dead, silent and expectant. A lone hawk hovered over the airfield, absolutely still as he faced into the wind. Jack, the tail gunner, said, "It would be nice if *we* could fly like that."

D for Dog eased around the perimeter track to the end of the runway. We sat there for a moment. The green light flashed and we were rolling—ten seconds ahead of schedule! The take-off was smooth as silk. The wheels came up, and *D-Dog* started the long climb. As we came up through the clouds, I looked right and left and counted fourteen black Lancasters climbing for the place where men must burn oxygen to live. The sun was going down, and its red glow made rivers and lakes of fire on tops of the clouds. Down to the southward, the clouds piled up to form castles, battlements and whole cities, all tinged with red.

Soon we were out over the North Sea. Dave, the navigator, asked Jock if he couldn't make a little more speed. We were nearly two minutes late. By this time we were all using oxygen. The talk on the intercom was brief and crisp. Everyone sounded relaxed. For a while the eight of us in our little world in exile moved over the sea. There was a quarter moon on the starboard beam. Jock's quiet voice came through the intercom, "That'll be flak ahead." We were approaching the enemy coast. The flak looked like a cigarette lighter in a dark room—one that won't light. Sparks but no flame. The sparks crackling just above the level of the cloud tops. We flew steady and straight, and soon the flak was directly below us.

D-Dog rocked a little from right to left, but that wasn't caused by the flak. We were in the slip stream of other Lancasters ahead, and we were over the enemy coast. And then a strange thing happened. The aircraft seemed to grow smaller. Jack in the rear turret, Wally, the mid-upper gunner; Titch, the wireless operator—all seemed somehow to draw closer to Jock in the cockpit. It was as though each man's shoulder was against the other's. The understanding was complete. The intercom came to life, and Jock said, "Two aircraft on the port beam." Jack in the tail said, "Okay, sir, they're Lancs." The whole crew was a unit and wasn't wasting words.

The cloud below was ten tenths. The blue-green jet of the exhausts licked back along the leading edge, and there were other aircraft all around us. The whole great aerial armada was hurling towards Berlin. We flew so for twenty minutes, when Jock looked up at a vapor trail curling across above us, remarking in a conversational tone that from the look of it he thought there was a fighter up there. Occasionally the angry red of ack-ack burst through the clouds, but it was far away, and we took only an academic interest. We were flying in the third wave. Jock asked Wally in the mid-upper turret and Jack in the rear turret if they were cold. They said they were all right, and thanked him for asking. Even asked how I was, and I said, "All right so far." The cloud was beginning to thin out. Up to the north we could see light, and the flak began to liven up ahead of it.

Boz, the bomb aimer, crackled through on the intercom, "There's a battle going on on the starboard beam." We couldn't see the aircraft, but we could see the jets of red tracer being exchanged. Suddenly there was a burst of yellow flame, and Jock remarked, "That's a fighter going down. Note the position." The whole thing was interesting, but remote. Dave, the navigator, who was sitting back with his maps, charts and compasses, said, "The attack ought to begin in exactly two minutes." We were still over the clouds. But suddenly those dirty gray clouds turned white. We were over the outer searchlight defenses. The clouds below us were white, and we were black. *D-Dog* seemed like a black bug on a white sheet. The flak began coming up, but none of it close. We were still a long way from Berlin. I didn't realize just how far.

Jock observed, "There's a kite on fire dead ahead." It was a great golden, slow-moving meteor slanting toward the earth. By this time we were about thirty miles from our target area in Berlin. That thirty miles was the longest flight I have ever made. Dead on time, Boz, the bomb aimer, reported, "Target indicators going down." The same moment the sky ahead was lit up by bright yellow flares. Off to starboard, another kite went down in flames. The flares were sprouting all over the sky—reds and greens and yellows—and we were flying straight for the center of the fireworks. *D-Dog* seemed to be standing still, the four propellers thrashing the air. But we didn't seem to be closing in. The clouds had cleared, and off to the starboard a Lanc was caught by at least fourteen searchlight beams. We could see him twist and turn and finally break out. But still the whole thing had a quality of unreality about it. No one seemed to be shooting at us, but it was getting lighter all the time. Suddenly a tremendous big blob of yellow light appeared dead ahead, another to the right and another to the left. We were flying straight for them.

Jock pointed out to me the dummy fires and flares to right and left. But we kept going in. Dead ahead there was a whole chain of red flares looking like stop lights. Another Lanc was coned on our starboard beam. The lights seemed to be supporting it. Again we could see those little bubbles of colored lead driving at it from two sides. The German fighters were at him. And then, with no warning at all, *D-Dog* was filled with an unhealthy white light. I was standing just behind Jock and could see all the seams on the wings. His quiet Scots voice beat into my ears, "Steady, lads, we've been coned." His slender body lifted half out of his seat as he jammed the control column forward and to the left. We were going down.

Jock was wearing woolen gloves with the fingers cut off. I could see his fingernails turn white as he gripped the wheel. And then I was on my knees, flat on the deck, for he had whipped the *Dog* back into a climbing turn. The knees should have been strong enough to support me, but they weren't, and the stomach seemed in some danger of letting me down, too. I picked myself up and looked out again. It seemed that one big searchlight, instead of being twenty thousand feet below, was mounted right on our wing tip. *D-Dog* was corkscrewing. As we rolled down on the other side, I began to see what was happening to Berlin.

The clouds were gone, and the sticks of incendiaries from the preceding waves made the place look like a badly laid out city with the street lights on. The small incendiaries was going down like a fistful of white rice thrown on a piece of black velvet. As Jock hauled the *Dog* up again, I was thrown to the other side of the cockpit, and there below were more incendiaries, glowing white and then turning red. The cookies—the four-thousand-pound high explosives—were bursting below like great sunflowers gone mad. And then, as we started down again, still held in the lights, I remembered that the *Dog* still had one of those cookies and a whole basket of incendiaries in his belly, and the lights still held us. And I was very frightened.

While Jock was flinging him about in the air, he suddenly flung over the intercom, "Two aircraft on the port beam." I looked astern and saw Wally, the mid-upper, whip his turret around to port and then look up to see a single-engined fighter slide just above us. The other aircraft was one of ours. Finally, we were out of the cone, flying level. I looked down, and the white fires had turned red. They were beginning to merge and spread, just like butter does on a hot plate. Jock and Boz, the bomb aimer, began to discuss the target. The smoke was getting thick down below. Boz said he liked the two green flares on the ground almost dead ahead. He began calling his directions. And just then a new bunch of big flares went down on the far side of the sea of flame and flare that seemed to be directly below us. He thought that would be a better aiming point. Jock agreed, and we flew on. The bomb doors were open. Boz called his directions, "Five left, five left." And then there was a gentle, confident, upward thrust under my feet, and Boz said, "Cookie gone." A few seconds later, the incendiaries went, and *D-Dog* seemed lighter and easier to handle.

I thought I could make out the outline of streets below. But the bomb aimer didn't agree, and he ought to know. By this time all those patches of white on black had turned yellow and started to flow together. Another searchlight caught us but didn't hold us. Then through the intercom came the word, "One can of incendiaries didn't clear. We're still carrying it." And Jock replied, "Is it a big one or a little one?" The word came back, "Little one, I think, but I'm not sure. I'll check." More of those yellow flares came down and hung about us. I haven't seen so much light since the war began. Finally the intercom announced that it was only a small container of incendiaries left, and Jock remarked, "Well, it's hardly worth going back and doing another run-up for that." If there had been a good fat bundle left, he would have gone back through that stuff and done it all over again.

I began to breathe and to reflect again—that all men would be brave if only they could leave their stomachs at home. Then there was a tremendous whoomp, an unintelligible shout from the tail gunner, and *D-Dog* shivered and lost altitude. I looked at the port side, and there was a Lancaster that seemed close enough to touch. He had whipped straight under us, missed us by twenty-five, fifty feet, no one knew how much. The navigator sang out the new course, and we were heading for home. Jock was doing what I had heard him tell his pilots to do so often—flying dead on course. He flew straight into a huge green searchlight and, as he rammed the throttles home, remarked, "We'll have a little trouble getting away from this one." And again *D-Dog* dove, climbed and twisted and was finally free. We flew level then. I looked on the port beam at the target area. There was a sullen, obscene glare. The fires seemed to have found each other—and we were heading home.

For a little while it was smooth sailing. We saw more battles. Then another plane in flames, but no one could tell whether it was ours or theirs. We were still near the target. Dave, the navigator, said, "Hold her steady, skipper. I want to get an astral site." And Jock held her steady. And the flak began coming up at us. It seemed to be very close. It was winking off both wings. But the *Dog* was steady. Finally Dave said, "Okay, skipper, thank you very much." And a great orange blob of flak smacked up straight in front of us. And Jock said, "I think they're shooting at us." I'd thought so for some time.

And he began to throw *D for Dog* up, around and about again. And when we were clear of the barrage, I asked him how close the bursts were and he said, "Not very close. When they're really near, you can smell 'em." That proved nothing, for I'd been holding my breath. Jack sang out from the rear turret, said his oxygen was getting low, thought maybe the lead had frozen. Titch, the wireless operator, went scrambling back with a new mask and a bottle of oxygen. Dave, the navigator, said, "We're crossing the coast." My mind went back to the time I had crossed that coast in 1938, in a plane that had taken off from Prague. Just ahead of me sat two refugees from Vienna—an old man and his wife. The co-pilot came back and told them that we were outside German territory. The old man reached out and grasped his wife's hand. The work that was done last night was a massive blow of retribution for all those who have fled from the sound of shots and blows on the stricken Continent.

We began to lose height over the North Sea. We were over England's shore. The land was dark beneath us. Somewhere down there below American boys were probably bombing-up Fortresses and Liberators, getting ready for the day's work. We were over the home field. We called the control tower, and the calm, clear voice of an English girl replied, "Greetings, *D-Dog*. You are diverted to Mule Bag."[Code for an airfield.] We swung around, contacted Mule Bag, came in on the flare path, touched down very gently, ran along to the end of the runway and turned left. And Jock, the finest pilot in Bomber Command, said to the control tower, "*D-Dog* clear of runway."

When we went in for interrogation, I looked on the board and saw that the big, slow-smiling Canadian and the red-headed English boy with the two weeks' old moustache hadn't made it. They were missing. There were four reporters on this operation—two of them didn't come back. Two friends of mine—Norman Stockton, of Australian Associated Newspapers, and Lowell Bennett, an American representing International News Service. There is something of a tradition amongst reporters that those who are prevented by circumstances from filing their stories will be covered by their colleagues. This has been my effort to do so.

[*Bennett survived the raid. He parachuted and was held prisoner by the Germans until May* 1945.]

In the aircraft in which I flew, the men who flew and fought it poured into my ears their comments on fighters, flak and flares in the same tones they would have used in reporting a host of daffodils. I have no doubt that Bennett and Stockton would have given you a better report of last night's activities.

Berlin was a kind of orchestrated hell, a terrible symphony of light and flame. It isn't a pleasant kind of warfare—the men doing it speak of it as a job. Yesterday afternoon, when the tapes were stretched out on the big map all the way to Berlin and back again, a young pilot with old eyes said to me, "I see we're working again tonight." That's the frame of mind in which the job is being done. The job isn't pleasant; it's terribly tiring. Men die in the sky while others are roasted alive in their cellars. Berlin last night wasn't a pretty sight. In about thirty-five minutes it was hit with about three times the amount of stuff that ever came down on London in a night-long blitz. This is a calculated, remorseless campaign of destruction. Right now the mechanics are probably working on *D-Dog*, getting him ready to fly again.

April 15, 1945

During the last week, I have driven more than a few hundred miles through Germany, most of it in the Third Army sector—Wiesbaden, Frankfurt, Weimar, Jena and beyond. It is impossible to keep up with this war. The traffic flows down the super-highways, trucks with German helmets tied to the radiators and belts of machine-gun ammunition draped from fender to fender. The tanks on the concrete roads sound like a huge sausage machine, grinding up sheets of corrugated iron. And when there is a gap between convoys, when the noise dies away, there is another small noise, that of wooden-soled shoes and of small iron tires grating on the concrete. The power moves forward, while the people, the slaves, walk back, pulling their small belongings on anything that has wheels.

There are cities in Germany that make Coventry and Plymouth appear to be merely damage done by a petulant child, but bombed houses have a way of looking alike, wherever you see them.

But this is no time to talk of the surface of Germany. Permit me to tell you what you would have seen, and heard, had you been with me on Thursday. It will not be pleasant listening. If you are at lunch, or if you have no appetite to hear what Germans have done, now is a good time to switch off the radio, for I propose to tell you of Buchenwald. It is on a small hill about four miles outside Weimar, and it was one of the largest concentration camps in Germany, and it was built to last. As we approached it, we saw about a hundred men in civilian clothes with rifles advancing in open order across the fields. There were a few shops; we stopped to inquire. We were told that some of the prisoners had a couple of SS men cornered in there. We drove on, reached the main gate. The prisoners crowded up behind the wire. We entered.

And now, let me tell this in the first person, for I was the least important person there, as you shall hear. There surged around me an evil-smelling horde. Men and boys reached out to touch me; they were in rags and the remnants of uniform. Death had already marked many of them, but they were smiling with their eyes. I looked out over that mass of men to the green fields beyond where well-fed Germans were ploughing.

A German, Fritz Kersheimer, came up and said, "May I show you round the camp? I've been here ten years." An Englishman stood to attention, saying, "May I introduce myself, delighted to see you, and can you tell me when some of our blokes will be along?" I told him soon and asked to see one of the barracks. It happened to be occupied by Czechoslovakians. When I entered, men crowded around, tried to lift me to their shoulders. They were too weak. Many of them could not get out of bed. I was told that this building had once stabled eighty horses. There were twelve hundred men in it, five to a bunk. The stink was beyond all description.

When I reached the center of the barracks, a man came up and said, "You remember me. I'm Peter Zenkl, one-time mayor of Prague." I remembered him, but did not recognize him. He asked about Benes and Jan Masaryk. I asked how many men had died in that building during the last month. They called the doctor; we inspected his records. There were only names in the little black book, nothing more—nothing of who these men were, what they had done, or hoped. Behind the names of those who had died there was a cross. I counted them. They totalled 242. Two hundred and forty-two out of twelve hundred in one month.

As I walked down to the end of the barracks, there was applause from the men too weak to get out of bed. It sounded like the hand clapping of babies; they were so weak. The doctor's name was Paul Heller. He had been there since 1938.

As we walked out into the courtyard, a man fell dead. Two others—they must have been over sixty—were crawling toward the latrine. I saw it but will not describe it.

In another part of the camp they showed me the children, hundreds of them. Some were only six. One rolled up his sleeve, showed me his number. It was tattooed on his arm. D-6030, it was. The others showed me their numbers; they will carry them till they die.

An elderly man standing beside me said, "The children, enemies of the state." I could see their ribs through their thin shirts. The old man said, "I am Professor Charles Richer of the Sorbonne." The children clung to my hands and stared. We crossed to the courtyard. Men kept coming up to speak to me and to touch me, professors from Poland, doctors from Vienna, men from all Europe. Men from the countries that made America.

We went to the hospital; it was full. The doctor told me that two hundred had died the day before. I asked the cause of death; he shrugged and said, "Tuberculosis, starvation, fatigue, and there are many who have no desire to live. It is very difficult." Dr. Heller pulled back the blankets from a man's feet to show me how swollen they were. The man was dead. Most of the patients could not move.

As we left the hospital I drew out a leather billfold, hoping that I had some money which would help those who lived to get home. Professor Richer from the Sorbonne said, "I should be careful of my wallet if I were you. You know there are criminals in this camp, too." A small man tottered up, saying, "May I feel the leather, please? You see, I used to make good things of leather in Vienna." Another man said, "My name is Walter Roeder. For many years I lived in Joliet. Came back to Germany for a visit and Hitler grabbed me."

I asked to see the kitchen; it was clean. The German in charge had been a Communist, had been at Buchenwald for nine years, had a picture of his daughter in Hamburg. He hadn't seen her for almost twelve years, and if I got to Hamburg, would I look her up? He showed me the daily ration—one piece of brown bread about as thick as your thumb, on top of it a piece of margarine as big as three sticks of chewing gum. That, and a little stew, was what they received every twenty-four hours. He had a chart on the wall; very complicated it was. There were little red tabs scattered through it. He said that was to indicate each ten men who died. He had to account for the rations, and he added, "We're very efficient here."

We went again into the courtyard, and as we walked we talked. The two doctors, the Frenchman and the Czech, agreed that about six thousand had died during March. Kersheimer, the German, added that back in the winter of 1939, when the Poles began to arrive without winter clothing, they died at the rate of approximately nine hundred a day. Five different men asserted that Buchenwald was the best concentration camp in Germany; they had had some experience of the others.

Dr. Heller, the Czech, asked if I would care to see the crematorium. He said it wouldn't be very interesting because the Germans had run out of coke some days ago and had taken to dumping the bodies into a great hole nearby. Professor Richer said perhaps I would care to see the small courtyard. I said yes. He turned and told the children to stay behind. As we walked across the square I noticed that the professor had a hole in his left shoe and a toe sticking out of the right one. He followed my eyes and said, "I regret that I am so little presentable, but what can one do?" At that point another Frenchman came up to announce that three of his fellow countrymen outside had killed three S.S. men and taken one prisoner. We proceeded to the small courtyard. The wall was about eight feet high; it adjoined what had been a stable or garage. We entered. It was floored with concrete. There were two rows of bodies stacked up like cordwood. They were thin and very white. Some of the bodies were terribly bruised, though there seemed to be little flesh to bruise. Some had been shot through the head, but they bled but little. All except two were naked. I tried to count them as best I could and arrived at the conclusion that all that was mortal of more than five hundred men and boys lay there in two neat piles.

There was a German trailer which must have contained another fifty, but it wasn't possible to count them. The clothing was piled in a heap against the wall. It appeared that most of the men and boys had died of starvation; they had not been executed. But the manner of death seemed unimportant. Murder had been done at Buchenwald. God alone knows how many men and boys have died there during the last twelve years. Thursday I was told that there were more than twenty thousand in the camp. There had been as many as sixty thousand. Where are they now?

As I left that camp, a Frenchman who used to work for Havas in Paris came up to me and said, "You will write something about this, perhaps?" And he added, "To write about this you must have been here at least two years, and after that—you don't want to write any more."

I pray you to believe what I have said about Buchenwald. I have reported what I saw and heard, but only part of it. For most of it I have no words. Dead men are plentiful in war, but the living dead, more than twenty thousand of them in one camp. And the country round about was pleasing to the eye, and the Germans were well fed and well dressed. American trucks were rolling toward the rear filled with prisoners. Soon they would be eating American rations, as much for a meal as the men at Buchenwald received in four days.

If I've offended you by this rather mild account of Buchenwald, I'm not in the least sorry. I was there on Thursday, and many men in many tongues blessed the name of Roosevelt. For long years his name had meant the full measure of their hope. These men who had kept close company with death for many years did not know that Mr. Roosevelt would within hours, join their comrades who had laid their lives on the scales of freedom.

Back in 1941, Mr. Churchill said to me with tears in his eyes, "One day the world and history will recognize and acknowledge what it owes to your President." I saw and heard the first installment of that at Buchenwald on Thursday. It came from men from all over Europe. Their faces, with more flesh on them, might have been found anywhere at home. To them the name "Roosevelt" was a symbol, the code word for a lot of guys named "Joe" who are somewhere out in the blue with the armor heading east. At Buchenwald they spoke of the President just before he died. If there be a better epitaph, history does not record it.

I believe that no mass journalism in history has lived up to its responsibilities as well as have American network television news organizations. But we need to find some innovations without lowering our standards. There is only a limited professional satisfaction in informing people who have gone to sleep.
    --Harry Reasoner, *ABC Evening News*, June 13, 1974.

60

Bernard Lucich

THE LUX RADIO THEATER

THE *Lux Radio Theater* of the Air began in New York in October, 1934, and ran for 21 consecutive years. Throughout its lifespan, the program was sponsored by Lever Brothers, makers of Lux Soap. During its beginning period, the program presented refurbished stage plays, usually very old ones. This first year, Lux Theater was on the NBC network on Sunday afternoons at 2:30. Then, in 1934, the program was replaced on NBC by the Radio Guild, and Lux moved to CBS at a new time and day—Monday evenings at 9:00. It remained at this time until the 1954–1955 season.

Later in 1935, the production of the show was handed over to Cecil B. DeMille, who moved the show to Hollywood, to present the "cream of Hollywood's crop of screen productions, neatly packaged and cased for delivery on the air." [1] Thus the idea of presenting radio adaptations of the best movies, using the original stars, was developed.

When the program was moved from New York, it had a regular audience of 13 million. The experts warned DeMille that no one would listen to one full hour of drama. DeMille replied, "Let's try anyway." Shortly afterward, the audience rose to over 30 million.

The show never used an original script. When asked why not, DeMille replied, "When you are giving a show for 30 million people, you don't dare be original. You have to know what you are showing is liked. It could only be your own opinion that an untried show was good." However, three best-selling stories—"Dark Victory," "How Green Was My Valley," and "This Above All" were used before pictures of them had been produced.

The show's plays were of all kinds; no concession was made to family tastes. Dramas, musicals and farces all were used. The most popular plays, however, were those which were supposed to appeal more directly to women: shows like "Dark Victory," "The Constant Nymph," and "Wuthering Heights."

The series drew constant raves from critics throughout these first 10 years that DeMille produced the program. Then in 1945, DeMille was replaced as producer by William Keighley. Keighley's attitude toward the show was that it was "good, solid, clean entertainment in which nothing is ever used to offend." [2]

When the *Lux Theater* series celebrated its 15th anniversary on the air in 1949, some statistics were collated. During the 15 years, over 500 top Hollywood stars had appeared in some 650 shows, with 39,120 pages of script, 14,344 musical cues, and 69,460 sound effects.

Many critics attribute the initial success of the series to Cecil B. DeMille. He seemed to be the perfect liaison man between the movies and radio since he had a background in both. In his capacity as producer, he also appeared as the "host" for every program. In 1945, DeMille left radio because of a fight with the American Federation of Radio Artists for refusing to pay a $1 union assessment for a political fund. This was when William Keighley became producer-host. Keighley formerly was a Hollywood producer and during the war served as a colonel in charge of the Army Air Force motion picture services.

George Wells was script writer for the first nine years of the series, but then left radio and went to write for the movies. Sanford Barnett, formerly a director, then took over Wells' position. Fred MacKaye, one of the regular actors on the show, then moved in as director.

DeMille asserted that no Hollywood stars of importance except Chaplin and Garbo had not been on the program at one time or another. Those who were most popular and consequently used most often were Bob Hope, Loretta Young, Barbara Stanwyck, William Powell, Walter Pidgeon, Greer Garson, Hedy Lamarr, Ronald Colman, Claudette Colbert, Don Ameche, and Fred MacMurray. Long lines of autograph hunters would wait for the stars to leave after the shows. Probably the lines were the longest for Roddy McDowall who appeared in "My Friend Flicka."

An attempt was always made to get the stars from the original show, but sometimes they were not available and substitutes were used. This fact wasn't advertised—in fact it was played down. However, occasionally DeMille did allow some mention of it on the show, as, for example, once Alan Ladd apologized for taking Humphrey Bogart's place in "Casablanca" when Bogart was in Italy.

It was difficult to get the stars to appear in the early years, for many of the big stars would not bother with radio at all. However, this was the area in which DeMille probably helped the program most by being able to convince these stars to appear. By the time DeMille left, the series had become well established and there was no problem getting the people to appear.

The *Lux Radio Theater* also had some "firsts" in regard to talent on the show. It broke ground in radio by casting such opera stars as Lawrence Tibbett, Lily Pons, and Helen Jepson in their first acting roles. The program signed radio comics Jack Benny and Burns & Allen for their "first dramatic parts." And Lux also induced Ronald Colman and Shirley Temple, "long holdouts from radio," to make their debuts on the air.

Each show generally had four rehearsals before the actual on-the-air performance. DeMille didn't work through the first three rehearsals. He would look over the script on Wednesdays, and then would not make an appearance until the full dress rehearsal on Sunday, given in the Vine Street Theater in Hollywood. DeMille's opening and closing remarks were prepared even though the radio audience thought they were extemporaneous.

Initially, the salaries paid to actors and actresses were low and the program had to depend on the nonfamous actors. For example, before Joan Fontaine and Alan Ladd were famous, they received $250 and $100 a show, respectively. However, by 1944, the top price for a star was $5,000. The cost of the program was then $30,000 per week, which includes the stars' salaries, DeMille's, and some 25 others who gave full- or parttime. De Mille's salary was tops of course, as his name became synonomous with the show. Later production costs of the program went up considerably as actors' salaries began rising. This fact was undoubtedly one of the reasons for the ending of the series some years later.

When the programs were done the first year at NBC, no studio audiences were permitted. The producer then, Vernon Radcliffe, felt that a studio audience would interfere with the actors' performances.[3] However, when the program moved to Hollywood, DeMille welcomed the studio audiences. The Hollywood Theater seated only 1,400, so that only a handful of the devoted audience could see the stars in the flesh. To make up to the audience, CBS then distributed brochures on stars' "mike mannerisms." Some of these included were: Bing Crosby—"Always rehearses with his pipe clenched between his teeth, even when singing; Robert Cummings—"Reads lines from a semi-crouch, like a boxer," Joan Crawford—"A microphone-clutcher"; Barbara Stanwyck—"A shoe-taker-offer"; and Don Ameche, who drank a pint of milk before every performance.

Once DeMille was snowbound on his ranch in Little Tujunga a couple of hours before he was due for the on-the-air performance. He borrowed a mule to take him to a place where he could rent a car, and made it to the studio on time. On another occasion, a bee stung a performer as she was entering the theater. She refused to go on until the bee was removed from the theater. The wife of a famous star, in her first radio performance, dropped her script and spent several seconds bewailing the fact before someone thought to turn off the mike.

During the years the *Lux Radio Theater* was on the air, it had the highest Hooper rating for its time period. Most of the time, no program was near it in popularity. The closest was in 1935–36 when *Lux* had a rating of 13.6 and the *Vick Open House* was at 12.7. From that time on, the *Lux Theater* almost doubled the rating of its nearest competitor. Probably the most successful of the competitors were *Dr. I.Q.* and the *Telephone Hour.*

For the first nine years it was voted the best radio dramatic show in the country by a poll conducted by a large New York newspaper. Radio and motion picture magazines also voted it tops in its field.

The 1954–1955 season was the final chapter in this dramatic series. The early 1950s witnessed the rise of television and the subsequent decline in the network radio night-time audience. Production costs were on the rise and the program could no longer draw enough of an audience to make it financially profitable. Another factor was that the *Lux Video Theater* began on NBC television in 1954–55 at a cost of $5.5 million a year.[4]

In 1955 the *Hallmark Hall of Fame* also went off radio after seven seasons and network radio was left without any "prestige drama." It was now the "Golden Age" of television drama.

61

Martin J. Maloney

THE RADIO MYSTERY PROGRAM

THE ACTIVE life of the U.S. radio mystery was approximately a quarter-century, from 1925 to 1950; this was followed by a few years of galvanic twitching by the ossifying programming department of the radio networks. But the last mystery series was gone long before Ma Perkins crumbled into dust during the difficult season of 1960–1961.

During recent years some of the original *Shadow* and *Green Hornet* programs have been syndicated and rebroadcast around the country; but this seems a display of antiquarianism, rather like listening to old Gallagher and Shean records on a 1921 windup Victrola.

If we contemplate the true and vital period of the radio mystery, from 1925 to 1950, and try to draw from our observations any conclusions of historic significance, we are likely to be driven back at once on the notions of Marshall McLuhan, who says, in a pair of seemingly (but only seemingly) contradictory aphorisms that (a) the content of a new medium is an old medium and (b) the medium is the message.

Reducing these gnomic utterances to the scope of our present inquiry, we might translate as follows. (A) Voice radio, when abruptly converted, around 1920, from a kind of superior telegraph to a means of public communication, had nothing to say—anymore than the telegraph itself had, in the day of Thoreau and Samuel F. B. Morse. Radio in the United States at once became a fad, a source of public amusement. And, like all new human institutions, radio marched backward into the future, sucking in its content from old vaudevilles, dramas, band concerts, minstrel shows, newspaper columns and dime novels. One of the delicacies it sucked in, from many sources, was the mystery story. (B) Once radio had drawn the mystery into its peculiar and special system, the content became the medium. The radio mystery was not print, film or theater, but radio—a special kind of communication in a special kind of language. There was nothing quite like it before, and—despite the inevitable tendency of the mass arts to adapt and plagarize—there has been nothing quite like it since.

The mystery story as it existed in 1920 was in one sense a very recent phenomenon, but in another a very old one. If we consider that the essential mythos of the story deals with flight and pursuit, with crime and punishment, which seems reasonable enough, then we are faced with instances ranging from the branded Cain to Captain Ahab and the monster whale, from Dante seeking Beatrice through Hell and Purgatory to the immortal stars and on to the search of Telemachus for his missing G.I. father. No doubt these great works set forth in palpable and varied forms a cluster of the most ancient human archetypes; but so does the Sherlock Holmes canon.

There are indeed occasional works and fragments produced before 1800 which are authentic enough mystery tales: the Old Testament tale of Daniel and the priests of Bal, an episode of Voltaire's "Zadig," are examples. But in fact, as a genre, the mystery story had to wait on the invention of a police force—a group of men professionally committed to solving puzzles involving human guilt, crime, and responsibility. Sir Robert Peel organized the first true police force in London, in the year 1829—the same year in which a young Baltimorean, Edgar Allan Poe, published a collection of poems called "Al Aaraf." Twelve years later, this same Poe published in *Graham's Magazine*, of which he was editor, a story of his own called "The Murders in the Rue Morgue." This was not only the first true detective story; it also presented readers with a pair of murders as gruesome and bloody as ever turned up in a pre-code comic book.

From this story—and from the other few which Poe wrote—came an amazingly durable and popular genre, somewhat slow in developing perhaps, but extremely long-lived. There were two important strands in the development. One originated with Conan Doyle's invention of Sherlock Holmes, who appeared first in the great *Study in*

Scarlet, in 1887. The other grew out of the dime novels—the cheap popular fiction of America's Gilded Age—which provided the world with Old Sleuth, Old King Brady, and Nick Carter. The influence of these stories, and their many imitations, was world-wide and enormous. With reference to Holmes, I need only refer you to the publication, in Heidelberg, 1914, of Freidrich Depkens' critical study called *Sherlock Holmes, Raffles und Ihre Vorgilder: Ein Beitrag sur Entwicklungsgeschichte und Technik der Kriminalerzählung.* And as for the dime novel heroes, I cite an anecdote told by the American lecturer Stoddard, as relayed by James Thurber: an American tourist in Paris around the turn of the century, when set upon by a gang of apaches, was able to disperse them in terror simply by calling out, "Je suis Nick Carter!"

So by the 1920s there was a rich, multi-lingual, multi-cultural pool of popular myths on the subject of crime and detection, dramatized in a hundred heroes, a thousand villains: Holmes and Professor Moriarity, Sir Denis Mayland Smith and the insidious Dr. Fu Manchu, Hercule Poirot and Inspector Hanaud and Charlie Chan. Most of these creations were of British and American provenance, and some were already finding their way from print into the film form. They were, of course, highly accessible to American radio, once the medium had gone through its early stage of simple faddishness and was able to offer reasonably sophisticated entertainments.

American radio encountered some serious early obstacles in doing dramatic performances of any sort. The earliest entrepreneurs hit on the simple idea of putting microphones on stage in a theater and broadcasting what happened when a play was performed. This technique, especially when combined with such classics of theater literature as "Craig's Wife," seem to have produced an effect so profoundly confusing that not even radio audiences of the early 1920s would hold still for it. The next radio assault on drama consisted, in effect, of simple vaudeville dialogue routines—usually dialect sketches—done in a studio. No special production was required. The routines had usually been well-tested on the vaudeville stage, and sometimes on records; the performers were vocally nimble, and they could be kept predictably on mike. Thus came into being, and a sort of immortality, *The Goldbergs* and the Correll and Gosden *Sam 'n' Henry,* later to be known as *Amos 'n' Andy.*

The mystery play was more difficult; on the stage and in films, it required a good deal of production machinery—for example, "The Cat and the Canary" and "Seven Keys to Baldpate." The production machinery for radio, such as sound effects, musical stingers and sound distorting devices, had to be invented. To the best of my knowledge, one of the earliest—perhaps the earliest—tries at the radio mystery was made on WMAQ, Chicago, in the mid-1920s. The station was then partially owned by the Chicago *Daily News*, so that the author of the drama, logically enough, was Robert Casey, who was better known as a foreign correspondent. This drama did employ sound effects—including, one hopes, a creaking door.

The last viable mystery series on network radio was *Yours Truly, Johnny Dollar*—one of the highly formalized, even ritualistic, private eye series which adorned the last days of radio network entertainment.*

Between Bob Casey's opus and *Johnny Dollar* came a rich offering of mystery series, most of them directly adapted from other media, and the rest—to put the matter politely—well within established forms in the genre. *Sherlock Holmes* was an obvious adaptation from print as were *Philo Vance, Mr. and Mrs. North, The Saint*, and *Murder and Mr. Malone*, and of course, *Dr. Fu Manchu*. *Nick Carter, Master Detective* came from the dime novels, via Street and Smith Publications; and I regret to say that there was a sort of spin-off of this series called *Chick Carter, Boy Detective*. (Chick was an adopted son of Nick.) The towering figure of *The Shadow* was developed in radio as a device for narrating mystery stories, but came alive with such vigor that he became the hero of his own tales and in addition kept a pulp magazine running for years. *True Detective Mysteries* and *Official Detective* came, more or less, from factual crime publications popular at the time, and *This is Your FBI* came ostensibly, from J. Edgar Hoover, who appeared on the first program of the series in 1945. Dashiell Hammett contributed *Sam Spade* and *The Thin Man*—and then, by a sort of natural dialectic, *The Fat Man*. When, toward the end of this historic period, it was discovered that Hammett actually understood the Marxist dialectic and thought rather well of it, these offerings disappeared abruptly.

Whatever the sources of these radio mysteries, they were rapidly converted into more-or-less pure radio. I think that the observation is quite true, and that the conversion or absorption worked in two ways, the ways being closely inter-twined: first, radio in working on these materials was wildly imaginative, or it was nothing; second, radio as a medium was as abstract as the paintings of a Bracque or a Picasso, and really could not be otherwise. What has happened to American radio, since the great transformation of the 1950s, is that it has been pushed into at least three rather specialized roles, two of which are not new. Top-40 radio has, as numerous critics have ob-

---

* But there were periodic revivals. ABC tried drama five nights a week in 1964 and NBC did several experimental suspense plays that same year. A number of 1950s programs enjoyed some popularity in syndication, 1963–1965, including *The Green Hornet, The Shadow, The Lone Ranger*, and several British productions. In 1973 a new series called *Zero Hour* produced by the Hollywood Radio Theatre began on Mutual and CBS introduced the seven nights a week *CBS Mystery Theater* in 1974.

served, become a jukebox into which you need not feed quarters; talk radio seems to be the modern equivalent of the old-fashioned partyline telephone; the rock stations appear to be creating a sort of total-environment sound narcosis, not unlike the shock and narcosis therapies of psychiatry, which is certainly new, and possibly artistically interesting, but which requires either great fortitude or the vigor of youth to endure. But radio from the late 1920s until the late 1940s was a *primary* medium of communication in the United States, not pressed into specialized roles of any sort, relatively free to develop according to its own requirements. What was the nature of these requirements, as revealed in the radio mystery drama?

First, abstractness. Radio in trying to depict human experience—the look and feel and taste of things, the appearance and actions of people—can only rely on human voices, manufactured or recorded sounds, and musical effects. We cannot see Holmes, or sniff the London fog; we can only hear the words exchanged, or a tugboat hooting on the Thames. Sometimes the abstraction was clumsy and naive, as in Pam North's classic and much imitated line: "Look out, Jerry! He's got a gun!" But the Shadow's line was infinitely better: "Who knows what evil lurks in the hearts of men?" And the creaking door on *Inner Sanctum* really did create a mansion, a whole universe, of pleasurable terror.

Jack Webb's *Dragnet* series came late to radio and pretended to a sort of super-naturalism, in which no cop scratched his head or handcuffed a suspect without the appropriate sound effect. But the series suggested its effects through highly skilled sound abstractions, all the same. There was one episode in which Friday and his partner, Sergeant Ben Romero, were after a salesman of pornographic comic books who was working the local schoolgrounds. They locate the fellow's room, and find a box full of his merchandise. Friday picks up a copy of one of the books and begins to turn the pages. Romero is looking over his shoulder. For at least two minutes you hear almost nothing but small sounds of rustling paper and half-articulate grunts. There may have been two intelligible lines of dialogue. It was a great radio scene.

Second, imagination. Radio of this sort was nothing if its abstract cues could not provoke a listener's imagination; and since radio was genuinely a mass medium, intended to reach almost everyone, the tendency was toward the wild, the fantastic, the weird. At its best the radio mystery was as formal and ritualized as a Chinese play—as in the case of private-eye dramas like *Sam Spade* and *Richard Diamond*—or it was completely out of this world, as in *The Shadow* or *Inner Sanctum*. Lamont Cranston did well enough in print, but he was really a creature of sound, as weird and impalpable as the friendly Blue Coal dealer who brought him to you on Sundays. Orson Welles may have thought that he was doing better radio in his *Mercury Theater* productions, but he wasn't. *The Shadow* was one of the high points in his career.

It is perhaps worth noting, that although the mystery story was naturally preempted by television when radio faltered, it has not done as well in the new medium, and has certainly not survived in the same form.

Watching the TV series, *Mission: Impossible*, I thought about a long-dead radio series written by Carleton E. Morse, called *I Love a Mystery*. It featured the adventures of three durable fellows who went around solving crimes and righting wrongs: namely, Jack Packard, who was bright; Doc Long, who could pick locks; and Reggie Yorke, who was very strong. They had a beautiful secretary named Gerry Booker, and see, the reason they were against wrong-doing was, they had met in this Chinese jail and survived the bombing of Shanghai, so they were against bad guys. The whole show made a lot of sense to me at the time; and while I was thinking about it, the *Mission: Impossible* people were wiring all these circuits together and cutting little holes in walls, and I'm not sure that even *they* knew what they were doing.

As McLuhan says, television is a cool medium, sometimes chilly. Radio in the 1930s and 1940s was something else again. I often miss it, especially the mysteries.

62

David T. MacFarland

UP FROM MIDDLE AMERICA:
THE DEVELOPMENT OF TOP 40

IN THE 1950s, as network radio service declined with the advent of television, local stations began to search for alternative programming. Every aspect of the business was changing. Audiences, sales, job opportunities, even the philosophy of program regulation were in upheaval. Many independent stations in the 1940s had been featuring "music-and-news," which was basically disc jockey programs interspersed with regular news reports.[1]

Top 40 as developed in the 1950s by the major radio station group owners was a refinement of music-and-news. Four station groups whose initial station purchases were primarily in the Midwest and South led the way: Todd Storz, Gordon McLendon, Gerald Bartell and the stations licensed to the Plough pharmaceutical firm.[2] Other station owners, many of whom were new in broadcasting, adopted Top 40 because it was inexpensive, seemed to interest a large audience, and certainly was easier to produce than traditional live programming. The latter was becoming less available both on networks and on local stations.

Disc jockey shows, although adopted by the networks for a brief period in the 1950s, had been local program fare throughout the history of radio. Several non-network "deejays" had also become nationally known for their chatter and platter selections. New York's independent WNEW featured Martin Block, who in 1935 began *Make-Believe Ballroom*. The *New Yorker* described Block's show as "gaily creating the illusion that the country's foremost dance bands are performing on four large stands in a glittering, crystal-chandeliered ballroom." In reality, the show came from "an unglittering studio that contains little more than a microphone flanked by two phonograph turntables." [3] Block's sincere, low-key approach earned him in excess of $100,000 a year in the mid-1940s, and spawned hundreds of imitators.

Top 40 eventually became associated with rock and roll music, but early practitioners varied their musical selections. They depended mostly on the popular hits of the day but used other music to broaden the audience appeal. Music selection was the major factor identifying a Top 40 format, although other program features were essential for the total program "sound." The leader in defining an explicit policy of record selection was the Storz station group.

The evolution of musical selection started in late 1949 on the Storz daytime station in Omaha (KOWH) which played only popular music.

"Music monitors" were hired by some stations to check the competition's playlist. Stations conducted surveys of record sales and juke box plays until they found that dealers and distributors were "hyping" the popularity figures to manipulate sales. Increasingly, station owners sought to avoid such manipulation by depending on national charts and newsletters to decide a record's popularity. Management's determination to be in control of music selection was in many cases an effective antidote to the conditions on which "payola" depended: i.e., the disc jockey choosing his own music.

A programmer worked for a "total station sound" and periodically would spend an entire day, often locked in a local motel room, monitoring his station, recording errors, preparing critiques on music selection, and evaluating disc jockeys. It became axiomatic that there should not be a moment of dead air and that no disc jockey should talk for more than a few seconds. It was the personality of the station, not the announcer, that was important. The sound had to be bright, involved, and constantly full of excitement—never a dull moment. The criterion for success was metro share, and disc jockeys were sometimes paid based on their ratings success. McLendon's stations were among those which conducted their own rating surveys and evaluated disc jockeys according to results.

SUMMARY OF DEVELOPMENT OF TOP 40 MUSIC POLICIES

Pre-1949 (and also after, on non-Top 40 stations)	—Currently popular music mixed with other types.
Late 1949—early 1950	—Omaha, KOWH, concentrates on pop music.
The first Top 40 Show —about 1953, with the purchase by Storz of WTIX, New Orleans—and also on KOWH, Omaha.	—Block-programming of hit tunes (but sometimes different versions); otherwise popular music.
(Date not certain)	—Selecting one "best" version of a hit song, to the exclusion of others.
(Date not certain)	—Playing from the Top 40 list outside of the "countdown" program block.
1956— first on KOWH and then on other Storz stations	—The true limited playlist—most popular records heard most often.

One of the keys to keeping the Top 40 sound consistent was a "clock hour" formula that specified every element of programming. In the case of music-and-news stations, the formula was so loose as to be virtually identical with the format—a wide variety of music, a disc jockey host, news, commercials, public service announcements, and a number of station promotions (or IDs). Segments on many early music-and-news stations were sponsored by one firm, with the music often selected *by* that firm. In contrast, the Top 40 station's strict formula was built around a "clock hour" which called for certain elements to occur at very carefully prescribed times. For example, a Top 40 station might specify that the song played at the "top" of the hour be a hit from the top ten and that its rhythm be uptempo. The next record might also be a hit, or perhaps a "hitbound" or a familiar "oldie," but whatever the variation, each different type of music to be played would be prescribed. In addition, stations with "clock" formats scheduled times for non-musical features such as weather, traffic reports, sports scores and even news bulletins. The "clock" format was later adopted by many stations that would not describe themselves as "formula" operations. One company actually sold a timer that flashed a light to remind the DJ to give the station call letters every few minutes and to keep the sound moving. For variety, singing jingles introduced almost every element. Singing time-signal tapes were also marketed with individualized call-letter identity.

Careful attention to programming—especially music—was only one reason for Top 40's success. Station promotion and publicity gimmicks helped boost ratings. So many stations copied successful Storz promotions that he had to introduce each new one on all his stations simultaneously. He ran a contest with $105,000 in prizes in Minneapolis and Omaha in 1956 that drew participants from all over the U.S. McLendon gave prize money to listeners with the right number on a car window sticker, threw cash off buildings, buried disc jockeys alive, and used variations of treasure hunts.

Most Top 40 stations emphasized local news, which then often forced other stations in the market to take measures to meet this challenge. Gaudy "news-mobiles," emblazoned with the station call letters, roamed the streets in search of local on-the-spot coverage of events. Many followed police radio closely and raced to the scene of crimes—occasionally arriving before the police. Sound effects, echo, and other gimmicks were used to add excitement.

Storz experimented to find the acceptable number of commercial minutes in an hour—settling on 18. Most local commercials were well-produced (often humorous or dramatic situations), musical, and above all fast-paced.

The purveyors of Top 40 were interested primarily in radio. While other radio station owners were acquiring television properties, and devoting more time, talent, and money to television, the Top 40 group owners were shifting radio properties in order to get the best facility for their sound. Top 40 came out of middle-sized markets, and out of middle America. The market and the station had to be big enough to afford expensive hardware, software, and personnel investment that the pioneers believed was necessary. Larger market old-line network affiliates would not take the chance of changing their entire programming overnight—risking everything on a new idea. The new Top 40 group owners bought the best power and frequency they could in the largest markets possible, but could not afford the 50,000-watt clear channel stations in the top 10 markets.

Stations programming music-and-news (or the later Top 40 specialization of it) provided a service that, unlike TV, newspapers, magazines or even earlier radio programs, demanded little concentration by the audience. The format was especially attuned to an increasingly mobile audience. Top 40 operators found that 50% of their audience was out-of-home.

The major Top 40 group owners centralized programming control. Some sent music play lists and packaged promotions to their stations. In other cases they tried to share new ideas among the group (via newsletters, etc.)

Top 40 group owners made heavy use of trade magazines to boast of their rating successes, thereby spreading news of Top 40's power to build audiences. Many of the imitators, especially in the small markets, ran their shows as cheaply as possible, rather than as attractively as possible. They failed by attempting to duplicate form rather than trying to understand function. However, the success of the specialized format in gathering large audiences encouraged other types of specialization and format experimentation. Country and Western, gospel, soul, all-talk, all-news, all "sweet" music—every one of the currently familiar format specializations had its genesis in the maverick sound that was Top 40 radio.

Stations in many countries—and even the BBC—imitated the sound. The success of Top 40, coupled with teenagers' increased spending power, encouraged a renaissance in the phonograph industry that eventually would see the new 45s displaced by sales of LPs. New music and novel promotion—the same two elements that propelled Top 40 to be the most-imitated radio format in the world— also were the factors behind the success of Elvis Presley, Dick Clark, Motown, the Beatles, folk rock, progressive rock, Drake-Chenault, and so much more. It had all come up from middle America.

63

Harrison B. Summers

PROGRAMMING FOR TELEVISION

IT IS MUCH too early [1944] to predict with definiteness the kinds of programs which television may offer its audience, five or ten years from today. Too little is known about the types of programs which are possible, or about the reactions of the television audience

Quarterly Journal of Speech, Vol. 31 (1945), pp. 44–47.

to such programs. From a technical standpoint, television is as far advanced as was radio ten or fifteen years ago; but television programming is still in the vague, uncertain trial-and-error stage that characterized radio in 1922 or 1923. The six television stations in operation today provide programs for a total of not more than 10,000 receiving sets. And since the novelty element in television is still strong—as it was in the case of radio twenty years ago—it is difficult to draw intelligent conclusions from the opinions expressed by those with access to television today, as to the probable reactions of the much larger television audience five or ten years in the future.

Based on the experiences of the television companies to date, several generalizations may be offered as to what kinds of television programs will be made available. The development of networks will make possible the telecasting of various special features: football games, basketball games, boxing matches, presidential inaugurations, national political conventions, the ceremonies attendant upon the opening of Congress, parades, mass meetings, and the like. Up to the present time, such special features have attracted greater interest from the television audience than any other type of program material, and they will doubtless continue to attract great interest in the future. However, the number of special features available for use on television will be limited; the day-to-day offerings of television stations must be made up of more prosaic materials.

From the television networks, programs will undoubtedly be made available that correspond to the more popular evening programs on radio networks today. Comedy programs, variety programs, various types of audience participation programs, and of course dramatic programs can be presented on television no less effectively than over radio—and in many cases, they should be far more effective on television. But even with networks established, the number of such programs offered by television may be somewhat more limited than some of us would expect, at least for the next several years. Network radio programs are expensive, but the cost of equivalent programs on television is likely to be even greater.

By way of comparison, consider the cost of an ordinary 30-minute radio dramatic program, and of the same program produced for television. On the radio, such a program calls for the services of a writer, of perhaps six actors, of a director, an announcer, a sound-effects man, a studio engineer, and someone to provide music for bridges or various musical effects. Once the program has been written, the production of the program involves the services of the actors and others for not more than two or two-and-a-half hours. Long rehearsals are not necessary; actors need not memorize their lines; and radio requires no scenery, no costuming, no make up.

On television, however, the number of man-hours necessary to present that same 30-minute program is infinitely greater. No more time is required for the work done by the writer, the announcer, the sound-effects man or the man who plays the electric organ. But actors must be costumed. Scenery must be constructed, painted, and set in place. Actors must memorize their lines. Stage business must be learned. The play must be rehearsed. And in some cases, 30-minute dramatic programs presented over New York television stations have required as much as ten or fifteen hours of rehearsal, before the camera. Instead of one engineer, the service of a whole battery of engineers is required: at least three camera men in the studio, three control-room engineers to handle the visual images from the cameras, one engineer to handle sound, and another engineer to act as "mixer," combining the various visual and sound ingredients into a single program. All of these engineers would have to be on hand during at least the last several hours of rehearsal. The tremendous increase in the number of man-hours required certainly means that costs of ordinary studio programs will be materially higher on television than on radio; consequently, the number of elaborate studio programs is likely to be limited. That will be true at least until television has become firmly established, with television receivers in several million homes and with advertisers willing to pay far more per thousand "listeners" for television broadcasts than they now pay for broadcasts on radio.

With reference to studio programs, too, one other factor must be considered. Certain programs heard over radio do not lend themselves well to the television situation. Psychological drama, for example, may be less effective on television than on radio; when sight is added to hearing, the impact of suggestion is correspondingly decreased. Comedy programs in which the humor is in any way subtle may likewise lose effectiveness on television. Generally speaking, television calls for physical action—action sufficiently marked as to be evident on an 18 by 24 inch screen. This may mean that most of radio's musical programs could not be transferred effectively to television. And individual programs of other types may be similarly affected.

There are many students of television who believe that for a number of years at least, 80 or 90 per cent of the television schedule will consist of two types of program material: talks, and motion pictures. By use of alternating long camera shots and close-ups, and particularly by liberal use of various visual material—maps, charts, pictures, actual objects brought to the studio—informative talks have made good material for television. Motion pictures, particularly short subjects, have also won favor with the television audience. Both types of programs have the advantage of being inexpensive to produce, and that may be an item of considerable importance during the early stages of the development of television.

One basic fact is already evident to those who have carried on experiments in the field of television programming. The span of attention of the television "listener" or viewer is limited. Television demands much more concentrated attention from those in its audience than does radio. And that sort of attention, after a time, requires effort on the part of the viewer. Consequently, television programs must be characterized by rapid changes. Just as in the motion pictures, changes of "scene" must be made frequently; and since television offers little opportunity to change the background setting during a single program, much use must be made of the device of switching from one camera to another, changing from long shots to close-ups, from front views to side views, and so on. Frequent change will be necessary whether the program is a football game, an elaborate dramatic production in a studio, or a news broadcast tracing the progress of the Allied armies in the Rhine valley.

64

Samuel Goldwyn

HOLLYWOOD IN THE TELEVISION AGE

MOTION PICTURES are entering their third major era. First there was the silent period. Then the sound era. Now we are on the threshold of the television age.

The thoroughgoing change which sound brought to picture making will be fully matched by the revolutionary effects (if the House Un-American Activities Committee will excuse the expression) of television upon motion pictures. I predict that within just a few years a great many Hollywood producers, directors, writers, and actors who are still coasting on reputations built up in the past are going to wonder what hit them.

The future of motion pictures, conditioned as it will be by the competition of television, is going to have no room for the deadwood of the present or the faded glories of the past. Once again it will be true, as it was in the early days of motion picture history, that it will

New York Times Magazine, February 13, 1949, pp. 15, 44, and 47.

take brains instead of just money to make pictures. This will be hard on a great many people who have been enjoying a free ride on the Hollywood carousel, but it will be a fine thing for motion pictures as a whole.

Within a few years the coaxial cable will have provided a complete television network linking the entire country. Whether the expense that is involved in producing full-length feature pictures for television can possibly be borne by advertisers or will be paid for by individual charges upon the set owners, no one can say today. But we do know that with America's tremendous technological capabilities and our ability to adjust to new situations, nothing will stand in the way of full-length feature pictures in the home produced expressly for that purpose.

Even the most backward looking of the topmost tycoons of our industry cannot now help seeing just around the corner a titanic struggle to retain audiences. The competition we feared in the past— the automobile in early movie days, the radio in the twenties and thirties, and the developing of night sports quite recently—will fade into insignificance by comparison with the fight we are going to have to keep people patronizing our theaters in preference to sitting at home and watching a program of entertainment. It is a certainty that people will be unwilling to pay to see poor pictures when they can stay home and see something which is, at least, no worse.

How can the motion picture industry meet the competition of television? Most certainly the basic business tactics—if you can't lick 'em, join 'em—apply in this case. If the movies try to lick television, it's the movies that will catch the licking. But the two industries can quite naturally join forces for their own profit and the greater entertainment of the public. Instead of any talk about how to lick television, motion picture people now need to discuss how to fit movies into the new world made possible by television.

Assuming that better pictures will be made, there remains the problem of how the motion picture industry is going to receive financial returns for pictures made for television. The greatest potentialities lie in a device called phonevision.

This device is not yet known to the American public because it has not yet been placed upon the commercial market, but to motion picture producers it may well be the key to full participation in this new, exciting medium of entertainment. Reduced to its simplest terms, it is a system by which any television set owner will be able to call his telephone operator, tell her that he wishes to see "The Best Years of Our Lives" (if I may be pardoned for thinking of my favorite picture), or any other picture, and then see the picture on his television set. The charge for the showing of the picture will be carried on the regular monthly telephone bill.

Phonevision is normal television with the additional feature that it can be seen on the phone-vision-television combination set only when certain electrical signals are fed into the set over telephone wires. No television set without the phonevision addition is capable of picking up phonevision programs, and no phonevision-television set can pick up such programs without those electrical signals supplied over the telephone wires on specific order.

It must be borne in mind that full-length pictures in the home are not necessarily something which will be realized in the immediate future. Despite the rapid pace at which we hurtle ahead, I am inclined to believe that the production of full-length pictures designed especially for home television will not become a practical reality for at least five to ten years more. Although phonevision seems to be ready for commercial adaptation today, it is obvious that no motion picture producer can risk the huge investment required for a full-length feature picture for television alone unless he has some reasonable assurance of recovering his costs.

In addition to producing for television, motion picture companies will undoubtedly make strenuous efforts to participate in the ownership and operation of television stations themselves. Already several of the larger companies have made extensive plans along these lines. An element which could blight the development of television would be the introduction into that field of monopolistic controls and practices similar to those which, in the motion picture industry, have hurt independent production. But this possibility should be reduced to a minimum by the fact that television-station ownership by theater companies and their affiliated interests, as well as others, will be limited by the Federal Communications Commission rule which provides, in effect, that no single interest can own more than five television licenses.

There is no doubt that in the future a large segment of the talents of the motion picture industry will be devoted to creating motion pictures designed explicitly for this new medium. As today's television novelty wears off, the public is not going to be satisfied to look at the flickering shadows of old films which have reposed in their producers' vaults for many years. Nor will the public be content to spend an evening looking at a series of fifteen minute shorts such as are now being made for television. There will be a vast demand for new full-length motion picture entertainment brought directly into the home.

The certainty is that in the future whether it be five or ten or even more years distant, one segment of our industry will be producing pictures for exhibition in the theaters while another equally large section will be producing them for showing in the homes. The stimulus of this kind of competition should have nothing but good results.

The people best fitted to make pictures for television will be those who combine a thorough knowledge of picture-making techniques with a real sense of entertainment values and the imagination to adapt their abilities to a new medium.

The weak sisters in our ranks will fall by the wayside. But no one in our industry who has real talent need fear the effects of television. I welcome it as opening new vistas for the exercise of creative ability, spurred on by intense competition.

I have always been basically optimistic about Hollywood and its potentialities. I see no reason to change my views now. I am convinced that television will cause Hollywood to achieve new heights and that, as time goes on, above these heights new peaks will rise.

65

Ted Nielsen

TELEVISION: CHICAGO STYLE

DURING THE LATE 1940s and early 1950s the centers of network television were located in New York or Chicago. Yet by 1959 it was impossible to find a network television program originating in Chicago, and aside from comments from television critics, no one seemed to notice. It wasn't the first time the city had been phased out during the later development of a communications form. From 1907 to 1917 Chicago was a motion picture production center, until the milder weather of the West Coast prompted that industry to move. In the early 1930s Chicago was the production center for network radio, but once again programs and personnel left for New York or Hollywood. No one was really surprised when it happened to network television.

But more than just quantity of television programming, Chicago had developed a style of television production, and this was also lost in its demise as a network center. The programs that came from Chicago had a distinctive approach to the medium, an original kind of creative effort that used television on its own terms rather than as a transmitting or reporting device for other entertainment or informational forms. In looking back, Chicago never was very effective with the "televised stage show" or "the televised radio program" or the "televised film." Production personnel there sought to develop and

Journal of Broadcasting, Vol. IX, No. 4 (Fall 1965), pp. 305–312.

maintain a "medium integrity" for this new kind of communication. Critics dubbed it the "Chicago Style."

The Beginnings (1929–1948)

Television actually began in Chicago in 1929, when NBC technicians wiring radio studios in the Merchandise Mart added heavy duty cables and television light outlets in the belief that the medium would need them one day.[1] In 1931 television broadcasting began on an experimental basis. That summer early viewers were receiving signals from the Chicago Daily News Station W9XAP and from the Zenith Radio Corporation station W9XZV. The first station on the air with regular programming was WBKB, owned by the Balaban and Katz Theatre chain. At the end of World War II, WBKB was operating 25 hours per month, with offerings primarily in the public service areas. The station staff included three news analysts who presented interpretations of the war with "maps, photographs, and animations."[2] In 1948, two more stations came on the air. In April the Chicago Tribune's WGN-TV and in September, the American Broadcasting Company's WENR-TV, WGN-TV became primarily affiliated with the Dumont Television Network. Chicago's fourth station, NBC's WNBQ, began regular programming in January of 1949. This station, more than any other, was the creative force behind the distinctive style of television production that came from Chicago during the early 1950s.

The most significant program debut for Chicago television was a section from an NBC Thanksgiving special in 1948. This was the network start for the children's puppet presentation *Kukla, Fran and Ollie,* broadcast from its local producer WBKB. On November 29 the program began to appear regularly on the midwest NBC network as part of *Junior Jamboree,* a children's production. It was the start of one aspect of the "Chicago Style" of television.

> Chicago spawned a great many radio programs in the early days and is showing some disposition to use its "think tank" in the video realm. Knowing it cannot hope to compete with New York or Hollywood in the realm of glamour, it is coming up with numerous idea shows. The loudest hosannas are directed to WBKB's puppet show, *Kukla, Fran and Ollie.*[3]
>
> It has a charm and spirit very much its own and in its unique blend of fantasy and realism illustrates how television can chart new courses in engaging make-believe.[4]

In 1949 the adult aspect of Chicago television began with the NBC series *Portrait of America.* The program took remote cameras into a different home each week, revealing the activities of a different family unit in its surroundings. All ethnic, racial, and socioeconomic levels were shown, with the program's emphasis on the small story of everyday life. The subject matter was handled with a direct simplicity and with a degree of reality to the television situation that became a mark of the "Chicago Style."

The Peak Years (1950–1954)

The 1950 fall schedule carried 13 network programs coming from Chicago. The schedule also listed NBC's *Garroway at Large*, destined to become the program typifying the "Chicago Style" of television production. The half hour variety program was originally used as a fill-in on the national schedule on Friday evenings, but was put on permanently following the acclaim on its temporary run. Critic Jack Gould's description provides a definition of the style.

> Its chief appeal is that it is designed for the home and not for a studio audience. . . . Mr. Garroway and his associates employ the camera as an artist does a brush and the effects they achieve are often startling in their originality and simplicity and often in their beauty.[5]

The informal style grew primarily from the combined concepts of the personnel involved in planning and production and, of necessity, from the limitations of WNBQ's physical plant. The original *Garroway at Large* set was a one-stage affair "used for cooking shows. The plan was to give the program informality by showing the mikes and the crew occasionally." [6]

Another of the significant aspects of Chicago television that was also implicit in *Garroway at Large* was that the programs were developed with a "medium integrity." The visual aspects and content of the subject areas were slanted for the new medium and its advantages and limitations rather than using film, radio, or stage techniques to achieve their ends. NBC, Chicago even had a set of rules for television productions.

> No show can have drapery backgrounds, because interesting sets are no more expensive; every show must have a design; never stage a scene in a living room unless it is a dramatic program; cameras must work for us instead of just recording what they see, as they are creative instead of reportorial.[7]

A third area was the low cost of production brought about by space limitations and the absence of credits of the more expensive kinds of name performers. In a cost analysis by *Television Magazine* in 1952, the most expensive Chicago origination was the *Wayne King Show* at $9,000 per program. *Kukla, Fran and Ollie* was produced for $3,000 per program in a time period costing $15,000. *Garroway at Large* had averaged between $5,000 and $6,000 per program in its early stages. ABC's *Super Circus* cost $12,000 for one hour, with

NBC's *Ding Dong School* low at $1,600 per half hour program.[8] As one article put it, "Ratings (of Chicago programs) are seldom startling, but very often the cost-per-1,000 is much lower than the network average."[9]

Programming for children was one of the creative areas of Chicago television. In 1950 *Kukla, Fran and Ollie* was given a Peabody award as "The Outstanding Childrens Program on Television." Awards were also given to Chicago's *Zoo Parade, Saturday at the Zoo,* the science program *Mr. Wizard,* the pre-schoolers' *Ding Dong School,* and the long running *Super Cicrus.*

Television dramatic productions were a second area in which Chicago television made distinctive contributions in approach to the medium. NBC's *Stud's Place,* a half hour weekly program set in an urban tavern, concerned the lives of the tavern owner, his employees, and their patrons. The actors worked from a general plot outline rather than from a script. They would discuss the program and work out lines from their knowledge and understanding of their roles in the various dramatic situations presented.

Another series on the same order was NBC's dramatic serial *Hawkins Falls,* based on the daily happenings in a small town as seen by the local newspaper editor. Settings were nonrealistic and acting and situations were low key. Concentration was on the characters and their relationships rather than on an action or highly dramatic format.

When Chicago failed in a television format, it seemed to be one that was someone else's style of presentation or an attempt to adapt another medium to television. NBC chose Chicago to originate the first hour of its new *Show of Shows* and flew in New York writers and cast to present the program. The critics were less than enthusiastic. One described the routine of the stage program as "awkward" and the choice of musical selections as "much too specialized." Chicago production people were also called to task for "lighting and camera work not up to network standards."[10] ABC's attempt to bring the radio version of *Don McNeill's Breakfast Club* to television met with a similar fate. "Since the *Don McNeill TV Club* is a duplicate of his radio show, it is much better when heard and not seen. It just doesn't seem appropriate as an after dinner liquor."[11]

A peak for Chicago television was reached in 1951 when 18 programs were being produced, with NBC's WNBQ leading the list with 11 productions. "Chicago seems to be way out in front . . . producing bold, new ideas . . . a point of view all its own."[12]

The End (1954–1959)

The first sign of a decline in Chicago fortunes came in 1951 when NBC announced the shortening of *Kukla, Fran and Ollie* to 15 minutes to make room for the variety/satire team of Bob and Ray.

The decision was explained by NBC on the grounds that sponsors could be found for the shorter segments of time on the program, but not for the entire half hour period. NBC president Pat Weaver replied to his critics,

> This is not a question of choosing one kind of entertainment over another. It is a question of making the form of the show fit the changing characteristics of the medium as it grows.[13]

A viewer expressed other ideas in a letter to the *New York Times:*

> Who are the myopic numbskulls with more authority than brains who would cram more baggy-pants comics, so called plunging necklines, horse operas and feeble crooners down our long suffering gullets? I hope the welkin rings with rage sent up by all righteously indignant viewers deprived of a really intelligent program.[14]

Critic Jack Gould also reacted:

> It is a disquieting phenomena that television never seems to have difficulty finding time for a few more vaudeville shows or where children are concerned, more Western movies. Yet when it comes to one show dedicated to the art of sheer make-believe and constituted to delight young and old . . . down comes the boom of the hucksters.[15]

The major blow to the development of the "Chicago Style" of television came in December of 1951 when NBC dropped *Garroway at Large* in favor of *The Red Skelton Show*. Garroway moved to New York to take over the *Today* show, and Ted Mills, Norman Felton, Bob Banner, Dan Petrie, and Bill Hobin—the nucleus of the Chicago NBC staff—moved out as well. Talent in Chicago began to move to the two coasts to find work in the new shows coming from studios in New York and Hollywood.[16]

Still, in 1953 Chicago ranked second only to New York in network originations. The biggest quantity decrease came in the fall of 1955 when no WGN-TV produced programs appeared on the Dumont network listings. NBC's *Hawkins Falls, Out on the Farm,* and *A Time to Live* were no longer listed. *Kukla, Fran and Ollie* had changed networks, appearing on ABC. By 1959 Chicago originations were gone from the schedule.

The post-mortem of Chicago television can get long and involved. Many factors contributed and many people had their views, within and without the industry. Some knew it was rating problems, others mentioned the exodus of key personnel to New York or Hollywood. Others felt that the advertisers and their agencies had failed to appreciate the gains inherent in the low key sell of the "Chicago Style." Advertising agencies did not have their main offices in Chicago while they conducted a great deal of their business on the two coasts. Film had begun to make itself known in television production and the advertiser was weaned away from live television to the profits in re-runs and the program control that recording offered. All of these factors, and probably many others, could and did have a bearing on the numerous decisions that took Chicago out of network television production.

The "Chicago Style" of television had built into it the seeds of its own destruction. The development of program production on the regional and local station level soon made the genre expendable. "Whatever good things have happened in Chicago, television-wise, could have happened in Atlanta or Minneapolis." [17] After the local stations had a chance to develop their own programming, the Chicago kind of low key, low budget, local talent approach was indeed being done over the country. The Chicago puppet shows, children's variety, and small variety programs, could be produced locally and profitably. *Ding Dong School, Kukla, Fran and Ollie,* or *Super Circus* could be duplicated locally quite easily. The basic forms of *Garroway at Large, The Ransom Sherman Show,* or the *Don McNeill TV Club* could be approximated by a local production effort. Of course the quality and creativity of the program forms that Chicago developed could not be duplicated, but their formats were actually more regional than national in character.

Discussion

Chicago network television developed in accordance with its position coaxially close to New York in the early television days, and in accordance with the philosophies and creativity of personnel at its stations. The Bob Banners, Ted Mills, and Bill Hobins combined to provide the wherewithall for a definitive style of production. The approach was low key and essentially visual and intimate. There was a "medium integrity" developed and maintained in a short period of time and with little time for preparation.

The tragedy of Chicago television was that it contained within its basic forms elements that could be duplicated on an individual station level. The big budgets and big stars of the coast network programs appealed to the national advertiser, while his local counterpart took advantage of the increased and varied productivity of his own regional outlets. There was no place left for Chicago in a national programming service. But if we are ever fully to investigate television in its own right, we must take account of the beginnings of the early Chicago productions. These producers had started on a path that has not yet been fully explored. The qualities of individual creativity, originality, and imagination that were present then must be inherent in any future development of the medium along its own lines.

66

Howard Blake

AN APOLOGIA FROM THE MAN WHO PRODUCED THE WORST PROGRAM IN TV HISTORY

WHAT *Gone With the Wind* is to the American novel and what *Life with Father* is to the American stage, *Queen for a Day*, I would guess, is to American broadcasting. *Queen* was one of the most popular of all radio-TV programs, and certainly the undisputed queen of the tearjerkers. Having been born on April 29, 1945, and dying on Oct. 2, 1964, *Queen* lived to be nearly 20. Money poured in (sponsors paid $4000 for a 1-minute commercial) and listeners tuned in (in 1955–56, *Queen* was daytime TV's all-time biggest hit: 13 million Americans watched it every day). And just because of its phenomenal commercial and popular success, a close look at this program, I am convinced, reveals with shining clarity the essential, sobering truth about radio and TV in these United States.

The format of *Queen for a Day* was simple but brilliant: Get believable women to tell their hard-luck stories over the air; let the audience choose the woman they think is most deserving; and then shower the winner with gifts. (Only be sure that the show doesn't pay for the gifts. Just let everybody *think* it does.)

The program would begin with its star, Jack Bailey, pointing straight into the camera and shouting, "Would *you* like to be Queen for a Day?" Then a parade of beautiful girls would trot by, each carrying a different gift (furs, dresses, TV set, etc.) to be presented to that day's Queen while an off-camera announcer extols how wonderful each gift is. Next, Jack Bailey interviews the day's candidates, asking each one what her personal wish is and why she wants whatever she wants. The last candidate makes her tearful plea, and then comes the voting—by audience applause. The applause meter appears on the screen. Jack stands behind the first candidate and recaps: "Candidate No. 1, who wants a trousseau for her daughter's wedding." Mild applause. "Candidate No. 2, who badly needs repair for her leaky roof before the rainy season starts." The applause is a little louder. "Candidate No. 3, whose mother is coming to spend her few remaining years with her, and she desperately needs a bed." The applause is tumultuous. Jack Bailey shouts, "It's No. 3!" The house comes down. Later, if No. 3 beats out two other contestants, a sable-collared red-velvet robe is placed around her shoulders, a jeweled crown is gently lowered onto her head, and Jack Bailey roars, "I now pronounce you—Queen for a Day!" Then, *ad infinitum* and *ad nauseam,* the Queen is shown all her gifts—not only the bed, but sheets, pillows, blankets, bedspreads, lamps, chaise lounge, bureau and so forth. The Queen dissolves into tears. Jack puts his arm around her. Women in the audience faint and ushers carry them to the rear of the theater. Finally Jack faces the camera, smiles his kindest smile, and says to the viewer, "Be with us again tomorrow when we'll elect another Queen. This is Jack Bailey, wishing we could make *every* woman Queen for a Day!"

For sheer psychological perfection, there was never a show like it.

When *Queen* made its debut on TV on Jan. 1, 1955, New York *Times* critic Jack Gould shrieked, "What hath Sarnoff wrought?!" Critics all over the country howled in similar protest, and the result was that the show became No. 1 in the ratings within 3 months.

Queen was hardly on the air 6 months when the network expanded it from 30 minutes to 45 minutes, a very unusual length for a show, yet in this instance quite logical. At $4000 for a 1-minute commercial, it brought NBC's potential annual take from the program up from $9 million.

The money didn't come only from advertisers like Proctor & Gamble and Alka-Seltzer. It also came from the companies that gave us free merchandise in return for plugs. For in addition to the merchandise they forked over, they had to cover the salaries of the beautiful girls who modeled the clothes we gave away and who displayed the other gifts. Oddly enough, the money paid for these models' fees also managed to be used for other expenses, like contributing to owner Ray Morgan's weekly $5000.

And so it came to pass that the more gifts we gave the Queen, the more money we made. We *loaded* the Queens with gifts—at the rate of a million dollars a year. Eventually what with the regular commercials and the gift plugs, only about 15 of the 45 minutes were left for the actual show—for Jack Bailey's interviews with the candidates and the voting for the Queen. The other 30 minutes were nothing but commercials and plugs.

But we had our integrity, I'll have you know. Other audience-participation shows chose their contestants after intensive interviews, wrote scripts for them to memorize, told them what answers to give the quiz questions, rehearsed them thoroughly in *how* to give those answers, and absolutely controlled who won and how much. None of this did we ever do. No candidate for Queen was ever planted, prompted, or rehearsed. Every candidate came from that day's walk-in audience. The Queen was chosen entirely by audience applause and this was never faked, or "sweetened," as the trade calls it, although that's easy to do. And it was a strict rule that the Queen was to be treated like a Queen during her 1-day reign and given everything the show promised her.

How holy can you get?

Our integrity, however, had limits. Our holiness had holes. When it came to picking the women to appear on the show, the general assumption was that we chose the most needy and deserving. But the most needy and deserving usually had to be dumped. A lot of the women desperately needed a doctor or a lawyer, for instance. We could never provide either because there was no way of telling what it might eventually cost. And no doctor or lawyer would work for free in return for a plug (we investigated). A candidate had to want something we *could* plug—a stove, a carpet, a plane trip, an artificial leg, a detective agency, a year's supply of baby food. And the reason she needed whatever it was had to make a good story. Some of the women were ugly, some were incoherent. They had to be dumped too, deserving or not. A woman with a wish like a wish any other woman had had recently was also out of luck. We had only one aim—to pick the woman who would provide the best entertainment.

Before the show, every candidate was given a "wish card" to fill out. The cards were numbered. Three of four members of the staff went through them before the show and passed likely ones to me. I picked 25. The 25 women were called on stage a few minutes before air time, and interviewed for a few seconds by Jack Bailey. Jack then chose the five with the best stories, and the best personalities, to be on the show. Complete phonies showed up once in a while, but Jack could smell a phony story instantly, almost every time.

The show had an embarrassing weakness. Only one of the five daily candidates could be elected Queen and have her wish granted. The other four, no matter how desperate their needs, supplied their share of the entertainment but had to settle for a small consolation prize—a radio, a toaster, a dozen pair of stockings. Sometimes they would burst into tears, but we never let the camera see that. Once the Queen was elected, the losers were deliberately ignored.

Occasionally a real good liar would get past Jack's sensitive nose and fool the audience as well. But we were protected. A clause in the release every candidate had to sign specified that if her story proved untrue she'd get nothing, and we had to exercise that clause a number of times.

For instance, one woman's wish was for round-trip tickets to Miami for herself and her 14-year-old son. Her mother was dying of cancer, the woman said, and had never seen her grandson. Tears rolled down her cheeks as she told all the heartbreaking details. Tears puddled the audience's seats too, and when it was time to vote, the applause for her almost broke the applause machine. It was a great show. But a neighbor of hers saw it and told the Queen's husband about it. The husband phoned us and said (1) they didn't have a son, and (2) his wife's mother had been dead for 10 years. His wife, he informed us, was having an affair with a friend of his, and she had been trying to find a way for the lovers to spend 2 weeks together in Miami. The husband wanted us to know that he wasn't in favor of it. We hated to buck a romance, but they didn't get to go.

We also had trouble whenever Jack went on vacation. Interviewing people is a most difficult art, and Jack has no peers. He learned his trade through years of work as a circus-carnival barker, an actor in stock, and a department-store salesman. The fact is that keeping an interview going without hesitating and stalling to think of appropriate questions takes experience, and innate genius to boot. Adolphe Menjou did the show for a couple of weeks and loved it. But he never knew the torture he put us through. He asked one woman about her husband's occupation. She replied, "He died in an automobile accident 4 months ago." Adolphe responded, "Wonderful! What kind of work did he do?" ("Wonderful!" is a stall word.)

Two imitations of *Queen* also turned out to be very successful— *Strike It Rich!* and Ralph Edwards' *It Could Be You.* But both expired long before *Queen* did. *Queen's* death was a lingering one and took years. The show started to breathe hard a few months after I got fired the first time (1956). ("What a coincidence!") I got fired because I wanted to make daring experiments with the format, convinced that we needed new surprises to keep boredom from descending over our audiences. Jack Bailey disagreed, and quoted Lucille Ball. Once one of Lucy's writers suggested some radical changes in her show, and she ordered: "Don't fuck around with success." So I left. I came back in 1957, thinking I would *now* be able to make innovations, but again Jack chickened out, and again I left. Ratings continued to drop. In the fall of 1959 ABC took over the show, and it lingered there for 5 years before finally giving up the ghost in October, 1964. If you want to be nasty about it, you can draw whatever conclusions you like from the fact that the show managed to last 6 more years without me.

Throughout my years with *Queen* I collected the "wish cards" that contestants submitted. I still have all the originals, and I read them over every once in a while.

Some of the wishes were pathetic:

> A bird for an old lady 94. She had one but it died. She does not realize it is dead. She keeps it in a cage, talks to it and takes it out and kisses its head.
>
> Some kind of car or hot rod or something to make my blind brother and crippled brother happy.

A typewriter or a recording machine. Because my husband hit me over the head with a shoe and completely paralyzed me for 7½ months. It left me with my right side paralyzed & I am a writer.

An artificial eye for my husband. Last winter his artificial eye (which he keeps in a small glass at night) froze and cracked. I have 16 children and No. 17 is coming up in the spring.

Services of a detective. My sister was murdered and I have been told she left money. Since it was in another state I have no way of knowing without help.

Urn to bury my mother. Her ashes have been in a vault and must be buried or they will throw them on the rose bush.

Have my front teeth put in. I am unmarried and have 1 child 10½ months. If I had my teeth fixed maybe I could get a husband to take care of my kid and self.

$100 for a divorce. Husband attempted rape on my 6 year old daughter, then left with money and car. Must be divorced so I can testify against him in court.

Mattress. My husband died on our bed April 28 and ruined our mattress.

Get a divorce. I want to divorce the man who ruined by life by taking me away from my home. He was 45 and I 14. Today I am on the street with 5 children and no husband. If I could divorce that monster perhaps the father of my 5 children would marry me.

Celotex sheets and carpenter. Due to a brain tumor, my husband went into a seizure and took his life with a deer rifle. The high-powered bullets pierced the ceiling and wall of the bedroom. I'd like to have it repaired.

Some of the wishes were not-so-pathetic:

To get "falsies" that won't blow up in the plane.

3 cases of I.W. Harper. My mother had heart trouble and her Dr. told her to take 2 jiggers every nite & she's always out of whiskie.

Bra for my daughter. Can't find one to fit or hold them up. I guess you know what I mean. She don't take after me.

I want a gun.

A parakeet that will talk. I have a husband but he won't talk. I am on my third husband have my eyes open.

100 lbs. corn sugar. 50 lbs. hops. My husband drinks too much regular beer & this would be cheaper if he made it himself.

Twin beds. My doctor said "Take it easy."

To be mother of our country. There is so much misunderstanding among us. I want my address & phone No. before the nation, so any one needing help with problems I will donate my services to free. I am just a usual lady & have time to help man kind.

To have my sister and her family analyzed, so the rest of us can live in peace.

A ticket to the Art Linkletter Show.

A Rolls-Royce with balloon tires for me. I'm *not* selfish.

All of these letters, I want to emphasize, were *typical,* not unusual. Sure, *Queen* was vulgar and sleazy and filled with bathos and bad taste. That was why it was so successful: It was exactly what the general public wanted. After all, the average American voted Warren G. Harding into office, reads the *Reader's Digest,* and made *Hercules Unchained* a smash movie. In the slightly amended words of H. L. Mencken, "Nobody ever lost money underestimating the taste of the American public."

To be honest, a few intellectual friends used to ask me, "Aren't you ashamed of producing a show like that?" I was never ashamed for a second. Somebody once asked novelist John P. Marquand how he could lower himself to write all those lightweight Mr. Moto mysteries for the *Saturday Evening Post.* Marquand pointed out that the stories obviously brought pleasure to many people, he got very good money for them, and he thoroughly enjoyed writing them. That's how I felt about producing *Queen for a Day.* I knew the show for what it was, but it seemed to bring pleasure to millions, helped a few (all right, mighty few), and it paid me a very good living. If all Americans—ad men, insurance brokers, lawyers—examined closely just how *they* make their livings, I think a high percentage would soon be on analysts' couches.

No, the show did not prove that there are good guys and bad guys, and the bad guys always eat up the good guys. I don't think there *were* any good guys. *Everybody* was on the make—we on the show, NBC and later ABC, the sponsors and the suppliers of gifts. And how about all the down-on-their-luck women who used to further our money-grubbing ends? Weren't they all on the make? Weren't they after something for nothing? Weren't they willing to wash their dirty linen on coast-to-coast TV for a chance at big money, for a chance to ride in our chauffeured Cadillac for the free tour of Disneyland and the Hollywood night clubs? What about one of the most common wishes they turned in? "I'd like to pay back my mother for all the wonderful things she's done for me." The women who made that wish didn't want to pay back their mothers at all. They wanted *us* to.

You *bet* they were on the make.

We got what we were after. Five thousand Queens got what they were after. And the TV audience cried their eyes out, morbidly delighted to find there were people even worse off than they were, and so *they* got what they were after.

Queen for a Day was a typical American success story. And if you don't like it, either try to change the rules of the game—or go back where you come from.

67

Ted Nielsen

A HISTORY OF
NETWORK TELEVISION NEWS

ON ELECTION NIGHT (1960) the news desk at NBC received a phone call requesting that the totals be kept on the screen longer as the caller was having a hard time copying them. He identified himself as The Associated Press.[1]

In the development of network television news, most of the advances have been brought about by the necessity of providing daily, visual reports of what is happening. "The daily news program commands the greatest attention of the staff, consumes by far the most manpower, and has created the organization which enables television to produce its special reports and offer live coverage of the big news events of the day." [2]

The Beginnings

Television news began on the experimental stations in the 1930s. A nine-hour report on WCBW, New York, on the day Pearl Harbor was attacked was the first television news instant special. At the time the CBS station was the only TV subscriber to the United Press radio wire and had a news staff of two. The station normally presented two 15-minute newscasts a day which were described as a "roundup of news, together with the latest bulletins and background developments." [3]

During the war, television broadcasting was cut back, but in 1943 the General Electric Company held a symposium to show newspaper editors how the new medium would cover the news. Printed pages of a special edition of the Schenectady *Times* were projected on screens, then stories, want ads, display ads, and comic cartoons. A financial story was illustrated by silver dollars to show the government's new tax proposal. A baby buggy offered for sale was wheeled into view. A war correspondent using a large map pointed out what the latest bulletins meant in geographic terms. "The re-enactment of the newspaper stories and features appeared remarkably natural on the screens of regular household television sets." [4]

In 1948 the first regularly scheduled television network news program was *CBS-TV News* with Douglas Edwards at 7:30 P.M. eastern time. In 1949 *NBC Newsreel* with John Cameron Swayze began at 7:45. Soon thereafter ABC and DuMont began early evening news reports. In 1958 ABC attempted a nightly program at 11:00, but the experiment was short lived.

Regular daytime news summaries began in 1951 and were expanded to a total of about six hours daily in the 1960s. Saturday news began in 1949 on NBC; CBS in 1950. Since 1965 ABC has presented an 11:00 P.M. newscast on Saturday and Sunday. Sunday news broadcasts were often wrap-ups of the week's events—*NBC News Film* began in 1948, *CBS News in Review,* and ABC's *Paul Harvey Reports.* Sunday has also been popular for news reviews and documentary magazine formats such as *Sunday, Outlook, Vietnam Report, Vietnam: The War This Week, Campaign and the Candidates, Frank McGee Report, 60 Minutes* and *Comment.*

Till 1963 when CBS and NBC moved to 30 minutes, the early evening network programs were 15 minutes in length. ABC began a half-hour report in 1967. At CBS the brevity of the 15-minute evening news programs was demonstrated by showing that the copy for Douglas Edward's program would fill only three columns of space on the front page of the *New York Times.* NBC offered 10- and 5-minute news reports as part of the *Today* program from its start in 1952. *CBS Morning News* began at 30 minutes (Mike Wallace, 1963–64) and went to an hour with Joseph Benti (later John Hart, then Hughes Rudd) March 31, 1969.

Titles of network news programs borrowed the "byline" from newspapers and were often changed—*CBS-TV News* to *CBS-TV News with Douglas Edwards* to *Douglas Edwards with the News* to *CBS Evening News* to *CBS Evening News with Walter Cronkite;* or *NBC Newsreel, The Camel News Caravan, The Huntley-Brinkley Report,* and *NBC Nightly News*—the latter introduced by the announcer as "reported by John Chancellor" and often including "David Brinkley's Journal." At ABC the anchorman chair was a revolving door for John Daly, Don Gardiner, Murphy Martin, Bob Young, Peter Jennings, Howard K. Smith, Frank Reynolds, and Harry Reasoner.

The number of stations carrying network news programs increased as more stations came on the air and the cables moved west. In 1951 Douglas Edwards was on 17 stations; *Camel News Caravan* on 21. In 1953 John Daly was on 33 ABC affiliates; Edwards on 53 CBS stations. By 1965 Peter Jennings, Walter Cronkite, and Huntley-Brinkley were carried on 106, 192, and 187 respectively. ABC's effort always suffered from lack of clearances—through the 1960s it was not carried by any affiliates in Ohio, which included several very large markets. After 1970 when Harry Reasoner joined Howard K. Smith on the *Evening News,* it received its highest ratings and more and more stations carried the program. In 1974 the number of affiliates carrying network evening news were ABC 191, CBS 194, and NBC 210.

News Gathering and Preparation

The development of radio news in the late 1930s and early 1940s provided the TV news base, especially the staff and overseas bureaus. In 1948 the major networks relied on their radio correspondents for the story and either contracted with foreign cameramen or with the national newsreel companies for the picture.[5] During the early stages of the Korean War in 1950, CBS used its radio men as cameramen to get footage for the television network.[6] NBC had separate radio and television personnel, and sent in three fulltime cameramen in addition to their own reporters on the scene. By 1954 CBS estimated a worldwide reporting staff of 200, including both full and part time stringers.[7] By 1961 the total had jumped to 700, including 38 full time correspondents, and 45 cameramen.[8] NBC's staff was developing at about the same rate, with ABC after a late start totaling 400, including stringers, in 1962.[9] In 1965, NBC President Robert Kintner observed:

> In a relatively brief time, we have built a news gathering, processing, and presenting organization with 800 employees scattered throughout the world, all of whom, except for a few stringers in remote spots, are fully employed by NBC and owe no allegiance anywhere else.[10]

In 1950 NBC maintained regular news bureaus in London, Paris, Bonn, and Tokyo. By 1960 they had added Havana, Rome, Moscow, Cairo, Athens, New Delhi, and Hong Kong. CBS matched these operations and added Beirut and Nairobi.[11] Key cities were often staffed with two or three men. ABC was late in developing foreign bases, but in 1960 added offices in Moscow, Berlin, Rome, Buenos Aires, and Mexico City.[12] In 1961 CBS added a bureau in Rio de Janeiro and named a new bureau chief for a Southeast Asia control point in Hong Kong.[13] In 1954 NBC announced new bureaus in Leopoldville and Ottawa, and in 1965 was reinstated in Moscow.

Domestic news gathering operations grew with the network news organizations. In 1948 CBS had a staff of 16 full time and four parttime employees, plus a film crew for New York news. By 1954 the network had a new staff of 100, operating out of New York, with NBC in 1961 indicating a New York-based staff of 325, including 26 national correspondents and 17 cameramen. In 1962 ABC increased its staff in its Washington bureau from 12 to 26. In 1962 CBS announced the formation of six domestic bureaus; New York for the Northeast; Chicago in the Midwest; Washington in the Mid-Atlantic states; Atlanta in the South; Dallas in the Southwest, and Los Angeles covering the West Coast, Hawaii, and Alaska. ABC and NBC maintain smaller bureaus, usually headquartered at their owned stations in the major market areas. These area correspondents make their reports through the home network station if time allows—if not, then through the nearest affiliate station.

After 1965 the Saigon bureaus of the networks became the largest outside of New York and Washington. At first, manned by correspondents from Hong Kong, Tokyo and other Asian bureaus and by stringers. Those included Charles P. Arnot and Lou Cioffi for ABC; Peter Kalisher, Adam Raphael, Murray Fromson, and Bernard Kalb for CBS; and James Robinson, Welles Hangen, John Rich, and John Sharkey for NBC.

American troops followed American advisers. The first Vietnam correspondents came as well—ABC: Malcolm Browne (from UPI), Roger Peterson and Ken Gale (from NBC); for CBS: Morley Safer, John Laurence, Dan Rather, and Don Webster; and for NBC: Garrick Utley, Jack Perkins, Dean Brelis and Ron Nessen. Many regular network correspondents took their turns reporting the war—for adventure, for career advancement, because it was expected and because they were journalists and it was the "oldest, permanent, floating story in the world." Most of the news "stars" would also make their tours. In all more than 150 correspondents, bureau administrators, and producers would work in Vietnam. From 1965 to 1972 each of the networks would maintain a staff of about 30 in Vietnam including five or six reporter-camera teams at an estimated cost of around $1,000,000 a year. In the early 1970s each of the networks was reported to have nine overseas film crews, not including Vietnam. The domestic news staff was growing, too. ABC had 16 fulltime domestic crews, CBS 25 and NBC 50—the latter including not just news but sports, special events, documentary and their five owned station staffs.

In 1971 it was estimated that NBC news (including sports) programming cost over $100 million each year for the television and radio networks and for the owned stations—nearly half for sports. The budget for the evening news, half hour, was about $9,000,000 or about $175,000 a week. The two-hour *Today Show* cost $5,000,000. NBC Radio Network's *News on the Hour* cost about $20,000 a week or $1,000,000 yearly. Some miscellaneous costs include $1,108,750 for satellite transmissions (1969), AT&T land lines $10 million, film stock and processing $3 million and nearly 200 film cameras costing from $1,000 to more than $12,000.[14]

The control point for network television news had always been at the network headquarter sites in New York. All of the correspondents and news materials from domestic and overseas sources are coordinated and channeled from these centers of operation. In 1948 for *CBS-TV News with Douglas Edwards* news decisions were made by a team consisting of the news coordinator, writers, a film editor, and a film librarian, Edwards and the director. In 1961 ABC carried an assignment editor, two news editors, five writers and three film editors for *John Daly and the News.*[15]

CBS in that same year had 30 writers and editors, and seven assignment editors to handle both its radio and televison news. NBC maintained a similar proportion of staff in 1961. By 1965 decisions on the *Huntley-Brinkley Report* were being made by six "senior people" with a total of 41 employed on that program alone.

The early editing personnel at the networks were "a mixture of experienced craftsmen from newspapers, wire services, radio news organizations, wire service picture desks, newsreels, and picture magazines." [16] Although the anchormen have, for the most part, strong broadcasting experience, the editors and reporters tend to come from newspapers and wire services.

In a 1961 poll of the network news departments by *Editor and Publisher,* CBS and NBC stated that seven of their eight top overseas correspondents came from the staffs of newspapers and national wire services. ABC sampled eight of its reporting staff at random finding five who had newspaper experience before entering broadcast news.[17] In 1965, all three of the White House network correspondents had early experience as newspapermen.[18] During the 1963 New York newspaper strike NBC hired newspapermen to help in a local expanded news effort. After the strike ended, the network retained seven of these people.[19]

Newsfilm and Facilities

The tools for part of the television news reporting job were in a mature stage of development even before the networks began transmitting in 1948. Newspapers and national wire services had laid down the facilities for getting the printed story out quickly and radio news during World War II had streamlined audio communication. The TV problem was getting motion picture news film on television rapidly.

The newsreel divisions of the national wire services provided the bulk of television news film in the beginning. In 1947 the Associated Press gathered material in its London and Washington bureaus and with the help of television stations in New York, Baltimore and Philadelphia aired the result—an experimental forerunner of the modern broadcast newsfilm.[20] The International News Service soon announced a daily service of newsreels for television,[21] and in 1948 the United Press and Fox Movietone News supplied a basic library of news footage, updating the material on a weekly basis. United Press then supplied an updated news script for the film morgue.[22] Stations continued to use still photos as backups for spot news items; a step toward "today's news today."

At the same time, the networks were building their newsfilm facilities to supplement wire service footage. In 1949 CBS received the bulk of their footage from Telenews, a newsreel company aligned with the International News Service, using its own camera crew in the New York area. NBC cooperated with 20th Century Fox to supplement its facilities in international and national coverage. ABC and Dumont made heavy use of newsfilm services.

The advent of the Korean War prompted both NBC and CBS to develop film coverage of overseas events. Soon the networks were receiving some 7,000 feet of film per week both from their camera crews and outside suppliers. CBS and NBC began to syndicate national and international film, for their owned stations and other local station's news programs as well. NBC discontinued its newsfilm syndication service in 1953,[23] but its prime news competitor CBS still offered its film service in 1966, taken mostly by independent television stations for national and international film coverage. Some NBC newsfilm is distributed abroad by Visnews.

Until 1961, ABC ordered sound and silent film from Telenews, or assigned one of its correspondents to meet the Telenews camera crew and cover the story. The appointment of James Hagerty to the ABC News vice presidency brought an effort to overhaul NBC and CBS in television newsfilm facilities. A fulltime ABC-TV camera division was formed, and special bureaus opened in Latin America.

In 1961, NBC shot some 5,600,000 feet of film for news. The news operations of NBC and CBS became the biggest film producers in the country.[24] The daily shipments of footage from the all-out network news coverage in Vietnam and the estimated NBC cost of $750,000 for direct coverage in 1965 indicate that the film facilities grew even more in the intervening four years.[25] By the 1970s it was estimated, for example, that NBC shot more than 25 hours of newsfilm everyday for news programs—or about 20 million feet.

In November 1965 NBC's news switched to color, CBS quickly followed, and ABC in 1967. From the mid-1960s nearly all newsfilm was in color as well.

In 1958 it took CBS three and a half hours to get a film story on the air that had been shot in the New York area. Much of the national newsfilm had to be flown to New York in the early days for transmission with often a 24-hour delay in getting to the air. In 1954 CBS cut the time to an hour and a half in New York. This time was cut even further through new processing techniques and the use of stations as transmission points. Switching around the network for film and tape pickups was pioneered by NBC on *The Camel News Caravan* in 1949,[26] and was adopted by CBS and ABC.

Overseas film production and delivery speed was a more complex problem. CBS in 1948 sometimes waited five weeks for film to cross the Atlantic to New York. The film of the Korean War in 1950 took three days to reach the United States audience. The CBS staff noted that it "must find ways of dating up film through the commentary." [27] In 1961, NBC newsfilm from Europe took six to 10 hours from the event overseas to the airing in New York. In 1966, film was relayed from Vietnam in 20 to 36 hours from shooting to showing on the air.

In 1961 NBC and the British Broadcasting Company combined forces to develop a slow-scan method of transmitting motion picture film by cable from Europe. A minute of film could be transmitted in 100 minutes, making possible the arrival of a normal report two or three hours after the event on the continent. In 1965 NBC created a special news unit utilizing communications satellites. At first the satellites were most frequently used to transmit reports from Vietnam—especially during Tet 1968—at a transmitter cost of about $3,000 for 10 minutes. By the 1970s the evening news casts would include satellite film reports almost every night from Asia, Europe and occasionally Latin America. In 1956 video tape was first used as a tool in network television news broadcasting on *Douglas Edwards and the News*. Video tape has been primarily used to delay broadcasts for transmission in various time zones throughout the country and to record live television pickups of news stories and on-going events for the evening programs. Live television coverage of spot news stories has been limited by the lack of mobility of facilities. In 1962 CBS announced a wireless portable television camera that would produce an air-quality picture under adverse lighting conditions. But it was not until 1970–71 that portable video cameras were experimentally used to regularly cover a story for the evening news (the Lt. Calley trial on CBS). Increasingly in the 1970s video cameras supplemented, but did not replace, film. By 1974 all three networks were using portable camera-VTR units, especially in Washington, and could broadcast live with portable cameras from a number of locations in the Capitol city.

With the end of American involvement in the Indochina war and growing domestic problems increased emphasis was put on domestic bureaus. In addition to bureaus within owned stations all three networks had an Atlanta bureau and one or more additional reporting teams in Miami, Houston and Dallas. NBC created a northeastern bureau separate from the New York operation with its own news manager, news editor, three correspondents and three field producers. In 1974 ABC, CBS, NBC each had a staff of about 50 and a budget of about $200,000 a week to produce the evening news programs viewed in about 25,000,000 homes each night.

When looking at the position of television news in 1957, CBS Vice President Sig Mickelson quoted Oliver Wendell Holmes to the effect that, "The great thing is not so much where we stand as in what direction we are moving." [28] The television news industry has the facilities, the craftsmen, and the support to do an effective and comprehensive job. Whether or not it will, isn't to be found in a chronicle of its material development, but at least we can see that the potential does indeed exist.

A 1949 CBS pilot for *Gunsmoke* sounded like the crime-detective programs of the era. Most of the action was carried by the central character talking to himself—after being hit on the head or shot. When it began on the radio November 29, 1952, Chester Proudfoot, Kitty Russell and Doc Adams helped with dialogue. The new program replaced Steve Allen on CBS radio and starred William Conrad later of *Cannon*. Jack Gould wrote that "*Gunsmoke* needs no picture," compared it to the BBC and praised the writing of John Meston and Leo Crutchfield. For the first TV episode "Matt Gets It," September 10, 1955, *Variety*'s review said: "In a showmanship fillip, John Wayne was called in to introduce the series, and worked in a 24-sheet for Arness that was done disarmingly." Gould pronounced it a "winner" and the star "appropriately rugged and noble." Dennis Weaver was Chester Goode, with Milburn Stone and Amanda Blake. Ken Curtis was introduced as Festus after Weaver left in 1963.

Table 25.

NETWORK RADIO EVENING PROGRAMMING

Figures show the number of quarter-hours of evening programming
per week on the national radio networks during the seasons indicated.

	1928	1931	1934	1937	1940	1943	1946	1949	1952	1955
VARIETY										
Comedy Variety	4	9	32	38	32	34	30	30	26	8
Semi-Variety	--	18	23	16	16	2	--	2	4	10
Amateur/Talent Var.	--	--	--	4	4	2	--	8	9	2
Country/ Variety	--	--	9	10	12	6	4	10	4	11
General Variety	10	16	14	24	16	21	22	4	4	25
Children's Variety	--	--	--	--	--	--	--	--	--	--
Magazine Format	--	--	--	--	--	--	--	--	--	--
MUSIC										
Musical Variety	34	75	64	56	59	60	63	52	29	76
Light Music	28	37	27	25	24	7	9	2	15	28
Concert Music	76	62	48	36	28	22	24	23	32	27
Records	--	--	--	--	4	--	--	--	10	4
DRAMA										
General Drama	--	--	2	8	14	12	18	20	16	6
Light/Drama	8	20	13	11	24	14	17	22	25	7
Women's Serials	--	--	15	--	--	--	--	--	--	--
Comedy Drama	--	18	8	34	21	20	40	35	33	16
Thrillers	--	9	34	25	40	35	57	68	91	62
Documentary	4	--	4	8	4	12	6	4	9	6
TALK										
Human Interest	--	--	6	16	10	10	11	8	6	2
Quiz and Panel	--	--	--	6	30	30	38	48	16	19
News and Commentary	4	13	27	34	56	65	77	50	83	82
Forums and Interview	2	5	--	8	13	12	14	13	10	17
Talk	4	14	14	14	38	8	21	22	18	21
Sports Play-by-play	--	--	--	--	3	--	3	3	6	26
Religious	2	14	5	5	5	11	5	3	--	10
TOTAL	176	310	345	378	453	383	459	427	446	465

Source: Computed by Lichty with C. H. Sterling from Summers, Radio Programs Carried on
National Networks, 1926-1956. Evening=after 6:00 p.m. Eastern time.

Ref: News content   Rounsaville Radio   WFUN

1. Lately a lot of material has been creeping into our news
   shows that does not belong there. Effective immediately
   kill all but the most major developments out of Saigon,
   Belfast etc. Stay away from D.C. stories on obscure
   economic indicators. All we should be interested in are
   the Consumer Price Index and unemployment figures. Kiss
   off politicals with a one liner. When we're out of the
   current campaign, kiss them off entirely.

                                              (continued)

Table 26.

NETWORK RADIO DAYTIME PROGRAMMING

Figures show the number of quarter-hours of weekday daytime
programming per week on the national radio networks during the
seasons indicated.

	1928	1931	1934	1937	1940	1943	1946	1949	1952	1955
VARIETY										
Comedy Variety	--	--	--	--	--	--	10	--	--	--
Semi-Variety	--	--	--	--	--	--	--	--	--	--
Amateur/Talent Var.	--	--	--	--	--	--	--	--	10	--
Country Variety	--	--	--	--	--	--	--	30	15	--
General Variety	--	--	20	30	42	62	55	55	65	121
Children's Variety	--	8	--	7	4	--	--	--	5	--
Magazine Format	--	--	--	--	--	--	--	--	--	--
MUSIC										
Musical Variety	--	--	--	8	--	5	10	20	10	41
Light Music	10	30	92	45	46	4	29	21	25	23
Concert Music	--	4	20	18	10	2	--	2	--	5
Records	--	--	--	--	--	--	--	15	30	28
DRAMA										
General Drama	--	4	8	4	--	--	--	--	--	--
Light/Drama	--	--	--	5	--	--	14	15	10	33
Women's Serials	--	--	43	154	305	200	200	165	175	130
Comedy Drama	--	--	9	5	5	--	10	10	--	--
Thrillers	--	--	13	27	20	25	50	40	35	12
Documentary	--	10	10	12	19	10	10	--	--	--
TALK										
Human Interest	--	--	5	12	4	--	45	85	50	35
Quiz and Panel	--	--	--	--	--	--	15	50	60	35
News and Commentary	--	--	--	29	10	49	51	35	30	63
Forums and Interview	--	--	--	--	--	--	--	--	--	--
Talk	31	96	91	83	68	33	44	54	40	18
Sports Play-by-Play	--	--	--	--	--	--	--	--	--	--
Religious	--	--	--	--	5	--	5	5	5	--
TOTAL	41	152	311	439	538	390	548	602	565	544

Source: Computed by Lichty with C. H. Sterling from Summers, Radio Programs Carried on
National Networks, 1926-1956. Daytime=before 6:00 p.m. Eastern time.

2. Emphasis should be placed on the following items:

a. Consumer
b. Public education
c. Quality police matter
d. Employment
e. Transportation

f. Environment
g. Aviation
h. Minorities
i. Yellow power

Consumer oriented stories include such items as the clear
meat packaging ordinance, consumer frauds, dangerous
items and substances, auto recalls and price gouging.

(continued)

Table 27.

NETWORK RADIO WEEKEND PROGRAMMING

Figures show the number of quarter-hours of weekend daytime programming per week on the national radio networks during the seasons indicated.

	1928	1931	1934	1937	1940	1943	1946	1949	1952	1955
VARIETY										
Comedy Variety	--	--	--	--	--	--	--	--	--	--
Semi-Variety	--	--	6	4	--	--	2	--	2	--
Amateur/Talent Var.	--	--	--	--	--	--	--	--	--	--
Country Variety	--	--	--	--	--	--	4	4	4	6
General Variety	--	--	4	6	12	8	6	2	10	17
Children's Variety	--	--	--	--	4	6	8	6	8	4
Magazine Format	--	--	--	--	--	--	--	--	--	39
MUSIC										
Musical Variety	--	4	13	10	2	13	13	4	8	32
Light Music	2	11	12	8	13	4	10	6	11	6
Concert Music	--	12	41	47	48	34	46	35	33	40
Records	--	--	--	--	--	--	--	2	--	--
DRAMA										
General Drama	--	--	--	--	4	--	2	--	--	--
Light/Drama	--	2	12	7	4	8	10	9	12	6
Women's Serials	--	--	1	--	--	--	--	--	--	--
Comedy Drama	--	--	--	--	--	--	2	6	--	--
Thrillers	--	--	5	4	2	4	10	10	20	10
Documentary	--	--	1	5	6	2	10	10	4	6
TALK										
Human Interest	--	--	1	4	6	--	2	4	--	--
Quiz and Panel	--	--	--	--	4	--	8	16	4	2
News and Commentary	--	1	1	8	4	9	9	12	9	12
Forums and Interview	8	--	2	2	7	8	10	7	11	12
Talk	2	12	8	12	17	11	18	18	18	18
Sports Play-by-Play	--	--	--	--	--	--	--	--	--	--
Religious	12	12	10	12	15	22	23	20	35	48
TOTAL	24	54	117	129	148	129	193	171	189	258

Source: Computed by Lichty with C. H. Sterling from Summers, <u>Radio Programs Carried on National Networks, 1926-1956</u>. Daytime=before 6:00 p.m. Eastern time.

Just about everyone has contact in some way with public education. The big ones here are busing, drugs in school, school money problems and school taxes.

When I say quality police matter, I mean I don't want to hear a robbery of under $1,000 or where someone didn't have the living hell beaten out of him and is consigned either to a wheelchair for the rest of his life or to a piece of the farm. In other police matters, I'm not interested unless they're dead. I don't want to hear fires unless the property loss is over $25,000 or if there is a nice crispy dead body inside.

"The Sunshine Group"

Table 28.

NETWORK RADIO PROGRAMMING SUMMARY

Figures show the number of quarter-hours of all programming
and the percent of that programming per week that was sponsored
on the national radio networks during the seasons indicated.

	1928	1931	1934	1937	1940	1943	1946	1949	1952	1955
ALL PROGRAMMING/QUARTER HOURS										
Variety	14	51	108	139	142	141	141	151	166	243
Music	150	235	317	253	234	151	204	182	203	310
Drama	12	63	178	309	468	342	456	414	430	294
Talk	65	167	170	245	295	268	399	453	401	420
TOTAL	241	516	773	946	1139	902	1200	1200	1200	1267
ALL PROGRAMMING/%										
Variety	6%	10%	14%	15%	12%	16%	12%	13%	14%	19%
Music	62	46	41	27	21	17	17	15	17	24
Drama	5	12	23	33	41	38	38	35	36	23
Talk	27	32	22	26	26	30	33	38	33	33
% OF PROGRAMMING SPONSORED										
Variety	100%	59%	71%	66%	54%	55%	68%	64%	54%	40%
Music	67	69	50	50	32	60	70	54	38	31
Drama	33	37	85	77	83	88	83	81	74	66
Talk	9	44	35	34	39	48	53	52	51	40
TOTAL % SPONSORED	51%	56%	55%	57%	56%	66%	69%	64%	57%	44%

Source: Computed by Lichty with C. H. Sterling from Summers, Radio Programs Carried on National Networks, 1926-1956.

Table 29.

THRILLER DRAMA, QUIZ, AND TALK PROGRAMS

Figures show a more detailed breakdown of the number of quarter hours of programming per week on the national radio networks in the categories: thriller drama, quiz and panel, and talk programs during the seasons indicated. Weekday daytime and weekend daytime were combined in this table.

	DAYTIME				NIGHTTIME			
	1932	1940	1948	1956	1932	1940	1948	1956
THRILLER DRAMA								
Crime/Detective	--	--	5	--	12	23	60	25
Action/Adventure	6	15	39	--	5	4	4	6
Western	--	5	5	12	2	8	8	2
Suspense	--	--	--	--	--	5	16	4
TOTAL	6	20	40	12	19	40	88	37
QUIZ PROGRAMS								
Audience Quiz	--	4	42	10	--	28	22	8
Comedy Audience Particip.	--	--	12	--	--	--	4	4
Panel	--	--	--	5	--	2	16	--
TOTAL	--	4	54	15	--	30	42	12
TALK PROGRAMS								
Comedy	27	11	--	--	6	--	1	--
Broadway/Hollywood Gossip	--	5	1	--	--	5	2	--
Sports	--	1	--	4	--	17	8	12
Farm	24	20	7	6	--	--	--	--
Homemaker	68	14	12	--	--	--	--	--
Miscellaneous	28	34	26	33	6	16	3	15
TOTAL	147	85	46	43	12	38	14	27

Source: Computed by Lichty with C. H. Sterling from Summers, Radio Programs Carried on National Networks, 1926-1956.

Table 30.

NETWORK RADIO NEWS PROGRAMMING--WORLD WAR II

Figures show the number of hours per year of news broadcasts by each of the four national radio networks--this includes regular newscasts, specials, bulletins and on-the-spot coverage.

	1937	1938	1939	1940	1941	1942	1943	1944
NBC Red	279	304	257	636	983	1280	1641	1726
CBS	405	389	491	769	829	1385	1454	1497
NBC Blue	274	222	310	681	796	836	909	1062
Mutual	NA	NA	193	310	840	1131	1370	1237
TOTAL			1251	2396	3448	4632	5374	5532

Source: Broadcasting, April 23, 1945, p. 23, from data supplied by the networks.

Table 31.

NETWORK RADIO NEWS PROGRAMMING--1974

Figures show the number of hours per week of news reporting, commentary-analysis, sports reporting, and other programming on the national radio networks.

	HOURS OF PROGRAMMING				
	News Reporting	Commentary/Analysis	Sports	Other	Total
ABC Information	13.0	1.3	3.0	3.8	21.1
ABC Entertainment	11.4	.4	1.4	5.0	18.2
ABC Contemporary	9.9	--	.7	2.6	13.2
ABC FM	9.1	--	--	.7	9.8
CBS	18.6	2.3	2.8	2.5	26.2
NBC	13.8	1.3	2.5	26.1	43.7
Mutual	36.9	3.4	1.6	5.4	47.3
Mutual Black	7.9	--	1.7	--	9.6
TOTAL	120.6	8.7	13.7	46.1	189.1
PERCENT	64%	5%	7%	24%	100%

Sources: Program schedules provided by the networks, January 1974, computed by Lichty and Topping. Other programming includes Monitor, forum and interview programs such as Face the Nation, cooking and advice, and religious. Not included are repeat feeds, closed circuit feeds of news material, news promotions, nor special events and sports play-by-play broadcast on an irregular basis.

Table 32.

RADIO STATION FORMATS

Figures show the % of stations in various format categories. Not all of the data are comparable as definitions of music and format varied. Some figures are for specific market categories. When available a further breakdown for "Other" is given at the bottom of this table.

	1964 AM & FM Large	1964 AM & FM Single	FM 1966 Market Top 50	FM 1966 Other	1968 Top 20 Mkts AM and FM	1970 FM	1971 Top 100 AM	1971 Top 100 FM	1972 Top 10 AM	1972 Top 10 FM	1972 11-110 AM	1972 11-110 FM	1973 AM and FM
Middle of the Road	12%	22%	49%	64%	40%	35%	21%	18%	25%	29%	26%	19%	22%
Top 40/Rock	10	9	15	4	15	17	27	25	20	13	24	15	26
Beautiful/Easy	22	21	30	23	13	22	17	39	8	28	6	29	8
Country	6	12	--	5	11	11	18	10	9	2	18	10	21
Black/Soul	5	1	--	--	7	1			10	4	7	4	14
Progressive	--	--	--	--	--	4			3	1	2	11	3
Other	45	35	6	4	14	10	17[a]	8[a]	25	23	17	12	6
TOTAL	100%	100%	100%	100%	100%	100%	100%	100%	100%	100%	100%	100%	100%
(Classical)						(1%)			(4%)	(11%)	(6%)	(5%)	(3%)
(Oldies)									(-)	(2)	(1)	(1)	
(Jazz)						(4)			(-)	(4)	(-)	(-)	
(Relig/Gospel)									(4)	(1)	(4)	(4)	
(Spanish)									(3)	(1)	(2)	(1)	
(Ethnic/Lang.)						(1)			(3)	(4)	(1)	(-)	
(News/Talk)						(1)			(11)	(1)	(3)	(1)	(3)

Sources: 1964: Broadcasting, 9/28/64, N=1,400; in this case only the % is for type of music only, excluding talk programming, it is not for format. 1966: NAFMB, National FM Programming Trends, 1967; N=244 for top 50 markets, 564 for other. 1968: Computed from Sponsor series on radio markets, N=1,076. 1970: NAFMB survey, Broadcasting, 10/26/70; N=1,365. 1971: Radio Programming Profile, reported in Broadcasting, 6/21/71; N=955 AM, 643 FM. 1972: Computed from Hamilton, Operating Manual for Starship Radio '72; top 10 N=159 AM, 100 FM, markets 11-110 N=901 AM, 549 FM. 1973: Computed from Broadcasting Yearbook, 1973, N=4,193. In all cases categories are not precisely the same as reported in the original sources, definitions varied and some re-categorization was necessary.
[a]Includes black, religious, and ethnic/foreign language.

Table 33.

NETWORK TV EVENING PROGRAMMING

Figures show the number of quarter hours of evening programming per week on the national television networks during the seasons indicated.

	1949	1952	1955	1958	1961	1964	1967	1970	1973
VARIETY									
Special/Varied	--	2	22	10	4	4	4	4	19
Comedy Variety	42	65	44	20	14	40	28	35	20
Amateur/Talent	8	14	6	6	--	--	--	--	--
Country Variety	6	--	4	4	--	4	--	8	--
General/Talk	--	--	30	35	35	39	42	26	48
MUSIC									
Musical Variety	15	26	8	40	18	28	16	24	12
Light Music	15	13	14	--	--	--	--	--	--
DRAMA									
General	24	54	80	50	28	60	8	34	24
Motion Pictures	34	--	--	--	--	16	48	72	101
Women's Serials	3	2	--	--	--	--	4	--	--
Action/Adventure	--	11	6	16	32	18	70	18	16
Crime/Detective	2	28	12	18	40	18	10	24	44
Suspense/Mystery	--	18	4	6	--	14	4	--	4
Westerns	--	6	6	40	54	34	38	22	12
Comedy/Situation	4	24	60	40	52	38	52	56	42
Animated Cartoons	--	--	--	--	6	2	--	--	--
QUIZ									
Audience Partic.	10	18	18	22	4	6	4	6	--
Human Interest	10	16	10	10	6	4	2	--	--
Panel Quiz	13	26	16	6	8	6	6	--	--
NEWS-INFO									
News	27	13	22	21	16	32	40	39	39
Forums/Interview	14	14	5	--	10	2	--	--	--
Documentary	4	2	10	12	28	16	12	8	8
OTHER									
Religious	--	4	2	--	--	--	--	--	--
Talk	30	10	5	--	--	--	--	--	--
Children's Shows	29	21	10	4	--	--	--	--	--
Sports	62	33	29	6	6	6	--	--	--
Misc.	10	7	--	--	--	--	--	--	--
TOTAL	362	427	423	366	361	387	388	446	392

Computed by Lichty, based on the third week in January.   Evening=after 6:00 p.m. Eastern time.

Table 34.

NETWORK TV DAYTIME PROGRAMMING

Figures show the number of quarter hours of weekday daytime
programming per week on the national television networks during
the seasons indicated.

	1949	1952	1955	1958	1961	1964	1967	1970	1973
VARIETY									
Special/Varied	--	--	--	--	--	--	--	--	--
Comedy Variety	--	35	--	--	--	--	--	--	--
Amateur/Talent	--	--	--	--	--	--	--	--	--
Country Variety	--	--	--	--	--	--	--	--	--
General/Talk	10	129	166	76	40	45	40	50	60
MUSIC									
Musical Variety	5	20	30	55	30	10	20	--	--
Light Music	10	5	--	--	--	--	--	--	--
DRAMA									
General	--	--	--	30	50	20	20	--	--
Motion Pictures	--	--	--	--	--	--	--	--	--
Women's Serials	--	30	84	65	100	70	110	158	160
Action/Adventure	20	--	--	10	20	--	--	--	--
Crime/Detective	--	--	--	--	--	--	--	--	--
Suspense/Mystery	--	--	--	--	--	--	--	--	--
Westerns	--	--	--	--	10	20	--	--	--
Comedy/Situation	--	--	--	10	50	50	50	60	20
Animated Cartoons	--	--	--	--	--	--	--	--	--
QUIZ									
Audience Partic.	20	28	40	80	10	120	128	68	130
Human Interest	15	1	20	45	50	20	20	--	--
Panel Quiz	--	--	--	--	--	20	10	28	10
NEWS-INFO									
News	--	10	--	5	9	24	22	26	25
Forums/Interview	--	--	--	--	--	--	--	--	--
Documentary	--	--	--	--	--	--	--	--	--
OTHER									
Religious	--	--	--	--	--	--	--	--	--
Talk	15	11	27	--	20	10	10	10	10
Children's Shows	10	15	32	25	15	20	20	20	20
Sports	--	--	--	--	--	--	--	--	--
Misc.	--	--	--	--	--	--	--	--	--
TOTAL	105	284	399	401	494	429	450	420	435

Computed by Lichty, based on the third week in January. Daytime=before 6:00 p.m.
Eastern time.

Table 35.

NETWORK TV WEEKEND PROGRAMMING

Figures show the number of quarter hours of weekend daytime
programming per week on the national television networks
during the seasons indicated.

	1949	1952	1955	1958	1961	1964	1967	1970	1973
VARIETY									
Special/Varied	--	--	6	10	--	--	--	--	--
Comedy Variety	--	--	--	--	--	--	--	--	--
Amateur/Talent	--	--	--	--	2	2	2	2	--
Country Variety	--	4	--	--	--	--	--	--	--
General/Talk	--	--	--	--	--	--	--	--	--
MUSIC									
Musical Variety	--	--	--	4	2	4	4	4	4
Light Music	--	--	--	--	--	--	--	--	--
DRAMA									
General	--	9	6	6	6	--	--	--	--
Motion Pictures	--	--	--	--	--	--	--	4	4
Women's Serials	--	2	--	--	--	--	--	--	--
Action/Adventure	--	6	6	--	6	8	--	2	--
Crime/Detective	--	--	--	6	2	--	--	--	--
Suspense/Mystery	--	--	--	--	--	--	--	--	--
Westerns	--	--	2	8	4	6	--	--	--
Comedy/Situation	--	6	--	--	--	2	--	2	2
Animated Cartoons	--	--	--	4	8	24	56	66	54
QUIZ									
Audience Partic.	--	--	--	2	2	4	4	--	2
Human Interest	--	2	2	--	--	--	--	--	--
Panel Quiz	--	2	2	2	--	--	--	--	--
NEWS-INFO									
News	--	1	1	2	2	2	--	--	--
Forums/Interview	--	12	18	8	6	4	6	6	6
Documentary	--	4	4	14	6	14	10	4	16
OTHER									
Religious	2	11	8	8	8	8	8	8	6
Talk	--	4	9	4	4	10	--	--	--
Children's Shows	8	26	22	6	16	4	4	4	4
Sports	--	--	13	22	26	30	38	42	46
Misc.	--	3	--	--	2	--	--	--	--
TOTAL	10	92	99	106	102	122	132	144	144

Computed by Lichty, based on the third week in January. Daytime=before 6:00 p.m.
Eastern time.

Table 36.

NETWORK TV PROGRAMMING SUMMARY

Figures below show the number of quarter hours and % of programming in the major program categories per week on national television networks, and the type of sponsorship of programs. Table 36 is continued on the next page.

	1949	1952	1955	1958	1961	1964	1967	1970	1973
ALL PROGRAMMING/ QUARTER HOURS									
Variety	66	249	278	161	95	134	116	195	150
Music	45	64	52	99	50	42	40	28	16
Drama	87	196	266	309	468	400	68	518	483
Quiz	68	93	108	167	170	180	174	102	142
News/Info	45	56	60	62	77	94	88	83	94
Other	166	145	157	75	97	88	74	84	86
TOTAL	477	803	921	873	957	938	970	1010	971
ALL PROGRAMMING/ PERCENT									
Variety	14%	31%	30%	18%	10%	14%	12%	19%	15%
Music	9	8	6	11	5	4	4	3	2
Drama	18	24	29	35	49	43	48	51	50
Quiz	14	12	12	19	18	19	18	10	15
News/Info	9	7	7	7	8	10	9	8	10
Other	35	18	17	9	10	9	8	8	9
TOTAL	99%	100%	101%	99%	100%	99%	99%	99%	101%
SPONSORSHIP/NUMBER OF PROGRAMS[1]									
Single Sponsor	33	85	75	59	25	13	8	3	--
Two Sponsors	--	5	25	41	44	16	12	2	--
Participating	1	4	5	11	29	50	66	78	70
TOTAL	34	94	105	111	98	79	86	83	70

Computed by Lichty, based on the third week in January. Cost as reported by producers in Broadcasting and Variety. Stations and ratings from A. C. Nielsen National Television Index, January Second Report each year; round to whole number.

[1]Information on sponsorship is ONLY for prime-time (7-11 ET) programs.

Table 36. (continued)

NETWORK TV PROGRAMMING SUMMARY

Figures below show the average cost of program production, live and video tape vs. film production, the number of network affiliates carrying programs, and the average rating for each network. All of this information is ONLY for prime-time (7-11 ET) entertainment programs.

	1949	1952	1955	1958	1961	1964	1967	1970	1973
AVERAGE PRODUCTION COST									
90-M Drama	$ 5,900	$35,900	$67,700	$84,000	$110,000	$181,000	$200,000	$300,000a	$342,500
60-M Variety	10,800	21,100	34,100	65,450	86,640	115,700	182,170	193,210	204,286
60-M Drama	3,800	16,700	24,600	44,100	63,000	120,810	176,520	203,610	213,636
30-M Variety						65,000		100,000	104,194
30-M Drama	3,500	13,200	26,100	36,200	42,270	59,030	88,690	103,960	
30-M Quiz	1,730	9,640	11,400	29,330	28,200	45,500	71,000	35,000	
Movies2					180,000	200,000	380,000	750,000	750,000
Movies for TV								400,000	418,333
LIVE/VTR OR FILM									
Live/VTR	34	78	65	42	17	25	19	22	12
Film	--	25	40	69	81	54	67	51	58
STATIONS CARRYING									
ABC	10	29	80	114	144	169	167	168	181
CBS	6	36	108	141	160	191	182	188	195
NBC	14	40	98	125	160	169	185	199	205
DuM	8	13	24						
AVERAGE RATING									
ABC		17	14	17	19	18	17	18	19
CBS		26	25	24	21	22	21	22	21
NBC		29	25	21	19	18	20	22	20
DuM		16	9						

2This is not the cost of production but the purchase or lease price for network showing. a1971.

3Through 1958 all the live/VTR were live, after that they were increasingly "live on tape" then more often edited tape. By 1973 there were no more live prime-time entertainment programs (during the January sample); and five sitcoms were produced on VTR.

Table 37.

NETWORK TV SPECIALS

Figures show the number and hours of prime-time special (not regularly scheduled) programming on the national television networks from mid-September to mid-June for the seasons indicated and for the total period 1948-1968.

	1949	1952	1955	1958	1961	1964	1967	1948-1968 TOTAL
Number of specials	44	30	49	107	260	130	175	2,388
Hours:Mins. of specials	64:35	28:45	50:00	101:25	223:45	159:30	199:25	2,279:55
CATEGORY:								
Musical Variety	5%	--	9%	13%	10%	16%	14%	14%
Comedy Variety	--	8%	11	14	9	4	6	8
All other Variety	22	34	6	5	4	27	--	4
'Prestige' Drama	--	--	2	7	6	1	5	6
All other Drama	7	--	14	27	15	7	21	14
Documentary	--	5	4	12	25	20	17	19
Political	19	8	15	2	15	3	6	9
News Actuality	--	7	1	5	10	7	14	10
Sports	36	3	29	4	2	6	5	6
All other Talk	11	35	19	11	4	9	12	10

Source: Robert Lee Bailey, "The Content of Network Television Prime-Time Special Programming: 1948-1968," *Journal of Broadcasting*, XIV, No. 3, pp. 325-336; tables adapted by Lichty and Topping. Also see, Bailey, "An Examination of Prime Time Network Television Special Programs, 1948-1966," Ph.D. dissertation, University of Wisconsin, Madison, 1967.

During the 1972-73 season the three networks broadcast 210 hours of specials (35 hours of that repeats) about evenly divided on the three networks with slightly more time on ABC. (*Variety*, July 4 and 11, 1973)

Table 38.

TELEVISION STATION PROGRAMMING

Figures show the % of programming in various categories for all
stations during the sample weeks for New York, Los Angeles and
Chicago in 1951, New York in 1952, New York in 1954, Washington,
D.C. in 1958, Los Angeles in 1960 and Washington, D.C. in 1970

	1951 NY	1951 LA	1951 CHI	1952 NY	1954 NY	1958 WDC	1960 LA	1970 WDC
Variety	24%	26%	16%	17%	11%	5%	5%	14%
Music	4	6	3	3	7	7	3	3
Drama	25	25	26	36	46	46	54	38
Quiz/Personality	11	8	14	9	10	9	6	8
News	6	13	6	6	6	4	5	9
Information/Talk	7	5	5	8	8	8	9	6
Religious	1	1	--	1	2	2	2	3
Children's	12	10	8	11	3	13	7	13
Sports	10	5	21	8	3	5	4	4
Miscellaneous	--	--	--	--	4	1	5	2
TOTAL	100%	100%	100%	100%	100%	100%	100%	100%

Sources: 1951, 1952, 1954: D. Smythe, New York Television January 4-10,
1951, 1952, National Association of Educational Broadcasters, August,
1952; D. Smythe and A. Campbell, Los Angeles Television May 23-29, 1951,
National Association of Educational Broadcasters, December, 1951;
D. Horton, H. Mauksch, and K. Lang, Chicago Summer Television July 30 -
August 5, 1951, National Association of Educational Broadcasters, n.d.;
H. Remmers and R. Mainer, Four Years of New York Television 1951-1954,
National Association of Educational Broadcasters, June, 1954.
1958, 1960: J. Brown, Inventory of Television Programming in Los Angeles,
April 30 - May 6, 1960, term paper, University of Southern California,
June 1960. 1970: H. Bourgeois, term paper, University of Wisconsin, 1970.

Table 39.

LIVE, FILM AND VTR PROGRAMMING ON TV NETWORKS AND STATIONS

Figures show the number of hours of programming each week for the national television networks, for network affiliated stations, and for non-network (independent) stations; and the % of network, syndicated, and local program which is network originated, syndicated, and locally produced.

	1953	1955	1958	1961	1964	1967	1970	1973
NETWORK PROGRAMMING								
Hours:Minutes/Week	184:15	222:30	205:30	227:00	228:20	261:33	270:25	249:46
Live	82%	87%	70%	27%	26%	47%	14%	21%
Film	18	13	24	35	37	23	36	32
Video Tape	--	--	6	38	37	31	49	47
NETWORK AFFILIATE STATIONS								
Hours:Minutes/Week	93:34	94:12	102:40	108:08	117:00	122:13	123:23	122:45
NETWORK PROGRAMS:	52%	51%	58%	62%	64%	65%	66%	64%
SYNDICATED PROGRAMS:								
Film for Television[1]	10	13	13	12	11	7	7	6
Motion Pictures[2]	17	16	16	13	10	10	9	7
Syndicated Video Tape	--	--	--	1	2	5	2	9
LOCAL PROGRAMS:								
Live[3]	21	20	13	10	11	10	10	9
Video Taped	--	--	--	2	3	3	3	2
Filmed	--	--	--	--	--	--	3	2
INDEPENDENT STATIONS								
Hours:Minutes/Week	50:57	41:43	74:12	90:19	72:18	78:44	88:37	101:27[a]
NETWORK PROGRAMS:[4]								12%
SYNDICATED PROGRAMS:								
Film for Television[1]	18%	21%	24%	40%	43%	21%	31%	26
Motion Pictures[2]	43	30	47	27	26	35	35	32
Syndicated Video Tape	--	--	--	5	5	15	15	13
LOCAL PROGRAMS:								
Live[3]	39	49	29	25	23	24	14	12
Video Taped	--	--	--	4	4	5	5	3
Filmed	--	--	--	--	--	--	1	2

Source: Broadcasting Yearbook, based on an annual survey, usually for June.
[1]"Film specially made for Tv," includes TV film made for syndication and increasingly since 1960 re-runs of off-the-network film programs made for TV. [2]"Film made for theatrical showing," usually motion pictures. [3]It is not clear but apparetly "live" includes "live-on-tape"--that is programs produced as if they were live with no stopping or editing but video taped for almost immediate (usually same day) broadcast, and those taped for delayed but same day showing to different time zones. [4]Network programming carried on non-network stations was not reported until 1972; it was 4%. [a]Figures for independent stations 1973 are different than reported in the Yearbook because of an apparent error in their table.

Table 40.

TELEVISION PROGRAM COSTS

Figures show the costs of producing a typical episode of five network drama programs.

	Typical Live Drama 1950 Half Hour	Typical Film Mystery 1952 Half Hour	Defenders 1961 Hour	Bonanza 1970 Hour	Typical Film Drama 1974[b] Half Hour
Script	$ 500	$ 1,000	$ 8,000[a]	$ 7,750	$ 7,500
Producer, Director	450	750	15,706	22,990	18,000
Miscellaneous	--	--	2,400	11,380	5,000
Cast	1100	2,750	17,500	55,885	27,000
ABOVE THE LINE	$2050	$ 4,500	$ 43,606	$ 98,005	$ 57,500
Production Staff	--	540	2,152	3,053	2,000
Camerman, Camera	--	800	3,704	5,379	2,500
Grips, Set Operations	--	250	3,300	6,869	2,000
Electrical	--	889	3,360	6,276	2,500
Scenery	--	--	6,000	4,479	3,500
Sound Recording	--	654	2,023	6,310	3,000
Makeup, Hair Dressing	--	238	815	4,199	500
Set Dressing, Props	750	550	3,537	5,722	2,500
Location	--	50	1,805	6,463	--
Transportation	--	200	925	1,511	1,000
Stage, Studio	--	850	4,525	13,550	15,000
Film Editing	--	875	2,590	8,704	4,000
All Other Costs: rerecord, stock, titles, royalities, wardrobe, misc.	4120	2,421	30,009	41,015	21,000
BELOW THE LINE	$4870	$ 8,317	$ 64,835	$113,530	$ 59,500
TOTAL FOR ONE EPISODE	$6920	$12,817	$108,441	$211,535	$117,000

Sources: "Television Program Costs," Sponsor, May 22, 1950: "What It Costs Producer To Make Typical Half-hour Mystery Film," Sponsor, March 10, 1952; "$108,441 For An Hour's Work," Television, September 1961; Morris Gelman, "Any Ceiling Ever On Program Costs?," Broadcasting, September 22, 1969 and "TV Costs: Dough-Re-Mi-Farther," Variety, September 12, 1973.

[a]Both The Defenders and Bonanza were more expensive than typical programs of these types; the budget for a script for the Defenders was about twice as high as for a typical hour drama which in 1961 was about $4,500.

[b]
This is based on the budget of an actual TV series--one without super-stars or exotic shooting locations--rounded to the nearest $500 in each category. Because budgets are compiled differently, the amount in the above categories may vary slightly from the original source.

PART SEVEN

AUDIENCES

Station	Location	Left Dial	Right Dial	Date
WNAC	Boston	16	17	Oct. 20 1924
WEEI	Boston	21	23	Oct. 20 1924
WGI	Boston	30	34	Oct. 21 1924
WGY	Schenectady	33	38	Oct. 21 1924
KDKA	Pittsburgh	23	26	Oct. 22 1924
WBZ	Springfield	24	29	Oct. 22 1924
WOR	Newark	36	40	Oct. 22 1924
WHN	New York	29	32	Oct. 24 1924

Station	Location	Left Dial	Center Dial	Right Dial	Date
WTAM	Cleveland	37	41¾	41¾	Dec. 4 1927
WKBW	Buffalo	5	6¼	6½	Dec. 4 1927
WOWO	Fort Wayne	7	8	8½	Dec. 6 1927
KTNT	Musketeen	11	12	12¾	Dec. 6 1927
WHK	Cleveland	12¼	14	14	Dec. 6 1927
KMOX	St. Louis	17¾	20	20	Dec. 6 1927
WSM	Nashville	24	27	27½	Dec. 6 1927

Station	Location		Center Dial	Date
WFI	Philadelphia		53.5	Sept. 24 1933
XEPN	Eagle Pass Texas		58.0	Sept. 24 1933
WLW	Cincinnati O.		69.5	Sept. 24 1933
XER	Mexico	Brinkley Hospital	73.0	Sept. 24 1933

—field book of E. O. Pray, kept in New Hampshire

This only goes to prove, my boy, all the intelligent people listen to Bergen.

> —Alexander Wollcott to Orson Welles after the "Invasion from Mars" broadcast.

The public is what we fly over.

> —Michael H. Dann, senior vice president, programs, CBS Television Network

TYPICAL OF predictions of the influence that broadcasting would have on society was this one from 1908:

> Manifestly, wireless telegraphy is destined to become a great civilizing and socializing agency, because the firmament of the world is the common property of all nations, and those who use it for signaling inhabit it, in a certain sense. When all nations come to inhabit the firmament collectively they will be brought into closer communion, for their mutual advantage. A new upper geography dawns upon us, in which there is no more sea, neither are there any boundaries between the peoples.[1]

No part of the broadcasting experience has been examined in America in more detail and more repetitiously than the audience. Estimates of the earliest broadcast audiences are more available than the circumstances surrounding the broadcasters themselves.

Estimates of the audience for the KDKA broadcast of the national election results in 1920 establish listeners at less than 1,000. These were the innovator listeners, with homemade equipment which was an undependable as early stations. In 1924 an estimated 20,000,000 or more persons listened to national election returns over more than 400 stations. Figures for the early homes are extremely tentative since a great many sets were made at home and not recorded by the manufacturers who were unable to keep up with the demand for radios.

There was high interest in radio among the young. *The American Boy* magazine was reporting to its readers in 1919 that the war restrictions had been removed from amateur radio.[2] The column was sandwiched between ads urging the readers to make big money raising rabbits, guinea pigs, bantams and squabs and encouraging boys to buy Brandes Wireless head sets.

In 1920 *Scientific American* described a "Portaphone which had been developed by the Bureau of Standards and which would allow the owner to receive music and news within a radius of 15 miles of the sending station."[3]

A 1922 Bureau of Standards letter circular showed how to construct an entire receiving station including five essential parts: the antenna, lightning switch, ground connections, receiving set and phone. The cost was as low as $6.00 but "a specially efficient outfit" cost about $15.00. A simple set was easy to make. Typically it had wire wrapped around a cardboard tube such as the Quaker Oats carton with a piece of tinfoil for the condenser. The crystaline detector was usually a piece of galena, silicon or carborundum that could be tickled by a piece of wire to find a sensitive spot. This wire was known as a "cat's whisker." With a set of earphones and a great deal of patience the listener could pick up local signals and could aspire to the goal set by *Radio Broadcast:*

Transoceanic signals have been received on crystal sets, but it is more to the credit of the skill and patience of the operator than to the efficiency of the crystal receiver.[4]

In the early years of broadcasting (1921–1924) two of the most popular brands of "factory wired radio music boxes" were Atwater Kent and Radiola. The latter was made by Westinghouse, General Electric and Radio Corporation of America. Most sets sold for $60 or more. Westinghouse introduced a set in June 1921—the Aeriola, Jr.—which sold for about $25.

The most important development to bring about mass produced inexpensive sets resulted from a present to a boy in Cincinnati. The son asked his father, Powel Crosley, Jr., for a "radio toy" in February of 1921. Crosley found that the cheapest set available was priced at $130. He built his son's present himself for $20. As a result he put two engineering students at work to bring his basic design to mass production. The result was a crystal set called the Harko which cost $20 across the counter, but later was reduced to $9. By July 1922 Crosley Manufacturing Company was reputed to be the world's largest producer of sets and parts.

The radio bug was biting young and old. The "Motorcycle Chums," "Go Ahead Boys," "Motor Boat Boys," "Air Service Boys," "Motion Picture Boys," "Moving Picture Girls," and "Ocean Wireless Boys," were joined in thrilling adventure by the "Radio Boys," "Radio-Phone Boys," and "Radio Girls." The "Radio Boys" had adventures under the sea, as flood fighters, with the border patrol, revenue guards, air patrol, and forest rangers, and in Alaska, darkest Africa, and on the Mexican border. The *1922 Montgomery Ward & Co.* catalogue devoted a whole page to radio accessories and half of another page to radio books.[5] *The Book of Rural Life,* an encyclopedia of "knowledge and inspiration," in 1925 devoted 20 pages to "The Story of Radio" including instructions for building a crystal set and a tube model.[6]

Montgomery Ward offered one radio book free:

The Radio popularity is sweeping the country like wild fire. People everywhere—men, women and children—are becoming radio fans. Everywhere people are talking about Radio—they know something about it—and want to hear more. It entertains. It fascinates.

The radiophone deserves your attention. It is one of the greatest marvels of the age. It does more than entertain, it instructs—it is a valuable business help, too. With it you may hear not only concerts, sport records, sermons and lectures but also Board of Trade and stock reports, news items and weather forecasts. It serves the farmer, the professional man and the merchant. It entertains and instructs the housewife, and the young folks—the entire family. Radio equipment and accessories have been crowding the market for the past several months. It is now easy to select an outfit which will meet exactly your individual needs. Send now for our new FREE Radio Book. We offer splendid outfits at surprisingly low prices. Write us for it—there is absolutely no obligation.[7]

In 1923 and 1924 more than 500 different models of receivers were introduced. Loudspeakers, the tulip type, were quite popular after their introduction in 1922. Radios with built-in speakers were becoming common in 1925.

In 1925 *Radio Broadcast* magazine began to examine some audience problems that reflected the growing importance of broadcasting. In April the magazine reported that "complaints are constantly coming . . . regarding failure of the radio programs published in the newspapers, to make clear what kind of performance can be heard." [8] In the same issue of the magazine a writer pondered the problem of how the local broadcaster can serve the distant listener and his obligation to provide that service.

Rapid consumer acceptance of radio was encouraged by marketing techniques. As an architect of radio promotion and advertising wrote in 1928:

> The unique difference with radio . . . was that whereas it took other industries from 5 to 20 years to reach a stage where all these marketing facilities could be employed on a national basis, radio found it necessary to adopt one after the other and, in the space of barely two years after its inception in 1920, it employed all these forces.[9]

It is difficult to speculate on the effect that radio had in replacing other media in the competition for time. Theater, in a slump, saw radio as a definite threat.

A noted singer of the day, Alma Gluck, mother of the television star of the 1960s and 1970s, Efrem Zimbalist, Jr., minced no words in describing the effect of broadcasting on record sales:

> Since the time a single record netted me sufficient to buy a private house on Park Avenue, receipts from royalties have fallen off precipitously, and all because of radio. The radio is a nuisance. They are perfectly darn foolish things to have around, and, besides the squawks, most of what one hears over the radio is terrible.[10]

Newspapers recognized the threat to their "extras" very early in the 1920s.[11] There was speculation that the radio public would become more attuned to listening than reading. However, in the 1920s more than one author agreed that "getting the news of the day by radio goes contrary to human nature." [12]

H. V. Kaltenborn believed that radio "cooperates rather than competes" with print.[13]

Radio was accused of affecting the nation in a number of ways. One author fully expected radio to bring "the best in music in all its forms performed by very good musicians." [14] Three years later one of the most popular song of the day was getting plenty of radio plays—"I Ain't Got Nobody" by the Coon-Sanders orchestra. By 1927 there was some reaction to the programming on radio which would echo in intellectual circles for years to come. The critic found radio "absolutely, utterly and completely devoid of vice." And he continued, "No possibility of the occurrence of the unexpected faces your poor radio reviewer. Year in, year out, radio pursues the even and spotless tenor of its ways." [15] It might have seemed dull to one author but to another it was the "The Alarm Clock of A Nation."

> Twenty years ago, if anyone had suggested that a great alarm clock, loud enough to reach out over thousands of miles, would be heard and heeded by millions some morning in the future, that suggestion would have been repudiated by the general public as a highly imaginative modern fairy story, the result of some unbalanced mentality.
>
> But now, radio waves carry an audible good-morning from coast to coast and from Maine to Florida. The world's largest gym classes gather around loud speakers in every state of the nation, while even isolated followers of the call of calisthenics stretch their sleepy bodies up in the cold fastness of the Canadian woods, in the lonely cabins of tramp steamers in mid-ocean and in the warmer habitations of Panama. More than a million people a day, over vast areas, willingly cut their morning slumbers and devote their stored-up energy to exercises which a few men in a few cities direct.
>
> For more than three years now, radio enthusiasts have been reaching out their arms for better health, bending their bodies for slimmer waistlines, riding imaginary bicycles on the parlor floor to change the pasty, white-faced look to one of rosy cheeks and brightened eyes.
>
> While station WOR was the pioneer in the idea of the morning round-up for gymnastics, the big chains of the country have adapted and developed the setting-up programs until now these opening broadcasts of the radio day are among the most popular features on the air.
>
> WEAF's hook-up carries the "Metropolitan Health Tower" classes to all parts of the country, while WOR, still active in the early-bird gym field, has enlisted the Colgate Company to sponsor its classes, holding its sunrise audience with the latest commerical effort to make loud-speaker athletes of its followers.[16]

Some were more reserved in their evaluations of the impact of radio. In the *American Journal of Sociology* Marshall D. Beuick discussed "The Limited Social Effects of Radio Broadcasting":

> The public has been led to believe that radio broadcasting is creating a social revolution. *One-fifth of the population are "lis-*

teners." —There are about 20,000,000 potential broadcast listeners and about 600 broadcasting stations, but they are only affecting markedly a limited group such as isolated dwellers. There are fundamental things in human nature that will prevent broadcasting from wielding any greater influence on us than the phonograph has. *Radio does not make us congregate.* —Radio does not satisfy man's desire to congregate with other persons in the mutual enjoyment of music, games, etc. *Broadcasting cannot compete with other amusements.* —Broadcasting does not encourage association or herding, and can, therefore, never compete injuriously with the theater, the concert, the church, or the motion picture. *Radio's greatest benefit is to isolated persons.* —It will, however, serve most effectively the sightless, the bed-ridden, the farmer, and the deaf.[17]

Thus, Beuick concluded:

Men must go among men. When they require this association they will seek the theater, the cinema, the church, the concert, the political meeting, and the lodge. These things radiotelephony cannot injure, because they have social psychological appeals of which broadcasting is almost entirely devoid.

The national radio conference which may be held in 1927 cannot change the status of broadcasting as a social force to any appreciable extent. It can deal only with technical rules and the reallocating of the etheric wave-lengths. Meantime the rural community will continue to benefit by broadcasting and the sophisticated city dweller will tire of the novelty.[18]

Commercial rating services did not gain prominence until radio had become a solid commercial success. Until this economic stability occurred at the national level in the early 1930s, stations depended for feedback upon fan mail, phone calls, and popularity contests conducted both by magazines and the stations themselves. One of the earliest recorded "program preference studies" was conducted in April of 1923 by a magazine published by WLW in Cincinnati. Readers of the *Crosley Radio Weekly and WLW Programs* magazine found a "ballot" entitled "Vote Now on Programs" followed by a list of 75 types of program—mostly variations of talk and music shows. Contests were conducted to discover the most popular station, announcer, band and the like.

By September 1923 there were more than 2,000,000 homes with radios. Three years later there were 5,500,000 households with sets—20% of U.S. homes.

Radio listeners in the first half of the 1920s were often concerned with the number of stations they could hear and not with the programs. Complaints came in when stations failed to give their location often since the "DXer" (person searching for distant stations) many times could hold the signal only a short time. Contests were conducted by radio clubs and magazines to find the DXing champions.

After 1925 most of the radios produced were suited to use with alternating current. Until this time sets used some sort of battery—many being powered by wet cell batteries which threatened to leak acid, keeping the set out of many living rooms. Even on the farms where sets were still being powered by batteries, radios were beginning to be "talking furniture."

In 1925 the radio columnist for *Theatre Magazine* confessed:

> When we first began to write about Radio, and mind you, this was something less than two years ago, we encountered a wrath-provoking tolerance on the part of our friends. There was on their faces and in their voices a curious expression we had never met with before. We have searched vainly for its counterpart and found it only the other day. It was in the eyes of a young college man who was being importuned to admire his sister's year-old-baby. The baby was a lovely pink-and-white scrap of lace and ribbons, but round its neck was fastened a wadded and saturated contraption known in the vernacular as a "bib," and from the corner of its rose-bud mouth trickled a little river which spread over its chubby chin and dripped onto the lingerie sponge on its chest. On the young uncle's face, as he gazed from rose-bud mouth to dripping chin, was that look of mingled admiration and disgust that greeted us when we said we had cast in our typewriter with Mike.
>
> "Oh, yes, we have a Radio," kind friends would say. "Billy made one in school and we keep it in the nursery."
>
> But during this past year everything has changed. Disguising its identity behind highboys and lowboys and console tables, Radio has emerged from the third-floor front and penetrated the drawing-room. Hiding its tubes behind mahogany panels and its loud speaker back of green or gold baize, it has suddenly become as much a part of a home as a hearthstone.
>
> All this is very encouraging to a Radio enthusiast and is quite in line with our hopes for the magic toy, but now, dear members of the *intelligentsia,* now that you have got it, what are you going to do with it? Are you going to be satisfied with the present system of procuring and presenting Radio entertainment or are you going to bend the force of public opinion so the Radio will be lifted to a place of stability and dignity? Great are the uses of advertising, but an artist like a professional man must advertise with restraint or even by circumlocution. There is nothing subtle about Radio publicity and at present publicity is the only bait which the studios can offer.[19]

Large cabinet sets with a single dial tuning and built-in speakers were the style of the late 1920s. Some were "audio centers" containing a phonograph, push button tuning and a shortwave band. It wasn't long before the DXing listener-in could hear police calls at one end of the dial and some sets in the 1930s had an input marked "television" next to the "phono" input on the back of the cabinet.

In the early 1930s television was still only seriously discussed in magazines like *Popular Mechanics.* But by 1938 TV sets were available with screens from three inches to 12 inches at prices ranging from $125 to $600.

The depression of 1929 lowered the market for radio set sales but manufacturing of table models continued in fewer varieties than before the crash. Total set sales dipped in the early 1930s but by 1935 had again reached the level of 1929. Car radios—of the tube type which drain heavily on the battery—were available in 1924 but became more common in cars in 1931. Rapid growth in car radio sales began in 1937.

Radio had become a part of American family life by 1935. Census figures of 35% set penetration in 1930 had risen to 65% in 1935. Listening was heaviest in the period from 6 p.m. to 10 p.m. with a peak about 7:30 p.m.

National ratings of programs had been started in 1930 by the Cooperative Analysis of Broadcasting (CAB). This organization used a "telephone recall method" of gathering audience information. The method, devised by Archibald Crossley, a marketing research expert, had interviewers phone listeners and ask them to recall which programs they heard the night before. Crossley ratings showed that in the 1930–31 season 53.4% of the homes telephoned recalled that they had heard *Amos 'n' Andy* the night before. Comedy was the favorite program type in the early 1930s. Eddie Cantor, *The Rise of the Goldbergs,* Ed Wynn, Jack Pearl, Burns and Allen and Joe Penner were favorites along with *Amos 'n' Andy.* Other popular programs included *Rudy Vallee Varieties, Maxwell House Showboat, Paul Whiteman Revue* and the drama program *First Nighter.* A poll of radio editors showed that in 1931 they preferred *Sherlock Holmes* and *March of Time* of the dramatic formats and agreed that *Amos 'n' Andy* was the foremost "dialogue" act.[20]

During the early 1930s there was some effort to survey audiences using the coincidental telephone method—"what station are you listening to now?" C. E. Hooper, Inc. adopted this method and offered monthly ratings starting in the fall of 1935. This method replaced the CAB ratings for sponsored network programs, when it was discovered that the Hooper survey indicated even bigger audiences than the CAB recall system.

Some important survey research was coming out of university departments. One series of audience studies began in the late 1930s and continued to the 1950s—by H. B. Summers and later Forest Whan at Kansas State.

In the middle 1930s comedians such as Jack Benny and Edgar

Bergen still had the highest ratings. *The Rudy Vallee Show* (which was similar to television's *Ed Sullivan Show*), *The Maxwell House Showboat, The Original Amateur Hour* and *Lux Radio Theater*, also brought in high ratings. Two singers, Kate Smith and Bing Crosby became established radio stars in the 1930s.

NBC sponsored a study in 1953 that indicated about 10% of autos had radios and were on an average of more than an hour each day—with two hours average in the summer. At home or in a car, by 1940 radio was affecting the American way of life, socially, economically, politically and to a lesser degree, educationally.

Paul Lazarsfeld in 1930 analyzing data from a survey of "northern states" found that radio was preferred for news in times of crises but the social scientist suspected that "radio broadcasting of a news event tends to encourage one to try to get more of the details from the newspaper." [21]

It was difficult to measure the effect of radio on the movies. But, as one theater-radio executive claimed in 1933: "Hard times have added millions of persons to the radio audience, while taking millions from the theatre audience." [22]

The beginning of World War II in 1941 affected radio in a number of ways. Set production tailed off the first two years of the war and in 1943 and 1944 there was no production of civilian sets at all. But the number of radio homes increased. The number of radio-equipped cars declined as did the number of cars.

The most popular shows during the war continued to be based on comedy with some musical appeal. Hooper ratings in the period were highest for Edgar Bergen, *Fibber McGee and Molly*, George Burns, and Jack Benny. Other comedy shows began to challenge the comedy leaders—Red Skelton, Bob Hope, Frank Morgan and Fanny Brice. Popular dramas were: *One Man's Family*, the *Aldrich Family* (one of the early successful situation comedies), *Mr. District Attorney* and the *Lux Radio Theater*. At the beginning of the war news broadcasts were at the peak of audience interest. However, as the war continued news broadcast ratings decreased. The decline in the interest in news was matched by a rise in the ratings of thriller and action dramas which were not war related such as *Mr. and Mrs. North* and *Nick Carter, Detective*.

There were a number of special events which brought high ratings. The morning President Roosevelt addressed Congress concerning the Japanese attack on Pearl Harbor, the estimated audience was 79% of U.S. radio homes. The following evening a fireside chat from the White House had a rating of 83.

Hooper ratings gave way to A. C. Nielsen ratings in 1945 as the major indicator of national radio audiences. The Nielsen Company used a mechanical recorder attached to sets in a sample of radio homes to indicate the hours and stations to which the set was tuned.

Set production began after the war and the public with war savings and scarcities of goods behind them began to buy sets to scatter in their homes. By 1950, 95% of the homes had sets—many with second and third sets. Comedy had not slipped with Jack Benny, Bob Hope, Red Skelton, Edgar Bergen, *Fibber McGee and Molly* and *Amos 'n' Andy* continuing as the most popular programs on the air. Other programs with high ratings in 1950 were *Arthur Godfrey's Talent Scouts, My Friend Irma* and *Stop the Music*.

In 1950 television already was making inroads into radio audiences but nevertheless radio set sales continued to expand. Television was the talk of the nation:

> How can a little girl describe a bruise deep inside?
> No, your daughter won't ever tell you the humiliation she's felt
> in begging those precious hours of television from a neighbor.[23]

Radio audience ratings plummeted from an average rating of 13 in 1948 to a rating of one in 1956. In the daytime the average rating in 1948 was seven, dropping to two in 1956; this despite a gain in the use of radio in the morning. Automobile traffic became a barometer of radio audience with peak listening during "drive time" in the 1960s. Auto and transistor radios certainly were of great importance in the number of persons listening to radio. No viable means of discovering the numbers in this mobile audience has been developed. Some estimates were as high as half the listening being done outside the home.

In the 1970s radio was truly ubiquitous. By the late 1960s FM radio became a bigger factor in set sales—especially in hi-fi phono combinations. In 1974 Pulse, Inc. reported that in more than half of the 150 largest markets FM saturation was above 90%; about 95% in 14 of those. More than 85% of all autos had radios and about one-fourth of all new auto radios included FM. For every person in the U.S. there were 1.8 radios—about 40% included FM—and half of all people had access to four or more radios including plug-in, portable, and auto sets. On the average about one-third of all adults listened to radio more than four hours each day; another third less than two hours. The heaviest listening was in the morning before breakfast when nearly two-thirds of all Americans used radio.

Early television sets were being purchased by middle income white urban parents with a median education (high school).[24] Set costs were rather high in 1947, with black and white receivers retailing for $280. Costs for small screens were less than $100 by 1966.

Early color sets were more expensive—at $500 to $600—and were still costing more than $200 for small portables in 1970. The introduction of the all-channel receiver—by law in 1962—seemed to have little immediate impact on the listenership to ultra high frequency stations.[25] In a mixed market—with both very high frequency and UHF stations—the VHF station was dominant, among other things because of the difficulty in tuning the UHF dial.

Community antenna television—using coaxial cable to carry signals to homes from community antennas—was an immediate boon to the UHF station, placing it in direct competition with the VHF station on the cable. Broadcasters, however, often viewed the cable as an undesirable middleman between stations and their audiences. The idea of the community antenna had been used as early as 1923 for radio. In 1950 antennas were set up for television—first only to guarantee a good signal for the nearest stations and later to supplement and broaden the number of stations available to the audience. After a halting start, and with considerable objections from radio and television stations CATV began to blossom in the 1960s and by 1974 there were about 5,000 systems in the U.S. serving more than 10% of all TV homes.

Nielsen reported the first TV ratings, for the New York area only, in 1948. The two highest rated programs were *Texaco Star Theater* with Milton Berle and *Toast of the Town* with Ed Sullivan. Berle stayed in the top-20 rated shows for the next seven years; Sullivan for more than 20.

A number of firms provided TV ratings and other audience data, but the field was dominated by A. C. Nielsen and the American Research Bureau. ARB dropped its national service in the mid-1960s to concentrate on local market ratings using the diary method to gather information. The notion of ratings as a part of decision making in programming matters was always irritating to some persons. This irritation erupted into charges of inaccuracy, too small samples, and mistakes. Investigations by the Federal Trade Commission and a congressional committee in the mid-1960s resulted in changes in rating methodology, self regulation, somewhat larger samples and the publishing of more specific data on sampling, methodology, and statistical estimates of accuracy. Other firms provided such services as data on program preferences (TVQ of Home Testing Institute) and pre-testing of programs and commercials (Schwerin and Audience Studies, Inc.).

Only two personalities have approached Ed Sullivan in the TV ratings race: Red Skelton and Lucille Ball (*I Love Lucy, The Lucy Show* and *Here's Lucy*).

The cycle of increasing and then declining ratings for TV shows was much faster than for radio. For example, in the 15 seasons from 1950–51 to 1965–66 only 35 programs were in the top 20 (average audience) more than four seasons—and more than half of those only four seasons.[26]

In the early 1950s variety programs were among the highest rated including the *Colgate Comedy Hour, Arthur Godfrey and his Friends* and *Talent Scouts*. Highly rated also were dramatic shows,

Fireside Theater and *Philco Playhouse* and boxing bouts sponsored by Gillette and Pabst.

Some game shows and human interest programs attracted large ratings in the mid- and late-1950s—Groucho Marx's *You Bet Your Life* (carried over from radio with high ratings from 1951 to 1958), *I've Got a Secret* and *This is Your Life. The $64,000 Question* and several imitators enjoyed brief popularity in the late 1950s.

Top rated shows in the late 1950s and early 1960s were dominated by Westerns and situation comedies. Those in the top 20 for four or more years include—*Gunsmoke, Wyatt Earp, Have Gun, Will Travel, Wagon Train, Rawhide, Bonanza, The Real McCoys, Andy Griffith, My Three Sons, The Beverly Hillbillies,* and *The Dick Van Dyke Show. Perry Mason* was also in the top 20 four years from 1959 to 1962.

Through the late 1960s and early 1970s *Gunsmoke,* Lucille Ball and *Bonanza* were front runners—with the last of the trio biting the dust of the Ponderosa spread in early 1973. Situation comedies, *My Three Sons* and the *Beverly Hillbillies* retained high ratings and were joined by *Gomer Pyle, U.S.M.C.* and *Family Affair.*

"Spin-offs" from popular situation comedies also ranked as rating leaders: *Gomer Pyle* and *Mayberry R.F.D.* from *Andy Griffith* and *Petticoat Junction* and *Green Acres* from the *Beverly Hillbillies.*

Under various titles (*Disneyland, Disney Presents, Walt Disney's Wonderful World of Color* and *Disney's World*) and in a format including cartoons, movies, and documentaries, Disney Productions had high ratings from 1954 into the 1970s.

In the early 1970s Monday night professional football and specials received high ratings but the most popular regularly scheduled programs were: *Laugh In,* Dean Martin, Flip Wilson, and *Hawaii 50.* Robert Young returning in the title role of *Marcus Welby, M.D.* established high ratings, matched against documentaries on the other networks. The leader in 1971–72 was *All in the Family* which led to a spin-off (*Maude*), and a spin-off from a spin-off (*Good Times*), and imitations (*Sanford and Son*). The strongest rating trend was the dominance of movies on networks every night of the week.

Popularity was not the only criteria for longevity. In January 1974 *Meet the Press* celebrated its 26th anniversary on television.

Christmas sales of color TV sets in 1966 were a bonanza. The number of color sets manufactured that year doubled the number produced in 1965. The number of color sets in homes rose almost 60% over the previous year. In 1970 a third of the homes had color TV and four years later it was two-thirds. Nearly one-half of all homes had more than one set in 1974. From 1965 to 1970 the Japanese-made share of the U.S. TV set market went from seven % to 29%. Of the small screen sets (less than 13 inches) 73% were imported.

68

Gerald Breckenridge

DIRECTIONS FOR INSTALLING AN AMATEUR RADIO RECEIVING TELEPHONE *

IN ORDER that the boy interested in radio telephony may construct his own receiving set, the Author herein will describe the construction of a small, cheap set which almost any lad handy at mechanics can build. Such a set should be sufficiently powerful to permit successfully picking up the concerts and other programme entertainments being broadcasted frequently by stations throughout the country.

First, draw the circle out with a compass to the 4 inch diameter on a heavy piece of cardboard, and then divide off the outside into seven divisions. Draw a light pencil line through each of these marks to the centre of the circle. Now with your scissors cut out the disc, after which you cut the slots 1½ inches deep.

The slots should be about one-quarter of an inch in width. Two such discs should be made and, when all cut out, should be given several coats of shellac to add stiffness and to improve the insulating qualities.

Now at your hardware dealer's buy one-quarter pound of No. 24 double, cotton-covered wire and proceed to wind the coils. Keep the windings even and avoid all joints throughout the length of winding.

When you have finished, mount the coils. Make sure that the windings on both coils run in the same direction. If you fail to do this, the set will not work.

For the detector, it is better to purchase a good make of galena detector at any radio supply store. If you are handy with tools, however, you can buy the galena and make your own detector. It will work with more or less satisfaction.

Your next need will be the condenser. The condenser consists of a series of aluminum plates, some of which are movable and the rest stationary.

Buy a small variable condenser. Its function is to tune the secondary circuit, which is accomplished simply by turning the knob.

The Radio Boys on the Mexican Border, New York: A. L. Burt Company, 1922, pp. iii–viii.

* Directions and instructions such as these appeared in many popular magazines—especially boys', science, and radio publications. Thousands of "how to do it" pamphlets and books about radio, were published. However, only this "Radio Boys" adventure, of nearly a score we know of, contained such a guide.

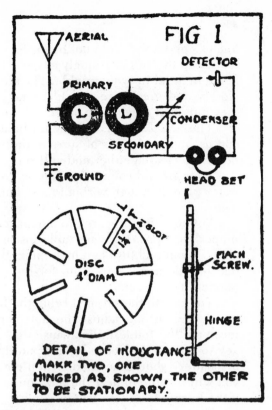

AERIAL

FIG 1

DETECTOR

PRIMARY

CONDENSER

SECONDARY

GROUND

HEAD SET

DISC
4' DIAM.

1¼" × ½ SLOT

MACH
SCREW.

HINGE

DETAIL OF INDUCTANCE
MAKE TWO, ONE
HINGED AS SHOWN, THE OTHER
TO BE STATIONARY.

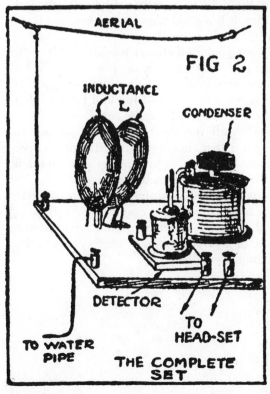

AERIAL

FIG 2

INDUCTANCE
L

CONDENSER

DETECTOR

TO WATER
PIPE

TO
HEAD-SET

THE COMPLETE
SET

Such a condenser could not be made without the use of a good set of tools, and the author strongly advises it be bought instead of made at home in order to avoid trouble. The aluminum plates are spaced very closely and great care should be taken to avoid bending them, as they must not touch each other.

The aerial for this set should be about 60 to 100 feet in length and as high and clear of surrounding objects as possible. A simple porcelain cleat at either end will serve to insulate it sufficiently.

Your ground connection can be made best by wiring to the cold water pipe, although wiring to a steam or gas pipe will do almost as well.

You are now prepared to mount the various instruments in their proper locations. For your table instruments, get a good pine board about seven-eighths of an inch thick. Buy four binding posts and use one for the aerial wire, one for the ground wire, and two for the phones or head set.

To operate the set, first bring the hinged coil of wire close up to the fixed coil and adjust the detector until you can hear in your receivers the loudest click caused by the turning on and off of the key to a nearby electric light. If no light is available, a buzzer and dry battery should be used. When the detector is properly adjusted you will be able to hear the buzz quite distinctly in the head phones if the buzzer is not too far away.

The actual adjustment of the detector is rather a delicate job, and once it is in the proper position it is a good plan to avoid jarring it, as it is liable to get out of adjustment very easily.

Once the sensitive spot on your detector is found, slowly turn the knob on your condenser and at some spot on it you should be able to pick up signals of some sort, either of radiophone or spark. If the set does not work, then go over all your wiring and be sure that the windings of the two coils are both running the same way.

The above set will work well for short distances, say up to twelve or fifteen miles. Beyond that, however, it will not receive music unless you have unusual facilities for putting up an aerial to a considerable height and well clear of surrounding objects.

Such a set should be constructed at a minimum of cost and may later, after you have become familiar with the operation of radio appliances, easily be converted into a set of much greater range by the use of a vacuum tube as detector and may even, by slight changes, be given the much desired regenerative effects.

69

"LISTENING IN,"
OUR NEW NATIONAL PASTIME

AMERICANS ARE a home-loving people. When the day's work is done, and the evening meal is over, the natural desire is to remain at home; one goes out merely to seek entertainment, recreation, and education which could not otherwise be had. There, perhaps, lies the secret of radio; for enterprising "broadcasters" bring to the ear, every hour and every day, wholly without cost to the "listener-in," a most amazing variety of entertainment and instruction.

No one knows how many thousand persons each night are informed, before and after a musical selection or a talk, that "This is WSB, the Atlanta *Journal*"; or "This is WHB, the Sweeney Automobile School, Kansas City"; or "This is WOO, John Wanamaker, Philadelphia"; or "This is WDAP, the Drake Hotel, Chicago." One station in Iowa mailed printed programs weekly until 30,000 listeners had asked for them; and then it quit issuing printed programs.

Who are these radio fans? Strange to say, they are not mechanics, even though every set requires a certain amount of installation and most sets are either home-made or home-assembled. Among the menfolk at an office with which the writer is familiar one in every three has a radio outfit. All were more or less home-made, no two are in any way alike, and every one gives satisfaction. Two of them regularly pick up broadcasting stations a thousand miles away. The most expensive set in the group cost less than $75, including telephone receivers and batteries.

Even an outfit of limited range will bring to one's sitting-room or fireside—through the turning of a knob or two, or the sliding of a cylinder—a variety of entertainment and instruction such as he could not himself have planned. Vocal and instrumental selections there are aplenty, as clear as though the artists were in the next room— solos, duets, quartettes, whole choruses, symphonies, and even operas. But besides those offerings the radio fan "gets" varsity football or baseball games and professional prizefights, described from field or ringside; he hears church services from beginning to end; he listens to a Shakespeare reading or to a speech. A modest companion outfit indoors will permit the radio fan to select, one at a time, the station or the message he wishes to hear.

Installing a home set is a short cut to neighborhood fame, a sure way to become known as a mechanical genius. But in truth no special knowledge is required. The novice needs to learn only one thing; Seek good advice, and follow it! A week of tinkering, off and on; and then a winter full of pleasant and profitable evenings at home.

70

Arthur Hornblow

WILL RADIO HURT THE THEATRE?

THAT THE INVENTION of the motion picture has worked incalculable harm to the legitimate theatre is beyond dispute.

Now the managers sense a more formidable peril in Radio, which furnishes an elaborate program which the potential theatregoer can enjoy free and without taking the trouble to leave his own fireside. Some managers, notably Arthur Hammerstein with *Wildflower,* Dr. Riesenfeld with his famous Rialto Symphony Orchestra and Dr. Rothafel, the celebrated "Roxie," with his Capitol "gang," claim good advertising results have been obtained from broadcasting their performances. Most producers, however, are bitterly opposed to it. Common sense tells anyone that broadcasting plays cannot possibly do the theatre any good. At best, the play gets over badly. It is heard, not seen. It is robbed of whatever enhanced value is derived from handsome costumes and beautiful stage settings, to say nothing of the pleasurable emotions and satisfaction the audience has in watching the movements, the gestures, the facil play of the actors. Frank Gillmore, speaking for the Actors' Equity Association, declared it the sense of his organization that Radio constituted a serious menace to the player's craft.

Little wonder that theatre managers took alarm. If people, sitting comfortably at home, can enjoy for nothing a gorgeous concert for which, at a box-office, they would have to pay $5 or $6 a seat, why should they go to the theatre? In fact, loss of attendance was immediately felt. Many plays for which it had generally been found impossible to buy seats, found themselves with empty rows.

Undoubtedly it is a serious situation, but who is to blame? The theatre manager, unmindful of his own shortcomings, attacks Radio.

Theatre Magazine, Vol. 41, No. 3, (March 1925), p. 7.

That, of course, is utterly foolish. Puny, impotent hostility was never a serious obstacle to human progress. Radio has come to stay. Its full possibilities, the benefits it will render to mankind, no one can foresee. If the theatre manager sees in Radio a dangerous competitor, he has an easy remedy. He must meet the threatened competition by improving the quality of his own entertainment. Give better plays— that is the answer. The managers, says William A. Brady, the veteran stage manager, are conceited ignoramuses. When one reads the record of this season's failures, we are tempted to think he is right. For one careful, conscientious producer, loving the art he serves, striving only to give the public the best, there are twenty others who are merely speculators, overbuilding, overproducing, putting on any kind of play, often with insufficient rehearsal, anxious for only one thing—to make money. For one real success this winter, how many plays have gone to the storehouse after a two-weeks' run? Even "The Road" has risen in revolt—in protest against poor companies and hurried, slovenly performances. Every day one hears of troupes closing or stranded for lack of patronage. When the legitimate theatre fails the "tall timbers," what is left but the movies and Radio? Bad plays, dirty plays, exorbitant prices of admission, the impossibility of getting good seats except on payment of an outrageous premium—all this has gradually disgusted the public with the theatre and made them welcome with open arms an invention such as Radio, which brings entertainment right to their door and charges nothing for it. The greedy, speculative manager alone is to blame for this new crisis threatening the theatre. His obstinacy, avariciousness, ignorance, pig-headedness has been Radio's opportunity.

71

James D. Young

IS THE RADIO NEWSPAPER NEXT?

THE FUTURE of the press lies in the air. Radio represents the one channel of news expansion not already developed to the full. When Fort Sumter was fired on in 1861, the Pony Express rode full tilt for a whole week to carry the news to California. Even then the telegraph

Radio Broadcast, September 1925, pp. 576–580.

wire, linked from pole to pole between skirmishes with Indians, was advancing across the continent. This was the eighth wonder of the world, surpassing all other wonders in the descent of man—a tiny thread of copper carrying sound unmeasured distances.

Then came the telephone. Its appearance was coincidental with the girdling of the globe by cable lines. But the last and greatest age of communication did not begin until three decades later, when crude instruments first feebly recorded wireless waves. The last ten years have served to improve radio to such an extent that man can instantly transmit his thoughts around the sphere.

But radio by no means is limited to the transmission of news between agents of the press. It is rapidly becoming a part of the press. We might call it an aerial edition and not be far in the wrong. More than fifty American newspapers send out bulletins at short intervals to the owners of radio sets both far and near, informing them of the latest decision of the British cabinet. That decision may not be half an hour old when some sheep herder in the backlands of Texas will learn that English labor has prevailed in its demands for better housing at state expense. Or the speeding waves of radio may convey word that Morocco is engaged in a new war. Even the gossip of Broadway and the last quotation on wheat are whisked around the world for all to hear.

This aerial edition of the press, usually issued every thirty minutes by the newspapers participating, offers possibilities which excel those of the established editions published daily by the great metropolitan plants. The instant communication of important matters to the whole body of mankind is now possible. Any great event that transpires to-day must be known within five minutes wherever men have ears.

The Influence of News Broadcasting on the Press

This new practice of instantaneous news broadcasting must essentially have a wide influence on the press. A dozen years ago the "extra edition" was the special marvel of the newspaper field. In some plants it was possible to produce such an edition within twenty minutes from the time of a world development. During the recent war these extra editions were almost an hourly event, particularly when the battle of the Marne hung in suspense and the Germans beat hard upon the door of Flanders.

Peace brought fewer editions and a steadier tone to the press. In the few years since 1918, radio broadcasting has developed so extensively and intensively that extra editions would lose much of their interest if the war were under way to-day. It might be argued that bulletins in front of newspaper offices whet the public appetite for news, instead of dulling its edge. But these bulletins are glimpsed by only a few thousands of people. And at best they are nothing more than skeletonized dispatches.

This is not the case with radio news broadcasting. When events justify, announcers inform a myriad listeners what has transpired. It is easy to read dispatches in full. Ordinarily news of the first rank arrives in short, pregnant messages. The man with a radio set may learn in the evening of some great event that his particular newspaper will not convey to him until the next morning. When an event of this kind is far distant—such as the Tokio earthquake—it frequently happens that a day or more will elapse before details begin to come through.

In view of all of these considerations, no one may doubt that radio is exerting a strong influence on the press, and the press certainly will have an equal bearing on radio. It would seem that the press has been somewhat backward in developing the possibilities of news transmission and broadcasting. Only a comparatively small group of American newspapers are using the international stations and there are but two press receiving stations in existence.

Publishers of small newspapers have found that radio broadcasting reduces interest in warmed over news. It is an old axiom of such newspapers that the scissors are mightier than the pen and seldom are the shears idle when a small paper is in the making. But the publication of matters already covered by some broadcasting station will not satisfy even country readers. The event may have been completed, perhaps wholly reversed, by the time that these papers appear.

Therefore small papers are beginning to suffer from radio competition. Even the papers in large cities will feel the stress of this competition as it expands. But we may be certain that the newspaper is a fixed institution. Although it may lose some of its claim to freshness, when news broadcasting becomes general, it will have wide opportunity to amplify and develop news. In a measure, the newspaper is likely to evolve along the lines of established magazine practice, departing somewhat from the breathless, last minute attitude that marks such a large section of the press. If that evolution ever comes about it will bring a large measure of relief to an abused public. We may conceive of the day when no paper can print such headlines as this one—"Burglar Slays Widow; Flees With Jewels"— for the excellent reason that it will be "old stuff." When the next edition comes out the burglar may be in jail, by the help of radio.

In the matter of broadcasting, first honors fall to the Chicago *Tribune,* which introduced the half hourly bulletin now sent out regularly from WGN in Chicago. Its bulletins are well known to a large section of the American public, furnishing a brief survey in terse language of just what is going on in the world.

KYW, also in Chicago, broadcasts the bulletins of the local Hearst papers, which further inform the public of the activities of its neighbors whether they happen to live in the next county or on the next continent. Even secret treaties and whispered understandings have drifted into this great hopper of news. Radio now supplements the press in disseminating such information everywhere. The man who runs need not pause to read. He can listen as he goes and take with him a concise, photographic mind picture of how the world is conducting itself.

Other papers in many states are broadcasting news by radio, ranging from such diverse communities as Detroit to Fort Worth. It is an odd phase of New York journalism that none of the country's greatest papers so far have embarked in news broadcasting. But the practice is growing daily, notably in cities of the 200,000 class, where life is not quite so busy as in the big centers, and people presumably have more time to heed the world's gossip. It is even said that farmers' wives have quit listening on the party line when Mrs. Jones calls up the grocer, preferring to get the latest word from Paris about this season's dresses. Radio news is broadly diversified, as it should be. It is a noticable reflection of the daily newspaper. First comes the "leader," the big story of the hour. Then the other news in a descending scale. Occasionally there is an editorial squib. The sports department, ordinarily the last in rank, frequently enjoys a larger number of minutes than all of the other departments joined together. The public may or may not care about the British cabinet decision and the new war in Morocco, but it always wants to know whether Babe Ruth has knocked another homer and if it really is true that poor old Ty Cobb has a "charlie horse" and must quit the game.

Such is to be the radio newspaper of to-morrow, or something approximating this brief glimpse. Perhaps it will have a fashion column and the busy housewife can note down the sizes and descriptions of new dresses. Conceivably the crossword puzzle will be a feature if the fad lasts much longer. We could draw our own squares and spend the rest of the night happily, after the announcer gave us a few instructions. In fact, the radio newspaper may be made almost anything that the public wants. Whatever this evolution is destined to be, the radio newspaper has become an accomplished fact. And certainly there is the call now for the latest bit of news.

72

Leslie J. Page Jr.

THE NATURE OF THE BROADCAST RECEIVER AND ITS MARKET IN THE UNITED STATES FROM 1922 TO 1927

"There probably has never been a scientific development that was as quickly translated into popular use as was radio broadcasting."

—Judge Stephen B. Davis, 1927

PROBLEMS IN transmission interference and the associated difficulties of broadcasting in the United States in the 1920's during the "period of confusion" have become a relatively well known phase of the history of broadcasting in this country. In spite of these problems, enthusiastic public interest in radio contributed to an abnormal growth of the receiver industry which added confusion to an already complex picture in the early years of broadcasting.

This increased popularity of radio in the early 1920's was accompanied by the sudden appearance of a large number of radio receiver manufacturing concerns destined to play an important part in the development of the receiver market in these formative years. Many of these companies were characterized by unethical operation which was seen by many as being a more serious threat to the future of broadcasting than station interference.

A statement by H. J. Kentner of the Better Business Bureau of New York partially indicates the extent of unsavory practices by manufacturers in 1922:

> This gentry (professional promoters) moved by the scores and hundreds into the radio field, organized companies and began campaigns for funds . . . descending upon the public with small, select armies of hair-trigger salesmen and with advertising of the "do-it-now" ballyhoo type.[1]

The seriousness of the situation had been recognized in an address made on July 26, 1922 at Washington where a meeting of radio manufacturers had been called to set up a National Radio Chamber of Commerce. Dr. L. duPlessus Clements spoke for Secretary of Commerce Hoover and urged manufacturers of wireless equipment to coordinate their various fields of activity.[2] With the organization of the National Radio Chamber of Commerce (not to be

Journal of Broadcasting, Vol. IV, No. 2 (Spring 1960) pp. 174–182.

confused with the N.A.B.) steps were taken to prevent further injury
to the receiver market caused by unscrupulous manufacturers. The
organization had as its purpose the function of serving as mediator
for manufacturer, broadcaster, and receiver owner. It was aimed at
including all manufacturers and broadcasters under regional
chambers of commerce with activities coordinated by a national
headquarters in New York. The president, W. H. Davis, expressed a
criticism that has been heard repeatedly by broadcasters since 1923:

> . . . the broadcasting of the trivial and the valueless have injured
> the business and unless remedied may ruin it.[3]

Another group in a position to deal more directly with the
buyers of receivers was the department store owners. Through their
organization, The National Dry Goods Association, a meeting was
called that was attended by representatives of five hundred department stores. Lew Hohn, managing director of the association said:

> Department store officials believe that they are essential to the full
> development of this trade, and are eager to establish broadcasting
> stations. The department store men want to make sure that only
> first-grade radio equipment is put on the market, so that, for ex-
> ample, a man will not spend $25.00 for a receiving set that he thinks
> will take messages from 200 miles away and then find that it will
> only cover 15 or 20 miles. As is natural in any boom business, infe-
> rior goods are being distributed in many cases, but the manufac-
> turers are ready to cooperate in remedying the situation.[4]

In the summer of 1923 one New York department store, Gimbel
Brothers, purchased from the Radio Corporation of America 20,000
Radiola R. C. receiving sets made by Westinghouse. The value of
these sets was not disclosed but at the current nationally established
list price the purchase was at least $3,000,000. An indication of the
rise in receiver use is found in increases in market value and number
of sets sold for representative years. H. L. Jome quotes a survey
made of the radio industry that placed the total value, excluding
tubes sold separately, at $43,460,676.00 in 1923. He further cites the
Radio Manufacturers Association's claim that ". . . the 1924 production of radio is approximately $400,000,000." [5]

How did the prospective buyer fit into the scheme of things at
this point? As the receiver became big business, he could purchase
an inexpensive set with a built-in crystal detector capable of receiving a continuous wave signal from a distance of about 100 miles or
radio-phone signals 25 miles or less from the sending station. Far superior to these crystal sets were the vacuum tube detectors which
required the use of two separate batteries, one each for filament voltage and plate current. These "A" and "B" voltages required critical
adjustment when supplying current to the receiver's tubes. One of

radio's earliest popular chroniclers, Austin C. Lescarboura, indicates that reception was never a matter of simply turning on the set and sitting back to listen.

> The radio amateur soon learns to arrange and rearrange his receiving equipment until he obtains the best results—if he is ever satisfied.[6]

In New York, Gimbel's was making it relatively easy for a set to be placed in the average living room. On May 5, 1925, the store began a sale of Freed-Eisemann Neutrodyne five tube receivers for $98.75 with a down payment of $ 15.00. This price included, in addition to the receiver, one "Prest-O-Lite" "A" battery of 90 amperes, two 45 volt "B" batteries, one phone plug, a complete antenna outfit, five vacuum tubes, and a choice of loudspeaker. The entire fifth floor of the store was given over to the sale and on the opening day 240 clerks sold 5,300 receivers. The sale was continued the next day with one change—closing time was 9 p.m. instead of midnight as on the first day.[7]

By May, 1925, 566 stations were broadcasting in the United States and its possessions and the *New York Times* of May 10th carried a story that gave a fairly reliable estimate of new receivers in operation.

> The sales manager of one of the largest radio corporations estimates at least 300,000 receiving sets have been placed on the market at reduced prices since April 1. The low prices are attributed to overproduction.[8]

The uncertainties that faced the buyer of a radio receiver had been lessened by mid 1925. Although sales continued to grow the rate of increase appeared to be much more stable. At the end of 1924 approximately 2,500,000 broadcast receivers were in use in the United States.[9]

Orrin E. Dunlap, Jr., then Radio Editor of the *New York Times*, pointed out that even though sets showed an improvement in physical appearance and simplified operation, there was nothing to be found that might be termed absolutely revolutionary. One feature that did create more than a passing interest was improvement in loud speaker design which was to result in increased use of boxed and cone type reproducers as opposed to the goose-neck horn.

From the beginning, receivers were either crystal sets or battery operated. However, attempts at production of a receiver using ordinary house current had continued and the 1925 shows did exhibit a few sets that enabled the buyer to dispense with the bulky batteries and their accompanying wires, acid, and general inconvenience. These sets were not seen, however, as offering any real competition to the battery operated sets.

Notwithstanding the progress made in meeting the problem of utilizing alternating house current in operation of radio receivers, there is no immediate sign that either storage or dry batteries are likely to be displaced to a very large extent. Some of the larger radio manufacturers, who have been developing radio receivers which will dispense with batteries, will this year for the first time place sets on alternating current. . . . These sets, however, are necessarily in the higher-price range, and are not likely to take the place of the popular battery sets.[10]

These predictions regarding the development of sets using alternating house current were not borne out. The following year as early as January, a set selling for $250.00 was put on the market by the MacLaren Manufacturing Company of New York. It used either AC or DC house current and had a built-in speaker.

Prior to 1925 the receivers had been designed primarily to amplify the signal as loud as was possible in order to get distant stations. Little thought had been given to tone quality or to appearance of the set. They had been very utilitarian in appearance, they required the use of a number of wires leading out from the cabinet to the batteries and various other parts such as the coils and condensers used to increase volume. The 1925 shows were presenting receivers that had a neater appearance. As one reporter of the events at the show put it: "Radio at the shows this year resembles a furniture display so much as it does an electrical exhibit." [11] The receivers were being advertised as appealing to an entire family, not only to the operator who must know how to manipulate all the knobs and controls necessary to tune the receiver; not unlike early television set operation.

The 1926 radio audience was estimated at 20,000,000 by *Radio Retailing* in a survey of manufacturers' sales. Their findings showed that:

The number of receivers in use is calculated at 5,000,000. The total retail value of radio equipment sold during 1925 is placed at $450,000,000. There are approximately 2,000 radio manufacturers, 1,000 radio jobbers, 31,000 radio retailers.[12]

The initial cost of the average 1926 receiver was $80.00, according to the findings of *Radio Retailing* which was reportedly based on a complete listing of all sets on the market. The results of this survey as reported in the *New York Times* also gave the average receiver five tubes, two stages of radio frequency, detector and two stages of audio frequency. By 1926 most of the tuning controls had been reduced to two. Earlier sets had used a voltage control knob for each tube. The average sale per customer was based on reports of five radio stores that were said to be representative. This credited the average sale at \$95.00 as compared with similar reports of \$51.88 in 1924 and \$16.22 in 1923.[13]

Unethical practices in marketing receivers and parts that had characterized the 1923 and 1924 periods had, by 1926, been largely overcome. Many of the marginal manufacturers had been weeded out as was predicted in 1925. However, some malpractices still faced the prospective receiver buyer. An example of one type of subtle practice engaged in by manufacturers is recorded by the Federal Trade Commission regarding false or misleading advertising. An unnamed company was distributing in interstate commerce sets equipped with cabinets advertised as "Beautifully finished mahogany" and "Built with mahogany legs."

> . . . when in truth and in fact the said cabinets, described as above, were not manufactured of mahogany but were manufactured of a wood or woods other than mahogany, finished to simulate mahogany.[14]

Practices such as this were counteracted by various means. In New York, Manhattan radio stores were trying to create a sense of responsibility and good practice in merchandising. They banded together to emphasize their methods and to stress their ". . . money back gurantees and the reliability of the apparatus they sell." [15] A week later a similar plan was adopted by Chicago dealers.

Some manufacturers who appeared to be in sound financial condition judging from their activity in the market, were forced to pass from the scene. One of these, the Music Master Corporation, went into the hands of temporary receivership. Its directors "admitted its insolvency, giving 'general depression' in the radio industry as the cause." The same fate was in store for the "Thermiodyne Radio Corporation which filed a petition in bankruptcy in the spring of 1926.

The early 20's had seen the sale of receiver parts in nearly every sort of establishment.[16] By 1925 these marginal dealers had given way to exclusive radio stores and as the market became more stable the final months of 1926 seemed to mark a new tendency in retailing. The summer slump in sales provoked a prediction for the future of radio stores by J. W. Griffin, president of a New York and Chicago radio retail organization. He said that stores selling radio sets exclusively would be a thing of the past "within a year or two."

> This is true because during the last three years the seasonal nature of radio has become more and more marked. The radio business as business probably begins about Columbus Day October 12, and it is pretty nearly all finished by St. Patrick's Day, March 17.[17]

Receiver sales began to rise in August of 1926 in keeping with the pattern that had been found in the preceding three years. The buyer and the dealer were apparently pleased with the merchandise for the coming 1927 season. It would appear that the summer of 1926 was a period of re-evaluation of receivers and their place as a commodity on the open market. Marginal manufacturers had been dropped and the industry was facing an era of stabilization. Sets had become much more standard in operation and in parts used. Manufacturers were still trying to bring down the cost of receivers that used regular house current and the over-all trend seemed to be toward greater prosperity for the industry and greater benefits for the buyer.

The tendency in set design at this point in their development was towards console models with indoor loop antennas. Most of them were not yet equipped with built-in loudspeakers. Service departments of radio dealers were finding that accessories such as batteries, tubes, and corroded connections at the antenna, were giving owners more trouble than the sets themselves.

The sixth season of broadcasting found that receiver manufacturers still in business had come into a period of leveling-off. During 1926 a total of 6,500,000 sets had been in use in the United States and the 1926 expenditures were said to be $506,000,000 by *Radio Retailing*. The owners of receivers had spent $1,490,000,000 for their sets from 1922 through 1926. By 1927 there had been a 24% radio saturation in the country and 29,000 retailers were selling sets supplied by 2,550 manufacturers through 985 wholesalers and distributors.[18]

With the establishment of the first network in 1926 and rapid technical improvements in transmission and receiving apparatus after 1927, the latter year marks the beginning of the broadcasting era and the end of a period of severe growing pains which were felt by the general public as well as the industry. This five year period witnessed the change in receivers from battery operated sets built with a complex assortment of components from numerous manufacturers to receivers largely standardized in construction and price. Broadcasting receivers had emerged from a public novelty to an indispensable utility.

This is the first national political campaign in which radio has played its part as a medium of public information. Undoubtedly, it will serve to minimize misrepresentation in the news columns of the press. The most reactionary newspapers will fear to twist facts which thousands of its readers receive directly by radio.

--Robert M. LaFollette, 1924.

73

W. F. Ogburn and S. C. Gilfillan

THE INFLUENCE OF INVENTION AND DISCOVERY

SEVERAL INVENTIONS were studied intensively to see how widespread were the social changes occasioned. One hundred and fifty such social effects were noted for the radio, and one of these, merely as an illustration, was further expanded into fifteen.

The statements of effects are collected under appropriate headings to facilitate reading. Some statements might equally well have been placed under different classifications. The numbering is largely for citation; some of the effects overlap; if those cited had been broken down into others, the list would have been longer.

EFFECTS OF THE RADIO TELEGRAPH AND TELEPHONE AND OF RADIO BROADCASTING

I. On Uniformity and Diffusion

1. Homogeneity of peoples increased because of like stimuli.
2. Regional differences in cultures become less pronounced.
3. The penetration of the musical and artistic city culture into villages and country.
4. Ethical standards of the city made more familiar to the country.
5. Distinctions between social classes and economic groups lessened.
6. Isolated regions are brought in contact with world events.
7. Illiterates find a new world opened to them.
8. Restriction of variation through censorship resulting in less experiment and more uniformity.
9. Favoring of the widely spread languages.
10. Standardization of diction and discouragement of dialects.
11. Aids in correct pronunciation, especially of foreign words.
12. Cultural diffusion among nations, as of United States into Canada and vice versa.

II. On Recreation and Entertainment

13. Another agency for recreation and entertainment.
14. The enjoyment of music popularized greatly.

Recent Social Trends in the United States, New York: McGraw-Hill Book Company, 1933, pp. 148–165.

15. Much more frequent opportunity for good music in rural areas.

16. The manufacture of better phonograph music records encouraged.

17. The contralto favored over sopranos through better transmission.

18. Radio amplification lessens need for loud concert voices.

19. Establishment of the melodramatic playlet with few characters and contrasted voices.

20. Revival of old songs, at least for a time.

21. Greater appreciation of the international nature of music.

22. Entertainment for invalids, blind, partly deaf, frontiersmen, etc.

23. With growth of reformative idea, more prison installations.

24. Interest in sports increased, it is generally admitted.

25. Slight stimulation to dancing at small gatherings.

26. Entertainment on trains, ships and automobiles.

IV. On Education

37. Colleges broadcast classroom lectures.

38. Broadcasting has aided adult education.

39. Used effectively in giving language instruction.

40. Purchasing of text books increased slightly, it is reported.

41. Grammar school instruction aided by broadcasting.

42. Health movement encouraged through broadcast of health talks.

43. Current events discussion broadcast.

44. International relations another important topic discussed, with some social effects, no doubt.

45. Broadcasting has been used to further some reform movements.

46. The government broadcasts frequently on work of departments.

47. Many talks to mothers on domestic science, child care, etc.

48. Discussion of books aids selection and stimulates readers.

49. The relationship of university and community made closer.

50. Lessens gap schooling may make between parents and children.

51. Provision of discussion topics for women's clubs.

52. New pedagogical methods, i.e., as to lectures and personality.

53. Greater knowledge of electricity spread.

54. The creation of a class of radio amateurs.

V. On the Dissemination of Information

55. Wider education of farmers on agricultural methods.
56. Prevention of loss in crops by broadcasting weather reports.
57. Education of farmers on the treatment of parasites.
58. Market reports of produce permitting better sales.
59. Important telephone messages between continents.
60. Small newspapers, an experiment yet, by facsimile transmission.
61. News to newspapers by radio broadcasting.
62. News dissemination in lieu of newspapers, as in British strike.
63. Transmission of photographic likenesses, letters, etc., especially overseas where wire is not yet applicable.
64. Quicker detection of crime and criminals, through police automobile patrols equipped with radio.

VI. On Religion

65. Discouragement, it is said, of preachers of lesser abilities.
66. The urban type of sermon disseminated to rural regions.
67. Services possible where minister cannot be supported.
68. Invalids and others unable to attend church enabled to hear religious service.
69. Churches that broadcast are said to have increased attendance.
70. Letter-writing to radio religious speakers gives new opportunity for confession and confidence.

VII. On Industry and Business

71. In industry, radio sales led to decline in phonograph business.
72. Better phonograph recording and reproducing now used.
73. Lowering of cable rates followed radio telegraph development.
74. Point to point communication in areas without wires.
75. The business of the lyceum bureaus, etc. suffered greatly.
76. Some artists who broadcast demanded for personal appearance in concerts.
77. The market for the piano declined. Radio may be a factor.
78. Equipment cost of hotel and restaurant increased.
79. A new form of advertising has been created.
80. New problems of advertising ethics, as to comments on competing products.
81. An important factor in creating a market for new commodities.
82. Newspaper advertising affected.

83. Led to creation of new magazines.

84. An increase in the consumption of electricity.

85. Provision of employment for 200,000 persons.

86. Some decreased employment in phonograph and other industries.

87. Aid to power and traction companies in discovering leaks, through the assistance of radio listeners.

88. Business of contributing industries increased.

VIII. On Occupations

89. Music sales and possibly song writing has declined. Studies indicate that broadcasting is a factor.

90. A new provision for dancing instruction.

91. A new employment for singers, vaudeville artists, etc.

92. New occupations: announcer, engineer, advertising salesman.

93. Dance orchestras perhaps not increased but given prominence.

IX. On Government and Politics

94. In government, a new regulatory function necessitated.

95. Censorship problem raised because of charges of swearing, etc.

96. Legal questions raised beginning with the right to the air.

97. New specialization in law; four air law journals existing.

98. New problem of copyright has arisen.

99. New associations created, some active in lobbying.

100. Executive pressure on legislatures, through radio appeals.

101. A democratizing agency, since political programs and speeches are designed to reach wide varieties of persons at one time.

102. Public sentiment aroused in cases of emergencies like drought.

103. International affairs affected because of multiplication of national contacts.

104. Rumors and propaganda on nationalism have been spread.

105. Limits in broadcasting bands foster international arrangements.

106. Communication facilitated among belligerents in warfare.

107. Procedures of the nominating conventions altered somewhat.

108. Constituencies are kept in touch with nominating conventions.

109. Political campaigners reach larger audiences.

110. The importance of the political mass meeting diminished.

111. Presidential "barn-storming" and front porch campaign changed.

112. Nature of campaign costs affected.

113. Appeal to prejudice of local group lessened.

114. Campaign speeches tend to be more logical and cogent.

115. An aid in raising campaign funds.

116. Campaign speaking by a number of party leaders lessened.

117. Campaign promises over radio said to be more binding.

118. High government officers who broadcast are said to appear to public less distant and more familiar.

X. On Other Inventions

119. Development stimulated in other fields, as in military aviation.

120. The vacuum tube, a radio invention, is used in many fields, as for leveling elevators, automobile train controls, converting electric currents, applying the photo-electric cell, as hereinafter noted. A new science is being developed on the vacuum tube.

121. Television was stimulated by the radio.

122. Developments in use of the phonograph stimulated by radio.

123. Amplifiers for radio and talking pictures improved.

124. The teletype is reported to have been adapted to radio.

125. Geophysical prospecting aided by the radio.

126. Sterilization of milk by short waves, milk keeping fresh a week.

127. Extermination of insects by short waves, on small scale, reported.

128. Body temperature raised to destroy local or general infections.

129. The condensor with radio tubes used variously in industry for controlling thickness of sheet material, warning of dangerous gas, etc.

130. Watches and clocks set automatically by radio.

XI. Miscellaneous

131. Morning exercises encouraged a bit.

132. The noise problem of loud speakers has caused some regulation.

133. A new type of public appearance for amateurs.

134. Some women's clubs are said to find the radio a competitor.

135. Late hours have been ruled against in dormitories and homes.

136. Rumor as a mode of expression perhaps hampered in broadcasting.

137. Growth of suburbs perhaps encouraged a little.

138. Letter-writing to celebrities a widespread practice.

139. Irritation against possible excesses of advertising.

140. Development of fads of numerology and astrology encouraged.

141. Automobiles with sets have been prohibited for safety, in some places.

142. Additions to language, as "A baby broadcasting all night."

143. Aids in locating persons wanted.

144. Wider celebration of anniversaries aids nationalism.

145. Used in submarine detection.

146. Weather broadcasts used in planning family recreation.

147. Fuller enjoyment of gala events.

148. Home duties and isolation more pleasant.

149. Widens gap between the famous and the near-famous.

150. Creative outlet for youth in building sets.

More Detailed Effects: For instance, item number 24 of the foregoing list, "Interest in sports increased, it is generally admitted," when analyzed in further detail shows fifteen further social effects, which are as follows: The broadcasting of boxing matches and football games tends (1) to emphasize the big matches to the neglect of the smaller and local ones, (2) increasing even more the reputation of the star athletes. In the case of football (3) the big coaches are glorified and (4) their salaries become augmented. (5) The attendance at colleges specializing in football whose football games are broadcast is increased. (6) Football practice in the springtime is thus encouraged and (7) the recruiting of prospective star players for college enrollment is fostered. (8) The smaller colleges or the ones with higher scholastic requirements tend to be differentiated as a class by contrast. (9) Boxing matches with big gates have accentuated trends in boxing promotion, notably the competition for large sums of money to the neglect of smaller matches. (10) Broadcasting of sports has led to a greater advertising of the climate of Florida and California, and (11) no doubt has aided a little the promotion of these two regions. (12) Broadcasting of sports has led to the developing of a special skill in announcing the movements of athletes not at times easy to see, a skill rather highly appreciated. (13) Athletic and social clubs with loud speakers have become popularized somewhat on the afternoons and evenings of the matches. (14) The broadcasting of baseball games is said to have bolstered the attendance, particularly by recapturing the interest of former attendants. (15) Another effect it is said has been the reduction in some cases of the number of sporting extras of newspapers.

If the other items in the list were further analyzed, as in the case of sports, the great influence of the radio on social change would be more truly appreciated. Such an expansion of other items would show more of the later derivative influences, such as the further advertisement of the climate of southern California, a derivative influence of the broadcasting of football games. There must be a vast number of these ramifying influences which, though minor, no doubt affect a good deal the daily lives of people.

Not only could the list be broken down in greater detail but it could also be shown that the various influences are felt at different times and in different degrees. Thus, the radio may help to destroy rural isolation but the farmers have lagged behind the city dwellers in buying radios. In general political campaign speeches may be more logical since the advent of the radio but some political broadcasters have not caught up with the times and still try oratorical effects.

74

Frederick H. Lumley

SYNOPSIS OF METHODS

IN THIS CHAPTER a few of the more useful methods of measurement are reviewed. For detailed considerations in carrying out these measurements, reference should be made to the appropriate preceding chapters.

For practical purposes many factors are important, as may be illustrated in the following case. A broadcaster wishes to determine the number of families listening to each of several different programs on a given day. The most accurate methods to determine to what programs any given family is listening are the simultaneous telephone survey and the recording device. The simultaneous telephone survey has the fault that the person interviewed may not be able to name the program or the station to which he and his family are listening. Furthermore, only telephone owners may be interviewed. The recording device notes all programs tuned in irrespective of whether or not the family is actually listening. Both methods are expensive, the first because a large number of persons must be interviewed to ob-

Measurement or Radio, Columbus: The Ohio State University, 1934, pp. 227–232.

tain an adequate sample for several programs, and the second because the equipment is costly.

The recall method of program identification is less accurate; listeners may forget programs they have heard on the previous day and may add the names of programs they usually hear. Nevertheless, one study has shown a significant relationship between the relative ranking of programs when information is obtained by the simultaneous method and the recall method. In recall interviews, all programs of the preceding day are investigated rather than the programs on at the time of the interview. This procedure lowers the cost per program considerably. Face-to-face recall interviews can be carried out more economically than can the face-to-face simultaneous interviews necessary to avoid telephone sampling bias. On the basis of these considerations, the broadcaster may decide that the recall method is a more practical if less accurate method to use in determining the number of families listening to the programs. Finally, the broadcaster may wish to determine, not the number of persons listening to the programs, but the impression which the names of the programs have created in the minds of the listeners after a period of time. In this case, the recall method becomes a more pertinent method than the simultaneous method.

The purpose of this rather lengthy discussion is to stress the fact that these methods have been ranked according to only one criterion. Three assumptions can be made in placing the methods. First, it is assumed that the bias inherent in each method is not of great importance. Otherwise, the rating of the methods would be primarily dependent upon the extent of this bias, and telephone interviews could only be admitted where they were shown to correspond with face-to-face interviews. Second, it is assumed that the information desired in surveys concerns actual listening and actual preferences rather than the radio-set owner's judgment of his own listening. Third, it is assumed that cost per unit of information is of secondary importance.

Mail Response

Free offers.—Little spontaneous mail response is received; therefore, it is usual to stimulate it in some fashion, such as making free offers. For purposes of measurement, the free offer should be closely related to the content of the broadcast and of little value aside from the program. Offers which fulfill these requirements are photographs of radio performers, copies of talks, bulletins related to the content of the talk, copies of the poems and songs used in the program, and schedules listing time and content of future broadcasts.

Spontaneous comments.—Occasionally, letters are received describing the help which radio programs have given in carrying out certain activities (housekeeping, farming, buying), or letters come in asking for information regarding such activities. The relation of these letters to other letters may be tabulated, and their content studied.

Mail Questionnaire

Station-listening questionnaires.—The mail questionnaire should be short and clearly worded. The Columbia Price-Waterhouse post-card questionnaire on station listening may be used as a standard. The questions asked are: "What radio station do you listen to most? Its call letters are————. What other station or stations do you listen to regularly?" Double government reply postal cards should be sent to every fiftieth home as listed in the city directory. Return cards should be keyed so that anlysis by economic levels is possible.

Recognition questionnaires.—In the recognition questionnaire, a number of programs, preferably not more than fifteen, are listed by full name on a return card, and the listener is asked to mark the ones he has heard. The accuracy of the results is not high, but the markings are at least indicative of what the listener thinks he would like to hear. It has been found that the mail questionnaire cannot be used profitably to have listeners write down the names of the programs they have heard.

General questionnaires.—Mail questionnaires may duplicate questions asked in personal interviews concerning the hours of listening, programs preferred, practices adopted; but they must be brief.

Personal Interview

General questions.—For fairly lengthy series of questions, the personal interview is the most practical method. Experienced interviewers, equipped with schedule cards, call at one in every fifty homes in specified areas. Introducing himself as a representative of a radio research organization, the interviewer asks:

> Do you have a radio?
> What stations do you usually listen to?
> At what hours do you usually listen during the morning? during the afternoon? during the evening?
> What types of programs do you prefer? dramatic programs, educational features (short talks, information), sports, music, women's features, children's programs, comedy, religious programs, news, special features (including talks by famous speakers, international broadcasts)?
> Have you obtained useful information from radio programs? If a housewife—to help you in cooking, care of the house, buying at stores, choosing what you read, caring for children?

There are, of course, many other questions which could be included in such interviews. Twenty-five questions are about as many as any interview should contain.

Roster method.—This is the recognition questionnaire presented personally. The complete list of all programs over several stations for a day can be printed in block form, and the person interviewed asked to identify the ones he has heard on the preceding day.

The personal interview may be employed to carry out both the simultaneous telephone survey and the recall survey described in the following section on telephone interviews.

Telephone Interviews

Simultaneous telephone interviews.—Telephone interviews recording actual listening are accurate but expensive. The customary form for the interview made at the time the programs are on the air goes:

> Good morning. This is the Radio Research Association. Would you mind telling me—
> 1. Have you a radio?
> 2. Was it turned on when you answered the telephone?
> 3. May I ask to what you were listening?
> 4. (If name of program is mentioned) Do you know what station that program is on?
> (If name of station is mentioned) What is the name of the program?

Sometimes the first and even the second questions are omitted to speed the interviewing. At other times, additional questions are asked as needed:

> 5. What advertiser is putting on the program?
> 6. What product does the program advertise?

For this sort of survey it is imperative that sampling be carried out by passing completely through the telephone book at frequent intervals to obtain numbers.

Recall interviews.—Telephone interviews regarding past listening are best typified by the Crossley interview. After a suitable approach, questions may be asked as follows:

> 1. Do you own a radio?
> 2. Was your radio turned on yesterday evening?
> 3. At what hours?
> 4. What programs did you hear?
> 5. What station carried this program?

The same questions are repeated for the afternoon and morning of the preceding day. The interviewing is best done in the morning between eight-thirty and eleven. By asking about evening programs first, the listener is more likely to be able to answer and thus start the interview properly.

General questions.—In a telephone interview, some of the same questions may be asked that are asked in the personal interview; the number of permissible questions is more limited and they should be more directly related to each other. The Columbia Price-Waterhouse questions on station listening may be asked by telephone.

Engineering and Mechanical Measurements

Signal strength.—In determining the physical coverage of stations, measurements of the signal strength and noise level in specified locations are indispensable.

Recording devices.—Devices to record the exact time at which radio sets are operated and name of the stations tuned in have been invented but are not yet in use. They will be useful in checking the results of other types of surveys.

In this summary, no attempt has been made to discuss the use of report forms, tests, or personal observation in measuring the effectiveness of radio. These methods are usually of service in special situations and can only be adequately discussed with reference to the peculiar conditions under which they are to be employed.

75

Frank N. Stanton

PSYCHOLOGICAL RESEARCH
IN THE FIELD OF RADIO LISTENING

WITH RADIO-SET ownership approaching the limits of population, the psychology of the radio listener practically becomes the study of the entire population. And because radio listening has come to be so interwoven in our daily behavior, we must necessarily delimit the scope of our discussion.

If we understand psychology to be the study of human behavior, then it seems to me our major interests in this case are in that segment of human behavior which is concerned with radio-listening

Educational Broadcasting 1936, Chicago: University of Chicago Press, 1936, pp. 1–12.

habits. By radio-listening habits I mean: who listens; where and when the individual listens; to what he listens; why he listens; what he does while he is listening; and how he is influenced by listening.

If you are an educator, your interests may center chiefly around the child as opposed to the adult, although we have many educators, especially in the field of radio, who are devoted to work at the adult level. On the other hand, the advertisers' emphasis, for the most part, is on the adult sections of the audience. Both, however, are vitally interested in examining listening behavior.

The questions of who listens, where, when, and to what are all psychological problems to be sure. But they are general in composition and so far have been left largely to the field of general measurement. My feeling is that psychology's contribution here should be largely one of technique.

Much has been accomplished in the past five years in an effort to establish the answers to who, where, and when. The dimensions on who and where are reflected by the present-day figures on radio ownership. Over twenty-three million homes have one or more radios [2]—that makes three out of every four homes for the United States as a whole. And 98 per cent of them are in working order. In addition, there are over three million automobile radios on the road.

Radio ownership, we find, is higher in the urban districts. In cities of over ten thousand population 93 per cent of the homes are radio-equipped. In an area such as the Middle Atlantic states there is 88 per cent ownership, while in the East South Central area, ownership drops to 44 per cent.[3]

The question, where, fades in significance from a research standpoint in the face of such overwhelming ownership figures. But these figures in themselves tell us little about the listener or the who aspect of our problem. Just because an overwhelming majority listens or can listen isn't enough. We must continue to collect information on the psychological characteristics of the total audience and relate these data to specific listening behavior.

On the question "When do they listen?" we have some general data by half-hour periods for the average weekdays, Saturdays, and Sundays. These data have been collected by Dr. Daniel Starch for the Columbia Broadcasting System over a three-year period and agree with the audience preferences as to listening periods generally, although there are occasions when the listening load is increased because of special programs. Furthermore, these data are available on urban listeners, broken down by daily periods for age, sex, and seasons of the year. It is my opinion that refinements in these measurements will come with time, until eventually they will include economic and population classifications. To be of maximum help psychologically, we should know something of the interests of the various groups as well.

From these data on "when listening takes place" we can establish figures for average radio use. During 1935 at least 77 per cent of all radios were in use sometime daily. And their operation averaged over four and one-half hours.[4] An indirect measure of this listening load is evidenced in the two hundred and fifty millions of dollars spent by listeners in 1935 for set repairs, tubes, and electricity to operate the radios.[5]

So much, then, for those dimensions. For me they constitute the rough plan or measurement of the audience. The detail and section work remains to be done. We turn now to the next question in our definition: "To what does he listen?" At this point we are able to go only part way in answering the question. This is because we have had to depend upon what people report they hear. (That is, until recently. I will mention the automatic recorders later.) Attempts to discover what is listened to, distort the picture if the surveys are made by unaided recall alone—that is, when one asks the listener, "What did you listen to this morning on your radio?" Such questioning lets the factor of memory creep in and tends to underestimate the newer and smaller programs, and even overestimate the big-name shows of long standing.[6]

In a small but representative sample of homes in an average city, radio use was measured—unknown to the listener—by an automatic recorder connected to the radio. The following day the listeners were questioned as to their previous day's listening experience. The results are interesting, for they demonstrate the memory loss very effectively. The subjects could recall correctly or account for about 31 per cent of the program time they had heard. However, when they were supplied with a list of all programs available to them the previous day they correctly identified 59 per cent of their listening experience, almost doubling the "pure recall" report—but still leaving 41 per cent unaccounted for! I should point out in passing that all the subjects in the experiment reported they were home during the period of observation.[7]

This memory discrepancy has been further demonstrated by telephoning homes and questioning the respondents on program reception at the time and then calling the same homes again the next morning. Roughly, only one-third of the previous evening's listening was reported correctly. The sad part—not strange, psychologically—was the lack of any constancy for the programs forgotten.[8]

Here, then, is a field open for careful experimentation designed to isolate the factors which contribute to this memory loss. Here are everyday problems in human learning and motivation which, when answered, may aid us in a more intelligent use of radio. But we have gone astray—we haven't answered the question: "To what does the audience listen?"

In order to get at the answer, we shall have to accept the results of the only extensive "unaided recall" survey now in operation. This is known as the Cooperative Analysis of Broadcasting.[9] We must accept it, primarily because it is the only one which may be considered nation-wide and deals with the entire radio day. It should be noted that this study is restricted to thirty-three major cities reached regularly by the three networks. From it I believe we can get some idea of what programs are listened to most. An analysis of the twenty programs having the largest audiences, from the most recent CAB report, reveals variety programs hold six places; comedy, five; popular music, three; classicial music and drama, two each; serials, one; with one program in a special division.[10]

Eleven of these programs were a full hour in length; eight were half-hour shows; and one was a quarter-hour program broadcast five nights per week. I do not cite these data to answer the question "What is listened to?" because at the present time we do not have a technique for giving the complete answer. They do indicate, however, the top-ranking programs that are pulling an audience and making an impression. They are not representative of all the audience because the interviews are conducted by telephone.[11] Furthermore, such data do not permit breakdowns of psychological interest such as age, sex, educational level, economic status, and the like.

With the use of automatic recording devices, which produce accurate evidences of listening both as to station and as to time, we may obtain, in the future, breakdowns that will reveal listening habits for various sections of the total audience.[12] These data will be available, however, only if the recording devices are used for survey work on much larger samples of the audience than are used for present surveys. This is necessary not only because present surveying techniques do not yield data on smaller communities, nontelephone homes, rural listeners, and the like, but also because the number of breakdowns necessary to produce adequate data for psychological analyses demands a larger sample. And this will make the results very costly, as one can readily understand, because of the initial cost of the devices and the installation charges.

Memory discrepancies will be eliminated, and we may be able to have accurate records of the programs tuned in. I say "tuned in" because there will be no way of establishing actual listening save by interview. Recorders are now in the experimental stages. Should they be used on an adequate scale, we shall be able to relate listening to certain data of a psychological nature which can be gathered on the same cases.

There will be some exceptions, of course. But the evidence will go a long way in telling us the answers to important questions. The exceptionally fine point in respect to radio listening and this type of mechanical measurement is that to listen one has to snap a switch—a manual act which may be recorded.

But the next question: "What does the listener do while the radio is in use?" does not lend itself to recording mechanisms. It is, however, as you all recognize, a very important psychological problem to both the educator and the advertiser. It is important because (and I think we are at liberty here to generalize on the basis of experiments in the field of learning) we know that conditions of attention vitally affect the material retained, whether it be some point in an educational lecture or the directions on how to enter a contest. Obviously, there must be certain periods of the day when the listener can give more attention to programs. This is due to his routine of living and is shown in the fluctuations in radio-set operation by periods of the day. But even we then have certain types of activity going on simultaneously with radio listening.

I attempted at one time to experiment with this problem by a mail questionnaire. Along with certain other data, such as age, sex, program preferences, and the like (I already had the data on set operation from my mechanical recorders), I asked listeners to indicate what they did while the radio was in use. The item read: "The radio is turned on while I—write—dance—dress—bathe—sew—eat—study—lie in bed—clean the house—read—play—iron—work—rest—talk—ride—cook—boat—and listen (that is, do nothing else)." There was space provided for additional activities, and the listeners were asked to check only those things they did regularly.

The results of this preliminary study on colistening activities reveal that four items—listening, eating, resting, and reading—received the highest number of checks for men. For women the story was different. They checked listening, sewing, resting, ironing, eating, cleaning, reading, and cooking. The women checked more and different items than the men. These sex differences are due largely to the types of work women perform during the day and also to the fact that women are home almost twice as many radio hours per day.[13] This study was mostly exploratory, but it does reveal possible fields for further psychological work.

From my definition of listening habits, so far, we have given our attention to who, where, when, to what, and how the individual listens. But a study of listening behavior, as pointed out earlier, takes in more than that. It includes the very important psychological questions; "Why does he listen?" as well as "What effect does listening have on his subsequent behavior?" To me those two questions contain enough problems to keep a whole corps of investigators busy. It isn't enough to know what programs are heard and preferred. We want to know why they are listened to and liked, and, furthermore, we want to quantify their influence.

First, why does one listen; then, why does one listen to certain programs? In the early days of radio the novelty factor was important. As time went on, listeners came to depend on certain features for entertainment and information. In additon, radio as a whole improved, including transmitters, receivers, and programs. Perhaps these are all reasons; frankly, I do not know. Surely there is scant research on the attraction of radio. Individuals will report listening and give the answers that they listen because of programs.[14]—even certain programs. But I do not know of any published research on why they listen to these particular programs, that is, what the motivation might be. Once the real motivating factors are isolated for various groups or sections of the audience, then educators and advertisers might put their time on the air to more efficient use.

In order to approach this psychological problem, it is not necessary to put on special programs, although they would help. There is a sufficient number of popular and moderately popular programs to begin work on at once. The exact technique is one that will probably take shape as the problem progresses.

Before talking about the question of listening results, there are some things which I should like to mention about listening in general. From the viewpoint of the life-cycle, understanding or social stimulation by listening precedes understanding by reading. We talk and listen before we read and write. Furthermore, one investigator has shown that, of the total time devoted to communicative behavior, adults spend 45 per cent in listening, 30 per cent in talking, 16 per cent in reading, and 9 per cent in writing.[15] Certainly, the use of the spoken word should be a factor to consider in the answer to this problem.

In addition, the variations and inflections of the human voice make it an excellent medium for conveying ideas to the listener. It is personal and extremely intimate, which may account for the results Carver secured, namely, that auditory suggestion is more powerful than visual.[16]

The next and final question is: "What is the effect of listening— does it alter our subsequent pattern of behavior, and, if so, how much?" There are many rough measures on this topic in the field of commercial broadcasting. The radio advertiser has for his objective the sale of certain products. If he can either control the other variables such as space advertising, seasonal sales fluctuations, and the like, or hold them constant statistically, he is able to put his finger on the sales contribution of the medium. That advertisers have changed or stimulated the buying habits of larger numbers by the effective use of radio is reflected in the increased business from year to year on the major networks.[17]

Educators have had similar but less frequent opportunities to institute similar measurements. Demand for books and information when related to special broadcasts is certainly an indication of radio's effectiveness.[18]

Some advertisers have had opportunities to check the auditory mode of sales stimulation against and in combination with other mediums.[19] However, there is considerable work in the experimental literature of psychology to throw light on this from a laboratory viewpoint. The findings of De Wick,[20] Stanton,[21] Cantril and Allport,[22] Carver,[23] and Elliott[24] clearly establish, I think, the superiority of the auditory method of presenting advertising copy as measured in terms of immediate and delayed recall and recognition. All these investigators worked with adults. Dr. Elliott did his first work on the problem under actual or "live" circumstances and then verified his results under rigid laboratory conditions.

Prior to 1932, other investigators tackled the problem of the "eye versus the ear" with different types of material, technique, and younger subjects as well. The results are conflicting. This may have been due to several things. In the first place, some investigators used numbers and "non-sense" material for their experiments, whereas the six workers already named confined themselves to advertising material employing fictitious brand names. Another difference may have been due to changes in research techniques. The early workers used very small groups of subjects; in one case only six subjects were used. Then, too, it hasn't been until recently that investigators could use the microphone and loud-speaker system. The early experiments did not even approximate the actual radio-listening situation.

Not all the recent work has been given over to measuring the effectiveness of advertising copy when presented visually and auditorially. Carver, whose work is reported in Cantril and Allport's book on *The Psychology of Radio,* conducted extensive experimentation on various other phases of the problem. His findings indicate: (1) that the effectiveness of listening is greater when the material is simpler; (2) that the effectiveness of auditory presentation is limited to meaningful and familiar material; for strange or meaningless material it is inferior; (3) that when difficulty of material and cultural level is constant, recognition, recall, and suggestibility are better after auditory presentation—comprehension, criticalness, and discrimination appear facilitated by reading; and (4) that the higher the cultural level, the greater the capacity to profit from auditory presentation—that is, up to a certain degree of difficulty, and then the advantage shifts to the visual mode.

Cantril and Allport also conducted experiments to determine the effects of certain broadcasting conditions.[25] They found that it was better to prepare a script in such a way that general ideas were followed by specific references or examples. Such passages were rated more interesting and were better recalled than general or concrete references. On the question of length of sentence, their work indicates that short sentences should be used where the material is highly factual because they are recalled better. Where the material is more interesting, the effectiveness of the shorter sentences disappears. The rate of speech they believe, on the basis of experimentation, should range between 115 and 160 words per minute. News material will suffer if presented less than 120 words per minute, but more difficult materials can be taken slower. They also found that, in general, repetition of material in programs aids understanding and retention, but it runs the risk of making the program uninteresting.

Another worker in this field, Wilke,[26] approached the problem of change or effectiveness by presenting propaganda to his subjects by the spoken and the printed word. After various exposures the subjects were given attitude scales in which the subject either agreed or disagreed with certain statements concerning the issue at hand. In this rather subtle way he succeeded in measuring the relative influence of each medium upon the subject's opinions. His results show that the situation in which the speaker is present is superior to the pure auditory and that both are superior to the pure visual experience.

Thus we see that what psychological evidence we have at our disposal at present sets up preliminary standards by means of which educators can best approach the use of radio. More research will serve to define further the advantages of radio in influencing human behavior until radio will come to fit into our educational pattern to the best advantage. There are gaps in our measurements of listening behavior, but with continued research we shall gradually emerge with educational as well as with advertising answers to: who listens, where he listens, when he listens, to what he listens, how he listens, why he listens, and, finally, how he is influenced by it.

Masscomm provides more "comm" of higher quality than "Mass" is willing to pay for. The difference (which is considerable) is subsidized by the business community through part of its advertising expenditure. The result, inevitably, is a measure of control reinforcing the industry's business orientation.   --R. S. Reid, Saskatoon, *Center Diary*, 1967.

76

Harrison B. Summers

SUGGESTIONS FOR IMPROVEMENT

THE FINAL question on the questionnaire form was "How could your favorite daytime station improve its program or give better service to its listeners?" Interviewers were instructed not to record any replies which were not given immediately by the person interviewed; the idea being to list only the attitudes strongly held by listeners, and which would probably be expressed without the listener having to "think things over" before replying.

Of the 1190 replies received and recorded, nearly one third related to advertising. The suggestion offered most frequently—by 293 listeners—was that the amount of advertising should be reduced. Another 21 listeners wished the length of the individual commercial reduced; and 32 suggested that advertising credits should not be inserted in the middle of a program, many mentioning specific news broadcasts, and others mentioning musical programs. Twenty-eight object to the character of the credits themselves, as "boresome," "cheap," "misleading," or being too extreme in their praise of the product. The remaining 33 were opposed to Sunday advertising, to advertising on religious programs, or to the advertising of cigarettes, tobacco, "quack patent medicines," or beer.

Suggestions relating to musical programs were offered by 136 listeners. Fifty want less "swing Music" or "jazz;" 29 want less "hillbilly" or "cowboy" music; the remaining replies were scattering, including requests for more variety in the type of music broadcast over some stations, including WIBW and KMMJ; the use of more variety in the numbers presented and avoidance of overworking certain numbers; use of more "old home songs;" and the use of more popular music during the daytime.

Serial dramatic programs received comments from 68 listeners; nearly all suggested that the number of serials on the air be greatly reduced. Others complained that there was too little originality or variety in plot, that the average serial contained too much tragedy, or that the triangle situation was being overworked on some of the shows.

Nearly 60 listeners asked for more programs of a religious nature; 25 wanting more religious programs or morning devotional programs, 27 asking for more religious music, and 2 suggesting that religious services be broadcast on Sunday evening.

Kansas Radio Listener Survey, Manhattan: H. B. Summers, 1938, p. 14.

News programs were mentioned by 51 listeners, including 20 who dislike insertion of advertising material in the middle of a news program. Fourteen asked simply for "more news broadcasts; while others suggested that crime news be played down or eliminated, that more national news be given and less time devoted to "trivial" items, or that more details or more comment be included in the news broadcast.

There was less objection to recorded and transcribed programs than might have been expected, only 11 objecting to the use of recordings, and 7 to the use of transcriptions. Reception conditions were the occasion for 41 suggestions, 34 listeners complained of too much interference at night, or that there are "too many stations," while the rest suggested that certain stations need greater power.

In the matter of broadcasting standards, 17 listeners ask for a greater number of "higher class" or "constructive" or "educational" programs; 12 others characterize present-day broadcasting as including too much "silliness," or too much "trash." Nineteen are opposed to dramatic thrillers; 4 others to dramatizations of crime. Ten others ask for "less vulgarity," "less profanity," or "less Hollywood."

Several interesting suggestions were made in relation to program production and the day's program structure; a total of 104 listeners dealt with one subject or the other. Six dislike the use of applause on programs; six others object to poor monitoring, so that musical and spoken portions of the broadcast vary in power. Twelve want better daytime programs; 9 others ask specifically for better programs at noon; 8 want more music—popular music—during the daytime. Seven complain of lack of variety in programs at a given time; or say that two good chain shows will come at the same hour, and nothing good at the next hour. A considerable number suggest changes in time of broadcasting of certain programs; 5 would have some of the afternoon dramatic serials shifted to the morning hours; 7 want Joe Nickell's night news broadcast, or some other late night news program, shifted to an earlier hour in the evening; 4 would like to have baseball scores about 7:00 in the evening; 18 would move the major programs to a later hour in the evening; while 4 want the late evening popular orchestra programs put on at an earlier hour. Exactly 11 suggest that there be fewer changes in time, of standard programs; 3 of them mention daylight saving time as a disrupting feature.

Other suggestions were scattered over a wide variety of fields. A number of listeners asked for "better talks" or for "more talks about national affairs;" a few object to broadcasting of political talks; a considerable number suggest that better quality programs and a higher type of talent be used during the daytime; several would have the Mexican stations eliminated; others suggest that either the day's broadcasting schedule be given more publicity in newspapers, or that coming features in the day's program be listed at fixed hours during the day by the stations themselves. One criticism of local shows offered by nearly 20 listeners was that the "chatter" or "would-be humor" of announcers or of participants in the show, between musical numbers, was much overdone; and several asked that dedications of numbers to listeners who write in be eliminated as a waste of time.

Included also were the usual comments favoring or condemning specific programs—"more Jack Benny," or "take the University of Nebraska programs off the air."

77

Herta Herzog

WHY DID PEOPLE BELIEVE IN THE "INVASION FROM MARS"?

THIS IS A REPORT [1] of thirty very detailed interviews which have been made in Orange, New Jersey. The respondents were, on the average, middle-class people and we learned before the actual interview from friends and neighbors, that they had been greatly affected by the broadcast.

The purpose of the interviews was to bring out those psychological aspects which would seem useful for an analysis of the whole event. Our thirty cases, of course, do not permit a reliable statistical evaluation. The results, however, are given in such a form that the reader can visualize how tables would look if the study were conducted on a broad basis.

An analysis of the total situation leads one to expect that the following psychological factors have to be considered:

a. What in the past experience or personality of our respondents made them inclined to become perturbed?

b. What in the program was especially conducive to taking it for a real news broadcast?

c. Which listener situations were especially likely to facilitate a misunderstanding of the program?

Memorandum to Dr. Frank N. Stanton, Director of Research, Columbia Broadcasting System, 1939, from Lazarsfeld and Rosenberg, *Language of Social Research,* © 1955 The Free Press.

d. How did people influence one another when they were listening in groups or got in contact with each other?

e. What possibilities of checking upon the nature of the broadcast did the listener have and what use did he make of these possibilities?

The sections of this report correspond to the points just enumerated and can be considered as tentative answers to these questions.

A. *The Time Is Out Of Joint*

The idea that everyone today is prepared to believe unusual and gruesome events is the theme which, in many variations, runs through the interviews. The interviews contain remarks like:

"The people's nerves are pitched up."
"These times are not normal."

Without being asked expressly, each respondent mentions at least one factor in his preceding experience which might have made him ready to take the program for a news broadcast. The following list of factors is arranged according to the frequency in which they have been mentioned:

The permanent talk about war
The strange developments of science
The recent floods
Religious beliefs
Individual experiences of a number of respondents

Very often one interviewee would give a number of concurrent factors which, in his opinion, made him susceptible to taking the broadcast seriously. The following pages include a number of quotations for each major group and an effort is made to put them in the correct psychological context.

The War Scare in Europe. The great majority of respondents mentioned, in one way or another, the recent political events. There are three different ways in which this factor seems to play a role. Some people point to the general atmosphere of uncertainty which has been created by the Czechoslovakia crisis and similar events.

"I have never been in any accident or catastrophe. But the war news has everybody so tense we more or less believe everything we hear. I could not believe the Martians were coming down but I thought it was some physical disaster and evidently the end of the world had come."

Other people seemed to feel more specifically that the political situation would make an invasion by an enemy quite believable.

"I was all excited and I knew that Hitler did not appreciate President Roosevelt's telegram a couple of weeks ago. While the United States thought everything was settled, they came down unexpected."

"The Germans or the Japs are the nations about which you hear things of that kind (poison gas attacks), and they do not need any reason for declaration of war. America is a fruitful country. If they want it, they will take it."

A third group feels that the special technique of relaying news over the radio prepared them to believe any bad news which would come to them in such a form.

"It was made up like a news flash exactly the way as it was made during the war crisis. I thought it was some sort of a disaster. One never knows what is going to happen these days."

Experiences with Science. That the political situation during the last years created a feeling of uneasiness, a readiness to be afraid, will not be a surprise. It is interesting to see, however, that the development of science of which we are so proud, in general, is also likely to create this potential anxiety.

Incidental reading about Mars is mentioned by quite a number of people in this connection. People have heard that Mars might be inhabited, that it is next to the Earth, Mt. Wilson Observatory was a familiar name to one respondent, "Life" had brought out pictures of how the world could come to an end, etc. Evidently the man on the street is sometimes more bewildered than elated by scientific progress. Mrs. C., it seems to us, formulates the psychological problems very aptly:

"I have no education. I do not know what can happen and what cannot. That's up to the scientist. I care for the children and my family. And if *he* says it happened! Also they mentioned those 'mirrors' of those armored men. Well, I learned about the Middle Ages. And I have seen an X-ray machine when my boy had a broken leg."

Buck Rogers and his feature stories in the newspapers are mentioned by several people. Is it the outcome of a spy scare that made Mrs. B. think for a moment that Buck Rogers had given the Mars people the idea to come to fight us?

"It's foolish I know, but somehow I thought: Buck Rogers had always put those things into the funnies. Maybe the Mars people have seen it. Maybe they are so smart and actually do it. Anything can happen and there is so much tenseness around anyhow."

It is quite likely that such a magic attitude toward science will prove, upon further study, a major determinant of the preparedness to believe in a real event. Some incidental information collected on people who did not get frightened shows that some training in the cultural evaluation of social or natural events was most likely to prevent people from believing in the disaster. It would at least be very valuable in case of further studies to check upon this point because of its implications for education toward rational behavior in emergencies.

Recent Natural Catastrophes. Some people feel that hearing of hurricanes and tidal waves contributes to giving a general feeling of lack of security.

"I hated to make myself think that the end of the world had come but there were such unusual things happening in the world, like floods, that I thought it was possible."

Religious Beliefs. Certain trends in religious thinking are another factor contributing to a general expectation of disaster. Evidently the religious aspect can either come in, in a rather rational way as exhibited by the first quotation or in an irrational and emotional way as exemplified by the second quotation given for this group:

"My husband and sons weren't as excited as I was but they had their doubts. They are both pretty calm people. While it was going on, they tried to figure it out. At the beginning of the broadcast, my older son said, "It sounds like a Buck Rogers story," but as time went on he became more convinced that it was real. He tried to explain to me while the excitement was on that that's the way the world balances itself—either by floods or wars and that this was some other form of God-sent elimination of people."

"I thought our Lord was punishing us for something we did to displease Him. I tried not to get panicky. You have to face things."

Individual Experiences. In addition to general influences like war and scientific awe and the natural catastrophes, and religious thinking, we find that a number of people had more special grievances into which the present event seemed to fit. Two active Republicans intimated that Roosevelt had so badly mismanaged foreign affairs that one could not be surprised if some foreign country had come and cracked down upon the United States.

A Jewish woman reports: "The first thing that came to my mind while my sister-in-law was talking was that there was an uprising against the Jews."

One respondent had heard recently of a meteor actually falling down in New Jersey and another heard a broadcast describing the explosion of an oil tank in Linden. So special events seem to have increased their preparedness for Sunday night. Occasionally, people would mention an incident immediately preceding the broadcast which increased their credulity later on: One man was just reading a mystery story when he tuned in during the program and one group of people had just been discussing natural catastrophes.

Altogether, one is surprised to see the great amount of *potential anxiety* which seems to be embedded in the minds of many of our respondents. Whether this feeling of insecurity is characteristic of all of us or whether it is especially great for those people who became disturbed by the broadcast cannot be decided without further research.

B. What Made It So Realistic?

The preparation of people to believe in a disaster is only one aspect of our problem. Another question is: What were the features of the broadcast which made it so believable? Each of our respondents gave his own impression of the program. The replies were classified in rather large units, not taking every single word but the main ideas expressed by the informants. Although people spoke a lot on this point, we were able to reduce each statement to two or three major features. For a classification of a greater number of cases the following list of features will probably prove helpful. They are ranked according to the frequency in which they were mentioned in our cases.

    a. The authenticity of places and persons mentioned.
    b. The technical realism of the performance.
    c. Some special sentences mentioned.
    d. Some more general aspects of the performance.

a. *Regarding Names.* Many people were especially impressed by the appearance of government officials or scientists. Some mentioned particularly that no federal official would get mixed up in something if it were not an authentic situation. Other people mentioned that they were especially impressed by the fact that names were so familiar, that they had been to all of those places, and that they were so nearby. Here is an especially interesting comment for this group.

"One thing was the local names. Watchung Mountains is a name known only to the people who live there. But by the way, I wonder if Welles did not want to give his wife's friends a thrill; he married a girl from my neighborhood."

b. *Regarding Technical Features.* These comments seem to be equally divided between those who say that interruptions in the night club and the shifting of the news flashes from spot to spot made the illusion so perfect; and those who mentioned acoustic items of the program. A majority of comments in the latter group mention the gasping voice of the announcer, his muffled scream when he was about to break down. Evidently the announcer is a cardinal feature in such a situation.

c. *Regarding Phrases.* For a psychological interpretation it should be worthwhile to study especially the phrases and actual quotations which people can remember as decisive features which made them believe in the broadcast. It is interesting, for instance, that the one statement of an "official" is mentioned several times. "It is incredible but true." It is psychologically quite understandable that people are more likely to believe a strange tale when the narrator himself stresses the incredibility. Many of the other sentences especially mentioned by our informants were those where the "government people" stressed that they would take the leadership in the emergency and give all necessary advice. If it could be proved in a larger study that just such remarks were important, it would point to an interesting psychological interpretation: in an emergency we are especially inclined to believe in people who promise that they will take from us and unto themselves the responsibility of coping with the situation.

d. *General Comments.* Of the cases belonging here the greater part said that they did not think there was any reason to doubt the broadcast; they felt that such a story was quite likely anyway. Some people mentioned the special confidence they have in radio as an institution. It should be worthwhile to quote a few comments made in this connection:

"We have so much faith in broadcasting. In a crisis it has to reach all people. That's what radio is here for."

"The announcer would not say it if it were not true. They always quit if something is a play."

"I put credence on news bulletins. I feel that the radio is the official organ to let people know of tragedies—this sort of broke my faith in radio."

"I always feel that the commentators bring the best possible news. Even after this I will still believe what I hear on the radio."

C. The Situational Context

How could they have believed it, was the question which a number of people asked after it was all over. And, indeed, neither the potential anxiety nor the realistic features of the program would fully account for the effect. We have to include in our analysis the special moment at which the people started to listen; here is a list of the main situations in the order of frequency in which they occurred in our sample.

> Dialed in by coincidence after the program had begun
> Family members or friends rushed in and made them listen
> Were urged over the telephone to listen
> Happened to enter a room where the program was on
> Listened from the beginning

As was to be expected, only a very few cases listened from the beginning among our respondents who were selected because they were known to have been upset. The majority were dragged into the situation by other people either directly or by telephone. Very revealing are those cases who heard from the beginning that it was a Mercury Theater Play because they evidently furnish examples of a loose kind of radio listening. They report that they did not listen very carefully and when the flashes came, they were so upset that they forgot what they had heard just a few minutes before. Relatively near to this psychological situation is the case of some people who had been listening to other programs when they were called to listen to WABC. Here again, the sudden impression of the flashes made them overlook the fact that everything was being carried on in an orderly fashion over the other station. (It might be, however, that the stressing of "scoops" in radio publicity made it plausible that one station reports the end of the world during the dance program of another station.)

D. *The Role Of Other People*

Our material does not permit us to do more than utter a few hunches as to how people mutually influenced each other. It seems that in most of the cases the husband behaved critically or at least much more calmly than the wife.

"My husband was so calm even when he thought that the end of the world was coming that he made me mad. He did not even put his arm around me."

"I got furious at my husband because he did not want to drive home quicker. . . . Then he stayed in the car to listen and I was pacing the floor inside."

On the other hand, when a man got panicky he seems to have especially impressed others in his environment. In one case a usually calm and intellectually conceited brother had telephoned and said very excitedly that he was leaving his home with his family. That a person who was considered apparently an intellectual authority told about the event evidently made for immediate acceptance. Another group of cases are those people who are usually sheltered and not used to making decisions of their own. When they happened to be caught by the broadcast without their usual guides the situation was especially difficult.

"I rushed downstairs to phone my husband to come home and decide what it was and what should be done. . . . Children were crying, 'Mother, where will we go? But I got them dressed and said, 'Wait until daddy comes, he will know.' "

Were people more likely to be scared when they tuned in for themselves or when other people made them aware of the event? Our evidence is contradictory. In some cases the excitement of others seemed to have increased the critical faculties of certain people; in other cases people felt they would never have believed it if they had been alone. On the other hand just because they were alone, some others were just in the mood to fall for exciting news.

E. *Everything Fits Into The Picture*

Altogether, it is one of the surest but, of course, most obvious results that most of those people who were upset had started to listen to the program after it had begun. The much more important psychological problem is to what extent people were able to check up on the authenticity of the broadcast. Here lies probably one of the most important aspects of the event from a social point of view: To what extent will an emergency deprive people of the intelligent use of a rational means of behavior?

Objectively, they could tune in to other stations, look into the newspaper, or check for information over the telephone. Most of the people did something of this kind but for a very interesting reason, only about half of them succeeded. The following list gives the main patterns in the order of frequency in which they occurred with our respondents:

Abortive check-ups were made which seem to prove that the program was a real broadcast.

Station identification or information from other people came so quickly that no major panic could develop in spite of the respondent believing the news.

People acted immediately under the impact of fear without further control.

The ten cases of people who checked up and found their suspicions corroborated show how great the danger is that a state of panic distorts our rational thinking. The issue is important enough to enumerate what happened in those cases:

One man mistook the sight of the neon lights in Newark streets as fire shining.

One woman looked out of the window and saw a "greenish eerie light" which later on proved to be the lights on the car of the maid who had just come home.

In two cases people were told over the telephone about the event and by coincidence tuned in to WABC for a check up. As a result, they had no more doubts.

In one case, the police were called so early that they had no information yet and were worried themselves.

In three cases a strange coincidence seemed to corroborate the fear of the one who tried to check up.

A boy telephoned to his mother at a party where she was supposed to be. When no one answered, he was sure that the fumes had overtaken all the people in that apartment. Later on, it turned out that the party had gone to an empty apartment in the same building where they could dance better.

In one home, there were two radios and the parents checked up on the radio of the boy; they knew that the boy always listened to Charlie McCarthy at this time Sunday night and when they heard the Mercury Theater program over the radio, they were sure that all stations carried the disaster.

One man looked at the newspaper and evidently got the wrong program because he found music announced for the time for which he was looking.

How definitely people interpreted all evidence in the light of their own apprehension is strikingly shown by the following two quotations:

> Mrs. B. tells: "We looked out of the window and Wyoming Avenue was black with cars. People were rushing away."
>
> Mrs. O. tells: "No car came down my street. 'Traffic is jammed', I thought."

There was no way out. Many cars or no cars, all seemed equally to indicate the worst.

The great role those abortive controls played has not been mentioned as far as we know in the newspaper discussions of the event. It seems to be a factor which could come out only from such a detailed kind of interview.

How about the five people who did not check up at all? One family was in a car and drove home horrified; they arrived there when the play was over. Two people ran out of the house immediately and stayed out until they finally learned that there was nothing to it. In two cases, the people just stayed paralyzed until the end of the program relieved them of the terror. In one of the cases, the respondent did not think he could tune in to other stations because the announcer had said that his station was the only one not yet destroyed.

F. The Thrill Of Disaster

The analysis of the factors leading to the "Mars scare" would not be complete if we did not point out some definite elements of enjoyment which radiate through a number of the reports we have collected. It is not alien to modern psychological theory to assume that interspersed in their experience of fear, people had experiences of relief and elation.

In some cases, the language of the respondents is astonishing. One woman tells how she and her husband were "glued to the radio." One young man did not turn to another station for a checkup because he did not want to miss anything. One man says that "although we were not scared, we could not stop listening."

In three cases, the people refused for quite some time after the broadcast to believe it was not true. It is almost as if they did not want to abandon something valuable and which they had to protect against the other people in their environment who wanted to rob them of it.

"They all dismissed it but I did not really believe that it was a play until I saw the newspapers the next morning. I went to bed still thinking that something was going to happen."

The following rather hazardous assumptions could be made and an example furnished here and there.

a) Some people felt important for participating in such a momentous event irrespective of the danger involved.

Mrs. C. says so explicitly:	"I urged my husband to listen and said it was a historical moment possibly and he would be sorry afterwards to have missed it."
Mrs. J., without knowing it, describes how she behaved as a messenger of great importance:	"I stood on the corner waiting for a bus and I thought that every car that came along was a bus and I ran out to get it. People saw how excited I was and tried to quiet me, but I kept saying over and over again to everybody I met, 'Don't you know that New Jersey is destroyed by Germans—it's on the radio.'"

b) Our daily lives are full of frustration and some people might have experienced the disaster as a release from all the prohibitions surrounding us.

Mrs. J. tells how she came home, knees shaking and hardly able to walk the stairs: "I looked in the icebox and saw some chicken left from Sunday dinner and that I was saving for Monday night dinner. I said to my nephew, 'We may as well eat this chicken—we won't be here in the morning.'"

c) In some cases where people felt personally worried, it might have been a relief to see one's own plight, so to say, taken over by the community. We do not have a case where that is expressed textually but the case of the Jewish woman mentioned previously comes very near to it: "I realized right away that it was something that was affecting everybody, not only the Jews, and I felt relieved. As long as everybody was going to go, it was better."

d) Finally, one cannot but feel that in a few cases an element of the sadistic enjoyment of a catastrophe is involved. One woman described how people were drowning "like rats" in the Hudson River and another said they were "dying like flies." Another woman was described by the interviewer in the following terms: "She is the kind that enjoys sensations (impressed by massacres in Spain). The expression on her face as she tells of her anxiety reveals her enjoyment." This report was given without any idea that in the final analysis we would look for this kind of evidence.

The following description of what was reported over the radio should be joy for any psychoanalyst: "They (the monsters) were like snakes—the little ones were crawling out of the pit and multiplying."

The most striking indication of such psychological implications is given by Mrs. S. Her behavior, as well as her wording, might intimate the voluptuous element we are thinking of: "Then, also, my husband tried to calm me and said, 'If this were really so, it would be on all stations,' and he turned to one of the other stations and there was music. I retorted, 'Nero fiddled while Rome burned.'"

78

G. D. Wiebe

THE ARMY-McCARTHY HEARINGS AND THE PUBLIC CONSCIENCE

DURING THE SPRING of 1954 the televised Army-McCarthy hearings created a nationwide sensation. Housewives neglected their housework, retailers reported decreased shopping, even theater owners noticed the drop-off in attendance during the days of the hearings. The Army-McCarthy hearings had loosed a wave of excitement and concern among many millions of people. It seemed that little else was talked about.

Among those who were especially devoted to civil rights and to the ideology of American freedom, there was the widespread hope, and even the belief, that the hearings would arouse the public to a ringing reaffirmation of traditional liberties and, correspondingly, to a mass rejection of Senator McCarthy for having encroached upon those freedoms in a bombastic and intemperate career which purported to expose Communist subversion.

With this belief as a hypothesis, a small sample study was conducted some sixty days after the close of the hearings. Twenty-one middle-class housewives and twenty-five middle-class shopkeepers were interviewed, half in a middle-sized city in Maine, half in a city of similar size in Kansas. Experienced interviewers, who had no special briefing beyond the instruction to encourage respondents to speak freely and at length, had the following questions as a general interview guide:

1. Would you please think back to *before* the Army-McCarthy hearings. How did you feel *then* about Senator McCarthy and his work?
2. How do you feel about Senator McCarthy and his work *now*? If the respondent indicated a clear change in feeling, he was asked:

Public Opinion Quarterly, Vol. IX (1958–1959), pp. 490–502.

3. As you think back to the hearings now, what comes to mind as the thing that changed your feelings? If he had not indicated a change in feeling, he was asked:

4. As you think back to the hearings now, what comes to mind as the most outstanding thing or the most important thing that happened?

Note that the first two items invite free experience about Senator McCarthy and his work. Respondents were provided with the opportunity to talk out their feelings, or the stereotypes with which they had chosen to affiliate themselves, regarding the man and his activities. Then, in the third or fourth item, attention was directed to the hearings, and presumably to the basic issues.

The central hypothesis was that responses would reveal strong support, either directly or by implication, for such values as the following:

1. It is wrong to assume guilt until innocence is proven.
2. It is wrong to require conformity through fear.
3. Assuming guilt by association is wrong.
4. It is wrong to encroach on freedom of speech.
5. It is wrong to condemn or to arouse suspicion against intellectuals, or other whole subgroups of the population.
6. A man should not be condemned or punished for action that was not culpable when it took place.
7. No one man or group of men should sit simultaneously as prosecutor, judge, and jury.
8. It is wrong to place a man's liberty, reputation, or job in repeated jeopardy on the basis of charges that have once been demonstrated to be groundless
9. It is wrong to require a man to testify against himself.

The hypothesis was conclusively rejected. The respondents did not talk about such values as these, either directly or by implication, often enough to justify reporting.

Dr. Samuel Stouffer reported results from a nationwide survey conducted *during* the hearings which tend to confirm our findings. Interviewers asked, "What kind of things do you worry about most?" Although the hearings were a nationwide sensation, Stouffer reports, "The number of people who said that they were worried either about the threat of communism in the United States or about civil liberties was, even by the most generous interpretation of occasionally ambiguous responses, *less than* 1%!" [1] Stouffer makes it clear that all mentions of the Army-McCarthy hearings are included in this less than 1 per cent. Apparently various subgroups of the public can share this involvement in an event while perceiving it in terms of quite different value systems.

A second hypothesis was that among the Senator's backers the hearings would have provided a shocking and vivid experience of infractions against ordinary decency; that since the Senator's targets in the hearings were men of prominence and distinction who were continuing in positions of trust under a highly popular Republican administration, they would not fit the "villain" role; and that many of the Senator's supporters would recoil and turn against him because of his tactics.

This hypothesis, though not completely rejected, found sparse confirmation. Following the hearings, our 46 respondents divided as follows: 25 were pro-McCarthy, 20 were anti-McCarthy, and 1 seemed to be genuinely neutral. According to their own reports of previous sentiment, only 2 had definitely changed their minds. Both had become anti-McCarthy as a result of the hearings, one because "Senators . . . shouldn't set themselves up as bigger than the government. . . ." and the other because Senator McCarthy wanted ". . . to have things in his own way like a spoiled child." There is a possibility that some respondents withheld their former feelings if the hearings changed their minds, but the social milieu would appear to have minimized this pattern. It had only gradually become apparent to the public that President Eisenhower, who enjoyed very high status as a national hero, was against the Senator. Numerous conservative Senators had turned against Senator McCarthy. So there was ego support in moving to an anti-McCarthy position. Furthermore, it is not easy to deceive an experienced interviewer during the whole of a discursive interview lasting thirty to forty-five minutes.

Although editorial opinion in the mass media had much to say about public opinion having been aroused and about a ground swell of protest, our small sample showed no such shift of position. Nor was this sample atypical in this regard. A nationwide poll by George Gallup in April 1954, before the hearings, showed 38 per cent Favorable to Senator McCarthy, 46 per cent Unfavorable, and 16 per cent No Opinion. In August, some two months after the hearings and at about the time our 46 interviews were conducted, Gallup reported 36 per cent Favorable, 51 per cent Unfavorable, and 13 per cent No Opinion. The hearings did not cause a definitive turnabout among the public. The Senator's supporters did not collectively turn their backs on him.

Some three years later, several months before Senator McCarthy's brief illness and death, Elmo Roper and Associates asked a nationwide sample this question: "Several years ago we heard a lot about Senator Joseph McCarthy of Wisconsin and his activities. But recently he has been much less prominent in the news. How do you feel now about Senator McCarthy and what he stands for? Do you approve, disapprove, or are you neutral about him?" The results were: Approve 16 per cent, Disapprove 20 per cent, Neutral 40 per cent, Don't know 24 per cent. So even at this late date, when Senator McCarthy's prestige, prominence, and power had long since disappeared, the relative proportions of pro and con opinion among the rank and file had changed little. The big shift was that more than half the pros and the cons had moved to the Neutral or No Opinion categories. What public spokesmen and the nation's leaders called a general repudiation of Senator McCarthy by the public was for the most part a repudiation among themselves. The dominant shift among the rank and file was that they turned their attention elsewhere. Although the hearings were fascinating to millions, they appear to have caused little change in position.

The two original hypotheses were rejected. Respondents had not perceived the hearings in terms of civil liberties, nor had pro-McCarthyites shifted, in any sizable proportion, to a position against him. Still the public fascination with the hearings was so intense, and was so clearly loaded with emotion and controversy, that one could hardly doubt that values were somehow deeply involved. But *what* values? What "rights" and "wrongs" did respondents use in structuring their reactions to the hearings?

Value Themes In The Survey Responses

The responses, which had been reported as nearly verbatim as possible, were searched phrase by phrase for value judgments. With the exception of one category of statements, every statement was tabulated that specifically expressed or clearly implied the feeling that something was right or that something was wrong. The exception was that large group of statements indicating that Communism or Communist subversion or infiltration was wrong. All 46 respondents stated or clearly implied their opposition to Communism and their approval of opposing it. Aside from these statements, 191 value judgments were recorded. No single value judgment was tabulated more than once for a particular respondent. Thus, if one respondent said the hearings were an unforgivable waste of time and later said that Mr. Welch should not have been permitted to delay things by asking the same question over and over, these statements were tabulated as a single instance of the value judgment, *It is wrong to waste time, to be repetitious.*

The value judgments reported below account for 132 of the 191. All values appearing in the protocols of 7 (15 per cent) or more of our respondents are reported. The remaining 59 value judgments are a widely scattered miscellany, including this comment from the proprietor of a paint and wallpaper shop:

No. 40 . . . I thought the TV hearings were an abomination for I called on a woman to talk to her about some wallpapering she had called me to consult her on. And she could not talk to me but kept her eyes glued to the hearings. She didn't know a word I was saying and so there was nothing to do but leave and ask her to be sure and call me after the hearings ended.

Specific value judgments emerged in responses to one of two questions. If the respondent had changed his mind about Senator McCarthy and his work during the hearings, his response was to this question: "As you think back to the hearings now, what comes to mind as the thing that changed your feelings?" If he did not indicate that he had changed his mind, his response was to this question: "As you think back to the hearings now, what comes to mind as the most outstanding thing or the most important thing that happened?"

There are one positive ("It is right") value theme, seven negative ("It is wrong") value themes, and two conflict value themes. In the last two instances, the same value was considered right by some respondents and wrong by others. Each value theme will be briefly discussed and illustrated. Then the findings will be summarized in tabular form.

Positive Value Theme. Among the things that are "right," a single theme stands out—The Lone Hero Theme: *It is right to be, or he is right because he is, selfless, dedicated, courageous, sincere, direct, determined, blameless. He sticks to his convictions, stands ready even if alone, in a good cause.*

This was the most frequently mentioned theme among the ten. It occurred in the responses of 18 people, 13 of whom were pro-McCarthy, 5 of whom were anti-McCarthy. This theme was used with reference to various participants in the hearings. As might be expected, it occurred most frequently with reference to Senator McCarthy, in the responses of his supporters. But it was also used with reference to other participants in the hearings. Our interest is not in the persons evaluated. It is in the fact that the theme frequently occurred as basis for establishing *rightness*.

Here are some examples:

> No. 3 . . . I think that McCarthy is bullheaded, but then a lot of people are, and if they want anything they are going to have to go after it in a bullheaded way. I don't believe that McCarthy and his fight against Communism can be swayed by anybody, regardless of their position or financial rating.
>
> No. 14 . . . I admire Stevens so much being the goat. Someone had to and he did it so gentlemanly. He was able to take it and I read that he had the flu during it and was running an extremely high temperature but it was all in the line of duty and he just took all that was heaped on his head and smiled. . . .

Negative Value Themes. The most frequently mentioned negative theme is that it is wrong to impede the lone hero: *They are* (he is) *wrong to condemn, pick on, misunderstand, beat down, interfere with, withhold information from, gang up on, be unfair to, a person who is pursuing a good end.* This theme occurred in the responses of 16 people, for example:

> No. 25. It showed that he could call anyone, no matter how important they were like the Army head, and scold them and no one could tell him to stop.
> No. 46. The most important thing that comes to my mind was the way that McCarthy was abused, and is still abused.

The second negative theme is that it is wrong to be weak: *He is wrong because he is weak, evasive, dependent, shifty, contradictory, afraid, incompetent.* Thirteen respondents mentioned this theme, for example:

> No. 43. I was ashamed about several things. . . First the Secretary of the Army was a sorry figure. He didn't have the forcefulness he should have to have a job like his. . . . Wishy-washy.
> No. 11. The most important and outstanding thing? Well, one of the things I noticed in particular was McCarthy's evasiveness with many of the witnesses.

The third negative theme, mentioned by 12 respondents, is that it is wrong for individuals to take precedence over, or be disrespectful of, the law: *It is wrong to be disrespectful of the dignity, to disturb the decorum, to depart from the precedents, of high office and constituted authority.* For example:

> No. 21. . . . it should be taken up before the Supreme Court so if there is anything, the judge can do something about it. The whole thing was a circus; it was a disgrace to this entire country.
> No. 17. I feel that his tactics on committees are improper for a Senator to use . . . he doesn't belong in the Senate at all . . . also I remember his taking undue advantage of the rules of the committee. . . .

The fourth negative theme, mentioned by 11 respondents, is that it is wrong to tell a lie: *He is wrong because he is dishonest; tells lies.* For example:

> No. 22. What I really think is if I was in authority in government, I would throw that guy out, as he was lying all the time and the people knew he was lying.
> No. 29. The most important and outstanding thing that happened during the hearings was the way they accused McCarthy of lying, because it was right in the newspaper.

The fifth negative theme, also mentioned by 11 respondents, is that it is wrong to waste time. Four of these eleven, and two others not among these eleven, also deplored the waste of money. But these statements were not in terms of the cliche, "a waste of time and money." The value judgments appear to have been in response to the tedium of legal or quasi-legal questioning and cross-examination: *It is (they are, he is) wrong to waste time, to be repetitious.* For example:

> No. 31. Well, I think both sides wasted an awful lot of time putting things into the records, deciding whether they should or not.
> No. 41. . . . so needless and proved to be nothing but time wasters.

The sixth negative theme, mentioned by 9 respondents, is that it is wrong to expose your own group to criticism: *It is wrong for Republicans to expose their party to its opponents, for officials to expose governmental errors to the public, for Americans to show other nations their culpability.* For example:

> No. 9. You can also add that he did a lot to pull down the Republican party in the eyes of the people, and I am a Republican.
> No. 38. . . . our own citizens became conscious of the inner workings of the government and it wasn't the nicest thing that they could learn. It is like a family washing too much of its linen in the public limelight. We should have kept much of it secret.

The seventh negative theme, mentioned by 7 respondents, is that it is wrong to evade guilt by attacking: *It is (they are, he is) wrong to attack a person in order to divert attention from one's own ulterior and venal motives:* For example:

> No. 36. McCarthy has to stop his work for hearings and answer charges and all that sort of thing and that is just throwing obstacles in his way so that he won't be uncovering more Communists. Some people are covering up for someone, that is sure.
> No. 14. McCarthy . . . must have had the blessing of those very powerful people whoever they are that were arranging for this show to go on while they accomplished some deviltry on the sidelines.

Conflict Value Themes. The values reported thus far are unambiguous among our respondents in the sense that there were no stated contradictions of them. For example, no one referred to deceit as right, etc.

There are two themes, however, that were considered right by some and wrong by others. The first was the conflict on the familiar issue of Ends and Means. Twelve respondents maintained that good ends justify the means. Nine respondents deplored ruthlessness as a means even to a laudable end. Here is an example of each side:

> No. 19. I approve of the way McCarthy has tried to get rid of Communism and he is only using some of their own tactics. As I

said before, they are using them over there in Russia, why shouldn't he use them?

No. 9. I feel that he would do anything he could to hurt anyone that wouldn't agree with him in any way.

There is a second conflict regarding the theme of Privilege Among Men. The responses suggest a pragmatic recognition that the law is differential in its application. Fourteen of our respondents state value judgments, not in terms of whether behavior is legal or not, but in terms of whether others have "gotten away with it" or whether others are "worse." The conflict then arises between those who identify with the aggressors: *Others have gotten away with it. Why shouldn't he (I)?* and those who identify with the aggressed against: *He won't let others (me) do it. Why should he get away with it?*

These references to the Privilege Among Men theme occur in the responses of 14 people. Seven are on one side, seven on the other. An example on each side follows:

No. 12. . . . he asked Stevens to give Schine a commission, which isn't wrong because it is being done every day.

No. 42. It seems so strange that he is so concerned with subversives and not want to follow the letter of the law himself. . . .

We have reported ten themes, each of which appeared in the responses of more than 15 per cent of our respondents (7 or more individuals among the 46). These findings are summarized in the table below.

Value Themes and Superego Formation

There were the values in terms of which our 46 respondents spoke.[2] They came into focus when it was realized that all of them have deep roots in the early *childhood* process of superego formation in our culture.

1. The lone hero theme suggests the familiar father figure; the great man, autonomous, righteous, powerful, loved, and feared. Deference toward father is among the first values introjected in childhood.[3]

2. The sin, and the danger, of impeding the father figure is, of course, at the very base of superego structure. Alternatively, children introject the "right" of opposition to being picked on, impeded, pushed around, when they are trying to do right.

3. The "wrong" of being weak, indecisive, inadequate, is a demon that stands between every child and his ambition for adulthood.

4. The "wrong" of disturbing or flouting the decorum of es-

NUMBER OF RESPONDENTS, IN A SAMPLE OF 46, WHO MENTIONED SPECIFIED VALUE THEMES

Value Themes	Number of Respondents
Positive:	
Lone hero	18
Negative:	
Impede lone hero	16
Weak	13
Disrespect of law	12
Deceit	11
Waste time	11
Expose own group	9
Evade guilt by attacking	7
Conflict:	
Means and ends:	
Ends justify means	12
Bad means discredit ends	9
Privilege among men:	
Identification with aggressor	7
Identification with those aggressed against	7
Miscellaneous	59 *
Total	191

* Among the values in this rather large residue labeled "Miscellaneous" were the following: 6 (already mentioned in passing) who deplored the waste of money, 5 who deplored the show of emotion, 4 who deplored the seeking of personal publicity, 4 who deplored and 4 who approved violation of secrecy.

tablished ways is introjected early in childhood and is a basic tool in the socializing process.

5. By the age of four, children in our culture know that it is wrong to tell a lie.

6. To waste time, to dawdle, to procrastinate, to delay—"just once more," "do it again," "in a minute"; children know these as preludes to arbitrary adult action in our time-driven society.

7. To "tattle," to "carry tales," to betray one's peers, is a "wrong" well introjected by the age of eight or nine.

8. The "wrong" of diverting the attention of authority figures from one's own wrongdoing by criticizing another is familiar to children as a form of cheating, of being afraid to "face the music." Guilt or anger, depending on whether a child is the exploiter or the exploited, are familiar to children involved in this mechanism, and these feelings, of course, bespeak the introjected "wrong."

9. The means-ends conflict pervades the formative years of childhood. On the one hand, an endless and complex code of man-

ners and methods must be learned. On the other hand, the tremendous status value of success—of getting the job done—tends to subordinate means to ends. Impulse gratification via means, softened by a socially desirable end, is an old story: "You always tell me to stop interfering with little brother (socially desirable end), so I let him play in the mud (impulse to see him in trouble)." But impulse gratification as an end, made permissible by impeccable manners, is hardly less common: "But I passed the candy first (impeccable manners) before I ate the little ones that were left (impulse gratification)."

10. The second conflict theme recalls endless examples in sibling and other childhood relationships: "They all were doing it, so I didn't think it would do any harm if I did too." "He started it." Or, on the other hand, "That's bad. If you do it I'll tell on you." "When I wanted to, you said it wasn't fair, so now you can't do it."

All these values that occurred most frequently in the statements of our respondents have obvious and numberless specific implementations in the socializing of children in our society. They are introjected. They become matters of conscience. These values, learned in a context of face-to-face relationships among members of the family and the home neighborhood provided the criteria, among our 46 respondents, for evaluating the hearings.

The Denial of Civil Rights in Early Superego Formation

Now consider the civil rights values listed earlier as they pertain to childhood.

1. Few, if any, children are consistently assumed to be innocent until guilt is proven. Most adults can recall childhood incidents when they were punished for the acts of siblings or friends. Most children have been scolded or otherwise treated as guilty when the real cause for the punishment was the parent's irritability. Children are frequently punished on evidence that would not stand up in court.

2. Every child learns conformity at least partly through fear of punishment.

3. Most children have been warned about, and punished for, associating with persons disapproved of by their parents.

4. No child enjoys freedom of speech.

5. Every generation of Americans has been notably better educated than the preceding generation. There is ambivalence on this score. Parents want their children to "get ahead." But superior education tends to weaken parental authority. And among members of a given generation, the minority with superior education are often perceived as threatening the majority's illusion of simple equality. In contrast with many cultures in which the highly educated are treated

with deference because of their education, in our society the highly educated have traditionally been regarded with an admixture of humor, skepticism, and suspicion. Both the "practical man" and the "rich man" outrank him. And if these "put the eggheads in their place," childhood training predisposes the rank and file to accept this as probably a good thing.

6. Most adults would have little trouble remembering childhood episodes followed by, "But you didn't tell me I couldn't." And then the parent: "Anyone your age knows better."

7. Every child is subjected to parents, and later to teachers, who sit simultaneously as prosecutor, judge, and jury. In fact this pattern has tended to seep, almost unnoticed, into the conduct of governmental agencies, bureaus, and commissions.

8. Most children become resigned to "double jeopardy" in those instances where wrongdoing is heard and judged first in Mother's "court," and then re-tried and re-judged when Father gets home.

9. The child in our society knows that refusal to testify against himself (confess) is the equivalent of refusing to tell the truth, which is, for practical purposes, lying.

These rights and guarantees, prominent among those referred to as civil rights, are not enjoyed by children in their relationships with authority figures. In fact, as we have seen, the denial of these rights, or at least substantial encroachments upon them, are introjected during the early years when the basic superego structure is formed. This is part of the socializing process and presumably contributes to the kind of adult maturity that makes our society a viable social system. Children can no more be guaranteed civil rights *vis-a-vis* their parents than adults can be guaranteed love and solicitude at the hands of civil authorities.

Discussion

At several points, the findings of this small sample study have been reported as corresponding rather closely with findings from nationwide samples. This similarity, on specified points, to the findings from nationwide samples by Stouffer and by Gallup somewhat enhances the stature of our small-sample findings. It must remain quite clear, however, that although our findings were prominent among our 46 middle-class people, they can be regarded only as *hypotheses* insofar as major patterns of reaction in the general population are concerned. With this reservation in mind, the small sample findings nevertheless suggest several points that have broad implications.

We hypothesize that civil rights are not generally introjected in our society and that when a public issue which apparently involves civil rights captures popular feeling there is a strong chance that the introjected values of childhood will provide the criteria for evaluating the issue. But, from the evidence at hand, a question arises as to whether even the word "evaluating" is appropriate. Many of our respondents seem not to have experienced the hearings as providing evidence on which to arrive at a decision. They seem rather to have handled the proceedings as events which required moral justification within the boundaries of preconceived decisions. These values of childhood morality would appear to have functioned, at least in many cases, as devices which endow psychological needs or emotional affiliations with moral legitimacy.

This pattern would leave power figures remarkably free of public criticism where political ideology is concerned. On the other hand, a public figure, though adhering to democratic political ideology, might arouse disabling public censure by comparatively trivial encroachments upon the values introjected during childhood. Our political liberties would appear, in a very real sense, to be perceived as guaranteed, owed to us, available on demand, but not sustained and nourished in the tissue of the body politic.

An autocracy, be it benevolent or despotic, projects the essentials of the child-parent relationship into the adult pattern of ruled and ruler. The introjected patterns of submission and obedience work in the direction of tranquility in an autocracy. But democracy and political liberty call for a break in this pattern. They call for a substantial degree of personal autonomy and responsibility as rewards for successful socialization during childhood. The rules of the game for this mature adulthood are collectively the ideology of democracy. And we hypothesize that our society has not provided for the introjection of these rules in a way that even approaches the success with which the interpersonal ethics of childhood are taught.[4]

It must be explicitly stated that a small but crucial minority of the population (probably less than 5 per cent) do appear to have introjected the political and civil principles that are the foundation of American freedom. They sense an encroachment upon a civil right, be it ever so distant and even if the victim is their enemy, as a direct and glaring threat to their own and every citizen's liberty. They are known by their works and are rare enough to be highly visible. Perhaps psychologist and sociologists will some day join forces and discover how this minority happens to introject these values. It is a challenging assignment.

At a less crucial level and quite aside from matters of political values, our findings suggest an interesting insight regarding sporadic outbursts of public indignation in which the heat often seems disproportionate to the fuel. Those who hold public office or work in the mass media know that while it is often difficult to stimulate tangible public response on important issues, it is also difficult to foresee when some apparently trivial point will release widespread public protest. Telephone switchboards light up and mail bags bulge because a radio or television panel participant, in the heat of discussion, utters a swear word. The issue at the nub of the controversy generally receives comparatively little comment from the public. The neckline of a female singer's dress can stir up a storm, but the quality of her singing gets comparatively little serious consideration. A passing comment by a wit on the too frequent rendition of a Christmas carol jeopardizes a television career. Rumors of pigeons or squirrels being shot on the White House lawn generate a true grassroots protest. Such outbursts of public indignation, when seen in terms of the present findings are not evidence of a capricious public. They are, rather, evidence of a public which is sure and articulate about one set of values, namely those introjected during childhood. It seems a likely hypothesis that if tangible personal benefits, perceived as such, are not at stake, the values introjected during childhood will take precedence over values that are presumed to be acquired later—values relating to such areas as aesthetics, economics, science, and politics.

Summary

1. Among the respondents in a small sample study, the Army–McCarthy hearings were not perceived or evaluated in terms of civil rights.

2. The hearings had relatively little effect in changing respondents' minds about Senator McCarthy.

3. The values in terms of which respondents judged the hearings were values that are generally introjected in our society during the childhood process of superego formation.

4. It is hypothesized that civil rights are typically not introjected during the childhood process of superego formation, that, in fact, encroachments upon these rights are characteristic of the process of socialization.

5. It is suggested that many instances of vigorous public response are motivated by inappropriate values and that our society has failed to provide systematically for the introjection of the values that are basic to political freedom.

79

Lawrence W. Lichty and Malachi C. Topping

A COLLEGE COMMUNITY
VIEWS THE FOURTH "GREAT DEBATE"

THE FOUR "Great Debates" of the 1960 campaign, as landmarks in broadcasting history, will long be considered as to their ultimate effect on the pattern of voting in the election of Senator John F. Kennedy to the presidency.

The fourth of the debates held in New York studios, October 21, 1960, was outstanding in that it unexpectedly gathered as large an audience as the record one for the first debate.[1]

To test an admittedly tenuous relationship between the broadcast and its effect on a very selective audience, a matching pair of semantic differential scales were administered to a group of married college students and their voting wives before and after the fourth debate. The object was to measure change in attitude toward both the candidates and some issues which had been brought up in the campaign prior to the debate.

METHOD AND SAMPLE

The Friday night of the fourth "Great Debate," prior to its broadcast in Columbus, Ohio, 164 persons, selected at random from the Ohio State University married student housing unit, were given attitude scale tests. The test sought to measure the attitude of respondents toward eight concepts—"Nixon," "Kennedy," "The Presidency," "Republican Party," "Democratic Party," "Federal Spending," "American Prestige," and "Television Debates." Each concept was followed by a series of 13 pairs of bipolar words.

The following Sunday, two days later, the same concepts were scored again by 114 of the original 164 respondents who were at home.[3] Fifty-six of these respondents (49.1%) indicated that they had discussed the Presidential campaign at some length between the end of the debate and the application of the test.

Ninety of those in the sample viewed all or part of the debate while 24 did not. The age of the respondents was predominantly "young adults"—79.2% in the 21–31 age group. The "non-stress" groups, as described by Barrow,[4] dominated the sample with 19 Protestant Democrats and only one Catholic Republican. Education, as might be expected, was advanced with 57.9% of the sample listed as college graduates. All but nine of the respondents had seen one or more of the previous debates.

The post-debate forms revealed little total group change in voting plans. Prior to the debate, 13.2% was undecided and after the broadcast the ratio had increased to 14% (a total change of one voter).

The sample was divided along party lines on "who made the most impressive showing in the fourth debate?" However, nearly a third of the Republicans (32%) felt that the two candidates came out "about even." An equal number of the Democrats was split between "Nixon" (17%) and "about even" (14.7%) in answer to the same question.

ATTITUDES TOWARDS CONCEPTS "NIXON" AND "KENNEDY"

Using the "good-bad" scale as a determinant for the evaluative factor and the "active-passive" scale for the activity factor, a number of attitude changes were revealed. According to a factor analysis reported in Osgood, the "good-bad" scale is considered the best determinant of the evaluative factor and the "active-passive" scale is distinctively loaded for the activity factor.[5]

The Evaluative Factor

In terms of "evaluation" on the "good-bad" scale, the term "Nixon" seemed to lose ground in five of six sex-political categories (Table 1). Only the Democratic women rated "Nixon" as more "good" after viewing the debate.

TABLE 1

THE EVALUATIVE FACTOR: CONCEPTS "NIXON" AND "KENNEDY" RATED BY 86 DEMOCRATS, REPUBLICANS AND INDEPENDENTS IN A COLLEGE COMMUNITY BEFORE AND AFTER VIEWING THE "FOURTH DEBATE"

Figures show the mean responses of men and women on a seven-point semantic differential scale.

(Good = + 3.00; Bad = − 3.00.)

	Nixon			Kennedy		
	Before	After	Change	Before	After	Change
DEMOCRATS						
Men (15)	+0.60	0.00	−.60	+1.27	+1.54	+.27
Women (12)	+0.09	+0.17	+.08	+1.42	+1.67	+.25
REPUBLICANS						
Men (21)	+1.86	+1.77	−.09	0.00	−0.57	−.57
Women (20)	+2.10	+1.95	−.15	+0.75	+0.25	−.50
INDEPENDENTS						
Men (13)	+1.08	+0.85	−.23	+0.77	+0.70	−.07
Women (5)	+0.20	0.00	−.20	+0.20	0.00	−.20

The concept "Kennedy" showed movement toward the "good" within the Democratic party—both men and women. He lost some ground with the opposition Republicans and with the Independents.

The Activity Factor

There were charges in the campaign that Senator Kennedy was impulsive—inclined to speak and act quickly before thinking.

TABLE 2

THE ACTIVITY FACTOR: CONCEPTS "NIXON" AND "KENNEDY" RATED BY 86 DEMOCRATS, REPUBLICANS AND INDEPENDENTS IN A COLLEGE COMMUNITY BEFORE AND AFTER VIEWING THE "FOURTH DEBATE"

Figures show the mean responses of men and women on a seven-point semantic differential scale.

(Active = + 3.00; Passive = − 3.00).

	Nixon			Kennedy		
	Before	After	Change	Before	After	Change
DEMOCRAT						
Men (15)	+0.40	−0.46	−.86	+2.67	+2.34	−.33
Women (12)	+0.62	+0.42	−.20	+2.84	+2.67	−.17
REPUBLICAN						
Men (21)	+1.72	+1.72	.00	+1.15	+1.18	+.03
Women (20)	+2.25	+2.45	+.20	+2.05	+1.85	−.20
INDEPENDENT						
Men (13)	+1.00	+0.93	−.07	+1.24	+1.39	+.15
Women (5)	+1.00	+0.40	−.60	+0.80	+1.00	+.20

After viewing the fourth debate, Republican women rated "Nixon" more "active"; there was no change in the Republican men. One of the other concepts included in the study was "The Presidency." The Republican category (men and women combined) had a mean rating of + 2.18 on the "active-passive" scale for "The Presidency." Thus while the shift for "Nixon" was towards the "active" among Republican women, the move was actually away from their ranking of "The Presidency." The Democrats and Independents ranked "Nixon" as more "passive" after viewing the television debate. In both cases this is away from their concept of "The Presidency."

Within his own party (for both men and women) "Kennedy" was ranked as more "passive" after the debate. But "Kennedy" was ranked as more "active" by Independents, slightly more "active" by the Republican men and less "active" by the Republican women.

Further, as "Kennedy" shifted to the "passive" end of the scale in his own party, he approached more nearly the Democratic concept of "The Presidency" on the "active-passive" scale. The Republican women also found "Kennedy" closer to their concept of "The Presidency" after the debate. Republican men were nearly unmoved in their concept of "Kennedy," ranking him slightly more "active."

Issues in the Campaign

Among the issues in the 1960 campaign were "Federal Spending" and "American Prestige." Vice-President Nixon repeated again in the fourth broadcast debate that the Democratic convention platform unrealistically called for more spending of federal money without increasing taxes. Further, the candidate opposed "Federal Spending" for teachers' salaries. Senator Kennedy had, on the other hand, been repeating a charge—which he re-stated in the fourth debate—that "American Prestige" was suffering abroad.

Federal Spending

The study showed a shift to the "bad" side for the concept "Federal Spending" in the minds of both Democrats and Republicans but a shift to the "good" for Independents (Table III). It should also be noted that Democrats generally thought "Federal Spending" was somewhat more "good" in the before test than Republicans.

American Prestige

The concept "American Prestige" showed a trend toward "bad" on the evaluative scale, indicating that Democrats, Republicans and Independents saw it in a more negative light than before the debate.

TABLE 3

THE EVALUATIVE FACTOR: CONCEPTS "FEDERAL SPENDING" AND "AMERICAN PRESTIGE" RATED BY 86 REPUBLICANS, DEMOCRATS AND INDEPENDENTS IN A COLLEGE COMMUNITY BEFORE AND AFTER VIEWING THE "FOURTH DEBATE"

Figures show the mean responses of the three political groups on a seven-point sementic differential scale.

(Good=+3.00; Bad=−3.00)

	"Federal Spending"			"American Prestige"		
	Before	*After*	*Change*	*Before*	*After*	*Change*
DEMOCRATS(27)	+ 0.82	+ 0.71	− .11	+ 0.60	+ 0.34	− .27
REPUBLICANS (41)	+ 0.57	+ 0.30	− .27	+ 1.61	+ 1.35	− .26
INDEPENDENTS (18)	+ 0.34	+ 0.73	+ .39	+ 0.62	+ 0.39	− .23

But Republicans thought that it was much better to begin with than did either the Democrats or Independents.

SUMMARY AND CONCLUSIONS

Early in the campaign Vice-President Nixon said that to win he would need to turn a number of Democratic and Independent voters to his support. The data in this study indicate that he was failing to do this the weekend of the fourth debate. He was able to reinforce viewers on the inadvisability of federal spending.

Kennedy's objectives in the campaign were different from Nixon's. The senator was more concerned with attracting and strengthening support in his own party which heavily out-registered the Republicans throughout the country. He improved the evaluation of himself in his own party for this sample. Further, he was able to dispel opposition charges that he was "immature" and inclined to "shoot from the hip," by convincing viewers he was less "active"— thus moving closer to his party's apparent image of the presidency.

The senator was more successful in changing opinion about American prestige than Vice-President Nixon was in manipulating attitudes toward federal spending.

By the time of the fourth "Great Debate," it was expected that voting intentions might already be set. However, this study indicates that there were changes in their attitudes toward the candidates and two of the issues in the campaign.

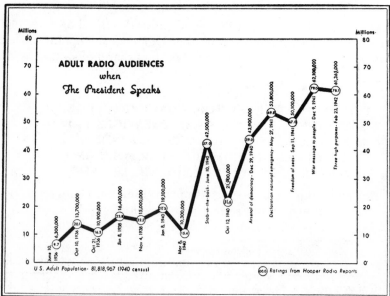

This chart in *Radio Audience Measurement* by Matthew N. Chappell and C. E. Hooper, Stephen Daye, 1944, shows the rising audience for FDR's radio speeches. His war message December 9, 1941, had an audience of 62,100,000.

Table 41.

RADIO SET SALES AND SATURATION

Figures show the number of radio receivers sold, the % manufactured outside the
U.S., the average cost, the % of all U.S. households with radio, and the total
sets available for use.

| | RADIO RECEIVER SET SALES | | | Homes | Auto Radio Set Sales | |
	Number Sold	Percent of Sets With FM / Imported	Average Cost	With Radio	Number	w/FM
1922	100,000		$50	0.2%		
1925	2,000,000		83	10		
1930	3,827,000		78	46	34,000	
1935	6,026,800		55	67	1,190,000	
1940	11,800,000		38	81	2,130,000	
1945	500,000		40	89	--	
1950	9,218,000	.02%	26	95	4,740,000	
1955	7,327,000	4% / 2	20	96	6,864,000	
1960	18,031,000	11 / 42	20	96	6,432,000	
1965	31,689,000	23 / 56	10	97	10,037,000	6%
1970	34,048,000	59 / 77[a]	11	99	8,145,000	14
1972	42,149,000	57		99	10,042,000	24

Source: Broadcasting Yearbook, Television Factbook, and National Association of Broadcasters.
[a]Imported does not include sets with a "domestic label" (U.S. name) but manufactured outside
the U.S.--total imports were actually 91% of the market in 1970.

John F. Kennedy held the first live TV Presidential press conference. The photo
above was one for August 29, 1963. Richard Nixon's 35th press conference October 26,
1973, was viewed by 63,900,000.

Table 42.

TV SET SALES AND SATURATION

Figures show the number of monochrome and color sets manufactured, the % manufactured outside the U.S. and the % with UHF, the average cost (manufacturer's value) of monochrome and color sets, and the % of U.S. homes with television, color, two or more sets and UHF.

	NUMBER OF SETS SOLD		PERCENT		AVERAGE COST		HOMES WITH			
	Monochrome	Color	Imported	UHF	Mono	Color	TV	Color	Multi	UHF
1946	6,000	--	--	--	$279b	--	.02%	--	--	NA
1950	7,355,000	--	--	--	190	--	9	--	1%	NA
1955	7,738,000	20,000	--	15%	138	--	65	.2%	3	11%
1960	5,709,000	120,000	--	8	137	$392	87	.7	13	8
1965	8,753,000	2,694,000	3%	100	104	356	93	5	22	16
1970	7,647,000	7,274,000	25[a]	100	81	324	95	39	33	63
1972	5,599,646	7,907,615	21	100	79	319	97	64c	44c	86c

Source: Broadcasting Yearbook, Television Factbook.

[a] Imported does not include sets with a "domestic label" (U.S. name) but manufactured outside the U.S.--total imports were actually about 35% of the market in 1970. b1947. c1974 ARB.

Table 43.

TELEVISION SATURATION

Figures show the % of U.S. households with television sets by region and by county size.

	1950	1955	1960	1965	1970
TV SATURATION BY REGION OF THE U.S.					
Northeast	24%	80%	92%	96%	96%
East Central	8	72	90	96	97
West Central	7	60	87	95	96
South	2	46	79	90	94
Pacific	9	64	88	93	95
TV SATURATION BY COUNTY SIZE					
A	21%	82%	93%	96%	97%
B	6	72	90	95	97
C & D	2	44	78	91	93

Source: A. C. Nielsen. A=all counties belonging to 26 largest metropolitan areas. B=counties over 120,000 not in A plus counties that are part of the metropolitan area of cities in B. C and D=all other counties.

Table 44.

AVERAGE RADIO AND TV USE PER HOUSEHOLD

Figures show the average amount of time radio and television are on in U.S. homes each day. Estimates put the out-of-home radio audience at 30 to 50% of in-home--the out-of-home audience is not included in the figures below. In the early 1970s about one-fifth of the population spent more than seven hours a day with TV, the other fifth watched less than a half hour.

	RADIO	TV
	Hours: Minutes	Hours: Minutes
1946	4:13	NA
1950	4:10	4:35 (1:12)[a]
1955	2:27	4:51
1960	1:40	5:03
1965	2:27	5:30
1970	NA	5:54
1972	3:24[b]	6:12

Source: A. C. Nielsen. Radio data was for various months, usually the spring. Average time listening to the radio 1965 is from a survey by R. H. Bruskin Assoc. by all persons 18 or older. TV data is the average for the year. [a]The average for TV viewing in radio homes (many of which did not have TV) was 1:12; the average for TV homes in 1950 was 4:35. [b]RADAR adults 18+ (not homes).

Table 45.

TOP RATED RADIO PROGRAMS--1930-1939

Figures show the ratings for sponsored radio programs in the Cooperative Analysis of Broadcastings top 10 for at least four seasons from 1930-1931 to 1938-1939 and the top five for at least three seasons during the daytime. Rating is generally for the season September to March.

Number of Seasons on the air		31	32	33	34	35	36	37	38	39
	EVENING									
27	Amos 'n' Andy	37	33	20	18	15				
16	Eddie Cantor		18	22	25	18	15	25	25	
10	Rudy Vallee	26	16	16	22	21	22	19	23	20
7	Maxwell House Showboat		19	24	24	20				
18	Burns and Allen				18	19		22	23	21
23	Jack Benny					17	26	33	36	36
16	Fred Allen					15	19	22	23	21
13	Bowes Amateur Hour						37	23	23	21
23	Bing Crosby						18	19	28	26
	DAYTIME									
9	Little Orphan Annie		6	6	6					
NA	Crummit and Sanderson		4	3			7			
18	Metropolitan Opera				13	13		11		
4	Today's Children						7	9	8	
NA	Magic Key of RCA						6	7		8

Source: Variety Radio Directory 1939-40. Summers, Radio Programs Carried on National Networks, 1958.

Table 46.

LARGEST TELEVISION AUDIENCES

Year	Special Event	% Homes Reached	Average Hours Viewed
1960	Election Returns	91.8%	4:30
1961	Kennedy Inaugural	59.5	
1962	Glenn Space Flight	81.4	5:15
1963	Death of President Kennedy	96.1	31.38
1964	Election Returns	90.6	2:51
1965	Gemini IV Space Walk	92.1	4:47
1966	Election Returns	84.4	6:10
1967	Johnson State of Union	59.6	
1968	Democratic Convention	90.1	9:28
1969	Apollo 11 on Moon	93.9	15:35
1969	Nixon Vietnam Address	61.6	
1973	Nixon Vietnam Truce Address	62.9	
1974	Nixon Resignation Address	60.3	

Date	Entertainment Program	Rating
Jan. 15, 1970	Bob Hope Christmas Show	46.6
Aug. 29, 1967	The Fugitive (last episode)	45.9
Jan. 14, 1971	Bob Hope	45.0
Feb. 9, 1964	Ed Sullivan (Beatles)	44.6
Jan. 16, 1972	Super Bowl VI	44.2
Jan. 8, 1964	Beverly Hillbillies	44.0
Apr. 4, 1970	Academy Awards	43.4
Feb. 16, 1964	Ed Sullivan (Beatles)	43.2
Jan. 15, 1964	Beverly Hillbillies	42.8
Jan. 14, 1973	Super Bowl VII	42.7

Source: A.C. Nielsen. For entertainment programs this list is only for sponsored programs July 1960 to November 1973 on individual networks.

Table 47.

TOP RATED TV PROGRAMS--1951-1970

The figures show 37 regularly scheduled sponsored network television programs that were in the A. C. Nielsen "Top 20" for four or more years based on average household audience in the second report for each January. List of programs from Nielsen; ratings added by LWL/MCT.

NUMBER OF SEASONS On Air[1]	In Top 15		51	52	53	54	55	56	57	58	59	60	61	62	63	64	65	66	67	68	69	70
15	5	Walt Disney													24	23		20	20	23		
10	6	Talent Scouts	42	54	58	44	33		30													
6	5	Colgate Comedy Hr.	44	44	53	39	24															
6	5	Milton Berle	63	51	55	40	34															
9	4	Godfrey and Friends	36	44	55	38																
22	14	Ed Sullivan	37			29	39	39							25	27	27	25	23	21		
19	16	Red Skelton		47	36			32	32		28	31	24	27	31	25	26	27	28	24	24	24
11	9	Jackie Gleason/H-moon				37	40	31							24	23	24	23	24	24		
13	6	Jack Benny					36	36	32					27		25	25					
5	4	Ernie Ford Show							31	30	27	27										
9	4	Your Hit Parade		29	36		32	28														
7	5	Fireside Theater	54	42	43	36		29														
7	4	Philco Playhouse	46	40	45	30																
8	6	I Love Lucy			51	69	58	49	44	45												
5	4	December Bride					34	36	36	30												
11	7	Danny Thomas							34	34	31	25	26	29	26							
6	4	Real McCoys								30	29	28	26									
9	10	Griffith/Mayberry											28	27	30	29	29	28	29	28	26	23
12	6	My Three Sons											27	24			24	25			22	21
8	8	Lucy Show/Here's													30	26	26	29	26	28	24	24
9	7	Beverly Hillbillies													38	40	27	28	24	23	21	
5	4	Dick Van Dyke													28	34	28	22				
6	4	Gomer Pyle														30	29		26	26		
12	6	Dragnet			50	54	42	35	31									22				
9	4	Perry Mason									27	28	24	27								
15	10	Gunsmoke							34	43	39	39	38	29	27					26	24	25
6	4	Wyatt Earp							30	32	30	25										
6	4	Have Gun, Will Travel								33	34	34	31									
8	4	Wagon Train									36	38	35	31								
7	4	Rawhide										25	27	24	22							
11	9	Bonanza											26	30	30	36	34	33	29		28	24
11	8	You Bet Your Life	36	32	45	44	41	31	31	30												
15	7	I've Got a Secret						33	34	33	34	39			25	25						
9	4	This Is Your Life					36	32	29		29											
8	4	Candid Camera											29	25	31	27						
16	4	Gillette Fights	41	39	41	29																
9	4	Pabst Bouts	35		41	32	34															

Source: <u>Nielsen Newscast</u> 19:1 (Spring 1970). The rating given is the Nielsen average audience rating for the 2nd reports for the months of October, January and April for each season averaged.
[1]Number of seasons on the air 1948-1949 to 1969-1970--total 22--compiled by Lichty; the Nielsen listing is only for 1950-1951 to 1969-1970. Only <u>Disney</u>, <u>Lucy</u> and <u>Gunsmoke</u> were still on in 1974.

Table 48.

CABLE TV SYSTEMS AND SUBSCRIBERS

Figures show the number of cable television (community antenna television) systems, the number of subscribers, average subscribers per system and the % of all U.S. homes that receive TV via cable.

	Systems	Homes	Average Subscribers/System	Percent U.S. Homes
1952	70	14,000	200	--
1955	400	150,000	375	.5%
1960	640	650,000	1,016	1
1965	1,325	1,275,000	962	2
1970	2,490	4,500,000	1,915	8
1974[a]	2,996	7,027,146	2,240	12[b]

Source: A. C. Nielsen in TV Factbook.   [a]Cable Sourcebook, 1974.   [b]ARB.

Table 49.

RADIO AND TELEVISION CREDIBILITY

"If you heard conflicting versions of the same story from these sources, which would you be most likely to believe?" (1939) "If you got conflicting or different reports of the same news story....which of the four versions would you be most inclined to believe...?"(1959, 1964, 1972)

Most Believable	1939	1959	1964	1968	1972
Radio	40%	12%	8%	8%	8%
Television		21	41	44	48
Newspapers	27	32	23	21	21
Authority you heard speak	13				
Magazines		10	10	11	10
DK, NA, "Depends"	20	17	18	16	13

Sources: 1939: Elmo Roper for Fortune reported in Peter, "The American Listener in 1940," Annals, January 1941; Elmo Roper and Burns Roper, "What people think of television and other mass media 1959-1972," New York: Television Information Office, May 1973. Other studies have shown somewhat different preferences depending on how the questions were asked, for a discussion see V. Stone, Journal of Broadcasting, XIV:1, p. 1.

Market quotations, produce and livestock reports, weather reports and other bits of information are sent out daily from WLW which is doing its part to mold the already rather homogeneous population of Cincinnati even closer--into a community that has community spirit and municipal pride developed to a high degree.   --Wireless Age, January 1923.

PART EIGHT

REGULATION

The law's the law, and that's that.

—Matthew Dillon

It could be no secret that the manager of a major New York TV station was speaking for a good part of the industry when he told an applicant for the post of program director: Your job here will be to protect this station's license. You'll have to take care of all that public affairs . . . (four letter word omitted).

—*Variety*, 1972

T HE UNITED STATES NAVY DEPARTMENT urged legislation for radio regulation as early as 1905 but it was not until the passage of the Wireless Ship Act of 1910 that radio telegraphy was legally acknowledged by the government. This law required "apparatus and operators for radio communications on certain ocean steamers" and "required wireless equipment on every passenger vessel carrying 50 or more persons . . . capable of transmitting or receiving a message over a distance of at least 50 miles." Power to make regulations for the execution of the act was given to the secretary of commerce and labor, who assigned the duties to the Bureau of Navigation.

This was replaced by the Radio Act of 1912 which contained additional provisions governing radio on merchant ships. It required two radio operators for each vessel navigating the oceans or the Great Lakes; and required that they stand watch. The Act of 1912 required stations and operators to be licensed but gave no power to make additional regulations to the secretary. This law was to remain the basis for the regulation of broadcasting until the passage of the Radio Act of 1927.

Without any real power to regulate, the staff of the Bureau of Navigation frequently tried to negotiate settlements among the operators of broadcast stations.

One agreement reached in Cincinnati provided that two stations would broadcast from 8:00 P.M. to 10:00 P.M. on different wave lengths for three consecutive months on Monday nights. Every fourth month on Mondays the stations would broadcast from 10:00 P.M. to midnight and other stations would be allowed to broadcast in the earlier time period. It was also arranged that one of the stations would share time with two other stations on alternate months for its broadcasts on Wednesdays—thus, station WMH would be on a different frequency on Wednesdays every other month.[1]

> Recently, a controversy over division of broadcasting time in Cincinnati was not promptly settled by the local Class B stations, two of which for several nights broadcast simultaneously on the same wavelength. The Department officials were asked in this and in one other similar case, "What are you going to do about it?" The answer was very simple, "Nothing".
>
> If two stations insist on killing themselves and each other, the Department is perfectly willing that they should do so but it will not allow this situation to interfere with public service. Two such disorderly patrons of the radio hotel will be permitted to settle their controversy outside. The wavelength which they should have agreed to share peaceably will very promptly be given to someone else who will use it in the public interest.
>
> Only one or two such examples will be ample to demonstrate to broadcasters that the public interest must be served. On no other basis can the radio broadcaster exist. On no other basis will he be permitted to retain his Class B license.
>
> The Department properly is insisting that each station maintain a certain technical standard of service and that it stay properly on its own wavelength. But the Department is equally emphatic that this is policing, not censorship.
>
> Judge Davis explains that neither he nor any one else in the Department is willing to assume that they know enough to determine on behalf of the public what may and what may not be broadcast. Whether such a station provides jazz or education, whether it runs from six o'clock to midnight, or from midnight to noon, is not defined or regulated in any way. The public is the judge, and the public makes its wishes known in no uncertain manner to the broadcast station which does or does not serve its needs or whims.[2]

The four national radio conferences held in 1922, 1923, 1924, and 1925 were largely responsible for the various radio control bills introduced into congress during the period—1921 to 1927. Many of the recommendations from the conferences made their way into the bill which finally became the Radio Act. The proposals for regulation came from a number of sources. Economist Hiram Jome, in proposing adoption of the British system, indicated that there should be regulation of point-to-point communication in addition to communication on wire and radio waves, anticipating the problems that were to come in wired television.[3] The spokesman for regulation to separate the government and the stations was Herbert Hoover, secretary of commerce. He made numerous attempts to get bills through Congress and probably was the architect of the American system of broadcasting.[4] In 1926 he was stripped of any authority he had been able to assume in broadcasting as secretary of commerce, by the Zenith decision.

> Alarmists predict chaotic days for radio. In Chicago courts, a decision has been rendered, confirming the obvious fact that there is no authority vested in the Department of Commerce or any other branch of the Government to prescribe a particular wavelength in the broadcasting channel to each station. Another decision, in the District of Columbia, makes it compulsory upon the Department of Commerce to issue broadcasting licenses to all who apply. An unconfirmed report from Chicago states that, acting in accord with these decisions, the Chicago Federation of Labor plans to appropriate WEAF's wavelength with a high power transmitter in that city. With radio neglected by Congress and the Department of Commerce defeated in the courts, Secretary Hoover would be justified in surrendering the control of radio to the tender mercies of anarchy.
>
> While it is possible that some of the 650 applicants for broadcast station licenses, emboldened by these courts decisions, may begin operating on wavelenths already in use, we feel certain that common sense will rule the situation. Even without legal control, the present set-up of wavelength allocation and regulation is sufficiently sound to survive a short period of self-government.
>
> But the failure of the legislative branch of our government to pass radio legislation, however imperfect, is not to be condoned. If a period of confusion arises, it will rightly be laid at the doors of our legislators who willfully mingled this non-partisan problem with political wrangles.[5]

The Radio Act was a compromise of a number of proposals. Many broadcasters were unable or unwilling to abide by the new FRC regulations. As problems in interference were cleared up the broadcasting regulators began to look at programming.

Radio Broadcast editorialized in July 1927 favoring program balance on stations saying that "There is no excuse for the existence of a station which serves only a special and limited interest—to the exclusion of general educational and entertainment services." [6] Two years later the Federal Radio Commission in the Great Lakes case would use similar language.

> Broadcasting stations are licensed to serve the public and not for the purpose of furthering the private or selfish interests of individuals or groups of individuals. . . .
>
> The entire listening public within the service area of a station, or of a group of stations in one community, is entitled to service

from that station or stations. If, therefore, all the programs transmitted are intended for, and interesting or valuable to, only a small portion of that public, the rest of the listeners are being discriminated against.[7]

The FRC also said it was up to program directors to "select entertainment and educational features according to the needs and desires of their invisible audiences" for "the sake of the popularity and standing of their stations."

The Radio Commission applied itself to a number of program problems including attacks on individuals, profanity, questionable medical advertising and the prescribing of medicine over the air.

The original legislation created only a temporary Radio Commission which was to clean up all the problems and then allow the commerce commission to administer radio. But it soon became obvious that the commission's work would never end. The FRC became a permanent body December 18, 1929.

The Communications Act of 1934 created the Federal Communications Commission (FCC) to replace the FRC. The new agency was also empowered to regulate point-to-point communications. The change was also desired by President Roosevelt to get a Democratic majority on the commission which he did by increasing the number of commissioners from five to seven and reappointing only two FRC commissioners.

Regulation of broadcasting seemed smooth in the 1930s. There still was an avoidance of censorship. The Federal Trade Commission, reviewed a total of more than 183,000 separate radio ads in 1934, seeking false and misleading commercial messages, but the results were not threatening to a free and uninhibited broadcasting climate.[8] There were ripples of protest. NBC got a "stiff scolding" from the chairman of the FCC in 1937 for a "serious offense against the proprieties" in a sketch featuring Charlie McCarthy, a dummy, as Adam and Mae West as Eve:

> WEST: "That's all right. I like a man that takes his time. Why don't you come home with me? I'll let you play in my woodpile . . . you're all wood and a yard long . . .
> CHARLIE: Oh, Mae, don't don't . . . don't be so rough. To me, love is peace and quiet.
> WEST: That ain't love—that's sleep.[9]

Miss West was not heard again on radio for years, whereas there was nothing done about Edgar Bergen without whom, as the dummy said in the skit, Charlie would be "speechless."

The surface of the broadcasting industry was placid but undercurrents of trouble were boiling—the new Federal Communications Commission talked tougher and there were "informal discussions" with stations. The regulation of stations was intensified as was a far-reaching probe of network practices which started in 1938 and ended in the sale of NBC-Blue which became the American Broadcasting Company. The Supreme Court upheld the commission's right to regulate network practices in 1943.

In 1946 the FCC issued its memorandum entitled *Public Service Responsibilities of Broadcast Licensees*–generally called the Blue Book—which "contended that too many stations had broken promises that accompanied their applications for a license regarding the program services they proposed." [10] Citing the legal precedents for regulation of programming, the memorandum gave some recommendations for good program service:

> Section Three of the *Public Service Responsibility of Broadcast Licensees* discussed the following aspects of public interest in program service: The Carrying of Sustaining Programs; The Carrying of Local Live Programs; Discussion of Public Issues; and, Advertising Excesses. The FCC listed the five distinctive and outstanding functions of the sustaining program:
>
> 1. To secure for the station or network a means by which in the over-all structure of its program service, it can achieve a *balanced* interpretation of public needs.
>
> 2. To provide programs which by their very nature may not be sponsored with propriety.
>
> 3. To provide programs for significant minority tastes and interests.
>
> 4. To provide programs devoted to the needs and purposes of non-profit organizations.
>
> 5. To provide a field for experiment in new types of programs, secure from the restrictions that obtain with reference to programs in which the advertiser's interest in selling goods predominates. [11]

The reaction to the Blue Book still can be heard in the corridors at state broadcaster association meetings.

Stations had been told not to editorialize in 1941. In 1949 the commission reversed this decision urging stations to become actively involved in issues. As more and more stations began to editorialize, the commission found it necessary to set out guidelines concerning fair play on controversial issues. This "Fairness Doctrine" was interpreted to require anti-smoking messages to match cigarette advertising which finally went off the air January 1, 1971. The doctrine, although it was not considered by the commission as a new concept, was viewed with trepidation by broadcasters. [12]

In 1958 FCC Commissioner Richard Mack resigned charged with wrong doing and two years later Chairman John Doerfer resigned, accused of accepting special favors from a broadcaster. It was a time of disclosure. In 1958 quiz programs on television were found to be rigged with many of the contestants, including Charles Van Doren, receiving help on questions. Meanwhile it was disclosed that many leading radio disc jockeys and some television performers were involved in "payola"—playing certain tunes for pay from record pluggers. It was an unpleasant period for broadcasting.

Broadcasters were not reassured in 1961 when the new chairman of the FCC told them that much of television programming was a "vast wasteland." [13] Chairman Newton Minow was heralding the start of a new era in broadcasting regulation—involvement in programming.

Broadcasters have had varying success with self-regulation. The National Association of Broadcasters began as a loose-knit organization of radio managers in 1923 and in 1929 adopted a simple code of ethics. In 1935 the association adopted new provisions, particularly in regards to advertising. In 1937 the NAB was reorganized as a stronger representative of broadcasting in order to deal with various business-wide problems such as unions and music licensing. In 1939 the code was revised again limiting advertising per hour. In addition the association urged broadcasters to ban sale of time for presentation of controversial issues. A ruling in 1945 by the FCC caused this ban to be lifted. The association adopted a seal which the broadcaster displayed if he followed the code. A code board passed on materials and monitored stations to be sure that the code was maintained.

As broadcasting began its sixth decade, its regulation was often as chaotic as during its first. The FCC had revoked the license of only 34 stations to 1960 but in the next decade would terminate 44 more. At the end of 1972 more than 140 petitions to deny licenses were on file with the FCC many from citizen groups—often minorities—with demands for fairer treatment, programming and employment.

Problems of the fairness doctrine and equal time for political candidates plagued broadcasters. Broadcasters expected better treatment under a Nixon commission, and often got it, but that same administration often attacked the networks for "bias" in news coverage. In 1969 the Nixon administration suggested a new Office of Telecommunication Policy within the White House; it was established in 1970. In 1972 the FCC—in a compromise struck with pressure from the OTP—assumed even more regulatory power over cable television primarily to protect the broadcasting industry.

Broadcasting had changed since 1922 when the commerce department announced two wave lengths for broadcasting; one for "government reports, such as crop and market estimates and weather forecasts" and another for "important news items, entertainment, lectures, sermons, and similar matter."

American society also had changed. In 1920 farm families represented 30% of the population; in 1970, five %. Throughout the 1920s radio had grown more "commercial" as audiences tuned in more expensive, entertainment programming. The ownership of stations changed, especially after the depression, with operators seeing their primary responsibility to their stockholders. But some critics, like controversial FCC commissioner Nicholas Johnson asked that our priorities be adjudged anew. Johnson argued that:

> The theory of the Communications Act was that the inherently oligopolistic structure of radio use necessitated a system of license for a limited term with no property rights accruing to the licensee. The radio spectrum was meant to be a resource owned and retained by the people. . . . Private interests could use the spectrum as proxies for the public, but in return for the right to sue for private gain they were to "pay" by performance in the "public interest." Congress clearly saw that the use of the spectrum without monetary payment might produce large returns for the private users. But Congress contemplated that the spectrum users, in exchange for the spectrum, would not simply profit-maximize as do other businesses. The concept was that operation in the public interest would preclude profit maximization by the spectrum used, and that the difference between a public-service operating level of profits and a theoretical level of maximum profits would be the price exacted for the use of the spectrum. It was thought that this system would produce benefits to the public in excess of the money that the public could have received from a sale of spectrum to a user with no public obligation.[14]

Throughout the history of the regulation of broadcasting it is difficult to quarrel with the theory or intent of most regulation. Clearly, the "public interest" has often been put first and espoused vigorously. But often the commission was less than aggressive in enforcing its own rules.

The words "public interest," "public convenience" and "public necessity" have appeared in various combinations in a rather wide variety of legislation and judical decisions. The first statute of this nature was enacted in New York in 1892 for railroads. In the Transportation Act of 1920, amending the Interstate Commerce Act, the device of a certificate of convenience and necessity was first applied to the requlation of interstate commerce.

--Louis G. Caldwell, *Air Law Review*, 1930.

80

Edward F. Sarno Jr.

THE NATIONAL RADIO CONFERENCES

THE GROWING interference of radio signals together with the inadequacy of existing legislation forced the government to take action to alleviate conditions. On February 8, 1922, President Harding at a Cabinet meeting instructed Secretary Hoover to call a meeting of both government and civilian experts in order to discuss the problems of radio and arrive at some recommendations for Congress to consider as possible new radio legislation. The government, at this time, was interested in preserving use of the ether both for national defense and for private commercial business.

Responsibility for the evergrowing interference of radio signals was laid at two distinct doors: amateur radio operators and broadcasters. Preconference plans proposed the restriction of amateur service in order to free more of the available channels for commercial purposes. When the First Radio Conference was called for February 27, 1922, the amateur organizations in the country raised storms of protest against possible government curtailment of their services. For example, one of the largest groups, the Hudson Radio Club of New York City, forwarded written protests to both President Harding and Secretary Hoover registering formal opposition to any plan to regulate amateur operations. They claimed that the increase of interference was not due to amateur involvement but rather to the poor quality of broadcast receivers used by the public. The amateurs asked that the government prove their guilt in the matter before enacting legislation. One of the loudest voices in support of the amateur position, Hiram Percy Maxim, president of the American Radio Relay League, blamed the proposed regulation upon pressure brought to bear upon the government "by big concerns which manufacture and sell wireless apparatus to 'broadcast listeners.' " [5]

The First National Conference was scheduled to follow a convention of the Third and Fourth Districts of the American Radio Relay League in Washington. As a result, about 1,000 amateurs were expected to remain in the Capital to witness the Conference. To promote cooperation of the amateurs in the problems of the Conference, a preliminary meeting was arranged between directors of the League and government officials in an attempt to devise some tentative plans acceptable to both sides. In addition, W. D. Terrell, Chief

Journal of Broadcasting, Vol. XIII, No. 2 (Spring 1969), pp. 189–202.

Radio Inspector of the Department of Commerce, spoke at the amateurs' convention and outlined to them a suggested grading system of amateurs with corresponding privileges. The chief result of the convention was a vote to recommend to the Department of Commerce that commercial broadcasters be assigned the 1000 to 1500 meter band of the spectrum (200 to 300 kc) and that amateur operators be assigned the 200 to 300 meter band (1000 to 1500 kc). This proposal was not accepted.

Conditions at the opening of the First Radio Conference were anything but cordial. About the only thing everyone agreed upon was the need to reduce the radio interference. Besides the amateurs' suspicion that their rights were about to be infringed upon, other factions disagreed upon specifically who should control radio. Fifteen official delegates attended the Conference; 10 representing governmental interests and five non-governmental interests, particularly in the fields of science and engineering. Conflict was evident between private and government interests. Large commercial concerns such at A T & T, General Electric, Westinghouse and RCA wanted the Commerce Department to control broadcasting and were decidedly against control by either the Navy or the Army. Navy representatives still claimed a vested interest in radio, due to their control of the medium during World War I, and the War and Agriculture departments also were anxious to expand their operations. Besides this, the Post Office department felt that since radio was a form of communication, it fell within its area of control much as did the mails, although Congress had rejected this contention a few years earlier. In short, attitudes of those attending the Conference were anything but conducive to reaching solutions to the problems which existed.

At the opening session, Hoover equated the necessity of reducing the existing radio interference with that of protecting the country's natural resources and praised the delegates for realizing that increased regulation was needed. He stressed that limited governmental control had become a "necessity to so establish public right over the ether roads that there may be no national regret that we have parted with a great national asset into uncontrolled hands." [6] Referring to amateur interests as "the small American boy with his wireless outfit," Hoover promised to protect such interests when legislation was drawn and pointed out to the delegates the important contributions amateur radio operators had made to the development of the radio art. Hoover felt much of the existing chaos in the airways could be eliminated by reducing the amount of advertising "chatter" and by discouraging the use of radio for other commercial purposes which could be as easily accomplished by other means of communication such as the telegraph or telephone. He emphasized the need for immediate legislation by pointing out that in less than one year the number of radio receivers had jumped from an estimated 50,000 to 600,000 sets.

In order to accomplish its objectives, the Conference was divided into three committees to sift the available information in hopes of arriving at some workable recommendations. These three groups, amateur, technical, and legislative, met after the opening sessions of the Conference had ended and submitted lengthy and detailed reports. The most important recommendations for broadcasting were reached by the Conference's Technical Committee. On March 10, 1922, they filed their results with Secretary Hoover. Although most of the major recommendations of the First National Radio Conference dealt with purely technical matters, it must be remembered that the basic problem of radio at that time was interference of signals and therefore there was a need for technical guidelines to correct the situation. The recommendations of the technical committee were used as the basis of a proposed bill introduced into the House of Representatives by the Honorable Wallace White of Maine early in 1923.[7] This bill subsequently was debated and passed in the House and was then referred to the Senate Committee on Interstate Commerce where it died.

Two factors made it clear in 1923 that a Second National Radio Conference should be called. The first reason was that the First Conference's proposed legislation had failed to pass Congress, while the second reason was that the chaotic conditions in the ether had grown to such immense proportions that something immediate "had to be done." On March 6, 1923, therefore, Secretary Hoover called for the Second Conference to begin on March 20th. The purpose of this Conference, with some 20 delegates, was to decide what temporary measures were needed to reduce radio interference before Congress got around to passing new legislation.

The number of broadcast stations in the United States had grown from 60 at the time of the First Conference to 581 by March, 1923, while radio receivers had increased from an estimated 600,000 to somewhere between 1½ million to 2½ million sets during the same period. Broadcasting used only two wave lengths at that time, 360 and 400 meters (833 kc and 750 kc). One of the primary considerations of the Second Conference, therefore, was to investigate means by which the allocations of channels to broadcasting might be increased. Strongest support was shown to the proposal that the government turn over part of their wave bands for public broadcasting. It was emphasized that unless more wavelengths were made available the larger stations could not continue programming as they did, because of the constant interference from the small stations.

While the First Radio Conference had been primarily concerned with technical standards to alleviate the interference problem, the Second Conference investigated other areas of concern to the broadcaster. Chief among these was the copyright problem. This issue was to become a major stumbling-block for succeeding Conferences and finally remained the only issue for which no recommendations could be agreed upon. The problem was introduced at the Second Conference by J. C. Rosenthal, general manager of the American Society of Composers, Authors, and Publishers. Speaking to the delegates, Rosenthal warned that unless broadcasters paid royalties to the owners of music copyrights, they would be prosecuted as being in violation of the Federal copyright statute. He stated that broadcasting had seriously damaged the sale of sheet music and recordings while radio had benefited from the use of copyrighted materials. Commenting on the point that broadcasters had hurt the value of record sales, George L. Israel, of a large Pittsburgh department store which advertised on radio, pointed out that record sales actually had increased by one-third in the country over the preceeding year. Undaunted, Rosenthal stated that about 50% of the broadcasters had begun negotiations with his group concerning the use of copyrighted materials and that evidence was being gathered on about 350 other broadcasters who either should pay or discontinue using the copyrighted materials. He added that the expected revenue to copyright owners represented by his group from broadcast royalties was $400,000 per year.

The Second Conference arrived at three conclusions concerning the 1923 broadcasting situation. First, it emphasized the need for discretion in granting licenses due to the limited number of channels available for broadcasting. Second, it recognized the uneconomic and tentative financial basis of the industry and suggested that a further increase of broadcast stations would only further worsen financial conditions. Third, the delegates urged that those persons in the different sections of the United States who had an interest in the medium meet with those individuals seeking to operate broadcast stations with the goal "that broadcasting conducted in each neighborhood by such a local association will receive public support and be handled in an economic and permanent fashion." [8] A fourth recommendation concerned the reclassification of broadcast facilities into three general classes. Explicit in the entire allocation plan was the belief that existing stations not be required to leave their currently designated wave lengths (unless they wished to do so) with the hope that eventually "stations can be gradually brought into accord without hardships." A fifth recommendation dealt with the assignment of short wave frequencies to help to relieve amateur congestion and interference. A sixth recommendation called for the equitable distribution of broadcast frequencies to the various areas of the country. Specifically, the plan suggested 50 territorial wave lengths approximately 10 kc. apart. The wave lengths of selected communities within each of five national zones were to be separated by approximately 50 kc. Seventh, the delegates to the Second Radio Conference defined the reading of letters or telegrams over the air as not to be point-to-point communication so long as the content of such was general in nature and the writer was not addressed in person. Eight, broadcast stations should be required to install equipment which would reduce interference. Specifically, the use of spark transmitting apparatus was to be discouraged. Ninth, it was suggested that amateur organizations should determine the time requirements of religious services and make arrangements with local broadcast stations for the transmission of these services.

As a result of the recommendations of the Second National Radio Conference, Representative White introduced a radio control bill, H.R. 7357, into the House in February, 1924.[9] This bill never was actually debated in Congress; it was almost immediately referred to the House's Committee on the Merchant Marine and Fisheries together with a recently passed Senate bill.[10] Both were never reported out of committee and consequently no legislation was enacted.

In the summer of 1923, the United States Court of Appeals for the District of Columbia ruled in the *Hoover v. Intercity Radio* case that the Secretary of Commerce could do little to regulate radio besides assign wavelengths. The court held that Hoover must issue licenses for wireless stations and determined that the Secretary of Commerce's function was purely ministerial and that he had no regulatory prerogatives.[11] This decision, and the failure of new legislation, made the calling of a Third Radio Conference inevitable.

At the opening evening's session of the Third National Radio Conference on October 6, 1924, Secretary Hoover stated its purpose as "to enable listeners, broadcasters, manufacturers, marine, and other services to agree among themselves as to the manner in which radio traffic rules may be determined." [12] Since the Second Conference, network broadcasting had made important advances. The AT&T network had just begun at the time of the Second Conference but during the following 18 months had proven itself as a possible means for a national system of broadcasting. Therefore, one of the major issues before the delegates to the Third Radio Conference concerned investigating the various available methods of station interconnection, chief among them being short wave relaying as developed by Westinghouse and the wired system employed by AT&T. In his opening remarks to the approximately 90 delegates, Hoover reaffirmed his philosophy that American broadcasting must be kept largely free from government control. He felt that this could best be accomplished by broadcasters themselves voluntarily setting up rules of operation with the single goal of public service. Hoover stressed the importance of broadcasting at the local level but also mentioned the necessity of bringing to the listeners "a hundred and one matters of national interest." This, he stated, only could be accomplished realistically through an organized national system of station interconnection. To this end, he recommended the formation of a mutual association of broadcasters, similar to existing press associations, to furnish programs of national interest and arrange for the transmission and distribution of programs among member stations.

Most of the first two days' proceedings at the Third Conference were spent in discussing a startling announcement made by David Sarnoff then Vice President and General Manager of RCA. On October 7, Sarnoff told the delegates that RCA planned to build a super-power broadcast station near New York City. He said that although the purpose of this particular station was to be entirely experimental, RCA was so confident of its ultimate success that it eventually planned to build a series of such stations in order to provide national coverage. Beyond this stage, there was also the possibility of international communication utilizing the super-power concept. After listening to Sarnoff's proposal, the delegates registered almost unanimous opposition. To many, RCA's plans sounded like an attempt to establish a monopoly of American broadcasting. Most vocal among the opponents was C. E. Erbstein, the owner of a small radio station in Elgin, Illinois. Erbstein argued that super-power stations would force smaller stations to increase their wattage not to better serve the public but because of forced competition caused by the power increase. Sarnoff answered that RCA's plan was to encourage rather than discourage local broadcasting. Super-power stations would not interfere with the effectiveness of local stations much as "national highways never obliterated the need for local roads." [13] Walter Strong, representing American newspaper publishers, suggested that the decision on whether or not to support super-power be delayed since there was no actual proof that better utilization of the power of present stations would not reach the distances proposed for super-power. Since the question of super-power could not be decided immediately, Hoover appointed one of the seven committees of the Third Conference to consider the problem.

Discussion of both wired interconnection and super-power had led to much concern on the part of the delegates about the danger of monopoly in American broadcasting. President Coolidge, speaking at the Conference on October 8, said that one of the benefits of increased governmental regulation was that it would permit the Department of Commerce to better insure against the danger of a few organizations gaining the control of the airwaves. Coolidge thought that the government should not operate its own stations in competition with private broadcasters, but rather act as the central authority in behalf of the public. In answer to a deluge of telegrams received in opposition to a broadcast monopoly, Secretary Hoover added that no present monopoly existed and with several alternative methods of interconnection available, no monopoly would be allowed in the future.

The Third Radio Conference completed its work on October 10, and submitted its list of recommendations to Secretary Hoover. Of those applicable to broadcasting, the following are most pertinent. First, members of the Conference were strongly opposed to monopolistic practices in the radio industry and stressed that the government should do everything in its power to prevent any such condition. Second, although the power of the Department of Commerce to regulate broadcasting should be extended, this control should be limited to technical areas and not extended to broadcast programs. In other words, the delegates were opposed to any form of government censorship. Third, the Conference recommended that national broadcasting through wired interconnection of stations be encouraged and developed. Fourth, experimentation in super-power be allowed under strict government surveillance. It was suggested that no final recommendation concerning super-power be made until these tests be completed. Fifth, the Conference recommended that the power of existing stations be increased, especially in areas where more power would enable rural listeners to receive the same information available to inhabitants of larger cities. Sixth, to prevent interference, the then-present broadcast band should be extended from 200 to 545 meters (550 to 1500 kc) and through a revision of the zoning system, the number of channels available for broadcasting should be increased by 30, thus bringing the total number of broadcast channels to 100. Seventh, it was suggested that the system of classifying and labeling stations be changed. One interesting note concerning the Third Conference was that while the first two Conferences had led to proposed legislation, no Congressional bill was drawn up on the basis of the findings of the Third Conference. This resulted from a letter written by Hoover to Representative White on December 4, 1924. In it, Hoover asked White not to introduce any control bill into Congress until some of the problems discussed at the Third Conference could be corrected. Hoover felt that although increased regulation was sorely needed, it would be unwise to propose it until more specific recommendations could be made.

Encouraged by the progress achieved in the first three Conferences but equally aware that major problems remained unresolved, Secretary Hoover felt compelled to call a Fourth National Radio Conference. More than 400 people attended these meetings. A mere 15 people three years before had grown to a multitude of delegates representing such varied interests as radio manufacturers, professional engineers, both government and public broadcasting, educators, amateurs, and an ever-growing number of concerned citizens interested in the proper role of radio as a societal institution. This last Conference between government officials and representatives of the broadcasting industry started on November 9, 1925, in Washington. At the opening session, Secretary Hoover asked the attendees to consider three questions as the basis of their work during the next few days. First, was it essential to limit the number of broadcast stations to prevent further congestion of the airwaves? Second, should the public interest as exemplified by service to the listeners be the basis for granting licenses? Third, should local committees, familiar with the needs of their own particular area, be appointed to help the Secretary of Commerce decide whom should be given broadcast franchises? The answer to the first question was obvious to the delegates. It was evident that there was not enough room on the airways for everyone who wanted to broadcast. The limited number of broadcast channels could not serve innumerable stations, even through geographical separation of facilities and elaborate time-sharing arrangements. One solution to the problem, which was rejected by the Conference, was to decrease the time of existing stations to one or two days a week in order to allow more stations to operate. The delegates felt that such a plan would only result in degenerated service to listeners. The Conference arrived at the conclusion that it was more desirable to have fewer stations broadcasting quality programming rather than many stations offering mediocre programs. The suggestion that the broadcast band be further widened was met with opposition. The majority of the delegates felt that if any more channels were allocated for broadcasting it would be unfair to other radio services which also had a legitimate right to use the spectrum. Hiram Percy Maxim, representing the American Radio Relay League, told the Conference that any further increase in the frequencies alloted to broadcasting would be unfair to amateur interests. Besides this reason, it was pointed out that the majority of receiving sets in use by the public were not capable of detecting radio signals outside the existing broadcast band. Therefore, the Conference favored the elimination of signal interference through limiting the number of stations on the air rather than increasing the number of available wave lengths. In answer to Hoover's second question of who should be allowed to broadcast, the opinions of the delegates seemed to be less consistent. They agreed with Hoover's suggestion that licenses should not be granted to everyone who could afford to build and operate a broadcast station, but rather should be granted on the basis of proposed service to the public. Beyond this, the delegates did little to spell out specific guidelines for Hoover to use in evaluating what constitutes "public service." In answer to Hoover's third question as to whether community groups should assist in processing an application, the delegates voiced negative opinions. They indicated that local involvement in the granting of licenses eventually would be subject to political control and thereby destroy the usefulness of the procedure.

Instructing the Conference to consider seriously specific recommendations which Congress might draw upon in drafting a radio control bill, Hoover asked the delegates to propose legislation only in those areas where industry self-regulation would not work. He reaffirmed his belief that broadcasters should solve their own problems where they could. H. M. Neely of Philadelphia suggested that broadcasters appoint a director to function in a manner similar to the Hays Office of the motion picture industry. One of the chief areas where self-regulation was supported was in the control of broadcast advertising. By 1925, it had become apparent to many that advertising had become the only logical means of supporting American broadcasting. While earlier Conferences, the Second in particular, had condemned advertising as the easiest way to destroy radio, the Fourth Conference felt the basic problem was one of control. While the delegates were still opposed to direct advertising or "any form of special pleading for the broadcaster or his products," [14] they did not object to what was referred to as indirect publicity. Hoover thought the broadcasters could control advertising if they distinguished between obtrusive direct advertising and unobtrusive publicity "accompanied by a direct service and engaging entertainment to the listener." [15]

Two other major issues were discussed at the Fourth Conference. The first was the super-power question which had been left unanswered at the Third Conference. Hoover reported that experiments carried out by RCA had proven successful and had done much to dispel the fear that super-power stations would blanket the signals of smaller stations. He mentioned that most of the mail received by the Commerce Department in response to super-power had been favorable and that more experiments were planned for the future. David Sarnoff added that as a result of super-power, "international broadcasting would soon be a reality" [16] and that already arrangements were being worked out with Great Britain and Germany for the exchange of programs.

The second recurring issue which became a major problem at the Fourth Conference was that of copyright. Although no definite agreements had been reached between the broadcasters and the copyright owners, conditions had worsened since the topic had been discussed at the Second Conference. The first legal test of whether the Copyright law applied to broadcasting was held in the U.S. District Court in New Jersey.[17] In this case, *Witmark v. Bamberger,* the court held that the broadcasting of copyrighted material without prior permission of the owner was a direct infringement of the law. A second major test occurred in Ohio where the U.S. District Court stated that broadcasting was not intended to be included in the meaning of "public performance for profit." [18] This decision was reversed, however, by the U.S. Circuit Court of Appeals [19] and on October 12, 1925, the U.S. Supreme Court refused to consider the broadcasters' appeal, therefore supporting the lower court's decision.[20] Since the courts had held that broadcasting was an infringement, the problem facing the delegates at the Fourth Conference was one of reaching terms for the use of copyrighted materials. In hopes of finding a solution to this controversy, Secretary Hoover prior to the Conference had appointed Judge S. B. Davis, Jr. to attempt to bring the two opposing factions together. One of the nine committees of the Conference was specially asked to consider the issue. After extensive study of the copyright question, Representative White, chairman of this committee, refrained from making any specific recommendations because of the evident diversity of opinions. His committee did outline certain principles Congress might follow in attempting to frame legislation pertaining to copyrights.

On November 11, 1925, the Fourth National Radio Conference submitted to Secretary Hoover a comprehensive program of legislation to amend the existing Federal law. The main points applicable to broadcasting were as follows. One, since the existing statutes were inadequate, Congress had the responsibility to enact further legislation to provide for the adequate administration of broadcasting. Two, in approving this legislation the doctrine of free speech should be held inviolate. Therefore, the law should concern itself with technical and administrative areas, rather than the censoring of broadcast programs. Three, although licenses should be awarded on the basis of public interest and contribution to the development of the art, broadcasters should not be required to devote their property to public use. This suggestion meant that broadcasting should not be thought of as a public utility as earlier Conferences had considered it. Four, that in times of national emergency the President should have power to take over the control of private stations with just compensation to their owners. Five, no monopoly in broadcasting should be permitted. Six, the Secretary of Commerce should be empowered to classify privately operated radio stations, to assign call letters, wavelengths, power, location, times of operation, character of emissions and duration of licenses. This recommendation applied only to private stations and gave the Secretary of Commerce no power over government-operated stations. Seven, licenses should be granted for a period of no longer than five years with renewal for the same period of time. Eight, the Secretary of Commerce should not change the original terms of a license application without due cause based on "public necessity." Nine, licenses should be revoked for (a) violation of the terms of the original application; (b) violation of any Federal law, international treaty or regulation of the Secretary of Commerce; and (c) failure to maintain operation without just cause. Ten, a construction permit should be required before an individual is authorized to build a station. Eleven, rebroadcasting of programs should be prohibited without the permission of the originating station. Twelve, the Secretary of Commerce should be empowered to make and enforce any regulations necessary to prevent interference to broadcast reception. Here, again, the delegates indicated that the government's regulatory powers should center on technical matters. Thirteen, existing stations should be given a reasonable time to conform to the proposed Act before being considered in violation of it.

The recommendations of the Fourth National Radio Conference were the basis of a House bill, H.R. 5589, introduced by Representative White in December, 1925.[21] This bill was to start the legislative chain-of-events that resulted in the passage of the Radio Act of 1927 . Between 1922 and 1925, these Conferences had served as the chief impetus of radio control bills submitted in Congress.

81

Marvin R. Bensman

REGULATION OF BROADCASTING BY THE DEPARTMENT OF COMMERCE, 1921–1927

THE DEPARTMENT OF COMMERCE throughout 1921 to 1927 regulated radio broadcasting under the provisions of the Radio Act of 1912. This regulation was under the direction of Secretary of Commerce Herbert C. Hoover and the staff of the Bureaus of Navigation and Standards. Because of the limited use made of radio prior to 1920 there had been no pressing need for further legislation. It became increasingly difficult to apply the law of 1912 to this new use of radio. Thus, attempts had to be made at the federal level to change the situation.

LEGISLATIVE ATTEMPTS TO CONTROL RADIO

Twenty bills were placed before the 67th Congress (1921–23); 13 proposed laws were submitted to the 68th Congress (1923–25);

and 18 bills were introduced to the 69th Congress (1925–27) all to regulate radio communication. Of these 51 bills only one was to pass both House of Congress—the Radio Act of 1927.

Secretary Hoover called the radio industry together for a series of conferences in 1922, 1923, 1924, and 1925 to seek advice on regulation and to formulate recommendations to Congress for legislation. The legislative suggestions from these conferences were acted upon by Congress in 1927.

The Department of Commerce's Commissioner of Navigation from 1908 to 1921, Eugene T. Chamberlain, had drafted a bill in 1915–16. With the coming of World War I this and other legislative attempts were laid aside. After the war, Senator Kellogg introduced this bill again as S. 1628.

A redraft of S. 1628 was introduced by Senator Kellogg in the Senate Committee on Interstate Commerce on April 20, 1922. This bill, S. 3694, had evolved in the legal committee of the First National Radio Conference of which Senator Kellogg was a member.

A similar bill was introduced into the House by Rep. Wallace H. White, Jr., on June 9, 1922. This bill, H.R. 11964, was also a product of the Radio Conference of which Representative White was also a member. The Committee on Merchant Marine and Fisheries January 2 and 3, 1923, redrafted Rep. White's bill and, as H.R. 13773, it was reported out of committee on January 16, 1923. The Radio Act of 1927 stems from this bill. It gave the Secretary of Commerce absolute discretion in issuing licenses. H.R. 13773 passed the House, but died in the Senate Committee on Interstate Commerce.

Early in 1924, Congressman White again introduced his bill, with slight changes, as H.R. 7357 and it was referred to the Committee on Merchant Marine and Fisheries. Almost concurrent with H.R. 7357, Senator Howell introduced into the Senate S. 2930 amending the Radio Act of 1912 to give the Department of Commerce powers it was already assuming. This piecemeal bill affirmed that the ether was a public possession and provided for limited grants for its use. S. 2930 quickly went out of the Committee on Interstate Commerce to the Senate floor where it was passed and referred to the House, April 7, 1924.

The Committee on Merchant Marine and Fisheries received the Howell bill and incorporated the provisions of H.R. 7357. This revised version was reported out on May 13, 1924, as H.R. 5589.

At this point Secretary Hoover withdrew his support from the proposed legislation to support the original Howell amendment as it appeared in S. 2930. Secretary Hoover felt that radio was developing too rapidly for comprehensive legislation to keep pace and recommended S. 2930 as a stop-gap measure. On January 23, 1925, H.R. 5589 was re-referred to committee where it died. By November of

1925 the broadcasting situation had worsened and without statutory authority the Department of Commerce ceased issuing licenses. Bitter complaints of discrimination ensued from applicants who had not received broadcast licenses.

H.R. 9108, the redraft of Representative White's former bill by the Committee on Merchant Marine and Fisheries was reintroduced and reported out of committee. It was withdrawn however, to eliminate a strong antitrust provision which Secretary Hoover opposed. Reintroduced as H.R. 9971, this bill was reported out of committee and, with slight amendment, passed the House on March 15, 1926.

S. 1754, a companion bill introduced in the Senate Committee on Interstate Commerce by Senator Clarence C. Dill, was redrafted as S. 4057. Before this bill could be reported out of committee the House passed H.R. 9971 and referred it to the Senate. The Senate Committee on Interstate Commerce then inserted S. 4057 as an amendment to H.R. 9971 and the Senate passed the revision on July 2, 1926.

There was further difficulty, however. The House bill vested the licensing function in the Secretary of Commerce, with appeals possible to a commission representing geographic sections of the country. The Senate bill placed licensing and appeal totally with a commission. On July 3, 1926, the conference reported disagreement and urged passage of a Senate Joint Resolution to preserve the status quo between Congressional sessions and until a compromise could be reached. S. J. Res. 125, which limited licenses to 90 days and required a waiver of any claim of right to any wavelength was quickly passed by both houses but not signed until December 8, 1926.

While the resolution was pending before committee, the United States District Court of Illinois held that a licensee using a wavelength and hours of operation other than those assigned by the Department of Commerce could not be prosecuted under the Radio Act of 1912. On July 8, 1926, Attorney General William Donovan ruled to the effect that, under the Radio Act of 1912 the Secretary had no authority to assign wavelengths, specify hours, limit power or duration of a license.

Secretary Hoover abandoned regulation. When Congress reconvened in December 1926, conditions were extreme enough to move it to action. The conferees brought out their bill January 27, 1927. The issue of commission versus Department of Commerce authority was compromised by vesting in the Department of Commerce authority of all functions except the primary licensing authority, which was vested in an independent commission. This licensing authority was limited to one year, after which all functions, except for revocation of licenses, would revert to the Secretary of Commerce. The commission would then assume an advisory and appellate role.

The House agreed on the conference report on January 29, 1927, the Senate concurred on February 18, 1927, and the bill to regulate radio was signed into law on February 23, 1927.[1]

REGULATORY ATTEMPTS TO CONTROL RADIO

While legislation was being considered by Congress the Department of Commerce proceeded to regulate broadcasting. This regulation was conducted as a background to the controversy and debate surrounding the form that such legislation should take. The Department of Commerce's daily regulatory activities influenced these deliberations.

Broadcast Regualtion and Policy from 1921 to 1924

The period 1921 to 1924 was the beginning of the broadcast era. The Department of Commerce began to license broadcast stations as "limited commercial stations" September 15, 1921. Apparently, no special license was required prior to that time for stations experimenting with broadcasting. Those stations which were so licensed could operate on only one frequency, 360 meters (832.8 kHz), which was to be utilized for "news, lectures, entertainment, etc." The wavelength of 485 meters (618.6 kHz) was allocated to any of these stations which wished to periodically transmit governmental reports such as weather and crop information.

The deputy Commissioner of Navigation, Mr. Arthur Tyrer noted:

> At the time Westinghouse representatives proposed to this office that they be given authority to broadcast music and other entertainment from several of their stations it was agreed that one wavelength only, that of 360 meters, would be assigned and for the purpose of preventing interference between the stations using the same wavelength they would necessarily have to arrange their schedules for different hours.[2]

While legislative attempts were being made to fashion a new radio law the Bureau of Navigation found itself facing increasing complaints of interference. Secretary Hoover, in his annual report of 1921 stated:

> The only justification for Federal regulation of radio communication lies in the fact that no such communication at all would be possible unless some authority determined the power and wavelengths to be employed by different stations and classes of stations in order to prevent mutual interference with the transmission

and reception of messages. Invention has already done much to reduce such interference and will doubtless do more, but interference is still the most important factor to be considered from the point of view of the practical use to-day of this indispensable means of communication.[3]

By the end of 1922 there were over 570 broadcasting stations licensed. Interference increased proportionately with the density of stations in a particular geographic area.

At first a major cause of interference appeared to be the amateur radio operator. The Bureau of Navigation issued an order January 1, 1922, forbidding amateur sending stations from transmitting until a solution to this problem could be reached. However, interference was not the sole reason for suspending amateur operations. The Commissioner of Navigation, Mr. David B. Carson stated:

> A number of amateur stations and other stations were beginning to broadcast phonograph records which had no real value as entertainment or instruction and which threatened to so seriously interfere with the higher classes of service that it was considered necessary to stop broadcasting by amateur stations until some plan can be arranged which will allow amateurs to do work of this kind, if it can be shown to be of value, on a wavelength just below or just above 200 meters (1499 kHz).[4]

The Bureau, January 11, 1922, provided an interpretation of "broadcasting" by authorizing the insertion of the following on all general and restricted amateur radio station licenses:

> This station is not licensed to broadcast weather reports, market reports, music, concerts, speeches, news or similar information or entertainment.[5]

Mr. Carson provided the *raison d'être* when he wrote:

> In the recent restriction placed upon amateur broadcasting this office did not lose sight of the recognized value of the amateur radio operator. The action was taken for the purpose of preventing interference and to stop broadcasting by amateurs of phonograph records, which are not enjoyed by the public but at times becomes annoying.[6]

Although "broadcasting" as a class of stations had begun September 1921 with the licensing of this class of station, this was the first time that it was made clear that no other class of station could provide the same type of programming to the general public. Thus, recognition of "broadcasting" as defined above dates from January 1922.

The Department of Commerce, while making such regulations found itself challenged in court on its powers to make any regulations. In the *Intercity Company Case* the Department had refused a license to a commercial wireless telegraphy company in 1921. This was following

> . . . a long period of experiment and investigation, during which time that company received all the assistance that could be given by this Department, as well as the assistance of others in the radio field, to remove, if possible, the aggravated interference that in many instances prevented the actual operation of government radio stations while . . . Intercity . . . was in operation.[7]

The courts ordered Secretary Hoover, November 18, 1921 to issue a license as:

> Only such regulations as are contained in the law itself were legal, counsel declared, and the court upheld this contention.[8]

The case was appealed but was not settled until 1924, when the Supreme Court dismissed the action as Intercity was no longer operating. However, Secretary Hoover and his staff had lost every appeal up to the Supreme Court and knew that they would likely lose before the highest court. The Intercity lawyer communicated the argument that:

> So long as the present statute remains in force, the right of the Secretary to refuse licenses, or to place other than statutory restrictions thereon, is continually brought up by applications. . . .
> These are powers arbitrarily taken and not given by statute, but exercised rather in anticipation of the passage of the new radio law.[9]

In some respects, this case contributed to the calling of the First National Radio Conference. Such a meeting had been requested by the Bureau of Navigation from 1921. Secretary Hoover went to the cabinet, February 7, 1922, to ask for such a conference two days after the Court of Appeals review of the case upheld the lower court decision on the Intercity case.

Secretary Hoover, in letters to those asked to attend the First National Radio Conference to be held February 27, 1922 suggested that their thoughts be formulated in three possible areas of solution to the problems facing broadcasting:

> First, an ideal solution, assuming suitable changes in the International Radio Convention and the U.S. radio law;
> Second, a solution compatible with the present International Convention, assuming that urgently needed changes in the U.S. law will be made; and,
> Third, an immediate solution which can be effected under the present law.[10]

The Department of Commerce had to settle for the third solution suggested, although it attempted to implement the second; a change in the U.S. law. However, as noted above Congress did not pass a new act so an immediate solution to the difficulties had to be implemented.

Time-sharing did not solve the interference problem as more and more stations went on the air in the same localities. Other plans were proposed. John F. Dillon, radio inspector in California, handed Mr. Hoover a letter March 1922 suggesting that the country be divided into zones, with different wavelengths allocated to adjacent areas, and "whenever necessary the same wavelength to be assigned to alternate zones, or to zones remotely situated." [11] Dillon, later named to the F.R.C. by Hoover, also suggested that each station be classified, "indicated by a letter of the alphabet, according to the character of the matter which it is engaged in broadcasting."

Another suggestion received by the Department was that the military should give up its reservation of 600 to 1600 meters (499.7 kHz—187.4 kHz). However the Department found heavy Navy opposition. [12]

As the level of interference increased in 1922 between stations operating on 360 meters John F. Dillon's suggestions were carried through. Mr. Carson proposed to Secretary Hoover that another wavelength be made available for broadcast purposes. To keep this wavelength from becoming as congested as 360 meters, the 400 meter wavelength [749.6 kHz] was set aside for a new class of radiotelephone broadcasting station which required more stringent technical capabilities and programming aspects.

The plan was proposed August 1922 to form Class A stations. August 5, 1922, Secretary Hoover returned the proposal to Commissioner Carson with the handwritten suggestion: "Regarding your memo attached. I think this is a good plan, but would suggest you call these Class B licenses instead of Class A." [13] It was hoped the Class B title would dissuade some broadcasters from considering such a license better than a Class A or C license.

William Terrell, chief radio inspector, was subsequently asked at a Congressional hearing, "What, if anything, did your department have to do with censoring the kind of speeches or music, or anything that went over the radio?" Mr. Terrell replied:

> We had not any legal authority to do that, and we, of course, could not do it. About the only thing I can say that would approach that was the creation of a special class of license known as Class B license under our administration. Under that class of license we would not permit the station owner—and he agreed to it—to use mechanical music, phonographs, and things of that kind. The reason we did that was because at the beginning all the stations were turning to entertainments, and at the beginning the people were appreciating it. But later they were tiring of it, and if we had not checked

it, it would have had an effect on broadcasting. So we created this special license, and they had to have talent.[14]

By October 1922 the Class B wavelength of 400 meters was becoming congested in the larger population centers as many stations complied with the more stringent requirements of that license. However, it was still felt that "separate wavelengths for each radio station is not practical." [15]

It had often been proposed by Westinghouse, Crosley and other broadcasting interests that stations be placed a few meters or frequencies apart and a zoning system be used so stations located at a distance from each other could utilize practically the same frequency. Thus, the Department of Commerce was aware that the most effective remedy for the continuing interference problem would be to remove the restrictions on the band of wavelengths reserved for military use. Non-broadcast stations could then be reallocated to that space and a broadcast band cleared elsewhere.

Commissioner Carson proposed from December 1922 that such a solution be sought. When Secretary Hoover learned, February 12, 1923 that there was no chance of the White-Kellogg bills passing the present session of Congress he telegraphed Chief Inspector Terrell from California, "Inasmuch as our legislation is not likely to go through, would it not be desirable to call a conference to consider what should be done by way of invasion of the Naval Reserve?" [16]

Such conferences began through the Interdepartmental Radio Advisory Committee, which consisted of all government departments with interests in wireless communication. Within the month of learning legislation would not be passed by Congress, Secretary Hoover also called the Second National Radio Conference "for considering legislation for lessening interference. Secretary Hoover also decided to utilize the conference in another way, as he advised those invited to attend, to devise some administrative measures for lessening interference in broadcasting.

Prior to the Second Radio Conference the Interdepartmental Radio Advisory Board reached an agreement with the Department of the Navy to relinquish its reserved frequencies. There was great public pressure upon the Navy to assist broadcasting and Captain Hooper, in charge of Naval Communications, supported this suggestion in order to obtain more modern equipment for the Navy.

When the Second Radio Conference convened March 21, 1923, the Department of Commerce was able to announce abandonment of group allocation on one frequency for a discrete frequency for each locality from a predetermined wave-band. May 15, 1923 the new wave-band opened for broadcast stations, with: Class A stations of up to 500 watts operating on 999.4 to 1365 kHz; Class B stations with power of 500 to 1000 watts operating from 870 to 999.4 kHz and 550 to 800 kHz; and Class C stations operating on one frequency of 832.8 kHz.

The Westinghouse Company was not satisfied with the new allocations as six stations were assigned KDKA's frequency in Pittsburgh and the surrounding area. Westinghouse executive H. P. Davis proposed to the Department of Commerce "national stations" to provide a "nation-wide service." [17] A frequency not used by any other station within the area covered by the new class was suggested. Thus, Class D (developmental) stations were introduced with requirements more stringent than the already overcrowded Class B stations. This class was restricted to stations conducting experimentation which were owned and operated by companies producing equipment for broadcasting purposes. At least three such stations were to be so classified.

The major problems during 1921 to 1924 were interference, increasing numbers of stations, and the difficulties of achieving legislation which would give the Department of Commerce discretionary powers to refuse to license all applicants. This period began the system of conferences to achieve some measure of voluntary cooperation, developed the broadcast band and brought about station classification by power and service rendered the public.

Regulatory Breakdown: 1924–1927

By May, 1924 the Bureau of Navigation staff realized that legislation would not be considered by Congress for that session. October 6, 1924 the Third National Radio Conference met and made recommendations to the Department of Commerce. Under the proposals, the broadcasting band was extended the 150 kilocycles over the recommendations of the Second Conference. However, the Bureau of Navigation did not implement this recommendation as receivers were not being built to receive this extra spectrum space.

It was anticipated that a two- or three-way time-sharing plan would be necessary as the only solution to the allocation problems. However, these steps were not sufficient. In December 1924 Class B stations were being assigned wavelengths in the Class A frequencies as spectrum space grew scarcer.

Secretary Hoover wrote Congressman White, December 4, 1924 withdrawing support of the bill and asked that his regulatory authority over wavelengths, power, apparatus and time of operation be legally established by an amendment.

Various industry leaders attacked such regulation, and it was "considered doubtful that there will be any important legislation dealing with the radio industry at the short session of Congress." [18]

Station applications continued and power increases were resulting in further congestion and interference. On January 31, 1925, a general reassignment of wavelengths separated all stations by 10 kilocycles. An experimental seven kHz separation had not worked as receivers were not sensitive enough to discriminate between stations that close in frequency. The radio inspector of Detroit noted:

> You have no idea of the number of obstacles we meet with every day in connection with broadcasting. We find people who absolutely refuse to cooperate with us and we do not seem to have authority under the existing law to compel them to do the things which they should do so that the public would benefit.[19]

By the end of 1925 the Bureau was sending letters to all applicants for broadcasting licenses that there was no longer any room for anyone on any frequency.

The Fourth Annual Radio Conference convened November 9, 1925. This conference approved the Bureau's decision not to license any further stations. Secretary Hoover said:

> I take pride in the fact that in this conference, made up as it was not only by representatives of the listeners, the amateurs, the great newspapers and magazines of the United States, but of the manufacturers and broadcasters, with millions of dollars invested in their enterprises at stake in this situation, not a dissenting voice was raised against the resolution by which they formally recognized that your (the listener's) interests are dominant in the whole situation.[20]

The conference also recommended that station classification be eliminated and Secretary Hoover remarked:

> From now on, all stations will be on the same basis. There is to be only one test, if Congress passes the necessary legislation, that is service to the listener, and this test will be applied to every station, big or little.[21]

The very success and popularity of broadcasting gave rise to its principal difficulty. As of January 1926 there was an average of six stations to the wavelength and over 300 applications were pending. It was this congestion and the decision to cease all licensing that made the voluntary efforts of the Department of Commerce fail.

Eugene F. McDonald, president of the Zenith Radio Company requested a license for a proposed station, WJAZ, June 1925. He was informed that no further frequencies were available in Chicago. He then asked for no more than two hours per week, 10 p.m. to 12 p.m. Thursday nights, when a frequency in use by WSAI, Cincinnati and KOA, Denver was free. After consultation with the companies involved the Department of Commerce allowed the license, Class D, provided "your avoidance of interference." [22]

McDonald soon asked the Department for more airtime and requested frequencies which were in use by Canadian stations and upon which no United States stations were assigned. This request was refused and legal action was threatened.

WJAZ began to operate on the reserved Canadian frequency of 910 kHz, which was being used by seven Canadian stations.

The Attorney General of the United States was asked to prosecute WJAZ as

> this case is the first serious instance which has arisen where a broadcasting station has persistently violated the laws and has caused widespread confusion and trouble in the air. The Secretary of Commerce regards this case as being of the greatest importance, both with regard to the maintenance of proper order in the air of this country and with regard to our friendly relations with the Canadian authorities.[23]

This unauthorized operation became known as "pirating" of an unauthorized wavelength. The Department of Commerce made it public that they felt "complete and utter chaos in the ether would result from an unfavorable decision in the McDonald case, at least until legislation is enacted granting authority to some agency to regulate radio." [24]

April 16, 1926, Judge Wilkerson announced his decision in the *United States vs. the Zenith Radio Corporation* case:

> There is no express grant of power in the Act to the Secretary of Commerce to establish regulations. The regulations subject to which the license is granted are contained in the fourth section of the Act.[25]

The conflict between the Intercity Radio Company case of 1923, which had indicated that although the Secretary could not refuse to license a station, he could assign a wavelength and power to prevent interference, and the Zenith WJAZ case of 1926 which, according to Department of Commerce solicitor Stephen Davis, took away the power to assign any wavelengths, left the Secretary of Commerce without judicial guidance.

The Secretary had no right to make any rules or regulations concerning broadcasting which were not specifically spelled out in the Radio Act of 1912.[26]

There is disagreement as to how much interference and actual "chaos" followed the Department of Commerce's relaxation of control. However, from July 1, 1926, to December 18, 1926, the Department was required to grant 126 new licenses (to total 642 stations). More than 91 stations changed wavelengths and about 132 stations increased power. By February of 1927 more than 210 new stations had been licensed from July 1, 1926, bringing the total number to 716.[27]

Secretary Hoover was strongly against an antimonopoly provision in any proposed law as "if applied to the Radio Corporation of America . . . it would mean the destruction of the international and transoceanic radio services which it now carries on with many parts of the world and upon which our people rely for valuable public service." [28]

Secretary Hoover also was against the concept of a communications commission. He wrote:

> The suggestion of a general commission, which would license and have regulatory power over all systems of communication, whether by radio or wire, including telephones, telegraphs and cables, raises extensive and serious questions, which have no place in a bill devoted to radio control.[29]

The compromise bill proposed a commission with authority to allocate wavelengths and assign licenses for one year, after which total control would be replaced in the Department of Commerce.

CONCLUSION

The Department of Commerce adapted its authority under the Radio Act of 1912 and (1) classified radio stations; (2) prescribed their service; (3) assigned frequencies; (4) cleared a broadcast band; (5) regulated and tested apparatus; (6) established zones and wavelengths for those zones; (7) made regulations to prevent interference; (8) advocated freedom from censorship; (9) helped settle on the phrase "public interest, convenience and necessity"; and (10) specified the role and makeup of the Federal Radio Commission formed by the Radio Act of 1927.

The Department of Commerce staff continually called for, revised, and developed the regulation upon which Congress finally acted. The Federal Radio Commission later was to formally codify most aspects of the regulation which had proven workable by the Department of Commerce's regulation of radio broadcasting. The main difference was that the FRC was given the legal power to codify, while the Department of Commerce implemented its regulation through cooperation and persuasion. In point of time, the Department of Commerce staff discussed, devised and implemented the regulation of radio prior to the passage of the Radio Act of 1927.

As a result of the Radio Conference called by this Department earlier in the present year, bills are now before Congress which promise to provide order instead of anarchy in the ether.
　　　　　--Herbert C. Hoover, secretary of commerce, 1922.

82

W. Jefferson Davis

THE RADIO ACT OF 1927

THE RADIO CONTROL BILL, as passed by Congress and signed by the President, is very frankly a compromise solution, and while not entirely adequate, it does, to some extent, represent a very substantial advance over the old law of 1912. It provides adequately for dealing with future stations, and by indirection meets to some extent the problems now confronting broadcasting.

The Radio Control Law has cured many of the defects in bills formerly proposed:

First: The preamble has omitted the declaration of ownership of the ether, and is proceeding properly under the commerce clause of the Constitution. The fundamental principle of the law, however, remains the same as expressed in the 1912 law:

> "No person * * * shall use or operate any apparatus for the transmission of energy or communications or signals by radio * * * except under and in accordance with this act and with a license in that behalf granted under the provisions of this act."

The corresponding paragraph of the 1912 law read as follows:

> "No person shall use or operate any apparatus for radio communication as a means of commercial intercourse except under and in accordance with a license revocable for cause in that behalf granted by the Secretary of Commerce on application therefor."

The language in both acts is similar in thought and the new law merely changes the details of administration.

Second: The license term has been fixed under the new law at three years instead of two.

Third: While there seems to be no provision for forfeiture of license for transfer for more than the value of the physical equipment, there is a limitation of the right to transfer a license, and the Commission might properly decline to acquiesce in such a transfer for any reason which it may consider proper.

Fourth: Navy stations are permitted to transmit newspaper and other private commercial messages at reasonable rates, but this provision is permissive only until such time when there are privately owned facilities for such business.

The law provides for a Commission to operate for the first year.

Virginia Law Review, Vol. CXIII (June 1927), pp. 616–618.

Thereafter the Secretary of Commerce will handle most of the problems which will arise, and the Commission will probably function only occasionally.

83

ACTION FROM THE RADIO COMMISSION

THE FEDERAL RADIO COMMISSION has begun suit against station KWKH, which it charges with the misdeed of using three times the power permitted by its license, for forty successive days. As a result, KWKH is liable to fines aggregating $20,000 at the rate of $500 a violation. If the Commission has a good case and wins out in the courts, it will certainly gain wide respect. The numerous violations of the Commission's regulation as to maintenance of assigned frequencies are likewise subject to fines of five hundred dollars a day. Certain stations frequently wander as much as ten kilocycles from their channels. The former WSOM, for example, was found at different times, within eight days, 24.8, 23.9, 12.5, and 16.1 kc. from its assigned channel.

The Commission, in a public statement, threatened to eliminate about twenty-five of the most flagrant wavelength wobblers but, as usual, grew softhearted in the end and gave them additional grace. Heterodyning is far too widespread to make listening to any but relatively nearby stations any very great pleasure.

The Commission's claim, however, that practically all heterodyning is due to frequency wobbling is not entirely founded on fact. There are altogether too many assignments of stations to the same frequency whose carrier waves are bound to create interference. The clearest broadcasting channels as a matter of fact, are at this time the higher frequencies between 1250 and 1500 kc. On these frequencies, we find mostly low-powered stations which do not interfere with each other.

The numerous hearings held in Washington, upon demand of some of the stations now assigned to these superior channels, are based on the fallacious superstition that the lower frequencies are the most desirable. At one time, when the lower frequencies were reserved for the better stations, while as many as twenty and thirty low- and medium-powered stations were huddled on the lower end of the broadcast band, the ambition to leave the higher frequencies was justified. Although conditions have changed, prejudice against the higher frequencies persists.

Mr. May, seeking a lower frequency for his advertising station, KMA, for example, testified before the Commission that it was a well known fact among radio engineers that the channels below 350 meters [857 kHz] were "practically no good for broadcasting purposes," although, as an expert brought out, KDKA, KOA, WBBM, WOK, and numerous other stations, occupying these allegedly unsatisfactory frequencies, have built up nationwide audiences.

The claim that stations do not "get out" on the very high frequencies is made because the public is not accustomed to looking for its programs on these channels. There are too few worthwhile stations using them. Why not assign a few really good stations to the higher frequencies, so as to distribute the public's attention throughout the broadcast band?

84

BROADCASTING BUNK

IN A FEW SPOTS over the United States local stations continue to pour forth filth and falsehood. In the obscure Kansas village of Milford, a blatant quack, one John R. Brinkley, whose professional record reeks with charlatanism of the crudest type, has for some years been demonstrating the commercial possibilities of goatgland grafting for alleged sexual rejuvenation. Brinkley's educational history is as shady as his professional record.

Brinkley, over his own broadcasting station, attempts to attract listeners by the kind of salacious innuendo concerning his methods that has brought millions to publishers of salacious periodicals. Far better might the United States Senate have concerned itself with such matters, than with its insistence that inspectors at our ports prevent the entrance into this country of Rabelais, Candide, or even the Decameron. At least the purchasers of those books know what they are getting, but in any home in the Southwest, the radio may snort into the family circle the news that Brinkley has reawakened the dormant sex desire of some ancient derelict by the injection of

The Journal of the American Medical Association, April 12, 1930, pp. 1146–1147.

some giblet-like mixture of glands. More recently Brinkley has extended his commercialization of medicine—via the radio—by prescribing for his unseen and unknown audience, and then entering into a financial arrangement with druggists whose professional standards are, apparently, as low as his own. Thus broadcasts station KFKB of Milford, Kansas.

In Iowa at Muscatine, over station KTNT, broadcasts a business man named Baker who is selling a cancer cure, with cigars and a cheap magazine as side lines. His cancer cure includes the old Hoxsey fake, originally promoted in Illinois, and apparently now resident also in Iowa. This nostrum for cancer is boomed by Mr. Baker over his radio station KTNT, which can be heard almost anywhere after 11 o'clock at night. This is exceedingly proper since it is the time of night when many devious and doubtful ventures are promoted. Over his privately controlled station Baker indulges in a repetition of much of the scandalous insinuation that proprietary manufacturers used back in 1905 when they first attempted to hinder the battle of the American Medical Association against the promotion of medical fraud.

The viciousness of Mr. Baker's broadcasting lies not in what he says about the American Medical Association but in the fact that he induces sufferers from cancer who might have some chance for their lives, if seen early and properly treated, to resort to his nostrum. The method can result in Muscatine, Iowa, as it did in Taylorville, Illinois—merely in death certificates signed by the physicians who have been so poor in finances and in morals as to sell their birthrights to Mr. Baker for his mess of garbage.

If the Federal Radio Commission wants to merit public confidence it must find some way to curb this type of broadcasting. If the association of broadcasters wants to retain public respect it must assure the public that the average home will be protected against this type of promotion over what should be a safe means of education and entertainment. If the states of Iowa and Kansas cannot protect surrounding states against this effluvium which emanates from within their borders, they are indeed to be pitied for their weakness and condemned for their crime against the great American public.

PLEASE ORDER YOUR MINIONS OF SATAN TO LEAVE MY STATION ALONE. YOU CANNOT EXPECT THE ALMIGHTY TO ABIDE BY YOUR WAVELENGTH NONSENSE. WHEN I OFFER MY PRAYERS TO HIM I MUST FIT INTO HIS WAVE RECEPTION. OPEN THIS STATION AT ONCE. AIMEE SEMPLE MCPHERSON. —Telegram to Secretary of Commerce Hoover.

85

Maurice E. Shelby Jr.

JOHN R. BRINKLEY: HIS
CONTRIBUTION TO BROADCASTING

JOHN R. BRINKLEY was the infamous "goat-gland-surgeon" who settled in Kansas after the First World War and bilked millions of dollars from unwitting patients with the treatment of diseased prostate
glands, which he claimed robbed the testes of vital functions. As a
treatment, Brinkley developed his "compound operation," a surgical
procedure intended to shrink enlarged prostates and to rebuild weakened testes. He achieved this latter objective by implanting the
gonads of a young Toggenberg goat inside the human scrotum. His
broadcasting station was an important adjunct to his fraudulent medical practice.

To reconstruct the early life of John R. Brinkley, one is forced to
rely heavily upon his biographer, Clement Wood. Brinkley paid
Wood $5,000 to write *The Life Of A Man*,[1] a book intended to build
Brinkley's image as a "rags-to-riches" doctor, who, born in poverty,
overcame fantastic obstacles to become one of the world's leading
surgeons. Some question exists as to whether he ever reached high
school, although Brinkley claims to have attended Tuckaseigee High
School in Beta, North Carolina. The school burned with the records
of his attendance.

Wood writes that Brinkley, in an effort to achieve his life-long
ambition to become a doctor, attempted to enter the School of Medicine at Johns Hopkins University at the age of 15. Rebuffed by the
school, barefoot and clad in overalls, Brinkley returned to the hills to
be a railroad telegrapher. After practicing medicine in North Carolina, Tennessee and Arkansas, Brinkley bought a diploma from the
Kansas City, Missouri Eclectic Medical University for $100. He
graduated in 1915, with a degree recognized by medical boards in
eight states. Licensed to practice medicine in Arkansas, he received
a Kansas license February 16, 1916, by reciprocal agreement. While
working as "plant surgeon" with Swift and Company in Kansas City
in 1916, he noted that of 5000 goats slaughtered, none was infected
with any disease that could be transmitted to human beings. Later
these observations influenced Brinkley in the development of his
"goat-gland" operation.

Brinkley was drafted into military service in 1917 and discharged "after a brilliant career"—he served one month. The Brink-
leys settled in Milford, a small, farm community in north central

Kansas, where he incurred debts of $60,000 in the construction of his new hospital. Brinkley hired a small platoon of publicists and began promoting his goat-gland operations. The publicity campaign paid off, and by 1923 Wood says that his debts had been repaid.

When he was experiencing financial difficulties, Brinkley recognized in radio a potential solution to his predicament. On a visit to Los Angeles, Brinkley observed the construction of station KHJ.[2] Brinkley obtained a broadcasting license for Milford from the Secretary of Commerce. In August 1923, he wrote to some prospective patients:

> . . . we are building a splendid brick building for the purpose of housing a Radio Broadcasting Station. This station will become one of the largest in the United States and its program will be available to people on either coast and beyond. The concert room will be larger and finer than will be found in the largest cities and the machinery is the best that money can buy. The programs will be in keeping with the modernity and progressiveness of this institution. Those of you who have receiving sets are invited to "tune in" for our concerts which will begin in October.[3]

Station KFKB (*K*ansas *F*irst, *K*ansas *B*est; "The Sunshine Station in the Heart of the Nation") with 1000 watts of power could cover much of the central United States. The station was licensed on September 20, 1923, and operated for almost two years.[4] In 1925, Brinkley's medical degrees were challenged on grounds that they had been granted by "diploma mills" and to off-set this he decided to get a license in England. Consequently, he sold the original KFKB on June 3, 1925 and left for London.[5] When he returned to the United States on December 25, 1925, he immediately began constructing another radio station, which was licensed as KFKB by the Department of Commerce on October 23, 1926.[6]

Apparently, the power and frequency for the second KFKB varied until the Radio Act of 1927 became effective and required stabilization. In January 1927 one of Brinkley's publicity flyers noted his frequency at 431.4 meters but indicated a future change to 428.3 meters. A letter of April 21, 1927, indicated that the station was operating at 219 meters, (1370 kHz) at 5000 watts. The Federal Radio Commission, however, said that on July 1, 1927, KFKB was supposed to be operating at 1240 kHz, 2500 watts from 7 a.m. to 7 p.m. and at 1500 watts after 7 p.m.[7] After November 1928, however KFKB operated at 265.3 meters (1130 kHz), 5000 watts of power.

Brinkley used his radio station as a lure to attract a very specific type of person to his hospital. He programmed KFKB to attract the listener that he needed most. One of Brinkley's innovations was the *Medical Question Box*, during which he answered letters from listeners. This program ultimately justified the Federal Radio Commis-

KFKB Program Log

April 12, 1930

5:00 A.M.   Lecture on Health.
5:30 A.M.   Uncle Bob Larkan and His Music Makers.
6:00 A.M.   Lecture on health and sanitation.
6:30 A.M.   Irish and his Uke.
7:00 A.M.   Hawaiian Music.
7:15 A.M.   McRee Sisters.
7:30 A.M.   Fenoglio and his Accordian.
8:00 A.M.   Prof. Gaston Bert's Language period.
8:30 A.M.   Dutch and his Uke.
8:45 A.M.   Uncle Bob and Sam McRee.
9:00 A.M.   Market reports, weather report, current news items, etc.
9.15 A.M.   Uncle Bob Larkan and his Merry Makers.
9:30 A.M.   Medical Question Box.
10:00 A.M.   Irish and Dutch accompanied by Evans Brown.
10:30 A.M.   Roy Faulkner.
10:45 A.M.   Fenoglio and his Accordian.
11:00 A.M.   Steve Love and Arthur Pizinger's Orchestras alternating.
12:30 P.M.   Medical Question Box.
1:00 P.M.   Uncle Bob and Sam McRee.
1:15 P.M.   Irish and his Uke.
1:30 P.M.   Albert Fenoglio and his Accordian.
1:45 P.M.   Hawaiian Music.
2:00 P.M.   Uncle Bob Larkan and His Music Makers.
2:15 P.M.   Albert Fenoglio and his Accordian.
2:30 P.M.   Medical Question Box.
3:00 P.M.   Evans Brown and his Accordian.
3:15 P.M.   Roy Faulkner.
3:30 P.M.   Uncle Bob and Sam McRee.
3:45 P.M.   Irish and his Uke.
4:00 P.M.   Uncle Bob Larkan and his Music Makers.
4:15 P.M.   Hawaiian Music.
4:30 P.M.   McRee Sisters.
4:45 P.M.   Evans Brown and his Harp.
5:00 P.M.   McRee Sisters.
5:15 P.M.   Hawaiian Music.
5:30 P.M.   Albert Fenoglio and his Accordian.
5:45 P.M.   Tell Me a Story Lady.
6:00 P.M.   Steve Love's Orchestra playing popular program.
6:30 P.M.   Arthur Pizinger's Orchestra playing concert numbers.
8:00 P.M.   Health Hints.
8:30 P.M.   Sign Off.[8]

sion in revocation of Brinkley's broadcasting license. Brinkley described the idea of the program:

> I began to receive an enormous amount of mail from people asking me about this thing and that thing and another thing. I couldn't answer it, and the only way it could be answered was to go on the radio and answer a good bulk of it, and in 1929 from answering those letters over the radio, the radio patients began to come to me because of radio advertising. You can readily understand that no living human being could answer three or four thousand letters a day. . . . Therefore, I conceived this idea: why not have a Medical Question Box over the radio like Doctor Evans of the Chicago *Tribune* did, and other people like Senator Copeland, and various magazines giving questions and answers.[9]

The *Medical Question Box* became so popular that druggists began to write that his medicines were in demand. He organized the National Dr. Brinkley Pharmaceutical Association, composed of 1500 area druggists. Members received number-coded "prescriptions." Brinkley read letters from listeners describing their symptoms for which he prescribed medicines by code number. Patients could purchase remedies at "Brinkley" neighborhood pharmacies. Brinkley would say:

> Here's one from Tillie. She says she had an operation, had some trouble ten years ago. I think the operation was unnecessary, and it isn't very good sense to have an ovary removed with the expectation of motherhood resulting therefrom. My advice to you is to use Woman's Tonic Number 50, 67, and 61. This combination will do for you what you desire if any combination will after three months persistent use.

> Now here is a letter from a dear mother—a dear little mother who holds to her breast a babe of nine months. She should take Number 2 and Number 16 and—yes—Number 17 and she will be helped. Brinkley's 2, 16, and 17. If her druggist hasn't got them, she should write and order them from the Milford Drug Company, Milford, Kansas, and they will be sent to you, Mother, collect. May the Lord guard and protect you, Mother. The postage will be prepaid.[10]

The author of *The Roguish World of Doctor Brinkley* estimates that Brinkley grossed $728,000 a year prescribing medicines that contained "little more than castor oil and aspirin." The program ran for 13 years.

Radio was only one part of the system. Brinkley's mode of operation was described by A. B. McDonald, a reporter with the *Kansas City Star*.

> The system begins with his radio. From morning to night it operates with orchestra, music, old fiddlers, singers and other entertainment.

> This entertainment corresponds to the banjo picker and singer of the street medical faker; it attracts the public and holds it for the ballyhoo of the faker himself and his lectures, the climax being the sale of his fake remedies.

> Brinkley's Ballyhoo is in his radio lectures each day. In these he describes the ailments of men, the symptoms of lost manhood and the sure remedy he has in his goat gland operation. He invites correspondence through the mails. . . . Once a person writes to Brinkley, he is doomed from then on to receive a deluge of pamphlets, testimonials and urging to go to Milford and be examined.[11]

In Brinkley's scheme, however, attracting an audience was only the beginning; the next step was to interest a sufficient number of listeners in receiving treatment at the hospital in Milford or at least in buying his patent medicines. Brinkley assigned this task to himself, taking to the air personally for a minimum of an hour and a half each day.

Brinkley's talks tended to be short on truth and logic and long on falsehoods and emotional appeals.[12] In a radio talk in 1929, Brinkley declared surgical operations perfectly safe in the hands of a competent surgeon but implied that early treatment of prostate trouble would aid recovery in every case. He claimed that tuberculosis of the prostate was increasing, as was massage of the prostate, concluding that prostate massage caused tuberculosis.

Brinkley sought credibility by using testimonials from satisfied customers. In a 1934 broadcast he turned to a testimonial letter from an "ordinary family man," a railroad employee, ill with headaches and back trouble, who could find no satisfaction with "big shot" doctors until:

> I figured this Doctor Brinkley was talking about something that had these other doctors bothered. I figured that Dr. Brinkley was writing these letters himself that he read over the air, and so, to check up, I took down the names and addresses of some of the men whose letter he read and wrote to 'em asking what they knew about it. To my surprise (sic), most of 'em answered me, and every mother's son that did answer was sure ace high for Dr. Brinkley and his treatment.[13]

The man went to Brinkley's hospital, received a "guaranteed" operation and returned to his wife and children a happier man. But he was puzzled by one thing:

> Now what I can't figure out is this: With this Dr. Brinkley pulling right down the main line, under full head of steam, and able to take care of all passengers, and right on schedule, why do so many of these regular members of the Doctor's Union try to run him in on a blind siding? That's what I don't understand.[14]

Brinkley insisted that the most qualified judges were the patients and the least qualified were legitimate medical doctors (the "doctors union"). Brinkley complimented the writer on the air for his intelligence and then launched an appeal for health and self preservation:

> Larry Reardon might have done just what a lot of men, who are listening to me tonight are doing—just sitting around worrying and suffering, and procrastinating and putting off coming to Dr. Brinkley, while your prostate keeps getting larger and larger, harder and harder, heading toward cancer; and your blood pressure gets higher and higher, and your old over-worked heart pounds louder and louder; and your poor kidneys are being abused and worked overtime trying to filter the poison out of your blood that the old diseased prostate keeps throwing into it.
>
> . . . Surely you will not keep postponing the reduction of your prostate until it is too late. You want to go through life, enjoy life, able to do your work—whatever kind it is. You want to go through your alloted span of life a whole man, not just a mere hollow shell, as you will if your prostate is cut out of you. If taken in time, it is useless for men to suffer the tortures of the condemned by prostate removal. Doctors of medicine used to think that when the prostate became infected, the only thing to do was to operate and remove it. . . . Dr. Brinkley set to work to discover some means of sufficiently reducing the enlarged and infected prostate and to clear the infection out of it . . .[15]

"Larry Reardon" was a name used by Brinkley to "protect" the man's identity. He treated more than 16,000 patients during his career at a gross income estimated to have exceeded 12 million dollars.[16] Brinkley claimed to have received 3000 letters a day as a result of his broadcasts, and *Radio Digest* awarded Brinkley a gold cup for running the most popular radio station in the United States. In another nationwide popularity poll, Brinkley collected 256,827 ballots, four times more than the nearest personality runnerup.

In 1930 the *Kansas City Star* began a series exposing Brinkley's profitable empire. The mounting campaigns against Brinkley by medical authorities and the *Star* took their toll on two fronts: the Kansas Medical Society issued formal notice on April 29, 1930 of its intentions to hold hearings on the revocation of Brinkley's medical license. Five days later, the Federal Radio Commission scheduled a hearing on the revocation of his broadcasting license.

Hearings on the broadcasting license convened on May 20, 1930. Although Brinkley boasted of plans to reserve an entire train to carry 1000 supporters to Washington with him,[17] only 35 persons made the trip.[18] The Federal Radio Commission charged Brinkley engaged in point-to-point communication illegally and that in advertising his medical remedies on the radio, he had perpetuated a fraud upon the public. Brinkley presented live witnesses and sworn affidavits that his treatments had been successful. He argued further that the Federal Radio Commission was trying to censor in violation of the Radio Act of 1927.[19]

When his broadcasting and medical licenses were in serious jeopardy Brinkley turned his eyes to the governship of Kansas, announcing his candidacy on September 23, 1930. During his first political campaign for the Governor of Kansas, Brinkley campaigned by radio four hours a day.[20] Francis Chase reported that KFKB was "opened wide to Brinkley's political orations," and that he "used radio mercilessly in his campaign to educate his followers to write in his name correctly on the ballot." [21] Brinkley would say: "Now friends, be sure that you don't write on the ballot the words, Doctor Brinkley, or John Brinkley or even John R. Brinkley. You must write this down as I say it—J. R. Brinkley, and don't put no M.D. after it." [22]

On Brinkley's radio station, campaign slogans saturated the schedule: "Let's pasture the goats on the statehouse lawn." "Clean Out, Clean Up and Keep Kansas Clean." "Only you and God will be in that voting booth." [23]

Brinkley's platform was: lower taxes, free medical care to the indigent, old age pensions for the blind and those who could not work, and a workingman's compensation law. He toured Kansas, speaking at fairs, picnics and rallies. KFKB entertainers went with him, performing such songs as *Kiss Me, The Wreck of Old 97, The Man of the Hour.* Occasionally his four-year-old son Johnny Boy would sing "Happy Birthday" to the children in the audience just as he did on the radio; or Mrs. L. McChesney, the "Tell Me A Story Lady," would tell the children a story. Brinkley would often be accompanied by a brass band and an old-time preacher who introduced him calling attention to his Christian virtues, his upstanding honesty and his dedication to public service. Then as uniformed nurses from his hospital passed out pamphlets to the audience, Brinkley would say: "The Democrats are saying the Republicans are crooked and no good and should be thrown out of office. The Republicans say the same thing about the Democrats. Why shouldn't you vote for me? I belong to neither party." [24] The rally ended with a prayer and a hymn.

If the will of the people had ruled in 1930, John R. Brinkley might have become Governor of Kansas. The final official count was Harry Woodring, Democrat 217,171; Frank Haucke, Republican 216,920; John R. Brinkley, Independent, 183,278.[25] Brinkley estimated that 50,000 votes had been discounted because his name had not been written in correctly upon the ballot. The *Chicago Daily News* said that somewhere between 10,000 and 50,000 votes for Brinkley had not been counted.[26] Others estimated between 25,000 and 30,000 votes for Brinkley were thrown out.[27]

The Federal Radio Commission voted 3-2 to deny Brinkley's

application for license renewal in June. He appealed the decision to the Federal Court of Appeals in Washington, D.C., but on February 2, 1931, the court upheld the Commission. The *Kansas City Times* announced January 22, 1931, that KFKB had been sold to the Farmer's and Banker's Insurance Company for $90,000.[28]

Brinkley turned to the task of saving his license to practice medicine in Kansas. He lost it on June 15, 1935, when the U.S. District Court at Topeka upheld the Medical Board on every point.[29]

During the Kansas gubernatorial campaign of 1932—the second time that Brinkley ran for governor—Brinkley was confined to buying time on other broadcasting stations in Kansas, having lost his license. He equipped a Chevrolet truck, called Ammunition Train No. 1 (there was no number two), with electronic equipment. On at least two occasions, his sound truck became a remote broadcasting unit and was connected to radio stations. The truck often played transcribed speeches by Brinkley to audiences while the doctor was campaigning in person elsewhere, usually accompanied by his old KFKB entertainers.[30]

In 1932 Brinkley, with his name printed upon the ballot, again ran a strong third. The results: A. M. Landon, Republican 278,581; H. H. Woodring, Democrat 272,944; J. R. Brinkley, Independent 244,607.[31]

By early 1931, Brinkley had devised still another broadcasting scheme: he would broadcast to the United States from across the border in Mexico by remote control from Milford.

When the United States government was aware of his intent the Department of State indicates that American diplomats tried to dissuade the Mexican government from granting Brinkley a broadcast license.[32] But the Mexicans had been excluded from talks between the United States and Canada over the allocation of frequencies and were not amenable to cooperate.[33] They licensed Brinkley's radio station XER at Villa Acuna, Mexico at 735 kHz with a power ranging somewhere between 75,000 and 500,000 watts.[34] The station went on the air in October 1931.

Telephone line charges from Milford to Mexico for the remote operation amounted to $100,000 per year. Brinkley moved his medical facility to Del Rio, Texas in November 1933 just across the border from XER.

Brinkley found little relief in Mexico from his troubles. In the ten years he operated XER and its successor XERA, he was harassed by Mexican authorities. In March 1931 the Mexican Immigration Department barred Brinkley from entering Mexico for any reason.[35] Brinkley merely telephoned broadcasts to the station from a remote studio inside the United States while he shifted some of the XER stock to Mexican authorities. The Mexican Department of Communications decided shortly that XER was operating within Mexican law and it remained on the air. In 1934, the Mexicans fined the owners of XER 600,000 pesos for illegally broadcasting medical advertisements and broadcasting in English by remote control without a permit. When the fines were not paid, XER was forcibly removed from the air. Brinkley countered by selling XER to the Compania Mexicanna Radioifusora Fronteriza, S.A. on March 29, 1934.[36] One judge ruled that the new company was not liable for the fine, another judge suspended the sale.[37] On November 17,1935, XERA, licensed to the Compania Radiodifusora Fronteriza, S.A., went on the air, replacing XER.[38] Brinkley still was in control of the station.

In 1937 the Mexicans placed an embargo on XERA but they were unable to expropriate the station until 1941. By that time, three international radio conferences had taken up the discussion of problems caused by Brinkley and other operators along the Mexico-U.S. border.

The impact of the Kansas broadcaster on regulation of radio was extensive. His defense of his KFKB license established the illegality of point-to-point communication in public broadcasting. Brinkley's charge that the commission was censoring his programs by looking into the content of the programs on KFKB was denied by a federal court, establishing another tenant in broadcasting law. In addition the Brinkley Mexican operation—along with that of another American border broadcaster Norman Baker—established a law which sought to control the production of programs for border stations. The success of XER gave Mexico leverage in negotiations with the United States to be recognized in international radio agreements.

He was a fountainhead of programming ideas and was a pioneer in new uses of radio for commercial gain. He gained grudging admiration from many of his adversaries including William Allen White who wrote: "Poor Brinkley, if only his head and his heart had been screwed on right."

86

Thomas W. Hoffer

TNT BAKER: RADIO QUACK

ON THE OLD bridge joining the State of Illinois with the Iowa river town of Muscatine, automobile traffic across the Mississippi was heavy. As dusk approached, the toll keeper could easily make out the long line of headlights streaming to the top of the bluff on the Muscatine side. There, on "KTNT Hill" nearly 32,000 persons gathered to watch Norman Baker and his medical wizards.

Days before the May 10, 1930 event, Baker told his midwest radio audience that he was going to show them the Baker cancer treatments. He was going to demonstrate that cancer was curable and give them some cheap thrills. One patient stepped forward. The treatment was administered. Another told the audience that her voice had been a mere whisper when she came to The Baker Institute; now she could speak clearly. Finally, a bandaged old man sat down in a chair on the platform. The crowd drew nearer. A Baker Institute physician removed the dressing and with a scapel he cut deep into the smelling flesh on the head of Mandus Johnson. Mr. Johnson leaned forward to show the top portion of his skull. The crowd gasped; someone fainted. Mr. Baker walked up to the microphone and told them that Mandus Johnson was at last cured of cancer.

When this event occurred, Norman Baker had been broadcasting for about five years on KTNT, a Muscatine, Iowa radio station which he said meant "Know The Naked Truth." Baker was one of the early "eccentrics" using radio to merchandise mail order goods and private opinions in an era when radio regulation was still unsettled. With a background in vaudeville (1897–1910) and business (1910–1924) he began regular programming on KTNT in late November 1925, mainly to promote his Calliaphone ("The newest Musical Tone in 40 Years") and mail order enterprises. Baker was 43 years old in 1925 when he started his personable radio talks, billed as "Mr. Baker, Himself." From 1925 to 1931, largely through the use of KTNT, he built a thriving group of business enterprises including a mail order house, auto service stations, cafes, a listener magazine, a daily newspaper and the Baker Institute, which had as its motto, "Cancer Is Curable." Despite increasing opposition among city officials, Baker's radio talks drew hundreds to Muscatine for his Sunday afternoon broadcast vaudeville performances on "KTNT Hill." *Radio Broadcast* in June 1927, observed:

> . . . From the Middle-west come many complaints regarding certain undesirable broadcasting stations which do nothing but inflict atrocious direct advertising upon listening audiences. Some of these stations are of considerable power and we have been able to hear them for short periods. The surprising thing about these disgraces is that the bargain corsets and harnesses which they offer are purchased by numerous dull-witted listeners who are thereby filling with numerous shekels the coffers of these miserable ether polluters . . .[1]

Most of Baker's mail order wares were obtained from various suppliers who put his name or the trade name "Tangley" on the sacks of flour, canned goods, first aid kits, radio receivers, coffee, brooms, alarm clocks, pig meal, mattresses, batteries and tires.[2]

When uncertainty over Herbert Hoover's authority to regulate radio broadcasting increased by mid-1926, Baker's radio talks included more editorials and personal attacks, airing the laundry of Muscatine politics to Iowa listeners. His occasional targets included the editor and publisher of the *Muscatine Journal*. A listener complained to Secretary of Commerce Hoover,

> . . . and he said Monday night, that it would be well for them to stay at home with their own wives and not visit other men's wives.[3]

By 1927, Baker's attacks also struck the American Telephone and Telegraph Company, the Federal Radio Commission, and the American Medical Association, whom he addressed as the "Medical Octopus." His talks contained homespun advice against immunization for smallpox in the Muscatine schools.

> . . . Yesterday . . . he talked about the horrors of vaccination . . . Told people how foolish they were to insist on tubercular tested milk, condemned one principal in one of the city schools in Muscatine, because of the fact that during a recent scarlet fever epidemic, she sent a child home because he was not vaccinated, and was counted a carrier. . . . No one escapes his tongue. Tonight I understand he is to "pan" our county officials because the sheriff has refused to give him a gun permit.[4]

By 1928, Baker survived a challenge to his KTNT frequency based on "public service" grounds and the public criticism concerning the content of his radio talks. Federal Radio Commissioner H. A. Bellows wrote Iowa Senator Smith Brookhart, who intervened in Baker's behalf, largely because KTNT extended airtime to the Senator.

> . . . Most of our correspondence regarding this station (KTNT) is from Iowa listeners who say that its service is a disgrace and want it completely taken off the air.[5]

But, the Federal Radio Commission was extremely reluctant to revoke licenses on the basis of broadcast content. The Radio Act of 1927 specifically stated that the Commission could not censor. Meanwhile, Baker had increased his radio staff to include a vaudeville comedy team called "Daffy and Gloomy," two blackfaced clowns hosting a children's program; but most of his employees were connected with the burgeoning mail order business.

Baker demonstrated his deft ability at saying one thing and doing another more than once. During the 1928 election campaign, he contracted with the Democratic National Committee to broadcast political programs for Al Smith. He turned the Democratic time schedules over to Republican representatives indicating that his political sympathies were with Herbert Hoover.

> I am going on the air with about one hour's talk each night after their (Democratic) talk is over and will do all I can to break down this campaign.[6]

The Democratic National Committee was furious when Baker's tactics were discovered.

> MANY COMPLAINTS RECEIVED DEMOCRATIC NATIONAL COMMITTEE RE INTOLERANT RELIGIOUS PROPAGANDA EMANATING FROM YOUR STATION AGAINST SMITH. REPETITION OF SUCH SUBJECT MATTER GROUND FOR CANCELLATION REMAINING FARM NETWORK SCHEDULES. SCOTT HOME BOWEN INC.[7]

Mr. Baker considered the telegram a compliment ". . . as to the force and power of KTNT." [8]

In early 1929, Baker imported two assistants from the Charles Othello Ozias cancer clinic in Kansas, considered by the American Medical Association to be a nest of quacks. Recognizing the utility of KTNT to promote a promising "medical business" Baker requested a power increase for his station but the FRC refused.

Baker's early afternoon radio talks "panned" the use of aluminum utensils, and advertised the Baker Institute, which now "cured" appendicitis, goiter and cancer ("without radium, x-ray or the knife"). His remedy for appendicitis was merely to apply a hot water bottle and "penetrating oil" to the painful spot, and the appendicitis would "unkink itself" by the next morning.[9] Baker continued to hammer away at the "radio trust," public utilities, aluminum utensils, tuberculin testing of cattle, the *Muscatine Journal* and the American Medical Association, whom he referred to as "The Amateur Meatcutters of America." For him "M.D." stood for "More Dough."

By 1930, the American Medical Association, *The Muscatine Journal*, the Iowa State Medical Society, and the State of Iowa began to gather evidence against Baker in an effort to persuade the Federal Radio Commission not to renew the license of KTNT, Baker's most important medium. The AMA Bureau of Investigation circulated pamphlets about medical quackery including the activities of Norman Baker, Harry Hoxsey and Dr. John R. Brinkley.

KTNT remained the center of Baker's propaganda efforts by parading patients to the microphone for testimonials and an abusive two-month campaign to persuade Muscatine residents to cancel their subscriptions to the *Muscatine Journal*. About 10% of 8,000 did. Shorthand stenographers, hired by the Muscatine County Medical Society, listened to Baker's talks to gather evidence.

. . . You doctors of Muscatine all the time hollering about deaths. One of you doctors got 11 deaths credited to you—more than I got with the thousands of patients . . . I counted them from the records of the courthouse . . . Why don't you cure your people instead of planting them in the graveyard? [10]

On Friday night, April 9, 1930, Baker and Hoxsey were in the radio station building atop "KTNT Hill." A car drove up and stopped. Mr. C. E. White, keeper of the Iowa-Illinois toll bridge, a few hundred feet away saw the action. A dog barked. Hoxsey went toward the window, peeking over the sill in time to hear gunfire. He saw three men. More gunshots were exchanged after Hoxsey drew out his revolver. The next morning, blood stains were discovered on the grass with evidence that the attackers dragged their partner away apparently wounded by Hoxsey. The Associated Press circulated the story. With the publication of the AMA editorial condemning Brinkley and Baker a few days later, there was some speculation that the AMA hired henchmen to finish off Baker and Hoxsey but Baker only said that the editorial might have prejudiced others against him. He did use the incident, through innuendo, to build more credibility in his propaganda about "persecution" by the AMA. Within three days, KTNT was turned into an armed camp, with hired guards patrolling the grounds, night lighting of the station exterior, and a machine gun set up near the entrance.[11]

The *Des Moines Register* investigated the Institute and reported that Baker's broadcast claims about curing cancer were false. Baker retorted by calling the paper ". . . cowardly, contemptible and dirty. . ."

To counter the unfavorable publicity, Baker staged outdoor "medical demonstrations." On May 10, 1930 the top portion of Mandus Johnson's head was removed and displayed to onlookers while Baker praised his physicians. The daytime radio talks continued, singling out Iowa Attorney General John Fletcher. Baker said,

He is too damn cowardly to come in and see if we are curing cancer at the Baker Institute; he is too cowardly to do it. I say Fletcher is one of the biggest cowards that ever drew breath in the State of Iowa and held a political job . . .[12]

The second medical show on May 30, 1930 drew an estimated 50,000 persons to Muscatine.

In September 1930, while Baker and Hoxsey were being tried together in the State of Iowa action against the Institute, Baker denounced his "partner", Hoxsey, over KTNT.

. . . In fact officials have been advised the prohibition officers have his name as a frequenter of road houses in this vicinity. . .[13]

Hoxsey later left Muscatine and eventually settled in Texas on some land a patient had given him in exchange for "medical" services. He struck oil and retired a millionaire.

While Baker's radio editorials spread to the pages of his new *Midwest Free Press* the Attorney General of Iowa obtained a successful appeal to the State of Iowa Supreme Court, reversing the earlier decision clearing Baker of practicing medicine without a license. To solve that problem, Baker leased his entire Muscatine hospital to a licensed physician.

In Washington, D.C., by February 1931, the Circuit Court of Appeals affirmed the FRC decision not to renew Dr. Brinkley's license for KFKB, thereby settling the Commission's authority to review past programming practices as an index of future performance. The FRC held hearings on Baker's KTNT in October 1930 and it seemed only a matter of time after the Brinkley decision that the KTNT license would not be renewed.

While the final decision was being deliberated, Baker involved himself in what was later called the "Cedar County Cow War" near Cedar Rapids, Iowa, which started in March 1931. Farmers were increasingly upset with the practice of having their cattle injected with tuberculin germs to determine if cattle were diseased. If the symptoms were present the cattle were promptly removed for slaughter. For those hard pressed to meet mortgage payments during the depression such practices contributed to rising frustrations among the rural folk. Baker, in a series of radio talks on the subject, fanned the smoldering dissension. Farmer's associations were independently formed and generally condemned the TB tests as inconclusive. In March, at the tiny rural community of Tipton, Iowa, 1500 farmers gathered at the Mitchell farm to prevent the state veternarian from completing his inoculations of suspected cattle. Baker reminded his listeners that ". . . the medical trust now takes in cattle victims as well as human beings." [14] On March 19, 4000 farmers took possession of the state house in Des Moines to present their position to the legislature.

On March 5, 1931, the FRC hearing examiner made his decision denying a renewal to KTNT; affirmed by the Commission on June 5, 1931. Baker gave his last talk over KTNT on June 12, 1930, before sign off. Complaining about high printing costs for the appeal, Baker attempted to enlist President Hoover's "help" and intervention, but the tactic was unsuccessful.

Baker, since early summer 1931, had traveled throughout Iowa to gain political support for KTNT's renewal; he spoke often of the farmer's plight and emphasized the bovine tuberculin inoculation of cattle as an appealing issue. Eventually, the crisis subsided.

In order to build a base for electioneering in 1932, he started a farmer's organization, but internal dissension involving Baker's personal ambitions limited its appeal to 10 dues paying members. In the meantime the *Midwest Free Press* became a weekly tabloid facing increasing demands from creditors.

Baker turned his attention to the pending lawsuit against the AMA; he was attempting to collect $600,000 from the association for alleged libel. The AMA successfully defended itself by demonstrating that Baker's "model" patients used for publicity purposes were either dead within five years of treatment or did not have what was medically defined as cancer in the first place. The AMA prevailed, but Baker managed to translate the trial results into favorable support among the gullible "common folks."

After the verdict and some haggling with his attorneys over their fees, Baker left for Mexico in March to build a high power transmitter at Nuevo Laredo. While there, the attorney general of Iowa discovered Baker's subterfuge of the leasing arrangement for the Baker Institute and other evidence indicating that Baker still controlled the hospital. This was considered tantamount to practicing medicine without a license. The Supreme Court of Iowa placed Baker in contempt and declared him a fugitive from justice. When his presence in Texas was discovered extradition proceedings were started. Fortunately for Baker, it was a short drive from his Laredo, Texas office to the XENT transmitter site 12 miles south of Nuevo Laredo.

The station was on a 75-acre plot. Immediately, Baker encountered electric power, labor and political problems which he solved with varying degrees of success. The *Midwest Free Press*, in Muscatine, still printed his weekly column and in it he promised to campaign against President Hoover largely because the President refused to intervene in the KTNT matter. The State Department sent an envoy to see Baker who reaffirmed to his superiors Baker's intent to finish XENT construction in time for the 1932 campaign. XENT would start from a 75 kw power plant base with additions enabling a 750 kw transmission when completed. Baker made friends with influential military men in the Mexican government and promised Spanish language programming attuned to the Mexican government's needs for educational and political messages.

The U.S. State Department through its ambassador in Mexico City attempted to convince Mexican authorities to delay XENT. On October 14, 1932, William R. Castle, the U.S. Under Secretary of State, wrote to Ambassador J. Reuben Clark Jr.:

> . . . It is believed that he can do a lot of damage as cranks of his kind always have a large following in our great country. Obviously the matter is very delicate but if there is any way in which you could bring about delay in the opening of the station for a month it would be a real help . . . [15]

Ambassador Clark's efforts were not successful. However, a new August 1932 Mexican broadcasting law required all stations to broadcast in Spanish; the border stations owned by Brinkley, Baker and others were exempted to some degree. Baker was required to broadcast about 25% of his programming in Spanish. Telephone connection to the transmitter across the border was prohibited but Baker planned to record his talks on discs in Laredo for replay on the other side of the border.

The 1932 elections passed and XENT was still silent due to technical problems, often directly caused by Baker when, for example, he poured cistern water into the cooling plant thereby corroding the most expensive parts.

Increasing apprehension concerning interference between high power Mexican and U.S. stations, and the border "renegades" beaming programs to U.S. and audiences from their Mexican sanctuary, created the conditions for the July 1933 North and Central American Regional Radio Conference in Mexico City. The Mexicans wanted more clear channels; U.S. broadcasters were reluctant to relinquish them. While limited agreements resulted from the conference, nothing was done concerning Brinkley's station, XER, nor Baker's silent XENT. Upon reading the newspaper accounts of the conference, Baker wrote President Roosevelt complaining about " . . . malodorous attempts . . ." to persecute Norman Baker.[16]

Finally, in October 1933, XENT started regular programming. Baker's ad agency in Muscatine released the news.

> . . . We shall strive to arrange our programs to make them different from the average program. There is no other station in the world equipped with a Calliaphone, which will give our programs individuality and a distinction that will prove pleasing.[17]

With only 75 kw, the maximum power ever reached by XENT, Baker's political tirades were heard during the nighttime hours by loyal listeners in Iowa. Baker told his listeners about his new hospital in Laredo, Texas, and his projected plans for another in the Ozarks, at Eureka Springs, Arkansas. He said the postal authorities were inspecting his mail for possible violations of the pure food and drug laws but the "medicines" shipped from Muscatine to Laredo had no labels claiming "cancer cures." Listeners also heard Baker's hired astrologers and "staff psychologists" who offered free advice and special publications if the listener would simply mail a small fee. Many did. In 1934, about $3400 was received from listeners; in 1936, the amount increased to $19,000. The biggest grosses were derived from Baker's hospitals in Muscatine and Texas. Through a complicated financial and organizational arrangement involving the Baker hospitals, an advertising agency in Laredo, Texas, and CIA

Enterprises, the holding company for XENT in Mexico, funds from the medical "business" were filtered across the border in cash after 1934. All of the money was formally listed as "advertising income" to XENT. In 1934, a paltry $23,000 was recorded; by 1936, $190,000 went into Baker's pockets.[18] The amounts increased to $1,700,000 by 1939.

Congress, concerned about the increasing advertising and political content thundering from Mexico, incorporated section 325 (b) into the 1934 Communications Act. Border broadcasters were prohibited from using studios and remote lines or recording apparatus on the U.S. side of the border for broadcast from Mexico (or Canada) without authorization of the FCC. The border stations were interfering with several U.S. stations, and the lack of progress in the 1933 Regional Conference made the legislation one of the few remedies available to the U.S.

Baker's radio talks were liberally spread throughout the XENT program schedule which included live and recorded material such as Hawaiian, Calliaphone, country and western, Mexican; accordian, and organ musical programs. The station operated only at night with flexible sign-on and sign-off times. Mr. Baker recorded some of his talks in his Laredo, Texas office, in violation of 325 (b), and these were broadcast from XENT during the late night hours.

XENT initially broadcast 6½ hours nightly; by 1936, the schedule was expanded to 15½ hours from 5:30 p.m. to 9:00 a.m. In 1936, Baker started a new Iowa political campaign. The station was changed from 1115 to 910 kHz and created more co-channel interference with U.S. stations. Internal political reasons appeared to be more important to the Mexican government than "radio diplomacy" since XENT frequently rebroadcast the output of XEO, a station owned and operated by the Mexican National Revolutionary Party.[19]

XENT continued to promote Baker's hospitals in Muscatine, Laredo, and plans for a new facility in Arkansas. Dr. Albert T. Cook, a highly respected surgeon in Laredo, Texas, complained to the AMA in Chicago about Baker's growing appeal in Texas. Dissatisfied with the AMA response, Dr. Cook developed inside contacts at XENT with a view toward citing Baker for a violation of Section 325 (b) of the Communications Act. During that evolution, Baker returned to Iowa to face the charges against him concerning the operation of the Muscatine clinic. He also laid plans to run for the Republican nomination for U.S. Senator from Iowa but his hope was merely to draw enough votes from the other contenders so as to force the matter to a convention vote. Upon his arrival, Baker staged another medical show on July 14, 1935 and received more public attention. Five months later, an indictment was returned by a Muscatine jury charging Baker with practicing medicine without a license. In the interim, Baker returned to Mexico in time to discover a plot to destroy the XENT transmitter.

A disgruntled XENT engineer told Marvin Lucke, an announcer and one of Dr. Cook's informers, he was going to tear out the wiring of the transmitter. With the damage done and XENT temporarily silent, the engineer and others quickly drove to the home of Dr. Cook, closely followed, in the style of a western chase scene, by Baker's lieutenants. By telephone, Baker prodded the Laredo county sheriff to surround the Cook home as the fleeing saboteurs drove up but no arrests were made. Within two weeks, XENT was on the air and Baker promptly "blasted" Dr. Cook and the AMA. By 1936, the *Midwest Free Press* filed for bankruptcy with several lawsuits initiated by creditors still pending. One of Baker's friends in Muscatine started another newspaper, *The Times*, in which Baker's senatorial candidacy was trumpeted to a limited audience.

Just before the campaign, in April 1936, Baker and others were indicted for violating the Communications Act involving the recording and transportation of content into Mexico for broadcast to the United States. This time Baker and two others spent a few days in jail until bail was arranged. Undaunted, Baker returned to Iowa to begin his spring 1936 campaign for the nomination. WOC in Davenport, at the last minute, decided not to allow him time which Baker had contracted for a few weeks earlier; a lawsuit was started. In June, another medical show was staged in Muscatine with "cured" patients paraded and political speeches given. But the June 1936 primary vote went to the incumbent Senator L. J. Dickinson. Baker placed fourth in a field of six candidates for the Republican nomination. His partner, Harry Fisher, placed second in his statewide race.

The criminal proceedings against Baker in Texas, involving the violation of Section 325 (b), went to trial on April 17, 1937. Baker and others were convicted but on appeal the convictions were reversed.

> The reversal ruling included an interpretation declaring the section concerning recording for foreign consumption as unconstitutional. The U.S. Supreme Court refused certiorari freeing Baker and leaving the constitutionality of Section 325 (b) in doubt.[20]

Baker attended to his new hospital in Eureka Springs while his recorded talks were broadcast over XENT from Mexico. More of them contained an anti-semitic tone, accusing Jewish doctors of being responsible for Baker's lack of recognition for his work in the field of cancer. A listener paraphrased Baker's remarks broadcast in 1938.

. . . That the Jews are killing people by their claiming to have a
cure for cancer and that all of them ought to be taken back to Germany and let Hitler do with them what he wants to . . .[21]

By July 1937, Baker's headquarters were moved from Mexico to
Eureka Springs. Business in Eureka Springs improved and Baker's
"messengers" made regular trips to Mexico turning over their cash to
the XENT "management." The Federal charges involving deception
with mailed advertising matter were tried in another emotion-packed
setting, Little Rock, Arkansas, during January 1940. Baker's lawyers
argued "good faith" as a defense. The verdict and subsequent sentence sent Baker and others to jail for four years. The Baker hospitals
were closed. During Baker's imprisonment XENT was operated by a
trusted subordinate, Thelma Yount, and in 1944 the station became
silent after the Mexican government did not renew the license. The
station property was sold to an unknown party for $100,000. Follow-
ing his release from prison in July 1944 Baker purchased an old
yacht and retired to Florida.

On September 14, 1958, Baker quietly died in his sleep following a stroke in a Miami hospital. Within hours of his death, a loyal
lieutenant rushed to his yacht *Niaguara,* and according to previous
instructions, ignited most of the remaining files of the Baker Enterprises. No one knew what became of the money Baker's messengers delivered to Mexico as a result of the Eureka Springs business
venture. No one knew or at least no one was talking. Baker, a prolific
letter writer, accidentally or intentionally overlooked one important
instrument, his will. Only about $60,000 was discovered in the estate
which was distributed among the Baker Foundation shareowners
and surviving kin.

87

Robert H. Stern

REGULATORY INFLUENCES UPON
TELEVISION'S DEVELOPMENT: EARLY YEARS
UNDER THE FEDERAL RADIO COMMISSION

IN 1928 the Federal Radio Commission, then in the second year of
its existence, reported that advances which recently had been made

American Journal of Economics and Sociology, Vol. 22 (1963), pp. 347–362.

in television were threatening to create "serious problems." The reference was to attempts that were being made to persuade the agency to authorize the initiation of a public broadcasting service for this medium.

Early the next year, evidently not yet satisfied that it knew enough to deal definitively with broadcast-band television, the commission held a scheduled public hearing and a few days after the hearing the agency announced it would continue to issue experimental licenses for operations under the same conditions as before.

In May 1929, it ordered that all experimental licenses would be issued for one year only, that each be required at a hearing to show:

1. That he intended to engage in *bona fide* experimental operations related to television,
2. That he had a definite program of research which was sufficiently advanced to require radio transmissions for further advances.
3. That he had apparatus suitably developed to be placed in operation.
4. That he had adequate financial responsibility, engineering personnel and sufficient equipment and facilities to carry out a research program . . .[13]

Under this policy the agency denied a large number of requests for licenses from applicants who appeared to be primarily interested in gaining a commercial foothold in television broadcasting rather than in carrying on experiments looking to its technical advancement.[14] It did not, however, enforce the policy as rigorously with regard to the requirement of a showing of previous experimentation as it did in respect to a requirement of valid intent.[15] This was perhaps owing to a reluctance to stack the deck in favor of the entrenched interests in the radio industry, or to appear to be doing so. By the end of the decade the movement toward commercial exploitation and the accompanying publicity process were gaining considerable momentum, and there was being projected to the public a vision of television convincing in its sharpness and detail. The stock market crash of October, 1929, did not shatter the vision; indeed it became for a time more poignant amidst disillusionment. From a wreckage of bright hopes this, at least, was carried into the next decade intact.

In 1930 several demonstrations were held, the reporting of which probably served to sustain confidence that steady progress was being made.[18]

Sometime in 1931 occurred the brightest moment in television's false dawn. Until then there had been, over a period of some four years, a more or less steadily increasing amount of attention devoted to it in the press and an intensifying sense of its imminent readiness. Expectations had been heightened by publicity, and publicity gen-

erated by expectations. Publicity and the entrepreneurial impulse
likewise had worked reciprocally upon each other. As long as commercialization of the art seemed ready to begin soon, parties hoping
to profit from it vied for attention to their own contributions to its development; others, recognizing that the advent of television would
pose a potential threat of technological obsolescence to fields where
they were already established, hastened to make for themselves a
place in it. When the dawning proved illusory a reaction of considerable severity occurred. The vision of television faded rapidly from
the public view, and numerous ventures for its development were
abandoned or curtailed. The *New York Times Index* for 1931 lists
about 100 items on television, for 1932 it has 41 items, for 1933 it has
23, and for 1934 it has 19. The *Readers' Guide to Periodical Literature* for the period 1929–32 carries 65 references, and 28 for
1932–35.[26]

Some of the causes of this reaction seem fairly clear. Where a
number of receivers were distributed during the high point of the
enthusiasm, as in Chicago, the public was disappointed in both
image quality and content. Although some attempts were made to
develop the techniques of live studio broadcasts by giving the camera a certain flexibility and breadth of vision, most stations limited
their transmissions to the faces of only one or two performers. Such
programs, the commission pointed out in its 1932 report, fell "far
short of what the public has been led to expect in the way of entertainment," especially considering that television would have to stand
comparison with talking pictures, the technical quality of which had
been improved steadily since their introduction a few years earlier.[27]
And it was not as if, while still in a stage of crude technical development, television could be put to important uses as a practical communications medium, as radio had been used in the pre-broadcasting
era. No such vital role immediately awaited television; its initial use
would be to entertain the public. For that, as *Fortune* pointed out
several years later in discussing the failure of television to take hold
during the early Thirties, novelty alone was not enough.[28]

The economic blight of the period as it wore on and worsened,
spread its pall also over television. For a time, as noted above, the
medium had attracted the more attention for its being an apparently
bright prospect in an otherwise bleak economic landscape; but as the
depression deepened, instead of intensifying their efforts toward the
improvement of the art when its current state of development proved
not good enough for commercial success, many companies that had
been active in the field were forced to abandon it or were pinched
into retrenchment. Regarding the impact of the depression upon the
radio industry, Maclaurin has noted that even such large, well-
financed organizations as General Electric, Westinghouse and the

Telephone Company cut their research budgets drastically, and that "in a period in which the emphasis . . . was in reducing costs, it was the research and development work on new products which suffered particularly." [29]

By 1933 a number of companies were reported by the Federal Radio Commission to have given up their licenses in the high-frequency band. It appeared, the agency said, as if the very high frequencies would be the final locus for television. In these frequencies, image quality was being steadily improved. Television was not regarded, however, as having progressed to a point which would justify the adoption of uniform technical standards. The final report of the body to Congress includes the observation that "although much progress has been made in the laboratory, visual broadcasting is still in the experimental stage." [30]

Of the influence of government upon the development of television in its early years, the first thing that should be said is that this influence began to be exercised in a pretty definite way before television came to be explicitly a matter of governmental concern. The legislative framework had been established and the regulatory pattern of control was already crystallizing when the problems of television were first seriously encountered by the responsible agency. The environment of early regulation, moreover, served to reinforce what had been a dominant influence on television's career before such control was instituted. This influence was the example of the spectacular success enjoyed by radio broadcasting upon its appearance at the beginning of the Twenties. The legislation which embraced television unawares was a product of the difficulties that had beset broadcasting because of its very success, and the regulatory scene that confronted television was a scene dominated by the business of serving broadcasting's needs. For many years thereafter—all of the period covered by this account—television was regulated by a body that had little time to devote to it, being preoccupied with other matters, and which possessed only very limited resources of expertness for coping with the problems arising from its peculiar technical character.

If over a period of several years the most profound governmental influences upon television's development were of the general charactershaping kind associated with the fact of radio broadcasting's dominance and the apparent, if tacit, assumption by government officials that television should naturally and properly grow as its image, the immediate and consciously applied influences guiding its development at this time were based upon considerations which were, willy-nilly, mainly technical. When allocations decisions had to be made there were, to be sure, broad social criteria hovering in the background. That television was worth developing was the inarticulate premise of any frequency assignment; and beyond that there needed to be some thought given to its needs relative to those of other services. But the controlling bases of decision were, nevertheless, the technical imperatives related to its own physical nature. Likewise, questions that arose early in respect to the authorization of certain systems for public use and the adoption of uniform system standards, though they were perceived to have ramifications beyond the purely technical, were in fact dealt with in the early years of regulation mainly by reference to considerations of technical adequacy and potentiality.

Whether on balance the regulatory authority was a force significantly hastening television's technical development or materially retarding it during the latter Nineteen Twenties and the early Nineteen Thirties, the record does not, in the opinion of this writer, unambiguously show. Pretty clearly it was not government but the tribulations of experience that caused the shift of attention from mechanical to electronic methods of image scanning, which proved later to be the key breakthrough in the technical advance. But a necessary concomitant of this was the movement upward on the frequency range where wider channels could be utilized. It may be said, at the least, that the commission, faced as it was by a lively demand by other services for television's lower experimental frequencies (i.e., in the high-frequency range of the spectrum), eagerly facilitated this upward movement. Earlier, the commission's encouragement of the exploration of the same high frequencies as a way of getting television away from the crowded broadcast band seems to have had similar reasons behind it. Again, what appears to have been a relatively strict application of a licensing policy which insisted that an applicant show intention and ability to advance the art technically as a condition of his grant may have helped to speed development by restricting the available channels to those who had some contribution to make. Finally, what of the weight and direction of influence upon development which was exerted by the Federal Radio Commission through its unwillingness to sanction various attempts to launch a regular television program service or to authorize the adoption of uniform transmission standards necessary for such service on a large scale?

One can only conjecture what the agency's course of action might have been if it had been confronted, say in 1930 or 1931, by a concerted drive on the part of the industry, accompanied by evidences of a genuine ground swell of public enthusiasm, for the inauguration of commercial television. Actually the agency seems to have escaped any really severe testing of this kind, possibly because the strongest organization in the field by then, RCA, was not heavily committed to the attempt to exploit mechanical scanning techniques but was involving itself deeply instead in work on electronic scanning methods that were clearly still several years away from any marketable results. Nevertheless, in view of the intimate relationship of system development of this sort and the frequency assignment availabilities upon which its practicability must ultimately depend, the agency may be credited by its persistent encouragement of work in the higher—and yet higher—frequencies with having helped to prepare its own avenue of escape, and with serving the public well thereby.

88

J. H. Ryan

RADIO CENSORSHIP "CODE"

PERHAPS THE MOST significant statement in the Code of Wartime Practices for American Broadcasters, issued in January of 1942 by the Office of Censorship is found in the second paragraph:

> ". . . and the following (Code) is intended to be helpful in systematizing cooperation on a voluntary basis during the period of emergency."

The Office shall merely act as a correlating branch of the broadcasters in the industry-wide effort to keep information of value to the enemy out of his hands.

We have no fear that censorship, as we intend to practice it in the radio industry, will do anything but teach Americans again that the best kind of radio is free radio. Each broadcaster is on his honor and on his nettle to keep his listeners honestly informed, but to tell his enemies nothing. He will find a way to do it. No one will ever be able to censor his ingenuity.

> The Code—Effective Jan. 16, 1942 Herewith is the text of a war-time code of practice for radio broadcasters, as issued January 16, 1942, by the Office of Censorship, Byron Price, Director. Statement embodied with the code, is included:

In wartime it is the responsibility of every citizen to help prevent the enemy, insofar as possible, from obtaining war, navy, air or

Jack Alicoate (ed.), *The 1942 Radio Annual,* New York: *The Radio Daily,* 1942, pp. 67–73.

economic intelligence which might be of value to him and inimical to our national effort.

The broadcasting industry has enlisted with enthusiasm in the endeavor, and the following is intended to be helpful in systematizing cooperation on a voluntary basis during the period of the emergency. Two possibilities exist:

(1) Enemy exploitation of stations heard only within our borders, to expedite the work of saboteurs, and

(2) Enemy exploitation of stations heard internationally (both short and long wave) to transmit vital information.

All American stations desire to prevent such exploitation. The statement herewith set forth is presented under three headings:

(1) News Programs.
(2) Ad lib programs.
(3) Foreign language programs.

News Program

It must be remembered that all newspapers, magazines and periodicals are censored at our national borders. No such post-publication censorship is possible in radio. Scores of stations operating on all classifications of frequencies are heard clearly in areas outside the United States. These stations especially should exercise skill and caution in preparing news broadcasts.

It is requested that news falling into any of the following classifications be kept off the air, except in cases when the release has been authorized by appropriate authority.

Weather Reports

(1) *Weather reports.* This category included temperature readings, barometric pressures, wind directions, forecasts and all other data relating to weather conditions. Frequently weather reports for use on radio will be authorized by the United States Weather Bureau. This material is permissible. Confirmation should be obtained that the report actually came from the Weather Bureau. Special care should be taken against inadvertent references to weather conditions during sports broadcasts, special events and similar projects.

Information concerning road conditions, where such information is essential to safeguarding human life, may be broadcast when requested by a Federal, State or municipal source.

(2) *Troop movements.* The general character and movements of units of the United States Army, Navy and Marine Corps, or their personnel, within or without the continental limits of the United States; their location, identity or exact composition, equipment or strength; their destination, routes and schedules; their assembly for

embarkation or actual embarkation. Any such information regarding the troops of friendly nations on American soil. (The request as regards location and general character does not apply to training camps in the United States, nor to units assigned to domestic police duty.)

(3) *Ships.* The location, movements and identity of naval and merchant vessels of the United States and of other nations opposing the Axis powers and of personnel of such craft; the port and time of arrival of any such vessel; the assembly, departure or arrival of transports or convoys, the existence of mine fields or other harbor defenses; secret orders or other secret instructions regarding lights, buoys and other guides to navigators; the number, size, character and location of ships in construction, or advance information as to the date of launchings or commissionings; the physical setup of existing shipyards, and information regarding construction of new ones.

(4) *Planes.* The disposition, movements and strength of army and navy units. The time and location of corps graduations or the equipment strength of any training school.

New Inventions

(5) *Experiments.* Any experiments with war equipment or materials, particularly those relating to new inventions. Any news of the whereabouts of camouflaged objects.

(6) *Fortifications.* Any information regarding existing or projected fortifications of this country, any information regarding coastal defense emplacements or bomb shelters; location, nature or numbers of anti-aircraft guns.

(7) *Production.* Specific information about war contracts, such as the exact type of production, production schedules, dates of delivery, or progress of production; estimated supplies of strategic and critical materials available; or nationwide "round-ups" of locally-published procurement data except when such composite information is officially approved for publication.

Specific information about the location of, or other information about, sites and factories already in existence, which would aid saboteurs in gaining access to them; information other than that readily gained through observation by the general public, disclosing the location of sites and factories yet to be established, or the nature of their production. Any information about new or secret military designs, or new factory designs for war production.

(8) *Casualty lists.* Total or round figures issued by the Government may be handled. If there is special newsworthiness in the use of an individual name, such as that attending the release concerning Capt. Colin Kelly, it is permissible material. Stations should use own judgment in using names of important personages from their own

areas killed in action. The Government notifies nearest kin BEFORE casualty's name is released to the press.

(9) *Release of figures on selective service enrollments.*

Unconfirmed Reports

(10) *Unconfirmed reports.* Reports based on information from unidentified sources as to ship sinkings or land troops reverses or successes should not be used. In the event enemy claims have been neither confirmed nor denied by established authority, the story ordinarily should be handled without inclusion of specific information; there should be no mention of ship's name—only its classification; there should be no mention of army unit designation—just its general description (tank, artillery, infantry, etc.). Commentators, through sensible analyses of reports from enemy origins, stressing the obvious fallacies, can do much to correct any false impressions which might be created.

(11) *Communications.* Information concerning the establishment of new international points of communication should be withheld until officially released by appropriate federal authority.

(12) *General.* Information disclosing the new location of national archives, art treasures, and so on, which have been moved for safekeeping; damage to military and naval objectives, including docks, railroads, or commercial airports, resulting from enemy action; transportation of munitions or other war materials, including oil tank cars and trains; movements of the President of the United States, or of official military or diplomatic missions of the United States or of any other nation opposing the Axis powers—route, schedules, or destination, within or without the continental limits of the United States; movements of ranking army or naval officers and staffs on official business; movements of other individuals or units under special orders of the army, navy or State Department.

Summation: It should be emphasized that there is no objection to any of these topics *if officially released.* These restraints are suggested:

(1) Full and prompt obedience to all lawful requests emanating from constituted authorities. If a broadcaster questions the wisdom of any request, he should take it up with the Office of Censorship.

(2) Exercise of common sense in editing news, meeting new problems with sensible solutions. Stations should feel free at all times to call on the Office of Censorship for clarification of individual problems.

Ad Lib Programs

Certain program structures do not permit the exercise of complete discretion in pre-determining the form they will take on the air.

These are the ad lib or informal types of programs. Generally they fall into four classifications:

    (a) Request programs.

    (b) Quiz programs (effective Feb. 1).

    (c) Forums and interviews (*ad lib*).

    (d) Commentaries and descriptions (*ad lib*).

As experience dictates the need of changes, they will be made, and all stations notified. Stations should make certain that their program departments are fully acquainted with these provisions.

(a) *Request programs.* Certain safeguards should be adopted by the broadcaster in planning request programs. It is requested that no telephoned or telegraphed requests for musical selections be accepted for the duration of the emergency. It is also requested that all mail bearing requests be held for an unspecified length of time before it is honored on the air. It is suggested that the broadcaster stagger replies to requests. Care should be exercised in guarding against honoring a given request at a specified time.

Special note is made here of "lost and found" announcements and broadcast material of a similar nature. Broadcasters are asked to refuse acceptance of such material when it is submitted via telephone or telegraph by a private individual. If the case involves a lost person, lost dog, lost property or similar matter, the broadcaster is advised to demand written notice. It is suggested that care be used by station continuity departments in re-writing all such personal advertising. On the other hand, emergency announcements asked by police or other authorized sources may be accepted. Announcements bearing official authorization seeking blood donors, lost persons, stolen cars, and similar material may be accepted by telephone, but confirmation of the source is suggested.

It is requested that announcements of mass meetings not be honored unless they come from an authorized representative of an accredited Governmental or civilian agency. Such requests should be accepted only when submitted in writing.

(b) *Quiz program.* It is requested that all audience-participation type quiz programs originating from remote points, either by wire, transcription or shortwave, be discontinued, except as qualified hereinafter.

Any program which permits the public accessibility to an open microphone is dangerous and should be carefully supervised. Because of the nature of quiz programs, in which the public is not only permitted access to the microphone but encouraged to speak into it, the danger of usurpation by the enemy is enhanced. The greatest danger here lies in the informal interview conducted in a small group—10 to 25 people. In larger groups where participants are selected from a theatre audience for example, the danger is not so great.

Care in Small Crowds

Generally speaking, any quiz program originating remotely, wherein the group is small, and wherein no arrangement exists for investigating the background of participants, should be discontinued. Included in this classification are all such productions as man-on-the-street interviews, airport interviews, train terminal interviews, and so forth.

In all studio-audience type quiz shows, where the audience from which interviewees are to be selected numbers less than 50 people, program conductors are asked to exercise special care. They should devise a method whereby no individual seeking participation can be GUARANTEED PARTICIPATION.

(c) *Forums and interviews.* This refers specifically to forums in which the general public is permitted extemporaneous comment; to panel discussions in which more than two persons participate; and to interviews conducted by authorized employees of the broadcasting company. Although the likelihood of exploitation here is slight, there are certain forums during which comments are sought "from the floor," or audience, that demand cautious production.

(d) *Commentaries and descriptions.* (*Ad lib*). Special events reporters are advised to avoid specific reference to locations and structures in on-the-spot broadcasts following air raids or other enemy offensive action. Both such reporters and commentators should beware of using any descriptive material which might be employed by the enemy in plotting an area for attack.

THE BROADCASTER IN SUMMARY, IS ASKED TO REMEMBER THAT THERE IS NEED FOR EXTRAORDINARY CARE ESPECIALLY IN CASES WHERE HE OR HIS AUTHORIZED REPRESENTATIVE IS NOT IN FULL CONTROL OF THE PROGRAM.

Foreign Language Programs

It is requested that full transcripts, either written or recorded, be kept of all foreign language programs; it is suggested that broadcasters take all necessary precautions to prevent deviation from script by foreign language announcers and performers.

Miscellaneous

Broadcasters are asked merely to exercise restraint in the handling of news that might be damaging, for the Army behind the Army represents a great force in the war effort. Radio is advised to steer clear of dramatic programs which attempt to portray the horrors of combat; to avoid sound effects which might be mistaken for air raid alarms. Radio is one of the greatest liaison officers between the fighting front and the people. Its voice will speak the news first. It should speak wisely and calmly. In short, radio is endowed with a rich opportunity to keep America entertained and interested, and that opportunity should be pursued with vigor.

89

Richard J. Meyer

REACTION TO THE "BLUE BOOK"

TO SAY THAT the 1946 FCC Report *Public Service Responsibility of Broadcast Licensees* created a furor is perhaps an understatement. Most of the inflammation came from within the ranks of the broadcasting industry. There were both good and bad reactions from the press; the government also responded. The public, whose interests were also at stake, reacted with its usual lethargy. The industry's initial attack on the "Blue Book" in March 1946 was amazingly mild compared with later. The single factor which re-directed the industry's ire from an inconstant Commission to an individual scapegoat was the release of *Radio's Second Chance*, in April of the same year. This book, authored by Charles A. Siepmann, set off the delayed reaction to the "Blue Book" which "let slip the dogs of war."

Initial Reactions

Broadcasting magazine, spokesman for the industry, carried a summary of the "Blue Book," with its proposals and conclusions, four days after the release of the FCC report. The article began with the statement: "The Federal government is going into the radio program business." [1] In the same issue, Judge Justin Miller, president of the National Association of Broadcasters, began his attack by saying that "the report overlooks completely freedom of speech in radio broadcasting which was a primary consideration in the mind of Congress when it passed the Communications Act . . ." [2] The following week *Broadcasting* reported that most broadcasters were opposed to the "Blue Book," but the feeling was that "there was nothing to get alarmed about." [3]

In the edition of March 18, 1946, *Broadcasting* began its edito-

Journal of Broadcasting, Vol. VI, No. 4 (Fall 1962), pp. 295–312.

rial campaign against the "Blue Book" and its authors. This aggressive action continued, week after week, without cessation until June 17, 1946. Thereafter, sporadic attacks appeared on *Broadcasting's* editorial pages. In *Broadcasting's* first anti-"Blue Book" comment, the headline read: "F(ederal) C(ensorship) C(ommission)." The editorial went on to say that:

> . . . Radio censorship is here . . . The charter upon which it is based was issued ten days ago by the FCC under the title of *Public Service Responsibility of Broadcast Licensees.* To accept lightly that charter . . . one must be blind to the implications within the document itself, and to the devious methods which contrived it. It has been carefully polished by the FCC's rhetorical experts in an attempt to justify its purpose . . . It is as masterfully evasive as it is vicious . . . the issues it projects are larger than broadcasting as a medium, are as large . . . as the welfare of democracy. For the meddling of Government in the instruments which enlighted public opinion is contrary to the precepts of the Constitution, and rebuts the fundamental thinking of our leaders from Washington to Truman. . . .

The editorial compared the FCC's tactics of "innuendo" with that of Herman Goering in building up the German Air Force. It hinted that the men of the FCC wanted to multiply their power and influence. The assault continued:

> . . . It is against this instinct that extremely foresighted men documented American freedom in a Constitution that stands as our nation's bulwark against tyranny. Have we forgotten so soon the fanatical Pied Pipers of destruction who led the German and Italian people down a dismal road by the sweet sound of their treacherous voices on a radio which they programmed? . . .

The *coup de plume* commented about the "Blue Book" statement that a station must operate in the "public interest." It asked:

> . . . Who shall determine the public interest? Forget what it is, since no one successfully has defined it. Whatever it is, who shall measure it? Is it in the public interest that Congress should defeat the GI housing bill? . . . Or that *Esquire* should publish the Varga girls? No one man, and no seven men, can answer such questions. The public determines what is in its interest and rejects that which is not. The public has not rejected American radio. . . . There is more at stake than the ultimate pattern of American broadcasting. There is at stake the pattern of American life, and you can find that truth in the charred ruins of a chancellory in Berlin.[4]

Another trade publication, *Variety,* took an altogether opposite stand regarding the "Blue Book." In its editorial of March 13, 1946, *Variety* stated that:

. . . The first fact radio must face is that broadcasting is made possible only by the use of a public commodity. In the past the industry has only paid lip service to the responsibility inherent in its use of this commodity. . . . Slowly but surely, over the past few years, over-commercialization has won out. Good taste, development of original radio technique and cognizance of public service programming have gone by the board. . . . Obviously the industry has brought upon itself the FCC proposals by its abuses, which were permitted to gain momentum simply because of a lack of policing. And it's obvious too, in the regulations that the FCC now suggests, there will be no excessive Governmental interference. The constitutionality of control that regulates freedom of expression affords a wider interpretation than that construed by the NAB. For in voicing the cry against the threat to this fundamental freedom, the NAB is obscuring the issue by resorting to frantic flag-waving. The Constitution requires a broader reading today than it did a century and a half ago in order to encompass this new field of expression—radio. . . .

The *Variety* editorial continued by claiming that if the public had been sufficiently vigilant and had availed itself of its prerogatives, it could have made the broadcasters "toe the mark." The commentary pointed out that if the broadcasting industry itself had been "sufficiently enlightened to become aware that it was nearing the danger point," the industry could have taken the steps that would have made the "Blue Book" unnecessary. *Variety* concluded that:

. . . It's apparent now that the industry has not exercised self-government, either of its own volition or by public pressure. . . . The FCC recommendations as such could well stand as a primer for the operation of a good radio station.[5]

In Chicago, radio advertising agency executives joined forces in condemning the "Blue Book."[6] Lewis H. Avery, president of Lewis H. Avery, Inc. (advertising agency), and former director of broadcast advertising for the NAB, "hotly attacked" the recent FCC program report. He accused the FCC of "imposing a diet of forced feeding on the American listening public."[7] Justin Miller, speaking at an NAB Meeting, expressed the hope (which he viewed as empty) that some broadcaster would defy the FCC openly, refusing the demand that program reports be made and thus bring the issue to court upon revocation of his license. "I don't advise that, however," he said. "The Court might uphold the Commission." Miller advised the broadcasters to speak their minds openly on the subject and not to hesitate in voicing their opinions to the FCC.[8]

Broadcasting admitted in an editorial that the "Blue Book" had one good feature. It was ". . . that the report will move broadcasters toward self-examination."[9] The next week, however, it maintained that ". . . until radio is 'as free as the press,' radio and the press and the motion pictures and all other media of expression are in jeopardy." [10]

Variety, on the other hand, thought that the "Blue Book" might influence broadcasters to keep institutional commercial programs, such as the General Motors "Symphony of the Air," on the air as "sustaining slots" even when the sponsors "bow out." [11]

Focus on Siepmann's "Radio's Second Chance"

The broadcasting industry found a scapegoat upon which to release its pent up aggressions in the person of Charles A. Siepmann, when his book, *Radio's Second Chance,* was released barely a month after publication of the "Blue Book." Siepmann's criticisms of the industry paralleled those of the FCC report, but went further. He attempted to answer all of the arguments raised by broadcasters in the history of American radio. Siepmann delivered a moving and poignant narration addressed to the American people; a plea to make use of the airwaves for some constructive purpose. Joseph K. Howard, reviewing the book in *Public Opinion Quarterly,* called it the first full-length critical study of American radio practice. He believed that the book might well have served as a manual for creation of an informed public opinion about the industry. Howard said that Siepmann had done all he could to arrest the dangerous drift of people accepting and even growing to like what they had gotten on radio.[12]

It was evident from the preface of *Radio's Second Chance* that Siepmann had anticipated the broadcasters' violent reaction. He spent ten pages proving that he was not against the American system of commercial broadcasting. He discussed his BBC background and mentioned that he was an American citizen. He realized that anyone of foreign origin who undertook criticism of an American institution was open to the obvious retort: "If you don't like it, why don't you go back where you came from?" Siepmann's reply was that ". . . the more recent the immigrant the more poignant and vital his stake in the living democracy of a nation which is his not by the accident of birth but by deliberate and thoughtful choice." [13] Siepmann also mentioned in the preface that he had been a special consultant to the FCC in July, 1945, and that he had drawn on studies, which he had made while he had served in that capacity, for material in several chapters of *Radio's Second Chance.*[14]

Variety was the first trade paper to comment. It stated that:

> . . . comment in the trade is growing on the irony of a man trained
> by and formerly an official of the BBC becoming years later, as an
> American citizen, a chief philosopher and ghost writer for a United
> States Government document ["Blue Book"] attacking the status

quo in American broadcasting. . . . Siepmann is thought certain to become . . . the plumed knight of radio's critical contigent.[15]

Broadcasting was not as kind. The headline of a story written by Robert K. Richards read: "Radio's Second Chance: Free to Broadcasters, $2.50 to Listeners—Blue Book Ghost Writer Gets Sponsor After Sustainer for FCC."

The article said that Siepmann had written *Radio's Second Chance* in "penetrating prose." It stated that the book represented "a legible and understandable presentation" of the arguments purveyed in the FCC report. Richards continued that:

> . . . This is a strange paradox that it should be legible and understandable; inasmuch as Mr. Siepmann wrote not only the book, but the Report. That he could contrive such a clearly enunciated prospectus as *Radio's Second Chance* and at the time have authored such gobbledygook as the FCC opus is high tribute to his versatility in letters. But there is enough in *Second Chance* to identify it as having come from the same mold as the FCC Report, although it may shine more brightly for having been burnished in Mr. Siepmann's Ivory Tower.[16]

The review accused *Radio's Second Chance* of being a "measured and cautious attack on American radio." It charged that Siepmann "got paid" while writing his book.[17] It went over the volume point by point in a militant manner. Richards concluded the analysis by remarking that:

> . . . No comment on *Radio's Second Chance* made here is intended to be prejudicial against Mr. Siepmann, who is an honorable man bent upon his own high designs. But comment will be labeled as prejudicial . . . against the manner in which the book emerged from the cloistered chambers which gave it birth. Inevitably it must be asked—is Charles Siepmann its father or is he a midwife who stood in patient attendance at the bower of Clifford J. Durr? [18]

An editorial, which appeared in the same issue of *Broadcasting*, claimed that the "mystery" of Charles A. Siepmann had been solved "by Mr. Siepmann himself." The opinion of the editor was that the magazine had conjectured in July, 1945, that the BBC program executive had been working on a program report which would represent the FCC's "formal move into censorship." The editorial concluded that ". . . American broadcasters who seek a clear conception of the motives behind the "Blue Book" will find the answer in *Radio's Second Chance*." [19]

Time magazine was impressed with *Radio's Second Chance*:

> Many doctors have diagnosed radio's ills; few have prescribed a cure. . . . Siepmann told radio how it could get well if it only half

tried. Like any competent physician . . . Siepmann began with a documented case history of his patient. For many a suffering listener, it was the best analysis of radio's excesses. . . .

Time concluded inimitably by saying that ". . . Professor Siepmann's brew was one cure-all that was not likely to get a radio sponsor." [20]

Defense and Debate

The NAB, represented by its president, Justin Miller, began a vicious attack upon Siepmann, the "Blue Book," the FCC, and all those who sided with them. The burden of the attack rested on the allegation that Congress did not intend to give the Commission authority to pass on program performance in making decisions on whether stations are acting, or will act, in the public interest.[21] Judge Miller described the FCC report as "an indictment of radio." He said that the FCC proposed to assert power over programs despite specific denial of that right in the Communications Act and under the Bill of Rights. He branded talk about "the people owning the air" as a "lot of hooey and nonsense." [22] Name calling by the NAB began in earnest. Siepmann was now referred to as "Radio's Cassius." [23] The FCC Commissioners were said to be "stooges for the Communists." FCC Chairman Charles R. Denny, Jr., stated that Miller called the "Blue Book" supporters, "obfuscators, intellectual smart-alecks, professional appeasers, guileful men, and astigmatic perverters of society." [24] Commissioner Clifford J. Durr was accused of being the "power" behind the "Blue Book." [25]

Siepmann agreed to defend the "Blue Book" in public debates. At one such event, he faced Justin Miller, before a meeting of the NAB Second District. Siepmann said the broadcasters misunderstood the FCC, which "always acts in default of action on the part of the industry." He stated that they now have a yardstick of what the FCC expects. Miller said that any American institution could be indicted if a one-sided picture were given and that no court would ever accept such a one-sided report.[26] In a debate between Siepmann and Sydney M. Kaye, vice-president of BMI, held at the Longacre Theatre in New York City, Siepmann again characterized the report as nothing more than a guide to lead stations toward a more mature attitude in programing. He said that the "Blue Book" would aid broadcasters to explore the cultural and educational possibilities and responsibilities of radio. Mr. Kaye reiterated the stand of the industry in claiming that any such improvements could be accomplished without the aid of any government agency and that the plan set forth in the book was a door opener which in the future could be applied to other arts and professions such as movies and newspapers.[27]

Justin Miller, in one of his cross-country speeches, answered the theory that radio was different from the press. Judge Miller was paraphrased in *Broadcasting*:

> . . . Except for use of mechanical devices for greater projection, Mr. Miller said that speech over radio does not differ from an address given from a platform, and alleged "difference" made by the device could as well be extended to include the megaphone, telephone, amplifier and other mechanical aids other than radio. Censorship of any, he said, would be just as much in violation of principles of free speech as restriction of a conversation in the home. . . .

Discussing the "Blue Book's" coverage of excesses of advertising, the NAB president said, "There is much to be done by broadcasters and by advertisers to improve the character and content of programs." He said that self-regulation by the industry "is the American way." [28]

Editorials

Meanwhile, the war of editorials was continuing. *Broadcasting* claimed that the FCC report ". . . was issued on March 7. On March 8, before most licensees knew exactly what had happened, it was put into effect. . . ." [29] The next week, the industry magazine foretold that the "Blue Book" would eventually apply to television program content and balance.[30] The following week, it pleaded hopefully: ". . . Somewhere there must be a radio Peter Zenger. . . ." [31] On May 6, 1946, *Broadcasting* stated:

> . . . Stations, in the aggregate, need make no apology for their public service. They should not for a second consider degrading their standards of program acceptance to a appease pressure groups or to satisfy the FCC. There's nothing wrong with commercial radio except the FCC's wholly fallacious definitions as set forth in the Blue Book which label anything sponsored as non-public service as iniquitous, and anything sustaining as beneficial.[32]

Variety's editorials took another viewpoint, and castigated some members of radio industry:

> The much-publicized FCC edict on programming, with its accompanying note of caution to broadcasters, has brought in its wake various shadings of finageling in an effort to make the record look good without hurting the purse strings. As one of the more alert radio execs put it: "If broadcasters put the same imagination and aggressiveness into honest-to-goodness programming as in the ingenious methods they use to beat the rap, radio would have a Utopian setup. . . ."

Variety illustrated a practice to which some stations around the country had resorted:

. . . In a move to avoid calling a lot of their record and e.t. musical shows "commercial" in terms of the new FCC program analysis form, they are double-and-triple spotting in the breaks, and running the programs as presumably "Sustainers" instead of "participating." This has resulted in recorded musical units of 13 to 13½ minutes length, with a cluster of commercial spots before and after. Naturally, on the FCC form, these will show up as "sustaining" programs since the commercial announcements aren't being run in the body of the program.[33]

The editorial in *Broadcasting* of May 13, 1946, attacked Commissioner Clifford J. Durr, who had been defending the "Blue Book."

. . . It is now evident that Clifford J. Durr is the FCC's knight errant. He sets forth with increasing regularity from the Commission's castle on the Potomac to protect the people against the horrible perpetrations of American broadcasters. He enters the joust in righteous splendor, garbed in an academic grey suit and gripping tightly in one hand—the Blue Book. And the banner he bears high—is it the white of purity, or is there a tint of pink? [34]

The following week's editorial in *Broadcasting* intimated that the public did not want, and would not listen to, public service broadcasts on Class "A" time. It said: "You cannot serve the public if the public isn't there." [35] Seven days later the president of the Australian Federation of Commercial Broadcasting, who was visiting the United States, was asked about the FCC's "Blue Book." He rejoined: "Why, that is the first step toward nationalization of American radio." [36] A week later, *Broadcasting* cited President Truman's use of radio for speeches as a sign of peacetime cooperation between broadcasters and government.[37]

The "Blue Book" was the topic of discussion between educators and commercial broadcasters at the Ohio State Institute for Education by Radio. *Variety* editorialized that:

. . . To the educator-in-radio it was obvious that he was being given the brush—even though with kid gloves. By once more having theory pooh-poohed when it tried to bid against working experience, a stalemate was affected. No attempt was made for an honest endeavor to accept the theory of statistics and classroom, or with an open mind to accept the workable contribution and go on from there. . . .

Variety pointed out that the same die-hards who had scorned the FCC also resented the "intrusion" of the educator element. The article concluded that:

. . . It all boils down to the basic difference between a communications medium and a business venture. Broadcasters and network officials know it's a business, and a mighty profitable one, which they operate very efficiently. On this premise they resent anyone coming in to advise them, or the fact that anyone can so presume in view of their own financial success. Neither harmony nor progress can result from this know-all attitude. . . .[38]

Judge Thurman Arnold defended the "Blue Book" in a speech. *Broadcasting* tore into him in a vicious editorial. It claimed that ". . . Somebody must have handed the venerated and hard-hitting judge the script." The article maintained that Arnold's speech was "the same production line job" that had been used by all those who had defended the FCC. *Broadcasting* speculated that it was an "even-money bet" that "those tinkling typewriter keys" that produced the "Blue Book" and *Radio's Second Chance,* had also "clicked off the rippling passages uttered by the Judge." [39]

Broadcasting concluded its weekly editorial attacks on the "Blue Book" and its intimations against Siepmann (which had begun on March 18) on June 17, 1946. Thereafter, the assaults were not presented as a regular diet, but merely as an extra-added dessert about once a month. The June 17 editorial summed up:

> . . . The Blue Book was conceived in the minds of men of Government. It was conceived spontaneously, with no audible demand from the public which should give impetus to reform if reform is indicated. It was written in great part by a man practiced in the Governmental radio art of Great Britian. It was installed in a *fait accompli* on March 7, and its effects were felt throughout broadcasting before licensees had received copies of it. We are opposed to the tactics which produced it. We are opposed to the way of life it portends . . .[40]

Siepmann, even before this violent outburst by *Broadcasting,* acknowledged that the magazine's blows had not all been "above the belt." He had remembered a statement by FCC Commissioner Ray Wakefield that large elements in the industry press had deliberately created distrust between the FCC and the working broadcasters.[41] Commenting on the NAB's attack on the "Blue Book," Siepmann propounded that the group scarcely even mentioned the subject of the FCC report. He said that ". . . Scarcely a word has been addressed to the defects in programming, with which the report is first and last concerned." He reminded the broadcasters of an important sentence from the "Blue Book" which invited comment from licensees and from the public. He claimed: "The industry's answer to this open invitation to reasoned and reasonable discussion has thus far been an appeal to the First Amendment of the Constitution." [42] He said that radio was too powerful to be entrusted to any single group without an overriding control.[43] In response to the name calling by Justin Miller, Siepmann replied in the understatement of the year:

. . . That a man with a distinguished public record should campaign on an issue of vital public importance in such terms as these
is perhaps the measure of declining standards in what I would call
the good manners of communication.[44]

Comments from Non-Industry Sources

Many newspapers and magazines around the country commented about the "Blue Book." *Collier's*, in its opposition, said that
the FCC was "up to its old tricks again, trying to interfere with the
content of radio programs." The national magazine claimed that
"Congress should long ago have taken away from the FCC its life-
and-death licensing power over radio, and confined it strictly to the
duties of an umpire among stations in the matter of assigning wave
bands." [45] *Life*, on the other hand, came out in strong defense of the
FCC report.[46]

The *St. Louis Post-Dispatch* commented that the NAB in the attack on the "Blue Book" seemed to regard the airwaves as a private
commodity, which they were not, and clothed its attitude in the
usual guise of solemn patriotism.[47] The *Chicago Tribune* characterized the report as "censorship through blackmail," while the *Philadelphia Inquirer* heartily endorsed the "salutary criticisms." The
Charleston (W. Va.) *Daily Mail* said that the good the "Blue Book"
might have accomplished was more than offset by the danger it
threatened.[48]

During the height of the "Blue Book" controversy, radio station
WJR (Detroit) sponsored a series of advertisements which appeared
in *Broadcasting* and *Variety*. The copy dealt with "FREE SPEECH
MIKE—Guardian of American Freedom." Quotations by famous
Americans on freedom of speech were used with the depiction of a
microphone in the guise of a young boy wearing the stars and stripes
and carrying the hat of Uncle Sam.[49]

United States Congressmen reacted in various ways to the "Blue
Book." Representative B. Carroll Reece of Tennessee, chairman of
the Republican National Committee, served notice that freedom
from program control by the FCC would be a major issue in the
forthcoming campaign. He declared the Commission "must have
tossed" the Communications Act "in the FCC's incinerator." He
charged the Commissioners "wrote their own law as to radio programming." [50] Reece also charged that "seven bureaucrats" had set
themselves up as "judge of what 70 million American radio listeners
should be allowed to listen to." He declared that the Republican
party was pledged to maintain the freedom of radio. *Variety* maintained that Reece's statements indicated that the GOP was "cuddling
up close" to the NAB in its troubles with the FCC. The paper

pointed out that Reece had not mentioned the fact that the "Blue Book" had been issued by a six-man Commission, "half of whom are Republicans, and there were no dissents." [51] Representative Andrew J. Biemiller (Democrat—Wisconsin) took issue with Representative Reece's charges that the FCC sought to control programs. "The facts do not support the gentleman's insinuations; . . . Responsible newspapers throughout the country have editorially complimented the Commission upon this report," he said, naming the *New York Times, St. Louis Post-Dispatch, Cleveland Plain Dealer, Washington Post,* and others.[52]

In another Capitol chamber, Senator Styles Bridges (Republican—New Hampshire) wanted to know why the FCC "saw fit to employ at an impressive salary, a person trained by the governmentally dominated British Broadcasting System which is opposed in principle and practice to our American system." He wanted to know also why Mr. Siepmann had access to "confidential files of the FCC—a privilege denied to the American public." The reply, sent by Charles R. Denny, Jr., acting FCC Chairman, stated that Siepmann was an American citizen; it gave his background; and it mentioned that Siepmann had been a special consultant to the FCC. The letter said that Siepmann had completed his assignment in "20 days and 6½ hours" and that the total amount paid to him was $670.17 in salary, with the amount for *per diem* expense "including time taken to travel $160.50." Denny stated that Mr. Siepmann was only "supplied with the files necessary and appropriate for his work in the Commission," and that any qualified person could have access to the files. The acting chairman sent a copy of the "Blue Book" with his answer to Senator Bridges with the remark: "I am sure you will find it interesting." [53]

Public reaction to the "Blue Book," as well as response from leaders of thought, was apathetic. Siepmann wrote that he was unaware of any concerted action on the part of those "non-profit organizations (whose interests this report bespoke) to let the FCC know that it had any solid body of opinion behind it." He said that at hearings before committees of the Congress concerned with radio "such organizations are generally conspicuous by their absence," and that it was deplorable that the organized voice of education was unheard in the controversy over the "Blue Book." [54]

The Commission on Freedom of the Press' Report on *The American Radio* (White Report) reported that after a year no broadcaster had been thrown off the airways for practices cited in the FCC report as being, in the Commission's view, contrary to "public interest, convenience, or necessity." White said that this did not mean that the broadcasters had successfully ignored the warning; on the contrary, it meant that the broadcasters had altered the practice complained of to a point where the Commission felt justified in setting down only six stations for hearings, and in granting license renewals to the first three to be heard. The White volume held that the "Blue Book's" labeling of "types" of radio programs and its discussion of "balanced fare" meant that ". . . the label is likely to look much more impressive in a logbook than the program sounds on the home receiver." It mentioned the likelihood of broadcasters incorporating in the titles of programs, subjects needed to round out the station's lack of program balance. White was disappointed that radio had not yet produced a Peter Zenger. He maintained that, beside the editorials in *Broadcasting*, the average broadcaster had remained in "bewildered silence." What worried White was that the radio industry had not fought the issue of "license-based-on-content" when it began with the Radio Act of 1927. The "Blue Book" was merely a "get-tough" policy based on the original law. The study concluded that the Communications Act without the "Blue Book" was, in so far as it touched on program adequacy, "a farce." [55]

Professor Elmer E. Smead pointed out, in his study of *Freedom of Speech by Radio and Television*, that the broadcasters used FCC program standards (set forth in the "Blue Book") to strengthen their applications against competitors. Thus they were taking the initiative in making program performance an issue in FCC license cases at the very time that the NAB was trying to get the industry to present a united front against FCC regulation of programs through its control of licenses.[56]

Effect of the "Blue Book"

In December, 1946, just nine months after the release of the "Blue Book," Siepmann considered the document "a collector's item" because the majority of radio listeners had neither seen nor read it. He recalled a statement made by the FCC Chairman, Charles Denny, who said: "We do not intend to bleach it ["Blue Book"]. Siepmann believed that the "Blue Book" produced some good results, although the only real legal "enforcement" test (the WBAL case) resulted in no action.[57] The radio documentary, in his opinion, was a partial answer to the insistence of the FCC that radio devote more and better time to programs in the public interest presented on sustaining time.[58]

Another beneficial effect of the "Blue Book" was the radio industry's continued approach to self-regulation. Members of the NAB proposed this method "for the continuing improvement of the American radio system." [59] In 1948, a new and more elaborate code than 1929 and 1939 editions went into effect.[60] The latter, according to Siepmann, was prodded by the "Blue Book" and public agitation. He concluded that had this code been drafted long ago, it would have made some of the strictures in the "Blue Book" redundant. Siepmann gave the NAB credit for conceiving the code, but hoped that listeners would help in its refinement and correction.[61]

Reaction to the "Blue Book" in 1947 became apparent when a bill to revise the Communications Act of 1934 was being considered by Congress. The NAB, according to Siepmann, seized the opportunity to press its case against the FCC and its "infamous" "Blue Book." [62] The following year, when the "Mayflower" decision was being discussed in Washington, Siepmann accused the propaganda mills of the NAB of working overtime to win adherents to a crusade "launched more than a year ago by its president, Justin Miller." He said that for Mr. Miller, the hearings were merely round two—"round one was the smear campaign against the FCC's Blue Book"—of a fight to the finish to strip the FCC of all power over radio stations' program service. Siepmann claimed that the ambition of the NAB was to relegate the FCC to the role of "a traffic cop" and to secure for radio "like freedom with the press and the movies." [63]

In 1949, Representative Forest A. Harness of Indiana, chairman of a special committee to investigate the FCC, was quoted in the *New York Times* as saying that he had found evidence to support the premise that publication of the "Blue Book" in 1946, "was a deliberate step toward government control of radio." The "evidence" was an allegation that a former employee of the BBC had prepared that report. Saul Carson, radio critic, discussing this Congressional Investigation stated that the rumor that the "Blue Book" was BBC-inspired was invented by commercial broadcasters. Carson claimed the rumor was given currency by NAB president, Justin Miller, whose career (Miller's) had been marked by "temperate" statements like: "The Blue Book was seized avidly by crackpots, communists, and rival advertising media, who proceeded to heap ridicule upon broadcasting and broadcasters generally." Critic Carson concluded his answer to "Capitol Hill" with this statement:

> . . . What broadcasting fears is not loss of freedom to broadcast but enhanced freedom to listen. The Blue Book not only chastized some broadcasters; it encouraged listeners to exercise their rights. Some listeners are doing just that; hence the disinternment of the Blue Book and the Siepmann "scandal." [64]

The United States Court of Appeals was the scene of a test which determined whether or not the FCC had the right to inquire into the amount of sustaining time proposed by an applicant for a radio license. The "Blue Book" went on trial two years after its release. A broadcaster, Bay State Beacon, Inc., argued that the First Amendment was being contravened and that Section 326 of the Communications Act prohibited censorship. The Court ruled in favor of the FCC. It said that Congress had delegated authority to the Commission to carry out the specific functions that called it into being.[65] The U.S. Supreme Court has not passed squarely on the legal issues raised by the opponents of regulation, although it has had opportunities to do so.[66]

Discussion

Despite the court's decision in favor of the FCC, despite the assertion of the FCC chairman that the "Blue Book" would not be bleached, despite the constant barrage of statements that the "Blue Book" had never been rescinded and that it was also applicable to television, Siepmann believes that "neither the letter nor the spirit of its regulatory decisions has since been honored by action on the FCC's part in its license-renewal policy." [67] The "Blue Book" is considered by the industry as a dead letter,[68] and its provisions have been "honored in the breach." [69]

Nonetheless, *Public Service Responsibility of Broadcast Licensees* remains as one of the most controversial documents concerning broadcasting in the United States.

90

Roscoe L. Barrow, et. al.

DEVELOPMENT OF TELEVISION: FCC ALLOCATIONS AND STANDARDS

THE IMPETUS to the commercial development of television came primarily from radio manufacturing and broadcasting firms. They conducted the technical research and development and operated the experimental television stations. By 1938, under the general aegis of the Radio Manufacturers Association (RMA), they recommended to the Commission adoption of transmission standards for the new medium.

The Commission, however, found the industry divided on the basic question whether television was ready for commercial broad-

Network Broadcasting: Report of the Network Study Staff to the Network Study Committee, Federal Communications Commission, Washington, D.C.: Committee on Interstate and Foreign Commerce, 85th Congress, Second Session, House Report No. 1297, 1957, pp. 17–31.

casting and also found the industry at odds as to transmission standards. Some (notably Du Mont, Philco, and CBS) believed that television had not reached the point where it could offer sufficiently attractive programing to justify commerical operation, and that standardization would result in the freezing of the art significantly below its potential. Others (led by RCA) were determined to proceed immediately with the launching of television on a broad scale.

The Commission, in 1940, turned to the RMA and cooperated with it in the formation of a National Television System Committee (NTSC), broadly representing national technical organizations and companies experienced in the television field. New transmission specifications were shortly drawn up acceptable to all sectors of the industry. These were formally adopted by the Commission in April 1941, and commercial operation of television stations was approved effective July 1, 1941. Eighteen channels, each 6 megacycles wide, were assigned to this service, extending from 50 to 294 megacycles. Two stations went into operation in New York (NBC and CBS) as of July 1, 1941.

Substantial development of the new medium was held up by the wartime freeze imposed in 1942 on station construction and set production. As of September 1944, 6 commercial stations were operating on a 4-hour-per-week basis. Approximately 7,000 sets were outstanding, and these were generally designed for reception of stations on frequencies below 90 megacycles.

2. *First television assignment plan, 1945*

On September 20, 1945, the Commission ordered a hearing to consider rules and regulations and standards of good engineering practice for television. Included in the order was a proposed plan for the assignment of the 13 VHF television channels among the 140 metropolitan districts. This assignment plan provided for larger metropolitan stations and smaller community stations; the intended minimum spacing for the metropolitan stations was 150 miles cochannel and 75 miles adjacent-channel spacing, but in some cases lower spacings were used; community stations were spaced 90 miles and 45 miles for co- and adjacent-channel separation. In this initial plan, New York was given four assignments. The maximum power to be permitted any station was to be limited to 50 kilowatts.

At the hearing, the Television Broadcast Association (TBA) presented an alternative assignment plan with the following major characteristics:

(a) Use of directional antennas to increase the number of assignments to larger centers.
(b) Reduction of cochannel and adjacent-channel minimum spacings to 85 and 55 miles.

(c) Lowering maximum power below 50 kilowatts.
(d) Providing for substantially uniform maximum power for all stations.
(e) Increasing the New York assignments to seven.

NBC and Du Mont gave testimony supporting the TBA assignment plan. Du Mont questioned the Commission's view as to the shortlived future of VHF television, maintaining that the television industry needed assurance that the allocations would remain for at least a decade and would not be eliminated at the first successful commercial operation in the UHF band.

Conversely, CBS and ABC stressed the undesirability of any extended operation in VHF. ABC proposed that after a short period of time, for example, 2 years, all commercial television should be transferred to UHF; that licensees of VHF television stations be required to carry on technical development work on the higher frequencies in a coordinated developmental program to be set up by the FCC; that the public be given adequate notice of the future changeovers; and that the industry promise to the public purchasing VHF-only receivers a liberal trade-in on future UHF sets.

The Commission, in its report of November 21, 1945, promulgated a revised table of assignments which adopted some of the recommendations of the TBA. The Commission added assignments in the eastern United States by closer spacings, and by limiting in many instances stations to less than 0.5 millivolts per meter contour. New York was thus given seven assignments. The Commission, however, rejected the use of directional antennas. Instead, it set up a plan whereby smaller communities would be assigned community stations with lower power and more limited coverage than metropolitan stations. All of the channels, except channel 1, were than made available for either metropolitan or rural stations.

The rules governing television stations were issued on November 28, 1945, and the Standards of Good Engineering Practices on December 19, 1945.

4. Hearing on deletion of channel 1, 1947–48 (docket 8487)

The rejection of the CBS color system in 1947 removed a major uncertainty in the plans of the VHF television group. Nevertheless, the Commission reiterated the desirability of moving to UFH as soon as possible, particularly as the sharing arrangements under which the VHF channels had been granted to television were resulting in serious interference to television reception. Thus, on August 4, 1947, the Commission issued a Notice of Proposed Rulemaking (Mimeo. 10421) proposing to delete television channel 1 and abolishing all provision for sharing television channels (except channels 7 and 8).

On May 5, 1948, the Commission issued its report in which it abolished channel sharing on all TV channels, deleted channel 1, and reiterated its statement of May 25, 1945, that a truly nationwide and competitive system must find its home higher in the spectrum. The Commission also announced that simultaneously it was issuing a notice of proposed rulemaking to change the television assignment table.

In the course of the hearing the TBA testified that a minimum of 15 commercial TV stations were on the air; that 176,000 receivers had been sold, and that receivers were being produced at the rate of 25,000 a month.

5. *Institution of general television hearings: Part 1, 1948 (dockets 8736, 8975, and 8976)*

In considering amendment of the assignment table, the Commission sought to obtain information relating to the interference existing on channels 2 to 13, and to consider the possibilities of establishing standards for the VHF band.

On June 20, 1948, the Joint Technical Advisory Committee (JTAC) was formed by the Institute of Radio Engineers and the Radio Manufacturers Association. The JTAC assumed many of the tasks of the RTPB which was dissolved on July 1, 1948. The first task undertaken by the JTAC, at the request of the Chairman of the FCC, was the collection of information on UHF television.

The hearing on May 5, 1948, dealt, first, with assignment of specific channels to specific communities. The assignment plan, incorporated in the Commission's rules since 1945, provided for 500 stations in the 140 metropolitan districts. In view of the growing interest in television, the Commission proposed an expanded television assignment plan with provision for over 900 stations to over 500 communities, including cities of population as low as 5,000. This expanded plan involved a more intensive utilization of the 12 VHF channels by narrowing station separations.

However, in the course of the hearing, testimony was introduced regarding the effects of tropospheric interference on existing and proposed allocations. At about that time, the Commission had completed a study based on signal measurements made over a number of years which also pointed to the need for greater, rather than less, station separations. As a result of this problem, the Commission called an FCC-industry meeting on September 13 and 14, 1948, at the conclusion of which the Commission announced that it would call an engineering conference to consider revision of the Commission's rules and standards. Pending the outcome of this conference, the Commission by its order of September 30, 1948 (the "freeze" order), called a halt in the processing of applications for new television stations. It was thought that the "freeze" could be lifted within 6 to 9 months. In fact, processing of new television assignments did not resume until July 1, 1952, almost 4 years later.

The complexity of the technical issues to be resolved was evident at the engineering conference held November 30–December 3, 1948. It was decided that before further progress could be made an ad hoc committee should be established to provide a basis for quantitative estimates of the effects of troposphere and terrain. A committee was formed of members of the Commission's Engineering Bureau, the Bureau of Standards, and consulting engineering firms. This ad hoc committee filed its report with the Commission on May 1949.

Meanwhile, the Commission went ahead on September 20–23, 1948, with a hearing (Docket 8976) to determine the utility of the UHF band for television broadcasting.

The JTAC, which had been asked to examine into the technical status of UHF, took the position that allocation standards for UHF could not be determined at that time because of insufficiency of data on field strength, service contours, and interference factors. It reported, further, that there was no commercial equipment for UHF available, and estimated that from 1 to 3 years would be required for the industry to design and produce such equipment. From the available data, the JTAC concluded that coverage comparable with that of the VHF service, using available or potentially available transmitter power, was not possible on the UHF frequencies with ground-based transmitters. JTAC suggested that the Commission set a hearing in approximately 6 months on the general UHF problem. It also made the following general recommendations:

> The JTAC recommends that the present 12 channels in the VHF frequency spectrum continue to be the backbone of the monochrome television system. It recognizes, however, that additional channels are necessary in order to provide adequate competitive service in certain areas. Therefore, it recommends that the Commission make plans to supplement the existing 12 channels with additional channels.
>
> The JTAC further finds that the place in the spectrum in which it is technically possible for 6-megacycle black-and-white television immediately to expand its number of channels is in the immediate vicinity of the present commercial channels. If this proves impossible, the future practicability of the use of the low end of the 475–890 megacycle band, for expansion of the monochrome service, should be thoroughly explored.

The TBA, in its testimony, recommended that commercial UHF operation not be approved without further experimentation. Meanwhile, the Commission should make clear that it would retain the 12 VHF channels as well as the UHF frequencies.

The RCA position was similar. It insisted that the 12 VHF channel allocation was basic; that the FCC should permit higher power for TV stations; that the Commission should make an exhaustive survey of the frequencies below 300 megacycles to determine whether additional channels for TV could be found; that the standards for UHF should be the same as for VHF; and that part of the UHF band be reserved for color development.

Du Mont, on the other hand, advanced the view based on its own field experimentation that UHF was immediately feasible for use in commercial monochrome television. Du Mont also stressed that full occupancy of the 12 VHF channels would not be practicable because of tropospheric interference, and that a nationwide competitive television service required at least 30 to 40 channels. Hence, Du Mont made the following recommendations:

(a) Retain the VHF stations then in operation.

(b) Leave construction permit holders untouched except those closer than approximately 160 miles cochannel or those in cities which could not be provided an adequate number of VHF assignments.

(c) Assign a minimum of 5 VHF stations to each of the 50 largest market areas, maintaining as large a separation as practical until the VHF channels were exhausted. These cities would be permitted high-powered transmitters to provide extensive coverage.

(d) Fill in all other cities with a sufficient number of UHF assignments to provide competitive service.

(e) Insofar as possible, there should be no mixing of VHF and UHF assignments in a single city. In this way, the cities with operating VHF stations would continue to have VHF-only receivers. Cities in which UHF stations were constructed in the future could have receivers built permanently for the UHF band.

(f) Finally, Du Mont recommended an FCC-industry conference to prepare and review an assignment plan utilizing the combined VHF-UHF frequencies.

In this hearing, two radically new transmission techniques were discussed, "stratovision" and "polycasting." As described by Westinghouse, which had engaged in the research, it was practicable to develop a system of airborne television, in which properly equipped planes circling about could provide extensive coverage of the Nation using a limited number of channels. With 5 channels, according to an estimate, service could be transmitted to about 80 percent of the cities of the Nation.

Polycasting was urged as another method of achieving widespread coverage. The principle involved was the use of a number of lowpower transmitters. A broad area might be served, for example, by using 4 transmitters on 2 frequencies, with each of the transmitters pointing in a different direction.

The hearing closed on September 22, 1948, and the Commission did not issue a report at that time.

6. Attempts to lift the "freeze," 1949–51

Early in 1949, the Commission had before it reports from three organizations dealing with the allocations and assignment problems: Ad hoc committee, JTAC, and RMA. The ad hoc committee report dealt mainly with VHF propagation and interference. It made no recommendations with respect to allocations.

The JTAC, on the other hand, urged that VHF be unfrozen; that UHF be assigned; that intermixture with VHF was inevitable; and that some wide-band UHF should be reserved for color.

The RMA also urged that VHF be unfrozen immediately and that UHF be assigned forthwith. In contrast with JTAC, it stressed the need for four assignments in every city that could support television economically but the RMA insisted that this must be done with a minimum overlap of UHF and VHF signals.

Several months later, in July 1949, the Commission set out proposed television standards and a nationwide assignment plan.

The Commission invited and received industry comments on its proposals. Considerable opposition was expressed to various aspects of the plan.

The Commission had set September 26 as the date for hearing on its proposals, but decided first to consider proposals for color television, before proceeding with the rest of the problem.

7. Hearing on color television, September 1949–October 1950

Considerable interest had developed in color; CBS took to the air with its new experimental 6-megacycle color system in July 1949; RCA claimed that it had a compatible color system; members of the Senate Interstate and Foreign Commerce Committee expressed the view that, if color were here, this was a crucial fact and every effort must be made to foster its acceptance. Accordingly, the chairman of the Senate Interstate and Foreign Commerce Committee appointed a committee of scientists under the leadership of Dr. Edward Condon head of the Bureau of Standards, to appraise the status of color and to estimate when it would be ready for practical use.

When the color hearing before the Commission began, it was estimated that the proceeding might last about 3 weeks. In fact, it lasted a year and provoked bitter controversy. Over the strong opposition of RCA and most manufacturers, the Commission adopted the field sequential system offered by CBS. This was a 6-megacycle system but had different characteristics than the existing monochrome standards (viz, 441 lines rather than 525 lines per frame) and was consequently incompatible with transmitters and sets in use. RCA contended that a compatible system was feasible and that its system had the potentiality for a high-definition, wide-screen color system. On October 10, 1950, the Commission adopted the CBS color system.

Before operation in color could begin, the Commission's decision was stayed by court injunction and the matter was litigated to the Supreme Court. Finally, on May 28, 1951, the Court upheld the FCC.

On October 19, 1951, the Director of Defense Mobilization addressed a letter to the president of CBS stating that since the national emergency required the conservation of critical materials, it was necessary to request industry to suspend plans for mass production of new products. Shortly thereafter, on November 21, the National Production Authority issued Order M-90 which expressly prohibited manufacture of sets designed to receive color television. On June 24, 1952, the NPA issued a revised order. In practical effect, however, no change resulted, and the incompatible color system came to an end.

8. *Third notice and sixth report, 1950–51*

After the color decision, the Commission resumed hearings, on October 16, 1950, on the television assignment and engineering standards. Considerable industry and political pressures were building up for lifting of the "freeze." Du Mont offered revised assignment plans which provided for four VHF or UHF assignments in most of the leading markets. These plans provided for more intermixture than in the original Du Mont plan, but less intermixture than in the FCC plan. RCA testified on the results of its UHF experimentation in Bridgeport and indicated that coverage was likely to be more limited than predicted. During this phase, the educational interests offered evidence as to their needs for reserved assignments. There was also important testimony on the technical side concerning the feasibility of offset carriers, which made possible closer spacing, and the need to guard against various types of interference in the UHF by spacing restrictions.

The Commission issued its third notice on March 21, 1951, which contained a new assignment table. Again opportunity was given for comments, but this time, pursuant to an order of July 25, 1951, the comments were to be submitted in writing. The third notice established a rule of thumb for the assigning of noncommercial educational reservations and, also, among other matters, clearly accepted intermixture of VHF and UHF channels in the same communities.

In subsequent months, the Commission conducted negotiations with the Canadian and Mexican Governments which provided for mutual protection of assignments along the borders. The Commission also analyzed the comments filed pursuant to the third notice.

Finally on April 11, 1952, the Commission issued the sixth report and order. Effective July 1, 1952, the Commission lifted the freeze which had lasted almost 4 years.

The salient features of the sixth report are as follows:

(a) An overall assignment plan attempts to assign the limited number of channels available for television as efficiently as possible from a technical standpoint.

(b) No existing VHF station was moved to the UHF, or moved to another community. To correct some substandard separations, 31 VHF stations were required to change channels within the VHF band.

(c) The entire UHF allocation for television from 470 to 890 megacycles, including 70 channels, was completely assigned.

(d) VHF assignments were distributed widely to provide an equitable distribution as among cities and States. At the same time, most of the VHF channels were assigned to larger cities above 50,000 population.

(e) UHF assignments were added to VHF so that larger cities could have an adequate number of outlets. In addition, UHF made possible the assignment of a first local station to over 1,000 communities.

(f) Each community with a radio station generally received a television assignment. Thus, hundreds of communities with less than 5,000 population received an assignment, usually in the UHF band except in the western regions where VHF was plentiful.

(g) Broadly speaking, the number of assignments was correlated with size of city. The criteria were as follows:

1950 population of cities (central city)	Number of assignments (VHF and UHF combined)
1 million and above	6–10
250,000–1 million	4–6
50,000–250,000	2–4
Under 50,000	1–2

(h) Most major communities were given a limited number of VHF stations; with the exception of New York (7) and Los Angeles (7) no city was assigned more than 4 commercial VHF stations. Moreover, only 7 communities were given as many as 4 commercial VHF assignments. The hope was that the strong demand for television would spill over into the UHF and thus lead to the quick conversion of existing sets to UHF and to production of new UHF receivers.

(i) Three zones were established with different minimum spacings. In Zone I, comprising broadly the Northern States, where population density is greatest and where large cities are most numerous, the minimum cochannel VHF spacing was reduced to 170. In zone II, the gulf area, minimum spacing was set at 220 miles because tropospheric interference was more likely and wider spacings were required to compensate for reduction in service areas caused by interference. The rest of the country was placed in zone III, within minimum spacing of 190 miles. It should be noted, however, that in each zone the great bulk of the actual separations between assignments was greater than the minimum specified.

(j) Increased heights and power were provided for both VHF and UHF. This had a very important consequence in the VHF of extending the service areas substantially beyond that contemplated in earlier planning. However, as a compromise measure, in zone I antenna heights with maximum power were limited to 1,000 feet.

(k) Each station in a region was given the possibility of having substantially the same coverage, since the same maximum and minimum powers were established. In addition, UHF stations were permitted substantially greater power than VHF stations in an attempt to compensate for the known coverage difficulties of UHF.

(l) Intermixture of VHF and UHF in the same community was accepted as an integral part of the assignment plan. This permitted maximum efficiency from a technical standpoint in the distribution of assignments. Also, it should be noted that the opponents of intermixture, such as Du Mont, would have provided most of the largest markets with VHF only. Nonintermixture would have meant that UHF would have been limited to markets overshadowed by VHF in large communities and, where such area intermixture did not exist, the UHF communities would have been of relatively limited economic significance. It is thus quite conceivable that nonintermixture would not have helped UHF nationally in any substantial degree. Stated another way, the alternative to intermixture was not nonintermixture, but a transition to UHF only (assuming that there was not enough space in the VHF for a nationwide competitive television system).

(m) A total of 252 assignments were made for noncommercial educational stations, divided as between 68 VHF stations and 174 UHF. A number of VHF assignments went to major communities (viz, Boston, Pittsburgh, St. Louis, New Orleans) where there were fewer than three VHF stations in operation at the time.

(n) The Commission did not use the protected service contour as in AM, but established standards of signal service. The "protection" any station had was the extent of its cochannel and adjacent-channel separations.

(o) A station was given relative freedom to locate in such a way as to provide service to more than one community, so long as it provided a signal of specific strength over the city to which it was assigned. Thus, a station assigned to a given community might locate its transmitter 20 or 30 miles out in order to cover nearby cities as well as the assigned community.

C. Resumption of Commission Processing of Applications

The Commission's sixth report provided that the Commission would begin processing applications for new stations or for changes in existing stations beginning July 1, 1952. When television application processing was resumed, more than 700 applications were on file and several hundred followed. The first group of applications were granted on July 11, 1952, when permits were issued for 18 television stations in various cities. The sharpest growth took place between 1952 and 1954, when the total number of stations on the air increased from 108 to 380.

91

Lawrence W. Lichty

MEMBERS OF THE FEDERAL RADIO COMMISSION AND FEDERAL COMMUNICATIONS COMMISSION 1927–1961

WITH OCCASIONAL exceptions in the past, FCC commissioners are rarely singled out to stand before the public. They are not asked to answer to a recognized constituency. Their terms exceed the span of those who appoint and approve them for office. Further, the collective nature of the Commission usually provides each member with a cloak of anonymity.

Information is presented on commissioner's length of service, age at the time of appointment, native geographical area, education, occupation, prior service in state and federal governments, prior service on the Commission, prior experience in broadcasting, occupation after Commission service, and publications.[1]

Since March 2, 1927, when President Calvin Coolidge appointed the original five members of the FRC, 43 men and one woman have served on either the FRC or its successor, the FCC [to 1961]. From

Journal of Broadcasting, Vol. VI., No. 1 (Winter 1961–62), pp. 23–34.

March 15, 1927, to July 10, 1934, 12 men served as FRC commissioners. Four of these men served, at one time or another, as chairman. With the exception of Admiral Bullard, who died after only eight months in office, all the chairmen of the FRC also served as regular members of that Commission.

Since July 11, 1934, 13 men have served as chairmen of the FCC. Seven of these men were also regular members of the Commission. In addition to these seven men, 28 other persons, including one woman, Frieda B. Hennock, have served as commissioners. Eugene O. Sykes and Thad H. Brown were members of both the FRC and the FCC, and Judge Sykes served as chairman of both bodies.

Length of Service

The length of time various commissioners have served on the FRC and FCC varies a great deal, but this can be misleading. The extremes run from Commissioner Paul A. Walker, who served for 19 years on the FCC, to Commissioners Hampson Gary and Charles H. King, who were members of the Commission only six months. It should be remembered that an appointee may be chosen to serve several full terms or the few remaining months of an unexpired term suddenly left vacant.

A full term for commissioners is seven years, but to 1961 only 12 members have served that long. Eight members have served less than one year; 14 members have served one to five years; 12 members have served five to 10 years; three members have served more than 10 years. This does not include those members presently serving on the FCC. One member, T. A. M. Craven was a commissioner from 1937 to 1944 and returned to the Commission in 1956, more than 12 years service. Commissioner Hyde has served 15 years and Commissioner Bartley, nine. The average length of service on the Commission has been about four and one-half years (54.4 months).

Age at Time of Original Appointment

The age of commissioners when appointed shows nearly as wide a range as their length of service. Commissioners Henry A. Bellows and Sam Pickard were only 31 years old when appointed. Commissioners Frederick I. Thompson, Anning S. Prall, and Frank R. McNinch were more than twice that old when they were appointed. At the time of their original appointment five members were under 35; 12 were 35 to 44; 15 were 45 to 50; eight were 55 to 60; and four were over 60 years of age.

Charles R. Denny, Jr., was the youngest member to have served as chairman. He was appointed acting chairman just two months before his 34th birthday and became chairman when he was 34.

Chairman Minow was named by President Kennedy a week before his 35th birthday.

Political Background of Commissioners

The Communications Act of 1934 requires that not more than four members of the FCC shall be members of the same political party. The FRC was composed of five members, and no more than three could be from the same party. Twenty-three Democrats, 19 Republicans, and two independents have been appointed to the Commission.

Caution should be exercised in relation to declared political affiliation with political "philosophy." Commissioner Craven, a registered Democrat, was a vehement antagonist of the tougher government regulation sought by President Roosevelt and Chairman James L. Fly, also a Democrat. Craven later opposed Democrat Newton N. Minow's regulatory philosophy regarding program content of broadcasting stations. Conversely, the "Republicanism" of Commissioner Ray C. Wakefield was frequently questioned; he was a strong supporter of federal regulation and a staunch defender of Chairman Fly.

The politics of the Commission chairmen thus far have always followed party lines. The first three chairmen of the FRC were Republicans appointed by Presidents Coolidge and Hoover. When Franklin Roosevelt was inaugurated, Democrat Eugene O. Sykes was named chairman. All the chairmen of the FCC under Roosevelt and Truman were Democrats; although an Independent, E. K. Jett, served as interim chairman for one month in 1944.

When Dwight D. Eisenhower became President in 1953, he named Rosel Hyde to be the first Republican ever to serve as chairman of the FCC. After Chairman Hyde, Republicans served as chairmen until President Kennedy's nomination of Newton N. Minow in 1961.

Most commissioners have had some prior political party experience before their appointment; as noted, there have been only two independents (Jett and Webster). In general, commissioners have had only minor or incidental dealings in politics. Few have come from high elective jobs. However, Commissioners Prall and Jones were congressmen; and Commissioners Wills and Case, governors.

A number of commissioners have been active campaign managers or assistants before their appointments. These include Commissioners Brown, Hanley, McNinch, Payne, Porter, Hennock, Lee, King, and Minow. Naturally, prospective appointees must be politically acceptable, as well as professionally competent, to win a nomination and Senate approval. Professor E. Pendleton Herring notes that "even the most able Commissioner would seldom have attained the position without political connections." [2]

Geographical Distribution

Five commissioners have come from New York, which is the greatest number from any state. Four have been residents of Texas and four of the District of Columbia. Ohio has had three members. Four states have had two members: California, Utah, Alabama, and West Virginia. The states of Maine, Vermont, Rhode Island, Pennsylvania, Indiana, Illinois, Michigan, Wisconsin, Minnesota, Nebraska, Kansas, Iowa, Maryland, Florida, North Carolina, Kentucky, Mississippi, Arkansas, Oklahoma, and Idaho have each contributed one commissioner. Twenty-three states have never had a resident on the Commission. Eighteen commissioners came from the Atlantic seaboard; only five from the Mountain or Pacific states. However, legal residence can be confusing. For example, Commissioner Hyde is legally a resident of Idaho, but he lived in the District of Columbia since 1924.

Under the Radio Act of 1927, members of the FRC had to actually reside in and represent one of five "radio zones" defined by that act. This is not a requirement under the Communications Act of 1934.

Educational Backgrounds

Viewed very broadly, members of the Commission have been professional men. Their training has been academic and legal rather than technical. Five of the commissioners had no formal college training. Seven attended college but did not receive degrees. However, three of these men, Commissioners Paul A. Porter, Rosel H. Hyde, and George H. Payne, received LL.B. degrees from other institutions. A fourth, Thad H. Brown, studied law in an office.

Two commissioners studied at normal schools, one in West Virginia (Fairmount), and the other in Nebraska (Fremont). Twenty-one commissioners were graduated with Bachelor of Arts, Bachelor of Science, or Bachelor of Philosophy degrees. Dr. Irvin Stewart received an A.B., a LL.B., a master's and a Ph.D. Charles H. King received a Master of Laws and Dr. H. A. Bellows earned a Ph.D.

The commissioners attended large and small, as well as private and public, schools. Only two schools can claim more than one commissioner as an alumnus. Commissioner Hyde attended Utah Agriculture College and Commissioner Lafount was graduated from that same institution. Four commissioners were graduated from the U.S. Naval Academy, one from the U.S. Military Academy, and one from the Coast Guard Academy.

More than one-half of the commissioners had some sort of legal training before their appointment to the FRC or FCC. Seventeen members of the Commission earned LL.B. degrees. Two were graduated with Doctor of Jurisprudence degrees. One attended but did not graduate from law school, and two studied in law offices. Clifford J. Durr, the only commissioner to do college work abroad, received a B.A. in Jurisprudence from Oxford (Queen's College). Just as in undergraduate training, the commissioners attended many types of law schools; large, small, night, and part-time as well. Three commissioners received their Bachelor of Laws from, and a fourth attended, Harvard Law School. No other law school can claim more than one graduate.

The education of commissioners seems to be representative of the various educational facilities available in the United States. Many attended local colleges; more than half sought graduate study or legal training, usually at more well-known institutions. Other commissioners read law privately or studied in an office. Several taught in universities at one time or another.

Occupational Backgrounds

Members of the FRC and FCC show as much variety in their professional careers as they do in their educational backgrounds—but some generalizations can be made. The "typical" commissioner had prior experience in law or government service before joining the Commission. It is also probable that he participated in politics and held prior office on the local, state, or national level. While many have taken some interest in politics (as noted above), the lawyer, jurist, educator, journalist, engineer or businessman has been more frequently appointed than the professional politician.

One-half of the commissioners (22) worked in law or government service as their primary occupation. Other primary occupational backgrounds have been divided between business, journalism and the military. Specifically, but just in terms of primary occupation, 11 commissioners have been from government service; 11 have had backgrounds in law; six have been in business, five have been journalists; five have been from the military, and two each have been educators, engineers or jurists.

It should be noted that a classification such as the above is only one view of the commissioners' backgrounds. For example, T. A. M. Craven's primary occupation before coming to the Commission was the naval service. Orestes H. Caldwell was a journalist, John S. Cross worked in government service and William D. L. Starbuck was an attorney. But all four of these men had excellent backgrounds in engineering. In reporting only a primary occupation, much of the depth of these men is lost.

Commissioner Craven was a radio officer in the Navy and chief engineer for the FCC before being named Commissioner. Commissioner Caldwell edited a variety of radio and electronic publications. Commissioner Cross studied electrical engineering at college and was Assistant Chief of Telecommunications for the Department of State. Commissioner Starbuck worked as an engineer for almost 20 years before becoming an attorney and specializing in radio patent law.

It should also be noted that the occupation "attorney" or "lawyer" is a very ambiguous definition of what a man does, since there is a great deal of difference between types of lawyers. Commissioner Starbuck was a patent attorney; Commissioner Lee served as an FBI agent and accountant. Commissioner Fly was a government attorney and argued the constitutionality of the Tennessee Valley Authority before the Supreme Court of the United States. Commissioner McConnaughey was a corporation lawyer for business firms in Cleveland. Chairmen Coy and Minow were assistants to state governors. Thus, more occupational information about the commissioners is necessary for a proper understanding of their backgrounds.

Prior Service with the Commission

Ten commissioners served with the Commission in some capacity prior to their appointment as members—usually in the legal or engineering departments.

Commissioners Craven, Jett, and Sterling were chief engineers. Commissioner Webster had been assistant chief engineer. Commissioners Denny and Hyde, who both served as chairman of the Commission, were general counsels to the FCC before their appointments. Commissioner Brown, a member of the FRC and FCC, was general counsel of the FRC before his appointment to that body. Commissioner Pickard was secretary to the Radio Commission before his appointment as a member of the FRC. Commissioner Bartley was with the FRC and was director of the FCC's original telegraph division from 1934 to 1937; he was appointed to the Commission in 1952. Commissioner Ford joined the FCC staff in 1947 as the first chief of the Broadcast Bureau's hearing division; he became a commissioner in 1957. Commissioner John F. Dillon, who served as one of the original members of the FRC until his death, had been a radio inspector for the Commerce Department before the Radio Commission was formed. Commissioner Gary was a member of the Commission and later worked on the staff. Mr. Gary was one of the original seven members of the FCC in 1934. After less than six months on the FCC, he resigned and was subsequently named general counsel to the Commission.

Prior Service in State and Federal Governments

Twenty commissioners had some previous experience in state governments. Six served on state public service commissions of various kinds. Two were governors, William H. Wills of Vermont and Norman S. Case of Rhode Island. Two were state jurists, and three served in their state's legislature.

Twenty-nine of the 44 commissioners served the federal government in other capacities before they came to the FRC or FCC. Seven of these were legal counsels; six served on other commissions or boards; and two served in the House of Representatives.

Only four commissioners had no previous service with state or federal government before their appointment to the Federal Radio Commission or Federal Communications Commission.

Prior Experience in Broadcasting

Twenty-four commissioners had some previous experience with broadcasting before becoming members of the Commission. As mentioned above, eight men had previous service with the FRC or FCC, and one was an inspector for the Commerce Department before the FRC was formed. Commissioners Coy and Bellows were radio station managers. Commissioner Caldwell, as previously mentioned, was the editor of numerous radio publications. Commissioner Bartley served with the National Association of Broadcasters and had earlier service as an executive with the Yankee Radio Network. Commissioner Pickard started a "college of the air" at Kansas State Agricultural College and broadcast farm programs to over 100 stations in the midwest for the U.S. Department of Agriculture.

Five commissioners had previous radio engineering experience in the military or in private business. Commissioner Lafount and his father owned a small radio equipment manufacturing company in Salt Lake City. Commissioner Merrill had been with the telephone branch of the War Production Board. Commissioner Cross had been with the telecommunications division of the State Department, with experience in the negotiation of international frequency allocation agreements.

Occupation after Commission Service

In order to obtain a more complete picture of the careers of FRC and FCC members, it is also necessary to look at their careers *after* they left the Commission, as well as their *prior* service. It will be remembered that some of the commissioners were comparatively young men when appointed to the Commission. Most of the members practice law or go into business (usually broadcasting) after they leave the Commission, generally following the occupation they pursued before joining the Commission.

In determining the occupation of commissioners after Commission service, it should be noted that 16 members have been excluded from the study. These are the seven commissioners presently in office, [1961] the four who died in office, and four members who retired. The remaining 29 members have been employed after serving on the Commission.

Fourteen former members resumed the practice of law after leaving the Commission. Most of these specialized in legal matters involving broadcasting. Six former members later worked in broadcasting. Commissioner Bellows went back to Minneapolis as manager of WCCO, later becoming a vice-president at CBS, and then did public relations work for General Mills until his retirement. Wayne Coy became a radio-television consultant with Time, Inc., and later a station owner in partnership with Time before his death in 1957. Charles R. Denny became a vice-president of the National Broadcasting Company. E.K. Jett is vice-president and general manager of WMAR-TV in Baltimore.

Before his death in 1952, Harold Lafount was a radio-television consultant for the Bulova Watch Company and an executive in several broadcasting companies. Sam Pickard, after leaving the FRC, became a vice-president at CBS and part-owner of an Albany, New York, radio station—which lost its license because he concealed his 24% interest in the station.

Commissioner Craven, after his resignation from the FCC in 1944, served as a vice-president of the Iowa Broadcasting Company (Cowles Publications), later serving as a consulting engineer with his own firm. In 1950 Mr. Craven was reappointed to the Commission.

Three former commissioners have taken jobs in government service and two others jobs in business other than broadcasting. Four former commissioners pursued occupations in education, journalism, and engineering. E. M. Webster, representing the latter, became an engineering consultant frequently working with broadcasters.

Publications

Publication of books and articles is sufficiently common among members of the Commission to give a tinge of scholarship to the group. Although the list is probably not complete, at least seven commissioners have published books. Three other members have written radio manuals. The commissioners also have a large number of popular and scholarly articles to their credit. Most common of the latter are articles for law journals or reviews—at least nine commissioners have written one or more legal articles.

Commissioners Bellows, Caldwell, Payne, Porter, Thompson, and Robinson were journalists sometime before their service on the Commission. Commissioner Ford was on the editorial staff of the *West Virginia Law Review* while he was in school there, and Newton Minow was editor-in-chief of the *Northwestern University Law Review*. Commissioner Payne wrote at least six books. One (*Fourth Estate and Radio*) is a compilation of various speeches he made discussing the role of the Federal Communications Commission. As an editor of the McGraw-Hill Publishing Company, Orestes H. Caldwell was in charge of a score or more publications at different times during his career. As a member of the original Radio Commission, he frequently wrote for the *New York Times* and other newspapers explaining the plans and policies of the FRC. Commissioner Robinson contributed to at least four different law journals. Commissioner Steward edited the special March 1929 issue of the *Annals of the American Academy of Political and Social Science* on "Radio." Commissioner Bartley wrote several articles for magazines explaining his position on the VHF-UHF dilemma. Commissioner Bellows edited and wrote numerous books, including a translation of Scandinavian poetry.

In general, the publications of these commissioners show evidence of their competence to deal with their responsibilities as commissioners. But none the less, while scholarship might be considered an important qualification for appointment to the Commission, the writing done by these members, for the most part, is incidental to their selection for the Commission. The average publication of commissioners is a legal explanation or clarification of their position while they are members of the Commission. But rarely does the wealth of experience and knowledge gained by commissioners while in office find its way into books written by those commissioners.

Summary

In summary, nearly all members of the Federal Radio Commission and the Federal Communications Commission (to October 1961) had service in federal or state government offices prior to their appointments. Lawyers have served more frequently than members from any other occupational group. Businessmen, journalists, career military officers, engineers, and educators have also been members. Commissioners, in general, have been appointed from relatively wide educational and occupational backgrounds and to some extent from a variety of geographical areas. None of the commissioners has left high management status in the broadcasting industry to serve on the Commission. However, several have gone from the FRC or FCC to high positions with one of the broadcasting networks, or have become station owners and/or operators. None of the members has come from the so-called "creative" or "artistic" area of broadcasting; i.e., writers, producers, performers, or directors. Some commissioners have been questioned as to their impartiality and/or honesty, and have resigned "under fire," but at this writing such charges have never been upheld by a court of law.

92

Lawrence W. Lichty

THE IMPACT OF FRC AND FCC COMMISSIONERS' BACKGROUNDS ON THE REGULATION OF BROADCASTING

EVEN A QUICK glance at broadcasting trade magazines will demonstrate the industry's deep concern with any change in the membership of the Federal Communications Commission. The reason for this concern seems obvious. Since 1927, when Congress created the Federal Radio Commission, the regulatory activities of the FRC and then the FCC have changed in direction and emphasis many times. Sometimes the Commission has been vigorously aggressive, while at other times it has been completely unobtrusive. Frequently the Commission has concerned itself with programing; while at other times it has been more concerned with engineering problems, the economics of broadcasting, or some other matters.

The thesis of this article is that these changes in the direction and emphasis of the Commission's regulation of broadcasting are a function of the members serving on the Commission at those specific times. Further, the personal experience, education, occupational background, and governmental philosophy of the members of the Federal Radio Commission and Federal Communications Commission directly influence the direction and emphasis of the agency's policies.

There are at least three ways of studying the decision making process: (1) "decision makers," their social and personal differences as related to the kinds of decisions they make; (2) "partisans in an issue," i.e. pressure groups, power structures, propaganda, and the like; or (3) the "decision making process," the effect of the internal

Journal of Broadcasting, Vol. VI, No. 2 (Spring 1962), pp. 97–110.

organization and the interaction between the decision makers as related to the outcome of the complex process of decision making. The present study depends primarily on the first of these approaches. This is not to say that the other approaches would not also be very fruitful. For example, the "partisans in an issue" approach might be very useful but such a study would, of necessity, require an exhaustive examination of the power structure of the broadcasting industry, Congress, the administrative branch of the federal government, and many other pressure groups, large and small. Such an all-inclusive study did not seem feasible. The "decision making process" approach might also be used but this method generally centers on one case or issue; thus it would not provide the continuity or long range view sought by this study.

An examination of the history of FRC and FCC regulation reveals, and strikingly so, that the major problems that now face the FCC seem to have been present from the birth of commercial radio in the United States. For example, the problems created by the limited amount of spectrum space, the problems of taste in advertising, classes of stations, signal interference, the problem of monopoly, censorship, editorializing, government regulation versus self-regulation, "public service" programing, the Commission's concern with programing balance, the Commission's concern with excessive amounts of advertising, violence and crime in programs, acceptability of programs for children—these are problems that have, in one degree or another, been the concern of the Commission since 1927. Even the problem of the television spectrum is not new. The FCC was concerned with video allocation not only in 1948 and 1941, but the FRC reported on the problem as early as 1928.[2] But from a standpoint of emphasis, the history of federal regulation of broadcasting may be characterized by several periods of development.[3]

Before 1927 there was practically no control of broadcasting. The Acts of 1910 and 1912 had given some control to the Commerce Department, but a federal district court ruling in 1926 completely stripped the Secretary of Commerce of his power to enforce the penalty provisions of the laws. Chaos reigned; stations changed frequencies and power at will. On February 23, 1927, a new radio act was passed and the Federal Radio Commission of five members created.

Establishing Technical Standards, 1927–1930

In 1927 the FRC began the job of untangling the mess. As the *First Annual Report* of the FRC states, "The work of the FRC from its first meeting, March 15, 1927, . . . was devoted almost exclusively to cleaning up the broadcast situation."[4] Slowly it reduced the number of total authorizations and thus greatly reduced interference, especially at night. In 1928 the FRC established a system of classification for stations that provided for local, regional, and clear channels. From the beginning the FRC specified frequency, location, and power and saw that they were strictly enforced.

The Federal Radio Commission, 1927–1930, was made up, to a large degree, of technical experts in radio. Four of the original five members can properly be described as radio pioneers. Chairman W. H. G. Bullard had been in charge of Navy Communications and an observer on the RCA Board of Directors. Orestes H. Caldwell had been an engineer and editor of numerous radio publications. Henry A. Bellows had been a station manager in Minnesota. Col. John F. Dillon had been a radio inspector for the Department of Commerce. One, Eugene O. Sykes, had been a lawyer.

Of the original members, only Judge Sykes served at length on the Commission. Two commissioners died shortly after their appointments. Two others, Commissioners Caldwell and Bellows, left to return to private business after technical chaos began to be remedied. According to Mr. Caldwell, "It was the purpose of most of us to get the job done and get home to our own occupations." [5] The two commissioners next appointed had broadcasting backgrounds. Sam Pickard had been an educational broadcaster in Kansas and for the Department of Agriculture; Harold Lafount had been a receiving set manufacturer in Utah. Six of the seven members of the Commission during this period, then, had prior experience in some phases of broadcasting; engineering, programming, or equipment manufacture.

The FRC and Important Legal Actions, 1930–1934

By 1929 the Commission had been challenged on a number of its decisions, rules and orders. Commissioners found an increasing necessity to defend their decisions in the courts. In 1928 the FRC had added a legal division as well as an engineering division to the already existing licensing division and press service. This was a time when the important rulings that might set precedence were coming before the commissioners. As McMahon has noted, "It (the FRC) immediately began to follow up the 'broad powers' concept of its enabling legislation by beginning to establish standards in specific cases which give notice to broadcasting interests concerning the type of service they might be expected to provide." [6] Dr. McMahon has listed six precedent-setting opinions in this regard. They are (1) the WCRW case, 1928; (2) the Schaeffer case, 1930; (3) the Dr. Norman Baker case, 1930; (4) the Dr. John Brinkley case, 1931; (5) the Rev. Schuler case, 1931; (6) and the Great Lakes Application decision, 1928.

During this period there was an increasing number of men with legal backgrounds on the Commission. William D. L. Starbuck had an engineering background, but after eighteen years as a mechanical engineer was admitted to the bar and specialized in radio law. Thad H. Brown had been the general counsel of the Federal Power Commission and general counsel for the FRC. Ira E. Robinson had been a judge in West Virginia and special assistant to the U.S. Attorney General. James Hanley had also been a lawyer. The only other member of the FRC not mentioned thus far, General C. McK. Saltzman who served from 1929–1932, had been with the Army Signal Corps and a delegate to several international radio conferences.

Thus, during the last year and a half of its existence, the FRC was composed of four lawyers and one radio equipment manufacturer, Harold Lafount.

Cleaning-up, 1934–1938

After the FCC took over, and under Chairman Anning S. Prall, the Commission seemed to get a little tougher especially in the area of programming. While it is true that the FRC had refused renewal for a number of broadcasters who were "medical quacks," "crackpots," and "swindlers" between 1928 and 1931, the FCC now concentrated its crack-downs on a limited number of stations. The Commission frequently warned stations about good taste in programs, fortune-tellers, astrologers, acceptable advertising, and the like. Many incidents during this time seem to have been personal crusades on the part of individual commissioners. Examples are the WMCA "Birconjel" opinion which was delivered after a hearing literally demanded by Chairman Prall, or Commissioner Walker's almost single-handed investigation of the telephone industry. Other opinions that reveal the tenor of Commission during this time are (1) the KFEQ (St. Joseph, Missouri) astrologer opinion; (2) the WAAT (Jersey City, New Jersey) race track information opinion; (3) WAAE (Hammond, Indiana) "Pur-Erg" advertising opinion; (4) WGBZ (York, Nebraska) "Texas Crystals" advertising opinion; (5) KFRC (San Francisco, California) "Marmola" dietary advertising opinion; (6) refusal to grant a station to a chiropractor opinion (Athens, Georgia); (7) KTWI (Twin Falls, Idaho) "Friendly Thinker" advice opinion; (8) NBC "Mae West" ruling; (9) Blue Network "Beyond the Horizon" opinion; (10) and the 1939 FCC memo on "undesirable program materials."

But even though the Commission was very vigorous during this time in its application of the law, coercion was used rather than the actual revocation of licenses.

The members of the Commission who served during this so-called "cleaning-up" period (1934–1938) can be characterized as lawyers and men with prior experience in government. Four of the eight commissioners during this time had experience as lawyers. Commissioner Gary had been practicing law for 12 years immediately preceding his appointment to the Commission, and later became general counsel. Commissioners Sykes, Brown, and Case had also practiced law.

All eight of these members had some previous experience in government service; Commissioner Gary had been a diplomat; Commissioner Prall had been a congressman; Commissioner Stewart had been in the Department of State; Commissioner Sykes had been a state judge; Commissioner Brown had been on the civil service commission in Ohio and general counsel for the Federal Power Commission and the FRC; Commissioner Payne had been a tax commissioner in New York; Commissioner Case had been the governor of Rhode Island; and Commissioner Walker had been a member of a state commission and a referee for a state court. Only Commissioner Walker had been serving on a public utilities regulation commission (the Oklahoma Corporation Commission) immediately before coming to the FCC.

Although the Commission had been involved with programing matters since 1927, it was only after technical matters had been resolved that programming was given concerted attention. It seems to have been important to the development of regulation during this period that the Commission was staffed with more men with legal experience.

Additionally, the "crusading" of the Commission seems to have been carried on the shoulders of a few commissioners. It has been stated that "FDR (President Roosevelt) for mysterious reasons packed the first FCC with political hacks and has-beens who were content to draw their paychecks." [7] This is an exaggeration and unfair to several of the dedicated members of that first FCC. But it is true that some of the first members of the FCC were older than the average commissioner has been, and several had been very involved in politics—they were strong supporters of Franklin Roosevelt—before their appointments.

The Period of "Trust-busting," 1939–1945

During the "trust-busting" era, the Commission forced NBC to sell its second network, ended dual ownership of facilities serving the same area, and sought wider diversification of media ownership.

On November 14, 1938, the FCC Network Inquiry Committee began to probe the network structure in broadcasting, prompted by complaints from the Mutual network. In June of 1940 the committee released its "sensational" report. The committee proposed licensing of networks, non-exclusive network contracts, changes in the option-time arrangement, and what the broadcasting industry generally opposed as "confiscatory control of contractual relations between networks and affiliates." In 1941 the FCC announced its "Chain Broadcasting Regulations" based on this report. In May of 1943 the Supreme Court of the United States upheld the network rules as constitutional. Additionally, during this period the FCC let it be known that it was generally interested in the wider diversification of the ownership of the mass media and it looked with disfavor towards the applications of owners of newspapers or other stations for new facilities. The FCC adopted the "duopoly rule" which stated that a person or company could not own more than one station that served substantially the same area. This was made effective June 1, 1944 and affected 40 existing multiple ownerships.

This period was most strongly influenced by two chairmen of the Commission, Frank R. McNinch and James L. Fly. Chairman McNinch had been a lawyer and had served on the Federal Power Commission before coming to the FCC. He was the FCC chairman when it first began its investigation of network practices. After Chairman McNinch's resignation, President Roosevelt appointed James Lawrence Fly chairman. Less than three years prior to his appointment to the FCC, Mr. Fly was the head of the legal department of the Tennessee Valley Authority. There he took charge of trial and appeal of a number of cases testing the constitutionality of TVA before the Supreme Court, just as he led the defense of the FCC's chain regulations.

In addition to these two chairmen, Commissioner Paul Porter had been with the Agriculture Adjustment Administration, and Commissioner Clifford Durr had been with the legal department of the Reconstruction Finance Corporation. The TVA, AAA and RFC were all newly created "New Deal" agencies. Further, Commissioner Paul Walker had been a member of a state public utilities commission and instituted the telephone investigation in 1935. Commissioner Walker was a member of the original network inquiry Committee in 1938. Commissioner Ray Wakefield had also been a member of a state commission—the California Railroad Commission.

It should be pointed out here that there was certainly not unanimity on the Commission in these matters. Commissioner T. A. M. Craven, former Navy and FCC staff engineer, was a member of the FCC at this time, but he strongly opposed the Chain Broadcasting Regulations as unconstitutional. He felt (and feels) that the FCC should never concern itself with the programming of stations. At this time he was in the minority.

It seems that this period of the Commission membership can be characterized by men with prior government service, especially men with public utility and "New Deal" agency backgrounds. Commissioners McNinch, Fly, Durr and Porter had been in the legal departments of such agencies. Commissioners Walker and Wakefield had been members of similar state agencies.

Emphasis on Public Service, New Radio Facilities, and TV Engineering Problems: 1946–1952

On March 7, 1946, the FCC issued a pronouncement entitled *Public Service Responsibilities of Broadcast Licensees*, which soon became known as the "Blue Book." This memo proposed no new rules or regulations but outlined what the Commission regarded as programming in the public interest. It is difficult to assess the exact affect of the "Blue Book." It was not a ruling or decision, only a memo stating the Commission's opinion. None the less, some of the commissioners felt very strongly about its issuance; it was passed unanimously. Clifford Durr, a commissioner at the time, says, "I strongly approved of the so-called 'Blue Book' . . . this expresses some of my philosophy about the regulation of broadcasting." [8] The "Blue Book" was taken quite seriously by the Commission and the broadcasting industry for several years, receiving a great deal of attention in the trade press, although later there seemed to be less emphasis on strict adherence.

Two other important developments took place during this period—the huge increase in radio authorizations and the "TV freeze." In 1945 there were 956 AM authorizations and 56 FM authorizations; by 1952 there were 2408 AM authorizations and 650 FM authorizations (falling from a high of 966 in 1949). Of course, there had been no construction during the war, but this was still a tremendous increase in the number of radio outlets. Working with a backlog of over a thousand applications, the FCC granted 64 FM stations and set hearings on 231 AM applications on one day.

Because of the confusion surrounding engineering standards and color television, the FCC declared the television "freeze" on new applications (but not on construction of stations already authorized) in 1948. In 1952 the freeze was lifted and the FCC's *Sixth Report and Order* provided a master plan for station allocations.

This period seems to be primarily influenced by former members of the FCC staff—engineers and chief counsels. Chairman Denny and Commissioner Hyde were both chief counsels of the FCC before their respective appointments to the Commission. Commissioners Jett, Sterling, and Webster were all on the FCC engineering staff before their appointments; Mr. Jett and Mr. Sterling as chief engineers, and Mr. Webster as assistant chief engineer. The backgrounds of these members can conceivably account for the emphasis given to the attempt to publicly state criteria for programming evaluation—the "Blue Book"—and the time given to the consideration of television engineering standards.

Other members of the Commission at this time included Chairman Albert Wayne Coy, who had been with the Works Progress Administration and White House Liaison Office, a journalist, and broadcaster; Commissioners Durr and Walker, previously mentioned above and both strongly in favor of the "Blue Book;" William H. Wills, former governor of Vermont, who served less than a year; Frieda B. Hennock, a New York attorney; and Robert F. Jones, an Ohio congressman.

Commissioner Jones dissented against the *Sixth Report and Order,* and Miss Hennock abstained from voting because she felt more provisions were needed for educational facilities. But Commissioner Hennock, the "evangelist of educational television," had succeeded in having one-tenth of the channels set aside for this purpose.

Moderate Regulation, 1953–1960

During this period a great deal of the Commission's time was taken up with new television applications and there was less concern with programming in the rush to get stations on the air. Radio was losing the limelight and the audience, and advertising revenue had leveled off to some extent. There was less FCC concern with both radio and television programming during this period. A majority of the commissioners during this time (McConnaughey, Doerfer, Hyde and Craven) could be said to subscribe to the principle, "The agency that regulates best is the agency that regulates least."

During this time a number of the commissioners had previous experience on state regulatory commissions. Commissioner Walker, previously mentioned, and Commissioner Merrill, a recess member appointed by President Truman, both had been on state commissions but served only briefly during this period and left the FCC in 1953. President Eisenhower's first three appointments to the FCC following his inauguration in 1953 were members of state public utility commissions. Chairman George C. McConnaughey served on the Public Utilities Commission of Ohio. Commissioner Richard Mack had previous service on the Florida Railroad and Public Utilities Commission, and Commissioner John Doerfer had been a member of the Wisconsin Public Service Commission.

Four commissioners during this time had previous service with the FCC; Frederick Ford, as chief of the hearing division of the Broadcast Bureau; Robert Bartley, as director of the telegraph division: Rosel Hyde, as chief counsel; and T. A. M. Craven as chief engineer and commissioner before he returned to private business. The two other commissioners during this period also had extensive government experience prior to their appointments. Robert E. Lee had been with the Federal Bureau of Investigation and the House Appropriations Committee. John S. Cross had been with the telecommunications section of the Department of State.

An Increased Emphasis on Programming, 1960

Under Chairmen Frederick Ford, and Newton Minow, the Commission seemed to shift to what they interpret as a more "vigorous application of the law." In addition to more stringent regulation, more emphasis seems to have been placed on programming considerations. Part of this emphasis was, no doubt, an effect of: the "rigged" quiz shows, "payola" scandals, and numerous congressional investigations of broadcasting. This change of emphasis was made more obvious by new Commission authority to (1) fine stations for infractions, (2) place stations on shortened license periods for infractions, and (3) adopt a new renewal form to include more detailed information about programming.[9]

Chairman Newton N. Minow favored "vigorous application of the law." [10] His early concern with the legality of the FCC's programming requirements in light of his legal background and his expressed concern over educational broadcasting (following his association with an educational film production company and Midwest Council for Airborne Television) seem to bear out the general thesis of this article. Further, it is clear that Minow's appointment tipped the balance in favor of tougher regulation. A station's license was set for a renewal hearing because that station allegedly failed to fulfill its programing promises made on its license application. According to *Broadcasting*, the hearing "would never have been possible without the chairman, the renewal hearing was ordered on a 4-3 vote." [11] [KORD, Pasco, Wa., the license was renewed July 1961.]

But despite these shifts in emphasis and swings from aggressiveness to quiescence, it is important to note that with few minor changes the federal law regarding broadcasting has remained the same since 1927. According to Sydney Head:

> That Congress was satisfied with both the Act itself and the Commission's basic interpretation is apparent from the fact that Congress made no major changes when the opportunity arose in 1934. . . .
> That the 1927 legislation has withstood the test of time and attacks from every imaginable source attests to the remarkable soundness of the work done by Congress . . . back in 1927, when broadcasting was in its infancy. Both wire and wireless communications have experienced enormous and revolutionary growth since then . . . Yet the Act has been flexible enough to foster and control these innovations.[12]

Summary

The thesis of this article is that the personal experience, education, occupational background, and governmental philosophy of the members of the FRC and FCC have overtly influenced the direction and emphasis of the agency's policies. The backgrounds of the 44 commissioners serving from 1927 to 1961 were relatively diverse. Yet, in each of the seven periods outlined above, the backgrounds of the commissioners were remarkably homogeneous.

Additionally, while there have been other influences and pressures on the FRC and FCC (e.g. the President, Congress, public opinion, and the broadcasting industry) in the absence of a specific definition of "the public interest, convenience or necessity," the regulation of broadcasting in America has been influenced to a measurable degree by the occupational backgrounds and political philosophies of these commissioners. For example, the "technical" period was dominated by members who had engineering backgrounds; the "trust-busting" era was characterized by attorneys experienced in government regulation.

Two former commissioners interviewed by the writer have indicated their support of this general thesis. In addition to the explanations offered above, McConnaughey stated that commissioners frequently depended on the opinions of their colleagues on the Commission in areas where a specific commissioner was an expert.[13] Further, Clifford J. Durr offered the explanation that commissioners were influenced by the "atmosphere" created by a particular group of commissioners at any one time." [14]

The other influences and pressures referred to might best be studied by the "partisans in an issue" approach described at the beginning of this article, while the interaction among the commissioners serving at one time would probably be studied most usefully as an example of "small group decision making." These other approaches to the study of the decisions made by the FRC and FCC, no doubt would shed even more light on the operation of the Commission. However, these three different but interrelated approaches cannot be as easily separated as implied here. It seems obvious that the pressures that befall the Commission and the interaction between the members are both dependent, to an extent, on the social and personal backgrounds of these commissioners.

Thus, while it is a gross oversimplification, it seems that the FRC and the FCC have had to face "universal" problems, or at least the same general problems, throughout the history of broadcasting. The problems they tackled and the solutions they proposed were due in part to the individual interests of commissioners. Many important decisions or changes were the result of a "crusade" by one

commissioner: Anning S. Prall pushed the clean-up in commercials
and programs in poor taste; Paul Walker conducted the telephone investigation; James Lawrence Fly was worried about monopoly and
diversification of ownership; Clifford J. Durr was strongly interested
in the "Blue Book" and public expression on politics; Miss Frieda
Hennock fought for educational television reservations; Robert Bartley is especially concerned with the UHF problem; Orestes H.
Caldwell concerned himself with establishing proper engineering
requirements; and Newton N. Minow was strongly concerned with
television programing and educational broadcasting.

One other point seems important here—the "Commission" has
frequently been criticized as if it were a static, permanent, and
unchanging body. However, this clearly is not the case. "The Commission" has been composed of men with diametrically opposed
ideas of the agency's proper role. There is no one "Commission" as
has been frequently described by its critics. Instead there have been
a number of "Commissions" at different times with divergent opinions as to how broadcasting should be regulated. This should be
remembered by all those who would criticize "the Commission" as
inconsistent and contradictory.

93

Don R. LeDuc

THE FCC: A THEORY OF
REGULATORY REFLEX ACTION

THE CHALLENGER—television—appeared on the verge of revolutionizing broadcasting, its innovations stimulating public interest
and growing investment support.[1] Despite popular enthusiasm the
Commission seemed wary, allowed 12 years to elapse before acting
upon the new medium's request for access on a commercial basis,
then revoked the grant only three months later.[2] Before the end of
the 1940s the Commission would impose a second freeze upon access, this one extending four years.[3] From a technological standpoint
the television systems of 1952 could have been operating in 1940;
with Commission support or even interest, possibly as early as 1937.[4]

Federal Communications Bar Journal, Vol. XXIII, No. 2 (1969), pp. 93–109.

The time lapse did not seem related to economic demand or scientific progress, but did parallel to a remarkable extent a general industry attitude favoring gradual phasing in of the new service.

The challenger—FM—appeared on the verge of revolutionizing broadcasting, its innovations stimulating public interest and growing investment support.[5] Despite popular enthusiasm the Commission seemed wary, responding to a request for access with a grant experts declared far too narrow and remote to sustain economic life.[6] When the new medium managed not only to survive but to show moderate signs of growth the Commission acted again, this time decisively. Sudden exile to a higher frequency rendered all receivers obsolete, decimating existing audience [7] The virtual death of FM at that time as an independent entity did not seem traceable to any flaws in its technology but rather was the result of regulation reflecting the broadcaster view that frequency modulation should remain a subsidiary method of transmission.

The challenger—Cable—appeared on the verge of revolutionizing broadcasting, its innovations stimulating public interest and growing investment support.[8] Despite popular enthusiasm the Commission seemed wary, its initial act upon assuming jurisdiction curbing signal importation into top 100 markets where 85 to 90% of the national audience was located.[9] Two years later it made such importation virtually impossible, denying new major market Cable systems the feature of program diversification essential in attempts to gain new subscribers.[10] Limitations upon Cable functions did not seem attributable to any factor other than the industry position that such systems should augment but never fragment broadcaster audiences.

The locale might be varied without altering the basic plot. When non-scheduled airlines appeared on the verge of revolutionizing the flight industry in the late 1940s, the CAB reacted by refusing them access to lucrative markets. When motor carriers appeared on the verge of revolutionizing the freight hauling business in the 1930s, the ICC reacted by bringing them within agency jurisdiction, blunting their threat to regulated railroads.[11] Nor is the pattern exclusively federal in operation, as surveys of state insurance and public utility regulators indicate.[12] It seems generally that in a closely supervised, limited access industry, regulatory attitude towards a challenger chills to the same degree that public enthusiasm warms.

These brief chronologies are advanced simply to furnish a point of departure, not a destination. Lacking depth and detail, they cannot establish any definite pattern of evolution for a competitor within a closely regulated environment. They may, however, provide a basic framework for comparing various administrative reactions to such competition. If, as the underlying studies seem to indicate, similar regulatory response has occurred at parallel stages in each challenger's progression regardless of any unique characteristics it possesses, the crucial determinant of reaction would appear to lie within the regulator, and the most significant factor its motivation for such behavior.

A composite description of typical agency relationships has been drawn from attributes present in all case histories examined. The functioning of this "typical agency" will be analyzed in terms of recent administrative behavioral research to discover what factors may shape regulatory attitude, and in turn, motivate particular reactions to challenge.

If such factors can be isolated and described the knowledge should not only broaden understanding of past administrative actions but allow the drawing of implications for future challengers as well. Admittedly, this technique cannot provide a definitive answer to any question posed purely in legal terms. However, if legal issues are determined by an agency whose structure and functions in themselves create certain biases in weighing evidence, then to ignore such influences would be to ignore reality. This approach, then, is not so much designed to supply answers as to stimulate a questioning of bureaucratic apparatus often accepted as a constant in legal equations.

THE TYPICAL AGENCY

Agency-Legislature

1) The agency has been granted broad authority to regulate a field demanding a fairly high standard of expert knowledge.

2) Because the legislature lacks such knowledge, it is unable to provide meaningful or comprehensive standards to guide the agency in its supervisory role.

3) Because the legislature lacks such knowledge, it is unable either to continuously monitor agency operation or to understand its needs. As a result, its policy fluctuates from customary neglect to occasional over-zealous interference.

a) During periods of neglect it fails to provide adequate funds or to enact legislation requested.

b) During periods of interference it treats the agency as an adversary, discouraging cooperation and information flow from the agency.

Effects of Agency-Legislature Relationship

An agency is basically "an organization that makes policy" [13] and if we presume an administrator intends to behave rationally,[14] he strives for some policy, some "verbal image of that portion of the good society relevant to the function of the bureau concerned, and the means of constructing it." [15] But the usual "public interest" and its statutory variants [16] give little direction. As David Truman points out:

> The administrator is called upon to resolve difficulties that were too thorny for the legislature to solve, and he must do so in the face of the very forces that were acting in the legislature. . . .[17]

As a result, the agency ultimately must set its own standards, formulate its own policy, and in general settle its own disputes, alienated from its natural governmental advisor. Lacking resources to conduct its own research, it must often turn to its regulated industry for data, tightening bonds of affinity as it loosens its ties with the legislature.

Agency-Public

1) Industry services regulated by the agency typically are not basic necessities directly related to specific needs, and thus "public interest" with respect to a particular service is difficult to define and protect.

2) The public, because of indirect impact of industry services, is largely apathetic and uninformed.

> a) Because of the lack of a single overriding interest of the public in functions of the complex industry, small vocal groups often speak for the public in divergent voices, a conflicting chorus providing no concensus.
>
> b) Because of this generally marginal interest, well organized pressure groups can often generate short term broad public support, not really representative of long term public sentiment.

Effects of Agency-Public Relationship

Most governmental agencies, especially those regulating complex, multi-faceted industries, no longer believe in the magic of the abstract phrase "public interest." As one scholar has written,

> Under democracy the public interest is based not upon the welfare of one class but the compounding of many group interests. . . . To hold out public interest as a criterion is to offer an imponderable. Its value is psychological and does not extend beyond the significance each responsible civil servant must find in the phrase for himself. Acting in accordance with this subjective concept the bureaucrat selects from the special interests before him the combination to which he gives official sanction.[18]

Over a period of time the typical agency comes to disregard expressions from the scattered and varied public special interest groups as unrepresentative, but it has no broader spectrum of opinion from which to determine true public needs. Ignored by the public it serves, and thus unable to measure popular sentiment, it is not surprising that "public interest" eventually is reduced to a ritualistic phrase sanctifying decisions reached on other grounds.

Agency-Industry

1) The typical agency has authority to grant or deny public access to members of the industry.

2) Because of this entry privilege, the agency asserts its right to intervene in industry functions.

3) Because industry and regulator are the only two groups deeply concerned about this area of enterprise, a certain community of interest is created in time, a commonality often heightened by industry self-policing and sharing of research data.

4) Lacking a means of determining either the wishes of the legislature or the needs of the public, the agency gradually begins measuring its own effectiveness in terms of industry stability and efficiency.

5) As this tendency increases, so does the trend towards intervention in matters the industry feels are purely internal affairs.

6) Intervention seems a function of the identification process, the agency fearing that business stability is too fragile an item to be entrusted to businessmen.

Effects of Agency-Industry Relationship

Professor Louis Jaffe describes the New Deal view of administrative process as

> . . . evolving through two stages, one merging imperceptibly into the other; first, the identification of the administrative process with the protection of the economically weak . . . and then, because private industry . . . appeared to fail in its organizing function, the assertion of government responsibility to plan for the well-being of the industry.[19]

Such paternalism is understandable either in terms of individual or group behavior studies. Each person needs some standard by which to judge his work and the efforts of the group with which he identifies.[20] A few, the dedicated artist, for example, may be able to apply internal criteria. But most of us lack sufficient confidence in our own judgment to be satisfied with such appraisal. Nebulous legislative direction and inarticulate public response create a standards vacuum which can be filled only through reference to the regulated industry. And yet such reference causes vulnerability because success or failure is subject to the skill and intelligence of others. Intervention is the only way to lessen this vulnerability an intervention which in itself increases identification with the regulated industry.

In his classic study, *The Independent Regulatory Commissions*, Robert Cushman expresses the view that both the Federal Radio Commission and the Federal Communications Commission have traditionally "followed a line of least resistance, assuming what is best for the radio industry must be best for the country." [21] What may seem at first glance a lack of integrity may simply reflect a lack of other clearer features by which to chart a regulatory course.

Agency-Challenger

1) The agency generally favors experimentation with new techniques and technology.

2) Agency staff administrators are usually most sensitive to the threat of competition, recommending curbs upon outside operations at the first instance of marginal operator complaint.

3) Agency leadership is usually slow in reacting to early warnings, complacent in their view that the regulated industry is capable of handling challenge unaided.

4) The first regulatory attempts usually reflect this lack of high level concern, specific in nature and designed to solve particular problems.

5) Initial under-reaction is customarily followed by over-reaction, denying access or halting other aspects of the competing operation until policy can be imposed after the fact.

Effects of Agency-Challenger Relationship

It is easy to attribute the violence of agency reaction to partisanship but the response might in some cases be more accurately labelled anti-competitive rather than pro-industry.

> The charge against the ICC and the CAB is that they are "industry minded." I would say that they are "regulation minded" . . . [C]ompetition became the equivalent of "chaos", of "waste", of "destruction"; regulation [would] assure neat, explicable, rationalized ordering. . . .[22]

Although positions of agency and industry may correspond in the face of outside threat, it is no indication that their interests are identical. Obviously, if an unregulated group can challenge and defeat the clientele industry, it would certainly reflect upon the ability of the agency. Even capture of one small portion of its domain would dilute authority, but if jurisdiction could be maintained, ownership of the facility would be a minor consideration.

Thus, while industry opposition is based upon protection of property, agency opposition may be based solely upon protection of its regulatory authority. As Professor Jaffe remarks:

> It is the way of the regulator to be mightly irritated by the peri-
> pherial which lies just beyond his grasp, because what goes on
> there appears to be precisely the cause of trouble in his own baili-
> wick.[23]

Once the challenger can be brought within regulator control, irritation is lessened. Some of the competitor's functions may be curtailed
in the interests of overall industry stability and harmony, but dismemberment usually proceeds at a leisurely pace, allowing internal
adjustments to be made.

Influence of Internal Factors

Predisposition against change exists within any administrative
agency prior to the application of outside pressure. Organizations
are, after all, only human creations subject to all the frailties of their
creators, including fear of the unfamiliar.

> An agency working with a stable program over a long period of time
> develops a definite philosophy and point of view. It develops strong
> tendencies to harmonize its present and past decisions. . . . By
> providing a rule of *stare decisis* it fills in most of the gaps of discre-
> tion left by formal controls, giving a safe way of exercising discre-
> tion and making decisions.[24]

Put in less diplomatic language, "tendencies towards inertia and
inflexibility are the natural and inevitable attributes of all bureaus;
creativity is not." [25]

An enterprise seeking entrance to a regulated domain through
use of new technology constitutes a threat to the status quo, forcing
modification of procedures or even reorganization. It enters the fray
with a legacy of antipathy, for change is a painful process in a large
agency, embodying interrelated alterations going on at different rates
of speed, with "patterns of extended drift, followed by intermittent
catch ups occurring at each depth of a bureau's structure." [26]

But it is usually fear, not pain of readjustment, which causes
strongest resistance to new technology, especially in the middle
ranges of the typical regulatory agency. Max Weber has written that
"knowledge is the basic source of power" [27] in bureaucracy, and a
threat to existing technology poses the same threat of obsolesence to
a bureau expert as it does to the industry. Even if his job is secure by
virtue of his civil service status, his prestige and the status of his particular section of the agency is endangered and thus, indirectly, his
chances of promotion.

The attitude of the middle staff is, of course, a significant factor
in determining general agency policy since "what an administrator
proposes to do . . . making his choice from among policy alterna-

tives is largely dependent upon his sub-ordinates." [28] Information
sent upward must be condensed, simplified, and reshaped at each
level. The ultimate reliance of Commissioners upon staff guidance is
well illustrated by an analysis of two alternative organizational plans
being considered by the FCC in 1950:

> They can organize the staff [and suffer delays] to have the assurance
> that the Commission will get a full disclosure of important consider-
> ations which they ought to take into account . . . or organize [for
> faster information flow] and take a chance that these men will not
> consciously prejudice the decision of the Commission by failure to
> make available the information . . . which they ought to consider.[29]

Thus, the Commission and the Congress were only following general
organizational policy in risking the second alternative.[30]

In addition to personal fears which might influence a staff
member to oppose a new competitor, there may also be factors in the
basic structuring of an agency which cause those favoring the status
quo to congregate in the middle of the hierarchy.

> The middle level of a bureau hierarchy normally contains a higher
> proportion of "conservers" than either the lowest or highest levels.
> At the lowest levels . . . new recruits are still imbued with ambi-
> tion and enthusiasm; the highest level contains many successful
> climbers and advocates.[31]

In line with this theory of middle conservatism is the view that,

> If a bureau fills high-level operations with officials who have di-
> verse viewpoints, or newcomers outside the bureau, it will carry out
> a much higher proportion of suggested changes than if it uses . . .
> those up from the ranks.[32]

Whatever motivational theory is advanced to explain this phenomena, the early antagonism of staff regulators towards each of the
challengers involved in this study, and the numerous directives prepared at this level advocating strict controls, seem to substantiate its
existence.

Perhaps the most serious limitation impairing the ability of a
regulatory agency to weigh the merits of new technology or techniques is lack of sufficient skilled personnel. The general statement
that,

> Decision makers have only limited capabilities regarding the
> amount of time they can spend making decisions, the number of
> issues they can consider simultaneously, and the amount of detail
> they can absorb regarding any problem [33]

is illustrated by Stern's description of television's neglect in the
1930s:

> Television was regulated by a body that had little time to devote to it, being preoccupied with other matters, and which possessed only a very limited resource of expertise for coping with problems arising from its peculiar technical nature.[34]

Lacking the resources to obtain such information, the F.C.C. had to place its reliance upon the industry, "whose presentation might not be altogether free from self serving coloration." [35] If this were a problem in the ordinary case, it became an almost insurmountable barrier when the industry was asked to provide data about a possible competitor. The Commission might attempt to equalize the bias by allowing the competitor to file similar information on its own behalf, but this procedure only doubled the paperwork for its limited staff without producing a unified impartial report.

In addition, lack of trained personnel may well be a factor in the administrative panic which precipitates a freeze. The sudden realization that regulatory responsibilities must be expanded without manpower either to formulate new policy or to supervise its implementation may result in the convulsive lunge to halt progress until the agency can begin to close the gap between technology and administration.

Individual traits of inertia, conservatism, fear; internal weaknesses limiting data available and hampering its interpretation—these are not characteristics of efficient operation. However, as Simon points out, the key to successful administrative policy is not efficiency but survival:

> To preserve its freedom an [agency] must to some degree adapt its program to various interests. To neutralize its enemies it must sometimes sacrifice elements in its programs that attract the most effective political opposition. Hence, organizations are in a continual process of adjusting to the political environment that surrounds them—an adjustment that seeks to keep a favorable balance of political support and political opposition.[36]

Weighed on a scale equating political pressure with virtue, the new competitor can cause only a slight fluctuation at best. Thus, in the larger arena as in the cloistered realm of staff administration, the very promise within the nascent quality of the competitor's development threatens its existence.

This brief exploration of administrative attitudes can only trace outlines of the most obvious configurations. However, even these clearly apparent features in themselves would seem to present a formidable barrier to progress.

The first factor standing out in bold relief is the isolation of the typical agency from governmental or public contact, and the effects of such isolation. Lack of either guidance or interest encourages customary rule, an accretion of traditions shaped by agency-industry interaction. The absence of statute necessitates rule by behavioral patterns; the absence of supervision allows their growth without form. Agency bureaucracy has a vested interest in maintaining this home-made legislation, created to reduce ambiguity in uncertain cases, and so resists any change in the industry which would threaten the structure. The outsider attempting to enter the industry finds the traditions hard to ascertain, difficult to use and impossible to change. As he slowly hacks his way through this jungle of unpublished but existing rule, he will cause new animosity with each blow of his knife.

The second element of importance is the schizophrenic nature of agency organization. Due to the characteristics of Civil Service employment, bureaucrats tend to cluster at certain levels, linked more closely to each other by mutual backgrounds and work than to the agency generally, or to its high command. These pockets of power can exert a great influence upon agency policy if strategically located and unified by like attitudes. Subject to only minimal supervision by officials usually much less conversant in the area of their expertise, the middle staff has a large field of autonomy and significant control over information and analysis received by agency chiefs. If this level is as strongly dedicated to preserving the status quo as studies indicate, the challenger enters each contest at a severe disadvantage.

Finally, there is the factor of the agency as a political institution, dedicated to balancing of interests rather than basic public policy, survival rather than efficiency. The undercapitalized and relatively unknown new competitor enters the struggle against the established industry poorly armed.

Each of these basic factors, then, and all the individual and group behavioral patterns, shape, motivate, and precondition the typical agency to oppose change and thus inhibit the new industry proposing or requiring change. The injustice is not so much in the fact that these basic human attitudes exist, but that they exist largely unrecognized in institutions whose primary societal function is to mediate objectively between competing parties.

Conclusion

> There's something fascinating about science. One gets wholesale
> returns in conjecture out of such a trifling investment of fact.

Mark Twain's comment may be uncomfortably close to describing this study, strewn as it had been with speculation and generalization. Generalization is always a painful process for our legal minds, trained and perhaps naturally inclined to brush past similarities or parallels in our quest for the elusive variant. "The single point upon which the cable controversy turned" and we have found the Grail, but it is possible the point appears singular only because of our focus.

In the distrust of broad outlines we may avoid one distortion of reality only to adopt another. For as no event is completely explained by others, neither is it completely isolated from them. If history is to some extent "philosophy taught by example," [37] discovery of its premises may require an extended vision of its process.

Viewed in this manner, the evolution of cable exhibits striking parallels to earlier challengers, few of its phases unusual, little of its history unique. The staff spearheaded the drive for full jurisdiction in 1966,[38] an effort culminating in what *Broadcasting* described as "The FCC Closes Its Fist Around CATV." [39] Perhaps because of the tardiness of federal intervention and the imminence of the threat,[40] cable's dismemberment stage does seem to have been distinctively severe. Effective denial of access to new systems seeking penetration of 153 major cities; administrative shutdown trapping more than 200 franchise holders in a limbo of undetermined rights; multiple docket hearings questioning validity of almost every phase of cable activity; in truth, it has been a rather unique reign of terror.[41]

The general outline seems in classic ICC-motor carrier tradition and once safely within the fold, cable's final share of broadcasting domain will be shaped not by technology, but its economic successes and political support.

In this broader view, then, opposition to cable and its predecessors does not seem traceable to nefarious interplay between agency and industry, but simply internal agency tendencies, stimulated by the particular configuration of challenging elements. However, lack of ulterior motive does not excuse lack of policy; denial of profit to entrepreneurs and denial of benefits to the public results despite purity of motive.

Regulatory opposition to challenge in itself is obviously neither erroneous nor unjust. Scientific and economic forces surge forward unencumbered by societal considerations which must influence governmental bodies. A segment of society relies upon continuation of the industry in its present form, and such indirect social impact is not the usual concern of business. A period of time could be prescribed for consideration of new competitor functions, but it should result from legislation, not visceral reaction.

If this analysis has some degree of accuracy, it will have more profound implications in years just ahead as technological advances emerge with greater and greater frequency. The point is not that technology should dictate law, but that laws, not behavioral patterns, should provide basic guidelines for integration of new forces into an evolving industry and society.

Table 50.

FCC LICENSE REVOCATIONS AND DENIALS--1934-1971

From its beginning to 1971 the Federal Communications Commission revoked or
denied the renewal of 87 broadcast station licenses--82 radio and five TV.
During the same period more than 40,000 broadcast licenses were issued and
renewed nearly all with no more than a cursory review.

Cause	Number	%
Misrepresentations to the FCC	40	22%
Unauthorized transfer of control/	32	18
False statements of control		
Failure to appear	10	6
Unauthorized discontinuance/abandonment	8	4
No evidence in support of application	5	3
Failure to file ownership/financial report	2	1
Improperly prepared application(s)	1	*
Censorship/violate political rules	2	1
Violations of duopoly rule	1	*
Double billing	1	*
Log alterations	2	1
Fraudulent contest(s)	3	2
False, fraudulent and misleading advertising	1	*
Indecent and vulgar material	1	*
Overcommercialization	1	*
Broadcast horse race information	1	*
Departure from promised programming	1	*
Violations of "fairness" doctrine	2	1
Personal attack	1	*
Violations in news presentations	1	*
"Irresponsible operation"	1	*
Technical violations	34	19
Character in question	19	11
Financially incapable	6	3
Blocking "strike" application	1	*
Diversification (WHDH)	1	*
	178	92%

Source: Abel, Clift, and Weiss, "Station License Revocations and Denials of Renewals,
1934-69," Journal of Broadcasting, XIV:4, pp.411-421; updated by Lichty and Topping
from FCC annual reports, 1969, 1970, 1971.
*Less than one %; thus, the total is less than 100%.

Table 51.

FINES AND SHORT-TERM RENEWALS

Since 1961 the Federal Communications Commission has had the power to assess forfeitures (fines) against stations of up to $10,000 and to grant short-term renewals rather that regular renewals. Figures show the types of stations and the reasons for fines (1961 to mid-1971) and for short renewals (1960-1972).

	FINES		SHORT RENEWALS	
	No.	%	No.	%
TYPES OF STATIONS				
AM	672	76%	116	74%
FM	187	21	28	18
TV	31	4	12	8
TOTAL	890	100%	156	100%
VIOLATION				
Failure to operate station as set forth in license (violation of broadcasting hours, power and presunrise)	89	8%	38	19%
Failure to observe provisions of the Act or rule or regulation of the Commission (filings, logging, un-licensed operators, etc.)	949	87	131	66
Violations of sponsor identification and "rigged" contest sections of the Com-munications Act	38	3	15	8
Violations of lottery, fraud, or obscene language sections of Title 18 of the United States Code	15	1	14	7
TOTAL	1091	99%	198	100%

Sources: Clift, Weiss and Abel, "Ten Years of Forfeiture by the Federal Com-munications Commission," Journal of Broadcasting, XV:4, pp.379-385 and Shelby, "Short-Term License Renewals: 1960-1972," Journal of Broadcasting, 18:3, pp. 277-288.

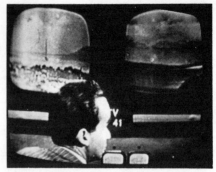

On the first *See It Now*, November 1951, Edward R. Murrow spoke from the CBS control room with director Don Hewitt at his back. Cameras showed the Pacific and Atlantic live.

On March 9, 1954, *See It Now* presented a number of excerpts from speeches by Joseph McCarthy and Murrow concluded: "This is no time for men who oppose Senator McCarthy's methods to keep silent, or for those who approve."

On April 6, 1954, McCarthy answered in a film produced at Fox Movietone with maps showing the spread of Communism.

In 1955 Murrow spoke of the dangers of Vice Presidential candidate selection.

Murrow with Louis Armstrong in 1956.

NOTES*

Part One/TECHNICAL

INTRODUCTION

[1] *Radio Broadcast*, September 1922.

[2] Lawrence E. Whittemore, "The Development of Radio," *The Annals of Political and Social Science* Vol. CXLII (March 1929), p. 4.

[3] C. Lloyd Egner, "Outline of the History of Electrical Transcriptions," (Broadcast Pioneers history project mimeographed paper No. 7) discusses the use Chevrolet made of the spot transcription on World Transcription Service.

[4] Robert A. Chipman, "De Forest and the Triode Detector," *Scientific American*, Vol. 212, No. 3 (March 1965), p. 99.

[5] Chipman, p. 100.

[6] David Sarnoff, Letter to E. W. Rice, Jr., Honorary Chairman of the Board, General Electric Company, June 17, 1922. From *Looking Ahead* (New York: McGraw-Hill Book Co., 1968), p. 42.

[7] Quoted in George Shiers, "The First Electron Tube," *Scientific American*, Vol. 220, No. 3 (March 1969), p. 104.

[8] Lawrence Lessing, *Man of High Fidelity: Edwin Howard Armstrong* (Philadelphia: J. B. Lippincott, 1956).

[9] See Edwin H. Armstrong, "Frequency Modulation and its Future Uses," *The Annals of Political and Social Science*, Vol. CCXIII (January 1941), p. 153 for his own account of the effort to get FM established.

[10] S. C. Gilfillan, "The Future of Home Theater," *The Independent*, Vol. LXXIII, No. 3333, (October 17, 1912), pp. 886–891.

[11] "The Jenkins 'Radio Movie' Reception Methods," *Radio News* (November 1928), p. 420.

[12] Owen P. White, "What's Delaying Television?" *Colliers*, XCVI (November 30, 1935), p. 10.

[13] I. R. Loundsberry, "Making Permanent Records of Radio Programs," *Radio Broadcast*, (September 1924), pp. 363–368.

* Please note that some footnote numbers are missing since parts of some articles were deleted in editing. However, in nearly all cases we have tried to incorporate important footnote material in other notes to cut as little information and as few references as possible.

645

3. Elliot N. Sivowitch, **A TECHNOLOGICAL SURVEY OF BROADCASTING'S PREHISTORY, 1876–1920.**

[1] E. N. Sivowitch, "Musical Broadcasting in the 19th Century," *Audio* (June, 1967), 19–23.

[2] Sivowitch, *Op. Cit.*; David L. Woods, "Semantics versus the First Broadcasting Station," *Journal of Broadcasting*, XI:3 (Summer 1967), 199–207.

[3] *Infra* (Section on DeForest). The Telharmonium was an "electrical music" generator.

[4] *Electrical Review*, 25 (Nov. 21, 1894), 259.

[5] William H. Ward, *Ward's Code of Signal Telegraph for Ocean Marine Service* (Auburn, N.Y.: W. H. Ward, 1858).

[6] Loomis Notebook, Mahlon Loomis Papers, Manuscripts Division, Library of Congress.

[7] Thomas Appleby, *Mahlon Loomis: Inventor of Radio* (Washington, D.C.: Loomis Publications, 1967), 101–104.

[8] No. 129971. Appleby feels that Loomis definitely radiated a signal with his apparatus, and received it with some type of rectifier action or magnetic detector effect in the galvanometer circuit.

[9] Samuel F. B. Morse had conducted experiments as early as 1842. See J. J. Fahie, *A History of Wireless Telegraphy*, (New York: Dodd, Mead & Co., 1902).

[10] Drawbaugh was a mechanic from Eberlys Mills, Pennsylvania, who worked on telephonic devices in the 1860s and 70s. He lost a legal decision to Bell by a very close margin. See Warren J. Harder, *Daniel Drawbaugh: The Edison of the Cumberland Valley* (Philadelphia: University of Pennsylvania Press, 1960).

[11] The "acoustic telephone" was essentially a "tin-cans-and-string" telephone for house-to-house communication. Believe it or not this type of device had some commercial application during the same time span as the first electric telephones, circa 1875–1895. Stubblefield had a patent on his device.

[12] Tom Hoffer, "Nathan B. Stubblefield and His Wireless Telephone," *Journal of Broadcasting*, Vol. XV, No. 3 (Summer 1971), pp. 317–329.

[13] Prospectus, Wireless Telephone Company of America, Clark Collection CWC 4-3340A. (See "note on sources" at end of footnotes).

[14] U.S. Patent No. 887,357 (May 12, 1908); Canadian Patent No. 114,737 (Oct. 20, 1908).

[15] The tendency to *radiate* increases as the square of the frequency.

[16] Nor the case of high-powered VLF stations used for communication with submarines, such as the Navy station at Cutler, Maine, which operates on 14.7 kHz. In this instance more than a megawatt of power is radiating from the antenna system.

[17] Charles Susskind, "Observations of Electromagnetic Wave Radiation before Hertz," *ISIS* 55 (March 1964), 32–42.

[18] *Ibid.* 37–39.

[19] *Marconi Wireless Telegraph Co. of America vs. De Forest Wireless Telegraph Co.* United States Circuit Court for the Southern District of New York. In Equity No. 8211 (1904).

[20] We are indebted to J. Brittain of the Georgia Institute of Technology for calling our attention to the early Stone experiments. See Clark Collection SRM 4-1230, John Stone Stone, Report (1892) Mechanical Department of American Bell Telephone Co. Also commentary in letter of Dec. 22, 1944 from Lloyd Espenschied to G. H. Clark, CWC 4-2839A. A published source is George H. Clark, *The Life of John Stone Stone* (San Diego: Frye and Smith Ltd., 1946), 35–37.

[21] Helen Fessenden, *Fessenden: Builder of Tomorrows* (New York: Coward-McCann, 1940), Chapter XV. See also R. A. Fessenden, "Wireless Telephony," *Transactions of the American Institute of Electrical Engineers, 1908*, Clark Collection CWC 135-178A.

[22] The distortion level, while less than that of the spark radiotelephone, was worse than that of the alternator.

[23] John Grant, "Experiments and Results in Wireless Telephony," *The American Telephone Journal*, (January 26 and February 2, 1907).

[24] Letter of January 29, 1932, Reginald A. Fessenden to S. M. Kintner, Vice-President, Westinghouse Electric & Mfg. Co. Clark Collection CWC 135-246A.

[25] Call Letters and Log Book of Francis Arthur Hart, 1906–1909. Smithsonian Institution Cat. No. 329,734. Hart also reports the DeForest arc experiments of March 20, May 7 and May 9, 1907.

[26] Lee DeForest, *Father of Radio* (Chicago: Wilcox-Follett, 1950), 221.

[27] H. J. Meneratti was wireless operator aboard the Ohio. The basic research material for this section is based upon his notes in the Div. of Electricity & Nuclear Energy files of the Smithsonian. See also data in the Clark Collection Class 134 History of Broadcasting and Class 135 History of Radiotelephony. A good published source is L. S. Howeth, *History of Communications—Electronics in the United States Navy* (Washington: Government Printing Office, 1963), 169–172.

[28] DeForest, *Op. Cit.*, 225; Georgette Carneal, *A Conqueror of Space* (New York: Horace Liveright, 1930), 205–209.

[29] R. A. Heising, *Montauk-Arlington Radio Telephone Tests of 1915* (1938), Clark Collection CWC 135-085A. A brief account of the tests is contained in: William Peck Banning, *Commercial Broadcasting Pioneer* (Cambridge: Harvard University Press, 1946), 6–7.

[30] DeForest, *Op. Cit.*, 338.

[31] U.S. Department of Commerce, *Commercial and Government Radio Stations of the United States* (1920).

[32] A full account of Elwell's role in radio engineering may be found in: *Pioneer Work in Radio Telephony and Telegraphy* by Cyril Elwell. (Smithsonian Institution: Clark Collection CWC 135-245A). A popularized though extensive account of West Coast developments may be found in Jane Morgan, *Electronics in the West: The First Fifty Years* (Palo Alto: National Press, Books, 1967).

[34] U.S. Department of Commerce, *Radio Stations of the United States* (1914 and 1915 editions).

[35] Eugene Lyons, *David Sarnoff: A Biography*. (New York: Harper & Row, 1966), 70–73; David Sarnoff, *Looking Ahead* (New York: McGraw-Hill, 1968), 31–34; Gleason Archer, *History of Radio to 1926* (New York: American Historical Society, 1938), 110–113.

[36] The complexities of the patent problem are told in W. Rupert MacLaurin, *Invention and Innovation in the Radio Industry* (New York: Macmillan Co., 1949).

[37] Letter of Jan. 31, 1922 from David Sarnoff to C. D. Young of RCA restates the "Radio Music Box" proposal, and discusses its previous introduction in 1915 as well as another memorandum of Jan. 31, 1920. Sarnoff does mention the lack of a suitable radiotelephone transmitter and compact receiver in the earlier period, inferring that this retarded the introduction of broadcasting. It might be argued, however, that had the industry responded with some inspiration to his initial proposal, some of the difficulties vis-a-vis the patent situation could have been resolved. In point of fact, the equipment needed for broadcasting was close to practical realization. The Bell System's radio-telephone tests of 1915 included oscillator, modulator and power amplifier tubes. DeForest's "oscillion" transmitting triodes were also available that year. Receivers such as the DeForest RJ-4 and RJ-5 audion detectors, with necessary receiving transformers were available in 1914 at prices in the $26–$40 category. These would fulfill the "Music Box" criterion, albeit with lack of sensitivity compared to later circuitry. As fate would have it, however, World War I provided the training ground for many of the first radiotelephone applications and for mass production of vacuum tubes, since manufacturers agreed to suspend any patent litigation for the duration of the war.

Note on sources: The Clark Collection of manuscripts and photographs is located at the Smithsonian Institution's Division of Electricity and Nuclear Energy. One of the most extensive collections of documents pertaining to the history of radio technology, it was compiled by George H. Clark (1881–1956), who was RCA's historian for more than 30 years. The Collection was used extensively by L. S. Howeth in his work (cited in footnote 27).

4. Thomas W. Hoffer, NATHAN B. STUBBLEFIELD AND HIS WIRELESS TELEPHONE

[1] *The Washington Post*, August 10, 1940. Nathan B. Stubblefield Papers, The University of Kentucky, Lexington, and the Chamber of Commerce Stubblefield Collection, Murray, Kentucky, hereafter cited as the Stubblefield Papers. The writer wishes to acknowledge the guidance and counsel of Dr. Lawrence W. Lichty, the University of Wisconsin, in the preparation and refinement of this paper, which originated in his History of Broadcasting seminar. The writer also wishes to acknowledge the help of Dr. Elliot N. Sivowitch, the Smithsonian Institution, for technical and bibliographic advice; Mr. James Johnson, Executive Director of the Chamber of Commerce at Murray, Kentucky, and Stubblefield historian for advice on "opposing arguments"; Dr. Don LeDuc, a lawyer and assistant professor at the Ohio State University, for some legal research; Dr. L. J. Horton, Director of Journalism at Murray State University, for advice; Mr. James Skelton, a student of electrical engineering at Michigan State University who is from Calvert City, Kentucky, for technical and patent data and Mr. Bernard B. Stubblefield, the son and trusted assistant of Nathan B. Stubblefield, for additional information valuable to this study.

[2] Rainey T. Wells, "Heard First Radio Broadcast," *The Fraternal Monitor* (undated).

[3] Anonymous, "Nathan B. Stubblefield, Inventor of Radio." Unpublished paper from the vertical file (undated), Library, Murray State University. The first published account of the Stubblefield system in a scientific journal was Waldon Fawcett's "The Latest Advance in Wireless Telephony," *Scientific American*, Volume 86 (May 24, 1902), p. 363. Trumbull White, in his book *The World's Progress in Knowledge, Science and Industry* (1902) wrote a full description of the Stubblefield experiments based largely on an account published in *The St. Louis Post Dispatch*, January 10, 1902. Other summary articles have been published since 1930 but these are mostly a rehash of the 1902 sources.

[4] Broadcasting means the dissemination of radio communications intended to be received by the public, directly or by the intermediary of relay stations. (U.S. Congress, The Communications Act of 1934, Public Law 416, 73rd Cong., Sec. 3.) There are various forms of radio communication and these are distinguished primarily by the way in which continuous radio frequency power generated in the transmitter is modulated. This investigation sought, in part, to discover evidence indicating whether Stubblefield's devices could generate radio frequencies. For a general overview of broadcasting's technical archaeology see Robert A. Chipman, "The Earliest Electromagnetic Instruments," *United States National Museum Bulletin* 240 Washington, D.C.: Smithsonian Institution, 1964), pp. 121–136; W. James King, "The Development of Electrical Technology in the 19th Century," *United States National Bulletin 228 (Papers 28 and 29)* (Washington, D.C.: Smithsonian Institution, 1962), pp. 231–331; George W. Pierce, *Principles of Wireless Telegraphy* (New York: McGraw-Hill, 1910), pp. 75–107; and R. A. Fessenden, "Wireless Telephony," a paper presented to the 25th annual convention of the American Institute of Electrical Engineers, Atlantic City, New Jersey, June 29, 1908.

[5] L. J. Horton, "Did He Invent Radio?" *Broadcasting*, March 19, 1951.

[6] Edward Freeman, "Stubblefield . . . and Radio," unidentified periodical article in the Stubblefield Papers.

[7] Note of A. H. Wear and Son, Murray, Kentucky, dated April 23, 1887. Stubblefield Papers.

[8] Telephone interview with Bernard B. Stubblefield, Florence, Mississippi, June 15, 1970. Bernard was the oldest surviving son of Nathan B. Stubblefield. According to Bernard, the "vibrating telephone" patent was the second of four U.S. patents his fa-

ther had ever obtained. The first patent was for a "lamp lighter." A third patent was approved for Stubblefield's electric battery, and a fourth was granted in 1908 for a wireless telephone system. A Canadian patent was granted for the wireless system about the time Stubblefield developed his 1908 device.

9 *The Evansville Press* (Indiana), January 17, 1937. Stubblefield Papers.

10 Jim Lucas, "He Helped Bring Radio into the Home, But—Tulsan Loses Millions," unidentified clipping in the Stubblefield Papers.

11 According to the 1902 *St. Louis Post Dispatch* story, and the report printed in White's book, Bernard ". . . would be able to carry out and finish the system of wireless telephony should the father die, so closely has he been allied with every step in its discovery and development." (White, p. 299.) Bernard was born in 1888. He lived in Murray, Kentucky until about 1915 when he joined the U.S. Army for about five years. Later, he settled in New York City engaging himself in a photostat business. He was never employed with any radio manufacturing, distributing or broadcasting business during the years following his brief Army career to his retirement some time in the 1950s. Bernard left New York and retired in Mississippi. Telephone interview, Bernard B. Stubblefield.

12 Letter of Byron F. Johnson to James L. Johnson, dated May 18, 1961. Stubblefield Papers.

13 *The St. Louis Post Dispatch,* January 19, 1902.

14 *Ibid.*

15 An account of the January 1, 1902 demonstration and Bernard's role in his father's work was contained in Edward C. Lambert, "Let's Hear It for Bernard Stubblefield!" *TV Guide,* October 10, 1970, pp. 18–20.

16 *The Washington Times,* March 21, 1902 and *The Evening Telegram* (New York City), March 21, 1902.

17 *The Washington Post,* August 10, 1940.

18 *Ibid.*

19 *The Evansville Press.*

20 M. T. McCarthy, (Murray) College News Staff, "Murray Woman Witnessed Demonstrations on the Potomac," Unidentified clipping, Stubblefield Papers.

21 Alvin F. Harlow, *Old Wires and New Waves* (New York: D. Appleton-Century Co., 1936), pp. 383–387.

22 Letter from the Arizona Corporation Commission to Tom W. Hoffer, dated May 14, 1968. The Wireless Telephone Company of America terminated following a 25-year statutory limitation on May 22, 1926.

23 According to L. J. Horton, the tests in New York City weren't as successful as those in the rural areas. *Evansville Press.*

24 *The Philadelphia Inquirer,* May 31, 1902. In another article, Stubblefield told reporters that his system utilized "earth currents." ". . . disturbance in the earth's magnetic field results and this disturbance . . ." is detected by another receiver. *The Philadelphia Press,* June 1, 1902; *The Philadelphia North American* May 31, 1902 and *The Philadelphia Times,* June 3, 1902.

25 Brochure, "The Wireless Telephone Company of America," Stubblefield Papers.

26 George W. Pierce, pp. 77–8.

27 Brochure, "The Wireless Telephone Company of America," undated. Stubblefield Papers.

28 Letter of Nathan B. Stubblefield to S. N. Turner, Secretary of the Wireless Telephone Company of America, dated June 19, 1902, Stubblefield Papers.

29 Unidentified clipping among the Stubblefield Papers.

30 *The Evansville Press.*

31 U.S. Patent No. 887,357 dated May 12, 1908. Serial No. 366,544 dated April 5, 1907. The omissions in the quoted text were numbers which referred to diagrams accompanying the letters patent.

32 *The New York Times,* January 11, 1913.

33 Unidentified newspaper clipping (1938) among the Stubblefield Papers.

34 Lucas.

[35] Letter of Conn Linn to Vernon Stubblefield, Murray, Kentucky, dated September 1, 1950. Stubblefield Papers. A Murray, Kentucky, AM radio station was licensed by the FCC in 1948. In memory of Nathan B. Stubblefield, the station signed on with the call, WNBS.

7. David T. MacFarland, TELEVISION: THE WHIRLING BEGINNING

[1] This and the next two subdivisions used in this article follow those given by John V. L. Hogan in his article, "The Early Days of Television" in the *Journal of the SMPTE*, Vol. 63 (November 1954), pp. 230–234. (SMPTE stands for "Society of Motion Picture-Television Engineers.")
[2] Orrin E. Dunlap, *The Outlook for Television* (New York: Harper and Brothers, 1932), p. 6.
[3] L. R. Lankes, "Historical Sketch of Television's Progress," *Journal of the SMPTE*, Vol. 51 (September 1948), p. 227.
[4] W. Rupert MacLaurin, *Invention and Innovation in the Radio Industry*, MIT Studies in Innovation Series (New York: Macmillan Company, 1948), p. 192.
[5] Richard W. Hubbell, *4000 Years of Television* (New York: G. P. Putnam's Sons, 1942), p. 57.
[6] Stanley Kempner, *Television Encyclopedia* (New York: Fairchild Publishing Company, 1948), p. 358.
[7] Kempner, pp. 100–101.
[8] Albert Abramson, *Electronic Motion Pictures* (Berkeley and Los Angeles: University of California Press, 1955), p. 19.
[9] J. C. Wilson, *Television Engineering* (London: Sir Isaac Pitman and Sons, Ltd., 1937), p. 3.
[10] Abramson, *Electronic Motion Pictures*, p. 30.
[11] *Nature*, No. 2016. Vol. 78 (June 18, 1908), p. 151.
[12] T. Thorne Baker, *Wireless Pictures and Television* (New York: D. Van Nostrand Company, 1927), p. 17.
[13] S. G. Sturmey, *The Economic Development of Radio* (London: Duckworth and Company, Ltd., 1958), p. 197.
[14] Sturmey, p. 195.
[15] Kempner, p. 238.
[16] C. J. Hylander and Robert Harding, Jr., *An Introduction to Television* (New York: Macmillan Company, 1941), p. 44.
[17] Sydney A. Moseley and Barton Chapple, *Television Today and Tomorrow* (London: Sir Isaac Pitman and Sons, Ltd., 1931), p. 143.

9. Robert H. Stern, TELEVISION IN THE THIRTIES

[1] On the status of television during the latter Nine Twenties and the early Thirties, particularly with respect to the response of the Federal Radio Commission to early attempts at commercial exploitation, see the author's "Regulatory Influences upon Television's Development: Early Years Under the Federal Radio Commission," *Am. J. Econ. Sociol.*, Vol. 22 (July, 1963), pp. 347 ff.
[2] It should be noted, however, that in the 1934 Act the regulatory agency was newly required "to study new uses for radio, provide for experimental use of frequencies, and generally encourage the larger and more effective use of radio in the public interest." Sec. 303(g).
[6] Zworykin traced his basic ideas for electronic television back to 1917, when he was in the employ of the Russian Telegraph and Telephone Company. In 1923, Westinghouse applied in Zworykin's name for a patent on the camera tube that incorporated some of the iconoscope's basic principles. The patent was granted in 1938, its issuance having been delayed for fifteen years by interference proceedings. W. MacLaurin, *Invention and Innovation in the Radio Industry* (New York, 1949), p. 200.
[7] A circumstance that may help to explain Sarnoff's intense interest in Zworykin's work was that well-publicized activities of experimenters working with mechanical-

scanning systems had begun to make it appear at this time as if the day of television's commercialization might not be distant. It should also be noted in this connection that until 1928 RCA had not itself engaged in experimental work in this field to any significant extent. At this period, while acting as sales agent and patent-holding company for its fellow members of the Radio Group, RCA did not possess an extensive research organization or manufacturing facilities of its own. In view of this arrangement, the fact that RCA-NBC engineers did commence experimentation with mechanical-scanning techniques in 1928 may be further indicative of that organization's anxiety lest it be left behind in the new field. The technical-industrial development of the period is further treated in R. H. Stern, "Regulatory Influences . . . ," op. cit.

[8] The realignment thus made was not to remain long in effect, being almost immediately challenged and eventually blocked by federal antitrust action. For an account of these events, see G. Archer, Big Business and Radio (New York, 1939), pp. 346–9, 382 ff.

[9] MacLaurin, op. cit., pp. 204–5.

[10] George Everson, The Story of Television (New York, 1949), Chapter 1.

[11] The patent on this system, the heart of which was the "image dissector," was issued three years later, RCA having failed in Patent Office interference proceedings to bring it under its patent domination (patent No. 1773980, August 26, 1930. RCA had contended that Farnsworth's system embodied principles earlier disclosed by Zworykin. The finding of the Patent Office was that Farnsworth and Zworykin had worked independently and that the image dissector utilized a principle of operation basically different from that of Zworykin's iconoscope. In consequence, Zworykin (RCA) and Farnsworth retained basic patents on alternative methods of electronic television transmission. MacLaurin, op. cit., p. 212. It cost the Farnsworth group about $30,000 to defend itself in these interference proceedings. Everson reports that to find the money was a "difficult and exhausting ordeal." Op. cit., p. 153.

[12] Ibid., p. 113. The mechanical systems then being demonstrated were capable of about 48- to 60-line definition.

[13] Ibid., Chap. 9.

[14] Most of the years 1931 and 1932 Farnsworth spent at the Philco laboratories in Philadelphia, an arrangement having been made through which Philco agreed to help finance Farnsworth's work in return for certain licensing privileges on Farnsworth's patents. This will be described further below in an account of Philco's entry into television.

[15] L. DeForest, Television Today and Tomorrow (New York, 1942), Chapter 13.

[16] By 1938 Farnsworth held 73 patents and had 60 applications on file. These applied to the image dissector, signal amplifiers, synchronization methods and other important components of a television system. Some of his inventions—for example, the electronic multiplier—were of considerable importance in the electronics field generally. MacLaurin, op. cit., p. 211.

[17] Everson, op. cit., pp. 243 ff.

[18] Ibid., p. 244.

[19] Ibid., p. 264. The year before the RCA cross-licensing agreement was made the Farnsworth company had undergone a major reorganization. A stock issue enabling Farnsworth to transform itself from purely a research organization to a manufacturing concern had been underwritten by the investment firm of Kuhn, Loeb and Company, which thus became influential in the company's affairs. Ibid., Chap. 26. Prior to the reorganization, impatient stockholders had prodded action whereby the company's patents were offered for sale both to RCA and Paramount Pictures. Neither company was willing to pay the asking price of almost $1,000,000. MacLaurin, op. cit., pp. 208–9.

[20] For the Farnsworth company, whose research expenses were mounting uncomfortably, the arrangement had much merit, especially since it was to retain control of patents secured on work done by Farnsworth at the Philco laboratories. Ibid., pp. 132–3.

[21] MacLaurin, op. cit., p. 208.

[22] Op. cit., p. 135.

[23] Note, however, that in 1940, at a time when the FCC had before it the question whether to authorize public broadcasting using certain standards and techniques proposed by the Radio Manufacturers Association, Philco opposed such authorization on the grounds that it had developed certain techniques superior to those proposed for adoption.

[24] Complaint of Philco Radio and Television Corp., filed in the Supreme Court of the State of New York, County of New York; *Philco Radio and Television Corp., vs. Radio Corporation of America et al.*, July 30, 1936. Quoted in F. Waldrop and J. Borkin, *Television: A Struggle for Power* (New York, 1938), p. 219.

[25] In 1931, CBS had 82 station outlets and time sales of about $10.4 million; NBC had 83 station outlets and time sales of about $20.5 million. FCC, *Report on Chain Broadcasting*, Docket No. 5060, May, 1941, pp. 17, 24.

[26] R. Hubbell, *4000 Years of Television* (New York, 1942), p. 97.

[27] *Ibid.*, pp. 98–9.

[28] *Business Week*, April 10, 1937, pp. 20–21.

[29] *Ibid.* Considering, however, that Columbia was acquiring its new transmitter by purchase from RCA, which was the only firm then able to supply such equipment, the independents in the field still had cause for only limited satisfaction.

[30] *Ibid.*, p. 21.

[31] This was the consent decree of 1932, in which RCA, General Electric and Westinghouse agreed to certain stipulations in order to avoid antitrust prosecution. Among the stipulations were that GE and Westinghouse should be able to re-enter the radio-receiver manufacturing field in competition with RCA after the lapse of two-and-a-half years following the time of the decree; that upon re-entrance their use of RCA patents would be on the same basis as that of any other RCA licensee. Archer, *op. cit.*, pp. 382 ff.

[32] *Fortune*, April, 1939, p. 172. Westinghouse, where Zworykin had done his pioneering work, does not appear to have had a significant role in the developmental work of the 1930s.

[33] FCC *Reports and Decisions* 308; also FCC *Second Annual Report*, 1936, p. 53.

[34] Testimony of A. T. & T. officials at an FCC Informal Engineering Conference in 1936 showed them to be not unaware of the potential threat to their company's position if an extensive radio relay system capable of similar services should be developed. Weldrop and Borkin, *op. cit.*, Chaps. 4, 8. It should be noted that during the middle '30s A. T. & T. was also locked in a struggle with RCA over the latter's attempt to lessen its domination of the business of supplying sound recording and sound reproduction systems to motion picture studios and exhibitors. Archer, *op. cit.*, Chap. 15 and pp. 393 ff; Waldrop and Borkin, *op. cit.*, Chaps. 12, 15.

[35] *Small Radio* (New York: Emerson Phonograph and Radio Corp., 1943), pp. 51–2; MacLaurin, *op. cit.*, pp. 140–1. *Cf. Ibid.*, p. 212 (note 44).

[36] *Fortune*, April, 1939, p. 176.

[37] MacLaurin, *op. cit.*, p. 219.

[38] See Hearings before the Committee on Interstate Commerce, U.S. Senate, 76th Cong., 3rd Sess., on S. 251, *Development of Television*, April 10, 11, 1940, p. 39. Also MacLaurin, *op. cit.*, p. 219.

[39] *Fortune*, April, 1939, p. 176. For several years it was a disputed question whether Paramount actually controlled DuMont. Rival interests claimed that it did; DuMont denied it. Finally, in December, 1948, the FCC ruled that Paramount clearly was in control, the issue having arisen in connection with the multiple-ownership rule for television broadcast stations.

[42] The survey report which proposed an entry into television in network radio broadcasting was prepared in 1937 for the Motion Picture Producers and Distributors of America, an organization then headed by Mr. Will Hayes. Interestingly, to prepare this report Mr. Hayes obtained the services of A. Mortimer Prall, son of the then chairman of the FCC, Anning Prall. A second report, done for the Academy of Motion Picture Arts and Sciences, saw no danger that television would burst unexpectedly upon an unprepared motion picture industry—but offered no preparedness program. See

John Western, "Television Girds for Battle," *Public Opinion Quarterly*, October, 1939, pp. 538–9; also Waldrop and Borkin, *op. cit.*, pp. 124 ff.
[43] However, see note 2 above, regarding a provision new in the 1934 statute, sec. 303(g), obligating the FCC to study new uses for radio, and so forth.
[44] In the 1927 legislation Congress directed the licensing authority (the Federal Radio Commission) to refuse broadcast licenses to parties finally adjudged guilty in a federal court of unlawful monopoly in the radio industry. The 1934 Act, in addition to repeating the earlier provision, declared that a court making such a finding of guilt against a licensee might itself revoke the license (sections 311 and 313).
[45] C. J. Friedrich and E. Sternberg, "Congress and the Control of Radiobroadcasting," *American Political Science Review*, Vol. 37 (October, 1943), pp. 803 ff., 810.
[46] *Congressional Record*, March 17, 1937, p. 2332, as quoted in Friedrich and Sternberg, *loc. cit.*, p. 810. These authors point out, however, that the actual number of legislators strongly pressing the monopoly issue was not large, and that there were also some who quietly did "a good deal of off-the-record work with the Commission for those who had important financial interests in the industry." *Ibid.*, p. 811.

11. Lynn A. Yeazel, COLOR IT CONFUSING: A HISTORY OF COLOR TELEVISION.

[1] Richard W. Hubbell, 4000 *Years of Television* (New York: G. P. Putnam's Sons, 1942), p. 35.
[2] John Swift, *Adventure in Vision* (London: Purnell & Sons, Ltd.), 1950, p. 40.
[3] Stanley Kempner, *TV Encyclopedia* (New York: Fairchild Publishing Co., 1948), p. 168.
[4] Swift, p. 108.
[5] Kingdon S. Tyler, *Telecasting and Color* (New York: Harcourt, Brace & Co., 1946), pp. 157–159.
[6] J. Richard Johnson, *Television: How it Works* (New York: John F. Rider Inc., 1956), p. 330.
[7] *Broadcasting* (October 28, 1946), p. 18.
[8] *Broadcasting* (November 4, 1946), p. 80.
[9] *Broadcasting* (December 16, 1946), p. 16.
[10] *Broadcasting* (February 3, 1947), p. 18.
[11] *Ibid.*, p. 72.
[12] *Broadcasting* (March 24, 1947), p. 14.
[13] *Ibid.*, p. 73.
[14] *Broadcasting* (October 4, 1948), p. 22A; William C. Eddy, *Television: The Eyes of Tomorrow* (New York: Prentice Hall, 1945), p. 137.
[15] *Broadcasting* (August 15, 1949), p. 42.
[16] *Broadcasting* (September 12, 1949), p. 66.
[17] *Broadcasting* (October 24, 1949), p. 50.
[18] *Broadcasting* (September 19, 1949), p. 48.
[19] *Broadcasting* (September 12, 1949), p. 66.
[20] *Broadcasting* (October 17, 1949), p. 47.
[21] *Broadcasting* (February 20, 1950), p. 77.
[22] *Broadcast News* (Vol. No. 127, August 1965), p. 22.
[23] Eddy, p. 37.
[24] *Broadcasting* (June 25, 1951), p. 25.
[25] *Broadcasting* (June 4, 1951), p. 4.
[26] *Broadcasting* (March 23, 1953), p. 58; and (March 30, 1953), p. 54.
[27] RCA-NBC, *Petition for Approval of Color Standards for the RCA Color Television System* (Washington, D.C.): RCA (June 25, 1953), pp. 4–6.
[28] *Broadcasting* (June 29, 1953), p. 33.
[29] *Broadcasting* (March 15, 1954), p. 99.
[30] RCA, pp. 360–368.
[31] *Broadcasting* (March 2, 1959), p. 76.

Part Two/STATIONS

INTRODUCTION
[1] David L. Woods, "Semantics versus the 'First' Broadcasting Station," *Journal of Broadcasting*, Vol. XI, No. 3 (Summer 1967), p. 202.
[2] R. Franklin Smith, " 'Oldest Station in the Nation?' " *Journal of Broadcasting*, Vol. IV, No. 1 (Winter 1959–1960), pp. 40–55.
[3] Austin C. Lescarboura, "The Gentle Art of Broadcasting," Scientific American, Vol. 126, No. 6 (June 1922), p. 376.
[4] J. Elliott Jenkins, "Highlights in the History of WDAP," *Radio Broadcast* (September 1923), p. 412.
[5] Orrin E. Dunlap, *The Outlook for Television* (Harper & Brothers, 1932), pp. 288–289.

12. Gordon R. Greb, THE GOLDEN ANNIVERSARY OF BROADCASTING
[2] From letter signed by Chas. D. Herrold, March 11, 1932.
[3] *Broadcast Reporter* (Jan. 2, 1933) quotes Fred J. Hart as saying the station would celebrate its 25th birthday on January 17; however, there is no evidence this date has any special significance.
[4] From letters dated March 25, 1940 and April 23, 1940.
[5] The act was approved Aug. 13, 1912. Herrold always claimed that his license in 1912 was the first to be issued to an actual radio telephone. Records show he filed application on Dec. 4, 1912.
[6] Oakland *Tribune* (July 4, 1948).
[7] Herrold's personal papers filled three large boxes. These were examined for the first time in 10 years by the author, together with his son, Robert R. (Herrold) True on Jan. 2 1959, and all radio contents were entrusted to the author for this study.
[8] From the author's tape-recorded interview with Newby, Jan. 9, 1959.
[9] Herrold, "90 Miles with a One-Inch Coil," *Modern Electrics* (October 1910), pp. 380–1. The statement appears, "With . . . the 7,000-foot aerial, phonograph music was easily transmitted from 15 to 20 miles . . ." Two aerials are described.
[10] From signed statements, many of them notarized, by Ray Newly, Terry Hansen, George W. Davis, R. S. Gray, James G. Hestwood and others. The author has examined personal records of W. W. Hanscom for 1912–17, in which, for example, he notes having heard the San Jose station on a daily basis, May 1–Oct. 24, 1913. These papers are preserved by Mr. and Mrs. Douglas Perham at their New Almaden (Calif.) Museum of Historic Properties. Mr. Perham has a large collection of original Herrold broadcasting equipment. San Jose City Historian Clyde Arbuckle also collects and exhibits Herrold material at the State House Replica Museum, located at the Santa Clara County Fairgrounds.
[11] Newby, *ibid.*
[12] From author's tape-recorded interview with Mrs. True, Jan. 2, 1959. She had not seen Newby in 30 years and did not know where he lived. So the cross-verification occurred without cues.
[13] This is 35 mm. film found among Herrold's personal papers and dates the event as 1914 or early 1915 by reason of the baby's age. Robert was born Sept. 5, 1914.
[14] The most important being that of George W. Davis, who was the N-W-T and T company vice president at the time.
[15] This report from the San Francisco *Examiner* (Sept. 6, 1912) amused Newby who recalled he often sang with the records, "just as the disc jockeys do today," he said.
[16] From correspondence by Baxter dated Jan. 3, 1913. (Copy available at the New Almaden Museum of Historic Properties.)
[17] From U.S. Naval Radio Service message, Mare Island, Sept. 18, 1913. Reception by Arlington is cited by Fred F. Wells, *Who is the Father of Radio Broadcasting?* (unpublished interview with Herrold), archives of the State House Replica Museum, San Jose, California.
[18] San Francisco *Call;* also San Francisco *Examiner* (Feb. 13, 1914).

[19] *Broadcast Reporter, ibid.* Also a notarized statement by R. S. Gray, Oakland attorney.

[20] Newby, *ibid.*

[21] From letter dated March 11, 1932.

[22] From speech quotation of De Forest, Sept. 7, 1940, copy of which is possessed by Ralph Brunton, Atherton, California.

15. R. Franklin Smith, "OLDEST STATION IN THE NATION"?

[1] E. P. Shurick, *First Quarter Century of American Broadcasting,* Midland Publishing Company, Kansas City, 1946.

[2] The material here was obtained from perusal of early editions of the *Radio Service Bulletins* of the Department of Commerce, Bureau of Navigation.

[3] The WHA historical marker is six feet tall, weighs 190 pounds, and stands near Radio Hall on the University of Wisconsin campus.

[4] Letter, L. L. Nettleton, Houston, Texas, to Professor Mack, November 13, 1958.

[5] Interview, C. M. Jansky, Jr. with writer, November 24, 1958.

[6] Copy of telegram to U.S. Department of Agriculture, Weather Bureau, Washington, February 15, 1923. Eric Miller files, University Department of Agricultural Journalism.

[7] *University Press Bulletin,* March 5, 1919, Archives, University Library.

[8] Letter, Malcolm Hanson to A. W. Hopkins, July 16, 1931, cited in unpublished paper, *Early History of WHA and History of the Farm Program* by Margary Stoll, 1945, page 9. WHA files.

[9] *Press Bulletin,* January 21, 1920.

[10] *Ibid.,* March 10, 1920.

[11] *Ibid.,* September 29, 1920.

[12] Letter, Malcolm Hanson to Mrs. Sara Terry, November 9, 1941. Hanson papers, Mass Communications History Center, State Historical Society, University of Wisconsin.

[13] *Press Bulletin,* January 19, 1921.

[14] Letter, Malcolm Hanson to Mrs. Lida Hanson, September 27, 1920. *Op. cit.,* Hanson papers.

[15] Letter, W. H. Lighty to Malcolm Hanson, March 12, 1930. WHA files.

[16] *Op. cit.,* Hanson letter to Hopkins.

[17] Typed questionnaire, undated, unsigned, WHA files.

[18] Unpublished paper, Malcolm P. Hanson, *Elementary Circular on Radio Communication,* February, 1922, page 3. WHA files.

[19] *Op. cit.,* Hanson letter to Hopkins.

[20] Letter, Professor Earle M. Terry, to Federal Radio Commission, October 31, 1928. WHA files.

[21] Unpublished, unsigned paper, *Notes on the University of Wisconsin Radio Station,* WHA, Madison, Wisconsin, February 26, 1925. WHA files.

[22] Unpublished, unsigned paper, *Background and Status of Administration and Financing of Radio Station WHA,* April 2, 1937. WHA files.

[23] Unpublished, unsigned paper, *Background Sketch of the Origin and Development of WHA,* December 20, 1929. WHA files.

[24] *Op. cit., Notes on the University of Wisconsin Radio Station,* WHA, Madison, Wisconsin.

[25] Letter, E. P. Shurick, to Professor Mack, November 11, 1958.

[26] Letter, Brigadier General David Sarnoff, Chairman of the Board, Radio Corporation of America, to writer, December 15, 1959.

18. Christopher H. Sterling, WTMJ-FM: A CASE STUDY IN THE DEVELOPMENT OF FM BROADCASTING

[2] Lawrence Lessing, *Man of High Fidelity: Edwin Howard Armstrong* (Philadelphia: J. B. Lippincott, 1956), pp. 193–194.

[3] *Ibid.*, p. 223.

[4] *Ibid.*, p. 230.

[5] *Ibid.*, p. 237.

[6] Gleason L. Archer, *Big Business and Radio* (New York: American Historical Company, Inc., 1939), pp. 424–425.

[7] The company produced and sponsored its first program over week-old WAAK, the first station in Milwaukee, in 1922. They built their own station WTMJ, in early 1927.

[8] Interview with Phillip Laeser, manager of *Journal* Radio and Television, Milwaukee, August 11, 1966.

[9] *Ibid.*

[10] The two Yankee network stations, the Hartford operation, and Armstrong's own W2XMN, preceded Milwaukee. Other applications were pending with the FCC. See Lessing, *op. cit.*

[11] Letter from Walter J. Damm, General Manager of WTMJ, to the Federal Communications Commission, April 8, 1941, p. 6.

[12] H. C. Brunner, "Selling FM to a City," *Radio and Television Retailing* (July, 1940), pp. 22–23.

[13] Letter from Walter J. Damm, exhibit 24.

[14] Lessing, p. 243.

[15] U.S. Federal Communications Commission, *Sixth Annual Report* (Washington, D.C.: Government Printing Office, 1940), p. 66. A number of stations also had "noncommercial educational" status. The *Journal of Broadcasting* has published verbatim extracts from FCC *Annual Reports* on the history of FM radio under the general title, "The Evolution of FM Radio." Material on the years 1935–1940 was published in Vol. 5, No. 2; 1941–1946 in 5:4; 1947–1950 in 6:3; and 1951–1956 in 7:4.

[16] *The Milwaukee Journal*, July 25, 1940, II, p. 1.

[17] Letter from John Guider, Hogan and Hartson Attorneys-at-Law, to FCC, March 26, 1941, p. 3.

[18] FCC, *Sixth Annual Report*, p. 68.

[19] U.S. Federal Communications Commission, *Ninth Annual Report* (Washington, D.C.: FCC Mimeo Print, 1943), p. 56.

[20] Letter from T. J. Slowie, FCC Secretary, to Journal Company, November 9, 1945.

[21] Thomas Porter Robinson, *Radio Networks and the Federal Government* (New York: Columbia University Press, 1943), pp. 62–63.

[22] U.S. Federal Communications Commission, *Order No. 79* (Washington, D.C., FCC Mimeo No. 48496), March 20, 1941.

[23] Murray Edelman, *Licensing of Radio Services in the United States 1927–47* (Urbana: University of Illinois Press, 1950), p. 108.

[24] Petition for Issuance of Construction Permit as Granted and Formal Reply to FCC Letter of April 4, 1941 (FCC File Nos. B4–PH6 and B4–MPH–2), April 12, 1941.

[25] *The Milwaukee Journal*, February 22, 1942, W55M Dedication Section, p. 5.

[26] *Ibid.*, August 23, 1942, Radio City Dedication Section, pp. 1, 10. The building twice expanded and still in use, is located in the northern part of Milwaukee.

[27] *Ibid.*, August 3, 1943, II, p. 1.

[28] Application of the Journal Company for Renewal of W55M License, February 19, 1943, Schedule I, Section 16.

[29] W. Rupert Maclaurin, *Invention and Innovation in the Radio Industry* (New York: Macmillan, 1949), pp. 230–231. Please note that there were a number of political and economic undertones to the Commission's actions.

[30] Interview with Phillip Laeser. Television interests were trying to obtain the 40 mc band for their own use.

[31] C. W. Carnahan, *et al.*, "Report on Propagation of 45.5 and 91.0 Megacycles between Richfield, Wisconsin, and Deerfield, Illinois, July 20, 1945 to September 20, 1945." Submitted to the FCC on October 1, 1945.

[32] U.S. Federal Communications, *Eleventh Annual Report* (Washington, D.C.: Government Printing Office, 1945), p. 19.

[33] *Ibid.*, pp. 20–21. See also Lessing, and Hearings on *Progress of FM Radio*, Senate Committee on Interstate Commerce, 80th Congress, 2nd Session.

[34] "FCC Allocates 88–106 Mc Band to FM," *Broadcasting* (July 2, 1945), p. 13.

[35] Lessing, pp. 258–259.

[36] Letter from T. J. Slowie, FCC Secretary, to Journal Company, September 12, 1945.

[37] Interview with Phillip Laeser.

[38] Application for Renewal of WTMJ-FM Station License, February 21, 1947, Section 15, Exhibit 1.

[39] *The Milwaukee Journal*, September 18, 1948, II, p. 5, and interview with Phillip Laeser.

[40] Interview with Phillip Laeser.

[41] *Ibid.*

[42] Interview with George Comte, Vice President and General Manager of *Journal* Broadcasting, Milwaukee, August 22, 1966.

[43] Letter from Frank E. Schooley, Director of University of Illinois Broadcasting, to writer, August 3, 1966.

[44] The two stations were WISN-FM and WEMP-FM, both affiliated with AM stations. WFMR came on the air as an independent station in Milwaukee in 1956.

[45] U.S. Federal Communications Commission, *Twenty-fourth Annual Report* (Washington, D.C.: Government Printing Office, 1958), p. 5.

[46] U.S. Federal Communications Commission, *Thirty-first Annual Report* (Washington, D.C.: Government Printing Office, 1965), p. 117. By this time, many AM stations were authorized to transmit during the daytime only.

[47] FCC, *Twenty-fourth Annual Report*, pp. 129–130.

[48] Interview with Robert Heiss, former manager of *Journal* Radio and Television, Milwaukee, August 10, 1966.

[49] *The Milwaukee Journal*, November 14, 1965, II, p. 1.

[50] *Milwaukee Consumer Analysis* (Milwaukee: Journal Company, 1959–1966).

19. Robert Pepper, THE PRE-FREEZE TELEVISION STATIONS

[1] The first two stations on the air July 1, 1941 were WNBT (NBC) and WCBW (CBS), both in New York. In addition, by the end of the war, four additional commercially authorized television stations were telecasting: WABD (DuMont in New York), WRGB (G.E. in Schenectady), WPTZ (Philco in Philadelphia), and WBKB (Paramount Pictures Corp. subsidiary of Balaban and Katz, Chicago). The three outstanding CP's belonged to KTSL (Don Lee in Los Angeles), WTMJ (the Milwaukee *Journal*), and WTZR (Zenith in Chicago that never made it on the air). In addition to the commercial authorizations four future commercial telecasters were telecasting with experimental authorizations: W6XAO (Don Lee in Los Angeles), W9XOI (Iowa State in Ames), W6XYZ (Paramount in Los Angeles), and W3XWT (DuMont in Washington, D.C.). Two experimental CP's became WLWT in Cincinnati and KDYL-TV in Salt Lake City. It is interesting to note that six of these first television stations were owned by television equipment manufacturers: RCA (NBC), Philco, DuMont, G.E., and Zenith.

   The information presented in this article was gathered primarily from *Broadcasting-Telecasting*, July 1947–July 1952, *Broadcasting-Telecasting Yearbook Number 1946–1953*, *Television Factbook 1972*, and *Federal Communications Commission 25th Annual Report*.

[2] Ownership is defined by owning or controlling 10% of the voting stock of the licensee.

[3] Erik Barnouw, *The Golden Web: A History of Broadcasting in the United States*, Vol. II—1933 to 1953 (New York: Oxford University Press, 1968), p. 225.

[4] The major television group owners were the Storer Broadcasting Co. (4 television licenses); Meredith Publishing Co. (3), Scripps-Howard Radio Inc. (3); General Tire and Rubber Co. (General Teledio Inc.) (3); Paramount Pictures Corp. (5 including DuMont's 3); AVCO Manufacturing Co. (4); ABC (5); NBC (5); CBS (3).

[5] *Broadcasting-Telecasting Yearbook* did not consider WTOP-TV a network owned-and-operated station because only 45% of the stock was owned by CBS (the remaining 55% was owned by the Washington *Post*); thus, it only considers 15 stations as being network owned-and-operated, instead of the 16 considered to be network O & O by the author.

Part Three/NETWORKS

INTRODUCTION

[1] David Sarnoff, *Looking Ahead* (New York: McGraw-Hill Book Company, 1968), p. 43.

[2] New York *Times* (September 14, 1926), p. 27.

[3] Bruce Barton, "There Will Always be Something New to Do," *The American Magazine*, Vol. CIV, No. 2, (August 1927), p. 16.

[4] Broadcast Pioneer, *NBC History*, 11a, p. 8.

[5] Ben Gross, *I Looked and I Listened* (New York: Random House, 1954), pp. 111–115.

[6] Federal Communications Commisson, *Report on Chain Broadcasting* (Washington: Government Printing Office, May 1941), pp. 103–110.

22. **Federal Communications Commission, EARLY HISTORY OF NETWORK BROADCASTING (1923–1926) AND THE NATIONAL BROADCASTING COMPANY**

[1] On January 4, 1923, a special circuit was set up between stations WEAF, New York City, and WNAC, Boston. A program originating at WEAF was then broadcast simultaneously by the two stations. See testimony of O. B. Hanson, NBC vice president and chief engineer, Transcript, p. 694: "Network Broadcasting" by Barrett and others in *Bell Telephone Quarterly*, vol. 13, pp. 81–82 (April 1934).

[2] The first broadcast stations licensed for regular operation were WWJ at Detroit on October 13, 1921, and KDKA at Pittsburgh on November 7, 1921. On November 2, 1920, however, station KDKA broadcast under a special license, the returns of the Harding-Cox election. See statement of M. H. Aylesworth in *Hearings on Confirmation of Federal Radio Commissioners*, before Senate Committee on Interstate Commerce, 70th Cong., 1st sess., February 4, 1928, p. 233.

[3] See *New York Times*, May 18, 1924, sec. VIII, p 3, for collection of opinions.

[4] Hanson Tr., p. 682.

[5] Hanson Tr., 688; *Radio Broadcast*, June 1924, pp. 130–132.

[6] *Report of Federal Communications Commission on Investigation of the Telephone Industry in the United States*, 76th Cong., 1st sess., H. Doc. No. 340 (1939) (hereinafter cited as F.C.C. *Telephone Report*), pp. 225–226; *Report of Federal Trade Commission on the Radio Industry*, 67th Cong., 4th sess. (1923) (hereinafter cited as F.T.C. *Radio Report*), pp. 47–48.

[7] The standard contract whereby the Telephone Co. sold transmitting equipment expressly provided that the purchaser was not to use the station for profit. *Radio Broadcast*, June 1924, pp. 130–132. It should be noted, however, that some independent stations operated in spite of the Telephone Co.'s claims. *Radio Broadcast*, June 1924, pp. 130–132. After April 18, 1924, some independent stations were licensed by the Telephone Co. to engage in "toll" broadcasting. Hanson, Tr. pp. 678 *et seq.*; F.C.C. *Telephone Report*, pp. 387–399.

[8] *Supra*, n. 1.

[9] Hanson Tr., p. 698. Station WGY was owned by General Electric Co. and stations KDKA and KYW by the Westinghouse Electric & Manufacturing Co.

[10] *Id.*, p. 699.

[11] F.C.C. *Telephone Report*, p. 388. WCAP discontinued operations in 1926. *Infra*, n. 24.

[12] Hanson Tr., p. 711.
[13] *New York Times*, October 24, 1924, p. 1.
[14] Hanson Tr., p. 717.
[15] Archer, *History of Radio to 1926*, p. 361.
[16] Archer, *Big Business in Radio*, p. 246.
[17] Station WJZ had originally been jointly controlled by Westinghouse and RCA. *RCA Annual Report for 1922*, p. 20. Its studios were originally located in Newark, but were moved to New York in 1922.
[18] Hanson Tr., p. 704.
[19] F.C.C. *Telephone Report*, pp. 390–392; Hanson Tr., p. 687. In general, this policy was to decline to furnish this service to broadcast-stations for network broadcasting and to pick up programs originating outside station studios, which was designed to protect the broadcasting activities and the patent position of the Telephone Co. In general, this policy was to decline to furnish this service to broadcasting stations which were not licensed under the Telephone Co.'s patents and to limit in various ways wire service supplied to licensed stations. For a discussion of the broadcasting activities of the Telephone Co., see F.C.C. *Telephone Report*, pp. 387–399.
[20] *Supra*, p. 5.
[21] Archer, *op. cit., supra*, n. 15, p. 304.
[22] *New York Times*, March 5, 1925, p. 5.
[23] F.C.C. *Telephone Report*, pp. 392–395; *Report on Communication Companies*, 73d Cong., 2d sess., H. Rept. 1273 (1934) (hereinafter cited as *Report on Communication Companies*), pt. 3, p. 4074.
[24] WCAP, the Telephone Co.'s station in Washington, had been sharing time with WRC, the RCA station in Washington. Following consummation of the agreement, WCAP discontinued operation and WRC took over its operating time and programs. *New York Times*, July 28, 1926, p. 33.
[25] F. C. C. *Telephone Report*, p. 394; Hanson Tr., p. 855.
[26] *Report on Communication Companies*, pt. 3, p. 1048.
[27] F.C.C. *Telephone Report*, p. 393.
[28] *Report on Communication Companies*, pt. 3, p. 4080.
[29] *New York Times*, March 5, 1925, p. 5. It was also estimated that about 4,800,000 persons heard the broadcast over the RCA network of four stations, WJZ, WBZ, WBC and WGY.
[49] Station WBZA, with a power of 1,000 watts, operates synchronously with WBZ.
[50] *Supra*, p. 11.
[51] After these arrangements had been voluntarily abandoned, the renewals were granted for reasons set forth in the orders and decision of the Commission. *In re Applications of Westinghouse Electric and Manufacturing Company for Renewals of Licenses* (stations WBZ, WBZA, KYW and KDKA), Docket Nos. 5823–5826, September 4, 1940; *In re General Electric Company* (WGY), *Application for Renewal of License and Auxiliary*, October 22, 1940, Docket No. 5822.
[52] The effective date of these contracts for the four Westinghouse stations was July 1, 1940, and for the General Electric station, October 1, 1940.
[53] *Radio Daily*, March 24, 1941, p. 1.
[54] *RCA Annual Report for 1940, passim*.

24. Federal Communications Commission, THE COLUMBIA BROADCASTING SYSTEM

[1] *Report on Communication Companies*, pt. 3, p. 4009.
[2] *Ibid.* Eleven years later the Columbia Phonograph Co. was acquired by the erstwhile subsidiary. On December 17, 1938, CBS acquired the Columbia Phonograph Co. together with three other phonograph record companies, from Consolidated Film Industries, Inc., for $700,000 cash. *Poor's Industrial Manual* (1938), p. 1270; (1940), pp. 790, 3023; *infra*, p. 25.
[9] Station WKRC in Cincinnati, which had been acquired by CBS in 1931.

[10] In California, the management activities of CBS with respect to both concert artists and radio artists are carried on through still another company, Columbia Management Corporation of California, Inc., which is owned jointly by CBS and Columbia Concerts Corporation. Columbia Management Corp. of California, Inc. performs a function in California similar to that carried on by Columbia Concerts Corporation and Columbia Artists, Inc. in other parts of the country.

[11] *Supra*, p. 17.

[12] In a suit by a minority stockholder in the Supreme Court of the State of New York it was alleged that a CBS director had purchased 20 per cent of the stock and subsequently sold it to CBS at a profit. The Court found for the minority stockholder and ordered the director to make restitution to CBS of $85,000. *Mason et al.* V. *Richardson et al.* New York Law Journal, March 5, 1941, p. 992, column 2. CBS attorneys have announced they would probably appeal the decision. *Broadcasting*, March 10, 1941, p. 58.

[13] *Poor's Industrials* (1940), p. 3023.

[14] *Broadcasting*, August 1, 1940, p. 21.

26. Federal Communications Commission, THE MUTUAL BROADCASTING SYSTEM

[1] On January 20, 1936, pursuant to an amendment of Mutual's corporate charter, the Crosley Radio Corporation, licensee of WLW, acquired five newly issued shares of Mutual stock. This ownership continued only until September 26, 1936, when Crosley returned the stock to Mutual.

[2] After this change the total issued capital stock of Mutual consisted of 100 shares which were held as follows: 25, WOR; 25, WGN; 25, Don Lee; 6, Colonial Network; 6, United Broadcasting Co.; 6, Cincinnati Times-Star Co.; 6, Western Ontario Broadcasting Co., Ltd.; 1, Fred Weber (qualifying share).

27. David T. MacFarland, THE LIBERTY BROADCASTING SYSTEM

A good brief treatment of LBS vis-a-vis baseball in "Liberty Chain to Air Major Games Over 250 Stations in 33 States." *The Sporting News*, March 1, 1950.

The expansion period of the network is covered in "LBS Expands" in *Broadcasting-Telecasting*, Feb. 27, 1950, p. 16, and in "Liberty Web Goes National," in *Billboard*, Feb. 25, 1950, p. 12.

Copies of Gordon McLendon's speech closing the Liberty Network and denouncing the Justice Department and the "baseball monopoly" have been available in the past from the McLendon Stations Headquarters, McLendon Building, 197 Elm Street, Dallas, Texas 75201.

An article titled "Liberty Suspends" appeared in *Broadcasting-Telecasting*, May 19, 1952, bargaining on page 25. This gives a brief history with more details about the waning days of the service.

Those wishing to investigate further the legal ramifications of doing "recreations" of sports events will want to refer to: (1) The WOCL "baseball recreation" decision in Newton, 2 FCC 381, 1936, and in 19 R.R. 606; (2) the KELP "recreations of major league baseball games" opinions in Liberty Broadcasting System vs. National League Baseball Club of Boston *et al.*, 7 R.R. 2164, 1952; and in Trinity Broadcasting Corporation, KELP 10 R.R. 279, 1954; and (3) the Fass "pirating of baseball play-by-play" decision in National Exhibition Co. vs. Fass (N.Y. Supreme Court), 11 R.R. 2086, 1955.

28. Hal W. Bochin, THE RISE AND FALL OF THE FOURTH NETWORK

[1] Gary N. Hess. "An Historical Study of the DuMont Television Network," (Unpublished Ph.D. dissertation, Department of Speech, Northwestern University, 1960), p. 216.

Part Four/ECONOMICS

INTRODUCTION

[1] *Ray-O-Vac Radio Manual & Broadcasting Station Directory* (Madison, Wisconsin: French Battery Co., 1925), pp. 28–39. (Directory supplied by Radio Digest "revised December 1925.")

[2] William Banning, *A Commercial Experiment* (Cambridge: Harvard University Press, 1946), p. 90.

[3] "Early Radio Sponsors Few, Far Between," *Broadcasting*, May 14, 1962, p. 139.

[4] Hugo Gernsback, "Who Pays for Radio Broadcasting," *Radio News*, Vol. 7, No. 5 (November 1925), p. 585.

[5] *Broadcasting*, May 14, 1962, pp. 139–140.

[6] "And Now a Word from Our Sponsor," *Broadcasting-Telecasting*, October 15, 1956, p. 110.

[7] H. D. Kellogg, Jr., "Who is to Pay for Broadcasting—And How," *Radio Broadcast*, March 1925, pp. 863–866.

[8] Speech at the Third National Radio Conference, October 6–10, 1924; see *Journal of Broadcasting*, Vol. IV, No. 2 (Spring 1960), p. 118.

[9] "Interesting Things, Interestingly Said," *Radio Broadcast*, July 1925, p. 341.

[10] Jennie Irene Mix, "The Listeners' Point of View," *Radio Broadcast*, February 1925, p. 685.

[11] "The March of Radio," *Radio Broadcast*, November 1927, p. 14.

[12] Orrin E. Dunlap, Jr., "Radio Advertising, Does It Pay?" *Radio News*, August 1928.

[13] Richard S. Nickeson, *The History of the Radio Commercial* (unpublished master's thesis, School of Journalism, University of Wisconsin, 1946), p. 198.

[14] Thomas T. Eoyang, *An Economic Study of the Radio Industry in the United States of America* (New York: Columbia University, 1936), p. 167.

[15] *Broadcasting-Telecasting*, October 15, 1956, p. 112.

[16] Kevin B. Sweeny, "How Radio Advertising Developed—Jingles, Humor, Stars who Sell Sponsor's Product Highlight 43 Years," *Advertising Age*, December 7, 1964.

[17] "George Washington Hill: Eccentric Genius," *Broadcasting-Telecasting*, October 15, 1956, p. 115.

[18] "Boxtops and Broadcasting," *Broadcasting-Telecasting*, October 15, 1956, p. 112.

[19] Nickeson, p. 200.

[20] Hadley Cantril and Gordon Allport, *The Psychology of Radio* (New York: Harper and Brothers, 1935), p. 246.

[21] J. A. R. Pimlott, "Public Service Advertising: the Advertising Council," *Public Opinion Quarterly*, Summer 1948, p. 211.

[22] "Television," *Life*, February 20, 1939, p. 49.

[23] Les Brown, *Television: The Business Behind the Box* (New York: Harcourt Brace Jovanovich, 1971), pp. 349–351.

[24] TVB data in *Backstage*, June 22, 1973.

[25] John Wallace, "Listener's Point of View," *Radio Broadcast*, December 1927, p. 141.

33. Hiram L. Jome, BROADCASTING AND ITS PROBLEMS

[1] See Hearings before House Committee on Merchant Marine and Fisheries, on H. R. 7357, a bill to regulate radio communication, March 11–14, 1924, p. 88. Testimony by Mr. Harkness, a vice-president of the Bell System. Mr. Harkness stated that the cost of operating WEAF for 1923 was about $250,000, and that the revenue to the company including that from its licenses to other companies, was "less than half that amount."

[2] Letter to writer, dated July 24, 1924.

36. John W. Spalding, 1928: RADIO BECOMES A MASS ADVERTISING MEDIUM

[3] Sydney Head, *Broadcasting in America* (Boston: Houghton Mifflin Co., 1956), p. 77.

[4] Ralph M. Hower, *The History of an Advertising Agency* (Cambridge: Harvard University Press, 1939), pp. 164–5.

[5] Gleason L. Archer, *Big Business and Radio* (New York: The American Historical Company, Inc., 1938), p. 246.

[6] Austin C. Lescarboura, "How Much it Costs to Broadcast," *Radio Broadcast*, September 1926, pp. 368–9.

[7] Archer, *op. cit.*, pp. 308–11.

[8] *New York Times*, December 23, 1928, ix, 8.

[9] Charles H. Stamps, "The Conception of the Mass Audience in American Broadcasting: An Historical-Descriptive Study" (unpublished Ph.D. dissertation, Northwestern University, 1956), p. 40.

[10] Bruce A. Linton, "A History of Chicago Radio Station Programming, 1921–1931, With Emphasis on Stations WMAQ and WGN," (unpublished Ph.D. dissertation, Northwestern University, 1955), pp. 162–3, 217, and 153.

[11] Head, *op. cit.*, p. 132.

[12] *New York Times*, September 16, 1928, xii, 1.

[13] O. H. Caldwell, "Radio Changes in Effect Today," *New York Times*, November 11, 1928, xi, 17.

[14] *New York Times*, November 25, 1928, xi, 16.

[15] Gleason L. Archer, *History of Radio to 1926* (New York: The American Historical Society, Inc., 1938), p. 254.

[16] Archer, *Big Business and Radio, op. cit.*, p. 90.

[17] *New York Times*, September 16, 1928, xii, 1.

[18] Advertisement, *New York Times*, April 20, 1924, ix, 12.

[19] Prices cited in advertisements, *New York Times*, throughout December, 1928.

[20] Quoted, *New York Times*, September 16, 1928, xii, 1.

[21] For a fuller description of the spread of broadcast radio receivers, see: Leslie J. Page, Jr., "The Nature of the Broadcast Receiver and Its Market in the United States from 1922 to 1927," *Journal of Broadcasting*, IV, 174–182 (Spring 1960).

[22] O. H. Caldwell, "The Radio Market," *Radio and Its Future*, ed. Martin Codel (New York: Harper and Bros., 1930), p. 206.

[23] O. H. Caldwell, *Radio and Its Future, op. cit.*, p. 206.

[24] Graham McNamee (with Robert G. Anderson), "You're On the Air," *Saturday Evening Post*, May 1, 1926, p. 14.

[25] Allan Harding, "Behind the Scenes at WOR," *American Magazine*, October, 1925, p. 154.

[26] "Sizing up the Radio Audience," *Literary Digest*, January 19, 1929, pp. 54–5.

[27] Linton, *op. cit.*, pp. 45–6.

[28] Cited by Hower, *op. cit.*, p. 164.

[29] Archer, *History of Radio to 1926, op. cit.*, pp. 342–3.

[30] American Telephone and Telegraph Company, press release, quoted, *ibid.*, p. 257.

[31] *Printer's Ink*, April 27, 1922.

[32] Banning, *op. cit.*, pp. 118 and 147. See also Archer, *History of Radio to 1926*.

[33] James P. Wood, *The Story of Advertising* (New York: The Ronald Press Co., 1958), pp. 405–8.

[34] James C. Young, "How Will You Have Your Advertising?" *Radio Broadcast*, December, 1924, p. 245.

[35] Linton, *op. cit.*, p. 84.

[36] Quoted, *New York Times*, November 15, 1931, ix., 8.

[37] "Radio Converts the Continent into an Auditorium," *Literary Digest*, December 4, 1926, p. 61.

[38] Llewellyn White, *The American Radio* (Chicago: University of Chicago Press, 1947), p. 61.

[39] "National Broadcasting Company, Inc.," *Fortune*, December, 1930, p. 70.

[40] Linton, *op. cit.*, p. 254.

[41] Merlin Aylesworth, "Radio is Classed as a Public Utility," *New York Times*, September 16, 1928, xii, 3.

[42] Linton, *op. cit.*, p. 211.

[43] Banning, *op. cit.*, pp. 147–8.

44 "Radio Magazine," *New York Herald*, January 20, 1924, sec. vii, and "Radio Programs for the Coming Week," *New York Times*, January 27, 1924, ix, 8.

45 Banning, *op. cit.*, p. 261.

46 *New York Times*, January 13, 1929, viii, 17.

47 Harrison B. Summers (ed.). *A Thirty Year History of Programs Carried On National Radio Networks in the United States* (Columbus: The Ohio State University, 1958), pp. 11–13.

48 "An Appraisal," *Fortune*, September, 1932, p. 44.

49 *Ibid.*

50 Advertisements, *Saturday Evening Post*, May 26, 1928, p. 103, and May 12, 1928, p. 133.

51 J. W. Spalding, "An Historical and Descriptive Analysis of the *Voice of Firestone* Radio and The Television Program, 1928–1959" (unpublished Ph.D. dissertation The University of Michigan, 1961), p. 190.

52 Summers, *op. cit.*, pp. 9–13.

53 Hower, *op. cit.*, p. 138.

54 Roy Durstine, "Audible Advertising," *Radio and Its Future, op. cit.*, p. 51.

38. Herman S. Hettinger, SOME FUNDAMENTAL ASPECTS OF RADIO BROADCASTING ECONOMICS

6 The World Broadcasting System also has developed a service of considerable importance to stations, especially smaller ones, in the form of a transcription library. Stations may use the programs in the library either upon the payment of a specified fee or the donation of a given amount of time. The programs may be sold to local advertisers for sponsorship. The National Broadcasting Company also has entered the transcription library field.

11 All information in this section either is based on the regular reports of advertising volume compiled and published by the National Association of Broadcasters, or is the result of special studies based upon reports of advertising collected in this manner.

12 These are all either 5,000 watts or better in power and constitute the clear channel and high-power regional group of stations.

13 Federal Radio Commission report in response to the Couzens-Dill Resolution. 72d Congress, Senate Document #137, p. 13.

14 A uniform contract adopted several years ago by the National Association of Broadcasters and the American Association of Advertising Agencies aided materially in minimizing uncertainty in this field.

39. David G. Clark, H. V. KALTENBORN AND HIS SPONSORS: CONTROVERSIAL BROADCASTING AND THE SPONSOR'S ROLE

1 The Kaltenborn papers are on file at the State Historical Society of Wisconsin, Madison, and fill more than 200 boxes. The author used the papers extensively in preparing a biography of the commentator.

2 Kaltenborn business papers, box 148.

3 Henry A. Bellows, memo to board of directors, General Mills, Dec. 13, 1938, box 148.

4 Kaltenborn script (typed transcript from a disk recording), Jan.1, 1939.

5 Bellows to Kaltenborn, Jan. 9, Jan. 18, 1939, box 148.

6 Wilbur Schramm and Ray Huffer, "What Radio News Means to Middleville," *Journalism Quarterly*, XXIII:2:178 (June, 1946).

7 Bellows to Kaltenborn, Jan. 24, 1939, box 148.

8 Rev. Thomas A. Lahey, C.S.C., Ph.D. to Bellows, Feb. 6, 1939, box 148.

9 Bellows telegram to Kaltenborn, Feb. 8, 1939, box 148.

10 Kaltenborn script, Feb. 12, 1939.

11 Bellows telegram to Kaltenborn, Mar. 7, 1939. Richard Barbour, public relations director of General Mills-Sperry, the West Coast division of the company, tried in the author's behalf in November 1966 to obtain relevant passages of the board's minutes. Though unsuccessful, Barbour (himself a member of the corporate structure, and

therefore eligible to examine the minutes) told the author that it was his informed guess the German bakers and not the Catholics constituted the primary threat. A check of religious affiliations revealed no Catholic clique of the size to which Kaltenborn alluded both in interviews with the author in December 1963 and for the Columbia University Oral History project.

[12] Bell to Kaltenborn, Mar. 8, 1939; Bellows to Kaltenborn, Mar. 27, 1939, box 148.

[13] Kaltenborn to Bellows, Mar. 29, 1939, box 148.

[14] Earl S. Grow, "A Dialogue on American International Involvement, 1939–1941, The Correspondence of H. V. Kaltenborn, His Sponsors, and His Public," unpublished Ph.D. dissertation, University of Wisconsin, 1964, pp. 334, 356.

[15] Francis H. Marling to H. V. Kaltenborn, June 8, 1939, box 148.

[16] Marling to Kaltenborn, Mar. 21, 1942, box 150.

[17] Kaltenborn to Marling, Mar. 23, 1942, box 150.

[18] Henry M. Dawes to Marling, Mar. 24, 1942, box 150.

[19] Kaltenborn-Pure contract, box 150.

[20] Dawes to Kaltenborn, July 3, 1942; Kaltenborn to Dawes, July 7, 1942, box 150.

[25] Kaltenborn, interview with author, December 1963.

[26] Homer T. Hirst, "Our Motive Had Much to Do with Self-Interest," *Journal of Broadcasting*, IX, 3:215 (Summer, 1965).

40. Harvey J. Levin, COMPETITION AMONG MASS MEDIA AND THE PUBLIC INTEREST

[1] Cities where the local daily or dailies are controlled by one publisher have grown, as a percentage of all newspaper cities, from 57% in 1920 to 92% in 1951. (See *Yale Law Journal*, 61:949, note 19.) Royal H. Ray estimates that at least 559 dailies disappeared through consolidation or merger between 1909 and 1950. Some 300 local combinations were also formed during the period. (Ray, "Concentration of Ownership and Control in the American Newspaper Industry," Ph.D. Columbia, 1951.)

[2] See U.S. v. Paramount Pictures, Inc., et al. 334 US 131 (1948).

[3] See FCC's Newspaper-Radio Hearings, in re: Orders 79 and 79-A (1941), Docket 6051, pp. 1370–90, 1720.

[4] Moreover, communities where the only newspaper owned the only radio station rose slightly from 8.7% of all radio communities in 1936 to 12.2% in 1950, although newspaper affiliated stations fell from 25.2% to 22.5% of all the stations on the air. (Data compiled from *Broadcasting* and *Editor and Publisher Yearbooks*.)

[5] The most spectacular development is the recent merger between the American Broadcasting Company, owning 5 radio and 5 TV stations and affiliated with 348, and United Paramount Theaters, Inc., operating outright some 650 theaters and holding minority interests in another 300. (See FCC, Dockets 10031, 10047, et al., and mimeo 83222, pp. 130–139.) Some experts feel that competitive pressures may force other theater owners to follow suit. (See Cmmr. Hennock's *Separate Views*, FCC-mimeo 8635, 2–9–53, pp. 22–3; also mimeo 81139, Oct. 3, 1952, pp. 164–5.

[6] See Docket 6051, pp. 830–63, 1370–90. More recently joint enterprises have been sued for attempting to "monopolize" the dissemination of news and advertising and for forcing joint rates on advertisers. (*Broadcasting*, Jan. 13, 1953, pp. 23, 32–33; Dec. 1, 1952, pp. 59–69; Nov. 24, 1952, pp. 71, 82.)

[7] A crucial question was whether UPT would really profit as much from enriching and developing TV programming transmitted to the home, as from treating TV as an adjunct to her older, more extensive theater properties and if need be restricting its growth. (See Hennock's *Separate Views*, FCC-mimeo 8365, pp. 12–17.)

[8] See Ernest W. Hocking, "Freedom of the Press," pp. 141–7. An anti-affiliation rule must be considered in the context of the First Amendment. Originally the latter sought to promote freedom of expression by protecting the individual speaker or transmitter from government restrictions. (Hocking, *op. cit.*, pp. 8–20; "A Free and Responsible Press," pp. 6–15.) Section 326 of the Communications Act reiterates the traditional proscription against government censorship. But freedom from government restraint does not sanction private restraint. Freedom of the press means "freedom for

all and not for some." (see 326 U.S. Reports at 17–23; also 52 Fed. Suppl. at 371–3, in the case of US v. AP, 1943). Freedom of media *from* governmental censorship, in short, does not mean freedom *to* suppress, distort or block the dissemination of news and comment. (See FCC mimeo 49–769 36009 on broadcast editorializing: "A Free and Responsible Press," pp. 15–19; Hocking, *op. cit.*, pp. 228–230). Indeed Congress made this clear in sec. 315 of the Communications Act, requiring equal time to all political candidates if *any* free time were given. The positive social basis for an anti-affiliation rule would seem similar: To prevent private restraints on the flow of ideas.

[9] For documentation of this point see Chapter II of the writer's study, "Cross Channel Ownership of Mass Media," University Microfilms, 1953, or Columbia University Library.

[10] By an "anti-affiliation" policy, we refer primarily to FCC's so-called Newspaper Rule. (See FCC, Public Notice 72993, Jan. 13, 1944; and *Yale Law Journal*, June 1950, pp. 1342–50).

[11] See Amer. Newsp. Pub. Assoc., *Proceedings*, 1930, pp. 209–10; 1931, p. 209; 1947, pp. 24–5; 1949, pp. 48–50; Docket 6051, pp. 1315–8, 1335–7, 2867–9. For full documentation of these "motives," see the writer's study "Cross Channel Ownership of Mass Media," Ch. III, esp. pp. 68–90; 93–4.

[12] See the writer's study, *op. cit.*, Ch. III, esp. pp. 68–99.

[13] For similar studies see Paul Neurath, "One Publisher Communities: Factors Influencing Trend," *Journ. Quart.*, 21 (Sept. 1944), pp. 217–244; Gerald and Ecklund, "Probable Effects of Television on Income of Other Media," *Journ. Quart.* 29 (Fall 1952), pp. 385–95.

[14] In 1930 many advertisers cut their newspaper outlays sharply at the same time they increased radio and even magazine appropriations. (ANPA, *Proceedings*, 1931, p. 209). Newspapers' share of advertising revenues going to newspapers, radio and magazines, fell from 80% in 1928 to 54% in 1947, while radio's rose from 1% to 25%. (Computed from data in U.S. Census, *Broadcasting Yearbooks*, and data from Dept. of Commerce.) The number of dollars spent on newspaper advertising per $1000 disposable income fell from 10.14 in 1928 to 6.00 in 1947, while the number spent on radio rose from .17 to 2.80 (*Ibid.*) Between 1929 and 1933 newspaper advertising revenues fell 40% with a 46% decline in national income, while radio revenues rose 112%.

[15] See Chart III in the writer's study, "Cross Channel Ownership of Mass Media," p. 140b.

[16] Our first test examined the degree to which levels of circulation per issue, per 1000 people, of English language dailies, in 48 states (X-1), are explained by levels of per capita income (X-2), and of radio homes per 1000 homes (X-3). We selected 1929, 1940 and 1947 as three significant points in radio's development. Similar tests were also conducted with advertising revenues of all newspapers per capita, as X-1. (Data for all tests here, unless otherwise noted, compiled from *Editor and Publisher Yearbooks*, U.S. Census, *Broadcasting Yearbooks*. All data appear in Appendices in "Cross Channel Ownership of Mass Media."

	Circulation		
	1929	1940	1947
r 12.3	.247	.385	.844
r 13.2	.323	.150	.837
	Advertising		
r 12.3	.300	.465	.553
r 13.2	.554	−.720	.414

r is the correlation coefficient—a concise numerical statement of the degree of closeness of relationship between two variables. r 12.3 states the closeness of relationship between income and circulation levels (or levels of advertising revenues), in 48 states, holding constant the factor of radio homes. r 13.2, on the other hand, depicts the relationship between levels of radio homes per 1000 homes and circulation (or advertising revenues), holding income constant. A negative sign indicates an inverse relationship.

[17] Here X-1 is the rate of change in circulation, per issue, per 1000 people; X-2, in per capita income; X-3, in radio homes per 1000 homes, 48 states, during three selected periods. We found:

	1929–1933	1937–1940	1941–1943
r' 1.2	.045 (.162)	.061	.173
r' 1.3	.011 (.063)	−.257	.243

(bracketed values are for 45 states with circulation *declines* during 1929–1933; 3 states had *increases* for reasons we could not ascertain)

r' (or rho) is the coefficient of rank correlation—a precise measure of the concordance between two sets of rankings. Here we ranked the 48 states in descending order, listing first the state with the greatest percentage decline in circulation and income and the greatest increase in radio homes, 1929–1933; and the greatest increase in each variable in the other two periods. r' 1.2 states the degree of correlation in 48 states between circulation and income ranks; r' 1.3 does the same for radio homes and circulation ranks.

[18] By *East* we mean the Middle Atlantic, New England, North Central and Pacific states, plus West Virginia and Maryland; by *South* we mean the Southeast, South Central and South West states; by *Central* we mean the remaining Mountain and West North Central states.

These areas were fairly homogeneous during the years studied, from the viewpoint of urbanization, average per capita income, average growth in radio homes per 1000 homes, average per capita circulation of newspapers, etc. Our findings follow:

	1929–1933		1937–1940		1941–1943	
	r'1.2	r'1.3	r'1.2	r'1.3	r'1.2	r'1.3
EAST	.6240	−.2240	.0090	−.5008	−.0935	.1409
SOUTH	−.1286	.1500	−.1607	−.2571	.5540	.5195
CENTRAL	−.4175	.1154	.3571	.2775	.3626	−.6401

Again rank order techniques were used. Ranks were arranged like those in footnote 17.

[19] For example, compare our findings in footnote 17 to those that follow:

	1929–1933		1937–1940		1941–1943	
	r'1.2	r'1.3	r'1.2	r'1.3	r'1.2	r'1.3
Circulation (36 cities)	.4300	−.1800	.2230	−.0140	.0811	−.0744
Advertising (23 cities)	.4100	−.0800	.1890	−.0560	.1124	−.1134

X-1 is 36 cities ranked according to the percentage change in city-zone circulation, per 1000 people, and estimates of advertising revenues per 1000 people (based on ad lineage and circulation figures). X-2 is ranking according to average per capita retail sales; X-3, ranking according to percentage change in radio homes per 1000 homes. We ranked first cities with the greatest decline (or least increase) in circulation or advertising revenues, the greatest growth in radio homes, and the lowest level of average per capita retail sales.

[20] See tables in footnotes 18 and 19.

[21] Data analyzed here were compiled from *Editor and Publisher* and from lists of suspensions prepared by Ray, *op. cit.*, Appendices. Suspensions were analyzed by chi-square. We arranged the data according to states experiencing changes in per capita in-

come greater and less than the median value of change, 1929–1933, 1937–1040, 1941–1943. A similar breakdown was made for states experiencing more and less growth in radio homes per 1000 than the median value of growth. (See "Cross Channel Ownership of Mass Media," Appendices C-1 and C-7).

22 See "Cross Channel Ownership of Mass Media," Table 19 and Appendix D-4.

23 See Allport, "Psychology of Radio," p. 244; also Docket 6051, pp. 3305–3340.

24 Docket 6051, pp. 199–200, 213, 218, 644.

25 Competitive advertising has been discussed by economists in many contexts. See J. M. Clark, "Social Control of Business," pp. 157–8; Veblen, "Theory of Business Enterprise," pp. 57–60; A. R. Burns, "Decline of Competition," p. 588; A. C. Pigou, "Economics of Welfare," pp. 57–60.

26 See Martin Codel, "FM and Television Digest," (hereafter called CODEL), Feb. 3, 1951, p. 10.

27 See Chart V in "Cross Channel Ownership of Mass Media," p. 151a and also Appendices D-2, E-1.

28 The problem of newsprint shortages is described by E. Emery, "History of the American Newspaper Publishers Association," pp. 164–6. Our hypothesis may explain the sudden sharp increase in national network revenues during the war. (See Chart VI, "Cross Channel Ownership of Mass Media," p. 162a; also Appendices D-2, E-1.) Changes in radio and newspaper advertising indexes on Chart II above, are equally suggestive, especially when we realize that radio's sharp wartime growth in revenues came virtually without any new increase of sets-in-use or of sets per family.

29 First we undertook a multiple correlation analysis with X-1 the levels of newspaper circulation per 1000 people in 27 TV cities, 1948; X-2, the levels of per capita retail sales (per capita income data are not available for cities); and X-3, TV sets per 10,000 people. We computed values of .237 (r 12.3) and .323 (r 13.2).

30 Here we computed a rank correlation coefficient measuring the relationship between 26 TV cities ranked according to the percentage change in circulation of dailies, X-1 (ranking first the city with the largest decline); and the percentage growth in TV sets per 10,000 people, X-3 (ranking first the city where sets grew the most). To ascertain the possible role of income we computed a second coefficient between X-1, above, and rankings according to levels of per capita retail sales, 1948, X-2 (the city with the lowest sales ranked first). Computed values were .8899 (r'1.2) and −.1292 (r'1.3). The second coefficient shows very weakly that cities where TV grew the *most* were those where circulation declined the *least*.

31 Analysis of standard stations reporting increases and decreases in revenues 1950/1949, by TV and non-TV markets, suggested a definite impact of TV. Computed x^2 was 7.84, significant on the .007 level. (See writer's study, op. cit., Appendix C-9, p. 263).

32 *Ibid.* Analysis of network stations and affiliates reporting profit and losses in 1950 by TV and non-TV markets, produced a X^2 value of 1.527—significant on the .23 level only. The same test, undertaken for non-network stations, produced similar results. In short, the data do not show significantly more stations with losses operated in TV areas.

33 Frederic Stuart computed values of .700 (r 12.3) and .230 (r 13.2) with X-1 as movie receipts per capita, 48 states, 1948; X-2, per capita income; X-3, TV sets per movie theater. (Stuart, "TV's Competitive Impact on the Movies," unpublished manuscript, Columbia Library).

34 Stuart analyzed 23 cities ranked according to the percentage decline in average gross movie receipts, 1946-1950, X-1 (ranking first the city with the greatest decline); and according to the number of TV sets per movie theater (the city with most TV sets ranked first). He computed a rank correlation coefficient of .38. When the number of stations operating in each city was taken into account, on the assumption that set owners were less likely to go to the movies the more stations they can hear, a coefficient of .59 was computed. In other words, cities where movie receipts declined the most seemed to be those where TV sets were most numerous.

35 r 1.3 was .9692 in a test where X-1 was the ratio of movie theaters operating in 1950

to those operating in 1946, 48 states; the state with the highest ratio ranked first; X-3, states ranked according to TV sets per capita in 1950, again the highest first. (Stuart, *op. cit.*) In other words where the number of theaters declined the most were those where TV grew the least.

[36] We found no evidence of an adverse impact of TV on newspaper circulation. See above, notes 29 and30.

[37] For example see *Broadcasting*, Nov. 15, 1948, p. 10 (survey conducted by Thomas Coffin, Hofstra College, Long Island); also Robert Alldredge, survey of TV's impact in Washington, D.C., summarized in CODEL, Feb. 4, 1950; also *Broadcasting*, Nov. 21, 1949, pp. 24, 45 (survey of advertising executives).

[38] The relationship between TV growth and decline in movie receipts does not seem quite so marked as the tendency for radio stations to report decreased revenues in TV (rather than non-TV) markets. (See above, notes 31 and 34.) More specifically, the value of r' 1.3 in Stuart's test, .38 is significant on the .05 level; the value of chi-square in Table 12—7.84—is significant on the .007 level.

[39] See Alldredge, *loc. cit.;* also Audience Analysis, *Broadcasting Yearbooks*, 1949, 1950; also Fact Finders Association, *op. cit.*, and survey by Thomas Coffin, *loc. cit.*

[40] See CODEL, Jan. 13, 1941, p. 11. Television is at present dependent on old film strips to fill much of its broadcast day. See also Merrill, Lynch, Pierce, Fenner and Beane, "Radio Television and Motion Pictures," Aug. 25, 1950, pp. 7–8; and "The Case for Filmed Television," *Broadcasting*, Jan. 26, 1953, pp. 77–8.

[41] See R. D. Levitt, "Advertising Agency and Advertising Selling," Oct. 1950, pp. 54–5, 128, 130; also CODEL, Sept. 23, 1950, p. 5; *Broadcasting*, April 30, 1951, pp. 29, 72; *Omnibook* News Dept., mimeo dated Jan. 16, 1951. These materials are also in line with Lazarfeld's conclusions about the mutual stimulation and complementary nature of books, movies, magazines and radio. (See "Radio Listening in America," pp. 4–9, tables 3–6).

[42] See *Broadcasting*, April 23, 1951, p. 36; *Editor and Publisher*, Jan. 31, 1953, p. 34.

[43] The comparative advantages of radio and newspaper rate structures are discussed in Borden, et al., *op. cit.*, pp. 210–218.

[44] There have been successive rate cuts on several occasions recently. (See *Broadcasting*, May 7, 1951, p. 23; April 30, 1951, pp. 23, 34, 36; April 23, pp. 15, 60, 90–1). Costs are also being reduced. (See *Broadcasting*, May 7, 1951, p. 87; Siepmann, Radio, Television and Society," p. 343.)

[45] See F. L. Mott, "Trends in Newspaper Contents," *Mass Communications* (ed. Schramm), pp. 337–345.

[46] This is apparent upón study of Mott's table of column inches going to different categories of news, features, etc. 1910–1940, decade years, in 10 leading metropolitan dailies. The 16 categories studied account for 56.3 per cent in 1910 and a full 91.2 per cent of total non-advertising space in 1940. See also Amer. Newsp. Pub. Assoc., *Continuing Studies of Newspaper Reading*.

[47] See ANPA, *Proceedings*, 1946, p. 19; 1948, pp. 188–190; also Emery, *op. cit.*, pp. 207–211. See also Lazarfeld's study for the ANPA. "Psychological Impact of Radio and Newspapers" (passim) and *Editor and Publisher*, Jan. 31, 1953, pp. 7, 34, 51.

[48] See Samuel Goldwyn, "Television's Challenge to the Movies," *NY Times*, March 25, 1950, magazine section; Paul Raibourn, "Television and Hollywood," *Elks Magazine*, April 1949. See also *Paramount Pictures*, Report to Stockholders Meeting, June 3, 1952, p. 3.

[49] See Bosley Crowther in *NY Times*, Oct. 7, 1951, theater section; March 16, 1952, magazine section, Leda Bauer, *Theater Arts*, Sept. 1951, p. 32.

[50] For example see Siepmann, *op. cit.*, pp. 343–8; Gilbert Seldes, "The Great Audience," pp. 181–191; Jack Gould, *New York Times*, Oct. 7, 1951. For a well-knit statement of obstacles to solvent "art theaters" see Arthur Mayer, "Hollywood Verdict— Gilt but Not Guilty," *The Saturday Review*, Oct. 31, 1953.

[51] See sources in notes 45–49. See also, Harriet van Horne, "Radio Grows Up," *Theater Arts*, May 1952, pp. 36, 98–9, wherein she describes the improved music, forums,

theater, educational programs and other radio fare. For a case study of one station, see *Broadcasting*, Feb. 2, 1953, pp. 80–82.
⁵² *Broadcasting Yearbook*, 1951, charts, pp. 30–31.

Part Five/EMPLOYMENT

INTRODUCTION

¹ William S. Hedges, "Just Another Fad," *American Heritage* (August 1955), p. 68.
² Graham McNamee, *You're On the Air* (New York: Harper & Brothers, 1926), p. 19.
³ "How One Ambitious Girl became Famous," *Radio Age* (April 1925), p. 27 and p. 64.
⁴ Charlotte Geer, "Roxy," *Theatre*, VLII (September 1925), p. 294.
⁵ Jennie Irene Mix, "Are Women Undesirable—Over the Radio?" *Radio Broadcast* (August 1924), p. 334.
⁶ Jennie Irene Mix, "How Shall We Get Great Artists to Broadcast?" *Radio Broadcast* (May 1924), p. 12.
⁷ "Galaxy of World Celebrities," *Radio Digest* (December 1928), p. 37.
⁸ Harold P. Brown, "Old Prejudice Dissolves—Radio Wins Stage Talent," *Radio Digest* (March 1929), p. 42.
⁹ Arthur Godfrey, CBS Radio Network, April 30, 1972, his last network radio broadcast (1942–1972).
¹⁰ Newton Minow, *Equal Time* (New York: Atheneum, 1964), p. 261.

44. F. G. Fritz, WENDELL HALL: EARLY RADIO PERFORMER

¹ Personal interview with Wendell W. Hall, Fairhope, Alabama, June 1967. Also see Francis Gerald Fritz, "Wendell Woods Hall An Early Radio Performer," (MA Thesis, University of Wisconsin, 1968).
² Erik Barnouw, *A Tower in Babel* (New York: Oxford University Press, 1966), p. 88.
³ Wilson J. Wetherbee, "Good Evening, Everybody! This is Station KYW," *American Magazine*, March 1924, p. 208.
⁴ Alfred N. Goldsmith and Austin C. Lescarboura, *This Thing Called Broadcasting* (New York: Henry Holt and Company, Inc., 1930), p. 97.
⁵ Wendell Hall manuscript collection, University of Wisconsin Historical Library, U.S., Mss, 50AF, Scrapbook 1.
⁶ Hall manuscript collection, Scrapbook 2.
⁷ Gleason L. Archer, *History of Radio to 1926* (New York: The American Historical Society, Inc., 1938), p. 361.
⁸ *The Radio Listener*, June 1926, in Hall manuscript collection, Scrapbook 2.
⁹ Ralph M. Hower, *The History of an Advertising Agency* (Cambridge, Massachusetts: Harvard University Press, 1939), p. 164.
¹⁰ Letter from T. J. McDermott, Senior Vice President for Media and Programming Services, N. W. Ayer & Son, New York, February 8, 1968 to Fritz.
¹¹ Robert T. Coldwell, "The Program as an Advertisement," in *The Advertising Agency Looks at Radio*, ed. by Neville O'Neil (New York: D. Appleton and Company, 1932), pp. 26–27.
¹² Hall manuscript collection, Scrapbook 2.
¹³ William P. Banning, *Commercial Broadcasting Pioneer: The WEAF Experiment, 1922–1926* (Cambridge, Massachusetts: Harvard University Press, 1946), pp. 153–154.
¹⁴ Lawrence W. Lichty, "The Nation's Station: a History of Radio Station WLW" (Ph.D. dissertation, The Ohio State University, 1964), pp. 131–132.
¹⁶ Wendell W. Hall manuscript collection, housed in the National Music Hall of Fame, Warren, Ohio, Scrapbook 2 (since moved to Florida, LWL).
¹⁷ Hall interview.
¹⁸ Akron *Times Press*, June 12, 1930, Hall manuscript collection, Scrapbook 1.

45. John Cogley, CLEARANCE AT CBS

[1] In 1953 Miss Ball, the top television star of the nation, suddenly became highly controversial when newspapers all over the country carried stories that in the mid-thirties, Communist meetings had been held at her home, that she had signed nominating petitions and had been listed as a member of the Communist Party's Central Committee of California. Miss Ball appeared before the House Un-American Activities Committee, told them of an eccentric grandfather and told the Committee that, as her husband put it, "There's nothing red about Lucy but her hair and even that's not real." The public, too, was satisfied and the "I Love Lucy" show continued to appear on CBS.

Part Six/PROGRAMMING

INTRODUCTION

[1] See Asa Briggs, *The Birth of Broadcasting* (London: Oxford University Press, 1961), p. 6.

[2] Edward Bellamy, *Looking Backward*, in a number of different editions.

[3] Reprinted in *Fifty Years of Popular Mechanics* (New York: Simon and Schuster, 1951), p. 140.

[4] "When de Wolf Hopper Broadcasted to His Biggest Audience," *Radio Broadcast*, (July 1922).

[5] Austin C. Lescarboura, "The Gentle Art of Radio Broadcasting," *Scientific American*, Vol. 126, No. 6 (June 1922), p. 377.

[6] Recounted in Sam J. Slatel and Joe Cook, *It Sounds Impossible* (New York: Macmillan Co., 1963), pp. 24–30.

[7] Ira A. Hirschman, "The First Symphony Broadcast," *Public Opinion Quarterly*, Vol. 13, No. 4 (Winter 1949–1950), pp. 683–684.

[8] Compiled from Goldsmith and Lescarboura, *This Thing Called Broadcasting* (New York: Henry Holt Co., 1930), pp. 99–101.

[9] "WLW in Class B; Honors Conferred on Crosley Station," *Crosley Radio Weekly*, II, 25 (June 4, 1923), p. 1.

[10] William Albig, "The Content of Radio Programs, 1925–1935," *Social Forces*, Vol. 16, No. 3 (March 1938), pp. 338–349; William Albig, *Public Opinion* (New York: McGraw-Hill, 1939), p. 347; and later editions of Albig, Modern Public Opinion. Harrison B. Summers, *Radio Programs Carried on National Networks, 1926–1956* (Columbus: Ohio State University, 1958).

[11] Samuel L. Rothafel and Raymond Francis Yates, *Broadcasting, Its New Day* (New York: The Century Co., 1925), pp. 45–46.

[12] John Wallace, "The Listeners' Point of View," *Radio Broadcast*, February 1926, p. 447.

[13] James C. Young, "New Fashions in Radio Programs," *Radio Broadcast* May 1925, p. 84.

[14] Windermere Hungerford, "How America is Turning to Radio and the Drama," *Radio Age*, December 1924, p. 36.

[15] Lawrence W. Lichty, "Radio Drama: The Early Years," *NAEB Journal*, July–August 1966, pp. 10–16.

[16] Charlotte Geer, "Summer Programming," *Theater*, Vol. XLII, No. 295 (October 1925), p. 37.

[17] *Radio Broadcast*, January 1926, p. 320.

[18] "Orchestras Dominate in All Radio Programs," *Radio Digest*, March 1928, pp. 32–33.

[19] "How *Amos 'n' Andy* Broke Conventions," *Broadcasting*, October 15, 1956, p. 212.

[20] "Big Radio Audience Follows Grid Games," *Radio Digest*, October 1927, p. 8.

[21] "Excitement Causes 12 Fight Fans to Drop Dead during Tense Description," *Radio Digest*, November 1927, p. 19.

[22] Ross Drachman, "Headline Hunting with Floyd Gibbons," *Radio Digest,* February 1930, p. 34.

[23] Lowell Thomas, *History as You Heard It* (Garden City, N.Y.: Doubleday and Company, 1957), pp. ix, 1; and see Lionel Crocker, "Lowell Thomas," *Quarterly Journal of Speech,* Vol. XXVII, No. 3 (October 1942), p. 298.

[24] Edgar Willis, "Sound Effects: A Look into the Past," *Journal of Broadcasting,* Vol. I, No. 4 (Fall 1957), p. 329.

[25] Robert B. Turnbull, *Radio and Television Sound Effects* (New York: Rinehart & Co., 1951), p. 183.

[26] J. Bryan, III, "Hi Yo, Silver," *Saturday Evening Post,* October 14, 1939, p. 131.

[27] Rudolph Arnheim, "The World of the Daytime Serial," in Paul F. Lazarsfeld and Frank N. Stanton (eds.), *Radio Research 1942-43* (New York: N. Duell, Sloan & Pearce, 1944), pp. 34–85.

[28] W. Loyd Warner and William E. Henry, "The Radio Day Time Serial: A Symbolic Analysis," *Genetic Psychology Monographs,* 37 (1948), pp. 3–71.

[29] "Never-Ending Serials," *Broadcasting-Telecasting,* October 15, 1956, p. 166.

[30] "Radio Covers Lindbergh Kidnapping," *Broadcasting,* March 15, 1932.

[31] Waldo W. Braden and Earnest Brandenburg, "Roosevelt's Fireside Chats," *Speech Monographs,* Vol. XXII, No. 5 (November 1955), p. 302. For the second conceptualization we are indebted to Lee S. Dreyfus.

[32] A. A. Schechter, *I Live on Air* (New York: Frederick A. Stokes, 1941) and Paul White, Jr., *News on the Air* (New York: Harcourt, Brace and Co., 1947).

[33] "Radio Carries on with Thrills in Directing Flood Rescuers," New York *Times* (January 26, 1937) and Martin Codel, "Nation Acclaims Radio for Flood Relief," *Broadcasting* (February 15, 1937), p. 20.

[34] Robert J. Landry, "Edward R. Murrow," *Scribner's* Vol. 104, No. 6 (December 1938), p. 8.

[35] H. V. Kaltenborn, *I Broadcast the Crisis* (New York: Random House, 1938), p. 6.

[36] Diane Brown, "A Description and Analysis of *The Free Company Presents* . . . (Master's thesis, University of Wisconsin, 1970).

[37] Hadley Cantril, "The Role of the Radio Commentator," *Public Opinion Quarterly,* Vol. 3, No. 4 (October 1939), p. 660.

[38] Kenneth G. Bartlett, "Radio War Programs," *Quarterly Journal of Speech,* Vol. XXIX, No. 1 (February 1943), p. 100.

[39] William Burke Miller, "Army Takes the Air," *Radio Age,* January 1943, pp. 11–14.

[40] William C. Ackerman, "The Dimensions of American Broadcasting," *Public Opinion Quarterly,* IX (1945–1946), p. 13.

[41] Robert Merton, *Mass Persuasion* (New York: Harper and Co., 1946).

[42] John Perry, "War Propaganda for Democracy," *Public Opinion Quarterly,* VI (Fall 1942), p. 439.

[43] Elmer Davis, "OWI Has a Job," *Public Opinion Quarterly* VII (Spring 1943), p. 13.

[44] W. W. Charters (presiding) "Radio Discussion in Wartime," in Josephine Maclatchy, (ed.). *Education on the Air* (Columbus: The Ohio State University, 1942), p. 38.

[45] Edward R. Murrow interviewed by Robert Trout, "Farewell to Studio Nine," CBS Radio Network broadcast, July 25, 1964, 9:05 EDT.

[46] Gilbert Seldes, "The Nature of Television Programs," *The Annals of the American Academy of Political and Social Science,* CCXII (1941), pp. 138–144.

[47] See John Gray Peatman, "Radio and Popular Music," in Paul F. Lazarsfeld and Frank N. Stanton (eds.) *Radio Research 1942-43* (New York: Duell, Sloan, and Pearce, 1944), p. 335–366; Kenneth Baker, "An Analysis of Radio's Programming," in *Communication Research, 1948–1949* by Paul F. Lazarsfeld and Frank N. Stanton (eds.) (New York: Harper and Brothers, 1949), pp. 51–72; and Elmo C. Wilson, "Measuring Radio News Since V-J Day," *Journalism Quarterly,* Vol. 23 (1946), p. 167.

[48] George A. Willey, "End of an Era: The Daytime Radio Serial," *Journal of Broadcasting,* Vol. V, No. 2 (Spring 1961), pp. 97–113.

[49] Frank L. Riggs, "The Changing Role of Radio," *Journal of Broadcasting,* Vol. VIII, No. 4 (Fall 1964), p. 332.

[50] Patrick D. Hazard, "Weaver's Magazine Concept: Notes on Auditioning Radio's New Sound," *Quarterly of Film, Radio and Television*, Vol. 10, No. 4 (Summer 1956), pp. 416–432; and "Cutaway GooGoo on Disc," *Harper's Magazine*, April 1956, pp. 78–79.

[51] "Early Birds on Modern Radio," *Sponsor*, May 28, 1962, p. 35.

[52] Lawrence Lichty, "Radio Programming in Megalopolis," unpublished paper, University of Wisconsin, 1965.

[53] Sherman P. Lawton, "Changes in U.S. Radio Programming—1960–1961," *Journal of Broadcasting*, Vol. VI, No. 4 (Fall 1962), p. 329.

[54] "Television and What the Motion Picture Industry is Thinking and Doing About It," *Hollywood Reporter* booklet, November 1948, reported in Orrin E. Dunlap, Jr., *Communications in Space* (New York: Harper & Row, Publishers, 1964), p. 247.

[55] Richard G. Lawson, "A Little Perspective, Please," *Journal of Broadcasting*, Vol. XV, No. 1 (Winter 1970–71), pp. 21–28.

[56] Reginald Rose, "TV's Age of Innocence—What Became of It?" *New York Times*, December 3, 1967.

[57] Maurice E. Shelby, Jr., "Children's Programming Trends on Network Television," *Journal of Broadcasting*, Vol. VIII, No. 3 (Summer 1964), p. 248.

[58] Sig Mickelson, "Growth of Television News, 1946–1957," *Journalism Quarterly*, Vol. 34 (1957), pp. 404–410.

[59] For an analysis of the telecasting of MacArthur's day in Chicago see, Kurt Lang and Gladys Engel Lang, "The Unique Perspective of Television and Its Effects: A Pilot Study," *American Sociological Review*, Vol. XVIII (February 1953), pp. 3–12; also reprinted in a number of mass communication readers including Schramm and Roberts, *The Process and Effects of Mass Communication* and Berelson and Janowitz, *Reader in Public Opinion and Communication*.

[60] Jim F. Palmer, "A Survey of Television News Over 39 Stations," *Journalism Quarterly*, Vol. 36 (1959), p. 451.

[61] Warren V. Bush, "The Test," *Television Quarterly*, Vol. IV, No. 3 (Summer 1965), pp. 21–27.

47. Lawrence W. Lichty, RADIO DRAMA: THE EARLY YEARS

[3] Donald W. Riley, "A History of American Radio Drama from 1919 to 1944," Ph.D. dissertation (The Ohio State University, 1944), 17.

[4] Donald W. Riley, *Handbook of Radio Drama Techniques* (Ann Arbor, Michigan: Edwards Brothers, Inc., 1946), 3.

[5] E. P. J. Shurcik, *The First Quarter-Century of American Broadcasting* (Kansas City, Missouri: Midland Publishing Company, 1946), 73.

[6] *Ibid.*

[7] Riley, "A History of American Radio Drama . . . ," 19.

[8] Shurick, 821.

[9] Riley, *Handbook of Radio Drama* . . . , 3.

[12] "Noted Musicians from Conservatory on WLW Program," *Crosley Radio Weekly*, I, 9 (November 20, 1922), 1.

[13] *Ibid.*

[14] Interview with Fred Smith, April 20, 1965, Cincinnati, Ohio.

[15] *Crosley Radio Weekly*, I, 9, 1.

[16] Interview with Fred Smith.

[17] "Radarios Included in Programs of WLW; Listeners Pleased," *Crosley Radio Weekly*, II, 17 (April 9, 1923), 1.

[21] Fred Smith, "Origin and Meaning of Radario Described by WLW Announcer," *Crosley Radio Weekly*, II, 22 (May 14, 1923), 1.

[22] *Ibid.*

[23] *Crosley Radio Weekly*, II, 17 (April 9, 1923), 1.

[24] "Authority on Radarios Writes Play Especially for Children: Will be Broadcast by WLW," *Crosley Radio Weekly*, II, 35 (August 13, 1923), 1.

[25] Shurick, 63–64.

26 "Will Direct Radarios on WLW," *Crosley Radio Weekly*, II, 42 (October 1, 1923), 1.

27 "Magazine Offers $100 in Prizes for Best Three Radarios," *Crosley Radio Weekly*, II, 28 (June 28, 1923), 5.

28 Riley, "A History of American Radio Drama . . . ," 21.

29 Shurick, 81.

48. David G. Clark, H. V. KALTENBORN'S FIRST YEAR ON THE AIR

1 Brooklyn *Daily Eagle*, April 22, 1922, p. 12.

5 Columbia University Oral History Project, typescript of interview with HVK, pp. 55–57; HVK, "On Being on the Air," ms. in Kaltenborn Collection, State Historical Society of Wisconsin, Madison, Wis.; interview with author.

6 *Ibid.*

7 *Ibid.*

8 *Eagle*, Oct. 24, 1923, p. 9.

9 *Ibid.*; HVK, *It Seems Like Yesterday* (New York, Putnam's, 1956), p. 52.

10 *Ibid.*

11 Letter files for November and December 1923 and January 1924, Kaltenborn Collection; interview with author.

12 Mrs. Francis Garmany, letter to HVK, in HVK scrapbook, "1920's" Kaltenborn Collection.

49. George A. Lundberg THE CONTENT OF RADIO PROGRAMS

1 The statistics of this study were compiled by my students in a course on *Public Opinion* at Wells College in 1927.

2 Willey, M. M. *The Country Newspaper*, pp. 24–32.

3 *Ibid.*, p. 123.

4 Benick, M. D. [*sic.* Beuick], "The Limited Social Effect of Radio Broadcasting," *American Journal of Sociology*, January, 1927, p. 616.

5 *Ibid.*

50. Lawrence W. Lichty and Thomas W. Bohn, RADIO'S *MARCH OF TIME*: DRAMATIZED NEWS

1 Theodore Peterson, *Magazines in the Twentieth Century* (Urbana, University of Illinois Press, 1964), 234–237 and 323–330. On the film MOT see T. Bohn and L. Lichty, "The March of Time: News As Drama," *Journal of Popular Film*, II:4 (Fall 1973), pp. 373–387.

2 Lawrence W. Lichty, " 'The Nation's Station,' A History of Radio Station WLW," (Ph.D. dissertation, The Ohio State University, 1964).

3 Lawrence W. Lichty, "A History of Radio Drama: Notes on the Early Years," *NAEB Journal*, July–August 1966, 10.

4 "Something Novel in a Program," *Popular Radio*, September 1925, 272. An interesting variation on the format and title was produced much later at KCET, Los Angeles. The program called *Newsical Muse* consisted of balladeer Len Chandler singing the week's news, with various satirical skits. Lew Irwin was producer and anchorman on the program which was on only 13 weeks in 1970. According to a letter from Richard Scott, executive producer, the title was arrived at "in blissful ignorance" of the *Musical News*, 1925.

5 We are grateful to Roy Larsen, Alex Groner, Celia Sugarman, and Marie McCrum of Time Inc. for providing us with corrections and additions. See Robert T. Elson, *Time Inc.* (New York: Atheneum, 1968) for a company history. Included is a short chapter on *MOT*, pp. 175–185.

6 Mrs. Smith (nee Majorie Garrigue) is a pianist; her sister is the poet Jean Garrigue.

7 Personal interview with Fred Smith, Cincinnati, Ohio, April 20, 1965; *New York Times*, September 30, 1928, IX, 17.

8 *OED*, Supplement Part 2 (L-Z), 70. "1930 *Observer* 28 September 21 Graham Mac-Namee, the newscaster of our American Newspaper newsreel, takes the part of the unseen dramatist."

9 Peterson, 329; *Time*, February 28, 1932, 24.

[10] Harrison B. Summers, *Radio Programs Carried on National Radio Networks, 1926–1956* (Columbus: Department of Speech, Ohio State University, 1958), 10.

[11] "Continuity Shop News," *Radio Digest*, May 1932, 40.

[12] Fred Smith, "Keeping Up with the March of Time," *Radio Digest*, May 1931, 24.

[13] Library of Congress, Copyright Office, *Catalog of Copyright Entries*, Part 3, Musical Compositions, Volume 25 (1930), No. 7, 1001.

[14] Smith, "Keeping up . . . ," 25.

[15] All of the information on the content of the first programs was taken from a disc recording of that program loaned by Martin Halperin to whom we are very grateful. The timing was from a tape dubbed from the original disc and thus there could be error in the speed of one or more disc playbacks or tape recorders.

Other actors who worked on *March of Time* included Jack Smart, Ted de Corsia, Alfred Shairley, Marian Hopkinson, Porter Hall, Barbara Bruce, John Battle, Jeannette Nolan, Ray Collins, Nancy Kelly, Arlene Francis, Kenny Delmar, Arnold Moss, Paul Stewart, Juano Hernandez, Dwight Weist, John McIntire, Billy Halop, Edmund Gwenn, Agnes Moorhead, Art Carney, Staats Cotsworth, Ed Jerome, Maurice Tarplin, Peter Donald, Elliott Reid, Martin Gable, Gary Merrill, Myron McCormick, Everett Sloane, and of course many others. Orson Wells first played on *MOT* in 1934 when he was 19 and from this role became an announcer in many commercials.

[16] Fred Smith, "Unique Psychology of 'The March of Time,'" *Broadcasting*, November 1, 1931, 13.

[17] *Time*, February 29, 1932, 32; *Time* did not begin a "Radio" section until May 16, 1938. It subsequently became "Radio and Television," 1948, "Television and Radio" 1957, and "Show Business" 1958.

[18] *Ibid.*

[19] "The March of Time," *Time*, February 29, 1932. Letters to the program were frequently published in *Time*.

[20] *Ibid.*

[21] *Time*, February 29, 1932, 32.

[22] Claudia Ann Case, "A Historical Study of the March of Time Program Including an Analysis of Listener Reactions" (M.S. thesis, The Ohio State University, 1943), 13–14.

[23] "Time Marches Back," *Time*, June 13, 1932.

[24] "Radio Innovation," *Time*, August 28, 1933.

[25] "March of Time Back," *Broadcasting*, October 15, 1934.

[26] "March of Time Weekly," *Broadcasting*, December 1, 1935, 59.

[27] Case, 33.

[28] "Radio Skit Causes Earhart Mixup," *New York Times*, July 10, 1937, 7; New York Times, July 11, 1937, X, 8.

[29] National Broadcasting Company in Case, 36–37; "March Resumed," *Time*, October 13, 1941, 56.

[30] Case, 79 and 71.

[31] *Broadcasting*, April 16, 1945, 18.

[32] In a *This Week* article about the film version of *March of Time* Nina Wilcox Putnam attributed the idea for *March of Time* to Roy Larsen. Larsen wrote Smith: "As you know I have always been anxious to give full credit for the idea of re-enacting the news on radio with which you were so happily inspired when you were working for me at *Time*." Mr. Larsen added, "As far as the working out of the idea for the half-hour drama, specific credit must be given to the group . . . who worked with it over a period of months." Letter from Roy Larsen to Fred Smith, March 26, 1936.

[33] Such as *News Drama*, WTCN, Minneapolis, 1935; *Headlines*, MBS, 1937–1938; *Radio News Reel*, NBC, 1937–1938; and *Front Page Parade*, WCCO, Minneapolis, 1939.

[34] Erik Barnouw, *A Tower in Babel* (New York: Oxford University Press, 1966), 278.

52. Sammy R. Danna, THE RISE OF RADIO NEWS

[22] Charnley, Mitchell V., *News by Radio*. New York: McGraw-Hill Book Company, Inc., 1948, p. 99.

[29] Mott, Frank Luther, *American Journalism*, New York: The Macmillan Company, 1962, pp. 679–680.

[36] Calibraro, Daniel D. *WGN: A Pictorial History*. Chicago: WGN, Inc., 1961, pp. 21–22.

[47] Summers, Robert E. and Harrison B. Summers, *Broadcasting and the Public*. Belmont, California: Wadsworth Publishing Co., 1966, pp. 307, 310.

[52] White, Paul, *News on the Air*. New York: Harcourt, Brace and Company, 1947, p. 32.

[57] White, *op. cit.*, p. 33.

[61] *Ibid.*

[62] *Ibid.*

[68] Raymond, Allen, "The Coming Fight Over News," *New Outlook*, June 1933, p. 15.

[72] "Broadcast Ban," *Business Week*, May 10, 1933, p. 16.

[80] "News and Comment from the National Capital," *The Literary Digest*, November 11, 1933, p. 12.

[81] "The Press and the Microphone," *The Christian Century*, November 22, 1933, 1462.

[82] Carskadon, T. R., "The Press Radio War," *The New Republic*, March 11, 1936, pp. 133–134.

53. Sammy R. Danna, THE PRESS-RADIO WAR

[2] Charnley, Mitchell V., *News by Radio*, New York: The Macmillan Company, 1948, pp. 16–17.

[9] Keating, Isabella, "Pirates of the Air," *Harper's Monthly Magazine*, September 1934, p. 467.

[11] White, Paul, *News on the Air*, New York: Harcourt Brace and Company, 1947.

[12] Magee, H. W. "Radio News Chasers," *Popular Mechanics*, March, 1934, pp. 386–389.

[13] "Radio News: Air Reporters Bow to Power of Press Radio," *Newsweek*, March 10, 1934, p. 21.

[18] "News on the Air," *Business Week*, March 24, 1934, p. 12.

[19] North, Anthony, "Extra! Extra!" *New Outlook*, April 1934, p. 14.

[20] "Press-Radio Competition Speeds Up Air News Reporting," *Newsweek*, June 2, 1934, p. 28.

[28] Whitmore, C. W. "Radio's Fight for News," *The New Republic*, February 4, 1935, p. 355.

[41] Latham, Frank, "The News War in the Air," *Scholastic*, January 11, 1936 p. 19.

[42] Carskadon, T. R., "The Press Radio War," *The New Republic*, March 11, 1936, p. 134.

[52] Rorty, James, "Radio Comes Through," *The Nation*, October 15, 1938, p. 372.

[55] "Trials and Tribulations of the Radio Reporter, a New Type of Correspondent," *Newsweek*, October 17, 1938, p. 32.

56. Ernest D. Rose, HOW THE U.S. HEARD ABOUT PEARL HARBOR

[1] Based on recordings of broadcasts at the Hoover Institute of War, Revolution and Peace at Stanford University.

58. George A. Willey, THE SOAP OPERAS AND THE WAR

[1] Nearly half of these, a total of 25, were on NBC.

[2] Address to a luncheon meeting of "The Pulse of New York," October 21, 1942.

[3] Savell, Isabelle, *New York Herald Tribune*, June 6, 1943.

[4] Van Horne, Harriet, *New York World Telegram*, October 17, 1942.

[5] "The Guiding Light," "Today's Children" and "Woman in White." In January of 1946 Miss Phillips added a fourth serial, "Masquerade."

[6] NBC Press Release, November 20, 1944 (mimeographed).

[7] Initially played by actor Richard Widmark.

[8] ". . . at least thirteen weeks." NBC Press Release, October 6, 1942 (mimeographed.) Also see CBS Press Release, September 30, 1942 (mimeographed.)

[9] In 1944 Miss Phillips had used these two programs together with their companion piece, "The Guiding Light," as an innovation having no connection with the war effort. At that time she experimented briefly in moving characters from one story to another, binding the three consecutive daily broadcasts into a unit.

[10] Many more were dropped than added during the same period; there was an overall decline from a total of 54 daily serials in 1941 to 38 in mid-1945. Of the thirty-one added during the war only eight were still on the air in January of 1946 and within a year this number had further been reduced to four: "Evelyn Winters," "Lora Lawton," "Perry Mason" and "Rosemary." For additional detail preceding and following the war see: Willey, George, "End of an Era: The Daytime Radio Serial," *Journal of Broadcasting*, Vol. V, No. 2, Spring 1964, pp. 97–115.

[11] Procter and Gamble was sponsoring ten daily serials at this time. In addition to "Brave Tomorrow" they presented "A Woman of America," "The Goldbergs," "Life Can Be Beautiful," "Ma Perkins," "Pepper Young's Family," "Perry Mason," "Right to Happiness," "Road of Life," "Vic and Sade."

[12] Enacted by Rev. Alfred Dorf, pastor of Our Savior's Church, Brooklyn. Actors Everett Sloane and Alexander Scourby were in the cast.

60. Bernard Lucich, THE LUX RADIO THEATER

[1] F. Daugherty, "He Sells Soap! DeMille's Lux Radio Theater of the Air," *Christian Science Monitor Magazine*, March 25, 1944, p. 8.

[2] "Teen-Ager: Lux Radio Theater," *Time*, October 17, 1949, p. 75.

[3] "Guild: Stage Stars Must Learn Acting Over Again for Radio," *Newsweek*, June 29, 1935, p. 29.

[4] "Lux Video Theatre Cost $5.5 Million First Year," *Broadcasting-Telecasting*, October 24, 1955, p. 35.

62. David T. MacFarland, UP FROM MIDDLE AMERICA: THE DEVELOPMENT OF TOP 40

[1] Based on David T. MacFarland, "The Development of the Top 40 Radio Format," (Ph.D. dissertation, University of Wisconsin, 1972).

[2] Todd Storz owned KOWH, Omaha; WTIX, New Orleans; WHB, Kansas City; WDGY, Minneapolis; WQAM, Miami; KOMA, Oklahoma City; and KXOK, St. Louis. Gordon McLendon owned KLIF, Dallas; WRIT, Milwaukee; KILT, Houston; WYSL, Buffalo, and others. Gerald Bartell and his family owned WOKY, Milwaukee; KCBQ, San Diego; WAKE, Atlanta, and others. The Plough pharmaceutical firm owned WMPS, Memphis; WJJD, Chicago; WCOP, Boston; and WCAO, Baltimore.

[3] "Profiles: Socko!" The *New Yorker*, July 29, 1944, p. 27.

67. Ted Nielsen, A HISTORY OF NETWORK TELEVISION NEWS

[1] Robert E. Kintner, "Broadcasting and the News," *Harpers Magazine*, April, 1965, p. 49.

[2] Sig Mickelson, "Growth of Television News, 1946–1957," *Journalism Quarterly*, Summer 1957, p. 305.

[3] CBS News, *Television News Reporting*, (New York, 1958), 3.

[4] *New York Times*, November 6, 1943.

[5] "The News by Television," *Newsweek*, February 2, 1948, p. 51.

[6] *Newsweek*, September 4, 1950, p. 48.

[7] "More Elbowroom for TV Newscasts," *Business Week*, March 13, 1954, p. 28.

[8] Phillip N. Schuyler, "TV-Radio Networks Budget $50 Million to Cover News," *Editor and Publisher*, August 19, 1961, p. 10.

[9] "News on Television," *Editor and Publisher*, June 30, 1962, p. 44.

[10] Kintner, "Broadcasting and the News," p. 52.

[11] Robert Shaplen, "A Farewell to Personal History," *Saturday Review of Literature*, December 10, 1960, p. 46.

[12] "News on Television," p. 44.

[13] *NBC News Release*, June, 1964.

[14] Alan Pearce, "What News Costs at NBC," *Broadcast Management/Engineering*, (January 1972), p. 24.

[15] Bob Siller, Ted White and Hal Terkel, *Television and Radio News* (New York, 1960), p. 189.

[16] Mickelson, "Growth of Television News," p. 307.

[17] "Newspaper Careers Lead to Stardom," *Editor and Publisher*, February 1, 1964, p. 14.

[18] "White House Reporters Ex-Newspapermen," *Editor and Publisher*, February 1, 1964, p. 14.

[19] "TV Plans for More News," *Editor and Publisher*, July 20, 1963, p. 18.

[20] *New York Times*, November 16, 1947, p. 79.

[21] *New York Times*, December 30, 1947, p. 40.

[22] *Newsweek*, September 4, 1950, p. 48.

[23] "Television Newsfilm Development," *Broadcasting*, June 2, 1958, p. 48.

[24] Albert Kroeger, "Banner Year for TV News," *Television Magazine*, Jan. 1966, p. 24.

[25] Albert Kroeger, "Vietnam, Television's Cruelest Test," *Television Magazine*, May 1966, p. 24.

[26] Flora Rheta Schreiber, "TV, New Idiom in Public Affairs," *Hollywood Quarterly*, 1950–51, p. 145.

[27] *Newsweek*, March 7, 1949, p. 59.

[28] Mickelson, "Growth of Television News."

Part Seven/AUDIENCES

INTRODUCTION

[1] Milton Percival and R. A. Jelliffe (eds.), *Specimens of Exposition and Argument* (New York: The Macmillan Co., 1908), pp. 45–46.

[2] "Radio Restrictions Removed," *The American Boy*, Vol. 21, No. 2 (December 1919), p. 55.

[3] "The Portaphone—A Wireless Set for Dance Music or the Day's News," *Scientific American*, CXXII, No. 21 (May 22, 1920), p. 571.

[4] Edgar H. Felix, "Care and Operation of a Crystal Receiving Set," *Radio Broadcast* (June 1922), p. 124.

[5] Montgomery Ward & Co. catalogue No. 97 (Chicago: Fall & Winter 1922–23. Reprinted in its original form, HC Publishers Inc., 1969), p. 540 and p. 428.

[6] *The Book of Rural Life* (Chicago: The Bellows-Durham Company, 1925), Vol. VIII, pp. 4602–4622.

[7] Montgomery Ward catalog No. 97, p. 539.

[8] "Newspaper Radio programs Are Incomplete," *Radio Broadcast* (April 1925), p. 1053.

[9] Pierre Boucheron, "Advertising Radio to the American Public," *The Radio Industry* (Chicago and New York: A. W. Shaw, 1928), p. 289.

[10] "Interesting Things Interestingly Said," *Radio Broadcast* (March 1926), p. 559.

[11] Hiram Jome, *Economics of the Radio Industry* (Chicago and New York: A. W. Shaw Company, 1925), pp. 273–274.

[12] Jome, p. 275.

[13] "The March of Radio," *Radio Broadcast* (April 1925), p. 1071.

[14] Charles Orchard, Jr., "Is Radio Making America Musical?" *Radio Broadcast* (October, 1924), p. 454.

[15] John Wallace, "The Listeners' Point of View," *Radio Broadcast* (March 1927), p. 473.

[16] Julie Showell, "Radio—The Alarm Clock of a Nation," *Radio News* (March 1928), p. 996.

[17] Marshall D. Beuick, "The Limited Social Effect of Radio Broadcasting," *The American Journal of Sociology*, January 1927, p. 615.

[18] Beuick, p. 622.

[19] Charlotte Geer, column in *Theatre Magazine*, XLII (July 1925), p. 292.

[20] Jack Foster, "Radio Editors Select an All-American Team," *Broadcasting* (December 15, 1931).

[21] Paul Lazarsfeld, *Radio and Printed Page* (New York: Sloane and Duell, 1930), p. 260.

[22] *Broadcasting-Telecasting* (October 15, 1956), p. 178.

[23] A 1950 advertisement by the American Television Dealers and Manufacturers reported in Hal Humphrey, "A Capsule History of TV," *Holiday*, 1967.

[24] Thomas F. Dernberg, Richard N. Rosett, and Harold W. Watts, *Studies in Household Economic Behavior* (New Haven: Yale University Press, 1958), pp. 41–42.

[25] Lawrence D. Longley, "The FCC and the All Channel Receiver Bill," *Journal of Broadcasting*, Vol. XIII, No. 3 (Summer 1969), pp. 293–301.

[26] Indelible Talent of 25 Years, *Broadcasting-Telecasting*, October 15, 1956, p. 158 and "Top Twenties Through the Years," *Nielsen Newscast*, October 1966, p. 5.

72. Leslie J. Page, Jr., THE NATURE OF THE BROADCAST RECEIVER AND ITS MARKET IN THE UNITED STATES FROM 1922 to 1927

[1] H. J. Kentner, "Ride to Riches with Radio; Some Get Rich Quick Schemes That Are all Bull and a Yard Wide," *Radio Broadcast*, II (March 1923), p. 398.

[2] *New York Times*, July 27, 1922.

[3] *Ibid.*, January 28, 1923.

[4] *Ibid.*, April 19, 1922.

[5] Hiram L. Jome, *Economics of the Radio Industry*, New York: A. W. Shaw Co., 1925, pp. 74–75.

[6] Austin C. Lescarboura, *Radio for Everybody*, New York: Munn & Co., 1922, p. 131.

[7] *New York Times*, May 7, 1925.

[8] *Ibid.*, May 10, 1925.

[9] *Ibid.*, June 29, 1925.

[10] *Ibid.*, September 13, 1925. This issue devoted sixteen pages to the shows.

[11] *Ibid.*

[12] *Ibid.*, February 14, 1926.

[13] *Ibid.*

[14] Quoted in U.S. Federal Trade Commission, *Federal Trade Commission Decisions*, XI (November 5, 1926 to January 29, 1928), p. 537. This bears a striking resemblance to a statement regarding misleading or confusing advertising of television console finishes in *Consumer Reports*, Vol. 24, No. 12 (December, 1959), pp. 628–629.

[15] *New York Times*, March 14, 1926. "A new association of radio dealers has been formed in Chicago to promote and uphold ethical standards of the trade." (*New York Times*, March 21, 1926).

[16] A. Henry, "Merchandising Radio," *Radio Broadcast* I (May, 1922), pp. 82–86. Henry points out that parts can be bought in hardware stores and drugstores. In his *Economics of the Radio Industry*, H. L. Jome mentions that "Every little village and hamlet has its dealer in radio, be it electrical shop, furniture store, or restaurant" (p. 73).

[17] *New York Times*, May 16, 1926.

[18] *Ibid.*, January 9, 1927.

75. Frank N. Stanton, PSYCHOLOGICAL RESEARCH IN THE FIELD OF RADIO LISTENING

[2] The number of families owning radio sets in the United States, January 1, 1936, was 22,869,000. This figure is the official estimate issued July 2, 1936, by the Joint Committee on Radio Research, which includes equal representation of the Association of National Advertisers, the American Association of Advertising Agencies, and the National Association of Broadcasters.

3 Columbia Broadcasting System, *Radio in 1936* (New York: Columbia Broadcasting System, 1936). (Sec. 1 of this report published separately, p. 18.)
4 *Ibid.*, p. 8.
5 *Radio Today*, II (January, 1936), 5. The following analysis of radio expenditures for 1935 was compiled by *Radio Today:*

5,700,000 radio sets, with tubes	$356,000,000
39,000,000 tube replacements	31,000,000
Electricity and batteries to operate 25,500,000 home sets	154,000,000
Repairs and servicing of sets (minus replacement tube sales;	68,000,000
Broadcasting time sold	86,000,000
Broadcast talent costs	25,000,000
1935 total	$700,000,000

6 For a discussion of the various techniques for measuring the radio audience see Frederick H. Lumley, *Measurement in Radio* (Columbus, Ohio: Ohio State University, 1934), Pp. vii + 318. Cf. also John J. Karol, "Measuring Radio Audiences," *Printers Ink Weekly*, CLXXVII (November 19, 1936), 44, 48, 52, 56.
7 Frank N. Stanton, "Checking the Checkers," *Advertising and Selling*, XXVI (December 19, 1935), 24, 44. A complete description of the recorders used in this survey is included in the report by Mr. Stanton. *A Critique of Present Methods and a New Plan for Studying Radio Listening Behavior* (Columbus, Ohio: Ohio State University Library, 1935), Pp. 244.
8 Pauline Arnold, "Sizing Up the Audience," *Advertising and Selling* XXI (June 22, 1933), 21, 22, 43.
9 The Cooperative Analysis of Broadcasting was inaugurated by 1929 by Mr. Archibald M. Crossley. Later, the Association of National Advertisers took over sponsorship of the surveys, and at the present time the CAB reports are issued under the supervision of a governing committee at two-week intervals. These reports are private and for subscribers only. The percentage ratings are based on all sets owned and indicate the size of the audience for various programs. The data are assembled by telephone interviewers located in thirty-three cities who call at four periods each day and ask the respondent what programs or stations he has listened to in the period preceding the call. Calls are made at the following times: 12:15 p.m., covering the period up to 12:00 noon of the same day; at 5:15 p.m., covering the period from 12:00 noon to 5:00 p.m. of the same day; at 8:15 p.m., covering the period from 5:00 p.m. to 8:00 p.m. of the same day; and at 9:00 a.m., covering the period from 8:00 p.m. to 12:00 p.m. of the previous day. The number of cities surveyed are as follows: Eastern Cities: 14; Southern Cities: 7; Midwestern Cities: 7 and Pacific Coast Cities: 5.
10 These data are taken from *CAB Report*, VII, 18, and are for the period ending November 24, 1936.
11 As of January 1, 1936, there were 11,100,000 residence telephones and 22,869,000 homes with radios.
12 At the present time there are two such recorders being readied for program and station measurement work. One is a product of Professors Robert F. Elder and L. F. Woodruff, of the Massachusetts Institute of Technology. One hundred of these "audimeters" were used in an experimental study over a ten-week period in the metropolitan area of Boston, November 3, 1935–January 11, 1936. Details of this study are reported by Professor Elder in *Broadcasting*, IX, No. 9 (December 1, 1935), II, 59; X, No. 2 (January 15, 1936), 9, 54; X, No. 5 (March 1, 1936), 7, 58; and *American Marketing Journal*, III, No. 1 (January, 1936), 41–46. The A. C. Nielsen Company of Chicago, is carrying on further experimental work with these devices, preparatory to setting up a regular service employing them to gauge listening in a series of cities.

The second instrument for automatically recording radio operation was designed by John Potter, of New York City. Preliminary work has been conducted on his recorder by Clark-Hooper, Inc., New York City, who have been licensed by Mr. Potter to use instruments of his design for radio survey work.

Both instruments give essentially the same data. Both may be left in use for periods of several weeks without attention. With proper installation they will provide objective records of when the radio was turned on and off, as well as the frequencies to which the radio was tuned. However, the manner in which the data are taken differs in the two instruments. Each recorder depends upon a small, noiseless, continuously running synchronous motor to drive a tape under styli at a constant rate of speed. Beyond this point the designs follow different principles.

The Elder-Woodruff recorder uses a mechanical stylus, which contacts the tape when the set is in operation. As the tape moves, a longitudinal line develops. The stylus is connected mechanically by means of a flexible shaft to the station selector of the receiver. When the set is tuned, the stylus moves laterally across the tape, depending upon the frequency of the station tuned.

The Potter device, on the other hand, uses a battery of electrothermal styli which remain in fixed positions over the tape. The recording tape is chemically treated to react to heat from the styli. One of them is designed to register set operation. The others (as many as ten) react when the set is tuned to certain predetermined stations. Since few families listen to more than seven or eight stations regularly, this device can be set to record the most popular stations heard in the community under observation. Potter employs an adjustable contacting device on the tuning shaft from which a multi-wire electric cable carries current to the styli to heat them for recording purposes. Here, then, is the essential difference: Elder depends upon mechanical transmissions of station tuning efforts, while Potter uses a multiple electric circuit.

[13] Frank N. Stanton, *A Critique of Present Methods and a New Plan for Studying Radio Listening Behavior*, pp. 175–78.

[14] At the Informal Engineering Hearing of the Federal Communications Commission, October 16, 1936, the writer reported the results of a survey designed to discover what station was listened to most and why. The survey was conducted by mail questionnaires in ten cities. The results are as follows: 64.9 per cent selected their favorite station because of the programs it broadcasts; 17.7 per cent because it is "easy" to get on their sets; and 17.4 per cent because it has the best programs and comes in "easiest."

[15] Paul T. Rankin, "Listening Ability," *Proceedings of the Ohio State Educational Conference, 1929* (Ohio State University, 1929), pp. 172–83.

[16] Hadley Cantril and Gordon W. Allport, *The Psychology of Radio* (New York: Harper, 1935), pp. 159–80. (Chap. ix, "Listening versus Reading," was written by Dr. Merton E. Carver.)

[17] Below are the gross network billings by years for the Columbia Broadcasting System and the red and blue networks of the National Broadcasting Company. These data are from the Publisher's Information Bureau, Inc., New York City.

1928	$10,227,731	1932	39,106,776
1929	10,096,365	1933	31,516,298
1930	27,594,090	1934	42,659,461
1931	37,502,080	1935	48,768,735

[18] Lumley, *op. cit.*, p. 166.

[19] Columbia Broadcasting System, *The Case of the Curious Footprints* (New York: Columbia Broadcasting System, 1936).

[20] Henry N. DeWick, "The Relative Recall Effectiveness of Visual and Auditory Presentation of Advertising Material," *Journal of Applied Psychology*, XIX, No. 3 (June, 1935), 245–64.

[21] Frank N. Stanton, "Memory for Advertising Copy Presented Visually versus Orally," *Journal of Applied Psychology*, XVIII, No. 1 (February, 1934), 45–64.

[22] *Op. cit.*

[23] Merton E. Carver, *The Comparison of the Mental Effects of Visual and Auditory Presentation* (Cambridge, Mass.: Harvard College Library, 1934), p. 345.

[24] Frank R. Elliott, "Memory for Visual, Auditory and Visual-Auditory Material," *Archives of Psychology*, No. 199 (May, 1936), p. 59.

[25] *Op. cit.*, p. 000. [sic]

26 Walter H. Wilke, "An Experimental Comparison of the Speech, the Radio, and the Printed Page as Propaganda, Devices," *Archives of Psychology*, No. 169 (June, 1934).

77. Herta Herzog, WHY DID PEOPLE BELIEVE IN THE "INVASION FROM MARS"?

1 Immediately after the Orson Welles broadcast on October 30, 1938—Hallowe'en— of "War of the Worlds" by H. G. Wells, Dr. Frank Stanton, Research Director of CBS, commissioned a study of reactions to the broadcast. Dr. Herta Herzog was in charge of the interviews for the Princeton Radio Project. This memo was written to Dr. Stanton summarizing information from the interviews. For a more complete analysis see: Hadley Cantril, Hazel Gaudet, and Herta Herzog, *The Invasion from Mars: A Study in the Psychology of Panic* (Princeton University Press, 1940); or (Harper Torchbooks, 1966). Cantril's book includes the script of the broadcast and the interview schedule.

78. G. D. Wiebe, THE ARMY-MC CARTHY HEARINGS AND THE PUBLIC CONSCIENCE

1 Samuel A. Stouffer, *Communism, Conformity and Civil Liberties*, New York, Doubleday, 1955, p. 59.
2 Fellow researchers might be interested in a personal note. When the original two hypotheses (reaffirmation of civil rights as values and large scale conversion of pro-McCarthyites to an anti position) were found to have been rejected, the data were laid aside. Months later, the content analysis just reported was undertaken with no special hypothesis in mind—simply out of a continuing irritation at not having found an understandable pattern in the data. What follows was completely unanticipated and falls into the category of research surprises, sometimes referred to as "serendipity."
3 "Introjection" is the process by which a "right" or a "wrong," usually defined and enforced as such by a parent, is so thoroughly learned that it becomes part of the conscience (superego).
4 Hyman and Sheatsley found that only about 20 per cent of a national sample could even identify the Bill of Rights. (Herbert H. Hyman and Paul B. Sheatsley, "The Current Status of American Public Opinion," Daniel Katz, editor, *Public Opinion and Propaganda*, New York, Dryden, 1954, p. 41.)

79. Lawrence W. Lichty and Malachi C. Topping, A COLLEGE COMMUNITY VIEWS THE FOURTH "GREAT DEBATE"

1 Theodore H. White, *The Making of a President 1960* (New York: Atheneum Publishers, 1961), p. 290.
3 Interviews were conducted by the writers with the assistance of Claire P. Topping, Neil J. Eskelin, and Wayne P. Warga.
4 Lionel C. Barrow, Jr., "Factors Related to Attention to the First Kennedy-Nixon Debate," *Journal of Broadcasting*, Vol. V, No. 3 (Summer 1961), p. 230.
5 See Charles E. Osgood, George J. Suci, and Percy M. Tannenbaum, *The Measurement of Meaning* (Urbana: University of Illinois Press, 1957), pp. 35–39.

Part Eight/REGULATION

INTRODUCTION

1 See Lawrence W. Lichty, "The Nation's Station: A History of Radio Station WLW," Ph.D. Dissertation, The Ohio State University, 1964, pp. 90–92.
2 R. S. McBride, "How the Government Is Regulating Broadcasting," *Radio Broadcast* (May 1925), p. 34.
3 Hiram L. Jome, "Public Policy toward Radio Broadcasting," *Journal of Land and Public Utilities Economics* (1925), pp. 198–214.

[4] "Hoover Set up American System for Radio," *Broadcasting* (October 26, 1964), p. 80.
[5] "Fourteen Years without Change in Radio Legislation," *Radio Broadcast* (September 1926), p. 372.
[6] "What the Radio Commission Is Accomplishing," *Radio Broadcast*, July, 1927, p. 139.
[7] Federal Radio Commission, *Third Annual Report* (Washington: Government Printing Office, 1929), pp. 32–34.
[8] Edwin L. Davis, "Regulation of Advertising," *Annals of the American Academy of Political and Social Science*, (January 1935), pp. 154–158.
[9] "Dummy and Dame Arouse the Nation," *Broadcasting-Telecasting* (October 15, 1956), p. 258.
[10] Richard J. Meyer, "The Blue Book," *Journal of Broadcasting*, Vol. VI, No. 3 (Summer 1962), p. 200.
[11] *Ibid.*
[12] Frederick W. Ford, "The Fairness Doctrine," *Journal of Broadcasting*, Vol. VIII, No. 1 (Winter 1963–1964), pp. 3–16.
[13] Newton N. Minow, *Equal Time* (New York: Atheneum, 1964), pp. 46–64.
[14] Nicholas Johnson, "Towers of Babel: The Chaos in Radio Spectrum Utilization and Allocation," *Law and Contemporary Problems*, XXXIV:3 (Summer 1969), p. 533.

80. Edward F. Sarno, Jr., THE NATIONAL RADIO CONFERENCES

[5] *New York Times*, February 17, 1922, 19.
[6] First National Radio Conference. *Minutes of Department of Commerce Conference on Radio Telephony*, 1922, 4–5 (mimeographed).
[7] H. R. 13773 (67th Congress, 4th Session), introduced and referred to the Committee on the Merchant Marine and Fisheries (64th *Cong. Rec.* 1617).
[8] *New York Times*, April 1, 1923, II, 6.
[9] H. R. 7357 (68th Cong., 1st Sess.), introduced and referred to the Committee on the Merchant Marine and Fisheries (65th *Cong. Rec.* 3294).
[10] S. 2930 (68th Cong., 1st Sess.), introduced by Senator Howell (65th *Cong. Rec.* 4915; passes Senate, 5737).
[11] *Hoover v. Intercity Radio Co.* (1923), 286 Fed. 1003.
[12] Third National Radio Conference, *Recommendations for Regulation of Radio* (Washington: Government Printing Office, 1924), 2.
[13] *New York Times*, October 8, 1924, 21.
[14] Fourth National Radio Conference, *Proceedings of the Fourth National Radio Conference and Recommendations for Regulation of Radio* (Washington: Government Printing Office, 1926), 18.
[15] *Ibid.*, p. 5.
[16] *New York Times*, November 11, 1925, 25.
[17] *M. Witmark and Sons v. L. Bamberger and Co.* (1923), 291 Fed. 776.
[18] *Jerome H. Remick and Co. v. American Automobile Accessories Co.* (1924), 298 Fed. 628.
[19] *Jerome H. Remick and Co. v. American Automobile Accessories Co.* (1925), 5 Fed. 2d 411.
[20] *American Automobile Accessories Co. v. Jerome H. Remick and Co.* (1925), 46 S.Ct. 19.
[21] H. R. 5589 (69th Cong., 1st Sess.), introduced and referred to the Committee on the Merchant Marine and Fisheries (67th *Cong. Rec.* 901; debated, 5474, 5485, 5585).

81. Marvin R. Bensman, REGULATION OF BROADCASTING BY THE DEPARTMENT OF COMMERCE, 1921–1927

[1] Joel Rosenbloom, "Authority of the Federal Communications Commission with Respect to the Programming of Radio and Television Broadcasting Stations" (FCC Mimeographed Document, No. 8674, September 27, 1957); reprinted in: John E. Coons

(ed.), *Freedom and Responsibility in Broadcasting* (Evanston: Northwestern University Press, 1961).

[2] Letter from Mr. Tyrer to Mr. Edwards, National Archives Record Group 173, December 16, 1921. Hereafter *NA* shall designate National Archives, Washington, D.C., and this shall be followed by Record Group number and date.

[3] "Ninth Annual Report of the Secretary of Commerce," U.S. Government Printing Office, 1921, p. 140.

[4] Memorandum from Mr. Carson to Assistant Secretary Huston, NA RG 173, January 27, 1922.

[5] Letter from Mr. Huston to Radio Inspectors, NA RG 40, January 11, 1922.

[6] Memorandum from Mr. Carson to Mr. Hoover, NA RG 40, February 20, 1922.

[7] Letter from Mr. Hoover to Mr. Versfelt, NA RG 40, November 22, 1921.

[8] *New York Times*, November 19, 1921, 10:1.

[9] Letter from Mr. Scofield to Mr. Beck, NA RG 60, August 25, 1924.

[10] Letters to Conference participants, Herbert Hoover Presidential Library 1-I/539, February 21, 1922. Hereafter the Hoover Presidential Library, West Branch, Iowa shall be designated as HHPL followed by file number and date.

[11] Letter from Mr. Dillon to Mr. Hoover, HHPL 1-I/539, March 27, 1922.

[12] Letter from Mr. Carson to Mr. Dillon, NA RG 173, October 26, 1922.

[13] Memorandum from Mr. Hoover to Mr. Carson, NA RG 40, August 5, 1922.

[14] *Hearings before the Committee on Interstate Commerce*, U.S. Senate, 71st Congress, 1st Session, May 24, 1929, p. 1071.

[15] Letter from Mr. Carson to Mr. Dillon, NA RG 173, October 26, 1922.

[16] Telegram from Mr. Hoover to Mr. Terrell, HHPL 1-I/538, February 21, 1923.

[17] Letter from Mr. Davis to Mr. Terrell, NA RG 40, April 9, 1923.

[18] *New York Times*, December 6, 1924, p. 4.

[19] Letter from Mr. Edwards to Mr. Horn, NA RG 173, February 11, 1925.

[20] "Radio Problems and Conference Recommendations—Address Broadcast from Washington, D.C.," HHPL, B-522A, November 12, 1925.

[21] *Ibid.*

[22] Letter from Mr. Davis to Mr. Marks, July 22, 1925, NA RG 173.

[23] Letter from Mr. Donovan to Mr. Olsen, January 14, 1926, NA RG 60.

[24] Press release of the Department of Commerce, February 11, 1926, NA RG 173.

[25] *U.S. v. Zenith Radio Corporation*, Docket No. 14257, April 14, 1926, NA RG 173.

[26] U.S. Attorney General. *Federal Regulations of Radio Broadcasting*, Opinions of the Attorney General, Vol. 35, 1926.

[27] Letter from Mr. Tyrer to Mr. Johnston, December 18, 1926, NA RG 40.

[28] Letter from Mr. Hoover to Mr. Sanders, February 1, 1926, NA RG 173.

[29] Letter from Mr. Hoover to Mr. Sanders, March 29, 1926, HHPL, 1-I/539.

85. Maurice E. Shelby, Jr., JOHN R. BRINKLEY: HIS CONTRIBUTION TO BROADCASTING

[1] Clement C. Wood, *The Life of A Man* (Ooshorn Publishing Company: Kansas City, Missouri), 1934.

[2] *Ibid.*, p. 135.

[3] The American Medical Association maintains an extensive file on John R. Brinkley. This quotation comes from a letter sent by the Brinkley-Jones Hospital Association signed by Ray P. Martin, Secretary. Undated, it was received by the AMA on August 17, 1923. Brinkley actually owned at different times two radio stations with the call letters, KFKB. The first station operated intermittently from September 20, 1923 to June 3, 1925 before it was sold. A station was re-licensed to Brinkley with the same call letters on October 23, 1926.

[4] *KFKB Broadcasting Assn. v. Federal Radio Commission*, 47F. (2d), 670, App. D.C., 1931.

[5] *Ibid.*

[6] *Ibid.*

[7] *Ibid.*

[8] *Transcript of Record, Court of Appeals of the District of Columbia, KFKB v. FRC, No. 5240*, April Term, 1930, pp. 255–256.

[9] Gerald Carson, *The Roguish World of Doctor Brinkley* (Rinehart & Company: New York), 1960, pp. 98–99.

[10] Carson, *op. cit.*, pp. 101–102. A number of these "advices" was introduced into the record during Brinkley's hearings before the FRC. A stenographer, Grace Dedrick, testified that she accurately transcribed some of Brinkley's answers to the letter on the *Medical Question Box* program. (FRC Docket No. 835, *op. cit.*).

[11] *Kansas City Star*, June 15, 1930.

[12] Anita Grimm Taylor, *Persuasive Techniques in Selected Speeches and Writings of John R. Brinkley*, Master's Thesis, Kansas State University, 1959, 50–58.

[13] Broadcast of Dr. J. R. Brinkley over Radio Stations KFBI and KFEQ, 6:15–6:45 a.m., November 26, 1934.

Few people who have heard John R. Brinkley on the radio disagree that he was an effective radio personality. His biographer, Clement Wood, called him "magnificent," "a student of human nature, a psychologist, a master showman." (Wood, *op. cit.*, p. 218). The American Consulate at Piedras Negras said that Brinkley was "an arresting and highly magnetic radio personality, which radiates confidence, faith and sincerity" (Letter to the Secretary of State, November 20, 1933). *Real America* recorded his delivery as being that of a "sincere minister" (July, 1933, p. 45). *Collier's* said: ". . . You heard him sigh between sentences, as though the woes, the heartaches and the mass anguish of the world are just too much for him." (January 16, 1932, p. 13). For a full discussion of Brinkley as a radio personality, see Ansel H. Resler, *The Impact of John R. Brinkley on Broadcasting in the United States*, Ph.D. dissertation, Northwestern University, 1958, p. 149.

[14] *Ibid.*

[15] *Ibid.*

[16] Carson, *op. cit.*, p. 10.

[17] *Kansas City Star*, May 10, 1930.

[18] *Kansas City Star*, May 18, 1930.

[19] See Federal Radio Commission, *In re Application of the KFKB Broadcasting Assn. (Station KFKB) for Renewal of License*, Docket No. 835, June 13, 1930.

[20] Carson, *op. cit.*, p. 162.

[21] Francis Chase, Jr., *Sound and Fury* (New York: Harper & Bros., 1942), p. 76.

[22] Carson, *op. cit.*, p. 159.

[23] *Ibid.*, p. 157.

[24] *Ibid.*, p. 159.

[25] *27th Biennial Report of the Secretary of State* (Kansas), 1929–30.

[26] Carson, *op. cit.*, p. 116.

[27] Don B. Slechta, *Dr. John R. Brinkley: A Kansas Phenomenon*, Master's Thesis, Fort Hays State College, 1952, p. 214.

[28] See also the *Davenport* (Iowa) *Times*, January 23, 1931.

[29] *Kansas City Times*, June 15, 1935.

[30] Carson, *op. cit.*, p. 170.

[31] *28th Biennial Report of the Secretary of State* (Kansas), 1931–32.

[32] These files, located in the Department of State, contain correspondence and materials exchanged between the U.S. Embassy in Mexico City and headquarters in Washington, D.C. In one letter, dated June 1, 1931, signed by W. R. Castle, Acting Secretary of State, instructions were given to J. Reuben Clark, Ambassador to Mexico, that "some measures should be taken to bring circumstances (of Brinkley's medical and broadcasting problems in the United States) to the attention of appropriate Mexican authorities."

[33] Carson, *op. cit.*, p. 179.

[34] Although XER was originally licensed by the Mexican Government for 75,000 watts (*Official Diary* of Mexico, August 29, 1931), Brinkley is said to have increased his power to 500,000 watts. He did apply to the Mexican Government in January 1932 for

permission to increase the power of XER to 150,000 watts, and authorization for another power increase to 500,000 watts.

35 In a letter to Vice President Curtis, dated October 9, 1931, one of Brinkley's representatives, John E. Singleton, Jr., states that "On March 12, 1931, the Immigration Department of the Mexican Government issued and directed to all Ports of Entry in Mexico its Order Number 47. This order stated that information had been furnished by the American Medical Association and the United States Federal Radio Commission that Dr. Brinkley's license had been revoked in the United States for practicing 'immoral' operations and that he was not to be permitted to enter Mexico under any conditions. Order Number 47 was cancelled on May 20th, 1931, but was reissued two weeks ago."

36 Resler, *op. cit.*, p. 149.

37 *Ibid.*, pp. 154–155.

38 *Ibid.*

86. Thomas W. Hoffer, TNT BAKER: RADIO QUACK

1 "Direct Advertising over the Air from Corsets to Calliopes," *Radio Broadcast*, June 1927, p. 81. The material for this paper is drawn from Hoffer, Thomas W., "Norman Baker and American Broadcasting," M.A. thesis, University of Wisconsin, Madison, 1969.

2 The name "Tangley" was derived from Baker's "mind-reading" vaudeville act which toured the midwest from about 1905–1910. Baker's assistant was "Madame Tangley" who, while blindfolded, demonstrated "psychic powers." "Madame Tangley" later became Mrs. Norman Baker; her real name was Theresa Pender. They were divorced in 1915. Baker's KTNT operations are summarized in Wolfe, G. Joseph, "Norman Baker and KTNT," *Journal of Broadcasting*, XIII (Fall 1968), 389–99.

3 Letter of Mrs. A. L. Branson, Muscatine, Iowa to Herbert Hoover, December 15, 1926. KTNT files, Record Group 173, the National Archives, Washington, D.C. (hereafter referred to as National Archives.)

4 Letter of Mrs. I. H. Schermer to Herbert Hoover, February 28, 1927. National Archives.

5 Letter of H. A. Bellows to Senator Smith Brookhart, undated. Hearings transcript, KTNT, Docket 83A, pp. 112–113. National Archives.

6 Letter of Norman Baker to Herbert Hoover, October 8, 1928. Hoover Presidential Archives, West Branch, Iowa.

7 Telegram of Scott Home Bowen, Inc. to Norman Baker dated October 25, 1928. Hoover Library.

8 Letter of Norman Baker to Herbert Hoover, October 25, 1928. Hoover Library.

9 Letter of Dr. Harold M. Camp to Dr. Morris Fishbein, the American Medical Association, Chicago, Illinois, December 28, 1929. Files of the AMA Bureau of Investigation, Chicago, Illinois.

10 Transcript of a radio talk by Norman Baker, KTNT, May 6, 1930. Docket 967, National Archives.

11 "Medical League Praises Cancer Cure," *TNT*, Vol. II, No. 4 (July 1930).

12 Transcript of a radio talk by Norman Baker, May 10, 1930. Docket 967, National Archives.

13 Harry M. Hoxsey v. Norman G. Baker (Petition at Law) filed in the District Court of Iowa in and for Muscatine County, October 24, 1930. Baker Papers. (Mr. Baker's remaining legal and personal papers were formerly held by his attorney, the late Charles P. Hanley, Muscatine, Iowa. These papers are currently in the custody of the author.)

14 "Norman Baker's Page," *TNT*, Vol. III, No. 2 (May 1931), 5.

15 Letter of William R. Castle to J. Reuben Clark, Jr., dated October 14, 1932. U.S. Department of State, Serial 812.76/151.

16 Alvin Winston (Clement Wood), *Doctors, Dynamiters and Gunmen* (Muscatine, Iowa: TNT Press, 1936), p. 437. Alvin Winston was a pseudonym. Clement Wood actually wrote Baker's biography distributed for $1 each as part of Baker's propaganda out-

put. Wood wrote Dr. Brinkley's biography, *John R. Brinkley, The Life of a Man*. Baker's letters to President Roosevelt were in the Roosevelt Presidential Library, Hyde Park, New York.

[17] News Release, October 1933. Baker Papers.

[18] *Thelma Yount (Universal Advertising Agency) v. Commissioner of Internal Revenue*, Hearings Transcript, pp. 353–355. 38 U.S. Board of Tax Appeals Reports 1457. Docket 87,404 and 89,595, retained by the Clerk, Tax Court of the United States, Washington, D.C.

[19] Letter of Ambassador Josephus Daniels to the Secretary of State, March 29, 1936. U.S. Department of State, Serial 812.76/207.

[20] Baker v. United States, 93 F.2d 332, 18 F. Suppl. 48; *Cert. denied,* 303 U.S. 642.

[21] Letter of Michael Eckstein, Attorney at Law, to Richard E. Gutstadt, Director, Anti-Defamation League, December 28, 1938, AMABI files.

87. Robert H. Stern, REGULATORY INFLUENCES UPON TELEVISION'S DEVELOPMENT: EARLY YEARS UNDER THE FEDERAL RADIO COMMISSION

[13] H. M. Smith, "The Regulation of Television," *Journal of Radio Law* (October, 1931), pp. 449–507, at 506–7.

[14] G. C. Gross in *U.S. Daily,* November 20, 1930.

[15] In one case of interest, involving an application of a subsidiary of the Columbia Broadcasting System, the Atlantic Broadcasting Corporation, for a station license in New York City, the commission reversed the report of its examiner, who had recommended that the applicant be given six months within which to make a showing of substantial research work in television and that only after such a showing should a license be issued, and granted the license apparently upon the basis of an assertion of valid intent.

[18] R. Hubbell, *4000 Years of Television* (New York, 1942), p. 94.

[26] Even in the amount of space devoted to television in the annual reports of the Federal Radio Commission one finds indication of a slackening of interest. The 1931 report carried something over a page on the subject; the 1932 report about three-quarters of a page; the 1935 report about one-third of a page.

[27] FRC, *Sixth Annual Report,* pp. 42–3.

[28] "Television: A $13,000,000 If," *Fortune* (April 1939), p. 54.

[29] Maclaurin, *op. cit.,* pp. 263–4.

[30] FRC, *Seventh Annual Report, 1933,* p. 31. The life of the Federal Radio Commission terminated with the passage of the Communications Act of 1934 which created in its place the Federal Communications Commission.

89. Richard J. Meyer, REACTION TO THE "BLUE BOOK"

[1] Robert K. Richards, "FCC Hits Programs," *Broadcasting*, XXX (March 11, 1946), 15 ff.

[2] *Broadcasting*, XXX (March 11, 1946), 15 f.

[3] *Broadcasting*, XXX (March 18, 1946), 15 ff.

[4] "Editorial," *Broadcasting*, XXX (March 18, 1946), 58.

[5] "Editorial," *Variety*, March 13, 1946, p. 35.

[6] Jean Eldridge, "Chicago Ad Men Decry FCC Report," *Broadcasting*, XXX (April 1, 1946), 77.

[7] "Avery Attacks FCC Program Report," *Broadcasting*, XXX (April 1, 1946), 18.

[8] Robert K. Richards, "NAB Districts Denounce FCC Blue Book," *Broadcasting*, XXX (April 1, 1946), 18.

[9] "Editorial," *Broadcasting*, XXX (March 25, 1946), 58.

[10] "Editorial," *Broadcasting*, XXX (April 1, 1946), 50.

[11] "Editorial," *Variety*, April 10, 1946, p. 35.

[12] Joseph K. Howard, "Review of Radio's Second Chance," *Public Opinion Quarterly,* X (Winter, 1946–1947), 593–596.

[13] Charles A. Siepmann, *Radio's Second Chance* (Boston: Little, Brown and Company, 1946), p. vii.

[14] *Ibid.*, p. vi.

[15] "Trade Brows Raised by Siepmann's Role in FCC Credo," *Variety*, April 3, 1946, p. 29.

[16] Robert K. Richards, "Radio's Second Chance," *Broadcasting*, XXX (April 8, 1946), p. 20 f.

[17] Siepmann actually had assembled one-third of the material for the book, having access to the FCC files, while he was in Washington. He did write the book at his farm in Newfane, Vermont, during the last half of 1945. Siepmann, personal interview, December 21, 1960.

[18] Robert K. Richards, "Radio's Second Chance," *op. cit.*

[19] "Editorial," *Broadcasting*, XXX (April 8, 1946), 46.

[20] "Cure-All," *Time*, XLVII (April 22, 1946), 62.

[21] Elmer E. Smead, *Freedom of Speech by Radio and Television* (Washington: Public Affairs Press, 1959), p. 105.

[22] "Miller Calls for United Radio Front," *Broadcasting*, XXX (April 15, 1946), 18 f.

[23] "Blue Book Controversy is IER Theme," *Broadcasting*, XXX (May 13, 1946), 25 ff.

[24] Smead, *op. cit.*, p. 94.

[25] "Durr Would Welcome Court Test of FCC Program Control," *Broadcasting*, XXX (May 13, 1946), 34 f.

[26] "Miller vs. Siepmann," *Broadcasting*, XXX (April 29, 1946), 106.

[27] "Blue Book Hits again at ACLU Forum," *Broadcasting*, XXX (June 3, 1946), 66.

[28] "Miller Calls FCC Advertising Threat," *Broadcasting*, XXX (July 1, 1946), 20 f.

[29] "Editorial," *Broadcasting*, XXX (April 15, 1946), 58.

[30] "Editorial," *Broadcasting*, XXX (April 22, 1946), 54.

[31] "Editorial," *Broadcasting*, XXX (April 29, 1946), 56.

[32] "Editorial," *Broadcasting*, XXX (May 6, 1946), 48.

[33] "Editorial," *Variety*, April 17, 1946, p. 33.

[34] "Editorial," *Broadcasting*, XXX (May 13, 1946), 58.

[35] "Editorial," *Broadcasting*, XXX (May 20, 1946), 50.

[36] "Editorial," *Broadcasting*, XXX (May 27, 1946), 56.

[37] "Editorial," *Broadcasting*, XXX (June 3, 1946), 50.

[38] "Editorial," *Variety*, May 15, 1946, p. 27.

[39] "Editorial," *Broadcasting*, XXX (June 10, 1946), 54.

[40] "Editorial," *Broadcasting*, XXX (June 17, 1946), 54.

[41] Siepmann, *Radio's Second Chance, op. cit.*, p. 237.

[42] Siepmann, "Storm in the Radio World," *The American Mercury*, LXIII (August 1946), 201–207.

[43] "Blue Book is Code, Not Regulation," *Broadcasting*, XXXII (Jan. 13, 1947), 20 f.

[44] Siepmann, "Radio," *The Communication of Ideas*, edited by Lyman Bryson (New York: Institute for Religious and Social Studies, 1948), Part XI, p. 181.

[45] "FCC Rides Again," an editorial reprinted from *Collier's* quoted in *Broadcasting*, XXX (April 22, 1946), 45.

[46] "Life Can be Beautiful," *Broadcasting*, XXX (May 20, 1946), 15.

[47] Siepmann, "Storm in the Radio World," *op. cit.*

[48] "Blue Book is Grist for Editorial Mills," *Broadcasting*, XXX (May 6, 1946), 67 f.

[49] *Broadcasting*, XXX (June 10, 1946), 69; *Variety*, March 13, 1946, p. 44; May 8, 1946, p. 39; June 5, 1946, p. 53.

[50] "Republican Chief Urges Free Radio," *Broadcasting*, XXX (April 8, 1946), 15 f.

[51] "Love Thy Freedom, Hate FCC," *Variety*, May 22, 1946, p. 32.

[52] "Biemiller Praises Aims of Blue Book," *Broadcasting*, XXX (May 27, 1946), 95.

[53] "Bridges Says Siepmann Was Paid $839," *Broadcasting*, XXX (May 20, 1946), 20 f.

[54] Siepmann, "Radio," *op. cit.*, pp. 191–194.

[55] Llewellyn White, *The American Radio*, A Report on the Broadcasting Industry in the U.S. from the Commission on Freedom of the Press (Chicago: The University of Chicago Press, 1947), pp. 193–198.

[56] Smead, *op. cit.*, p. 95.

[57] Station WBAL (Baltimore) had been cited in the "Blue Book" as an example of a station in default of its promises to the FCC. An FCC decision was considered difficult, since the station's license had been renewed in 1942—after the start of the FCC's period of analysis. In addition, the WBAL frequency was claimed at the renewal time by columnists Drew Pearson and Robert S. Allen, who quoted the "Blue Book" as evidence of WBAL's inability to serve the public interest. Siepmann, in an article ["Radio's Operation Crossroads," *Nation*, CLXIII (Dec. 7, 1946), 644–645] pleaded with his readers to take an avid interest in this test case, to offer testimony, that here was a rare opportunity to test democracy's workings. He said that the greatest weakness in our system of broadcasting was the indifference of the public to the possibilities of radio service. WBAL's owners (the Hearst Corp.) was turned down by the FCC on a petition to postpone the hearing and "correct" the "Blue Book." ["WBAL Plea Denied," *Broadcasting*, XXXII (Feb. 10, 1947), 86]. Although for a time it appeared as if the FCC had decided to apply "Blue Book" principles, WBAL's license was renewed and it is still licensed to the Hearst Corp.

[58] Charles A. Siepmann and Sidney Reisberg, "To Secure These Rights: Coverage of a Radio Documentary," *Public Opinion Quarterly*, XII (Winter 1948–1949), 649–658.

[59] "Industry Self-Regulation is Proposed," *Broadcasting*, XXX (May 6, 1946), 77.

[60] Elmer E. Smead, *op. cit.*, p. 97.

[61] Siepmann, "New Wine in Old Bottles," *Nation*, CLXV (September 27, 1947), 312–313.

[62] Charles A. Siepmann, "Radio: Tool of the Reactionaries," *Nation*, CLXV (July 5, 1947), 15–16.

[63] Charles A. Siepmann, "Shall Radio Take Sides," *Nation*, CLXVI (Feb. 21, 1948), 210–211.

[64] Saul Carson, "The Embattled Listener," *New Republic*, CXX (Jan. 17, 1949), 27–28.

[65] Sidney W. Head, *Broadcasting in America* (Boston: Houghton Mifflin Company, 1956), p. 335, n. 6.

[66] Elmer E. Smead, *op. cit.*, p. 113.

[67] Siepmann, *Radio, Television and Society* (New York: Oxford University Press, 1950), p. 37.

[68] *Ibid.*, p. 336.

[69] Siepmann, "Moral Aspects of Television," *Public Opinion Quarterly*, XXIV (Spring, 1960), 12–18.

91. Lawrence W. Lichty, MEMBERS OF THE FEDERAL RADIO COMMISSION AND FEDERAL COMMUNICATIONS COMMISSION 1927—1961

[1] Complete lists of all former and present commissioners, their state of residence, political affiliation, and term of office are found in most industry reference books. *Annual Reports* of the Commission normally contain this information. The biographical information for commissioners was obtained from standard published biographies, newspapers, trade magazines, and from FCC publications and news releases. Additional information was obtained from correspondence and interviews with twelve former or present members of the Commission.

[2] E. Pendleton Herring, *Public Administration and the Public Interest* (New York: McGraw-Hill, 1936), quoted in Robert E. Cushman, *The Independent Regulatory Commission* (New York: Oxford University Press, 1941), p. 682.

92. Lawrence W. Lichty, THE IMPACT OF FRC AND FCC COMMISSIONERS' BACKGROUNDS ON THE REGULATION OF BROADCASTING

[2] *Second Annual Report of the Federal Radio Commission* (Washington: Government Printing Office, 1928), p. 4. See also: John M. Kittross, "Television Frequency Allocation Policy in the United States" (Ph.D. dissertation, University of Illinois, 1960).

[3] For a history of the regulation of broadcasting, see several of the following:

Lawrence F. Schmeckebier, *The Federal Radio Commission* (Washington: Brookings Institute, 1932).

Elmer E. Smead, *Freedom of Speech by Radio and Television* (Washington: Public Affairs Press, 1959).

Llewellyn White, *The American Radio* (Chicago: The University of Chicago Press, 1947).

Robert S. McMahon, *Regulation of Broadcasting: Half Century of Government Regulation of Broadcasting and the Need for Further Legislative Action* (Washington: Government Printing Office, 1958).

Paul Clifton Fowler, "The Formulation of Public Policy for Commercial Broadcasting by the Federal Communications Commission" (Ph.D. dissertation, Indiana University, 1957).

Murray Edelman, *The Licensing of Radio Services in the United States, 1927 to 1947* (Urbana: The University of Illinois Press, 1950).

Henry Hottmann, "Some Problems of Regulation of Radio Broadcasting" (Ph.D. dissertation, University of Colorado, 1947).

Walter B. Emery, *Broadcasting and Government: Responsibilities and Regulations* (East Lansing: Michigan State University Press, 1961).

[4] *First Annual Report of the Federal Radio Commission* (Washington: Government Printing Office, 1927), p. 1.

[5] Letter from O. H. Caldwell, February 21, 1961.

[6] Robert Sears McMahon, "Federal Regulation of the Radio and Television Broadcast Industry in the United States 1927–1959 with Special Reference to the Establishment and Operation of Workable Administrative Standards" (Ph.D. dissertation, The Ohio State University, 1959), p. 51.

[7] *Newsweek*, September 11, 1961.

[8] Letter from Clifford J. Durr, February 27, 1961.

[9] *Broadcasting*, April 10, 1961.

[10] *Ibid.*

[11] *Ibid.*, March 27, 1961.

[12] Sydney W. Head, *Broadcasting in America* (Cambridge: Houghton Mifflin Co., 1956), p. 134.

[13] Interview with Mr. George C. McConnaughey, February 28, 1961.

[14] Interview with Mr. Clifford J. Durr, April 26, 1961.

93. Don R. LeDuc, THE FCC: A THEORY OF REGULATORY REFLEX ACTION

[1] For an example of this early enthusiasm, see "Radio Finds Its Eyes," *Saturday Evening Post*, July 27, 1929, p. 12. The *New York Times Index*, 1931, lists 100 entries under the subject heading "Television." For a more general treatment of popular interest, see R. Stern, "Regulatory Influences Upon Television Development," 22 *American Journal of Economics and Sociology* 347–62 (1963).

[2] FRC General Order 55, December 22, 1928; 3 FRC Ann. Rep. 55–56 (1929); FCC Docket No. 5866, February 29, 1940, 5 Fed. Reg. 933 (withdrawn May 22, 1940). For a more detailed analysis, including 1936 and 1939 experimental rules, see H. Warner, *Radio and Television Law* 620–67 (1953). Also, Hearings on S. Res. 251 Before the Senate Committee on Interstate Commerce, 76th Cong., 2d Sess. (1940).

[3] 13 Fed. Reg. 5182 (1948); In the Matter of Amendment of Section 3, 606 of the Commission's Rules and Regulations, Sixth Report and Order, 1 R. R. 91:601 (1952). An interesting sidelight on television ownership during the freeze: 87 of the 108 stations authorized and on the air during the period were owned by licensees of AM radio stations.

[4] R. Stern, "Television in the Thirties; Development, Control and Government Concern," *American Journal of Economics and Sociology* 285–302 (1964).

[5] For an example of this early enthusiasm, see "Revolution in Radio," *Fortune*, Octo-

ber, 1939, pp. 86–87; W. Maclaurin, *Invention and Innovation in the Radio Industry* (1949).

[6] W. Maclaurin, supra note 5, at 229–30. See also Hearings on "Certain Charges Involving Development of FM Radio and RCA Patent Policies" Before the Senate Committee on Interstate and Foreign Commerce, 80th Cong., 2d Sess. (1948).

[7] FCC Docket No. 6651; for statistical information on the rise and fall of FM, see 24 FCC Ann. Rep. 131 (1958).

[8] For examples of this early enthusiasm, see "Strong Reception Throughout the U.S.: The Market for CATV Is Growing," *Barron's*, Sept. 12, 1962, p. 51; T. Murray, "The Golden Antenna of CATV," *Dunn's Review*, May 1965, p. 44; "CATV, The Communication Revolution," *Television Digest*, July 26, 1965, p. 2.

[9] 2 FCC 2d 725 (1966). No importation of distant signals into top 100 markets unless hearing proves lack of economic impact or is waived by Commission.

[10] 15 FCC 2d 417 (1968). No importation without retransmission agreement beyond maximum determined by market size. With January 17, 1969 clarification in Docket 18397, program by program agreement required from owner of rights.

[11] "The Effective Limits of the Administrative Process," 67 *Harv. L. Rev.* 1105–58 (1954), discusses each of these agencies in some detail.

[12] For a general discussion of regulatory reaction to change see R. Lorch, *Democratic Process and Administrative Law* (1969). For past reaction of state insurance department to new contracts and insurers see E. Paterson, *The Insurance Commissioner in the United States* (1927).

[13] K. Davis, *Administrative Law and Government* 11 (1951).

[14] H. Simon, *Administrative Behavior* XXIII (1957). Simon argues that meaningful analysis can only be predicated upon the theory that an administrator is neither purely emotional nor purely rational. He intends to be rational and task-oriented. But because of his limited knowledge of all options and all possible ramifications of his actions, he is less than completely rational, but more than completely emotional; a "psychological theory with room for rational behavior."

[15] A. Downs, *Inside Bureaucracy* 237 (1967).

[16] As an example of such variation, Title 47 specifies the standard as "public interest" in §§201(b), 215(a), 221(a), 222(c)(1), 221(e)(1), 415(a)(4), 319(c), 315; "public convenience and necessity" §314(f); "interest of public convenience and necessity," §214(d); "public convenience, interest and necessity," §§303, 307(a); "public interest, convenience and necessity," §§307(d), 309(a), 316(a), 319(a); "public interest, convenience or necessity," §§307(d), 311(b), 311(c)(3). From the above, it seems obvious that no ritual phrase was standardized to impart a particular legal meaning.

[17] D. Truman, *The Government Process* 443 (1951).

[18] P. Herring, *Public Administration and the Public Interest* 337 (1936).

[19] L. Jaffe, 337 (1936), supra note 11, at 1107.

[20] H. Simon, supra note 14, at 97.

[21] R. Cushman, *The Independent Regulatory Commission*, 730–31 (1941).

[22] L. Jaffe, supra note 11 at 1112.

[23] Id. at 1135.

[24] H. Simon, supra note 14, at 543.

[25] A. Downs, supra note 15, at 204.

[26] Id. at 206.

[27] See C. Jacob, *Policy and Bureaucracy* 36 (1966).

[28] W. Boyers, *Bureaucracy on Trial* 51 (1964).

[29] S. Hnyeman, *Bureaucracy in a Democracy* XII (1950).

[30] 66 Stat. 712–713.

[31] A. Downs, supra note 15, at 99. See generally, H. Simon, supra note 14, for the same view.

[32] Id. at 203.

[33] Id. at 26.

[34] R. Stern, supra note 1 at 361.

[35] Id. at 349.

[36] H. Simon, supra note 14 at 388.

[37] Dionysius, *Ars. Rhetorica*, XI, 2.

[38] "Up for Action, Tough Cable Rules. What Staff Wants FCC to Do," *Broadcasting*, February 7, 1966, p. 27; "Forbid Big City CATV, FCC Staff Urges," *Television Digest*, February 7, 1966, p. 1.

[39] *Broadcasting*, March 14, 1966, p. 48.

[40] Subscriber growth rose at a rate of more than 20% per year during the past decade; up 33.2% from 1965 to 1966 from 1,575,000 to 2,100,000 homes.

[41] 153 cities comprise the top 100 market ARB listings incorporated in the "Notice of Inquiry and Notice of Proposed Rulemaking" in Docket 18397 (December 13, 1968). Waiver statistics for top 100 markets are projected from the FCC 1968 Annual Report, p. 135. Dockets referred to include pay TV carriage, 11279; cross-ownership, 17371; telephone connections, 18509; distant signal, 17438; business radio, 17824; and notice requirements, 18416; among others.

BIBLIOGRAPHY

This is a brief bibliography of sources for more information on the history of broadcasting. Its organization parallels that of the book. Its primary purpose is for those doing further research—a starting point only. Only books that are histories, or that describe broadcasting at a particular time in its history, are listed. When reprints or revised editions are available we have tried to note them. Except for early technology, only American broadcasting is covered. Many more references are given in the notes immediately preceding this section. There is little annotation, assuming that those who use this bibliography have read the text. What follows, then, should lead the researcher to other resources.

Some items have cross references or are listed in chronological order for convenience. For some government documents a shortened title is given to save space. Of all House, Senate and FCC reports, only a very small number can be listed; including the most important and those with the best summary information. City of publisher is given only for foreign sources.

A number of radio and TV stations have published histories which are picture stories with little or no analysis. More than a score of M.A. and Ph.D. theses are station histories cited in the indices published in *Journal of Broadcasting*.

Radio and television programs are available for purchase or rental, or trade from a number of sources. See, "Sources for Research and Teaching in Radio and Television History," in Perry, Edward, *Performing Arts Resources*. Theater Library Association and Drama Book Specialists, 1974.

For example, send for catalogs from: Radiola, Box H, Croton-on-Hudson, New York, NY 10520 or Old Time Radio, Inc. 618 Commonwealth Building, Allentown, PA 18101. Also see Schwann Long Playing Record Catalog for a list of spoken and dramatic records including radio programs such as the Orson Welles *Mercury Theater* "War of the Worlds" on Audio Rarities; or collections of program excerpts such as those offered by Longines Symphonette, Larchmont, NY 10538. A number of film companies have TV programs for rental or purchase, especially documentaries.

The compiling was made easier and more complete by the work of C. H. Sterling—as research assistant to Lichty compiling other bibliographies which were consulted, as friend, and as editor of *Mass Media Booknotes*.

TECHNICAL

Abramson, Albert. *Electronic Motion Pictures: A History of the Television Camera.* University of California Press, 1956.

Appleby, Thomas. *Mahlon Loomis: Inventor of Radio.* Loomis Publications, 1967.

Baker, Thomas T. *Wireless Pictures and Television.* London: Constable, 1926.

Baker, W. J. *A History of the Marconi Company.* London: Methuen, 1971. St. Martin's Press, 1971.

Battison, John H. *Movies for TV.* Macmillan, 1950.

Benson, Thomas W. *Fundamentals of Television.* Mancall Publishing, 1930.

Blake, G. G. *History of Radio Telegraphy and Telephony.* London: Chapman and Hall, 1928.

Clarkson, R. P. *The Hysterical Background of Radio.* J. H. Sears, 1927.

Coe, Douglass. *Marconi: Pioneer of Radio.* Julian Messner, 1943.

Collins, A. Frederick. *Experimental Television.* Lothrop, Lee & Shepard, 1932.

Crawley, Chetwode. *From Telegraphy to Television.* London: Warne, 1931.

De Forest, Lee. *Father of Radio: The Autobiography of Lee De Forest.* Wilcox and Follet, 1950.

De Forest, Lee. *Television Today and Tomorrow.* The Dial Press, 1942.

Dunlap, Orrin E. *Communications in Space: From Wireless to Satellite Relay.* Harper & Row, 1962. . . . : *From Marconi to Man on the Moon,* 1970.

Dunlap, Orrin E. *Marconi: The Man and His Wireless.* Macmillan, 1937. Arno reprint.

Dunlap, Orrin E. *Radio and Television Almanac.* Harper & Brothers, 1951. A chronology of electronic developments.

Dunlap, Orrin E. *Radio's 100 Men of Science.* Harper & Brothers, 1944. Chronological descriptions. Reprinted by Arno.

Dunlap, Orrin E. *The Future of Television.* Harper, 1942; revised, 1947.

Dunlap, Orrin E. *The Outlook for Television.* Harper & Brothers, 1932. Arno reprint.

Dunlap, Orrin E. *The Radio Manual.* Houghton-Mifflin, 1924. The first of his 13 books on radio.

Dunlap, Orrin E. *The Story of Radio.* The Dial Press, 1927, 1935.

Erickson, Don V. *Armstrong's Fight For FM Broadcasting: One Man vs Big Business and Bureaucracy.* University of Alabama Press, 1973.

Everson, George. *The Story of Television: The Life of Philo T. Farnsworth.* Norton, 1949.

Fahie, John Joseph. *A History of Wireless Telegraphy, 1838–99.* Edinburgh: William Blackwood and Sons, 1899; revised 1901.

Federal Trade Commission. *Radio Industry.* GPO, 1923. Patent control, government documents.

Fielding, Raymond. *A Technological History of Motion Pictures and Television.* University of California Press, 1967. Articles from *The Journal of The Society of Motion Picture and Television Engineers.*

Gelatt, Roland. *The Fabulous Phonograph From Edison to Stereo.* Appleton-Century, 1965. Summary, particularly of phonograph as home music instrument before radio.

Goldmark, Peter C. *Maverick Inventor: My Turbulent Years At CBS.* Saturday Review Press, 1973. Color TV controversy, LP and EVR.

Greenwood, Harold S. *A Pictorial Album of Wireless and Radio 1905–1928.* Floyd Clymer Publications, n.d. reprinted and expanded as McMahon, Morgan E. *Vintage Radio 1887–1929.* Box 2045, Palos Verdes Peninsula CA 90274.

Harlow, Alvin. *Old Wires and New Waves: The History of the Telegraph, Telephone and Wireless.* Appleton-Century, 1936. Arno reprint.

Hilbrink, W. R. *Who Really Invented Radio.* G. P. Putnam's Sons, 1972. For young readers.

Howeth, L. S. *History of Communications-Electronics in the United States Navy.*
    Government Printing Office, 1963.
Hubbell, Richard W. *Four Thousand Years of Television.* London: George G. Harrap,
    1946.
Jacot, B. L. and Collier, D. *M. B. Marconi: Master of Space.* London: Hutchinson,
    1935.
Jolly, W. P. *Marconi.* Stein and Day, 1973.
Lessing, Lawrence. *Man of High Fidelity: Edwin Howard Armstrong.* Lippincott,
    1956. Inventor of FM.
Levin, Harvey J. *The Invisible Resource: Use and Regulation of the Radio Spectrum.*
    The Johns Hopkins Press, 1971.
Maclaurin, William Rupert. *Invention and Innovation in the Radio Industry.* Mac-
    millan, 1949. Arno reprint.
Marconi, Degna. *My Father Marconi.* McGraw-Hill, 1962.
Maxwell, James Clerk. *A Treatise on Electricity and Magnetism.* Volumes I and II.
    Unabridged republication of the last, third revised edition [1891]. Dover Publica-
    tions, 1954.
McMahon, Morgan E. *Radio Collector's Guide 1921–1932.* Box 2045 Palos Verdes
    Peninsula, CA 90274. Reprinted and expanded from Langley, Ralph H. *Set Cata-
    log and Index.*
Moseley, Sydney A., and McKay, Herbert. *Television: A Guide for the Amateur.* Ox-
    ford University Press, 1936.
OTP. *The Radio Frequency Spectrum: United States Use and Management.* Office of
    Telecommunications Management, Executive Office of the President, July 1969.
    Especially on use since 1960.
Pierce, George W. *Principles of Wireless Telegraphy.* McGraw-Hill, 1910.
Reade, Leslie. *Marconi and the Discovery of Wireless.* London: Faber and Faber,
    1963.
Susskind, Charles. *Popov and the Beginings of Radiotelegraphy.* San Francisco Press,
    1962.
Tiltman, Ronald F. *Baird of Television.* London: Seeley Service, 1933.
Tiltman, Ronald F. *Television for the Home.* London: Hutchinson, 1927.
Tyler, Kingdon S. *Telecasting and Color.* Harcourt, Brace, 1946. Mostly CBS system.
Zworykin, V. K., and Morton, G. A. *Television: The Electronics of Image Transmis-
    sion.* John Wiley & Sons, 1940.

STATIONS

Banning, William Peck. *Commercial Broadcasting Pioneer: The WEAF Experiment
    1922–1926.* Harvard University Press, 1946.
Cherington, Paul W., Hirsch, Leon V., and Brandwein, Robert. *Television Station
    Ownership: A Case Study of Federal Agency Regulation.* Hastings House 1971.
Evans, James F. *Prairie Farmer and WLS: The Burridge D. Butler Years.* University of
    Illinois Press, 1969. To 1948.
Frost, S. E. *Education's Own Stations.* University of Chicago Press, 1937. Arno re-
    print.
Johnson, Joseph S. and Jones, Kenneth K. *Modern Radio Station Practices.* Wads-
    worth, 1972. Programming and management.
Kurtz, E. B. *Pioneering in Educational Television.* State University Iowa Press, 1959.
    W9XK, WOI-TV.
Lutz, William W. *The News of Detroit.* Little, Brown, 1973. Information on WWJ.
Perry, Dick. *Not Just A Sound: The Story of WLW.* Prentice-Hall, 1971.
Quaal, Ward L., and Martin, Leo A. *Broadcast Management: Radio-Television.* Hast-
    ings House, 1968.
Quinlan, Sterling. *The Hundred Million Dollar Lunch.* J. Phillip O'Hara,
    1974. WHDH case.
Reinsch, J. Leonard, and Ellis, Elmo Israel. *Radio Station Management.* Harper &
    Brothers, 1948, 1960.
Roe, Yale. *Television Station Management: The Business of Broadcasting.* Hastings
    House, 1964.

Sanger, Elliott M. *Rebel in Radio: The Story of WQXR.* Hastings House, 1973.
Sill, Jerome. *The Radio Station: Management, Functions, Future.* George W. Stewart, 1946.

NETWORKS

Barrow, Roscoe L., *et al. Network Broadcasting: Report of the Network Study Staff to the Network Study Committee.* Federal Communications Commission, 1957. Also House of Representatives, 85th Congress 2d Session. Report No. 1297.
Burtin, Cipe Pineles. *The Visual Craft of William Golden.* George Braziller, 1962. Created advertising and promotional material for CBS-TV 1947 to 1959, pictures.
CBS. *Network Practices.* Columbia Broadcasting System, 1956. Memo to Senate Commerce Committee; on proposed regulation.
Federal Communications Commission. *Report on Chain Broadcasting.* Commission Order No. 37. Docket 5060. GPO, May 1941.
Johnson, Nicholas. "Broadcasting in America: The Performance of Network Affiliates in the Top 50 Markets." Federal Communications Commission Reports (42 FCC 2d), August 10, 1973. An analysis of programming, minority employment, ownership filed as a dissenting opinion to the 1973 renewal of licenses for Arkansas, Louisiana and Mississippi.
Robinson, Thomas Porter. *Radio Networks and the Federal Government.* Columbia University Press, 1943.
Slate, Sam J., and Cook, Joe. *It Sounds Impossible.* Macmillan, 1963. Informally written history of radio, especially network, to 1960s.

ECONOMICS

Agnew, Clark, and O'Brien, Neil. *Television Advertising.* McGraw-Hill, 1958.
Aly, Bower, and Shively, Gerald D. *A Debate Handbook on Radio Control and Operation.* University of Oklahoma Press, 1933. See Buehler.
Arnold, Frank A. *Broadcast Advertising: The Fourth Dimension* (Television Edition). Wiley, 1933.
Bellaire, Arthur. *TV Advertising: A Handbook of Modern Practice.* Harper & Brothers, 1959.
Bogart, Leo. *Strategy in Advertising.* Harcourt, Brace & World, 1967.
Brown, Les. *Televi$ion: The Business Behind the Box.* Harcourt Brace Jovanovich, 1971. Network TV in 1970.
Buehler, E. C. *American vs. British System of Radio Control.* H. W. Wilson, 1933. Arguments for national debate topic.
Della Femina, Jerry. *From Those Wonderful Folks Who Gave You Pearl Harbor: Front-line Dispatches from the Advertising War.* Simon and Schuster, 1970. Pocket Books, 1971.
Diamant, Lincoln. *Television's Classic Commercials: The Golden Years, 1948–1958.* Hastings House, 1971.
Dunlap, Orrin E. *Advertising by Radio.* Ronald Press, 1929.
Dunlap, Orrin E. *Radio in Advertising.* Harper, 1931.
Dygert, Warren B. *Radio As An Advertising Medium.* McGraw-Hill, 1939.
Eoyang, Thomas T. *An Economic Study of the Radio Industry in the United States of America.* RCA Institutes Technical Press, 1937.
Evans, Jacob A. *Selling and Promoting Radio and Television.* Printers' Ink, 1954.
Federal Communications Commission, Engineering Department. *Report on Social and Economic Data Pursuant to the Informal Hearing on Broadcasting,* Docket 4063, Beginning October 5, 1936. Government Printing Office, 1938. Station classification, location, finances.
Federal Radio Commission. *Commercial Radio Advertising.* GPO, 1932. Reply to Senate questions, tables.
Felix, Edgar H. *Using Radio in Sales Promotion.* McGraw-Hill, 1927.

Garver, Robert I. *Successful Radio Advertising with Sponsor Participation Programs.* Prentice-Hall, 1949.

George F. Baker Foundation. *The Radio Industry.* A. W. Shaw, 1928. Lectures to Harvard Business School by those in industry.

Hettinger, Herman. *A Decade of Radio Advertising.* University of Chicago, 1933. Arno reprint.

Jome, Hiram L. *Economics of the Radio Industry.* A. W. Shaw, 1925. Arno reprint.

Midgley, Ned. *The Advertising and Business Side of Radio.* Prentice-Hall, 1948.

NAB. *Broadcasting in the U.S.* National Association of Broadcasters, 1931. Argument of U.S. vs. British "system."

Ogden, Warde B., *The Television Business: Accounting Problems of a Growth Industry.* Ronald Press, 1961.

Ogilvy, David. *Confessions of an Advertising Man.* Antheneum, 1963. Dell, 1964.

Oxenfeldt, Alfred R. *Marketing Practices in the TV Set Industry.* Columbia University Press, 1964.

Radio As An Advertising Medium. Metropolitan Life Insurance Company, 1929.

Stevens, Paul. *I Can Sell You Anything: How I Made Your Favorite TV Commercials with Minimum Truth & Maximum Consequences.* Peter H. Wyden, 1972.

U.S. Attorney General. *Report to the President on Deceptive Practices in Broadcast Media.* GPO, 1959.

Waldrop, Frank C. and Borkin, Joseph. *Television: A Struggle for Power.* William Morrow, 1938. Arno reprint. Opposes control by large corporations; reviews radio patents, corporations.

EMPLOYMENT

Allen, Steve. *Mark it and Strike It: An Autobiography.* Holt, Rinehart, and Winston, 1960.

Allen, Steve. *The Funny Men.* Simon and Schuster, 1956. Profiles on comedians.

Arnold, Frank A. *Do You Want To Get Into Radio?* Frederick A. Stokes, 1940.

Bannister, Harry. *The Education of a Broadcaster.* Simon and Schuster, 1965. Autobiography of WWJ, Detroit, manager and NBC vice president.

Barber, Red. *The Broadcasters.* Dial Press, 1970. On sports broadcasting.

Bentley, Eric. *Are You Now or Have You Ever Been: The Investigation of Show Business by the Un-American Activities Committee, 1947–1958.* Harper, 1972.

Bentley, Eric. *Thirty Years of Treason: Excerpts from Hearings before the House Committee on Un-American Activities, 1938–1968.* Viking, 1971.

Berg, Gertrude. *Molly and Me.* McGraw-Hill, 1951. Autobiography of broadcasting actress.

Bouck, Zeh. *Making A Living in Radio.* McGraw-Hill, 1935.

Brokenshire, Norman. *This is Norman Brokenshire: An Unvarnished Self-portrait.* D. McKay, 1954.

Burlingame, Roger. *Don't Let Them Scare You: The Life and Times of Elmer Davis.* Lippincott, 1961.

Cantor, Muriel G. *The Hollywood TV Producer: His Work and His Audience.* Basic Books, 1971.

Carroll, Carroll. *None of Your Business: Or My Life With J. Walter Thompson* (Confessions of a Renegade Radio Writer). Cowles, 1970.

Chesmore, Stuart. *Behind the Microphone.* Thomas Nelson & Sons, 1935. Autobiographical.

Cogley, John. *Report on Blacklisting II Radio-Television.* The Fund for the Republic, 1956. Arno reprint with Miller, Merle. *The Judges and the Judged,* 1952 under the title *Blacklisting: Two Key Documents.*

Correll, Charles J. *All About Amos 'n' Andy.* Rand McNally, 1929. History and scripts.

Correll, Charles J. *Sam 'n' Henry.* Shrewsbury, 1926. Story from scripts.

Edwards, Frank. *My First 10,000 Sponsors.* Ballantine, 1956. Autobiography of news commentator.

Eichberg, Robert. *Radio Stars of Today.* L. C. Page, 1937. Biographies of radio stars.

Faulk, John Henry. *Fear On Trial.* Simon and Schuster, 1964. Blacklisting, 1957.

Firth, Ivan, and Erskin, Gladys S. *Gateway to Radio*. Macaulay Co., 1934.

Fulton, Eileen, and Bolton, Brett. *How My World Turns*. Warner, 1973. TV soap operas.

Gibbons, Edward. *Floyd Gibbons: Your Headline Hunter*. Exposition Press, 1953.

Hill, Edwin C. *The Human Side of the News*. Walter J. Black, 1934.

Higby, Mary Jane. *Tune in Tomorrow*. Cowles, 1968. Memoirs of star of *When A Girl Marries* and other soaps.

Husing, Ted. *Ten Years Before the Mike*. Farrar & Rinehart, 1935.

Husing, Ted and Rice, Cy. *My Eyes Are in My Heart*. Random House, 1959. Hillman, 1961. Autobiography continued.

Kendrick, Alexander. *Prime Time: The Life of Edward R. Murrow*. Little, Brown, 1969.

Lent, Henry Bolles. *This Is Your Announcer*. Macmillan, 1945. Career of announcer.

Lyons, Eugene. *David Sarnoff*. Harper & Row, 1966.

Maier, Paul L. *A Man Spoke, A World Listened*. McGraw-Hill, 1963. Biography of Dr. Walter A. Maier of *The Lutheran Hour*.

Marcus, Sheldon. *Father Coughlin: The Tumultuous Life of the Priest of the Little Flower*. Little, Brown, 1973.

McBride, Mary Margaret. *Out of the Air*. Doubleday, 1960. Autobiography of radio talk personality.

McCarthy, Joe. *Fred Allen's Letters*. Doubleday, 1965; Pocket, 1966.

McNamee, Graham. *You're on the Air*. Harper & Brothers, 1926. Autobiography of announcer.

Miller, Merle. *The Judges and the Judged*. Doubleday, 1952. Arno reprint.

Morella, Joe, and others. *The Amazing Careers of Bob Hope: From Gags to Riches*. Arlington House, 1973.

Nelson, Ozzie. *Ozzie*. Prentice-Hall, 1973.

Sarnoff, David. *Looking Ahead: The Papers of David Sarnoff*. McGraw-Hill, 1968.

Sevareid, Eric. *Not So Wild a Dream*. Knopf, 1946. Autobiography, especially reporting WWII.

Stern, Bill. *The Taste of Ashes: An Autobiography*. Henry Holt, 1959.

Strainchamps, Ethel (ed.). *Rooms with No View: A Woman's Guide to the Man's World of the Media*. Harper and Row, 1974.

Swing, Raymond. *Good Evening! A professional memoir*. Harcourt, Brace and World, 1964. Autobiography of news commentator.

Thomas, Bob. *Winchell*. Doubleday, 1971.

Treadwell, Bill. *Head, Heart and Heel*. Mayfair Books, 1958. Biography of "Uncle Don."

Vallee, Rudy. *My Time is Your Time*. Obolensky, 1962.

Vaughn, Robert. *Only Victims: A Study of Show Business Blacklisting*. G. P. Putnam's Sons, 1972.

Whelan, Kenneth. *How the Golden Age of Television Turned My Hair to Silver*. Walker, 1973. Reminiscence, CBS producer-director.

PROGRAMMING

Ace, Goodman. *Ladies and Gentlemen—Easy Aces*. Doubleday, 1970.

Allen, Fred. *Treadmill to Oblivion*. Little, Brown, 1954.

Allen, Fred. *Much Ado About Me*. Little, Brown, 1956.

Andrews, Robert Douglas. *Just Plain Bill, His Story*. David M. Kay, 1935. Life of a soap opera hero.

Arlen, Michael J. *Living-Room War*. Viking, 1969; Tower, 1969. Collection of articles from *New Yorker*, many on television and the Vietnam war.

Averson, Richard, and White, David Manning. *Electronic Drama: Television Plays of the Sixties*. Beacon Press, 1971.

Barnouw, Erik. *Handbook of Radio Writing*. Little, Brown, 1946. Illustrations of specific writing techniques.

Barrett, Marvin. *Survey of Broadcast Journalism 1968–1969*. Grosset & Dunlap, 1969.

Barrett, Marvin. *Survey of Broadcast Journalism 1969–1970: Year of Challenge, Year of Crisis*. Grosset & Dunlap, 1970.

Barrett, Marvin. *Survey of Broadcast Journalism 1970–1971: A State of Siege.* Grosset & Dunlap, 1971.

Barrett, Marvin. *Survey of Broadcast Journalism 1971–1972: The Politics of Broadcasting.* Thomas Y. Crowell, 1973.

Belz, Carl. *The Story of Rock.* Oxford, 1969; revised 1972.

Berg, Gertrude. *The Rise of the Goldbergs.* Barse, 1931.

Bickel, Mary E. *George W. Trendle: An Authorized Biography.* Exposition Press, 1972. Producer Lone Ranger, Sgt. Preston, Green Hornet.

Blair, Cornelia. *The Nora Drake Story.* Duell, Sloan & Pearce, 1950. Depiction of a soap opera heroine's experiences.

Bliss, Edward. *In Search of Light: The Broadcasts of Edward R. Murrow 1938–1961.* Knopf, 1967.

Bluem, A. William. *Documentary in American Television: Form, Function Method.* Hastings House, 1965.

Bluem, A. William. *Religious Television Programs: A Study of Relevance.* Hastings House, 1969.

Blum, Daniel. *A Pictorial History of Television.* Chilton, 1959. Bonanza reprint.

Boyd, James. *The Free Company Presents.* Dodd, Mead, 1941. Pre-WW II Scripts.

Bryant, Ashbrook P. *Television Network Program Procurement Part I and II.* Second Interim Report by the Office of Network Study (Docket 12782). Federal Communications Commission, GPO, 1963, 1965. Also Committee on Interstate and Foreign Commerce, 88th Congress, 1st Session, House Report 281.

Buxton, Frank, and Owen, Bill. *The Big Broadcast—1920–1950.* Viking Press, 1972. List of programs, stars, details.

Buxton, Frank, and Owen, Bill. *Radio's Golden Age.* Easton Valley Press, 1966; enlarged edition *The Big Broadcast.*

CBS. *We Take You Now To . . .* Columbia Broadcasting System, 1937. Compilation of remote broadcasts.

CBS. *Vienna: March 1938.* Columbia Broadcasting System, 1938. Some excerpts of broadcasts.

CBS. *Crises: A Report from the Columbia Broadcasting System.* Columbia Broadcasting System, n.d. Munich crises, 1938, broadcasts, analysis.

CBS. *Church of the Air.* Columbia Broadcasting System, 1941.

CBS. *CBS News on D-Day.* Columbia Broadcasting System, 1945.

CBS. *From D-Day Through Victory in Europe.* Columbia Broadcasting System, 1945.

CBS. *From Pearl Harbor Into Tokyo.* Columbia Broadcasting System, 1945. Bulletins, commentaries, speeches on CBS.

CBS. *10:56:20 PM 7/20/69.* Columbia Broadcasting System, 1970. "The historic conquest of the moon as reported to the American people by CBS News."

Charnley, Mitchell V. *News By Radio.* Macmillan, 1948.

Chayefsky, Paddy. *Television Plays.* Simon and Schuster, 1955. Six, including "Marty" and "The Bachelor Party" and notes.

Chester, Edward W. *Radio, Television and American Politics.* Sheed & Ward, 1969.

Childs, Harwood L. and Whitton, John B. *Propaganda by Short Wave.* Princeton University Press, 1942.

Cohn, Nik. *Rock from the Beginning.* Stein & Day, 1969. Pocket Books, 1970.

Corwin, Norman Lewis. *More by Corwin.* Henry Holt, 1944.

Corwin, Norman L. *Thirteen by Corwin.* Henry Holt, 1942.

Corwin, Norman. *This is War!* Dodd, Mead, 1942. Thirteen 1942 broadcasts.

Coutler, Douglas. *Columbia Workshop Plays.* Whittlesey House, 1939.

Darrow, Ben H. *Radio: The Assistant Teacher.* R. G. Adams, 1932.

Darrow, Ben H. *Radio Trailblazing: A Brief History of the Ohio School of the Air and its Implications for Educational Broadcasting.* Columbus, Ohio: College Book Company, 1940.

de Antonio, Emile, and Talbot, Daniel. *Point of Order: A Documentary of the Army-McCarthy Hearings.* W. W. Norton, 1964. Also film that can be rented.

Dryer, Sherman H. *Radio in Wartime.* Greenberg, 1942.

Eisen, Jonathan. *The Age of Rock: Sounds of the American Cultural Revolution.* Vintage, 1969.

Ellison, Harlan. *The Glass Teat: Essays of Opinion on the Subject of Television.* Ace, 1970. TV columnist, Los Angeles *Free Press.*

Fadiman, Clifton. *Prize Plays of TV and Radio, 1956.* Random House, 1957. Live TV Scripts.

Fenin, George N., and Everson, William K. *The Western: from Silents to Cinerama.* Bonanza Books, 1962.

Foote, Horton. *Three Plays.* Harcourt, Brace and World, 1962.

Friendly, Fred W. *Due To Circumstances Beyond Our Control . . .* Random House, 1967.

Galanoy, Terry. *Tonight!* Doubleday, 1972. Late night TV show.

Gaver, Jack and Stanley, Dave. *There's Laughter in the Air.* Greenberg, 1945. Radio comedy scripts.

Golenpaul, Dan. *Information Please!* Random House, 1940.

Gordon, George N. and Falk, Irving A. *On the Spot Reporting: Radio Records History.* Julian Messner, 1967.

Gordon, George N. and Falk, Irving A. *TV Covers the Action.* Julian Messner, 1968.

Harmon, Jim. *The Great Radio Comedians.* Doubleday, 1970.

Harmon, Jim. *The Great Radio Heroes.* Doubleday, 1967. Ace, 1967.

Harris, Michael David. *Always on Sunday—Ed Sullivan: An Inside View.* Meridith, 1968.

Herzberg, Max J. *Radio and English Teaching: Experiences, Problems, and Procedures.* D. Appleton-Century, 1941.

Hickock, Eliza Merrill. *The Quiz Kids.* Houghton-Mifflin, 1947.

Hirsch, Paul. *The Structure of the Popular Music Industry: The Filtering Process by Which Records are Preselected for Public Consumption.* Institute for Social Research, University of Michigan, n.d. c. 1968.

Hubbell, Richard W. *Television Programming and Production.* Murray Hill Books, 1945.

Jares, Joseph. *What Ever Happened to Gorgeous George?* Prentice-Hall, 1974. Wrestling on television.

Johnson, William O. *Super Spectator and the Electric Lilliputians.* Little, Brown, 1971. TV and sports.

Kaltenborn, H. V. *I Broadcast the Crisis.* Random House, 1938. CBS scripts September 12, to October 2, 1938.

Kaltenborn, H. V. *It Seems Like Yesterday.* G. P. Putnam's Sons, 1956.

Kaltenborn, H. V. *Kaltenborn Edits the News.* Modern Age Books, 1937. News reports, 1936.

Kaufman, William I. *Great Television Plays.* Dell, 1969. Including "Requiem for a Heavyweight" by Rod Serling, "Twelve Angry Men" by Reginald Rose, and "The Final War of Olly Winter" by Ronald Ribman.

Kirby, Edward M. and Harris, Jack W. *Star-Spangled Radio.* Ziff-Davis, 1948. Radio in US, and reporting WW II.

Koch, Howard. *The Panic Broadcast.* Little, Brown, 1970. On "War of the Worlds" by the script writer.

Lackmann, Ron. *Remember Radio.* G. P. Putnam's Sons, 1970. Scrap book of memorabilia.

Lackmann, Ron. *Remember Television.* G. P. Putnam's Sons, 1971. More memorabilia.

Lawton, Sherman P. *Radio Continuity Types.* Expression Co., 1938.

Lee, A. M. and Lee E. B. *The Fine Art of Propaganda: A Study of Father Coughlin's Speeches.* Harcourt, Brace, 1939. Institute of Propaganda Analysis.

Leroy, David J., and Sterling, Christopher H. *Mass News: Practices, Controversies, and Alternatives.* Prentice-Hall, 1973.

Lesser, Gerald S. *Children and Television: Lessons From Sesame Street.* Random House, 1974.

Levenson, William B. and Stasheff, Edward. *Teaching Through Radio and Television.* Rinehart, 1952.

Liss, Joseph. *Radio's Best Plays.* Greenberg, 1947. By MacLeish, John Mason Brown, Teichmann, Lampell, Benet, Corwin, Barnouw, Al Morgan, Faulk, and others.

Lord, Phillips H. *Seth Parker and His Jonesport Folks, Way Back Home.* John C. Winston, 1932.

Lyle, Jack. *The News in Megalopolis.* Chandler, 1967. Radio and TV news, Los Angeles, 1964.

Malone, Bill C. *Country Music U.S.A.: A Fifty-year History*. University of Texas, 1968.

Mattfeld, Julius. *Variety Music Cavalcade: 1920–1961—A Chronology of Vocal and Instrumental Music Popular in the United States*. Prentice-Hall, 1962.

Mayo, John B. *Bulletin from Dallas: The President Is Dead*. Exposition Press, 1967. "The story of John F. Kennedy's assassination as covered by radio and tv."

McGinniss, Joe. *The Selling of the President 1968*. Trident, 1969.

McMahan, Harry Wayne. *TV Tape Commercials*. Hastings House, 1960.

Michael, Paul, and Parish, James Robert. *The Emmy Awards: A Pictorial History*. Crown, 1970.

Miller, Merle, and Rhodes, Evan. *Only You, Dick Daring! Or How To Write One Television Script and Make $50,000,000*. William Sloane, 1964. Background, planning for a TV pilot.

Mitchell, Curtis. *Cavalcade of Broadcasting*. Follett, 1970. Summary and pictures, 1920 to 1970.

Morgan, Edward P. *Clearing the Air*. Robert B. Luce, Inc., 1963. 120 news commentaries.

Murrow, Edward R. and Davis, Elmer. *This Is London*. Simon and Schuster, 1941. Broadcasts August 1939 to December 1940.

Murrow, Edward R., and Friendly, Fred. *See It Now*. Simon & Schuster, 1955. Pictures, descriptions.

National Broacasting Company. *There Was A President*. Ridge Press-Random House, 1966. Assassination of President Kennedy.

NBC. *NBC and You*. National Broadcasting Company, 1944.

Oboler, Arch. *Free World Theater: Nineteen New Radio Plays*. Random House, 1944.

Oboler, Arch. *Plays for Americans*. Farrar & Rinehart, 1942. Radio dramas written for and dedicated to the war effort.

Polsky, Richard M. *Getting to Sesame Street: Origins of the Children's Television Workshop*. Praeger; Aspen Program on Communications and Society, 1974.

Rhymer, Mary Frances. *The Small House Half-way Up In The Next Block: Paul Rhymer's Vic and Sade*. McGraw-Hill, 1972. Soap opera scripts.

Rolo, Charles J. *Radio Goes to War: The Fourth Front*. G. P. Putnam's Sons, 1942.

Rose, Reginald. *Six Television Plays*. Simon and Schuster, 1956.

Rubin, Bernard. *Political Television*. Wadsworth, 1967. Summary 1960–1964.

Ryan, Milo. *History in Sound: A Descriptive Listing of the KIRO-CBS Collection of Broadcasts of the World War II Years and After in the Phonoarchive of the University of Washington*. University of Washington Press, 1963.

Saerchinger, Cesar. *Hello America*. Houghton Mifflin, 1938. (European edition as *Voice of Europe*, London: Gollancz, 1938). Foreign correspondent.

Schechter, A. A. and Anthony, Edward. *I Live On Air*. Frederick A. Stokes, 1941. NBC Radio News history.

Serling, Rod. *Patterns*. Simon & Schuster, 1957. Four TV plays.

Settel, Irving. *A Pictorial History of Radio*. The Citadel Press, 1960. Grosset & Dunlap, 1967. First edition to the 1950s, and some on the 1960s.

Settel, Irving. Best TV Humor of 1957. Ballantine Books, 1957.

Settel, Trudy and Irving. *The Best of Armstrong Circle Theatre*. Citadel Press, 1959.

Settel, Irving. *Top TV Shows of the Year 1954–1955*. Hastings House, 1955. Includes *The Honeymooners*, *See It Now* on McCarthy, *Kraft Television Theatre*, *What's My Line*, *Home*, others.

Sevareid, Eric. *In One Ear*. Knopf, 1952. Radio broadcasts.

Sevareid, Eric. *This Is Eric Sevareid*. McGraw-Hill, 1964. Broadcasts and articles.

Shaw, Arnold. *The Rock Revolution*. Macmillan, 1969. Paperback Library, 1971.

Shulman, Arthur, and Youman, Roger. *How Sweet It Was: Television: A Pictorial Commentary*. Shorecrest, 1966.

Shulman, Arthur, and Youman, Roger J. *The Television Years*. Popular Library, 1973. Also magazine format, Popular Library, 1974. Pictures.

Siepmann, Charles A. *Radio in Wartime*. Oxford University Press, 1942.

Siepmann, Charles A. *Radio's Second Chance*. Little, Brown, 1946. Criticism following author's work on "The Blue Book."

Simon, George T. *The Big Bands*. Macmillan, 1967.

Small, William J. *Political Power and the Press*, W. W. Norton, 1972. Particularly on "The Selling of the Pentagon."

Small, William J. *To Kill A Messenger: Television News and the Real World*. Hastings House, 1970.

Spivak, John L. *Shrine of the Silver Dollar*. Modern Age Books, 1940. On Father Coughlin.

Stambler, Irwin, and Landon, Grelun. *Encyclopedia of Folk, Country and Western Music*, St. Martin's Press, 1969.

Stedman, Raymond William. *The Serials: Suspense and Drama by Installment*. University of Oklahoma Press, 1971.

Summers, Harrison B. *Radio Programs Carried on National Networks 1926–1956*. Department of Speech, The Ohio State University, January 1958. Arno reprint. Listing of network radio programs, sponsors, ratings.

Summers, Robert E. *America's Weapons of Psychological Warfare*. H. W. Wilson, 1951.

Swing, Raymond. *How War Came*. W. W. Norton, 1939.

Swing, Raymond. *In the Name of Sanity*. Harper & Brothers, 1946.

Swing, Raymond. *Preview of History*. Doubleday, Doran, 1943.

Taylor, Sherril W. *Radio Programming in Action: Realities and Opportunities*. Hastings House, 1967.

This Is War. Dodd, Mead, 1942. Scripts.

Thomas, Lowell. *History As You Heard It*. Doubleday, 1957. Abstracts of daily news broadcasts 1930 to 1955.

Thomson, Charles A. H. *Television and Presidential Politics: The Experience in 1952 and the Problems Ahead*. The Brookings Institution, 1956.

Thurber, James. *The Beast in Me and Other Animals*. Harcourt, Brace, 1948.

Vidal. Gore. *Best Television Plays*. Ballantine Books, 1956.

Wade, Robert J. *Staging TV Programs and Commercials*. Hastings House, 1954.

Wagner, Paul H. *Radio Journalism*. Burgess Publishing, 1940.

Weinberg, Meyer. *TV in America: The Morality of Hard Cash*. Ballantine, 1962. On the quiz show scandals.

West, Robert. *So-o-o-O You're Going On the Air*. Rodin Publishing, 1934.

Whitfield, Stephen E., and Roddenberry, Gene. *The Making of Star Trek*. Ballantine, 1968.

White, Paul. *News on the Air*. Harcourt, Brace, 1947. How-to-do it, but some history, especially CBS News.

Williams, John R. *This Was Your Hit Parade*. John R. Williams, 1973. List of songs on the program, 1935–58.

Winick, Charles, and others. *Children's Television Commercials: A Content Analysis*. Praeger, 1973.

Wolf, Frank. *Television Programming for News and Public Affairs: A Quantitative Analysis of Networks and Stations*. Praeger, 1972.

Wood, William A. *Electronic Journalism*. Columbia University Press, 1967. General survey, short case study on civil rights coverage.

Wylie, Max. *Best Broadcasts of 1938–39*. McGraw-Hill 1939.

Wylie, Max. *Best Broadcasts of 1939–40*. McGraw-Hill, 1940.

Wylie, Max. *Clear Channels: Television and the American People*. Funk & Wagnalls, 1955. First big attack on TV commercials and smoking.

Yellin, David. *Special: Fred Freed and the Television Documentary*. Macmillan, 1973.

AUDIENCE

Baker, Robert K. and Ball, Sandra J. *Mass Media and Violence, Vol. IX: A Report to the National Commission on the Causes and Prevention of Violence*. GPO, 1969.

Bogart, Leo. *The Age of Television: A study of viewing habits and the impact of television on American life*. Frederick Ungar, 1956. Data on early TV audiences. Revised 1958; reprinted and updated 1972.

Bower, Robert T. *Television and the Public*. Holt, Rinehart and Winston, 1973. Replicates Steiner, 1963.

Cantril, Hadley. *The Invasion From Mars: A Study in the Psychology of Panic With the complete script of the famous Orson Welles Broadcast*. Princeton University Press, 1940; Harper Torchbook, 1966.

Cantril, Hadley and Allport, Gordon W. *The Psychology of Radio*. Harper & Brothers, 1935. Arno reprint.

CBS. *Radio in 1937*. Columbia Broadcasting System, 1937.

Chappell, Matthew N. and Hooper, C. E. *Radio Audience Measurement*. Stephen Daye, 1944. Especially on coincidental telephone, Hooperating, method.

Committee on Interstate and Foreign Commerce, House. *Evaluation of Statistical Methods Used in Obtaining Broadcast Ratings*. GPO, 1961.

Cunningham & Walsh. *First Decade of TV in Videotown*. Cunningham & Walsh, 1957. TV use in New Brunswick, N.J.

Department of Health, Education, and Welfare. *Television and Growing Up: The Impact of Televised Violence*. GPO, 1972. "Report to the Surgeon General . . . from the Surgeon General's Scientific Advisory Committee on Television and Social Behavior."

Elliot, William Y. *Television's Impact on American Culture*. Michigan State University, 1956.

Glick, Ira O. and Levy, Sidney J. *Living with Television*. Aldine, 1962. Summary of a number of audience studies.

Greenberg, Bradley S., and Parker, Edwin B. *The Kennedy Assassination and the American Public: Social Communications in Crisis*. Stanford University Press, 1965.

Klapper, Joseph T. *The Effects of Mass Communications*. The Free Press, 1960. Summarizes a number of studies; proponent of limited effects of media.

Kraus, Sidney. *The Great Debates: Background—Perspective—Effects*. Indiana University Press, 1962.

Lang, Kurt, and Lang, Gladys Engle. *Politics and Television*. Quadrangle, 1968. See especially "MacArthur Day in Chicago" and "The Televised Conventions: 1952."

Larsen, Otto N. *Violence and the Mass Media*. Harper & Row, 1968.

Lazarsfeld, Paul F. *Radio and the Printed Page*. Duell, Sloan, Pearce, 1940.

Lazarsfeld, Paul F., Stanton, Frank. *Radio Research: 1941*. Duell, Sloan and Pearce, 1941.

Lazarsfeld, Paul F., and Stanton, Frank N. *Radio Research: 1942–43*. Duell, Sloan and Pearce, 1944.

Lazarsfeld, Paul F., others. *The People's Choice: How The Voter Makes Up His Mind in a Presidential Campaign*. Duell, Sloan and Pearce, 1944. 2nd Columbia University Press, 1948.

Lazarsfeld, Paul F. and Field, Harry. *The People Look at Radio*. University of North Carolina Press, 1946.

Lazarsfeld, Paul F. and Kendall, Patricia L. *Radio Listening in America: The People Look at Radio—Again*. Prentice-Hall, 1948.

Lazarsfeld, Paul F., and Stanton, Frank. *Communications Research 1948–49*. Harper & Brothers, 1949.

Liebert, Robert M., Neale, John M. and Davidson, Emily S. *The Early Window: Effects of Television on Children and Youth*. Pergamon, 1973. Summarizes most of same material as Surgeon General's report, 1972. Evidence for some effects.

Lumley, Frederick H. *Measurement in Radio*. The Ohio State University, 1934. Arno reprint.

Mayer, Martin. "How Good Are Television Ratings?" Television Information Office, 1966. Also see "How Good Are Television Ratings? (continued . . .)" TIO, n.d. [1969]. "Television Ratings Revisited . . . : A further look at television audiences" TIO, 1971.

Melody, William. *Children's TV: The Economics of Exploitation*. Yale University Press, 1973.

Mendelsohn, Harold. *Mass Entertainment*. College & University Press, 1966. Summary of entertainment, sociological and psychological functions.

Mendelsohn, Harold and Crespi, Irving. *Polls, Television, and the New Politics.* Chandler, 1970.

Merril, I. R. and Proctor, C. H. *Political Persuasion by Television: Partisan and Public Affairs in the 1956 General Election.* Department of Television Broadcasting, Michigan State University. WKAR-TV Research Report 565M.

Merton, Robert K., Fiske, Marjorie, and Curtis, Alberta. *Mass Persuasion.* Harper and Brothers, 1946. Study of Kate Smith War Bond drive.

Porter, James P. (Entire issue, 20 articles on radio audiences and effects) *The Journal of Applied Psychology.* XXIII (1939).

Schramm, Wilbur, others. *Television in the lives of Our Children.* Stanford University Press, 1961.

Schramm, Wilbur, Lyle, Jack and Pool, Ithiel de Sola. *The People Look at Educational Television.* Stanford University Press, 1963.

Steiner, Gary A. *The People Look At Television: A Study of Audience Attitudes.* Knopf, 1963.

REGULATION

Brindze, Ruth. *Not To Be Broadcast.* Vanguard Press, 1937. Charges business and government censorship of broadcasting; examples.

Carson, Gerald. *The Roguish World of Doctor Brinkley.* Rinehart, 1960.

Committee on Commerce, Senate. *Fairness Doctrine.* GPO, 1968. Includes historical review.

Committee on Interstate and Foreign Commerce, House. *Regulation of Broadcasting: Half A Century of Government Regulation of Broadcasting and the Need for Further Legislative Action.* (85th Cong. 2nd Sess.) GPO, 1958. Written by Robert S. McMahon, often referred to as the McMahon Report, a summary of legislation and proposed legislation for broadcasting.

Communications Act of 1934 with Amendments and Index Thereto. Government Printing Office.

Congressional Research Service, Library of Congress. Congress and Mass Communications: An institutional Perspective. GPO, 1974.

Cox, Kenneth A. and Johnson, Nicholas. *Broadcasting in America and the FCC's License Renewal Process: An Oklahoma Case Study.* Federal Communications Commission, 1968. Information on ownership and programming.

Cox, Kenneth A. and Johnson, Nicholas. *Renewal Standards: The District of Columbia, Maryland, Virginia and West Virginia License Renewals (October 1, 1969).* Federal Communications Commission, 1969. Public Notice 42255. Ownership, employment, programming.

Davis, Stephen. *The Law of Radio Communication.* McGraw-Hill, 1927.

Edelman, Murray. *Licensing of Radio Services in the United States: 1927–47.* University of Illinois Studies in the Social Sciences, Vol. XXXI, No. 4, 1950. Published Ph.D. dissertation.

Emery, Walter. *Broadcasting and Government: Responsibilities and Regulations.* Michigan State University Press, 1961; revised 1971.

Federal Communication Commission. *Sixth Report and Order* (52-294). GPO and *Television Digest,* April 14, 1952. Final TV allocations.

Federal Communications Commission. *Public Service Responsibilities of Broadcast Licensees.* (Public Notice 95462). GPO, 1946. ("Blue Book")

Gillmor, Donald M. and Barron, Jerome A. *Cases and Comment on Mass Communications Law.* West, 1969.

Interstate and Foreign Commerce, House. *Television Inquiry.* (84th, 85th, 86th Cong.) GPO, 1959–1960. I and II:UHF-VHF Allocations; III: Subscription Television; IV: Network Practices, V, VI and VIII: Allocations and VII: The Television Rating Services.

Kahn, Frank J. *Documents of American Broadcasting.* Appleton-Century-Crofts, 1968. 2nd, enlarged edition, 1973. Laws, FCC and court decisions.

Kittross, John M. and Harwood, Kenneth. *Free and Fair: Courtroom Access and the*

Fairness Doctrine. Association for Professional Broadcasting Education, 1970. Selections from the *Journal of Broadcasting.*

Krasnow, Erwin G. and Longley, Lawrence D. *The Politics of Broadcast Regulation.* St. Martin's Press, 1973.

Lamb, Edward. *No Lamb for Slaughter: An Autobiography.* Harcourt, Brace, & World. 1963. Blacklisting, the FCC and a licensee.

Lamb, Edward. *Trial by Battle: The Case History of a Washington Witch-Hunt.* The Fund for the Republic, 1964.

Le Duc, Don R. *Cable Television and the FCC: A Crisis in Media Control.* Temple University Press, 1973.

Levin, Harvey J., *Broadcast Regulation and Joint Ownership of Media,* New York University Press, 1960.

Minow, Newton. *Equal Time: The Private Broadcaster and The Public Interest.* Atheneum, 1964. Speeches.

NAB. *Broadcasting and the Bill of Rights.* National Association of Broadcasters, 1947. Defense of broadcast against proposed changes in Communications Act.

Nelson, Harold L. and Teeter, Dwight L. *Law of Mass Communications: Freedom and Control of Print and Broadcast Media.* Foundation Press, 1969.

Noll, Roger G., others. *Economic Aspects of Television Regulation.* The Brookings Institution, 1973.

Schmeckebier, Laurence F. *The Federal Radio Commission: Its History, Activities and Organization.* The Brookings Institution, 1932.

Schwartz, Bernard. *The Professor and the Commissions.* Knopf, 1959. Congressional investigation of FCC 1958, scandals.

Snead, Elmer E. *Freedom of Speech by Radio and Television.* Public Affairs Press, 1959.

Summers, Harrison B. *Radio Censorship.* H. W. Wilson, 1939. Reference Shelf V. 12, No. 10.

Summers, Robert E., *Wartime Censorship of Press and Radio.* H. W. Wilson, 1942. Reference Shelf V. 15, No. 8.

Winston, Alvin. *Doctors, Dynamiters, and Gunmen: The Life Story of Norman Baker.* Muscatine, Iowa: TNT Press, 1934, 1936. "Alvin Winston" was Clement Wood (see below) who wrote a foreword to his own book which he calls a "brilliant biography, written by one of America's most caustic pens."

Wood, Clement C. *The Life of a Man.* Kansas City: Ooshorn Publishing Company, 1934. Promotional biography of Dr. John R. Brinkley.

GENERAL AND MISCELLANEOUS

Ace, Goodman. *The Book of Little Knowledge.* Simon and Schuster, 1955. Articles, criticism, *Saturday Review,* 1951–1955.

Alford, W. Wayne. *NAEB History: 1954–1965.* National Association of Educational Broadcasters, 1966. See Hill.

Archer, Gleason L. *Big Business and Radio.* The American Historical Company, 1939. Arno reprint. Radio, 1926–1939; and some new information to supplement Archer, 1938.

Archer, Gleason L. *History of Radio to 1926.* The American Historical Society, 1938. Arno reprint. Important source, well documented.

Bagdikian, Ben H. *The Information Machines: Their Impact on Men and the Media.* Harper & Row, 1971. Broadcast news.

Barnouw, Erik. *A Tower in Babel: A History of Broadcasting in the United States to 1933.* Oxford University Press, 1966.

Barnouw, Erik. *The Golden Web: A History of Broadcasting in the United States 1933–1953.* Oxford University Press, 1968.

Barnouw, Erik. *The Image Empire: A History of Broadcasting in the United States from 1953.* Oxford University Press, 1970.

Bickel, Karl A., *New Empires: Newspapers and the Radio.* J. B. Lippincott, 1930.

Chase, Francis. *Sound and Fury: An Informal History of Broadcasting.* Harper & Brothers, 1942.

Codel, Martin. *Radio and its Future.* Harper & Brothers, 1930. Arno reprint. Collection of articles by industry leaders.

Cole, Barry. *Television.* The Free Press, 1970. Selections from *TV Guide.*

Crosby, John. *Out of the Blue: A Book About Radio and Television.* Simon and Schuster, 1952. Articles, criticism, New York *Herald-Tribune,* 1946 to 1951.

Dulles, Foster Rhea. *A History of Recreation: America Learns to Play.* Appleton-Century-Crofts, 1965.

Eddy, William C. *Television: The Eyes of Tomorrow.* Prentice-Hall, 1945.

Federal Council of Churches of Christ in America. *Broadcasting and the Public.* Albingdon Press, 1938.

Felix, Edgar H. *Television: Its Methods and Uses.* McGraw-Hill, 1931.

Frost, S. E. *Is American Radio Democratic?* University of Chicago Press, 1937.

Goldsmith, Alfred N., and Lescarboura, Austin C. *This Thing Called Broadcasting.* Henry Holt, 1930. Description, comprehensive.

Green, Abel, and Laurie, Joe. *Show Biz from Vaude to Video.* Henry Holt, 1951. From *Variety,* 1905 to 1950. General summary on the entertainment business.

Gross, Ben. *I Looked and I Listened.: Informal Recollections of Radio and TV.* Random House, 1954, revised, 1970. Radio columnist, New York *Daily News.*

Head, Sydney W. *Broadcasting in America: A Survey of Television and Radio.* Houghton-Mifflin, 1956, revised 1972.

Hill, Harold E. *The National Association of Educational Broadcasters: A History.* NAEB, 1954. See Alford.

Hutchinson, Thomas. *Here is Television.* Hastings House, 1946, 1950.

Kempner, Stanley. *Television Encyclopedia.* Fairchild, 1948.

Koenig, Allen E. and Hill, Ruane B. *The Farther Vision: Educational Television Today.* University of Wisconsin Press, 1967.

Land Associates, Herman W. *The Hidden Medium: A Status Report on Educational Radio in the United States.* National Association of Educational Broadcasters, 1967.

Landry, Robert J. *This Fascinating Radio Business.* Bobbs-Merrill, 1946. History and status of radio to WW II.

Lohr, Lenox B. *Television Broadcasting: Production, Economics, Technique.* McGraw-Hill, 1940.

MacLatchy, Josephine. *Education on the Air.* Ohio State University, annual, 1930 to 1944. Proceedings of Institute for Education by Radio.

Mayer, Martin. *About Television.* Harper & Row, 1972.

Paul, Eugene. *The Hungry Eye.* Ballantine Books, 1962. "An Inside Look at TV: The shows, the personalities, the fabulous incomes and fantastic costs."

Porterfield, John, and Reynolds, Kay. *We Present Television.* W. W. Norton, 1940.

Powell, John Walker. *Channels of Learning: The Story of Educational Television.* Public Affairs Press, 1962.

Public Television: A Program for Action. Harper & Row; Bantam, 1967. "The Report of the Carnegie Commission on Educational Television."

Reck, Franklin R., *Radio from Start to Finish.* Thomas Y. Crowell, 1942. History of industry to 1941.

Rothafel, Samuel L., and Yates, Raymond Francis. *Broadcasting: Its New Day.* The Century Co., 1925. Arno reprint. Summary of the radio "industry" in 1925.

Schubert, Paul. *The Electric Word: The Rise of Radio.* Macmillan, 1928. Arno reprint.

Seldes, Gilbert. *The Public Arts.* Simon and Schuster, 1956. See particularly on Berle, Benny, Gleason, Murrow, color and UHFs.

Shayon, Robert Lewis. *Open to Criticism.* Beacon Press, 1971. Collection of *Saturday Review* pieces, some unpublished; on criticism.

Shayon, Robert. *The Crowd-Catchers.* Saturday Review Press, 1973.

Shurick, E. P. J., *The First Quarter-Century of American Broadcasting.* Midland Publishing Company, 1946. Chronologies for 26 categories of subject matter about radio.

Skornia, Harry J. and Kitson, Jack William. *Problems and Controversies in Television and Radio.* Pacific Books, 1968. Collection of articles.

TV Guide Roundup. Holt, Rinehart and Winston, 1960; Popular Library, 1961. Also see Cole.

Tyler, Kingdon S. *Modern Radio.* Harcourt, Brace, 1947.

Udell, Gillman G. *Radio Laws of the United States: 1972 Edition.* GPO, 1972. 1910–

Waller, Judith C. *Radio: The Fifth Estate.* Houghton Mifflin, 1950.

White, Llewellyn. *The American Radio.* University of Chicago Press, 1947. Arno reprint. Report on broadcasting of the Commission on Freedom of the Press, with a good historical summary.

BIBLIOGRAPHIES

Barcus, F. "Bibliography of Studies of Radio and Television Program Content, 1928–1958," *Journal of Broadcasting.* Vol. IV, No. 4, Fall 1960, 355.

"Books About Radio," *Radio Broadcast,* September 1922, pp. 441–442.

Broadcasting Yearbook. Chronology of year 1937–1939; highlights and headlines; 1941–1947; major trends, events 1957–1971; several special chronologies.

Cooper, Isabella. *Bibliography on Educational Broadcasting,* University of Chicago Press, 1942.

Journalism Quarterly. Regular bibliographies of periodicals, books, etc.

Journal of Broadcasting. Bibliographies on special subjects, theses, etc. See index XV:4 (Fall 1971)

Lichty, Lawrence W. *World and International: A Bibliography.* Association for Professional Broadcasting Education (now Broadcasting Education Association), 1970.

Shiers, George. *Bibliography of the History of Electronics.* Scarecrow Press, 1972. See especially for list of periodicals, biographies, technical history.

Rose, Oscar. *Radio Broadcasting and Television.* H. W. Wilson, 1947.

Topicator. Monthly, quarterly, annual listings; index for a score of broadcasting and advertising periodicals. 1965–

PERIODICALS

Air Law Review. 1930–

Billboard. Music, radio programming. 1894–

BM/E Broadcast Management/Engineering. 1965–

Broadcasting. Combined with *Broadcast Advertising, Broadcasting-Telecasting,* 1945–1957. 1931–

Broadcasting Yearbook. Annual. 1935–

Cable Report. Earlier part of *Chicago Journalism Review.* 1973–

College Radio. Campus stations. 1963–

Educational Broadcasting Review. Formerly *NAEB Journal.* 1967–1973.

Electronic Age. Earlier *Radio Age.* 1941–

Federal Communications Bar Journal. 1937–

Federal Communications Commission. *Annual Report.* GPO, annual, 1935 to 1955 reprinted by Arno Press.

Federal Communications Commission Reports. GPO. FCC orders and reports.

Federal Radio Commission. *Annual Report.* GPO, annual, 1927 to 1933. Reprinted by Arno Press.

Federal Register. GPO. FCC proceedings.

Film Quarterly. Earlier *Hollywood Quarterly, Quarterly of Film, Radio and Television.* 1948–

FM and Television. Also titled *FM Electronic Equipment Engineering and Design Practice, FM Radio Electronic Engineering and Design, FM Radio Electronics, FM-TV, FM-TV Radio Communications,* and *Communications Engineering;* absorbed into *Radio-TV News.* 1940–1952.

Journal of Broadcasting. Broadcast Education Association, formerly Association for Professional Broadcasting Education. 1957–

Journal of the SMPTE. Society of Motion Picture and Television Engineers. 1916–

Journalism Quarterly. Association for Education in Journalism. 1924–

Mass Comm Review. Mass Communications and Society Division, Association for Education in Journalism. 1973–

Mass Media Booknotes. Monthly listing, reviews, new books; special bibliographies. Write C. H. Sterling, Department of Radio-Television-Film, Temple University, Philadelphia, PA 19122. 1969–

Media/scope. Standard Rate and Data Service. 1957–1967.

NAEB Journal. National Association of Educational Broadcasting. 1957–1967.

Nielsen Newscast. A. C. Nielsen Company. 1951–

Old Timer's Bulletin, The. Antique Wireless Association. 1959–

Pike and Fischer. *Radio Regulation.* Digests and summaries of cases. See *RR Consolidated Digest* for 1927–1963, *RR Current Digest, Second Series* for 1963–

Printer's Ink. 1888–1967. Now *Marketing Communications.*

Public Opinion Quarterly. 1937–

Public Telecommunication Review. Formerly *EBR.* 1973–

QST. American Radio Relay League. 1915–

Radio Age. 1922–1928.

Radio Broadcast. 1922–1930.

Radio Guide. Also *Radio and Amusement Guide, Movie and Radio Guide.* 1931–1943.

Radio Retailing. Also *Radio and Television Retailing.* 1925–1953.

Sponsor. 1946–1968.

Telefilm Magazine. Title varies. 1956–1963.

Television. 1944–1968.

Television Almanac, annual, Quigley Publications, Producers, stars, business and advertising information.

Television Digest. Title varies. 1945–

TV Communications. Cable TV. Also published *CATV.* 1963–

Television Factbook. Annual.

Television Quarterly. National Academy of Television Arts and Sciences. 1962–1970, 1972–

Topicator. Index of broadcasting and advertising. 1965–

Variety. 1905–

For more details on a periodical check *Ulrich's International Periodicals Directory.* To find libraries that have specific periodicals see *Union List of Serials.*

INDEX

T

W

Combining a skillfully edited anthology of 93 selec-
·tions (one-third never before published) with
commentaries by the authors, this unique source
book provides a comprehensive description and
analysis of broadcasting in America from its prehistory to 1975. It is the most up-to-date, complete
and accurate single volume on the development
of radio and television now available.

The arrangement is in eight parts, each preceded by an essay giving a general overview of
that area of broadcasting:

Technical—Stations—Networks—Economics
Employment—Programming—Audiences—Regulation

Augmented by accounts of broadcasters,
journalists and others, the scholarship of leading
teachers of mass communications provides details
of many of the most significant facets of radio
and television. Thus, this book serves not only to
explicate the complex history of broadcasting but
relates its development to other mass media. It
will serve as a handbook on research techniques
and sources, and as a guide to much that remains
to be studied.

More than 50 original tables give information
on the number and type of stations, the economics
of broadcasting, the history of programming and
audiences, including ratings of the most popular
programs. A bibliography of over 500 items, as
well as many others contained in the notes for the
articles, provides the most detailed starting point
available to lead the researcher to other sources.
Illustrations include a concise explanation of how
radio, FM and TV work, and some 70 photographs
of the most important television programs are included — all taken off the TV screen.

A second, chronological table of contents and a
comprehensive index will help readers look for
specific information.